Claiborne County, Tennessee, Marriages 1838 – 1891

Two Volumes in One

By

Byron Sistler and Barbara Sistler

Janaway Publishing, Inc.
2012

Claiborne County, Tennessee, Marriages 1838-1891. Two Volumes in One.

Copyright © 1983-1984, by Byron Sistler

ALL RIGHTS RESERVED. Written permission must be secured from the
publisher to use or reproduce any part of this book, in any form or
by any means, including electronic reproduction,
except for brief quotations in
critical reviews or articles.

Originally published as two books:
Claiborne County, Tennessee, Marriages 1838-1868. 1983
Claiborne County, Tennessee, Marriages 1868-1891. 1984
Nashville, Tennessee
1983 and 1984

Reprinted by

Janaway Publishing, Inc.
732 Kelsey Ct.
Santa Maria, California 93454
(805) 925-1038
www.JanawayGenealogy.com

2012

ISBN: 978-1-59641-279-8

Made in the United States of America

Claiborne County, Tennessee

Marriages

1838 – 1868

Byron and Barbara Sistler

Byron Sistler & Associates, Inc.
1983

Claiborne County, Tennessee, Marriages 1838-1868

Copyright © 1983 by Byron Sistler
All rights reserved.

Originally printed, Nashville, 1983
Byron Sistler and Associates, Inc.

Janaway Publishing, Inc.
2412 Nicklaus Dr.
Santa Maria, California 93455
(805) 925-1038
www.JanawayPublishing.com

2007

ISBN 10: 1-59641-077-9
ISBN 13: 978-1-59641-077-0

Made in the United States of America

CLAIBORNE COUNTY, TENNESSEE MARRIAGES

1838-1868

Where two dates appear on an entry, the first one is the date license was issued, the second (in parentheses) the date marriage was solemnized. If only one date, the marriage took place the date of issuance, did not take place or there was no return to the courthouse.

We were not able to obtain originals from the marriage books for the period prior to December 1850, so copied them from the WPA books prepared in the 1930s and 1940s from those originals. They include a number of errors, either in the reading or transcribing of the records, but we do not know where the originals are, if indeed they are still extant. They are not available at the Tennessee State Library and Archives.

Marriages starting December 1850 have been copied by us directly from microfilm of the original books.

Byron Sistler
Barbara Sistler

Nashville, TN
August, 1983

Note: Since preparing this booklet we have been told that the marriages for 1838 to 1850 have been preserved in their original form and can be found at the Courthouse in Tazewell.

The Sistlers
May, 1989

Abs, Robert A. to Mary E. Bussel 2-20-1854
Adams, Joshua to Timpa? Smith 10-3-1843 (11-2-1843)
Admes?, E. C. to Ruthy Hockins 12-4-1858
Ales, John W. to Sarah Willis 11-8-1866
Alexander, John to Olive Root 3-5-1842 (3-10-1842)
Alexander, William B. to Louisa Hodges 10-2-1847 (10-7-1847)
Allen, Alexander to Laura Patterson 4-18-1868 (4-22-1868)
Allen, George to Emaline Pitman 8-3-1850 (8-7-1850)
Allen, John to Martha Gideans 3-31-1838 (4-1-1838)
Allen, Stephen to Mary Rhea 4-5-1838
Allin, Enas to Sarah Lay 1-23-1850 (1-24-1850)
Alston, J. W. to Melvina J. Haynes 11-4-1865 (11-5-1865)
Alton, Stokley to Susanah Carpenter 10-7-1844 (10-8-1844)
Anderson, John W. to Sarah Ann Brantley 3-12-1851 (3-13-1851)
Anderson, W. M. W. to Elizabeth Johnson 10-12-1850 (10-13-1850)
Arber, William to Juicy Taylor 1-22-1842 (1-23-1842)
Ares, Elemuel H. to Sophia Liford 9-18-1851 (9-20-1851)
Aries, Jessee to Sarah Carter 8-1-1859
Armstrong, Stephen to Mariah Cloud 12-20-1867 B
Arnel, Samuel to Rachal Rolin 11-24-1846 (11-25-1846)
Arnold, Samuel to Emeline Guy 8-15-1868 (8-16-1868)
Arnold, Stephen to S. M Perman 11-2-1853 (11-3-1853)
Arnwine, Isaac W. to Phebe E. Lewis 12-14-1867 (12-19-1867)
Arthur, Ambrose to Susan Hall 9-19-1838
Arwine, F. to P. Farmer 8-6-1858 (8-8-1858)
Atkins, Scott to Emeliza Hall 11-8-1854
Atkins, Seth to Nancy Jane Malacott 3-21-1859
Ausben, William to Mary J. Baless 4-15-1867 (4-16-1867)
Ausmus, Benjamin to Barbry Hunter 5-20-1863 (5-22-1863)
Ausmus, Benjamin to Elizabeth Proffit 8-24-1857
Ausmus, Henry to Matilda Bowlinger 1-3-1854
Ausmus, Hiram to Sarah Balinger? 5-15-1850 (5-20-1850)
Ausmus, Thos. to Mary Emily (Polly) Rogers 3-4-1853
Austin, Fredrick H. to Martha A. Hodges 5-15-1867
Avonin, Hyram to Nancy Rosan Culm 8-30-1865 (9-3-1865)
Ayers, Henry to Lack G. Marcum 11-20-1848 (11-24-1848)
Ayers, Jacob Washington to Elizabeth J. Collensworth 1-4-1853 (1-5-1853)
Ayers, John W. to Luhamy Hawkins 11-17-1859
Ayers, William to Jeminia Hatfield 4-22-1843 (4-23-1843)
Badwor?, D. B. to P. Whiteted 9-20-1852 (9-23-1852)
Bailey, William to Elizabeth Hoskins 2-1-1844
Bailey, Wm. to Merica Marcum 12-30-1865
Bailey?, Collin? to Mary A. Smith 11-1-1842 (11-2-1842)
Bainman, Isaac to Rachel Stansbery 1-31-1859
Bains?, Robert S. to Nancy L. Shomate? 9-6-1845 (9-7-1845)
Baker, Briant to Martha J. Locke 2-9-1838 (2-14-1838)
Baker, C. to Luckrisha? McGee 11-24-1845 (11-27-1845)
Baker, Charles to Elizabeth Brooks 10-24-1843
Baker, Elihugh to Marcynann Read 3-10-1838 (4-7-1838)
Baker, Henry to Anny Harris? 7-16-1842 (7-19-1842)
Baker, Jno. J. to Hannah Standerfe? 6-11-1840
Baker, John M. to Mariah Hurst 12-5-1855
Baker, John to Permdy Vanoy 2-21-1838 (2-22-1838)
Baker, John to Polly Ramsey 9-15-1850
Baker, Nelson to Sinda Williamson 5-7-1854
Baker, Thomas to Ann Sumptre 8-7-1858
Baker, Thomas to Elizabeth Sumpton no date (summer 1859?)
Baker, Tipton to Susan Billingsly 11-25-1847 (11-26-1847)
Baker, William to Frankey I.? Mills 9-26-1849
Baker, William to Nancy Ponder 1-20-1851
Baldridge, Thos. to Martha Wilbourne? 8-16-1850 (8-17-1850)
Bales, Daniel B. to Lucinda Pruett 6-22-1867 (6-27-1867)
Bales, Ewing to Cathrine Lenard 8-21-1853 (9-8-1853)
Bales, Fidelio to P. A. Neil 2-15-1853
Bales, Jonathan to Sarah A. Crockett 9-4-1855 (9-27-1855)
Bales, S. to M. J. Lockmillor? 5-16-1846 (5-17-1846)
Bales, Wm. P. to Russilla Ann Houston 6-4-1850
Baley, Charles to Mary Ball 10-5-1841 (11-7-1841)
Baley, Jobe to Mary Minton 1-28-1857
Baley, Jove to Jemima Minton 3-16-1867 (3-17-1867)
Balis, Abraham to Elizabeth Pressley 11-28-1849 (11-29-1849)
Ball, Evan to Jane Hamlin 11-17-1866 (11-25-1866)
Ball, George W. to Nancy Haskins 3-24-1858
Ball, John T. to Ellender Colston 8-17-1866 (8-20-1866)
Ball, John to Esther Hoskins 2-11-1867 (2-14-1867)
Ball, John to Rachel E. Lock 5-11-1843 (5-14-1843)
Ball, Lemuel to Ann Eliza Powers 1-18-1849
Ball, Pridmore to Nancy Ball 7-28-1838 (7-29-1838)
Ball, Samuel L. to Sarah Ball 1-21-1868 (1-26-1868)
Ball, Tilmon D. to Elizabeth Ball 4-24-1845
Ball, William F. to V. A. Cottrell 3-11-1850 (3-19-1850)
Balloo, Peter to Rebecca Dowys? 9-10-1838 (9-15-1838)
Bannum, Bolivar to Mary A. Gillasie 10-28-1865 (10-29-1865)
Barker, Joel to Susan No? 2-14-1845
Barlet?, Martain to Ann McNeil 1-7-1843 (1-8-1843)
Barnard, Anderson to Mary A. Singleton 7-9-1847 (7-10-1847)
Barnard, James to Malissa Michel 1-21-1851 (1-3?-1851)

Barnard, James to Rebecca Bartlett 4-23-1851 (4-29-1851)
Barnard, Jas. to Emaline Mathis 3-30-1858
Barnard, John to Lewisa Davy 11-21-1858
Barnard, Johnathan to Clary Hill 2-22-1846 (2-27-1846)
Barnard, Jonathan to Lemira Barnard 2-12-1849 (2-13-1849)
Barnard, Sterling? J. to Nancy Mason 1-25-1845 (1-27-1845)
Barnard, Wiley to Malissa Lawsan? 6-19-1847
Barnes, John to Mary Willis 10-24-1851 (10-26-1851)
Barnes, Wm. to R.? Grace 5-9-1846 (5-17-1846)
Barnett, A. to ____ Baughman 11-25-1850
Barnett, John to ____ Leake 3-30-1865 (3-31-1865)
Barns, William R. to Olley Mapels 8-1-1866 (8-13-1866)
Barns?, John to Rosemial? Grace 1-14-1842
Barren, William to Nancy Jane Burns 8-18-1847 (8-20-1847)
Bartlet, Claiborne to Lucy C. Blancet 7-20-1854
Bartlet, Wiley to Sarah Ruth no date (Dec 1859?)
Barton, George to Matilda Jackson 7-25-1848
Bauels, T. J. to M. E. Bartlett 4-11-1858
Baxter, J. W. to Mary Owens 8-20-1865 (8-30-1865)
Baylay?, William to Zilpha J. Frasher 6-25-1849 (6-26-1849)
Bayless, Daniel to Catharine Biggs 10-29-1866
Beach, Henry to Mourning Parrott 11-14-1846 (11-23-1846)
Bean, Reuben to Malinda Vitatoe 3-13-1867 (3-14-1867)
Beard, A. M. to Nancy Green 2-26-1852
Beard, Robert to Martha Davis 7-20-1850
Beason, John to Emiline Smith 8-15-1866 (8-16-1866)
Beaty, William to Catharine Minton? 12-26-1842
Beeler, Bowyer to Rebecca Lewis 2-2-1850 (2-21-1850)
Beeler, Daniel to Melvina Ballinger 1-29-1867 (1-31-1867)
Beeler, F. to M. Bowman 4-15-1853 (4-21-1853)
Beeler, Jesse F. to Polly Beeler 2-18-1839 (2-22-1839)
Beelon?, Joseph to Hariet Branscome 3-5-1849 (3-8-1849)
Beelor, George W. to M. Cardwell 1-18-1853 (1-19-1853)
Belamy, John D. to Jane Cline 10-2-1855
Bell, B. T. to T. A. Mize 12-14-1852 (12-19-1852)
Bell, W. S. to C. Gibson 8-9-1853
Bell, Wm. S. to Caroline Gibson 7-9-1853 B
Bellema, John to Elisabeth Shoemaker 1-20-1851 (1-21-1851)
Belvin, James to Nancy Dobkins 1-30-1839
Berry, Benj. to Sarah Ellerson 10-3-1853 (2-24-1854)
Berry, Henry to Louisa Ellerson 11-20-1855
Berry, Jackson to Elizabeth Eads 9-18-1849 (9-19-1849)
Berry, John F. to Amanda Nash 11-23-1846 (11-24-1846)
Berry, John F. to Susan A. Moses 2-14-1850
Berry, John to Harrett Kid 12-27-1837 (12-29-1837)
Berry, John to Sarah West 8-26-1858
Berry, Nelson to Joannes? Pain 6-20-1843
Berry, Prior L. to Malinda Ausmus 10-1-1856
Berry, William E. to Malinda Cannon 2-22-1868 (2-25-1868)
Biggs, John to Nancy Idle 5-23-1859
Billingly, George M. to Eliza Shumate 8-9-1842
Billingsley, Linneius? to Polly Hunter 12-26-1845 (1-4-1846)
Bingham, Lafayett? to Rebeckah Baker 6-3-1846
Black, Edward to Franky Brownlow 12-18-1839 (12-22-1839)
Black, J. W. to Susan Maples 7-14-1855
Blackburn, W. A. L. to Sarah A. Graham 9-1-1857
Blackomone?, Wm. H. to E. Winn 3-9-1846 (3-18-1846)
Blancet, Wm. to L. Bartlett 1-14-1854
Blancit, Emanuel to Luvana Norman 2-16-1859
Blancit, James M. to Sarah Wells 3-3-1859
Blancit, James to Polly A. McBee 7-16-1859
Blankinship, Charles to Susanah Little 7-21-1838 (7-22-1838)
Blankinship, William to Belenda Burgin 10-7-1842
Blansett, Elias to S. McClelland 9-30-1853 (10-2-1853)
Bolinger, Isaac to Elizabeth Right 1-13-1842 (1-22-1842)
Bolton, James P. to Martha J. Parks 3-15-1867 (3-21-1867)
Bomon, Daniel to July A. Leach 6-10-1865 (6-22-1865)
Boruff, Valentine to Sarena Beelar 11-18-1852 (11-21-1852)
Bowman, Anderson to Martha Leach 1-16-1855 (1-21-1855)
Bowman, Daniel to July A. Leach 6-10-1865
Bowman, Elisha to Lucinda Bradin 12-26-1850
Bowman, Nelson C. to Martha L. Rogers 12-23-1847
Bowman, Nelson to T. ? Wilson 6-26-1867
Bowman, Wm. to Mary Ann King 10-2-1846 (10-7-1846)
Brachett?, Felix to Neoma Howel? 8-13-1846
Brack, Ervin to Eliza F. Cook 8-22-1856
Braden, Cornelius to Susanah Ausmus 1-22-1839 (1-29-1839)
Braden, Elijah to Lucinda Lynch 2-5-1850 (2-10-1850)
Braden, George to Lucinda Hunacutt 5-12-1853 (5-28-1853)
Braden, James to Sarah Waddy 10-13-1838
Braden, Jno. to Respy Lynch 12-11-1838
Brader, David to Martha Collins 5-13-1865
Bralock, Hubbard to Catharin Graceclose 12-10-1842 (12-12-1842)
Branbury, David to Nancy Branbury 5-22-1853
Branscome, Joseph to Rachel Dunn 12-15-1849 (12-20-1849)
Bransom, J. to A. Cupp 12-9-1852
Bratcher, John to Mary Malicoat 10-16-1852

Bray, Abejah? to Polly Webb 1-4-1838 (1-10-1839?)
Bray, Edward to Emily Campbell 8-10-1850 (8-11-1850)
Bray, Hugh G. to Elisabeth Campbell 1-19-1856
Bray, Thos. P. to Lavesa Holt 7-22-1843 (7-24-1843)
Breeden?, Russel to Sarah Day 5-13-1847 (5-14-1847)
Breeding, Andrew J. to Mary Pitman 5-19-1847
Breeding, Neil to Rebecca Hurst 4-23-1850 (4-28-1850)
Breeding, Russel to Mary I. Dinsmore 2-3-1849
Breeding, Samuel to Sarah Evans 9-6-1852 (9-7-1852)
Breeding, Thos. W. to Margaret Johnson 2-13-1852 (2-15-1852)
Bremmer, Reuben to Cathrine Sheare 10-17-1853 (10-19-1853)
Brent, John M. to Virginia Hurst 1-14-1856 (no return)
Brewer, James to Mary Jane Brewere 7-20-1838 (7-22-1838)
Brewer, Levi to Sally Johnston 3-6-1838
Brewer, M. to M. J. Hopper 2-14-1853 (2-17-1853)
Brewer, Major to Mary Marler 1-22-1845 (1-26-1845)
Brewer, Thos. to Anna White 9-20-1844 (9-21-1844)
Brewor?, Russel to Polley Cloud? 11-4-1844 (11-7-1844)
Brians, Henley C. to Eliza W. Holley 12-25-1866
Bridine?, John T. to Catharine Davault 2-6-1854
Bright, John to Mary Hardy 1-9-1850 (1-10-1850)
Brink?, John to Elejiceia Spiers 6-7-1845
Brock, Andrew J. to Sarah Day 12-13-1841 (12-16-1841)
Brock, John to Melvina Nicely 6-1-1839 (6-3-1839)
Brock, John to Sarah Longworth 12-22-1849 (12-23-1849)
Brocks, Gideon to Winney Hurst 8-19-1841
Brogan, Alvis to Jane Rows 4-27-1853 (4-30-1853)
Brogan, Alvis to Malinda Walker 9-21-1847 (9-23-1847)
Brogan, Asa to Leta Sharp 2-4-1850 (2-7-1850)
Brogan, Franklin to Martha J. Dykes 3-4-1857
Brooks, A. to E. Whitaker 11-15-1852 (11-18-1852)
Brooks, Alexander to Mary J. Brooks 12-19-1855
Brooks, Andrew to Elizabeth Chadwell 4-1-1856 (4-10-1856)
Brooks, Andrew to Mary J. Brooks 8-16-1848
Brooks, Armstrong to E. Chadwell 6-14-1858
Brooks, B. to M. S. E. Rowlette 9-28-1839
Brooks, Calvin to Judah E. L.? Estice 11-7-1843 (11-8-1843)
Brooks, Clinton to Rutha M. Hobbs 7-6-1866 (7-8-1866)
Brooks, David to Malinda Proffet 5-10-1854 (1?-11-1854)
Brooks, David to Nairvsty? Hill 4-23-1858 (5-25-1858)
Brooks, Doctor to Melvinia Wilson 1-21-1868 (1-22-1868) B
Brooks, Geo. W. to Cathrine Zicks 4-3-1848
Brooks, James F. to Sarah Fultz 11-1-1866 (11-4-1866)
Brooks, James P. jr. to Martha Moore 8-5-1858
Brooks, Jeremiah to Margaret Brooks 8-4-1851 (8-5-1851)
Brooks, John H. to Matilda Longworth 1-11-1848
Brooks, John M. to Nancy J. Brooks 3-16-1867 (3-17-1867)
Brooks, Levi to Emily A. Campbell 7-1-1848 (7-5-1848)
Brooks, Levi to Lucinda Brooks 12-14-1850 (12-15-1850)
Brooks, Nathaniel to Lucinda Dobkins 7-27-1850 (7-28-1850)
Brooks, Preston to Lucy Ann Campbell 6-15-1857
Brooks, Robert A. to Nancy Furgerson 3-27-1867 (3-31-1867)
Brooks, Thos. to Catharine Brooks 7-15-1847
Brooks, Thos. to Sarah Johnson 3-12-1856
Brooks, Traves to Elizabeth Whitecar 2-8-1843
Brooks, W. P. to Minerva A. Goins 4-25-1857 (4-26-1857)
Brooks, Zachariah to Sarah Whitaker 10-19-1853 (10-20-1853)
Brown, Henry A. to Catharin Cheek 5-6-1840
Brown, John to Virginia Rowlett 9-28-1853
Brown, James to Elizabeth Chick 11-11-1848
Brown, John to Martha Short 3-15-1867 (3-17-1867)
Brown, Michail T. to Polly Smith 7-21-1858 (7-25-1858)
Brown, William to Nancey? Wien? 2-2-1849
Bruce, James to Nancy Wright 12-25-1864 (12-28-1864)
Bruden?, Tennessee to Elizabeth Day 7-4-1839
Bruice?, Jesse to Deborah Crank? 5-21-1842 (5-22-1842)
Bruister, Wm. M. to Sarah R. Cadle 2-5-1857
Brummit, Campbell? to Mahaley Townsley 6-19-1847 (6-22-1847)
Bruster, John to Nancy Grubb 6-2-1851
Buchanan, John A. to Sarah Calar? 10-18-1842 (10-23-1842)
Buchanan, Toney to Tilda Buchanan 1-25-1866 B
Buchanan, Walter R. to Darcus Kincaid 7-23-1855 (7-27-1855)
Buck, William to Emaline Baltrip 5-4-1845 (5-7-1845)
Buck, Wm. to Emeline Baltrip 5-8-1845 (5-7?-1845)
Buis, Henry to Elizabeth Heil 8-16-1866 B
Buise, Joseph to N. Kesterson 6-16-1853
Bull, Britton to Elizabeth Wolf 10-31-1866
Bull, Calvin to Elizabeth Parm 9-21-1857
Bull, Calvin to Martha Barnard 10-26-1853 (10-27-1853)
Bullard, B. P.? to B. A. Gibson 4-7-1858
Bullard, Boyer to Mildred Lanham 1-25-1848 (1-?-1848)
Bullard, C. B. to Rebecca Hodge 11-10-1838
Bullard, Henry to Celia Haynes 9-26-1853
Bullard, Isaac to Tempia Catharine Worwick 9-17-1866
Bullard, Joseph H. to Manery? Dobkins 7-20-1848
Bullars, Isaac to Rebeca Perlina Gibson 5-13-1854
Bullen, James to Rinda Rosenbalm 10-8-1853

Bully, Philip to Manervy Jennings 1-22-1845
Bunch, D. W.? to Sarah West 4-7-1858
Bunch, Green B. to Morning Bunch 5-23-1855
Bunch, John to Adaline Bunch 10-5-1866 (10-4?-1866)
Bunch, Joseph to Wilmirth? Harral 7-28-1842
Bunch, M. V. to M. J. Hopson 1-2-1856 (2-7-1856)
Bunch, M. V. to Mary J. Hopson 2-2-1856
Bunnels, John to Perlina Kerby 1-29-1866
Burch, Bazebel to Candus McNealance 10-11-1851 (10-17-1851)
Burch, Bezeet? to Mary Tucker 6-11-1842 (6-14-1842)
Burch, Brazeal to Elmeda A. Jenkins 4-7-1851
Burch, John to Mary Willis 12-30-1841 (1-2-1842)
Burch, Reubin to Pheeby Harrell 7-2-1845 (7-3-1845)
Burch, Thomas to S. E. Goin 10-12-1857
Burchett, Benjamin to Elisabeth? Ann Ray? 12-26-1845 (12-30-1845)
Burchett, D. M. to Abagil Litrell 3-5-1858
Burchett, D. N. to Abigale Litrell 3-5-1858
Burchett, James D. to Cinthy M. Johnson 9-6-1845 (9-11-1845)
Burchfield, H. to Jane Graham 7-2-1846
Burchfield, Henry A. to Polly A. Phelips 4-15-1843 (4-16-1843)
Burchfield, Jeremiah to Sarah Welch 2-21-1849
Burchfield, Madison to Nancy Casady 9-9-1852
Burchfield, Martain to Susan Bull 4-2-1842
Burchitt, Ekils? to Leor? Anderson 1-23-1846 (1-25-1846)
Burk, D. D. to M. Yoakum 5-17-1858 (5-23-1858)
Burk, James to Nancy Mays? 10-22-1842
Burk, John Jesse to Penelopa Brogan 12-28-1852 (12-30-1852)
Burk, Johnson to Jane Redmon 2-10-1855 (9-8-1855)
Burk, Presley G. to Martha Grimes 8-23-1854 (8-24-1854)
Burket, James to Lidda Green Lee 5-18-1850
Burket, Ralph to Orlena Lee 5-2-1850
Burket?, William to Lidia? McMillion? 2-1-1847
Burnet, Allen to Viney Martain 5-9-1840
Burnett, James H. to Elizabeth Simmons 4-25-1868 (4-26-1868)
Burnett, John to Emaline Sharp 1-8-1856 (1-10-1856)
Burton, William to Malisa Carpenter 10-3-1844
Bush, Enoch to Agga Vance 11-19-1838 (11-20-1838)
Bush, Isaac to Mary Hale 10-2-1867 (10-3-1867)
Bush, James to Avda Bush 11-13-1856
Bush, John to Mary A. Good 7-27-1867 (7-29-1867)
Busick, Alfred to Sarah Ann Haris 11-1-1858
Bussel, Matthew to Lurana Joihnstan 5-24-1838
Bussel, McDaniel to Emaline Baltrip 4-2-1852 (4-4-1852)
Bussell, Charles to Surrena Meeler 10-9-1838
Bussell, James to Louiza Butcher 5-1-1867 (5-3-1867)
Bussell, Seabord to Mollie Lambert 4-7-1867 (4-28-1867)
Bussle?, Bird to Susan Baltrip 6-3-1842 (6-8-1842)
Bussle?, Charles to Sidney Ann Jones 11-16-1843 (11-17-1843)
Butcher, Elisha to Jane Calestane? 11-28-1843 (12-1-1843)
Butcher, Elonza D. to Martha Jane Vaughn 6-11-1849 (6-12-1849)
Butcher, Jas. to Ruth Jackson 5-19-1838
Butcher, Joseph to Ruthy Jackson 5-19-1838
Butcher, Wornick to Jane Harper 5-17-1867 (5-18-1867) B
Cade, Sinclar to Elly Baker 2-18-1840 (2-22-1840)
Cadle, A. M. to Catharine Redmon 12-31-1867
Cadle, Abraham to Eliza J. Childers 2-24-1851 (2-26-1851)
Cadle, Druciller to William Grace 1-18-1845
Cadle, George to Margret Ann Sprinkles 6-5-1859
Cadle, Green B. to Elisabeth J. Moore 5-9-1848
Cadle, Hamilton to Sarah A. Denham 12-23-1858
Cadle, James P. to Lucinda Rose 6-25-1853 (6-26-1853)
Cadle, M. B. to C. Sauls 4-17-1859
Cadle, Mark to Mary Covy 8-6-1838 (8-9-1838)
Cadle, Martin (Marcus) to M. (Martha) Clark 2-10-1858 (2-11-1858)
Cadle, Martin to Martha J. Bruster 2-19-1838
Cadle, Matthew to Jane Vaughn 9-1-1866 (9-6-1866)
Cain, J. F. to N. Kincaid 10-26-1853 (11-3-1853)
Cain, John S. to Barberry Lynch 2-8-1850 (2-12-1850)
Cain, Nathaniel D. to Mary Sharp 2-25-1843
Cairdny?, Thos. to Sarah Chumley 11-5-1855
Callahan, David to Malvina Dulin 1-18-1854 (1-19-1854)
Callep, Hiram to Martha Hampton 10-18-1855
Campbell, A. to Levisa? Campbell 10-2-1844 (11-2-1844)
Campbell, Barnet? to Jane Kesterson 3-26-1840
Campbell, Benjamin F. to Elizabeth J. Lanham 11-20-1866
Campbell, Benjamin to Louisa Eastridge 9-28-1842 (9-29-1842)
Campbell, E. to Emaley Hazelwood? 6-24-1845 (6-4?-1845)
Campbell, Eldridge to Sarah Walker 8-31-1842 (9-1-1842)
Campbell, George W. to Mary L. Roberts 1-14-1868 (12?-16-1868)
Campbell, George to Nancy Eastrage 2-10-1842
Campbell, Hawkins to Sarah Henderson 8-16-1854
Campbell, Isaac A. to Martha Williams 12-8-1866 (12-25-1866)
Campbell, Isaac A. to Ruth Hoskins 12-25-1854 (no return)
Campbell, James to Melvina Whitaker 8-14-1843 (8-15-1843)
Campbell, Jas. P. to Nancy E. Estep 10-30-1865 (11-2-1865)
Campbell, John to Mary Ann Chadwell 5-15-1850 (5-16-1850)
Campbell, Oliver to Sarah Lewis 2-9-1854

Campbell, Thos. to M. Campbell 2-18-1853
Campbell, William P. to Elisabeth Masengale 1-5-1856 (1-6-1856)
Camran, William to Rachel Hart 11-5-1849 (11-10-1849)
Candy, Wm. H. to Louisa Barnard 12-25-1838
Cane, Eli D. to Cleressey? Lamone? 7-31-1846
Cane?, Hugh to Orlina? Ritter 12-24-1839
Canner?, James to Elisabeth? Lenard? 1-27-1849 (1-28-1849)
Cannon, William to Fanny McNeelence? 8-9-1848
Canter, William J. to Eliza Robinson 2-28-1842
Cantwell, Andrew to Louiza Smith 5-24-1867 (5-26-1867)
Cape?, David to Sally Hamons 6-15-1846
Capps, David B. to Nancy Hurst 3-17-1842
Capps, William to Lucinda Collins 11-10-1857 (11-?-1857)
Capps, Wm. to L. Collins 11-10-1858 (11-13-1857?)
Capps, Wm. to Louisa E. Jones 9-4-1850
Carden, Joseph to Adalade B. Noel 5-2-1849
Carder, Richard to Polly Grimes? 10-4-1841 (12-22-1841)
Cardwell, David to Elizabeth Cailor 3-26-1850 (3-20?-1850)
Cardwell, Obediah to Martha L. Thompson 3-8-1842
Cardwell, Reuben to Luritta Sanders 10-29-1844 (10-31-1844)
Carell, Jas. to Elvira? M. Herrell 10-27-1845
Carmac, Isaac to Camfred Hail 3-14-1838 (3-27-1838)
Carmach, Enan to Polly Cox 8-26-1853
Carmack, Abraham to Delila? A. Dunn 10-21-1848 (10-22-1848)
Carmack, Enoch to Sally Campbell 12-17-1858
Carmack, Even to Elizabeth Lunday 12-8-1858
Carmack, Jacob to Sarah J. Fults 2-4-1851
Carmack, Levi to Mary Rollins 9-15-1847 (9-20-1847)
Carmack, M. to S. A. Barnes 3-5-1858?
Carmack, Martin to Ann Barns 3-5-1858
Carmack, Wiley to Elender Magard 12-2-1856
Carmack, William to Nancy Cocks 9-23-1847 (9-7?-1847)
Carman, William H. to Mary Ann Large 10-20-1858
Carmon, John to Phebe Price 10-3-1849 (10-4-1849)
Carmon, William to Alzira Crutchfield 3-12-1867 (3-14-1867)
Carpenter, Anderson to Syntha A. Hopson 5-12-1843 (5-18-1843)
Carpenter, George W. to Malissa Bunch 7-7-1857
Carpenter, Jas. R. to Mary Ward 1-12-1864
Carpenter, Jas. to Letia Shelton 6-6-1852 (6-8-1852)
Carpentr?, Anderson to Polla Burton 9-3-1844
Carr, Benj. F. to Sarah C. Sharp 11-28-1863 (12-6-1863)
Carr, D. A. to Mary A. Hopper 2-8-1866 (2-9-1866)
Carr, David F. to Mary M. Runions 11-5-1866 (11-25-1866)
Carr, James M. to Jane Hodge 4-12-1844 (4-14-1844)
Carr, James to Charlota J. Cloud 7-10-1848 (7-13-1848)
Carr, John H. to Mahala Seals 4-24-1850 (4-26-1850)
Carr, John H. to Mary Briant 7-27-1844 (7-28-1844)
Carr, John H. to Nancy Venable 6-7-1866
Carr, L. R. to N. Kelley 6-19-1852 (12-16-1852)
Carr, Lafayett M. to Martha J. Yoakum 11-21-1859
Carr, R. Y. to Mary Bales 2-3-1857
Carr, William M. to Emily Kilbert 1-20-1855 (1-25-1855)
Carr?, David W. to Orlena Lewis 11-4-1857
Carral, Gustavis to Margaret McMahan 8-1-1865
Carrel, Augustus to M. Herrel 7-4-1853
Carrell, A. to R. S. Herrell 12-18-1851
Carrell, Augustus to Mary Herrell 7-4-1853
Carrell, Henry to Elvira Cadle 9-1-1851 (9-4-1851)
Carrell, James C. to Sarah Elizabeth Ales 8-13-1868
Carrol, John J. to Mary J. Sawyers 7-17-1848 (7-19-1848)
Carroll, Henry to Mary England 9-1-1849 (8?-3-1849)
Carroll, James to Mary Poor 2-7-1855 (2-8-1855)
Carroll, William H. to Nancy Bawldridge 10-8-1849 (10-11-1849)
Carroll, William to Mary E. Mundy 7-7-1851 (7-17-1851)
Carroll, William to Polly Hamelton 10-24-1839 (10-31-1839)
Carroll, William to Polly Slatten? 2-8-1839 (2-21-1839)
Carrons, Nelson to Catharine Woollem 4-13-1854 (4-14-1854)
Carson, Samuel M. to Harriet D. Short 8-15-1853
Cartar?, Georg to Eliza Jane Carter? 1-28-1845 (1-29-1845)
Carter, Alexander to Rachael Lassey 11-16-1841 (11-21-1841)
Carter, Benjamin S.? to Nancy Carter 10-22-1843 (10-23-1843)
Carter, James C. to Nancy E. Cunningham 2-24-1868 (2-25-1868)
Carter, James M. to Winna Bunch 10-11-1865 (10-13-1865)
Carter, James to Mary M. G.. ? ? 1840 (10-?-1840)
Carter, Joseph to Ellis George 1-23-1848 (1-27-1848)
Carter, Sterling B. to Margret Cole 1-18-1847 (1-19-1847)
Carter, Thos. M. to Nancy A. Thompson 8-19-1855 (8-21-1855)
Cartor, Georg? to E. J. Harris 1-28-1845
Casada, John A. to Mary M. Walker 1-2-1867 (1-3-1867)
Casey, Simpson to Elizabeth Dulin 5-21-1850
Cash, Andrew T. to Martha C. Roberts 2-28-1865 (3-1-1865)
Cash, Thompson H. to Mary M. Davault 8-16-1859
Cass, J. M. to L. J. Margraves 2-24-1853
Cassel, James to Manilia Martin 12-28-1867 (12-29-1867)
Cassel?, J. S. to Nancy Hopper 8-28-1845
Cassle, John R. to Judy Ann Wright 2-15-1840 (2-18-1840)
Cavit, Richmon to Nancy Johnson 8-21-1856 (8-24-1856)

Cawood, John to Marlena Vanbebber 7-12-1843
Cawood, Wm. H. to Ruthy J. Sharp 9-18-1858
Caymard?, James to Polly Ann Sharp 12-9-1846
Cazort, Wiley to Nancy Hollon 2-27-1848 (2-29-1848)
Cazort?, Wiley to Nancy Hollon 2-27-1848 (2-29-1848)
Cerrel, Elias to Elizabeth Jane Bullard 1-15-1868 (1-16-1868)
Chaden, Spencer to Polly Weir 11-17-1842 (11-20-1842)
Chadwell, Alexander to Emeline Davisson 9-22-1866 (9-23-1866)
Chadwell, Alexander to Margaret Linsa 2-24-1855 (2-25-1855)
Chadwell, David to Fanna Humphria 5-15-1853 (5-17-1853)
Chadwell, David to Matilda J. Gilpin 10-23-1857
Chadwell, David to Nancy Rennels 3-26-1850 (3-28-1850)
Chadwell, George F. to Cornelia Robinson 9-12-1867
Chadwell, George to Malissa Murphey 10-11-1856
Chadwell, James B. to Sallie Baker 3-13-1867
Chadwell, Pleasant to Elizabeth Bowman 3-13-1838
Chadwell, S. to M. Campbell 1-26-1853 (1-27-1853)
Chadwell, Thomas to Margret J. Grimes 12-25-1858
Chadwell, William to Martha Brown 6-8-1868 B
Chadwich, John Y.? to Malvina White 7-26-1847 (7-29-1847)
Chadwich?, Josiah to Temprance Presley 1-13-1847 (1-14-1847)
Chance, Evean to Nancy Isral 12-3-1859
Chance, John to Margha Susong 2-22-1853 (2-24-1853)
Chance, Samuel to Elizabeth Curry 1-30-1858
Chance, Stephen to Margaret Jones 2-13-1856
Chany?, John to Margret Renolos 7-20-1845
Chapman, John to Susanah Chadwell 5-29-1845 (6-8-1845)
Chapman, Joshua H. to Margarett Ellis 2-8-1844
Cheatham, John W. to Tempey A. Goin 10-30-1866 (10-31-1866)
Cheek, Granville? A. to Elisa Hurst 11-20-1839 (11-21-1839)
Cheek, James to Luiza Gilpson 1-30-1865
Cheek, Nelson to Nancy Sutton? 12-12-1847 (12-13-1847)
Cheek, Robert to Peggy Cox 9-22-1849
Chesnut, Frankliin to Cathrine Brigman 7-17-1848
Chick, James to Mary Cox 6-6-1856
Chick, Jefferson to Priscella Fulks 4-19-1843 (4-20-1843)
Chick, William to Mary Cox 2-5-1845 (2-6-1845)
Childers, Jesse to Permela C. Grubb 2-26-1855
Childs, James O. to Elisebeth J. Hosford 1-8-1855 (1-9-1855)
Chittam, Wesley to Malinda Neil 3-26-1850
Chittan, James to Nancy Peck 9-13-1848 (9-16-1848)
Chittum, William to Malissa Munday 8-5-1848 (8-8-1848)
Chumbly, William to Mary A. Wallen 6-21-1851
Chumley, Daniel to Matilda Briant 3-3-1855 (3-4-1855)
Chumley, William to Sarah Datsan? 10-6-1846 (9-5-1846?)
Cimen, James H. to Fanny Hurst 3-29-1854 (3-24?-1854)
Clap, Boston to L. Carrell 2-21-1853 (3-?-1853)
Clapp, Boston to Lidda Cornell 11-4-1854
Clapp, Boston to Nancy Flinchum 7-23-1855 (7-26-1855)
Clapp, John W. to Elizabeth Hughs 11-11-1851
Clapp, Thomas to Nancy Hughes 11-21-1854 (11-22-1854)
Clark, Elisha to Pheba James 10-29-1846 (11-1-1846)
Clark, Elisha to Sarah Bundon 11-14-1858
Clark, John to Lucy Poor 1-13-1868 (1-14-1868)
Clark, Joseph to Nervesta Morrison 3-16-1867 (3-17-1867)
Clark, Leftrage to Mary Shoemaker 3-12-1844
Clark, Riley to Emily Chumbly 1-1-1850
Clarkson, William to Martha Clarkson 7-30-1843
Clarrick?, Thomas to Susannah Doolin 11-26-1842
Claxton, Henry to Nancy Mannon? 2-21-1843
Clemmons, John to Nancy Ellison 7-22-1854 (7-24-1854)
Clevelan, William M. to Eliza A. Jennings 4-17-1850
Cline, D. C. to R. C. Herrell 12-18-1852 (12-28-1852)
Cline, D. T. to Wineford M. J. Moody 10-12-1857
Cline, Daniel C. to Elizabeth Posey 10-7-1855 (10-30-1855)
Cline, William E. to Mary Mason 3-28-1854 (3-30-1854)
Cline, William E. to Susan Parry 11-17-1855 (11-18-1855)
Cloud, B. F. to Elisabeth? M. Shultz 12-29-1845
Cloud, B. F. to Nancy Middleton 5-10-1850 (5-14-1850)
Cloud, Benjamin to Mariah Barnard 7-19-1842 (7-21-1842)
Cloud, Elnathan to Polly Ritter 1-30-1847 (1-?-1847)
Cloud, John to Adaline Campbell 4-5-1850 (4-7-1850)
Cloud, Prior I. to Emily A. T..... ? ? 1855 (? ?? 1855)
Cloud, Saml. to Peggy Bowyers 5-15-1839
Clouse, Adam to Temperance Eastridge? 4-18-1840 (4-25-1840)
Clouse, John to Sally Fletcher 10-17-1839
Clouse, William to Louvania C. Culbyhouse 2-1-1868 (2-2-1868)
Clouse, William to Rachel S. Wilson 7-9-1845 (7-11-1845)
Clouse, William to Susana E.? Culeyhouse 7-31-1867
Code, Samuel D. to Sarah Code 12-21-1841
Coffer, Thomas to Matilda Cox 7-24-1854
Cogar, J. H. to Rhoda Jane Cawood 10-30-1854 (11-1-1854)
Cole, B. H. M. to Mary E. Butcher 7-23-1849
Cole, George to Martha Baker 2-14-1842
Cole, Henry to Elizabeth Scritchfield 10-13-1851 (10-17-1851)
Cole, Henry to Ellander Hatfield 8-31-1859
Cole, Isreal to Frances Jane Louden 10-17-1848

Cole, Michal to Elizabeth Bundren 4-1-1851 (4-17-1851)
Coleman, Alvis P. to L. M. Riley 10-18-1853
Coleman, Henry F. to Matilda Parkey 2-15-1867
Coleman, Sterling G. to Elisabeth Jane Hobbs 7-10-1845 (7-13-1845)
Coles, Isral to Sarah A. Peck 6-13-1849 (6-14-1849)
Collens, William P. to Louisa Robinson 2-22-1854
Collensworth, Coventan to Jane Jones? 1-30-1839 (1-31-1839)
Collings, J. W. A. to Franky J. Tresley 11-24-1860
Collins, A. to L. Ingram 10-14-1857
Collins, Abadiah to Polly Smith 12-20-1839
Collins, Alexr. to Margaret Collins 5-13-1840
Collins, Anderson to Letty? Bray 11-27-1841 (11-28-1841)
Collins, Arthur to Silvey Bruer? 1-17-1848
Collins, Brison to Eliza Camier? 2-2-1843
Collins, Caloway to Ann Collins 6-16-1857 (6-17-1857)
Collins, Crispin to Prudy? Collins 1-19-1843 (1-22-1843)
Collins, Dowel to Nancy Johnson 8-4-1856 (8-28-1856)
Collins, Emanuel to M. Roden 3-31-1853 (4-3-1853)
Collins, Hamilton to Eliza A. Smith 1-29-1868
Collins, J. L. to M. J. Miller 3-31-1857
Collins, James to Josephin Ingram 4-5-1858
Collins, Jesse to Cintha Smith 8-17-1838 (8-18-1838)
Collins, John A. to Lucinda Weaver 2-6-1854 (2-14-1854)
Collins, John C. to Jincy C. Fowler 2-25-1856 (2-28-1856)
Collins, Joseph to Elander Mise 10-12-1854 (10-14-1854)
Collins, Leroy to Louiza M. Collins 11-8-1867
Collins, M. C. to Mary Capps 12-19-1865 (12-25-1865)
Collins, Nathan to Jemima? Mays 3-7-1843
Collins, Paschal to Nancy V. Denham 9-26-1866 (9-27-1866) B
Collins, Stewart to Catharine Colliins 3-8-1845 (3-9-1845)
Collins, Thos. to Berthena? Presley 1-29-1847 (1-31-1847)
Collins, Wayde to Nancy Gibson 10-11-1856
Collins, Wiat to F. Collins 4-20-1853 (4-21-1853)
Collinsworth, Abraham to Nevesta Parks 2-25-1855 (2-26-1855)
Collinsworth, Farwick to Lucy A. Rowlet 3-10-1851 (3-11-1851)
Collinsworth, William to E. Wallen 10-4-1853 (10-5-1853)
Collinsworth, Wm. F. to Louisa Roland 11-2-1850
Collons, J. L. to M. J. Miller 3-21-1857 (3-23-1857)
Color, Thomas to R. Gwin 7-29-1858
Colson, John C. to Catharin Smith 11-20-1843 (12-25-1843)
Colson?, Thomas to Manervay Bales 1-30-1850 (2-3-1850)
Colston, Henry to Mary Day 12-24-1853
Colwell, Samuel to Amelia York 4-19-1849
Combs, Bartholomew to Louiza Daniels 4-24-1867 (4-25-1867)
Combs, John to Manda M. Hamlin 9-7-1867 (9-8-1867)
Condrey, Thos. to Sarah Chumley 11-5-1855
Condry, H. to Elizabeth Richardson 1-10-1852
Conner, Benjamin F. to Martha Virginia Ely 11-3-1866
Connor, Jno. to Eliza Zeck 10-5-1838 (10-7-1838)
Consley, G. B. to L. G. Sharp 6-30-1865
Cook, Claiborne to Emely E. Cook 3-31-1866 (4-1-1866)
Cook, Joab to Sarah Smith 8-30-1855
Cook, M. A. to D. L. Jones 11-23-1846
Cook, Marquirus to Mary Ousley 5-23-1852
Cook, Morwrixes? to Elizabeth Hamelton 1-5-1854 (1-6-1854)
Cook, P. to N. L. Cook 12-24-1851 (12-25-1851)
Cook, Reuben M. to Nancy N. Whitaker 1-18-1848 (1-19-1848)
Cook, William A. to Elisabeth Dotson 1-15-1856 (1-16-1856)
Cook, William A. to Sarah Hamilton 2-15-1855
Cope, Anderson to Emeline Davault 1-11-1867 (1-13-1867)
Corbin, William W. to Mary Jane Sanders 10-9-1855 (10-10-1855)
Corman, John to Rebecca R. Moody 4-24-1851
Cornelson, Alexander to Mary M. Jones 12-2-1853 (12-3-1853)
Corrbin, George C. to Melvina Sanders 9-3-1859
Cosbey, William to Eliza Whitaker 3-18-1865 (3-22-1865)
Cosby, D. to E. Massengale 10-4-1852 (10-12-1852)
Cosby, John to Sarah Massingale 7-4-1859
Cosley, Shadrick to Mary Butcher 10-30-1858
Cotterell, Fountain to Ellender C. Anderson 8-17-1867 (8-20-1867)
Cotton, Nathan to Julian Mize 9-2-11867 B
Cottral, Presley to Elisabeth? Owens 8-24-1844 (8-25-1844)
Cottrell, Moses to Mary Woodson 2-15-1856
Cowan, C. H. to Elizabeth Murphey 3-3-1866 (3-6-1866)
Cowen, John to Elisabeth Grace 1-19-1856 (1-22-1856)
Cowen, S. A. to Abagal Townsley 11-18-1862 (11-20-1862)
Cox, Christian to Lucy Mason 9-18-1854 (9-19-1854)
Cox, Francis to Mary J. Keck 12-6-1854
Cox, Jas. to Elizlabeth Oaks 10-5-1865 (10-27-1865)
Cox, John to Neely Sharp 12-21-1846 (12-22-1846)
Cox, Newton A. to Martha J. Murphey 1-8-1868 (1-9-1868)
Cox, Thomas to Barthena Hill 1-10-1840 (1-12-1840)
Cox, W. R. to N. R. Goforth 10-20-1864 (10-23-1864)
Cox, Wiley to Mahala J. Cox 5-9-1868 (5-10-1868)
Cox, William to Elisabeth? Hoskins 2-18-1846 (3-5-1846)
Cox, William to Elizabeth Rector 12-4-1839
Cox, William to Luhany Thompson 12-31-1839 (1-1-1840)
Cox, William to Nancy Sullivan 10-21-1867 (10-23-1867)

Cox, William to Sarah Hail 9-16-1867 (9-17-1867)
Cox, Wm. to E. Hoskins 2-18-1846
Cox, Wm. to Jane Coleson 1-15-1859
Crabtree, Job B. to Martha Magard 6-18-1867 (6-20-1867)
Crabtree, John B. to Minerva Butcher 9-21-1855 (9-23-1855)
Crabtree, Joshua to Susan Tate 2-11-1853 (2-12-1853)
Crabtree, Joshway to Susan Tate 2-11-1854 (2-12-1854)
Crabtree, Richard D. to Ledna A. Hamilan? 4-18-1854 (4-21-1854)
Crabtree, Richard to Betsy Ann Grimes 8-16-1849 (8-17-1849)
Crabtree, Richard to Mary Balls 8-3-1846 (8-4-1846)
Crafford, Thos. to Mary Eads? 1-15-1847 (1-17-1847)
Craft, Stephen to Jane Roson 12-28-1867
Crawford, James D. to Tempe A. Surber 12-22-1854 (12-24-1854)
Crawford, Josiah to Sally Shofner 7-21-1849 (7-22-1849)
Cress, J. to Sarah Wells 4-12-1858
Cress, John S. to Sarah A. Snaveley 9-8-1867
Cress, Nathaniel to Nancy Vanderpool 1-25-1851 (2-2-1851)
Criger, Daniel to Jane Grosse 12-24-1866 (12-27-1866)
Crisp, John W. to Mary? Havely? 7-4-1845 (7-8-1845)
Crockett, Andrew J. to Sarah J. Browen 6-14-1856
Crockett, R. E. to S. McWilliams 8-31-1852 (9-4-1852)
Croft, Stephen to F. Drummons 5-30-1853 (5-31-1853)
Cromwell?, A. F. to M. A. Scofield? 11-19-1844 (11-21-1844)
Crouch, Hiram to Elizabeth J. Taylor 9-7-1857
Croushorn, Wm. H. to Sarah J. Davis 9-9-1856
Croxdale, W. to M. Peck 9-24-1852
Culvyhouse, Wm. S. to Hester A. Jones 8-18-1855
Cumming, Jas. to E. Nelson 5-24-1858 (5-25-1858)
Cuningham, Prior to M. A. Dobkins 6-29-1844
Cunningham, Calvin to Mary A. Richardson 8-19-1859
Cunningham, Francis to Nancy F. Eastes 11-12-1856
Cunningham, J. to Nancy Cardwell 12-23-1844
Cunningham, James P. to Orleana Jane Adams 10-8-1849
Cunningham, John to Silvena Burchet 8-30-1855
Cunningham, William to Martha Hicks 12-18-1843 (12-22-1843)
Cup, George W. to Catharin Wilson 12-7-1841
Cupp, A. Ham to Susan Scrichfield 8-2-1854
Cupp, Abram to Lousa Hopper 4-12-1852
Cupp, Aham to Frances J. Collins 1-14-1868
Cupp, Daniel to Nancy Parker 12-4-1845 (12-6-1845)
Cupp, Isaac to Mary Jane Daniel 4-5-1858 (4-11-1858)
Cupp, Jacob to Mary A. Falkner 12-22-1848
Cupp, Ransam to Sarah Lynch 7-8-1839 (7-14-1839)
Cupp, Ransom to C. Vance 3-7-1853 (3-8-1853)
Curtis, Monroe to Lundy Huff 12-24-1850
Dalton, C. J. to Charlottee Singletree 11-14-1856
Daniel, Georg to Feba Cuff 10-15-1864 (10-16-1864)
Daniel, John L. to Nancy M. Daniel 2-7-1855 (2-8-1855)
Daniel, William to Mary Liford 1-11-1847 (1-12-1847)
Davault, Henry C. to Louiza Carpenter 8-10-1868 (8-13-1868)
Davault, Martin V. to Martha Vance 4-9-1868 (4-10-1868)
Davault, Pryor to Marry Ward 9-16-1858
Davault, Pryor to Mary Bundren 3-28-1868
Davis, Andrew J. to Sarah Priddy 3-12-1852 (3-14?-1852)
Davis, Benjamin F. to Catherine E. Lewis 8-24-1853 (8-25-1853)
Davis, C. J. to M. A. Breeding 8-5-1858
Davis, Edmon to Ackey? Jones 4-15-1845
Davis, Ephriam to Lucinda Richie 12-14-1866 (12-16-1866) B
Davis, Henry to H. A. Buckanan 6-16-1852 (6-18-1852)
Davis, Heston to Lucinda Lewis 12-2-1845 (12-4-1845)
Davis, Isaac to Mary Harman 12-13-1854 (no return)
Davis, Jacob to Elen Pridda 5-7-1850
Davis, James H. to Belenda Crumbly 11-2-1838 (11-4-1838)
Davis, John A. to Sarah Buckhanan 8-8-1843
Davis, John W. to Margret J. Smith 3-16-1868 (3-28-1868)
Davis, John W. to Sarah England 8-22-1865 (8-24-1865)
Davis, Johnson to Emaley Lee 2-9-1847
Davis, Preston to Frances Hatfield 9-19-1867 (9-26-1867)
Davis, Preston to Frankey Hatfield 9-19-1867
Davis, Russel to Elisabeth Sowder 2-18-1856 (2-22-1856)
Davis, Thomas J. to Susan Mealer 3-18-1864 (3-19-1864)
Davis, Walter to Catharin Pearson 12-20-1842 (12-22-1842)
Davis, William G. to Virginia A. Grantum 3-16-1858
Day, C. M. to Sarah Ann McCrary 4-22-1856
Day, Charley M. to Hannah Guthery 12-15-1843 (12-17-1843)
Day, Enas to Nancy Dougherty 1-29-1845 (1-30-1845)
Day, Enas? to Mary Parker 4-22-1842
Day, Enos to Margaret Linsey 3-1-1858
Day, George to Rhoda Ford 11-29-1854 (11-30-1854)
Day, James A. to Sarah Epps 7-30-1867
Day, John E. to Mary C. Roddy 12-23-1855
Day, John to Martha Bartlett 9-2-1855
Day, Lewis to Polly Evans 1-11-1842 (1-23-1842)
Day, Noah to E. (Elvereen) Treese 9-1-1853
Day, Ransam? to Catharine Bowman 11-25-1843 (11-28-1843)
Dean, William E. to Mary Moore 3-7-1843
Dean, William P. to Rachel Salyers 1-15-1850

Deane, John W. to M. Shelvy 8-18-1859
Deans, Christopher to Eliza Toney 6-12-1847 (6-16-1847)
Deans, William to Patsy Bundren 1-12-1848 (2-2-1848)
Dearnal, Wm. to Elizabeth Roark 8-20-1838 (8-21-1838)
Deaton, Wm. H. to Almira A. Murphey 1-18-1868 (1-19-1868)
Debusk, James to Achsah J. Jones 12-15-1856
Deen, Robert to Matilda Hatfield 3-1-1856 (4-4-1856)
Denham, William to Belinda Anderson 12-31-1867 (1-2-1868) B
Denny, Andrew to Esther Brewer 12-10-1866
Denny, John to Nancy Bullard 2-20-1847 (2-21-1847)
Devault, George to Margret Wircick 10-6-1847
Dickinson, Benjamin to Matilda Garnett 6-21-1849
Dickinson, William to Margret Cauk? 9-16-1845
Dickson, George A. to Elizabeth Hale 7-1-1859
Dikes, James to Mary Holton 1-14-1850 (1-17-1850)
Dikson, William to Mary England 9-4-1865 (9-7-1865)
Divine, John W. to Ada M. Newlee 4-17-1865 (4-17-1865)
Dobbs, Ephraim to Mahala Dinkins 4-20-1850 (4-21-1850)
Dobbs, Jas. to Sally Brooks 8-5-1852 (8-5-1853?)
Dobbs, John to Mary Peck 3-9-1852 (no return)
Dobbs, Parrish to Nancy M. Poor 10-10-1860
Dobkins, Alexe to Mary Ann Neil 3-18-1839 (4-2-1839)
Dobkins, Solomon to Nancy Adams 10-10-1850 (8-11-1850)
Dodson, Jno. C. to Barthina Dobkins 10-19-1839
Dodson, Lasarus to Rebecca Freeman 6-21-1839 (6-29-1839)
Doiel, Henry to Nancy Croxdale? 2-24-1846 (2-26-1846)
Doriant, Lawson to E. J. Fortner 1-14-1853 (1-166-1853)
Dosier?, Joseph to Barthena Barnet 7-1-1844 (7-20-1844)
Dosset, Jas. to Phebe Lynch 2-11?-1840
Dosset, Wm. to B. Dougherty 1-12-1853 (1-13-1853)
Dotson, Henry to Tabitha Patterson 12-12-1865 (12-27-1865) B
Dotson, William to Mary J. Kulley? 12-19-1848 (12-25-1848)
Dougherty, Albert to Matilda Overton 10-4-1847 (10-7-1847)
Dougherty, Ezekiel to Mary Furry 8-30-1838 (9-4-1838)
Dowel, Calvin to Nancy Johnson 7-15-1847 (7-15-1847)
Dowell, William to W. Smith 10-22-1853
Doyby, Stokley to Ledia Woodard 4-13-1847 (4-15-1847)
Doye, John to Polly Western 12-18-1846 (12-20-1846)
Doyle, James to Louisanna Green 10-10-1849
Drake, James to Rachel Totten? 9-4-1842
Drummond, Stephen to Polly Cupp 3-24-1842
Drummonds, Anderson to Susannah Ritter 3-13-1848 (3-19-1848)
Drummons, Jacob M. to Sarah E. Collens 2-23-1867 (2-24-1867)
Dulin, McKenna to Eliza Kesterson 4-17-1850
Dulin, William to Elender Fielos? 7-25-1844
Dum?, Thos. to Elizabeth M. Brandscombe 1-30-1847
Dun, Madison to Cathrine Hunter 5-6-1867 (5-7-1867)
Duncan, Wm. M. to Arah J. Simmons 8-1-1867 (8-4-1867)
Dunkin?, Andrew J. to Mary Venable 6-26-1847 (5?-27-1847)
Dunn, Benj. to S. J. Miller 10-11-1852
Dunn, Henry A. to Elizabeth Anderson 10-28-1843 (11-23-1843)
Dunn, Madison to Prissella Branscomb (no date) (with 3-1858)
Dunn, Nathaniel to Malinda Jennings 4-26-1845 (4-27-1845)
Dunn, Wm. B. to Nancy Sharp 11-30-1844 (12-4-1844)
Dunn, Zephaniah to Nancy Ragan? 7-28-1848 (8-6-1848)
Dunsmore, D. R. to Virginia Breeding 1-13-1868 (1-16-1868)
Dunsmore, E. H. to L. Brewer 1-1-1854
Dunsmore, E. H. to Salla Breeden 1-1-1855 (no return)
Dunsmore, P. to B. A. Hysyes? 4-2-1850 (3?-3-1850)
Dunsmore, Preston to Beste A. Hodges 2-2-1850
Dunsmore, Wiley to Amanda Stone 10-18-1859
Duygns?, P. P. to Emily Wilson 4-13-1844
Dykes, Fidello to Betsey Ann Harrison 10-8-1855 (10-11-1855)
Dykes, Ryley to Lewrittey? Holton 2-17-1845
Dykes, William to Eliza Brasher 10-2-1843
Dykes, Wm. R. to Phebe Jane Rossin 10-1-1851 (10-5-1851)
Eads, Jesse to Anna Rector 1-23-1851 (1-24-1851)
Eads, Thomas to Matilda Braden 1-4-1854 (1-7-1854)
Eads?, Thos. to Sarah Weever? 8-17-1846 (8-18-1846)
Eapps, John to Margret Willcox 11-24-1860
Earls, Thomas to S.? Reed 5-3-1858
Early, Martin to Nancy M. Yeary 2-15-1867 (2-17-1867)
Eastes, Elisha to N. Collins 7-1-1853 (8-1-1853)
Eastes, John J. F. to Rebecca Friar 8-15-1849 (8-16-1849)
Eastes, Joseph to Priscilla Cox 5-24-1849
Eastrage, Isaac to Noomy? Powers 12-29-1841
Eastrage, John to Margaret Sierben 10-16-1856
Eastrage, Timothy to Lucy J. Furgason 11-23-1850
Eastrage, Timothy to Thurisa Ann Lane 11-4-1856 (11-6-1856)
Eastrage?, Noah to Millay Pridemore 12-30-1845 (1-4-1846)
Eastridge, Isaac to Matilda Stephens 4-23-1867 (5-19-1867)
Eastridge, John to E. Bruster 11-9-1852 (11-11-1852)
Edens, William to Mary Herrell 11-11-1855
Edmonson, Elijah to Patia Owens 8-20-1868 (8-21-1868)
Edmonston, J. H. to Martha Devenport 4-5-1854 (4-6-1854)
Edunsmore, William to Luritta Breeding 11-24-1855 (11-25-1855)
Edwards, Henry? to Sarah Williams 11-8-1844 (11-10-1844)

Edwards, James F. to Malenda McNeil 2-10-1842
Edwards, James to Sinda Hunter 8-27-1856
Edwards, Jeptha? to Sarah Matilda Goforth 4-23-1842 (5-16-1842)
Edwards, Joseph to Phoebe Sparks 3-13-1848 (3-14-1848)
Edwards, Martin J. to Dicy M. Lynch 12-4-1867 (12-5-1867)
Edwards, Owin to Fanny Smith 9-13-1843 (12-11-1843)
Edwards, Spencer to Mahala Cook 7-19-1866 (7-22-1866)
Edwards, Spencer? to Antamasa Odell 10-28-1841
Eldridge, Ransom to Martha Harris 9-5-1857
Eldridge, Wm. to Ruthy Owin 1-23-1844 (1-25-1844)
Eldrige, James to Masora Rowwlet 2-5-1853
Eldrige, King to Sarah Mink 11-21-1848
Elison, John to Sarah E. Jones 4-3-1854 (4-7-1854)
Elleron, McKindry to Manervy Lynch 9-15-1849 (10-2-1849)
Ellerson, J. to Nancy Whitaker 4-14-1857
Ellerson, Jeremiah to Minervy Lyons 9-17-1856
Ellis, Alexander to Margret McMahon 1-31-1857
Ellis, Danl. W. to Cathrine Gibson 12-22-1851
Ellis, J. H. to Margaret Furry 2-21-1840 (12-23-39)[sic]
Ellis, J. T. to Mary J. White 11-9-1864
Ellis, James H. to Margaret Furry 12-21-1839
Ellis, John to Hanah Fauche? 4-12-1846 (4-13-1846)
Ellis, Samwell P. to Meala E. Qualls 6-10-1854
Ellison, Asa M. to Selia C. Rogers 3-19-1867 (3-20-1867)
Ellison, George to Susan Ellison 12-6-1854 (12-7-1854)
Ellison, Henry to Elizabeth M. Odel 10-10-1851
Ellison, Hiram to Martha Clemmens 8-5-1857 (8-6-1857)
Ellison, Jeramiah to Sousan Lambert 11-23-1859
Ellison, Wiley to Nancy Carrell 8-21-1867 (8-24-1867)
Ellison, William to Sarah Carnell 8-28-1866 (9-30-1866)
Elrod, Rowen to Martha Davis 1-18-1847 (1-21-1847)
Ely, Anneas to Jane McCrary 5-27-1843 (5-28-1843)
Ely, Columbus to Nancy Riley 5-22-1865 (5-25-1865)
Ely, S. P. to Margaret Willing 6-5-1865 (6-6-1865)
Ely, Wm. to Susan Childers 5-29-1851 (5-20-1851)
Ely?, Elias to Jerusha Billingsly? 11-7-1845 (11-9-1845)
England, Alexander to Susanah Mays 2-22-1847 (3-4-1847)
England, Ezekial E. to Caroline Myers 7-25-1854 (7-27-1854)
England, I.? to L.? Norvell 1-16-1852
England, J. M. to Lucy A. Graham 1-31-1866
England, James A. to Nancy Williams 12-9-1867 (12-11-1867)
England, Jas. C. to Minerva Soard 9-20-1865 (9-21-1865)
England, Pleasant to Martha Quarles 7-12-1855
England, Thomas to Rachel Fergerson 9-9-1859
England, William to Lydia Ann Lambert 10-11-1843 (10-14-1843)
Epison, Thos. to Elizabeth Rowe 1-31-1840 (2-6-1840)
Epperson, John W. to Martha Allen 1-21-1867 (1-22-1867)
Epperson, William C. to Nancy L. Epperon? 10-16-1863
Epperson, William T. to Linda Ann Jones 9-30-1854
Epperson, Wm. C. to Nancy L. Hopson 10-14-1853 (10-16-1853)
Eppes, Edward E. to Catharine L. Fugate 11-22-1866
Epps, George to Margaret Southern 11-20-1855 (11-22-1855)
Epps, William to Lucy Janes? Evans 5-2-1843
Epps, William to Matilda Dickinson 2-2-1859
Erles, Nathaniel to Bisa Hatfield 3-21-1851 (3-22-1851)
Erls, Wm. to Elizabeth Maloney 5-23-1866
Estep, Jacob W. to Mourning E. Daniel 11-6-1866 (11-8-1866)
Estes, Lazarous to Elizabeth Vanoy 2-6-1867
Estice, David to Mary Householder 1-2-1844
Estice, Elisha to Mariah Jones 10-17-1843 (10-18-1843)
Estrage, M. to W. A. Ausmus 11-10-1864
Evans, Alfred to Sarah McNew 6-23-1847 (6-22?-1847)
Evans, George to Eliza Day 1-30-1844 (2-1-1844)
Evans, Henry to Luritta Willis 9-24-1854
Evans, J. L. to M. V. Sewell 6-16-1852 (6-17-1852)
Evans, John to Elizabeth Mason 2-5-1852
Evans, John to Malasha Hurst 7-15-1849
Evans, Lafayette to Sarah Huff 11-11-1848
Evans, Nelson to Elisabeth? Hurst 11-7-1845 (11-9-1845)
Evans, Newton A. to Elizabeth J. Crockett 3-7-1848
Evans, Ricahrd T. to H. A. Corban 6-18-1857
Evans, Thomas to Nancy Day 4-20-1850 (4-21-1850)
Evans, Tipton to Linda R. Fugate 1-30-1850
Eversal?, John to Nancy Ann Duff? 9-30-1846
Falkner, John to Lucinda Hollan 1-10-1849 (1-14-1849)
Farby?, David to Elisabeth? Hopkins 8-14-1846 (8-16-1846)
Farmer, Aquillah? to Emaley? Lathan? 6-29-1846
Farmer, James to Sarah Arwine 11-23-1859
Farris?, Joseph to Catharin J. Hopkins 5-16-1842 (5-17-1842)
Fawbush, Lewis to Neppy Dickinson 9-5-1867 B
Fergerson, Anderson to Malissa J. Shelby 2-1-1868 (2-2-1868)
Fernay?, James F. to Perlina Cain 1-21-1844
Fields, Abner to Julia Morris 1-31-1846
Fields, Edwards to Orlena Hix? 9-11-1849 (9-17-1849)
Fields, James D. to Rhoda Fullington 2-21-1852
Fields?, George to Polly Willis 11-2-1846 (12-20-1846)
Fips, Peter to Julia A. Lockwood 4-29-1846 (4-30-1846)

Flecher?, John to Ivey Ann Lanham 12-21-1846 (12-24-1846)
Flemming, Charles to Elizabeth Lovel 3-31-1855 (4-7-1855)
Flemming?, Marcus to Mary Owsley 9-1-1843 (10-2-1843)
Fletcher, James to Rachel M. Monday 7-25-1868
Fonel, Wesley to Melvina Holton 4-28-1865 (5-1-1865)
Forber, George to Loucy Southern 11-15-1839
Ford, Green B. W. to Nancy Lynch 6-15-1839 (6-?-1839)
Ford, Greenberry to Catharine Thompson 1-14-1838
Ford, Hyram to Cathrine Carrell 4-15-1860
Ford, Isaac N. to Catharine M. Mountain 11-28-1853 (12-1-1854?)
Ford, Isaac to Mary Day 1-5-1863 (1-6-1863)
Ford, James T. to Margret K. Moody 1-10-1848 (1-13-1848)
Ford, John to Nancy Jane Pike 4-29-1867
Ford, William B. to ____ Smith 12-16-1847 (12-19-1847)
Forde, Richard B. to Elizabeth R. Mountain 9-24-1855
Fordy?, James to Emily C. Evans 8-22-1844
Forgerson, Eligah to Nancy W. Mayers 5-25-1858 (5-31-1858)
Forgerson, James to Sarah Bussel 10-15-1853 (10-16-1853)
Forgerson, John to Lavina Semmonds 9-12-1839
Fortner, Elisha to Sarah Day 12-4-1858
Fortner, Isah M. to Nancy M. Hollinsworth 9-17-1858 (9-21-1858)
Fortner, Jas. to Nancy Goins 9-1-1852 (9-2-1852)
Fortner, Jesse to Elizabeth Isaacks 1-29-1839
Fortner, Reason M. to Mary E. Fortner (was Evans) no dates (before 1869)
Fortner, S. to O. Holton 8-11-1853 (8-14-1853)
Fortner, Solomon to O. Holton 7-11-1853
Fostnez?, Preston to Rachael Johnson 8-16-1841
Fox, A. to M. Fox 5-1-1858
Frasher, L. W. to N. Wells 10-8-1857
Freeman, Hu L. to Pheoba England 3-1-1852
Freeman, Hugh L. to Sarah J. Day 10-4-1866
Friar, Geo. H. to Zhynettie Brooks 1-24-1852
Friar, Henry H. to Minervy J. McVay 1-19-1867 (1-20-1867)
Friar, Thos. to Martha J. Runnions 2-3-1848 (2-4-1848)
Friar, Timothy to Mary Whiteaker 8-3-1843
Friar, Z. to Harriet Roberts 8-21-1859
Frior, George to Nancy E. Monday 2-3-1851 (2-5-1851)
Fritts, Henry to Sarah Burchett 11-3-1845 (11-19-1845)
Frost, William S. to Vina J. Baker 9-11-1846 (9-13-1846)
Fudington, J. to Febe C. England 3-31-1857
Fugate, Eli to Lelitha Wolven 1-31-1842 (2-1-1842)
Fugate, Hendly? to Rebecco Parkey 4-18-1843 (4-20-1843)
Fugate, John to Elizabeth Caly 7-3-1865 (7-6-1865)
Fugate, John to Mary E. Overton 2-5-1851 (2-6-1851)
Fugate, Lee to Mildred Denham 1-31-1867 B
Fugate, Martain to Lucinda Martain 11-25-1856 (11-27-1856)
Fugate, Wiley to Catharine Coleman 2-12-1867 B
Fulkerson, Samuel to Rebecca Woodson 3-18-1868 (3-19-1868) B
Fulks, David to Nancy Woatan? 10-17-1843 (10-18-1843)
Fullington, David to Polly Townsley 3-1-1856 (3-2-1856)
Fullington, Elisha to Malilsa Branond 8-29-1851 (9-2-1851)
Fulp, A. to E. Fulp 7-30-1852 (8-1-1852)
Fulp, John to Mary J. Gooman 11-10-1864 (11-29-1864)
Fulp, Wm. G. to Maria Kelley 11-20-1851
Fulps, Solomon to Franky Moore 7-31-1852 (8-2-1852)
Fulps, Volentine to Ann Beeler 7-7-1851 (7-13-1851)
Fulta, Francis M. to Malinda Murphey 10-2-1856 (10-3-1856)
Fulth, H. W. to Mary H. Simons 12-5-1864 (12-6-1864)
Fults, Fredrick to Emaley Nunn? 7-25-1846
Fults, John to Malissa Murphey 11-15-1846
Fultze, John to Emly Runions 3-5-1865
Furry, Hiram to Levisa Maurae 8-17-1842
Furry, Randolph to Mary Welch 4-6-1838 (4-7-1838)
Gains, William to Elizabeth Bunch 8-25-1843 (8-27-1843)
Gallion, Franklin to Rachel Crigor 4-27-1854 (5-7-1854)
Galyon, B. F. to Malese? Breeding 1-5-1855 (1-3?-1855)
Gambral, Martin to Sarah Walland 8-20-1851
Garland, J. to M. Bussle 11-10-1852 (11-12-1852)
Garland, Samuel to Pheba Peck 2-20-1862 (2-24-1862)
Garland, Wiley F. to Sarah A. Shransbule 3-12-1855 (3-13-1855)
Garland?, Lewis to Rebecker? Lockoral? 9-16-1844
Garlin, Wiley to Sarah E. Hurst 6-2-1859
Garrett, John D. to Jemima Davenport 7-29-1852
Garrett, Robert to Nancy Spurlock 9-18-1850
Garrett, William to M. J. Devenport 5-22-1853
Garrison, Jacob to Sarah Hurst 1-20-1851 (1-23-1851)
Gase, Stephen to Mary A. Burch 9-17-1853 (9-18-1853)
Geabolf?, Jesse J. to Prissilla Evans 7-24-1839 (7-28-1839)
Gentry, Isaac to Margret Burk 4-4-1859
Gibbs, Carroll to Martha Owens 12-21-1845 (12-23-1845)
Gibbs, James B. to R. Madux 4-26-1859
Gibbs, Wm. to Barbery Sutton 8-10-1844 (8-12-1844)
Gibert?, William to Mary Ann Jackson 3-26-1842
Gibson, Drury D. to Claricey? Knight 1-28-1847
Gibson, Ewing to Frances Reed 9-2-1853
Gibson, Hillary to Mary Ann Guthrie 2-25-1856 (2-28-1856)
Gibson, Isaac to Cathrine Biggs 6-17-1850
Gibson, Isom to Elizabeth J. Burch 1-1-1844 (1-2-1844)
Gibson, James J. to Malinda Persifield 3-9-1867 (3-10-1867)
Gibson, James to Mary Province 9-23-1847
Gibson, John to Pheoba Dobbs 4-30-1852 (no return)
Gibson, Thomas to Celia Roberts 7-21-1856 (7-22-1856)
Gibson, Thomas to Margret McNeil 1-5-1859
Gibson, William F. to Elizabeth Dutton 4-1-1844
Gibson, William R. to Mary Catterell? 3-18-1843 (3-21-1843)
Gibson, Zack S. to Margaret E. Miller 11-2-1851
Gibson?, Saviour? to Milley Willis 12-29-1842
Gilbert, D. I. to Nancy Ann Rice 1-15-1845 (1-17-1845)
Gilbert, Thomas to Lutissia Moore 2-21-1865
Gilbert, Thos. to Malvina Edwards 11-24-1847
Gillenwater, W. S. to Mar Parrott? 2-21-1846
Gipson, Mastin to Dosha Scott 12-23-1846 (12-24-1846)
Givens, Alexander to N. Evans 5-22-1853
Givin, George to Sally Ferrell 2-16-1839 (2-17-1839)
Glanden, Silas to Sarah Williams 9-7-1839 (9-8-1839)
Glenn, Robert to Margaret Weir 10-26-1843
Goforth, James to Sarah Jane Jones 9-15-1842
Goforth, Preston C. to Louisa Brogain 12-28-1842 (1-4-1843)
Goforth, Preston C. to Malinda? Hunucutt? 7-23-1845 (7-24-1845)
Goin, Andrew J. to Martha J. Goin 5-4-1867
Goin, C. to M. A. Lewis 1-20-1862 (1-24-1862)
Goin, Caleb to Elizabeth A. McVay 1-28-1864
Goin, Charles to Matilda Southern 3-12-1868 B
Goin, Henry to Sarah Ann Jackson 9-8-1868 (9-10-1868) B
Goin, James K. to Elizabeth A. McVay 12-6-1865 (12-7-1865)
Goin, John B. to Louiza M. E. Fortner 10-21-1867 (10-24-1867)
Goin, John to Fanny Raney 10-27-1859
Goin, John to Jane Keck 6-30-1863
Goin, M. C. to Winna R. Sharp 9-3-1855
Goin, Matthew to Sarah Buchanan 3-12-1868 B
Goin, Phillip to Ellender Bollinger 9-18-1866 (9-20-1866)
Goin, Thomas J. to Elizabeth Frith 7-17-1868 (7-25-1868)
Goin, Thomas to Martha J. Johnson 2-9-1859
Goin, Wm. to Mary J. Soweler 11-6-1865
Going, John L. to Cass? Ann Going 7-27-1843 (7-30-1843)
Goins, D. to S. Rosan 1-10-1852 (1-1?-1852)
Goins, Eli to Rachel Edwards 8-8-1849 (8-9-1849)
Goins, John to Elizabeth Goins 4-4-1851 (4-30-1851)
Goins, Madison to Sophia Jane Webb 2-19-1855 (2-22-1855)
Goins, Wilson to Mildred Killion 1-15-1857
Good, Lafayett to Martha Johnson 10-7-1867 (10-8-1867)
Gooden, Ezekiel to Tempy? A. Cain 9-18-1842
Goodin, Ezekiel to Licha? Falkner 3-26-1848
Goodman, Malin to Louisa E. Wooderd 2-5-1856 (2-14-1856)
Goss, William to Marthy Wellman 5-19-1865
Gourley, Robert J. to Elizabeth Harrell 7-10-1858
Gowens, Uriah to Rebeca Goodman 4-7-1854 (4-13-1854)
Gowin, Benjamin F. to Mary Lake 11-28-1853
Gowin, Isaac to Mary Vanoy 12-19-1839 (12-22-1839)
Gowin, Nelson to Polly Putchard? 10-8-1839 (10-10-1839)
Gowin, Sturling to Mary Keck 10-2-1839
Gowins?, Urior? to Nancy Gowins 9-26-1846 (9-27-1846)
Gowns, Ralph to Mary A. Goodman 5-11-1854
Grabill, Isaac to Nancy Russell 10-25-1848 (10-26-1848)
Graham, Francis to Jucy White 7-16-1855 (7-19-1855)
Graham, Henry H. J. T. to Mary Garrett 2-27-1868 B
Graham, Hugh to Rachel Hopper 12-9-1847
Graham, Lafayette to Eliza Burk 1-16-1855 (1-17-1855)
Graham, William to Polly Sweet 12-4-1847 (12-5-1847)
Graham, Wm. to Margaret Clark 5-21-1855
Grammer?, John W. to Sarah E. Littral 7-22-1847 (7-25-1847)
Grant?, E. S. to Elizebeth Chumley 12-6-1858
Graves, Caloway to Souson Hunter 9-6-1858
Graves, Hugh H. to Elizabeth Renols 12-14-1850 (12-31-1850)
Graves, Jesse to Serrena Cain 11-26-1867 (11-28-1867)
Graves, John to Lucindy Hurst 5-23-1840
Graves, John to ____ Willson 10-7-1844 (10-13-1844)
Graves, Peter to E. E. White 12-6-1851 (12-28-1851)
Graves, Sebastian to Mary Moyers 3-17-1851 (3-18-1851)
Graves, Wm. to B. Lynch 5-26-1858
Gray, John E. R. to Rachael Williams 1-13-1839
Gray, W. A. to Anna Clapp 1-26-1859
Grayson, Thos. M. to Cristeena Davis 1-23-1857
Green, Andrew J. to Rachel Serber 4-15-1857
Green, James D. to Lucy Ann Lanham 12-2-1843 (12-3-1843)
Green, John to Mohaby? Goins 4-14-1845 (4-4?-1845)
Green, John to Susannah Shelby 1-17-1844 (1-18-1844)
Green, William to Mary Jane Lanham 8-14-1838 (8-16-1838)
Greenlee, Joseph to M. A. Young 9-2-1859
Greenlee, Saml. J. to Sarah Stansbury 11-13-1865 (11-27-1865)
Greer, Calaway to Angeline Burchfield 2-13-1867 (2-14-1867)
Greer, James K. to Sarah A. Kelley 6-6-1868 (6-7-1868)
Greer, Robert to Thursa Ann Evans 10-18-1845 (10-12?-1845)
Greer, W. W. to Nancy Ousley 2-22-1867 (2-23-1867)

Greer, W. W. to Sarah Johnston 11-10-1854 (11-12-1854)
Greer, Washington to Mary Roland 12-29-1855 (1-1-1856)
Greer, Wm. jr. to Martha Guy 12-22-1863 (12-24-1863)
Gregery, John to Eliza A. Lewis 8-24-1859
Gregory, Elijah to Nancy Ragan? 8-1-1848 (8-18-1848)
Griffin, James F. to Elizabeth Minton 7-11-1868 (7-15-1868)
Griffin, Joseph to Martha M. Turner 12-3-1867
Grimes, Henry to Martha Short 9-13-1852 (9-14-1852)
Grimes, Isaac A. to Thursy England 9-5-1838
Grimes, James to Mary Pridemore 10-31-1844 (11-3-1844)
Grimes, James to Matilda Leford 9-29-1841 (9-30-1841)
Grimes, Jno. to Cathrine Christa 5-4-1852 (5-6-1852)
Grimes, John M. to Emily Rose 9-11-1847
Grimes, John to E. Hatfield 6-4-1845 (6-5-1845)
Grimes, Lewis C. to Sela Sharp 12-4-1854 (12-5-1854)
Groseclose?, Adam to Sophia Snavely 4-6-1840 (4-8-1840)
Grub, John to Sidna Walker 2-10-1857
Grubb, Thomas to Margret Chumley 11-23-1859
Grubb, Jno. to Emiline? Sweet 4-10-1845
Guim?, Isaac to Lousa Marie? Willis 1-21-1849 (1-23-1849)
Guthry, William to Rebecca Lickliter 5-18-1839 (5-19-1839)
Guy, James to Nancy Duncan 9-1-1866 (9-2-1866)
Guy, John to Margart Fullington 1-22-1856
Guy, William to Martha Bammell 7-27-1865 (8-6-1865)
Guy, Wilson to Boni Hill 9-12-1865
Hacker, John to Lety Smith 9-22-1849 (10-5-1849)
Hacker, William to Mary A. Goin 2-23-1865 (2-26-1865)
Hale, George to Ann Cheek 12-24-1855 (12-25-1855)
Hale, James to Sarah J. Cox 9-25-1853
Haley, John to Sarah Burk 1-8-1857
Hall, Elisha to Jane Goins 9-29-1847
Hall, George to Louiza Williams 11-11-1867
Hall, Hugh to Eliza Nunn 11-14-1857
Hall, John W. to Martha Roberts 9-23-1847
Hall, Robert H. to Sarah E. Wilson 7-18-1857 (7-22-1857)
Hall, Thos. to Martha J. Leath 7-30-1856
Hamblin, Daunt to Elizabeth Davis 11-11-1856 (11-16-1856)
Hamblin, Leroy to Juda Hamblin 4-21-1845? (4-23-1846)
Hamblin, R. to Anna Bowman 2-12-1852 (3-4-1852)
Hamelton, G. W. to Elisabeth? Lambert 12-3-1845
Hamelton, George to Julia Ann Cadle 7-23-1848 (7-27-1848)
Hamelton, Joshua to Elzera Collensworth 10-27-1838 (10-29-1838)
Hamelton, Wm. to Nancy Hamelton 4-26-1839 (4-30-1839)
Hamilton, Andrew J. to Elizabeth Green 12-29-1866 (1-1-1867)
Hamilton, James C. to Martha A. Day 9-9-1867 (11-7-1867)
Hamilton, Tilmon A. to Catharine R. Scott 10-20-1866 (10-28-1866)
Hammack, Isaac to Charity Hopper 6-11-1856 (6-14-1856)
Hammock, Sterling to Mary Jourden 10-26-1843
Hammon, Moab? to Elizabeth Seal 5-5-1842 (7-10-1842)
Hamons, William to Elender Hamons 1-8-1850
Hampton, Samuel to Eliza Barnes 4-13-1868 (4-16-1868)
Hanes, Hugh to Mary McVay 7-28-1854
Hansard, Abner C. to Mary A. H. Marcum 10-11-1842
Hansard, Joseph K. to Florintha J. Burchfield 6-15-1866 (6-21-1866)
Hansard, Wm. B. to E. [Elizabeth] Lane 4-30-1853 (5-1-1853)
Harden, Wm. to Monday Needham 9-10-1855 (9-27-1855)
Hargraves, Watesel to Elizabeth Redrick 5-20-1868 (5-22-1868)
Harlis, James to Susan Mahane? 6-15-1847 (6-17-1847)
Harmon, Andrew J. to Benny Branscomb 11-13-1843 (11-16-1843)
Harmon, Dulany P. to Catharine Simmons 5-2-1867 (5-3-1867)
Harmon, J. M. to Nancy A. Simons 7-18-1865 (7-20-1865)
Harmon, Thos. A. to Catherine Hunsford 1-3-1866 (1-4-1866)
Harmon, Wm. L. to Martha E. Cloud 7-19-1855
Harp, James to Nancy Tate 7-15-1850
Harp, Jesse to Alendor P. Thomas 10-31-1856 (11-6-1856)
Harp, Joseph to Elizabeth Davis 4-29-1858
Harp, Nelson to Hoday? M. Day 11-25-1858
Harp, William A. to Harriett M. Bowman 9-29-1867
Harpe, Benager to Elizabeth Sowder 4-18-1848 (4-19-1848)
Harper, James L. to Sarah Laffoon 7-1-1853
Harper, James L. to Sarah Laffoon 8-1-1853 (8-2-1853)
Harper, John to Manda Birdine 12-25-1866 (12-27-1866) B
Harper, Lenard G. to Louisa Carpenter 11 5 1848
Harper, Richard H. to Frankey Hopper 5-19-1849 (5-24-1849)
Harper, Richard to Milley McVay 4-7-1848
Harper, Wm. H. to H. Wells 9-17-1853 (9-18-1853)
Harral, A. to B. Sword 10-20-1857
Harrel, Noah to Nancy E. Green 3-14-1850 (3-17-1850)
Harrell, A. W. to Malinda L.? Bartlett 1-1-1849 (1-5-1849)
Harrell, Alexander to Lidda Presly 5-20-1846 (5-21-1846)
Harrell, G. W. to Nancy Baker 9-10-1858
Harrell, James C. to Eliza Hurst 3-17-1859 (3-23-1859)
Harrell, Montgumry to Mary E. Reece 11-28-1859
Harrell, Richard to Manday Hurst 8-25-1859
Harrell, Robert to Mahala Hurst 1-5-1850 (1-6-1850)
Harrell, Sylvester to Lugana Nunn 7-20-1848
Harrell, William L. to Mary Brooks 1-1-1868 (1-3-1868)

Harris, Martin to Rhoda Dougherty 8-303-1839 (8-20-1839)
Harris, R. F. to Jane Cowan 10-6-1857
Harris, S. E. to M. B. Yeary 12-5-1851
Harris, Samuel to H. (Hanah) Lawson 7-12-1853 (7-13-1853)
Harris, Samuel to Sela Geoge 9-27-1850
Harris, William to Mary Bolton 12-17-1856 (12-21-1856)
Harris, Wm. P. to E. J. Camin? 1-27-1846 (1-28-1846)
Harrison, V. to E. A. Rowson 12-7-1857
Harrison, Werley to Eliza A. Rosan 3-5-1856 (3-9-1856)
Harry, Henry F. to Minervy J. Bartley 2-21-1843 (2-28-1843)
Harvey, John to Louiza Hodges 7-25-1867 (7-28-1867)
Harvey, Zoe to Barbery Collins 7-2-1856
Harvy, Thomas to Matilda Lakins 7-26-1856
Hase, William to Sarah A. Brooks 7-9-1849 (7-10-1849)
Hash, Dunkin to Maranda Howell 10-29-1858
Haskins, Benjamin F. to Hester A. Buchanan 1-7-1851
Hatchell, William A. to Mary Wright 2-19-1868 (2-20-1868)
Hatfield, Adam to Mary Davis 10-7-1839 (10-13-1839)
Hatfield, Andrew to Rachel Loson 9-2-1850 (9-5-1850)
Hatfield, E. W. to Catharine Minton 7-13-1865 (7-12-1865)
Hatfield, Francis M. to Lucinda Kestrson 9-23-1854 (9-27-1854)
Hatfield, Greenberry to Cathrine Hatfield 8-31-1852 (9-1-1852)
Hatfield, Henry to Emily Davis 11-13-1841 (11-21-1841)
Hatfield, Henry to Sarah Davis 1-7-1867 (2-24-1867)
Hatfield, Joseph to Elizabeth Standsford 1-1-1868
Hatfield, Lynch to Hella Hatfield 9-10-1852
Hatfield, Lynch to Jane Dodson 2-24-1840 (2-27-1840)
Hatfield, Lynch to Sarah Brooks 12-17-1867 (12-19-1867)
Hatfield, Moses to Sarah Grimes 6-17-1847 (6-20-1847)
Hatfield, Ralph to Elizabeth Ann Worrick 1-25-1843 (1-26-1843)
Hatfield, Thomas to Nancy J. Upton 7-4-1850 (7-6-1850)
Hatfield, William to Sallie Morgan 5-16-1868
Hatfield?, Walter? to Polly Hurst 4-10-1845
Havely?, Charles H. to Louisa Parker? 8-11-1846
Havlaen?, Nathaniel S. to Sarah M. Poindexter 4-18-1849
Hawkins, Eli to Sarah Burns 7-1-1844
Hayes, Green Berry to Elizabeth Shelton 10-19-1867 (10-20-1867)
Haynes, H. to Caroline Davis 7-31-1852 (8-1-1852)
Haynes, John to S. J. Patten 10-29-1852
Hayse, Calvin to Nancy Vermillion 1-10-1853 (1-11-1853)
Hayse, Rice to Sarah Fultz 4-7-1854
Hayse, William R. to Adaline Devault 2-5-1849 (2-22-1849)
Hazs, Jos. to S. McAnnaly? 2-15-1845
Hedrick, Elijah to Susan Hall 4-12-1855 (4-13-1855)
Heller, Hiram to Nancy Herron 10-9-1866 (10-19-1866)
Hellon?, Arnold? to Nancy? Turnbull 6-3-1844 (6-20-1844)
Hellon?, Peter to Emaline Helton? 1-14-1849 (1-18-1849)
Helton, Silas to Elizabeth Lay 12-22-1865 (12-24-1865)
Helton?, Mathew A. to Nancy Thacker 11-18-1846 (11-26-1846)
Henderson, Christian to Emelia Parton 1-17-1839 (2-9-1839)
Henderson, Thos. to Emly Hurst 4-11-1854
Henderson, William to Eliza Bagwell 1-14-1856 (1-15-1856)
Hendrick, Fealix to S. A. Thacker 7-19-1853
Hendricks, F. to S. A. Thacker 7-19-1853
Henson, Robert to Barbara Hunter 10-19-1851
Hepsher, Henry to Angelina Miller 2-7-1851 (2-27-1851)
Hermen?, James to Susan Vaughn 2-17-1847 (2-18-1847)
Hernen?, Baley to Roddy? Baley 11-29-1846 (11-29-1846)
Herrall, James C. to Rachel Herrall 1-28-1843 (1-29-1843) *
Herrell, Anderson W. to Eliza Cunningham 6-26-1847 (6-26-1847)
Herrell, Montgomery to Pertilly? Brooks 12-3-1846
Hester, Jackson to Emeline Stillwell 10-25-1866 (10-25-1866)
Hetton, Alson? to Carolinle Helton 1-25-1843 (1-26-1843)
Hickle, John to Lousa Harrel 6-25-1853 (7-7-1853)
Hicks, James M. to Lucy Green 7-4-1849 (7-10-1849)
Hicks, John to Jane Prisley? 8-3-1844 (8-5-1844)
Hicks, John to Manerva Brooks 12-13-1865 (12-14-1865)
Hicks, John to Sally Large 8-3-1846
Hicks, R. to L. J. Poore 2-15-1858 (3-11-1858)
Hicks, Robert to L. J. Poor 2-15-1858 (3-11-1858)
Higgins, James to Elizabeth Cadle 7-27-1853 (7-28-1853)
Hill, Alexander to Elisabeth? Brooks 2-15-1848
Hill, David to Mary Jane Manon 5-26-1855
Hill, Edward N. to Julia A. Brown 9-24-1844
Hill, Elvis to Ann Hopper 12-9-1847 (12-14-1847)
Hill, Enoch to Elizabeth Bussell 11-12-1851 (11-16-1851)
Hill, Geoge to Nancy Presley 11-22-1855
Hill, Haisel? to Permelia? Sharp 8-16-1847 (8-26-1847)
Hill, Mariel to Louisa Day 1-11-1847
Hill, Zachariah T. to Susan C. Hill 8-13-1868
Hinshilder?, Matthias? to Nancy Marcu 11-23-1843 (6-10-1844)
Hipsher, Arnal to Mary Hall 10-18-1854 (10-19-18540)
Hobbs, John A. to Francis Wolf 8-9-1857
Hobbs, Solomon D. to Selina Marcum 2-5-1851 (2-7-1851)
Hodge, James C. to Elizabeth Davis 10-3-1857
Hodge, Wm. to Mariah Cloud 10-8-1844 (10-10-1844)
Hodges, Elbert S. to Sarah Jane Tucker 4-9-1851 (4-10-1841)

Hodges, Elijah to Elisabeth Hodges 12-16-1847
Hodges, Fielding? to Teney? Shelton 1-1-1848 (1-5-1848)
Hodges, Granville to Margaret Jennings 7-31-1857
Hodges, Henry C. to Manervy Devault 8-23-1849
Hodges, James to Ann Epperson 4-5-1855
Hodges, John to Alley Cuningham 3-26-184 (3-28-1849)
Hodges, Pleasant M. to Orleana Cloud 12-30-1848
Hodges, Preston to Margret Eppes 1-25-1866 B
Hodges, William to Mahala Hurst 3-27-1868
Hodges, Wm. B. to Lucy Shoemate 7-15-1856
Holden, W. to D. Etter 2-2-1848 (2-3-1848)
Holden, Washington to Deaner Etten 1-2-1846
Hollan, Elisha to Eliza Oliver 9-26-1848 (9-27-1848)
Holland, Mageror to Nancey Willis 1-25-1859
Holland, William to Elizabeth Earles 8-30-1854 (8-31-1854)
Hollensworth, Madison to Mahala Maddy 9-12-1838 (9-18-1838)
Holliway, Isaac to Martha Ausmus 8-3-1868 (8-27-1868)
Holt, Jackson to Minervy Trease 9-22-1857
Holt, Kindruk? to Polley? Sumpter 2-15-1845 (2-20-1845)
Honeycut, Austin to Rebecca Robinson 5-14-1839
Honeycutt, James M. to Nancy Woodward 3-4-1850
Honeycutt, Moses to Hannah Beeler 2-15-1842 (2-20-1842)
Hood, John to M. J. Priddy 7-27-1852
Hooker, J. C. to Susan Hopper 8-30-1865
Hooper, Daniel to Rachel Hunter 9-25-1850 (9-26-1850)
Hooper, Jessee to Jane Pall 2-15-1838
Hooper, Spenser to S. Wagener 8-9-1858
Hooper, Wilbourne to Nancy Rutledge 5-2-1850
Hopkins, Arthor? to Nancy Jones 5-9-1844 (5-11-1844)
Hopkins, Isaac to Nancy Ann Pew 4-22-1843 (4-30-1843)
Hopkins, J. R. to Elisa? Hopkins 9-27-1845
Hopkins, James M. to Rebecca Baker 12-8-1843 (12-9-1843)
Hopkins, Jobies? to Juda Bishop 6-25-1846 (6-28-1846)
Hopkins, N. to Malinda Jones 8-28-1846
Hopkins, Stephen to ----- Maniak 11-15-1839
Hopkins, Stuphin? to Mary Ann Hopkins 6-7-1843
Hopper, Alferd to Elizabeth A. McBee 3-22-1853 (3-24-1853)
Hopper, Benjamin F. to Anna Edwards 3-8-1867 (3-30-1867)
Hopper, C. J. to Monerva Keck 9-4-1865 (9-5-1865)
Hopper, David to Malinda Dunn 9-26-1855 (9-30-1855)
Hopper, Henry to Josephen Seals 7-3-1868 (7-4-1868)
Hopper, Jeremiah to Abigail? Fulps 5-22-1839 (5-24-1839)
Hopper, Jesse to Sarah Flinchum 1-24-1867
Hopper, Silas to Jane Reason 12-13-1865 (12-14-1865)
Hopper?, Jesse to Eliza Wells 8-2-1845 (8-3-1845)
Hopson, Daniel to C. Carter 3-25-1853 (3-26 1853)
Hopson, David R. to Eliza Rosebalm 5-17-1851 (6-1-1851)
Hopson, Harid? to Sarah A. Bunch 4-7-1847 (4-8-1847)
Hopson, Harrod to Elisabeth M. Ritter 12-23-1847
Hopson, J. to Eliza True 6-12-1852
Hopson, James to Martha Wills 10-26-1844
Hopson, John to Sarah Flemings 4-27-1855 (4-29-1855)
Hopson, Miland to Jane Bull 1-26-1856 (1-27-1856)
Hopson, Richard to Hanner? Ritter? 7-15-1845
Hopson, Thomas B. to Margaret Stansbury 2-12-1856 (2-14-1856)
Hopson, William to Chloe? Bowers 12-23-1847 (12-26-1847)
Hopson, William to Elizabeth Herral 7-5-1843 (7-6-1843)
Hopson, Wm. Y. to J. Ritter 3-2-1853 (3-3-1853)
Hornis?, William to Mary Cane? 7-11-1844
Horvell, John A. to Perlina Welch 4-4-1868 (4-9-1868)
Hose, Ransam? to Jane Freeman 11-25-1845
Hosford, F. M. to L. Cadle 12-17-1852 (12-22-1852)
Hoskins, Heram to Kissash Locke 1-3-1838 (1-4-1838)
Hoskins, Hiram to Polly Henderson 6-8-1844 (6-10-1844)
Hoskins, James to Margaret Henderson 4-20-1856 (4-21-1856)
Hoskins, Levi to Elizabeth A. Britton 8-14-1866 (8-21-1866)
Housholder, A. J. to M. C. Marcus 9-24-1844 (9-24-1844)
Houston, J. to N. Ausmus 3-10-1858
Houston, John to Mary Keck 2-12-1866 (2-15-1866)
Houston, John to Nancy Gollehorn 5-11-1868 (5-14-1868) *
Houston, John to Nancy King 12-23-1846 (12-27-1846)
Houston, R. to S. C. Bull 1-4-1858
Houston, W. J. to M. Fox 9-16-1857
Houston, Wm. to Elizabeth Honeycutt 10-11-1841 (10-14-1841)
Howerton, David to Eliza West 10-17-1866 (11-2-1866)
Howerton, Green B. to Mary E. Mullens 2-5-1868 (2-6-1868)
Howerton, James to Malinda Maiden 5-31-1855 (6-3-1855)
Howerton, John to Polly Stansbury 9-24-1856 (9-25-1856)
Howerton, R. to S. C. Bull 1-4-1858
Hubbard, Andrew to Sarah Stowers 7-14-1843 (7-18-1843)
Hubbard, Wiley to Sarah Lyncy 12-6-1854 (12-2-1854)
Hubbrt?, Samuel to Mary Parton 1-22-1845 (3-22-1845)
Huddleston, Benjamin L. to Sarah Vanderpool 5-19-1845 (5-24-1849)
Huddleston, David to Peggy Seals 10-16-1839 (10-17-1839)
Huddleston, David to Telitha? Vanderpool 10-23-1849 (10-24-1849)
Huddleston, Flemman? to Elizabeth White 10-26-1843 (10-26-1843)
Hudson, Elijah to Rebecca J. Norvell 12-19-1843

Huffaker, Wiley to Rachael Alexander 11-21-1851
Hughs, James H. to Mary J. Jones 12-29-1863
Humfleet, Jacob to Nancy Jones 1-27-1851
Hunnacutt, Alvis to Martha Preslee? 7-18-1849 (7-19-1849)
Hunt, James C. to Caroline Kesterson 12-29-1852 (12-30-1852)
Hunter, Henry to Susanah Ausmus 9-5-1854
Hunter, James to Nancy Brooks 12-8-1841
Hunter, James to Thirsa McVey? 10-10-1849 (10-12-1849)
Hunter, Jordan to Sarah Edwards 8-26-1859
Hunter?, Judan? to Jane Hicks 11-15-1844 (11-18-1844)
Hurst, Aaron to Elmira Ritter 1-27-1840
Hurst, Amariah to Mary Ann Williams 12-19-1839
Hurst, Andrew to Mary Evans 10-23-1853
Hurst, Eldridge to Martha Stanerford 8-1-1867 (8-9-1867)
Hurst, Floid to Charity Breeding 11-1-1855
Hurst, George to Nella Maden 10-4-1856
Hurst, H. to S. Stone 3-6-1846 (3-8-1846)
Hurst, Henley to Jane Bunch 5-10-1855
Hurst, Isaac M. to Fanny B. Stone 6-7-1855
Hurst, James D. to Elisabeth M. Farmer 11-25-1848 (11-26-1848)
Hurst, James to Polly Cookard? 6-22-1842
Hurst, James T. to Rhoda J. Harrell 9-21-1867 (10-9-1867)
Hurst, L. to S. Miller 3-24-1846 (3-36-1846)
Hurst, Lisay? to Eliza James 4-12-1843
Hurst, Mark to Margaret Nave 12-22-1854 (1-12-1855)
Hurst, Milton to Emaley Miller 1-20-1847 (1-21-1847)
Hurst, Prior L. to Lucy J. Hodges 5-24-1856 (5-25-1856)
Hurst, Robert to Loisa Bunch 11-24-1857
Hurst, Robert to Sarah Neil 9-29-1842
Hurst, Robet to L. Bunch 11-24-1857 (11-26-1857)
Hurst, Roland to Sallie A. Chadwell 8-8-1866 (8-9-1866)
Hurst, Squire C. to Neely Sharp 2-24-1840 (2-27-1840)
Hurst, T. L. to Louisa Pittman 2-11-1852 (2-12-1852)
Hurst, William S. to Catharine Day 5-18-1859?
Hurst, William to Mary Eastis 1-2-1851
Hurst, William to Mary Lynch 5-24-1856 (5-25-1856)
Hurst, William to Sarah Cemor 1-27-1842
Hutson, E. to Mary Bowman 12-21-1838 (12-25-1838)
Hynes, Alford to Bartheny Hawthorne 9-11-1865 (9-18-1865)
Inkelbary, Wm. C. to Lucy Jinnings 8-9-1858
Inman, Caswell to Ester Woodson 11-4-1865 (11-19-1865)
Itson, William to Polly Sullivan 8-7-1850 (8-8-1850)
Jackson, Benjamin to Mary Ayers 3-12-1842 (3-13-1842)
Jackson, Ed to Sarah Ann Buchanan 1-23-1866 B
Jackson, Edward to Martha A. Graham 11-27-1867 B
Jackson, Franklin to Nancy Hargis 4-1-1855
Jackson, James to Martha Jane Lee 12-5-1853 (12-6-1853)
Jackson, Jefferson to Ruth Roland 8-7-1856 (8-10-1856)
Jackson, John S. to S. M. Willson 7-17-1858
Jackson, John to Sarah Colson? 4-6-1843 (4-15-1843)
Jackson, Pleasant B. to Frances Easley 8-31-1854
Jackson, Wilson to Sarah Brownlow 8-22-1854
Janes, David to Pheba Spark 10-23-1855
Janes, E. E. to Elizabeth J. Yaden 10-24-1855 (10-25-1855)
Janeway, Samuel to Mahala Walker 10-19-1867 (10-20-1867)
Janeway, William to Pricila? Vance 11-6-1845 (11-9-1845)
January, Joab to Amanda M. L. Ward 11-23-1843
January, Joseph to Mary J. Helms 2-9-1852 (2-12-1852)
Jarnigain, J. to Rebecca Bullard 10-20-1855 (1-21-1855)
Jene?, M. to E. Dorethy 3-28-1846 (4-4-1846)
Jennings, A. M. to Sarah Hodge 5-17-1858 (5-23-1858)
Jennings, D. A. to Julia Sewell 10-20-1865 B
Jennings, George W. to Ellender Waller 3-2-1844 (3-3-1844)
Jennings, James R. to Louisa Campbell 2-20-1840
Jennings, Jno. to Mary Moore 7-23-1838
Jennings, John M. to Mary Berry 7-20-1867 (7-21-1867)
Jennings, John S. to Ellender Johnson 5-21-1867
Jennings, John to Mary Branson 11-12-1865
Jennings, John to Mary Jones 3-23-1855 (3-25-1855)
Jennings, Royal to Nancy Kerby 4-6-1866 (4-8-1866)
Jennings, Samuel to Elizabeth Gray 4-7-1866 (4-9-1866)
Jennings, William D. to Martha A. Vance 10-31-1867
Jessee, F. J. to L. J. Thompson 9-22-1857
Jessee, Isaac M. to Martha E. Ousley 10-19-1867 (10-24-1867)
Jinkins, Elbert to Elizabeth Smith 1-15-1868
Jinnings, D. to Leuisey Davis 8-19-1858
Johnson, Ambrous to Mary Southern 12-1-1841 (12-2-1841)
Johnson, Andrew J. to Mary Southern 8-1-1867
Johnson, Claiborne to Martha Cormeny 11-6-1867 (11-7-1867)
Johnson, George R. to Minerva Miller 10-5-1856
Johnson, George to Elizabeth West 6-7-1855
Johnson, George to M. Barnard 3-7-1853 (no return)
Johnson, H. A. to Judy? Parratt 12-18-1846 (12-18-1845?)
Johnson, Isaac M. to Nervesty M. Suthern 2-26-1859
Johnson, Isaac to Sarah J. Smith 8-8-1852
Johnson, James P. to Marlenia Goin 6-18-1868 (6-20-1868)
Johnson, James to Mary Hoskins 10-10-1866 (10-11-1866)

Johnson, Joel to Julyann Overholt 7-27-1859
Johnson, Joel to Sarah Raider 1-2-1854 (no return)
Johnson, John to Elender Barnet 1-18-1849 (1-19-1849)
Johnson, Jos. M. to Rebeckey Hix 1-10-1846
Johnson, Joseph P. to Elender E. Goins 1-29-1850
Johnson, Joseph to Elizabeth Brown 6-30-1866 (7-1-1866)
Johnson, Pharore to Miley Barnard 7-21-1851 (7-22-1851)
Johnson, William H.. to Martha E. Vitetoe 11-26-1868 (11-29-1866)
Johnson, William to Sarah Fortiner 3-1-1841
Johnson, William to Sarah Fortner 2-23-1842 (3-1-1842)
Johnston, Thos. J. to Eliza J. Graham 4-17-1839
Joice, James to Nancy Stuart 11-21-1855 (11-22-1855)
Jone, Wiley to Huldy Devault 1-13-1866 (1-14-1866)
Jones, Abraham to Sarah Furry 9-1-1838
Jones, Alexander to Mary J. Robertson 6-8-1867 (6-20-1867)
Jones, Andrew C. to Eliza Lee 9-14-1847
Jones, Arthur L. to Mary Dobins 11-28-1849
Jones, Arthur to Nancy N. Chadwell 6-2-1856
Jones, D. W. to Elizabeth? Davis? 5-4-1844 (5-5-1844)
Jones, Daniel to Ann Jane Cook 9-1-1847 (no return)
Jones, Elihu to Elmirah Powell 5-2-1840
Jones, Elijah to M. E. Cook 12-23-1858
Jones, George W. to Elender Chumbley 10-14-1850
Jones, Henderson to Elizabeth Simmerman 3-21-1853
Jones, Hezekiah to Nancy Shipmon 12-5-1866
Jones, James to Sarah V. Fullington 8-7-1856
Jones, Jesse L. to Martha Welch 6-30-1838 (7-3-1838)
Jones, John C. to Louisa Johnson 9-13-1854 (9-14-1854)
Jones, John M. to M. L. Moore 10-28-1858
Jones, John T. to Elisabeth Fisher 9-6-1856
Jones, John to Lurina Lanham 8-4-1854
Jones, Johnston to Rhoda Burnt Vigger? 2-27-1839
Jones, Lewis to Nancy Jennings 6-28-1851 (7-17-1851)
Jones, Mark to Sally Laffoon 1-7-1847
Jones, Moses to Polly Callor 1-1-1851 (1-2-1851)
Jones, Randolph to Melvina Patterson 8-26-1867 (9-5-1867) B
Jones, Roblins? to Chariity Snuffer 5-18-1844 (5-20-1844)
Jones, Sasival? to Amanda Sowder 9-25-1852 (9-26-1852)
Jones, Thomas to Eliza Mitchell 11-6-1867
Jones, W. H. to Mahulda Carpenter 12-29-1865 (12-29-1865)
Jones, William W. to L. J. McBee 1-13-1853
Jones, William to Mariah Cadel 10-5-1844 (10-6-1844)
Jones?, Elijah to Sally Lea 2-9-1844
Jonns, W. B. to Lucenta Evans 9-23-1865 (9-26-1865)
Keck, A. to Cathrine Shofner 1-17-1855 (12-18-1855)
Keck, Danl. to Cementha Whited? 7-16-1839 (7-18-1839)
Keck, Eli to Catherine Dunn 2-8-1866 (2-8-1866)
Keck, Fredrick to Mary Shofner 12-21-1854 (12-28-1854)
Keck, Henry to Elizabeth Edwards 5-17-1839 (5-19-1839)
Keck, Jasper to Mary T. German? 9-4-1861 (9-15-1861)
Keck, John D. to Mary Johnson 5-30-1868 (5-31-1868)
Keck, John to Rebecca Yaden 4-14-1843
Keck, M. to E. Toin 1-30-1846 (1-31-1846)
Keck, Madison to Anah Sowders 2-3-1866 (2-8-1866)
Keck, Mathew to Orlena Brogan 8-31-1857 (9-1-1857)
Keck, Newton to Sarah E. Johnson 3-16-1868 (3-25-1868)
Keck, Sterling to Harriet M. Harmon 10-11-1866 (10-18-1866)
Keck, William to Margaret Davy 12-19-1866 (12-23-1866)
Keites, John to Jane Heller 9-20-1865 (9-21-1865)
Kelley, John A. to Catharine B. Hurst 12-27-1866
Kelley, John H. to Ann Jane Sewell 7-11-1849
Kelley, Mathis to Martha Fulkerson 10-27-1866 B
Kelly, B. L. to Sarah F. Grazy? 9-27-1852
Kelton, Silas T. to Jane Perry 3-9-1865
Kerby, Anderson to Martha Vidtoe 3-25-1865
Keribey, Wiley to Anna Vance 11-23-1859
Kesterson, Wm. to Adaline Fusan 9-20-1854
Kesterson?, Reubin to Adaline? Henderson 8-26-1845
Ketrom, Wm. H. to Margret Patterson 1-13-1866 (1-18-1866)
Ketron, Allen to Elizabeth Hatfield 2-8-1865
Kibert, James A. to M. Day 3-8-1853
Kibert, Lewis to Malinda Garland 6-28-1852 (6-30-1852)
Kibert, Samuel to Eliza Butcher 6-6-1853 (6-7-1853)
Kibert, Samuel to Elizabeth Marsh 1-28-1867 (1-31-1867)
Kibert, Wm. to Susan Arnel 4-1-1846 (4-5-1846)
Killeren, Wm. to Iselee Day 10-25-1864 (10-25-1864)
Killian, Daniel to Milla Eastrage 7-14-1854 (7-16-1854)
Killion, Andrew to Samiramiss? Lanham 2-15-1846
Killion, James S. to Elizabeth Bullard 1-23-1867 (1-24-1867)
Killion, John to Hetty Ann Evans 6-24-1868 (6-25-1868)
Killion, John to Matilda Lanham 5-29-1846
Killion, John to Mohaley McBee 5-10-1865
Killion, R. to A. Inklebarger 9-17-1856
Killion, Robert to N. A. Inklebarger 9-17-1856
Killion, Robert to N. A. Inklebarger 9-17-1856 (9-21-1856)
Killion, Thomas C. to Mary Rossan? 6-11-1842 (6-12-1842)
Kincaid, James M. to Olivia P. Moss 3-3-1856

Kincaid, Jerry to Mary Kincaid 3-8-1866 (3-16-1866) B
Kincaid, John W. to Margaret Huff 8-19-1857
Kincaid, Marshall L. to L. B. Miller 9-30-1857
Kincaid, Sterling C. to Sarah Woodson 9-15-1847 (not executed)
Kincaid, Sturling C. to Thursey Miller 3-17-1858
Kincaid, Wm. C. to M. A. Moss 7-18-1858
Kindred, Richard to Sidney Eperson 9-9-1865
King, Alvin to Mary Siler 7-19-1853 (7-22-1853)
King, Daniel to Cathrine Stansbury 10-6-1857
King, E. to E. Buice? 2-9-1846 (2-12-1846)
King, H. C. to Eliza Neil 2-18-1852
King, Howard to Fama Collins 12-24-1850
King, Samuel to Murica Jane Vanbeber 6-1-1865
King, Solomon to Nancy Wilson 8-16-1853 (8-18-1853)
King, Spencer to Emaline Hamblin 10-11-1848 (10-12-1848)
King, Thomas to Harriett Bowman? 11-11-1848
King, William F. to Sarah J. Bowman 1-1-1857
King, William to Anna Smith 9-8-1856 (9-8-1856)
King, William to Nancy Braver? 12-28-1841 (12-29-1841)
King, Wm. to Susan Maples 8-5-1852
Kinningham?, William to Susan Baker 3-27-1848
Kirby, Elisha to Lucinda Rice 11-2-849 (11-3-1849)
Kirby, S. B. to Louza Helton 9-29-1865 (10-1-1865)
Kirkpatrick, William to Louisa Evans 11-18-1841
Kivett, Hiram A. to Emely J. Stine 12-14-1867 (12-29-1867)
Kivett, Hiram J. to Maneva Ausmus 3-5-1868
Kivit, John Z. to Elizabeth E. Hall 8-24-1857
Knight, Richard to Julia A. Buchanan 11-28-1867
Knuckels, Henderson to Elizabeth Honeycutt 9-27-1866
Korly, C. to Nim? Smith 11-10-1864
Kyle, Franklin to Mariah Phillips 5-13-1867 B
Lacock, John to Alisey Howerton 9-9-1856 (9-11-1856)
Laffoon, Drewrey to Manervey Stone 12-19-1850
Laffoon, John E. to Rosa A. Powell 2-1-1851 (2-2-1851)
Lake, Dolin to Ester Hale 5-1-1854 (5-2-1854)
Lake, Elisha to Alpha Ann Thomas 3-8-1853
Lamar?, Samuel to Rebecca Montgomery 7-5-1842
Lamare, Wm. to Labitha Robinson 2-24-1838 (2-27-1838)
Lamb, Dawson to Geminia Jackson 7-15-1850
Lamb, Noah to Sally Shoftner 7-30-1855 (8-1-1855)
Lambert, B. to S. Furgerson 7-16-1854 (7-18-1855?)
Lambert, Benjamin to Sarah Furgerson 7-16-1854
Lambert, James J. to Polly Ann Roward 10-11-1843 (10-14-1843)
Lambert, John to Martha E. England 1-24-1843 (1-25-1843)
Lambert, John to Mary Vance 9-1-1854
Lambert, Joseph to Milla Whitaker 8-5-1854 (8-6-1854)
Lambert, Joseph to Nancy Elerson 12-27-1855
Lambert, Wayman to Nancy Southern 2-12-1839 (2-19-1839)
Lambert, William to Susan Hill 12-30-1854 (1-4-1855)
Lamdon, John to Susan Massa 7-29-1854 (8-2-1854)
Landers, Jackson to Mary E. Willialms 6-27-1842 (6-30-1842)
Lane, G. W. to Margaret Lane 9-1-1865
Lane, H. to Lucyann Chadwell 12-19-1857
Lane, J. W. to Elizabeth Bullard 1-21-1864
Lane, James to Mary J. Myers 12-28-1864 (12-27-1864)
Lane, John L. to Elizabeth Sowder 10-4-1838 (10-14-1838)
Lane, Samuel to Sarah Keith 12-27-1849
Lane, William B. to Thersa Ann Willis 8-4-1849 (8-5-1849)
Lane?, Robt. B. to Martha Jane McNew 2-20-1840 (2-27-1840)
Lanham, Abel to Ann Killion 2-15-1846
Lanham, Eldrage? H. to Perlina Henderson 9-10-1845 (11-11-1845)
Lanham, Stokely R. to Caroline Henderson 6-2-1842
Lanham, Thos. J. to Eliza Green 7-25-1838
Lankford, John to Ruthy S. Rowland 1-25-1844 (1-26-1844)
Lankford, Thos. to Minerva Sullivan 6-26-1856 (6-29-1856)
Larance, Wm. T. to Almiry Griffen 11-17-1859
Large, J. C. to Eliza J. Hollansworth 9-5-1859
Large, J. C. to S. J. Richardson 11-28-1851 (11-24-1851)
Lastly?, William to Elizabeth Crabtree 12-25-1839
Latham, John to Phibi Dobkins 8-24-1839
Laughmiller, James to Mahaly I.? Stublefield 1-30-1848 (2-10-1848)
Lavson?, Drury to Mary Ann Lewis 1-19-1846 (1-20-1846)
Lawson, D. to D. Tinn? 8-10-18 (8-11-18)
Lawson, Greenberry to Lavina Carter 4-12-1844 (4-16-1844)
Lawson, Nathan to Elvisy? Mason 6-8-1844 (6-9-1844)
Lawson, S. to A. Brooks 5-27-1852
Lawson, Thos. to Hetty Moor 8-7-1845
Lawson, Thos. to Sarah Lawson 1-27-1846 (1-30-1846)
Lawson, Wm. B. to Catherine Daniels 9-4-1851 (9--24-1851)
Lay, James to Eliza Woodson 8-26-1856 (8-28-1856)
Lay, Jesse to Sarah Shelby 9-6-1845 (7-3-1846)
Lay, Joseph to Mary Minton 12-20-1865 12-21-1865
Lay, Rufus N. to Mary E. McClary 2-24-1852 (2-29-1852)
Lay, Thos. N. to Cintha A. Rice 3-28-1856
Lay, Wateel to Milley Chumbley 4-9-1850
Laycock, Williamson to Elizabeth Russell 11-13-1839 (12-13-1839)
Laycock, Wyley to Louisa Ray 8-1-1838 (8-12-1838)

Lea, James to Catharine Howerton 11-4-1843 (11-9-1843)
Lea, Stephen to Sarah Scritchfield 3-12-1851 (3-13-1851)
Lea, Wm. A. to Matilda J. Vaughn 3-2-1858
Lea, Wm. J. to M. J. Vaughn 3-2-1858 (3-4-1858)
Leach, David to Cathrine Proffit 11-30-1850
Leach, Jacob to S. S. Beeler 8-19-1858
Leach, Wm. F. to Elizabeth Hunter 7-10-1857 (7-16-1857)
Leach?, John M. to Trifany? Bruce 9-30-1842 (10-2-1842)
Lebow, Royal to Rawsy? Sanders 10-23-1839 (12-15-1839)
Ledbetter, J. L. to Aati? M. Tulnies? 8-25-1861 (8-25-1862)
Lee, A. to J. McDaniels 8-12-1852 (8-13-1852)
Lee, Bowling to Elizabeth Howard 7-2-1852 (7-2-1852)
Lee, Curtis to Martha Alferd 5-30-1852 (no return)
Lee, Gabril to Rebecka Lee 9-23-1858
Lee, James to Jane Pridemore 11-10-1866 (6-16-1867)
Lee, Pearvan? to Polly Bray 2-14-1839 (2-21-1839)
Leffue, John T. to Sarah Hodges 9-21-1867 (10-16-1867)
Leforce, J. B. S. to Nancy Buchanan 6-11-1868
Leforce, James to Elizabeth Hatfield 7-3-1865 (7-6-1865)
Legeor?, William to Vina Hurley? 8-27-1842 (8-28-1842)
Leicey, Andrew to Margarett Thompson 8-3-1867 (8-4-1867) B
Lenard, Patrick to Nancy Lambert 11-22-1867 (11-28-1867)
Lenvar?, J. M. to B. Davis 10-13-1852
Lewis, Abraham to Lucy Campbell 11-8-1859
Lewis, George M.? to Cyntha Fulps 9-16-1848 (9-17-1848)
Lewis, George W. to Eliza A. Thompson 6-24-1848 (6-25-1848)
Lewis, Isaac to E. King 2-24-1858
Lewis, J. M. to S. Russel 11-27-1852 (11-28-1852)
Lewis, John to Ann Walker 1-24-1853
Lewis, Samuel to Syntha Thomas 8-16-1867 (8-22-1867) B
Lifard?, James N. to Manervy Hatfield 4-29-1843 (4-30-1843)
Liford, ----- to Soperia? Grace 6-12-1843
Liford, Wm. P. to Sarah Pew 8-23-1851 (8-24-1851)
Lingar, John to Sarah Chumbly 1-27-1838 (2-13-1838)
Lingar, Lewis to Sarah Litterele 12-4-1867 (1-12-1867?)
Lingar, Robt. to Elizabeth A. Greer 11-12-1865 (11-13-18650)
Links, James to Jane Baily 1-26-1856
Litrell, Samuel to Ann Shumate 12-30-1838 (12-31-1838)
Litrell, Wm. H. to Rachel Pridemoore? 12-19-1842 (12-25-1842)
Litterall, Isaac to Mary Burchett 2-7-1859
Litterrell, Jonathan to Sarah Bane 12-31-1866 (1-1-1867)
Littrell, Daniel to Nancy A. Hinton? 6-28-1850
Littrell, John A. to Sarah Hamblin 9-25-1856
Loc?, John to Susan Harris 2-21-1865
Lock, Parks to Margaret Leonard 1-19-1855
Lock, Samuel to Cary Ayrs 6-28-1856 (6-29-1856)
Lock, William to Sarah Carroll 4-5-1844
Loe, John to Susan Harris 2-21-1865
Loftis, Hosea D. to Eliza J. Billingsby 9-29-1866 (10-7-1866)
Logans, John H. to Mary J. Debusk 8-20-1868
Longworth, F. to S. Hatfield 4-29-1858
Longworth, George to Mary A. Barker? 2-25-1847
Longworth, James to Elizabeth Carmack 3-15-1854 (3-19-1854)
Longworth, William to Jane Brown 8-12-1854 (8-16-1854)
Loop, John W. to Lucy Jane Walker 3-5-1867
Lorton, John to Eliza Halton 12-2-1850 (2-20-1851)
Lorton?, John to Elizabeth Ellis 10-14-1843 (10-17-1843)
Louder, P. to J. Tucker 7-12-1852 (7-15-1852)
Louis, William to Elizabeth Howel 4-2-1850 (4-2-1859)
Louthr?, Jas. to Mary Hatfield 5-9-1846
Love, M. W. to L. J. Brown 9-3-1857
Lovel, William H. to Louiza C. Moore 7-4-1868 (7-5-1868)
Lovelace, Willialml to Martha Cardwell 1-3-1867
Loves, Esom to Anny Grocecloce? 3-29-1844
Lowe, J. M. to Delila Morris 9-9-1844
Lucker?, Lewis to Calvina Lee 12-17-1849
Lunday, John to Rachel Snavely 12-20-1843 (12-21-1843)
Luster?, Henry P. to May Ann Cadle 4-30-1840 (5-1-1840)
Luster?, Robert C. to Julia Hamelton 1-18-1850 (marr, no date)
Lynch, Andrew J. to Hariet E. Monday 5-16-1851 (5-18-1851)
Lynch, David to Nancy Lynch 12-28-1843
Lynch, Isaac R. to Caroline Robertson 1-1-1867 (1-3-1867)
Lynch, Jeptha to Loisa Davis 11-4-1846 (11-5-1846)
Lynch, Jesse to Lavina Ford 6-15-1839 (6-18-1839)
Lynch, John B. to Anna Williams 12-20-1854
Lynch, John to Elizabeth Kesterson 8-8-1850
Lynch, John to Mary Wamiers? 6-28-1846 (7-3-1846)
Lynch, John to Nancy White 8-19-1865 (8-20-1865)
Lynch, Riley H. to Perlina Stone 10-30-1856
Lynch, Sanford Ciseroe to Susan McBee 1-25-1868 (1-27-1868)
Lynch, Sterling W. to Sinda Hunter 12-12-1854
Lynch, William W. to Sarah Hunter 8-17-1847 (exe, no date)
Lynch, William to Martha McClellan 12-4-1850
Lynch, Wm. .D. to Cathrine Salyers 2-4-1856 (2-14-1856)
Lyngar?, James H. to Eliza Sharp 9-6-1856 (9-7-1856)
Maddox, George W. to Melvina England 6-9-1865
Malicoat?, Anderon to Elizabeth Bundren 2-9-1844

Malone, H. to J. Culberson 8-28-1852 (9-2-1852)
Malone, John B. to Elizabeth Ousley 2-18-1852
Malone, John to Sarah Sharp 2-1-1844 (2-8-1844)
Malone, R. to Esther Beeler 11-24-1865 (11-30-1865)
Manawy, Jacob to Nancy Chance 1-20-1854
Mannon, Andrew to Martha J. Estep 10-4-1866 (10-10-1866)
Mannon, Mark? to Mary A. Dulin? 2-15-1847
Maples, Edmon to N. Hamach 3-26-1853
Maples, James to Mary A. Strevels 9-28-1850
Maples, John to Elizabeth Bruor 11-28-1854 (11-30-1854)
Maples, Wm. to Betsy Hammock 9-25-1841 (9-30-1841)
Marcum, George to Nancy Elizabeth Bales 2-4-1846 (2-7-1846)
Marcum, J. M. to Nancy George 4-6-1851 (4-7-1851)
Marcum, John to Abigail Sutton 11-9-1850
Marcum, John to Rebecca A. Simmons 1-13-1852
Marcum, Squire to Mary H. Roger 10-1-1867 (10-3-1867)
Marcum, Wm. A. to Mary Thomas 3-15-1851 (3-16-1851)
Marcum?, Alford to Levina? R. Thomas 11-7-1845 (11-9-1845)
Marian?, Elijah to Nancy Gilbert 1-16-1845 (1-19-1845)
Marion?, A. to S. Hall 11-18-1845
Marlar, Daniel to Milia J. Leforce 8-23-1867 (8-12-1867)
Marlom, Thomas to Catherine Cross 9-9-1849 (9-12-1849)
Marlor, Allen to Effa Huddleston 8-12-1851 (8-28-1851)
Marlow, John to Venila Late? 5-16-1842 (5-25-1842)
Marr, Nathaniel to M. Like 3-7-1853
Marsee, Joseph S. to Susan E. Hyden 1-1-1868
Marsee, Joseph to Susan E. Hyden 1-1-1868
Marson, M. to M. A. Parrott 2-12-1855 (2-15-1855)
Martain, James M. to Susannah Gibert? 3-27-1842 (3-30-1842)
Marteal, William to Malinda Hooper 1-20-1844 (1-21-1844)
Martin, James T. to Mary A. Hill 2-28-1865 (3-1-1865)
Martin, John H. to Sarah Jones 1-3?-1859
Martin, Wm. to Sidna McClary 1-25-1853 (1-6-1853)
Maser, Michael to Sally Graves 4-18-1840 (5-3-1840)
Mason, John T. to Hessie S. Wilson 8-18-1866 (8-19-1866)
Mason, R. F. to Healen Vanbibber 9-27-1851 (10-1-1851)
Mason, Wm. to C. J. Sharp 12-11-1851
Massa, Jacob to Elith Brummet 10-29-1850 (10-31-1850)
Massengale, Hiram D. to Susan M. Maples 11-19-1857
Massengle, Calvin to Louisa Roark 1-27-1849
Massengle, J. M. to Winna Vannoy 12-28-1855
Massingale, G. to M. Owens 3-3-1852 (3-6-1852)
Massingale, Isaac to Sarah Collins 4-15-1851 (4-16-1851)
Massingille, J. Calvin to Luticia Williams 11-9-1851
Mathes, Jno. D. to Mary Ann Mason 3-26-1839
Mattox, Geoge W. to Melvina England 6-9-1865 (6-11-1865)
Maupin, David C. to Mary A. Rogers 8-20-1867 (8-22-1867)
Maupin, Frank to Bettie Bowman 5-19-1866 (5-20-1866)
Maville, William to Amy Wilder 6-10-1865
Mayers, James L. to Amy Rogers 12-7-1867 (12-12-1867)
Mayes, James K. P. to Elizabeth Dunn 7-31-1866 (8-5-1866)
Mayes, James to Eliza Jones 11-3-1865
Mays, Jerrice? B. to Carolina Treese? 1-21-1842 (1-30-1842)
Mays, John to Lucinda Johnson 10-30-1843 (11-7-1843)
Mays, Thos. to E. Lawson 2-21-1846
Mays, Wm. H. to Mary A. Goins 5-23-1853 (5-24-1853)
Mayse, David to M. Richerson 10-6-1855
Mayse, J. to R. C. Yeaden 8-6-1857
Mayse, Johnson to Manerva Hopper 6-29-1857 (7-2-1857)
McAfee, Moses to China Wallen 11-22-1844
McAfee?, James to Elizabeth Minton 8-29-1845 (8-30-1845)
McAmis, A. A. to Matilda? Weir 1-8-1840 (1-9-1840)
McAnelly, Hamelton to Winny Simmons 2-5-1842 (2-6-1842)
McAnelly, James to Manila Mitchel 1-22-1842 (1-26-1842)
McAnlush?, William A. A. to Emaley? Black 8-30-1846
McBee, Burton to Mary A. Burk 1-1-1848 (1-3-1848)
McBee, Calvin to Emeline McBee 11-27-1846 (1-10-1847)
McBee, Claiborne to Sementha Hurst 2-25-1840
McBee, Gamon to Polly Wood 10-14-1851 (10-16-1851)
McBee, Ganeum to Rebecca Fulps 7-16-1849
McBee, Granville to Caroline Moore 9-13-1847 (9-16-1847)
McBee, Houston to Lucinda Owens 2-28-1848 (3-9-1848)
McBee, Isaac to Sarah Blancet 5-6-1865 (5-7-1865)
McBee, John to Mary A. Sevord 1-18-1853 (1-19-1853)
McBee, Prior L. to Sufphronia C. Meyers 12-14-1867 (12-15-1867)
McBee, Prior to Bethena Lewis 9-18-1851
McBee, Samuel to Alemida? Stubblefield 7-21-1849
McBee, Samuel to Nancy I. Lewis 11-6-1849
McBee, William C. to Permelia Greer 12-10-1839 (12-15-1839)
McBee, Wm. to Lilly J. Owens 9-29-1849 (10-5-1849)
McCankey?, S. to M. Davis? 11-15-1845 (11-23-1845)
McCard?, James T.? to Mary Ann Collins 2-18-1844
McCarty, James to Margaret McFarlin 1-20-1842 (1-21-1842)
McClane, Thomas to Susan Crutchfield 2-21-1838 (2-22-1838)
McConnel, A. to Sarah Graves 3-19-1840 (3-13?-1840)
McCrary, Cleveland to Elizabeth Lay 11-?-1849 (12-16-1849)
McCrary, George to Elender Venable 11-17-1849 (11-18-1849)

McCrary, J. to M. Webb 8-30-1852 (8-31-1852)
McCrary, N. to Norciss Willson 4-29-1844 (4-30-1844)
McCrary, Peter to N. Venable 2-12-1853 (2-13-1853)
McCullough, Samuel to Elizabeth Fairchilds 1-24-1843 (1-26-1843)
McCullum?, James to Polly Gray 3-15-1847 (3-22-1847)
McDaniel, Wm. B. to Rachel M. Meyers 10-5-1866 (10-11-1866)
McDermott, Thomas to Ann Kirkpatrick 4-19-1865
McDonal, Mathew C. to Menervy J. Shoemate 12-9-1846 (12-17-1846)
McFarland, William to Susannah Hopper 9-2-1847
McGinis, Robert to Martha Slone 12-11-1854 (12-14-1854)
McGinnes, James to Sarah M. Harrell 10-30-1867 (10-31-1867)
McGonigal, Henry to Agness Norris 5-15-1843 (5-26-1843)
McHenry, Wm. to Sally Huffaker 2-25-1839 (2-28-1839)
McKamy, Daniel to A. Thomas 9-25-1865
McKee, Wm. to Gemmima E. Greenlee 12-21-1855
McKeehan, James D. to Mary Chadwell 6-12-1866 (6-14-1866)
McKenny, James to Elizabeth Mills 8-31-1850 (8-12-1852)
McKinney, Samuel P. to Elizabeth A. Thomas 9-25-1865 (9-28-1865)
McMahon?, John to Elisabeth Wilson 5-19-1849
McMakan, John to Nancy Cloud 12-2-1838 (12-6-1838)
McNeal, William to Nancy Gilbert 12-6-1839
McNeel, J. F. to Matilda J. McNeil 11-3-1865 (11-9-1865)
McNeelance, Wm. to N. A. [Nancy] Herrell 3-18-1853 (3-20-1853)
McNeil, William H. to Nancy J. Fletcher 8-14-1867 (8-22-1867)
McNeil, William to Nancy L. Carter 12-22-1849 (12-27-1849)
McNew, Isaac to Mary Ann Arwine 4-1-1845
McNew, John F. to Harriett L. Rogers 12-28-1867 (12-29-1867)
McNew, Wm. J. to Caroline M. Rogers 4-26-1845 (5-1-1845)
McNew?, Jno. to Louisa Hurst 4-11-1840
McQuary, John to Mary Goin 12-29-1865 (12-30-1865)
McVey, Clinton to Rhoda Bray 2-13-1858 (2-14-1858)
McWilliams, Joseph to Moholey? Chumbley 5-28-1844 (5-29-1844)
McWilliams, William N. to Emaley Brusten 5-11-1849 (5-24-1849)
Meelor, John to Elizabeth Jane Woodson 2-18-1848 (3-19-1848)
Meotor?, William to Ally Slotton 8-24-1842 (10-25-1842)
Messer, Andrew to Polly Nealley 8-10-1859
Messer, Hiram to Mary Doke 3-4-1848
Messer, Hiram to Mary Smith 8-28-1848 (8-29-1848)
Messer, Tillford to Martha Brackett 11-3-1866
Meyers, Abraham to Phebywathy Altemere Simmons 3-11-1853 (3-13-1853)
Meyers, Isom L. to Martha M. Needham 2-24-1866 (3-1-1866)
Michel, John M. to Thursa M. Moppin 3-11-1857
Michel, John to Elizabeth Kesterson 11-20-1855 (11-22-1855)
Miles?, Benjamin D. to Harriet Grantham 9-25-1841 (9-26-1841)
Millar, Thomas to Cordaline Belvins 1-5-1857
Miller, George W. to Lucy King 5-9-1840
Miller, Isaac to Louisa Cloud 6-17-1845
Miller, J. to V. E. Jones 8-1-1853
Miller, James M. to Martha Miller 1-30-1868 (2-3-1868)
Miller, Jurean to V. E. Jones 7-1-1853
Miller, Leander to E. C. Dickinson 8-26-1851
Miller, Leander to Nevesta Mason 7-10-1854 (7-11-1854)
Miller, Pleasant to Winney Runnalds 1-14-1840 (1-23-1840)
Miller, Wm. J. L. C. to Isabella F. Scott 12-11-1863 (12-29-1863)
Miller, Wm. S. to Missouri A. Young 12-1-1866 (12-5-1866)
Miller?, David to Ann Runolds? 11-13-1841 (11-28-1841)
Miller?, Russell to Polly Smith 3-10-1840
Millis, J. B. to Elizabeth Johnson 12-22-1844
Mills, Henry to Mahaley Hill 2-1-1847
Mills, James to Sarah Lawson 12-21-1839
Mills, Reubin to S. Autton? 5-2-1845 (5-4-1845)
Mills, William to Rhoda Lawson 12-19-1839
Mink, Saml. O. to Mary A. V. Rector 11-8-1865 (11-20-1866?)
Minks, Phelin to Anna Brewer 11-11-1843 (11-18-1843)
Minor, W. to J. Blumer 12-11-1852
Minter, Landon C. to Mary A.? Buchanan 1-15-1867 (1-30-1867)
Minter?, Landax? C. to Mary Montgumary? 4-4-1842 (4-5-1842)
Minton, Ebenezer to B. Ball 9-27-1853 (9-28-1853)
Minton, J. to Mary C. Parsen 11-7-1864 (11-8-1864)
Minton, James to Elender Herrell 9-30-1847 (10-?-1847)
Minton, John to Evaline Lyncy 5-15-1850
Minton, John to Sary Reed 7-11-1843
Minton, J. J. to Martha Reed 4-26-1866
Minton, Philip to Rachel M. Hodges 10-4-1849 (10-5-1849)
Minton, Samuel L. to Ceseer? Susong 9-13-1850 (10-3-1850)
Minton, Vardamon to Nancy Locke 8-25-1838
Minton, William to Polly A. Ousley 11-1-1848
Mise, William to Narcissa Mise 12-18-1854 (12-21-1854)
Mize, Calvin to Mary Mize 11-15-1856 (11-25-1856)
Mize, Jos. to Sarah Woods 7-28-1853 (no return)
Mize, Littleton to Elizabeth Wilson 2-16-1851 (2-27-1851)
Molana?, John to Bilenda? Hopkins 12-16-1843 (12-17-1843)
Mole, Elihue H. to Hariet Baldwin 5-26-1856
Moles, Gabriel H. to Martha E. Epperson 1-16-1867 (1-17-1867)
Moncy?, John J. to Louisa Owen 5-29-1847
Monday, T. J. to M. Brooks 9-6-1852 (9-8-1852)
Monday, William L. to Margret R. Norvell 8-22-1850

Mongomry, John T. to Rebecca Grantham 4-28-1865 (4-31?-1865)
Monk, James M. to Manila Bray 2-21-1842 (2-22-1842)
Monor?, Nicalis? to Polly Strevels? 4-13-1847 (4-15-1847)
Monsy, Perry to Sarah Lorton 3-3-1856 (3-4-1856)
Montgomery, James to Manila Sensabaugh 4-11-1858
Moody, A. V. B. to Louisa Venable 12-28-1854
Moody, Joseph to Martha A. Smith 1-10-1856 (1-24-1856)
Mooney, James to Elizabeth Goin 12-13-1858
Moor, John to Permealy? McMahan 6-26-1846
Moor, Samuel to Polly Beeler 7-19-1839 (7-20-1839)
Moor, Shadrick to Polly Ann Oneil 4-7-1845 (4-12-1845)
Moor, Tilman H. to Mary A. Burket 12-29-1849 (12-25?-1849)
Moore, Chastin? S. to Nancy W. Jones 11-27-1841
Moore, Hubberd to Lucind Staneford 2-21-1865
Moore, Joseph to Manervy Greer 1-19-1843
Moore, N. H. to Mary E. Lorton 8-13-1857
Moore, Nathan H. to Sarah Ann Thompson 7-25-1844
Moore, Wm. to Ellen Patterson 6-5-1852 (6-6-1852)
Mopin, Overton to Mary Jones 9-20-1853 (10-?-1853)
Morgan, Madison to Emily Murphey 6-19-1867
Morgan, Preston to Effy Field? 4-13-1839
Morgan, Willson to Lucresa Lewis 7-15-1853 (7-16-1853)
Moritz, J. D. to Amelia Soullivan 6-8-1866 (6-9-1866)
Morris, Daniel to Nancy Mayes 6-23-1865
Morrison, Daniel to Nancy Hayse 6-23-1865
Morrison, James to Vesty Young 7-21-1857
Morseless, M. P. to Mary E. Simpson 5-10-1865
Moss, John to Olivia Treece 11-27-1867 (11-28-1867)
Moss, R. M. to M. S. Ball 1-23-1853 (1-24-1853)
Moyer, Vincent to Jane Fulp 3-19-1842 (4-14-1842)
Moyers, Cany to Sarah Smith 7-15-1846
Moyers, Henry P. to Syntha Ann Lane 2-8-1868 (2-9-1868)
Moyers, Hesakiah to Rachel Harison? 3-1-1849 (3-4-1849)
Moyers, Isham to E. Poor 11-7-1859
Moyers, John C. to Mary L. Moss 9-21-1867 (9-22-1867)
Moyers, Joseph B. to Livisa? Ausmus 9-22-1842 (9-27-1842)
Moyers, Joshua to Sindney Bunch 9-3-1850 (9-4-1850)
Moyers, Marion to Mary A. Carr 12-7-1858
Moyers, Volentine to Sarah J. Snitchfield 10-19-1852
Moyers, William N. to H.? Moyers 5-14-1840
Moyers, William to Susanah Bowman 11-19-1844
Mulhohs, A. I. to Mary McConkuy? 7-27-1844 (8-1-1844)
Mullens, Eldrage? to Nancy O. Carpenter 3-17-1848
Mullins, Moses B. to Mary Subar 3-3-1865 (4-6-1865)
Munday, Pleasant C. to Elizabet? Williams 10-9-1841 (10-17-1841)
Munday, William L. to Margret R. Norvell 2-14-1850
Munday, William to Mary Ann Abs? 2-20-1854
Munday, Wm. to Mildred Grows 12-13-1853 (12-?-1853)
Murphey, Brownlow to Millia Butcher 6-24-1867 B
Murray, James H. to Elizabeth Brigmon 10-3-1846
Murry, Edmund to Polly Welch 8-2-1850 (8-1?-1850)
Murry, W. to Lucinda Townsly 5-20-1858
Mussey?, John to Cynthia M. Tucker 10-10-1850
Myers, Carey to Pasefy Timey? Lewis 1-29-1849 (2-1-1849)
Myers, G. W. to Martha F. Guinn? 9-26-1850
Myers, John to Arminda Carpentur? 10-9-1843 (10-19-1843)
Myers, Newton to Tabitha Furgeson 12-18-1854 (12-24-1854)
Myes, Hugh to Mary Myes 1-11-1854 (1-12-1854)
Mynett, Andrew to Elizabeth Doset 1-29-1838 (2-1-1838)
Myres?, Isham to Charlotta Ritter 4-21-1846 (4-22-1846)
Napeer, Edmand to Matilda Fly 10-21-1843
Nash, Henry to Emily b. Rogers 12-6-1848 (12-14-1848)
Nash, Wm. to Charity Brewer 5-20-1858
Nash, Wm. to Manda Nash 5-9-1846
Nave, Wm. to Angeline Hurst 12-12-1854 (12-12-1855?)
Neal, John O. to S. S. Bullard 2-22-1853
Neal, Joseph to Margaret Margraves 11-?-1849 (11-29-1849)
Neal, Robert to Cornelia Rose 12-18-1854
Needham, George B. to Martha Jane Mays 9-3-1842 (9-11-1842)
Neely, James F. to Sarah J. Denney 3-5-1868
Neil, Ellerlley? to Caroline Masan 4-18-1847 (4-1?-1847)
Neil, Royal to Mary Hodges 3-1-1843
Neil, William to Margaret E. Graham 9-11-1919
Nelson, John B. to Sarah Meyers 3-24-1858
Nelson, John to Emaline Lankford 4-14-1856
Nelson, John to Margret Shofny? 5-26-1846
Nelson, William to Louisa Odel 3-22-1856 (3-23-1856)
Nevels, Bishop to Mary J. Brown 9-16-1865 (9-21-1865)
Newby, Jas. to Virginia A. Powers 8-3-1852
Nice, James to Mary A. Hurst 1-21-1857 (1-27-1857)
Nicely, David to Polly Nance 2-8-1848 (2-17-1848)
Niel, Joseph B. to Lizzie Robertson 7-24-1856
Niel, Thomas J. to Martha J. Bullard 1-27-1857
Nighbert, Hugh to Manirvy? Smith 1-29-1839 (1-30-1839)
Noe, Randolph to Elsebeth Hobbs 1-9-1855
Norris, Obediah to Rebecca Brandsan 6-18-1839 (6-20-1839)
Norris, Reubin to Nancy A. Moor 9-1-1845

Northern, Ephraim to Mary Collins 8-26-1867 (8-29-1867)
Norton, Thomas to Manerva Clemings 3-25-1868 (3-26-1868)
Norton, William H. to Martha A. Walker 3-1-1848 (3-5-1848)
Norton?, James W. to T. Green 6-12-1848 (6-15-1848)
Norvell, B. F. to Mary England 9-19-1851 (9-23-1851)
Norvell, William to Elizabeth Rolin 7-30-1850 (8-4-1850)
Nuckels, John to Jane Bray 11-11-1842 (11-15-1842)
Num?, Silvester? to Levisa Herrell 11-12-1845
Nun, Elisha to Ollie Koiner? 2-9-1861 (2-11-1861)
Nunn, Abner to Margart Harrell 12-15-1838
Nunn, Calloway to Mary M. Waller 8-13-1857
Nunn, Elisha to Effy Huddleston? 8-1-1838
Nunn, Frustan to Elisabeth? Ward 2-17-1848
Nunn, Harry to Tabitha Bunch 8-5-1848 (8-6-1848)
Nunn, M. B. to Elisabeth? Forgerson 11-26-1845 (11-28-1845)
Nunn, M. B. to Elizabeth Ellerson 10-17-1853 (10-20-1853)
Nunn, M. B. to Sarah Furgeson 4-7-1849
Nunn, Phaskil B. to Mary Nunn 2-21-1856
Nunn, Russel to Flurrender Nunn 11-24-1841 (11-25-1841)
Nunn, Silvester to Levica Herrell 11-12-1845 (11-13-1845)
Nunn, Silvester to Margaret Nunn 7-28-1852 (7-29-1852)
Nunn, Sterling to Angeline Vennoy 12-25-1848 (1-4-1849)
Nunn, Sterling to Mariah Herrell 4-19-1850
Nunn, Sterling to Martha J. Herrell 10-4-1850 (10-5-1850)
Nunn, William to Delpha Nunn 8-25-1846 (8-27-1846)
Oaks, William to Lucinda Willis 9-26-1851 (9-28-1851)
Odel, M. L. to Serena Hopper 10-22-1856
Odel, William to Polly Arwine 10-18-1856 (10-23-1856)
Odell, E. J to Haner? Williams 1-8-1848 (1-13-1848)
Odle, Wm. L. to Sarah A. Overlay? 8-28-1854
Olinger, Adam to Margaret McCollum 8-24-1857
Osborn?, James H. to Elizabeth Jane Marcum 12-31-1844 (1-1-1845)
Otey, William R. to Frances A. Cadle 11-12-1866 (11-15-1866)
Ousley, James K. to Mary Edmonson 10-5-1867 (10-10-1867)
Ousley, Mathew to Susannah Ellison 8-17-1857 (8-19-1857)
Ousley, Shermon W. to Margaret M. Kelly 12-19-1856
Ousley, Spencer to Susan Skaggs 10-17-1849 (10-21-1849)
Ousley, T. A. H. to Watstill Tomlinson 5-7-1852 (5-9-1852)
Ousley, Wm. to D. M. Moore 5-7-1852
Overbey, Smith to America Jackson 10-27-1857
Overcash, Caleb to Elizabeth Mosley 4-16-1867 (4-5?-1867)
Overholser, John to Amanda Rittere 1-25-1859
Overton, Albert D. to Mary Ann Fugate 9-24-1866 (9-2?-1866)
Overton, Hiram to Malinda Wilson 1-17-1867 (1-18-1867) B
Overton, M. to C. Riley 1-27-1846 (1-28-1846)
Overton, Melburn to Martha Jane Kesterson 1-29-1868 (1-30-1868)
Overton, Milburn to Elisabeth S. Parkey 10-26-1846 (10-28-1846)
Overton, R. F. to M. J. Mason 6-9-1865 (6-11-1865)
Overton, R. F. to Martha Jane Mason 6-9-1865 (6-11-1865)
Overton, Robert R. to Mary A. Parkey 9-18-1866 (9-2?-1866)
Overton, Wm. L. to Rachel Fugate 6-8-1840
Owens, Archable? to Tabitha Eldrage? 8-24-1844 (8-29-1844)
Owens, Doctor H. to Jane Chick 1-22-1850 (1-23-1850)
Owens, Elias to Elizabeth Johnson 7-28-1854
Owens, Ellis to E. Johnson 1-28-1854 (1-29-1854)
Owens, George B. to Lucy J. Runion 11-20-1854
Owens, Jacob G. to Nancy Niel 11-29-1853
Owens, James R. to E. Whitaker 1-25-1853
Owens, James to Jane Lee 9-1-1853 (no return)
Owens, John to Orlena J. Fults 12-4-1846
Owens, John to Sarah Readman 2-10-1855 (2-13-1855)
Owens, John to Susan M. Hardy 11-22-1847 (11-25-1847)
Owens, Joseph to China Parton 1-27-1853 (1-30-1853)
Owens, Peter to Lucida Eastes 12-10-1849 (12-12-1849)
Owens, Rodden F. to Amanda Ferrell 5-25-1848
Owens, Roman to Abigal Frier 1-17-1848 (1-18-1848)
Owens, William to Sarah Vane 8-5-1844 (8-6-1844)
Owens, Wm. to Elizabeth Hays? 10-11-1843 (10-12-1843)
Owsley, John to Polla? Powell 8-29-1844 (9-22-1844)
Owsley, Wm. to Matida? Herrel 2-25-1845
Pace, Edwin to Mary Hill 10-7-1853
Pace, Wm. A. to Elizabeth Lawson 10-20-1854 (11-6-1854)
Painter, David to Margrett Woodard 4-7-1856 (4-10-1856)
Painter, James to R. M. Speak 9-19-1853 (9-22-1853)
Painter, John to Rachal Fox 12-27-1852 (1-4-1853)
Palmer, Jesse Green to Sarah Sharp 1-14-1843 (1-?-1843)
Pane, Thos. C. to Jane Burkhart 6-2-1854 (6-6-1854)
Parker, A. I.? W. to Mary Tony 11-7-1846 (11-8-1846)
Parker, Andrew H. to Rebecca Harp 9-10-1856
Parker, Benjamin to Elizabeth Mayes 8-29-1865 (8-31-1865)
Parker, John B. to M. B. Hawley? 9-21-1845? (9-6-1846?)
Parker, John to Susan Proff 1-8-1852
Parker, William to Elizabeth Vermillion 3-21-1848
Parkey, Hugh to Elisabeth A. Fugate 11-11-1856 (11-20-1856)
Parkey, M. G. to R. Fugate 4-16-1859
Parkey, Peter to Sarah Croxdale 12-14-1850
Parkey, Thos. to Polly Edwards 3-34?-1848

Parkey, William to Martha Ann Martin 2-15-1846
Parks, George to Mary Ann Lawson 11-25-1858
Parks, Robert G. to Mary Jane Haynes 5-5-1857 (5-19-1857)
Parks, Simpson to L. T. Nove? 8-20-1845 (8-21-1845)
Parks, W. F. to Marthena McClellan 12-20-1851 (12-28-1851)
Parrat?, Wm. to M. E. Bales 10-7-1844 (10-10-1844)
Parrett, Allen to Sarah Hyslep 12-6-1854 (12-10-1854)
Parrot, Ledford to M. Marcy 3-7-1853 (3-10-1853)
Parrott, Benjamin to Eliza Thomas 1-18-1867 (1-28-1867)
Parrott, John R. to Martha J. Parrott 2-18-1857 (2-19-1857)
Parrott, Taylor to Mary Vanbebber 11-10-1867 B
Parsons, Richard B. to Sallie M. Clark 5-7-1867 (5-9-1867)
Partan, Calvin to Milly Bray 2-20-1842 (2-26-1842)
Parten, James to Jane Jackson 2-21-1844 (2-22-1844)
Parton, L. to N. Cadle 11-6-1859
Parton, Pharo to Polly Wombels 4-10-1856 (4-12-1856)
Patterson, Robert E. to Mary L. Houston 10-8-1857
Patterson, Wm. H. to C. H. Graham 9-1-1859
Paul, Joseph to Nelly Ann Daniels 12-3-1865 (12-7-1865)
Paul, Wm. J. to Abagil S. Daniel 9-24-1866 (9-27-1866)
Payne, D. F. to A. E. Kinser 6-29-1865
Payne, Joel to Sarah A. King 11-5-1853
Payne, Wm. G. to Roday? H. Marcum 7-23-1845
Peace?, Benajah to Elizabeth Fusian 10-1-1839? (10-7-1838)
Peace?, Simon? to Ginsy Balloo 10-1-1838 (10-10-1838)
Pearmon, Samuel to Charlotta Pridemore 9-1-1868 (9-3-1868)
Pearson, William E. to Minda Sanders 4-18-1867
Pearson, William to S. Smithe 5-12-1858
Peck, Canady to Elizabeth Hill 4-27-1857
Peck, John to Jane Fullington 7-3-1855
Peck, Robert to Eliza Beuchen 4-6-1859
Pendleton, Wilborn to Anna Huddleston 10-2-1849 (10-4-1849)
Penington, Jeremiah to Mary E. Rose 8-3-1867 (8-4-1867) B
Perce, Alexander to Presellar Mayers 9-19-1857
Perkeyfile?, James to Dicey? Wilborne? 10-17-1845 (11-10-1845)
Perkins, F. to Nancy McKehan 1-17-1839 (1-9?-1839)
Perry, Paul to Sallie Ann Barger 6-16-1855 (6-17-1855)
Perry, R. H. to M. Almis 6-11-1853 (no return)
Persifall, James A. to Matilda Hurst 9-19-1853
Person, Pleasant H. to Martha Davis 9-23-1848
Person?, Sterling to Elizabeth Davis 12-8-1849 (12-9-1849)
Pheleps, W. B. to Charity Owsley 11-12-1837
Phellps, Andrew to Martha J. Gowin 12-5-1837
Phillips, Andrew to Elinor Goins 4-25-1857 (4-26-1857)
Phillips, F. B. to Dasha Kitinger 5-12-1856 (5-18-1856)
Pierce, Robert to Louiza Myers 4-29-1867
Pike, Benjamin to Elizabeth Wells 12-15-1848 (12-17-1848)
Pike, Jacob to Barthene Jones 10-29-1846 (11-1-1846)
Pillian, John to Sarah Carter? 10-30-1845 (11-2-1845)
Pillian, Thomas to Minta Mannan 10-18-1851 (11-6-1851)
Pirkins, Felix to Nancy McKehan? 1-17-1839
Plank, Christian to Mary McNiel 3-8-1852 (3-11-1852)
Plank, Henry to R. McVay 4-7-1853
Plank, James W. to Mary Jane Edwards 9-28-1848
Pleming, Samuel W. to Lavina Sanders 12-19-1839
Poor, B. to M. E. Herell? 6-14-1845
Poor, Edward to Mary Morris 4-5-1856 (4-10-1856)
Poor, Isaac W. to Caroline England? 7-25-1867 (8-1-1867)
Poor, Isaiah C. to Amilia A. Carrell 7-25-1868 (7-26-1868)
Poore, Henry to Vina Calone 3-10-1849 (3-11-1849)
Poore, Isaac to M. W. Greenlee 7-3-1865 (7-19-1865)
Poore, J. W. to Melvina Poore 3-13-1858 (3-15-1858)
Porrott?, Wesley to Catharine Jennings 9-7-1844 (9-8-1844)
Posey, Ensley to Amada Kelley 7-30-1868 B
Posey, Juballee to Perlina Atkins 8-20-1859
Powel, Richard to Nancy Jones 1-12-1847
Powell, George to Loucinda Hopper 11-22-1839 (11-23-1839)
Powell, George to Mary Owens 9-12-1843
Powell, Harvy to Sally Mcbee 5-3-1838 (5-6-1838)
Powers, Thomas 2-9-1847 (2-11-1847)
Powers, Michel? to Leeby? Ann? Murphy 1-26-1846 (2-6-1846)
Presley, Josiah to Sarah Clapp 11-15-1865 (11-17-1865)
Presley?, Elias to Jane A. Calon 9-19-1849 (9-20-1845?)
Presnell, Elisha A. to Mary D. Ely 8-16-1853
Presnell, Isaac to V. M. Greer 8-5-1858 (8-12-1858)
Presnell, Nathaniel to Eliza Jones? 2-10-1842 (2-11-1842)
Price, James to Pheby Hicks 2-1-1849 (2-8-1849)
Price, William to Deby Large 9-11-1845
Price, Wm. H. to Cathrine Baley 8-15-1853
Pridda, Franklin to Elizabeth Parker 1-20-1854 (1-21-1854)
Pridda, George W. to Perlina Gains 12-17-1853
Pridda, Lewis C. to Elen Davis 4-28-1850
Prideman, Jonathan to Elizabeth Roland 12-30-1852 (1-1-1853)
Prideman?, James M. to Levina Lock 10-30-1847 (10-31-1847)
Pridemoore, George W. to B. Scritchfield 7-4-1853
Pridemore, A. I. to Malinda Eastrage 8-5-1844 (8-18-1844)
Pridemore, G. W. to Barthena Scrichfield 10-9-1854 (10-10-1854)

Pridemore, John W. to Elizabeth Crabtree 3-4-1868
Pridmore, Jo Hiram? to Esther? Hoskins 6-11-1840
Proffit, Enoch to Mary Beeler 7-10-1857 (7-14-1857)
Provance, Wm. to Serena? Russell 2-20-1846 (2-22-1846)
Province, Jno. to Susanah Baley 1-19-1839 (1-20-1839)
Province, John to Margaret Bishop 10-4-1841 (10-10-1841)
Pugh, James M. to S. J. Graceclose 1-15-1853 (1-23-1853)
Pugh, Nicholas S. to Eliza Marcum 10-25-1856 (11-26-1856)
Purkeyfile?, John to Patcy Seals 1-10-1846
Qualls, George M. to Polley McVay 2-14-1854
Quay, Robert to Sarah Caroll 1-7-1838
Rader, Danil to Martha Hollins 5-13-1865 (5-14-1865)
Railey, Daniel to Elizabeth Berry 3-22-1851
Rainey, Ezekiel to Fannie Marion 7-11-1868 (7-26-1868)
Ramsey, Calvin to Polley? Crumbley 10-12-1846 (10-14-1846)
Ramsey, Jos. to Margaret Baker 6-2-1845 (6-8-1845)
Ramsey, Josiah to Elizabeth Sims 2-23-1845 (3-2-1845)
Ramsey, William to Catharine Hatfield 2-6-1868
Ramsey, Wm. to Nancy Clause 12-10-1839 (12-11-1838)
Ramsy, Rial to Nila Collens 1-6-1854 (1-7-1854)
Raney, Ezekiel to Omey Gons 2-1-1853
Raney, John to Ann Yaden 5-31-1854 (6-1-1854)
Raney, William J. to Malinda Goins 10-30-1856 (11-3-1856)
Rannins?, Latan to Becky Hammack 7-18-1846 (7-19-1846)
Rawlet, Wm. T. to Elizabeth Brown 12-12-1859
Rawson, Ire to Jane Wilcock 10-29-1857 (11-1-1857)
Ray, David to Betsy Maples 2-9-1839
Ray, John to Emily Davis 2-1-1844 (2-3-1844)
Rector, Jesse to Susannah Rector 9-2-1839 (9-3-1839)
Redman, David to Mary ann Carmack 9-5-1841
Redman, George to Elisabeth B. Burk 11-1-1855 (11-3-1855)
Redmon, Caswell to Cathrine Willson 10-11-1856
Redmon, Franklin to Anna? Murry 1-7-1846 (1-15-1846)
Redmon, Jacob to J. Letterrell 12-26-1866 (12-27-1866)
Redmon, Pallestine L. to M. Ball 8-21-1853 (8-22-1853)
Redmon, Thos. to Martha J. Carr 1-4-1850 (1-6-1850)
Redmond, James F. to E. L. Mathis 7-24-1858
Reed, Eleane? to Nancy Maden 1-25-1847 (1-26-1847)
Reed, Jacob to Milly Webb 12-31-1846
Reed, Samuel to Sarah Lee 12-7-1846
Reen, David to Viny Hopper 11-17-1865 (11-24-1865)
Renfro, Moses J. to Mary Ann Danahoo 1-28-1843
Renolos?, Henry to Chaniy? Preday 10-13-1844
Retherford, William F. to Leta S. Shoemate 4-7-1859
Retter, Moses to Rhoda Carr 1-5-1842 (1-6-1842)
Reynolds, Parker D. to Nancy England 9-19-1865 (9-28-1865)
Rhea?, Lewis? to Margarett Latan? 11-14-1842 (11-22-1842)
Rice, C. F.? to Dicey? M. Rogers 1-28-1847
Rice, Clinton Y. to Nancy Hurst 7-25-1854 (7-26-1854)
Rice, Harper to Eliza Hurst 12-30-1848 (12-31-1848)
Rice, James L. to Nancy N. Whitaker 1-10-1859
Rice, James S.? to Bartheny Nunn 6-20-1842
Rice, James to Susan Arnold 10-13-1854 (10-15-1854)
Rice, John L. to Mary Bingham 9-29-1854
Rice?, Elbert to Emily L. Taker 2-14-1850
Richardson, John to Mary L. Davis 2-13-1868
Richardson, Wm. to Martha A. Garull 9-19-1853
Richerson, John to Louisa J. Forgerson 12-24-1852 (12-26-1852)
Richie, Matthew to Louiza Jones 3-30-1867 (4-7-1867) B
Rider, George F. to Mary Sulfrage 1-14-1867
Right, Greenberry to Sarah? Jane Hopper 11-23-1841 (11-25-1841)
Rigsbee, James H. to Lucy Jane Neal 7-21-1868 (7-26-1868)
Rigsby, Thomas to Martha York 7-30-1866
Riley, Nelson to Jane Willson 5-29-1851
Ristan, John to Jane McCulla 2-1-1856 (2-4-1856)
Ritchards, George W. to Mary Jane Wyeman 3-7-1859
Ritchie, Harvey to Lucy A. Mason 6-11-1867 (6-20-1867)
Ritchie, James to Barbary Parkey 7-7-1840
Rite, Green B. to Sarah A. Hix 3-8-1855
Rite, Thomas to Mary Sexton 9-8-1849 (9-15-1849)
Rite, William M. to Mary Linch 6-5-1849 (6-6-1849)
Ritter, Aaron to Bethena Posey 9-13-1853
Ritter, Henry to Unica Hopson 12-17-1853 (12-18-1853)
Ritter, John to Syntha Hurst 7-24-1839
Ritter, William to Barbra Hollin 11-27-1846
Rivett, Hiram A. to Sarah Lynch 10-15-1856
Roach, Mathias C. to Susannah King 7-25-1855 (7-29-1855)
Roark, James to Sarah Freyor 7-28-1855 (7-29-1855)
Roark, John T. to Mary A. Patterson 7-8-1867 (7-11-1867)
Roark, John to Martha J. Jones 3-6-1854 (3-10-1854)
Roark, John to Turressy Murphey 11-10-1857
Roarkes, James to M. A. Morison 5-1-1865 (5-4-1865)
Roarks, John to K. Masingil? 3-2-1846 (3-5-1846)
Roarks, Timothy to Polly Williams 3-12-1840
Roberson, Daniel to Nancy Lemar 9-20-1843
Robert, James A. to Mary Jane Poor 2-19-1856
Roberts, Hiram C. to Susan Adams 12-14-1866
Roberts, Nicholas M. to Martha Thomas 9-10-1848 (9-20-1848)
Robertson, Allen to Elizabeth Bolinger 4-20-1842
Robinson, Alexander to Lina Gibson 12-26-1867 (1-10-1868) B
Robinson, Ezekiel to Winney Vandergriff 11-15-1849
Robinson, James to Elizabeth Honeycutt 8-26-1839 (8-27-1839)
Robinson, John to Lerinda? Hurst 12-17-1847 (12-23-1847)
Robinson, John to Louisa Sharp 9-21-1839 (9-22-1839)
Robinson, Nelson to E. M. Henderon 2-24-1853
Robinson, Thomas to Nancy Hunter 1-18-1842 (1-23-1842)
Robinson, Wiatt J. to Polly Williams 10-12-1839
Robinson, Wm. to Rebecca Rogers? 9-10-1839 (9-17-1839)
Robinson, Woodbery to Nancy Evans 10-18-1849 (10-26-1849)
Roe, Benjamin J. to Ulinney Debusk 2-12-1868 (2-13-1868)
Rogan, Theophilus to Mary Louisa Graham 12-14-1853
Rogers, Camador to Mary Grimes 3-25-1849 (3-26-1849)
Rogers, Canada to Nancy Malinda Vanbeber? 10-2-1846
Rogers, Cornelius to Manery? Bowman 6-19-1845
Rogers, F. H. to Emaley? Beelor? 11-14-1845
Rogers, G. W. to Elizabeth Perry 4-22-1859
Rogers, Henderson to Anna Caywood 9-13-1848 (9-28-1848)
Rogers, Hugh L. W. to Barbara Caywood 9-12-1843 (10-5-1843)
Rogers, James K. to Eliza Lajasce? 6-17-1842
Rogers, M. M. to Mary White 11-16-1846
Rogers, William to Lucy Moor 1-5-1839
Rogers, Wm. M. to Susan Paul? 2-26-1840
Rogers, Wm. to Lucy Moor 1-5-1839 (1-6-1839)
Rogers, Wm. to Reeny Howerton 11-10-1865
Roland, D. to S. Collinsworth 2-22-1856 (2-24-1856)
Roley, Vincen to Tempy? Davis 8-21-1844
Rollens, James to B. Crigger 1-26-1859
Romines, William to Polly Presly 10-12-1839 (10-13-1839)
Roolin, M. to E. Campbell 8-6-1858
Rosan, James to Angelina Sanders 12-4-1848 (12-10-1848)
Rosan?, Asa to Emaline Mallicoat 3-23-1849 (3-25-1849)
Rose, G. W. to A. J. Cadle 12-17-1852 (12-22-1852)
Rose, J. to M. A. Wilsono 9-13-1854
Rose, James to Jane Guy 1-8-1866 (1-26-1866)
Rose, Jefferson to Sarah Brock 8-23-1842 (8-24-1842)
Rose, John to Louisa Willis 9-7-1865
Rosenbalm, George P. to Nancy J. Hopson 4-9-1857
Rosenbalm, Hamilton to Eliza A. Phelps 9-1-1866 (9-2-1866)
Rosenbalm, Harrell to Emly Hurst 3-29-1859
Rossan, Fidelio to Julia A. Maticks 3-10-1857
Rossan?, Joshua to Elizabeth Laarakge 1-17-1844 (1-18-1844)
Roth, Philip to Malvina Hunnacott 2-20-1855
Roust, Henrey to Freely Beelor 11-6-1855
Rowatt?, Morris P.? to Darkey Campbell 9-26-1843 (9-27-1843)
Rowe, Washington to Margaret Smith 1-9-1840 (1-10-1840)
Rowe, Wiley to Emaley Person 1-5-1847 (1-6-1847)
Rowlan, Samuel E. to Mary Green 2-22-1867 (2-24-1867)
Rowland, Creed to Emaline Smith 12-17-1842 (12-22-1842)
Rowland, Michael to Emely Adams 12-29-1866 (1-7-1867)
Rowlett, Jesse B. to Louisa Jones 2-20-1856
Rowlett, Luther R. to Rebecca Yerra 8-26-1856
Rowlett, Macknep to Nancy Brooks 7-31-1838 (8-1-1838)
Rowson, Ire to Jane Wilcocks 10-29-1857 (11-1-1857)
Royston, James C. to Martha Willson 1-15-1859
Ruha?, Robert to M. J. King 3-24-1846 (4-1-1846)
Runions, James C. to Martha M. Fortner 2-5-1856
Runnolds, John to Rebecca Sourd 11-26-1867
Runnyans, Charles W. to Jane Eastus 8-27-1839
Russel, A. S. to Edney I. Neil 1-11-1845 (1-16-1845)
Russel, A. to Nancy Lynch 12-12-1855 (12-16-1855)
Russel, James L. to Catherin L. Sharp 12-20-1845 (12-25-1845)
Russell, James to Susan Hedrick 6-11-1866
Russell, Jason to Elizabeth Reyers 6-15-1858
Russell, Joseph to Mary T. Yoakum 10-25-1859
Russell, Josiah to Elizabeth Gentry 8-13-1839
Rutherford, Wm. to Rachael Smith 10-9-1841 (10-10-1841)
Rutledge, Caleb W. to Eliza Ann Berry 9-20-1843
Rutledge, Nelson to Mary Killian 3-14-1857
Rutledge, T. to P. Baldwin 5-4-1853
Rutledge, William to Nancy Blanton 11-30-1861
Ryans, J. M. to Ann Debusk 10-3-1865 (10-5-1865)
Salyers, Crage to Elizabeth Chumbley 4-5-1854
Sampson, Nutan to Minerva Kellams 10-18-1855
Samuel, David A. to Ruth Green 9-14-1852
Sanders, David to Polly Geasley 8-5-1850 (8-7-1850)
Sanders, Hemelton to Anjaline Maden 7-30-1850 (8-1-1850)
Sanders, Jno. to Arrena Bundren 12-24-1838 (12-25-1838)
Sanders, Robert to Mary England 1-20-1844 (1-21-1844)
Sanders, Rubin R. to Mary C. Carter 3-23-1865 (3-24-1865)
Sands, James H. to Lucy Killin 12-12-1867
Sands, Jas. P. to Nancy Simmons 12-2-1856
Sands, John to Sarah A. Poore 12-14-1858 (12-18-1858)
Sane, G. W. to Margaret Lane 9-1-1865 (9-3-1865)
Saunders, John L. to Margret N. Stone 11-20-1865 (11-22-1865)

Saville, John F. to Margaret R. Davis 5-23-18687
Sawyer, Andrew to Elizabeth Arney 2-7-1865
Sawyers, Ambrose to Elizabeth Jones 5-27-1848 (5-30-1848)
Sawyers, John M. to Marian J. E. Martin 4-3-1849
Sawyers, Thos. L. to Louisa Dobbs 7-30-1839
Sawyers, William to Elizabeth Shoemate 11-24-1854
Scalf, Ira to Nancy McVay 1-27-1854 (2-2-1854)
Scalf, Miles J. to Martha E. Qualls 7-10-1854 (no return)
Scalf, Miles to Catherine Self 9-14-1854
Scalf, Richard to Jane Perry 3-1-1852 (3-2-1852)
Scott, E. L. to C. Rose 5-2-1853 (5-3-1853)
Scott, John to Vina Brooks 6-10-1848 (6-11-1848)
Scott, Joseph G. to M. Niel 2-3-1853
Scott, Nathaniel M. to Elisabeth? Yaunce? 11-24-1845 (12-4-1845)
Scrichfield, William to Mary A. Collins 6-3-1856 (6-5-1856)
Seafield?, Jesse to L. Callaham? 3-28-1846 (4-4-1846)
Seal, Enos to Miscelany Sutton 3-11-1867 (3-19-1867)
Seals, G. G. to Lucinda Mayes 10-15-1856 (11-19-1856)
Seals, Marshal to Louisa Houston 9-4-1850
Seals, Noel to Elizabeth Southers 4-25-1866 (5-10-1866)
Seals, R. S. to Martha Lewis 10-6-1855 (10-7-1855)
Sebolt, A. to N. Harkins 1-31-1852 (2-1-1852)
Sensabagh?, John L. to Manila McAnalla? 6-7-1847 (6-9-1847)
Sephis, Joseph to Elizabeth Salyers 3-24-1859 (no executed)
Sevier, Wm. R. to Louisa A. Evans 12-26-1864
Sewell, H. to S. J. Coterell 4-22-1858
Sexton, William to Jane Strifle? 4-20-1839 (3-?-1838?)
Shanon?, Wm. to Milly? Rhey 12-7-1844 (12-8-1844)
Sharp, Ambris? to Elisabeth Shofney? 12-15-1847 (12-16-1847)
Sharp, D. to E. Heath 1-1-1852 (1-8-1852)
Sharp, Daniel to Caraline Nash 12-27-1852
Sharp, Esaw to Tabitha? L. Toliver 3-1-1842 (3-6-1842)
Sharp, George W. to Rebecca Bryant 8-29-1851
Sharp, H. M. to Matilda E. Jones 3-15-1850 (3-19-1850)
Sharp, Henry H. to Rachael Caywood 8-12-1854 (8-21-1854)
Sharp, Henry to Cathrine Sowder 12-22-1849 (1-1-1850)
Sharp, Henry to Cela Freemon 7-5-1838 (7-6-1838)
Sharp, Isaac H. to Nancey E. White 3-5-1866 (3-15-1866)
Sharp, Jacob to Elizabeth Nash 3-13-1840
Sharp, Jonathan to Margret Elviny? Lynch 1-5-1846 (1-8-1846)
Sharp, Joseph D. to Elizabeth Coward 3-18-1854 (3-23-1854)
Sharp, Joseph to Mary Jane Sowder 11-7-1851 (11-11-1851)
Sharp, Larkin? D. to Nancy Janeway 6-19-1847 (6-20-1847)
Sharp, Levi to Elizabeth Graves 1-18-1840 (6-30-1840)
Sharp, Mathew to Manerva Carr 12-4-1849 (12-6-1849)
Sharp, Wiley to Matilda Wood 10-22-1851 (9-20-1849)
Sharp, William K. to Mary Lemara 9-15-1849 (9-20-1849)
Sharp, Wm. C. to Elizabeth Mason 9-27-1851 (10-2-1851)
Sharp, Wm. H. to Elender? Oaks 4-18-1845 (4-20-1845)
Shaw, John M. to Emaline Mayabb 3-7-1854
Shaw, John M. to M. J. Ryan 11-15-1853
Shaw, Wm. to L. A. [Lucy A.] Brown 4-23-1853 (4-26-1853) *
Shaw?, John M. to Manerva J. Waters 8-1-1865 (8-2-1865)
Sheffle, Wm. D. to M. L. Becknel 9-5-1855
Shelby, John to Nancy Sheckels? 10-23-1844 (10-27-1844)
Shelly, James to Annice Seals 10-23-1847 (11-4-1847)
Shelton, Anderson to Mary Hurst 11-12-1859
Shelton, Eli to Mahaley? Moser? 4-3-1847 (4-4-1847)
Shelton, John H. to Sarah E. Hurst 10-14-1867 (10-17-1867)
Shelton, Joseph to Martha Ann Griger 4-27-1868
Shelvy?, Isaac to Leor? Capps 4-27-1847 (4-29-1847)
Sherman, Thompson to Elizabeth England 1-8-1844 (1-9-1844)
Sherp?, Richard G. to Margaret Ellerson 6-8-1854 (6-10-1854)
Shields, James T.? to Mary A. Glenn 5-11-1848
Shilby, Jacob to Mailda Scalf 8-14-1851
Shishen, John M. T. to Letta Warnacutt 5-31-1848
Shoemaker, Samuel to Mahala Hodges 1-4-1851
Shoemate, Mark to Elza Davis 10-8-1866 (10-11-1866)
Shomate, Bales to Rebecca Lolson? 3-4-1850 (3-7-1850
Shomate, John W. to Berrelvy? Billingsly 5-15-1846
Shomate?, L. B. to Louisa Hodges 4-4-1846 (4-5-1846)
Short, Calvin to Maiah Jones 6-21-1854 (6-26-1854)
Short, Greenberry to Catharin Ferrel 7-13-1842 (7-14-1842)
Short, Wm. to (see Wm. Shaw)
Shultz, Martin V. to Margret V. Dunsmore 11-13-1850
Shumate, Isaac to Catherine J. Freemana 10-8-1851 (10-9-1851)
Shumate, Thomas T. to Elizabeth Conner 12-31-1866 (1-1-1867)
Simmions?, Enoch C. to Patey? Davis 9-4-1847 (9-5-1847)
Simmons, Albert to Mary Roland 12-30-1852
Simmons, James R. to Elisabeth J. Roberts 4-7-1856 (4-8-1856)
Simmons, James to E. A. Thompson 10-8-1845 (10-9-1845)
Simmons, James to Levina Hatfield 7-14-1854
Simmons, John to Abby Harpa 7-31-1857 (8-11-1857)
Simmons, John to Emaly? Stone 1-1-1849 (1-22-1849)
Simmons, John to Mary M. Lambert 3-3-1851 (3-5-1851)
Simmons, Joseph to Martha England 8-5-1865 (8-24-1865)
Simmons, Robert to M. A. Green 7-1-1853

Simmons, Thomas to Orlena Jones 1-28-1851
Simmons, Wesley to Nancy Owens 8-2-1849 (8-3-1849)
Simons, H. C. to S. Radner 11-10-1864
Sims, James H. to Mary E. Lakins 1-3-1868
Singleton, James to Caroline Barnard 12-9-1847 (12-11-1847)
Singleton, Jeremiah to Lotty Carpenter 11-30-1838 (1-22-1838)
Singleton, Richard to Rachael Cumber? 10-20-1839
Sivil, Timothy G. to Emly J. Cadle 1-1-1867 (1-3-1867)
Slatton, John to Molinda? Chumbly 9-6-1845
Slatton, Nicolis to Lucinda Cardwell 5-2-1856 (5-7-1856)
Slauter, Jacob S. to Sarah E. Hopkins 12-15-1866 (12-20-1866)
Slone, James to E. Wolfenbarger 12-9-1845
Slvan [sic], Hiram to Mary Ellis 9-4-1851
Smiley, Jacob to Suanah? Wilburn? 3-27-1844
Smith, Absalom G. to Mary Davis 2-5-1857 (2-22-1857)
Smith, Alvis to Malinda Berry 6-22-1867 (6-24-1867)
Smith, Andrew B. to Ann Hobbs 8-27-1847 (8-29-1847)
Smith, Berrill? to Faney? ----- 12-22-1846 (12-23-1846)
Smith, Constantin? to Mary Moor 2-6-1847 (2-11-1847)
Smith, Constentine to Emely Brooks 8-28-1866
Smith, Elijah to Susan Roberts 2-17-1854 (11-5-1854)
Smith, Franklin M. to Elizabeth Alexander 3-5-1842 (3-8-1842)
Smith, G. W. to Matilda Lane 1-7-1839 (1-13-1839)
Smith, George to Sarah A. Hurst 5-12-1852
Smith, Harvy to Druciler Goinbral 9-23-1844
Smith, J. H. to Nancy A. Edny 6-27-1865 (7-1-1865)
Smith, J. W. to Lucinda Ford 11-7-1848 (11-9-1848)
Smith, J. W. to Sarah F. Moyers 6-12-1865 (6-15-1865)
Smith, James A. to Nancy E. Ellison 10-30-1846
Smith, James A. to Sarah A. Wright 3-31-1868 (4-2-1868)
Smith, James F. D. S. to Manervy Jane Harrison 4-25-1853 (4-28-1853)
Smith, James L. to Louiza M. Collensworth 8-20-1867 (8-21-1867)
Smith, Jirriael? to Mary Ann Fletchere 12-25-1843 (12-27-1843)
Smith, John M. to Selina Leavis? 3-29-1851 (4-4-1851)
Smith, John to Rena Barnard 5-16-1855 (5-17-1855)
Smith, John to Sarah C. Bulb 4-22-1855 (not exec.)
Smith, Moses to Polly Kesterson 3-24-1849 (3-26-1849)
Smith, Robert to Mary Smith 2-13-1867 (2-15-1867)
Smith, William L. to Elizabeth Ann Sharp 2-19-1856
Snavely, Adam Y. to Angeline Clarkson 2-20-1867
Snavely, James to Martha? Year? 7-11-1845 (7-17-1845)
Snavely, Jonas to Lena? Fletcher 8-3-1850 (8-4-1850)
Snavely, Leander to Elizabeth Mustart 9-9-1865
Snider, J. T. to Catharine Cardwell 10-8-1866 (10-9-1866)
Snider, James H. to Sallie McBee 1-31-1867 (1-31-1867)
Snider, John A. to Nancy J. Stone 12-26-1863 (12-31-1863)
Snodgrass, James to Cathrine S. Thompson 1-7-1856 (1-8-1856)
Snow, Cyrus A. to Frances C. Thompson 11-22-1867 (11-23-1867)
Sourd?, Henry to Rebecca Hacker 11-3-1851 (11-4-1851)
Southerland, Joel to Martha Hamelton 4-14-1842
Southern, Garett to Elizabeth Willis 6-26-1850
Southern, Garrett to Elizabeth Willis 7-16-1850 (7-17-1850)
Southern, Isaac to Sarah Chadwell 11-7-1843 (10?-8-1843)
Southern, Joseph to Jennetter Brooks 11-19-1849
Southern, M. D. to Mary Nave 1-29-1856
Southern, Robert to Martha Ann Henderson 5-31-1849
Southern, Stephen to Polly Lambert 8-13-1839
Sowder, Adam to Anna Dunn 10-9-1855 (10-15-1855)
Sowder, Daniel F. to Nancy Willis 1-16-1847 (2-21-1847)
Sowder, Henry M. to Rachel Ausmus 12-6-1847
Sowder, Jacob to Matilda Ausmus 3-13-1848 (3-16-1848)
Sowder, Michael to Mandy Lea 9-28-1843
Sowder, Peruda to Elisabeth Ausmus 4-2-1849 (4-6-1849)
Sowder, Richd. to Sidney Lin? 2-17-1840 (5-17-1840)
Sowder, William H. to Adeline Buchanan 1-2-1868
Sowder, William to Elizabeth Turner 5-9-1857
Sowder, Wm. to Sarah Brummit 4-6-1846 (4-9-1846)
Sparks, Preston to Mary Eley? 1-24-1849
Sparks, Thomas to M. D. Ely 12-5-1859
Sparks, Wm. H. to Mirah Goins 10-8-1851
Speer?, Arthur to Mary Margraes 4-13-1842 (4-14-1842)
Spillars, Daniel to Julia Qualls 4-18-1850
Spillers?, James to E.J. Qualls? 7-8-1847
Spradling, William to Mary Carpenter 10-31-1850
Sproles, John to Sarah Bales 11-18-1843 (11-23-1843)
Sprowls, Thomas to Mary Jinkins 2-12-1868 (2-14-1868)
Stamper, Calvin to Elizabeth J. Higginbottom 9-1-1857
Stanaford, S. to M. M. Eastis 6-3-1858
Standafer, William to Elisabeth Jones 3-5-1847
Standefer, Jobe C. to Amanda Dunsmore 7-16-1866
Standifer, William to Mary Bolin 9-4-1867
Standley, Scott to Elizabeth Warf 8-27-1868
Standsbery?, William A. to Elisabeth? Carnard? 7-20-1846 (8-21-1846)
Stansberry, Jas. to Catharine Barnard 1-11-1839 (1-13-1839)
Stansbury, Riley to Elizabeth Webb 1-15-1848
Stanter, Shelton to Nancy Taylor 12-21-1863
Stephens, Richard to Rebecca Smith 8-25-1852

Stern, Edward to Elizabeth H. Evans 12-26-1867
Stewarts, H. to S. Morris 11-30-1852
Stokeley, Edward W. to Louisa Barnard 9-24-1865 (9-21?-1865)
Stone, Robert to Margret Thompson 9-9-1859
Stone, S. W. to C. J. Mason 6-19-1865
Stout, James M. to Sarah Crage 6-28-1846 (11-29-1846)
Strevels, John to Mary Ann Sherac? 10-19-1849 (10-21-1849)
Strevels?, William to Lidaey? Lane 1-3-1846 (1-3-1845?)
Strevle, William to Nancy Lane? 5-11-1842 (5-15-1842)
Stuard, Martin to Rhoda J. Hubbard 9-30-1867
Stuart, Isaac to Sarah Hurst 6-24-1849
Stuart, Joseph to Mary Willson 11-6-1859
Sufrage, John to Salla Calline 9-19-1844
Sulfradge, Mc. to Mary A. Collins 8-14-1867 (8-15-1867) B
Sulfrage, Andrew to Margaret Cook 9-17-1851 (9-18-1851)
Sulfrage, Fannister to Mahala Odle 5-5-1866 (5-6-1866)
Sulfrage, John to Emanda Cook 3-29-1856 (3-30-1856)
Sulfridge, William to Martha Seebolt? 3-30-1850
Sulfrig, C. Q. to Nancy Frith 2-5-1862 (2-7-1862)
Sulivan, John to Lucindy Davis 10-19-1842 (10-20-1842)
Sullivan, Calvin to Lucinda Englebarger 10-6-1866 (10-7-1866)
Summermon, Adam to Jane Carpenter 6-29-1839 (6-30-1839)
Sumpter, Geo. to Lucy Hoult 7-26-1838
Sumpter, Henry to Ann Doolen 4-12-1839
Sumpter, John to Milla Jones 5-8-1855
Susong, Jacob to Polly Wheelor 11-29-1854 (11-30-1854)
Sutteen, Daniel to Malissa Grimes 7-28-1856
Sutten, Robert to Lucy Muncy 9-30-1838
Sutton, George to Martha Englent 2-25-1851 (8-12-1851)
Sutton, John to Sarah Pridemore 12-4-1844 (12-16-1844)
Sutton, Thomas to Matilda Brown 12-21-1855 (12-25-1855)
Sutton, Thomas to Olive Mayer 11-2-1859
Sutton, William to Louiza Williams 10-16-1867 (10-20-1867)
Sutton, Zackariah to Lucy Ann Eastrage 10-24-1844
Swann?, John L. to Elisabeth? E. Eve 7-23-1846 (8-2-1846)
Sweet, Binson? to Rebecca Prestley 11-27-1848
Sweet, D. B. to M. A. Moor 12-31-1852
Tackett, Oliven to Nancy Hall 12-12-1839
Tackitt, D. B. to Martha J. Dougherty 2-27-1855
Taff?, Thos. B. to N. I. Kellons? 10-4-1845 (10-5-1845)
Taff?, Wilson to Margaret Worley 6-14-1842 (6-15-1842)
Taillor, Wm. to A. McGeorge 2-26-1858
Tailor, G. to Cathrine Grimes 2-21-1853
Tailor, Wm. to Agness McGeorge 2-26-1858
Tanny?, Alexander to Elisabeth? Clapp 8-22-1848
Tapp, Daniel to Martha Overbay 6-9-1866 (6-10-1866)
Tass, Lewis to Mary Simpson 1-12-1865 (12-12-1865)
Taylor, Elijah to Nancy Write 9-10-1844
Taylor, James H. to Eliza Cloud 9-2-1854 (9-3-1854)
Taylor, James H. to Sarah Vanaver 11-1-1855 (11-4-1855)
Taylor, James P. to Sarah Nevels 4-8-1867 (4-14-1867)
Taylor, James to Debah Bourman 12-18-1858
Taylor, Jas. W. to Susan Chadwell 1-9-1839 (1-10-1839)
Taylor, Joel to Sary? Ann Ritter 1-15-1847
Taylor, Leander to Nancy Lawson 3-25-1868 (3-26-1868)
Taylor, Nelson to Louisa Nunn 9-10-1838
Taylor, Sampson to Polly Miller 7-27-1839
Taylor, William H. to Catharine Marlar 1-21-1867 (1-25-1867)
Taylor, William to Elizabeth Chadwell 2-15-1867 (2-17-1867)
Teague, Calvin to Jane Buchanan 7-21-1858
Teague, Joshua to Nancy Harp 10-31-1856
Thacker, John to Elizabeth M. Toney 6-28-1854
Theirs, Daniel to Kisicror? Kawin 9-23-1847 (9-24-1847)
Thomas, Allen to Elisebeth Hazelwood 3-3-1855 (3-26-1855)
Thomas, Carter to Darcas Jones 9-21-1866 (10-7-1866) B
Thomas, Elijah to Nancy Rebecca Greer 11-21-1867 (11-24-1867)
Thomas, George M. to Martha A. Main 4-1-1868 (4-9-1868)
Thomas, George W. to Deborah Rose 3-1-1856
Thomas, John to Milly Kirk 10-22-1846 (10-24-1846)
Thomas, John to Pheby Large 2-15-1846
Thomas, Joseph to Catharine Wirich 5-28-1839 (5-8?-1839)
Thomas, Joseph to Sarah Ann Kirk 5-7-1846 (5-?-1846)
Thomas, Samuel to Nancy Snow 2-9-1847 (2-11-1847)
Thomas, Wm. to A. Bowden 5-8-1838?
Thompson, A. J. to Susanah Eastridge 9-3-1866 (9-14-1866)
Thompson, Caleb N. to Clementin N. Henderson 8-10-1848 (8-11-1848)
Thompson, John F. to Melley? Harris 10-7-1842 (10-8-1842)
Thompson, Robert M. to Mary A. Burchfield 1-10-1867
Tolbert, Davis to Abigail Marcum 4-25-1868 (5-7-1868)
Toney?, William F. to Orleany Johnson 5-5-1849
Townsley, William H. to Tennessee R. Smith 4-15-1868 (4-16-1868)
Townzeen, Preston to Deliza Lay 3-31-1855
Tramel, Wm. to Margaret Wilson 1-21-1852 (1-22-1852)
Tredaway, Alfed to Rebecca Gresly? 11-3-1849
Trent, Cornelus to Tebitha Scalf 1-6-1854
Trent, Zackariah to Matilda Scelf? 2-12-1850
Trese, Jefferson to Cristiniy? Wilson 2-19-1842

True?, James to Nancy Pitman 12-15-1841 (12-17-1841)
Tucker, Mathew to Mary Oaks 1-27-1846 (1-28-1846)
Tucker, Paschal to Rhoda Dees 2-24-1844 (2-29-1844)
Tuder, Harmon to Sarah Nuckles 5-18-1854
Turnbull, James to Mary Raby 12-4-1845
Turner, Christopher to Mary Fortner 10-12-1859
Turner, Jac to Mollie Lane 12-30-1865 (12-31-1865)
Turner, Joel to Mary Sharp 11-14-1845 (11-19-1845)
Tyar, Daniel to Nancy Simmons 9-20-1865
Ulright, George F. to Sarah Ausmus 1-30-1867 (2-3-1867)
Upton, Edward to Malinda Saler 7-22-1859
Upton, Gainford to Lewisa Green 3-23-1859
Upton, Geo. J. to Catherine Moore 10-1-1851 (10-3-1851)
Upton, John to Mary Rogers 7-7-1851 (7-9-1851)
Upton?, James to Elender Dulin 11-27-1853
Upton?, Wm. to Polly Burns 6-13-1849 (6-15-1849)
Vanbebber, A. to Louisa Lee 2-25-1848
Vanbebber, Isaac to Sarah Hamelton 7-23-1839 (7-30-1839)
Vanbebber, J. M. to Hina M. Yoakeem 12-1-1851 (12-14-1851)
Vanbebber, James to Elizabeth Snuffer 12-30-1839 (2-14-1841?)
Vanbebber, John M. to Elisabeth Beilor 8-19-1856
Vanbebber, John M. to Manervia J. Kincaid 4-12-1843 (4-?-1843)
Vanbebber, R. to Jane Susong 1-19-1858 (1-20-1858)
Vanbebber, Robert to Margaret J. Susong 1-19-1858 (1-20-1858)
Vance, Daniel to Martha Hurst 9-25-1856 (10-2-1856)
Vance, Prior L. to Catherine Felps 2-19-1850 (2-22-1850)
Vanderpool, John to Manervy Smith 3-18-1843
Vandevarter?, Larkan to Ony? Slaven? 4-5-1842 (4-7-1842)
Vandeventer, Robert to Rachael Kelly 6-19-1859
Vanforkis, Robert to Emly Cross 5-1-1865 (5-4-1865)
Vannoy, William L. to Levinda Venoy 12-10-1847
Vaughn, Jacob to Patsy L. Greenlee 11-15-1851 (11-18-1851)
Veatch, Philip to Vineny Nunn 3-20-1842 (6-20-1842)
Venable, B. to V. O. Acreer 8-7-1852 (8-10-1852)
Venable, James to Louisa McCrary 7-23-1846
Venable, Wm. to Jane McNeil 2-1-1846
Venany?, Joel to F. Crumbley 1-18-1845
Venoy, William J. to Matilda Fox 10-15-1853
Venoy, William L. to Lucy S. Venoy 11-29-1849 (12-1-1849)
Vickery, F. H. to Eliza J. Burch 9-27-1852
Wadkins, Joseph to Catharine Thomas 1-9-1838
Wagby?, John to Eliza Vanbebber 8-19-1850 (8-15?-1850)
Waggoner, James to Lucinda Ashten 2-12-1853
Waggoner, Thomas to Lucinda Batton 8-30-1852 (3?-30-1852)
Waggoner?, William? to Lucinda Braden 1-7-1843 (2-19-1843)
Walker, Elihue to Barberry Parks 10-4-1856 (10-5-1856)
Walker, Franklin to Letla Brogans 9-24-1851 (9-25-1851)
Walker, Henry to Lucenda Dougherty 7-20-1839 (7-21-1839)
Walker, Isaac to Alyra? Rice 3-8-1848 (3-9-1848)
Walker, Jacob to Louisa Lewis 11-26-1846
Walker, Jacob to M. Davis 11-9-1846
Walker, James to Mary Ann Campbell 7-2-1849
Walker, James to Mary Ann Campbell 7-20-1849
Walker, John W. to Lucretia Campbell 7-21-1850
Walker, John to Lucinda Atkins 9-10-1856 (9-12-1856)
Walker, Jonathan T.? to Amanda J. Tussey? 12-23-1843 (12-25-1843)
Walker, Samuel to Louisa Parks 3-13-1848 (3-16-1848)
Walker, Thomas B. to Elizabeth Nash 9-15-1842
Wallace, George Washington to Molinda Hendrix 10-16-1841 (10-17-1841)
Wallace, William C. to Elisebeth Helms 12-28-1854 (1-2-1855)
Wallar, Isaac to Manirva Sumpter 12-2-1844
Wallen, Joseph to Manda Simmons 12-2-1858
Waller, James to Livisa? Liford 12-5-1843 (12-10-1843)
Waller, William N. to Martha Bundren 1-1-1856 (1-27-1856)
Wallie, Wm. H. to Mary Ann Mitchel 9-19-1844 (9-22-1844)
Wallin, James F. to A. E. McKeehan 1-7-1856
Wallin, John to Elizabeth Billingsley? 5-8-1843
Wallis, Thomas to Lurinda Sanders 10-6-1848 (10-8-1848)
Wallon, E. V. to Jane Graham 12-30-1846
Warick, Henry to Mary Burch 6-5-1847 (6-6-1847)
Warnicutt, William to Letty Ward 12-21-1842 (12-23-1842)
Warrin?, Thomas to Eleana? Smith 12-9-1844 (12-12-1844)
Waters, Lemuel to Nuvena Hurst 7-26-1858 (7-27-1858)
Watson, Calvin to Elizabeth Cupp 2-3-1865 (2-4-1865)
Watson, Nathaniel to Maoma Browning 4-10-1865
Watts, Wm. E. to Belinda Ely 11-28-1863 (12-1-1863)
Waymires, Joseph to M. Lewis 9-28-1858
Webb, Iredale to Dicy Lee 5-19-1840
Webb, Larkin to Peggy Lea 2-26-1839 (2-28-1839)
Webe, William to Nancy Bray 2-24-1854 (lic. ret'd.)
Welbourn, Claborne to Polly Gibert 4-13-1839 (4-14-1839)
Welch, Calvin to Elzabeth Brooks 12-3-1867 (12-5-1867)
Welch, J. M. to S. Welch 3-7-1846 (3-8-1846)
Welch, John H. to Susanah Brooks 1-30-1840
Welch, William to Clarkis Scivofield? 3-29-1843
Welch, William to Luritta Ramsey 4-16-1839 (8-18-1839)
Wells, George T. to M. E. Jennings 9-1-1853

Wells, James to Margret Young 3-30-1856
Wells, John to Elisabeth Green 6-14-1856 (6-16-1856)
Wells, William to Elizabeth Cress 4-5-1851 (4-6-1851)
Wereman?, Hiram C. to Hannah Province 2-1-1844 (2-22-1844)
Wesley, Solomon? to Sarah J. Richardson 11-28-1849
West, Chesley to Sally Barnard 5-12-1840
West, Geo. W. to Nancy O. Carpenter 1-9-1864
West, John A. to Mary K. Rosenbalm 2-2-1857 (2-5-1857)
West, Joseph Anderson to Susanah Posey 1-6-1848
West, William to Luvernia C. Barnard 7-31-1868 (8-9-1868)
West?, Matin? H. to Malinda Jane Posey? 5-29-1846 (5-31-1846)
Wetherford?, David? to Elisabt? Presby 6-8-1846
Wheelar, J. M. to Mary Susong 11-8-1856 (11-9-1856)
Wheeler, Thomas J. to Frances J. McHenry 9-20-1839 (10-8-1839)
Wheelus, Wm. to Polly Legeer? 4-1-1839 (4-11-1839)
Whicker?, Zachariah to Martha Hurst 7-18-1849 (7-11?-1849)
Whitaker, James C to Elizabeth Fullington 12-16-1858
Whitaker, Rice to Patsy Vermillion 2-1-1853
Whitaker, Timothy to Sarah Southern 11-30-1841 (12-1-1841)
Whitaker, Wm. to Mary Hatfield 10-8-1851 (10-9-1851)
White, Beverly P. to Helen G. White 11-24-1867
White, F. S. to E. C. Harda 5-21-1851 (6-20-1851)
White, Fidelio to Mary E. Perry 3-15-1851 (3-18-1851)
White, Hugh G. to Magret Powers 9-17-1850
White, Jas. S. to Emly Hardy 6-21-1851
White, John E. to Elizabeth G. Brawler 3-31-1859
White, John M. to Charaty? Chadwich? 10-22-1846
White, John to Margaret Patterson 9-26-1851 (9-27-1851)
White, John to R. Hobbs 12-14-1847
White, Joseph to Mary McHenry 6-28-1847 (7-1-1847)
White, Joseph to Olivia Moss 10-10-1855 (10-11-1855)
White, Lee? to Margaret McNielin? 6-16-1842
White, Thos. C. to Roda V. Lane 2-5-1851
White, Wm. T. to Minerva H. Leach 12-2-1854 (no return)
White, Wm. to Sarah Mason 12-15-1841 (12-26-1841)
White, ___ S.? to Emily J. Wanocott 7-24-1843 (8-3-1843)
Whiteaker, Matthew to Rosanah Willis 6-12-1866 (6-14-1866)
Whiteaker, Matthew to Sarah Ann Estice 6-6-1843
Whiteaker, Timothy to Margaret Patterson 4-15-1867 (4-16-1867)
Whited, Sylvester to Jane Wells 10-11-1853
Whitemore, James to Jane Nisbert? 10-15-1864 (10-31-1864)
Whiteted, William to Mary Keck 8-14-1848 (8-16-1848)
Whiteted?, Wm. to Frances Cyraus 6-1-1842 (6-21-1842)
Whitted, Alvis to Rachael Russel 1-24-1852 (1-30-1852)
Wiat, Samuel to Delila Lee 5-1-1851 (5-6-1851)
Wiers, William to Martha Brown 11-17-1856
Wilbern, William to Manervy Seals 1-24-1843 (1-29-1843)
Wilborne, Henry to Margret Devault 11-21-1850
Wilborne, William to Delpha Masan 7-29-1846
Wilburn, Lewis to Sarah Hatfield 10-7-1867 (10-12-1867)
Wilcocks, L. H. to Margarett Mattocks 11-10-1857 (11-15-1857)
Wilcoks, L. H. to M. Mattocks 11-10-1857 (11-15-1857)
Wilcox, J. G. to A. J. Williams 12-19-1865 (ret. no ctf.)
Wiley, F. H. to Sarah Harmon 10-5-1865
Wilkerson, Martin to Mary Ramsey 3-16-1868 (3-18-1868)
Williams, Albert to Tabitha Wilson 12-5-1867
Williams, Andrew to Catharine Ritter 6-20-1846 (6-21-1846)
Williams, David to Ann Mayes? 7-8-1848 (7-13-1848)
Williams, George W. to Eliza Williams 7-24-1867 (7-28-1867)
Williams, George W. to Martha Teague 8-26-1867 (8-29-1867)
Williams, George W. to Mary West 7-20-1867 (7-21-1867)
Williams, J. to E. Lake 2-3-1852
Williams, James A. to Elizabeth Rosanbalm 7-13-1867 (7-18-1867)
Williams, James to Polly Ann Bullard 1-20-1846
Williams, John G. to Laverta Campbell 7-19-1852
Williams, Silas H. to Elizabeth Bartlet 3-29-1851 (4-3-1851)
Williams, Silas to Levisa? Willis 1-14-1843
Williams, W. D. to Mariah Harp 9-5-1865 (9-21-1865)
Williams, William to Sintha Roarks? 7-2-1845 (7-3-1845)
Williamson, Albert G. to Sarah A. Rogers 8-25-1866
Williamson, Albert to Catharine McNew 5-19-1854 (5-21-1854)
Willis, Bartlett to Mary Hurst 3-20-1855
Willis, Bartley to Elizabeth Divault 8-28-1858
Willis, Bartley to Louisa Jennings 6-6-1857
Willis, David to Olly Quarles 11-10-1859
Willis, Docker to Mary Condry 9-14-1854
Willis, E. D. to Faney B. Hurst 4-13-1868
Willis, E. D. to Orleany Lanham 1-18-1845
Willis, Flemon to Mary J. Harper 11-13-1849
Willis, James A. to Matilda Holt 2-24-1856 (3-4-1856)
Willis, Levi to Jane Woshawm 11-18-1859
Willis, Levi to Mary A. Hollan 12-1-1856
Willis, Moses to Jane Moore 1-17-1852 (1-18-1852)
Willis, Patrick to Elizabeth Ann Pitman 12-13-1845 (12-14-1845)
Willis, Skelton to Marium Crumpley 2-15-1868 (2-16-1868)
Willis, W. to V. Hurst 6-18-1852 (6-24-1852)
Willis, William C. to Elixna? King 1-20-1842 (1-21-1842)

Willis, William to Elisabeth Lanham 1-14-1851 (1-15-1851)
Willson, Jacob to Nancy J. Stinner 5-5-1865
Willson, James to Rachel Litterall 7-21-1859
Willson, Owen to Eliza Jane Moor 7-9-1846
Willson, Wm. S. to Rachal Painter 2-23-1857
Wilmer, John R. to Eliza T. Townsel 11-9-1859
Wiloby, Preston to Parkey Davis 11-9-1857
Wilson, Alexander to Dithula Mize 1-3-1867 (1-4-1867) B
Wilson, Elihu to Harriet Wilson 1-19-1867 B
Wilson, George W. to Cerena Hurst 1-26-1850 (1-27-1850)
Wilson, J. S. to B. Miller 9-6-1852
Wilson, Jacob to Martha C. Rite 6-17-1868 (6-28-1868)
Wilson, Jesse to Franky Laws 2-23-1857
Wilson, John to L. J. Hurley 10-7-1853 (10-9-1853)
Wilson, John to Martha Davis 4-10-1867 (4-11-1867)
Wilson, Mitchel A. to Martha Davis 4-10-1867 (4-11-1867)
Wilson, Wm. A. to E. C. Sharp 9-22-1851
Wilson, Wm. to Permila? Kincaid 12-3-1839
Winegar?, David to Mary Yearry 12-4-1843 (12-7-1843)
Winter?, Jefferson to Susanna Beeler 11-26-1836
Wireman, Wm. C. to Eliza A. Welch 4-23-1852
Wolfenbarger, Peter to R. Collins 9-4-1850 (9-9-1850)
Wolfenbargor, Jacob to E. Rogers? 8-27-1845 (8-28-1845)
Woodall, Bluford? to Nancy Toney? 1-11-1845 (1-12-1845)
Woodard, Alexander to Martha Bobit 1-18-1842 (4-4-1842)
Woods, Jas. to Sarah Moshy? 5-16-1846 (5-17-1846)
Woods, John to Christiana Scalf 7-24-1851
Woods, John to Martha? C. Powers 6-26-1845 (6-25?-1845)
Woods, S. A. to H. R. Honeycutt 11-3-1852 (11-4-1852)
Woods, Silas D. to Emily Ferrile 3-3-1840
Woodson, John F. to Eliza Fernell 2-8-1848 (2-9-1848)
Woodson, Marshal to Fany Harkins 7-16-1852
Woodson, Morgan J. to Elizabeth Ramsey 9-28-1849
Woodson, Robert C. to Lucy Jane Fugate 10-3-1849 (10-4-1849)
Woodson, Samuel to Anny Scott 9-15-1866 B
Woodson, William to Lucy A. Hoskins 5-20-1868 (5-23-1868)
Woodward, Calvin C. to Nancy Williams 8-18-1842 (8-20-1842)
Woodward, Solomon L. to Matilda A. Riggs 4-26-1851 (5-1-1851)
Woollum, Israel K. to Elizabeth York 7-4-1867
Word, George R. to Olleiy? Daey? 2-7-1848
Wright, Abraham to Telitha Proffett 8-8-1863 (8-10-1863)
Wright, John W. to Elizabeth Grimes 7-6-1868 (7-9-1868)
Wright, Luke to Sarah A. Day 1-14-1868 (1-19-1868)
Wyatt, Francis M. to Margaret E. Poor 7-27-1868
Wyatt, John to Elizabeth Doty 9-30-1842
Wyatt, Josiah to Jane Jones 5-28-1849 (5-31-1849)
Wyatt, William to Susan Grigery 11-18-1846 (11-8?-1846)
Wylie, Frank H. to Sodnia? Davis 3-6-1852 (3-11-1852)
Yaden, Benjamin A. to Eve Hunter 3-27-1843 (4-2-1843)
Yaden, J. M. to L. Goins 8-11-1853 (8-12-1853)
Yaden, J. M. to Lucinda Goins 7-11-1853 (8-12?-1853)
Yearey, Houston to Margaret Mize 12-24-1866 (1-25-1866) B
Yearry, Henry to Rachel J. Dannel 5-14-1854 (5-28-1854)
Yeary, Adam C.? to Matilda E. Estept 1-9-1856 (1-13-1856)
Yeary, James W. to Susan Sutton 1-25-1848
Yoakum, Ewing to Martha Vanbebber 3-15-1845 (3-27-1845)
Yoakum, Isaac to Jane White 6-18-1859
Yoakum, Isaac? to Emily Ann Lane 6-26-1848 (7-1-1858)
Yoakum, Marcillis to Catharine Ellison 7-30-1859
Yoakum, Robert to Lucinda Jennings 6-19-1856 (6-20-1856)
Yoakum, William R. to Sophiah W. Moss 3-1-1859
Yoakum, William? W. to Nancy Poff 9-26-1850 (12-30-1850)
York, Archa T. to Hester Hurst 10-18-1859
Young, B. F. to Ann Knuckles? 6-3-1843
Young, David to Orlena Schrichfield 2-4-1856 (2-5-1856)
Young, James M. to Minerva Barnard 4-21-1855 (4-24-1855)
Young, Leander to Mary Zick 4-8-1851 (4-13-1851)
Young, Mathew to Ann M. Hutcherson 7-3-1854 (7-4-1854)
Young, Thos. to Becky Hix 9-5-1857
Young, William to Jane Carpenter 7-18-1839
Zicks, Thos. to Cacey? Thacker 2-24-1849 (2-25-1849)
____, John to Fereby Crabtree 1-22-1842
____, Jonathan C. to Nancy Mattox 11-18-1841 (11-19-1841)
____, Josiah? to Polly Hopkins 6-20-1846
____, Willis C. to Nancy Angel 7-17-1845

-----, Faney? to Berrill? Smith 12-22-1846 (12-23-1846)
Abs?, Mary Ann to William Munday 2-20-1854
Acreer, V. O. to B. Venable 8-7-1852 (8-10-1852)
Adams, Emely to Michael Rowland 12-29-1866 (1-7-1867)
Adams, Nancy to Solomon Dobkins 10-10-1850 (8-11-1850)
Adams, Orleana Jane to James P. Cunningham 10-8-1849
Adams, Susan to Hiram C. Roberts 12-14-1866
Ales, Sarah Elizabeth to James C. Carrell 8-13-1868
Alexander, Elizabeth to Franklin M. Smith 3-5-1842 (3-8-1842)
Alexander, Rachael to Wiley Huffaker 11-21-1851
Alferd, Martha to Curtis Lee 5-30-1852 (no return)
Allen, Martha to John W. Epperson 1-21-1867 (1-22-1867)
Almis, M. to R. H. Perry 6-11-1853 (no return)
Anderson, Belinda to William Denham 12-31-1867 (1-2-1868) B
Anderson, Elizabeth to Henry A. Dunn 10-28-1843 (11-23-1843)
Anderson, Ellender C. to Fountain Cotterell 8-17-1867 (8-20-1867)
Anderson, Leor? to Ekils? Burchitt 1-23-1846 (1-25-1846)
Angel, Nancy to Willis C. _____ 7-17-1845
Arnel, Susan to Wm. Kibert 4-1-1846 (4-5-1846)
Arney, Elizabeth to Andrew Sawyer 2-7-1865
Arnold, Susan to James Rice 10-13-1854 (10-15-1854)
Arwine, Mary Ann to Isaac McNew 4-1-1845
Arwine, Polly to William Odel 10-18-1856 (10-23-1856)
Arwine, Sarah to James Farmer 11-23-1859
Ashten, Lucinda to James Waggoner 12-2-1853
Atkins, Lucinda to John Walker 9-10-1856 (9-12-1856)
Atkins, Perlina to Jubalee Posey 8-20-1859
Ausmus, Elisabeth to Peruda Sowder 4-2-1849 (4-6-1849)
Ausmus, Livisa? to Joseph B. Moyers 9-22-1842 (9-27-1842)
Ausmus, Malinda to Prior L. Berry 10-1-1856
Ausmus, Maneva to Hiram J. Kivett 3-5-1868
Ausmus, Martha to Isaac Holliway 8-3-1868 (8-27-1868)
Ausmus, Matilda to Jacob Sowder 3-13-1848 (3-16-1848)
Ausmus, N. to J. Houston 3-10-1858
Ausmus, Rachel to Henry M. Sowder 12-6-1847
Ausmus, Sarah to George F. Ulright 1-30-1867 (2-3-1867)
Ausmus, Susanah to Cornelius Braden 1-22-1839 (1-29-1839)
Ausmus, Susanah to Henry Hunter 9-5-1854
Ausmus, W. A. to M. Estrage 11-10-1864
Autton?, S. to Reubin Mills 5-2-1845 (5-4-1845)
Ayers, Mary to Benjamin Jackson 3-12-1842 (3-13-1842)
Ayrs, Cary to Samuel Lock 6-28-1856 (6-29-1856)
Bagwell, Eliza to William Henderson 1-14-1856 (1-15-1856)
Baily, Jane to James Links 1-26-1856
Baker, Elly to Sinclar Cade 2-18-1840 (2-22-1840)
Baker, Margaret to Jos. Ramsey 6-2-1845 (6-8-1845)
Baker, Martha to George Cole 2-14-1842
Baker, Nancy to G. W. Harrell 9-10-1858
Baker, Rebecca to James M. Hopkins 12-8-1843 (12-9-1843)
Baker, Rebeckah to Lafayette? Bingham 6-3-1846
Baker, Sallie to James B. Chadwell 3-13-1867
Baker, Susan to William Kinningham? 3-27-1848
Baker, Vina J. to William S. Frost 9-11-1846 (9-13-1846)
Baldwin, Hariet to Elihue H. Mole 5-26-1856
Baldwin, P. to T. Rutledge 5-4-1853
Bales, M. E. to Wm. Parrat? 10-7-1844 (10-10-1844)
Bales, Manervay to Thomas Colson? 1-30-1850 (2-3-1850)
Bales, Mary to R. Y. Carr 2-3-1857
Bales, Nancy Elizabeth to George Marcum 2-4-1846 (2-7-1846)
Bales, Sarah to John Sproles 11-18-1843 (11-23-1843)
Baless, Mary J. to William Ausben 4-15-1867 (4-16-1867)
Baley, Cathrine to Wm. H. Price 8-15-1853
Baley, Roddy? to Baley Hernen? 11-29-1846 (11-29-1846)
Baley, Susanah to Jno. Province 1-19-1839 (1-20-1839)
Balinger?, Sarah to Hiram Ausmus 5-15-1850 (5-20-1850)
Ball, B. to Ebenezer Minton 9-27-1853 (9-28-1853)
Ball, Elizabeth to Tilmon D. Ball 4-24-1845
Ball, M. S. to R. M. Moss 1-23-1853 (1-24-1853)
Ball, M. to Pallestine L. Redmon 8-21-1853 (8-22-1853)
Ball, Mary to Charles Baley 10-5-1841 (11-7-1841)
Ball, Nancy to Pridmore Ball 7-28-1838 (7-29-1838)
Ball, Sarah to Samuel L. Ball 1-21-1868 (1-26-1868)
Ballinger, Melvina to Daniel Beeler 14-9-1807 (10-14-1007)
Balloo, Ginsy to Simon? Peace? 10-1-1838 (10-10-1838)
Balls, Mary to Richard Crabtree 8-3-1846 (8-4-1846)
Baltrip, Emaline to McDaniel Bussel 4-2-1852 (4-4-1852)
Baltrip, Emaline to William Buck 5-4-1845 (5-7-1845)
Baltrip, Emeline to Wm. Buck 5-8-1845 (5-7?-1845)
Baltrip, Susan to Bird Bussle? 6-3-1842 (6-8-1842)
Bammell, Martha to William Guy 7-27-1865 (8-6-1865)
Bane, Sarah to Jonathan Litterrell 12-31-1866 (1-1-1867)
Barger, Sallie Ann to Paul Perry 6-16-1855 (7-1-1855)
Barker?, Mary A. to George Longworth 2-25-1847
Barnard, Caroline to James Singleton 12-9-1847 (12-11-1847)
Barnard, Catharine to Jas. Stansberry 1-11-1839 (1-13-1839)
Barnard, Lemira to Jonathan Barnard 2-12-1849 (2-13-1849)
Barnard, Louisa to Edward W. Stokeley 9-24-1865 (9-21?-1865)

Barnard, Louisa to Wm. H. Candy 12-25-1838
Barnard, Luvernia C. to William West 7-31-1868 (8-9-1868)
Barnard, M. to George Johnson 3-7-1853 (no return)
Barnard, Mariah to Benjamin Cloud 7-19-1842 (7-21-1842)
Barnard, Martha to Calvin Bull 10-26-1853 (10-27-1853)
Barnard, Miley to Pharore Johnson 7-21-1851 (7-22-1851)
Barnard, Minerva to James M. Young 4-21-1855 (4-24-1855)
Barnard, Rena to John Smith 5-16-1855 (5-17-1855)
Barnard, Sally to Chesley West 5-12-1840
Barnes, Eliza to Samuel Hampton 4-13-1868 (4-16-1868)
Barnes, S. A. to M. Carmack 3-5-1858?
Barnet, Barthena to Joseph Dosier? 7-1-1844 (7-20-1844)
Barnet, Elender to John Johnson 1-18-1849 (1-19-1849)
Barns, Ann to Martin Carmack 3-5-1858
Bartlet, Elizabeth to Silas H. Williams 3-29-1851 (4-3-1851)
Bartlett, L. to Wm. Blancet 1-14-1854
Bartlett, M. E. to T. J. Bauels 4-11-1858
Bartlett, Malinda L.? to A. W. Harrell 1-1-1849 (1-5-1849)
Bartlett, Martha to John Day 9-2-1855
Bartlett, Rebecca to James Barnard 4-23-1851 (4-29-1851)
Bartley, Minervy J. to Henry F. Harry 2-21-1843 (2-28-1843)
Batton, Lucinda to Thomas Waggoner 8-30-1852 (3?-30-1852)
Baughman, _____ to A. Barnett 11-25-1850
Bawldridge, Nancy to William H. Carroll 10-8-1849 (10-11-1849)
Becknel, M. L. to Wm. D. Sheffle 9-5-1855
Beelar, Sarena to Valentine Boruff 11-18-1852 (11-21-1852)
Beeler, Ann to Volentine Fulps 7-7-1851 (7-13-1851)
Beeler, Esther to R. Malone 11-24-1865 (11-30-1865)
Beeler, Hannah to Moses Honeycutt 2-15-1842 (2-20-1842)
Beeler, Mary to Enoch Proffit 7-10-1857 (7-14-1857)
Beeler, Polly to Jesse F. Beeler 2-18-1839 (2-22-1839)
Beeler, Polly to Samuel Moor 7-19-1839 (7-20-1839)
Beeler, S. S. to Jacob Leach 8-19-1858
Beeler, Susanna to Jefferson Winter? 11-26-1836
Beelor, Freely to Henrey Roust 11-6-1855
Beelor?, Emaley? to F. H. Rogers 11-14-1845
Beilor, Elisabeth to John M. Vanbebber 8-19-1856
Belvins, Cordaline to Thomas Millar 1-5-1857
Berry, Eliza Ann to Caleb W. Rutledge 9-20-1843
Berry, Elizabeth to Daniel Railey 3-22-1851
Berry, Malinda to Alvis Smith 6-22-1867 (6-24-1867)
Berry, Mary to John M. Jennings 7-20-1867 (7-21-1867)
Beuchen, Eliza to Robert Peck 4-6-1859
Biggs, Catharine to Daniel Bayless 10-29-1866
Biggs, Cathrine to Isaac Gibson 6-17-1850
Billingsby, Eliza J. to Hosea D. Loftis 9-29-1866 (10-7-1866)
Billingsley?, Elizabeth to John Wallin 5-8-1843
Billingsly, Berrelvy? to John W. Shomate 5-15-1846
Billingsly, Susan to Tipton Baker 11-25-1847 (11-26-1847)
Billingsly?, Jerusha? to Elias Ely? 11-7-1845 (11-9-1845)
Bingham, Mary to John L. Rice 9-29-1854
Birdine, Manda to John Harper 12-25-1866 (12-27-1866) B
Bishop, Juda to Jobies? Hopkins 6-25-1846 (6-28-1846)
Bishop, Margaret to John Province 10-4-1841 (10-10-1841)
Black, Emaley? to William A. A. McAnlush? 8-30-1846
Blancet, Lucy C. to Claiborne Bartlet 7-20-1854
Blancet, Sarah to Isaac McBee 5-6-1865 (5-7-1865)
Blumer, J. to W. Minor 12-11-1852
Bobit, Martha to Alexander Woodard 1-18-1842 (4-4-1842)
Bolin, Mary to William Standifer 9-4-1867
Bolinger, Elizabeth to Allen Robertson 4-20-1842
Bollinger, Ellender to Phillip Goin 9-18-1866 (9-20-1866)
Bolton, Mary to William Harris 12-17-1856 (12-21-1856)
Bourman, Debah to James Taylor 12-18-1858
Bowers, Chloe? to William Hopson 12-23-1847 (12-26-1847)
Bowlinger, Matilda to Henry Ausmus 1-3-1854
Bowman, Anna to R. Hamblin 2-12-1852 (3-4-1852)
Bowman, Bettie to Frank Maupin 5-19-1866 (5-20-1866)
Bowman, Catharine to Ransam? Day 11-25-1843 (11-28-1843)
Bowman, Elizabeth to Pleasant Chadwell 3-13-1838
Bowman, Harriett M. to William A. Harp 9-29-1867
Bowman, M. to F. Beeler 4-15-1853 (4-21-1853)
Bowman, _____, _____ to _____ _____ _____
Bowman, Mary to E. Hutson 12-21-1838 (12-25-1838)
Bowman, Sarah J. to William F. King 1-1-1857
Bowman, Susanah to William Moyers 11-19-1844
Bowman?, Harriett to Thomas King 11-11-1848
Bowyers, Peggy to Saml. Cloud 5-15-1839
Brackett, Martha to Tillford Messer 11-3-1866
Braden, Lucinda to William? Waggoner? 1-7-1843 (2-19-1843)
Braden, Matilda to Thomas Eads 1-4-1854 (1-7-1854)
Bradin, Lucinda to Elisha Bowman 12-26-1850
Branbury, Nancy to David Branbury 5-22-1853
Brandsan, Rebecca to Obediah Norris 6-18-1839 (6-20-1839)
Brandscombe, Elizabeth M. to Thos. Dum? 1-30-1847
Branond, Malilsa to Elisha Fullington 8-29-1851 (9-2-1851)
Branscomb, Benny to Andrew J. Harmon 11-13-1843 (11-16-1843)

Branscomb, Prissella to Madison Dunn (no date) (with 3-1858)
Branscome, Hariet to Joseph Beelon? 3-5-1849 (3-8-1849)
Branson, Mary to John Jennings 11-12-1865
Brantley, Sarah Ann to John W. Anderson 3-12-1851 (3-13-1851)
Brasher, Eliza to William Dykes 10-2-1843
Braver?, Nancy to William King 12-28-1841 (12-29-1841)
Brawler, Elizabeth G. to John E. White 3-31-1859
Bray, Jane to John Nuckels 11-11-1842 (11-15-1842)
Bray, Letty? to Anderson Collins 11-27-1841 (11-28-1841)
Bray, Manila to James M. Monk 2-21-1842 (2-22-1842)
Bray, Milly to Calvin Partan 2-20-1842 (2-26-1842)
Bray, Nancy to William Webe 2-24-1854 (lic. ret'd.)
Bray, Polly to Pearvan? Lee 2-14-1839 (2-21-1839)
Bray, Rhoda to Clinton McVey 2-13-1858 (2-14-1858)
Breeden, Salla to E. H. Dunsmore 1-1-1855 (no return)
Breeding, Charity to Floid Hurst 11-1-1855
Breeding, Luritta to William Edunsmore 11-24-1855 (11-25-1855)
Breeding, M. A. to C. J. Davis 8-5-1858
Breeding, Malese? to B. F. Galyon 1-5-1855 (1-3?-1855)
Breeding, Virginia to D. R. Dunsmore 1-13-1868 (1-16-1868)
Brewer, Anna to Phelin Minks 11-11-1843 (11-18-1843)
Brewer, Charity to Wm. Nash 5-20-1858
Brewer, Esther to Andrew Denny 12-10-1866
Brewer, L. to E. H. Dunsmore 1-1-1854
Brewere, Mary Jane to James Brewer 7-20-1838 (7-22-1838)
Briant, Mary to John H. Carr 7-27-1844 (7-28-1844)
Briant, Matilda to Daniel Chumley 3-3-1855 (3-4-1855)
Brigman, Cathrine to Franklin Chesnut 7-17-1848
Brigmon, Elizabeth to James H. Murray 10-3-1866
Britton, Elizabeth A. to Levi Hoskins 8-14-1866 (8-21-1866)
Brock, Sarah to Jefferson Rose 8-23-1842 (8-24-1842)
Brogain, Louisa to Preston C. Goforth 12-28-1842 (1-4-1843)
Brogan, Orlena to Mathew Keck 8-31-1857 (9-1-1857)
Brogan, Penelopa to John Jesse Burk 12-28-1852 (12-30-1852)
Brogans, Letia to Franklin Walker 9-24-1851 (9-25-1851)
Brooks, A. to S. Lawson 5-27-1852
Brooks, Catharine to Thos. Brooks 7-15-1847
Brooks, Elisabeth? to Alexander Hill 2-15-1848
Brooks, Elizabeth to Charles Baker 10-24-1843
Brooks, Elizabeth to Calvin Welch 12-3-1867 (12-5-1867)
Brooks, Emely to Constentine Smith 8-28-1866
Brooks, Jennetter to Joseph Southern 11-19-1849
Brooks, Lucinda to Levi Brooks 12-14-1850 (12-15-1850)
Brooks, M. to T. J. Monday 9-6-1852 (9-8-1852)
Brooks, Manerva to John Hicks 12-13-1865 (12-14-1865)
Brooks, Margaret to Jeremiah Brooks 8-4-1851 (8-5-1851)
Brooks, Mary J. to Alexander Brooks 12-19-1855
Brooks, Mary J. to Andrew Brooks 8-16-1848
Brooks, Mary to William L. Harrell 1-1-1868 (1-3-1868)
Brooks, Nancy J. to John M. Brooks 3-16-1867 (3-17-1867)
Brooks, Nancy to James Hunter 12-8-1841
Brooks, Nancy to Macknep Rowlett 7-31-1838 (8-1-1838)
Brooks, Pertilly? to Montgomery Herrell 12-3-1846
Brooks, Sally to Jas. Dobbs 8-5-1852 (8-5-1853?)
Brooks, Sarah A. to William Hase 7-9-1849 (7-10-1849)
Brooks, Sarah to Lynch Hatfield 12-17-1867 (12-19-1867)
Brooks, Susanah to John H. Welch 1-30-1840
Brooks, Vina to John Scott 6-10-1848 (6-11-1848)
Brooks, Zhynettie to Geo. H. Friar 1-24-1852
Browen, Sarah J. to Andrew J. Crockett 6-14-1856
Brown, Elizabeth to Joseph Johnson 6-30-1866 (7-1-1866)
Brown, Elizabeth to Wm. T. Rawlet 12-12-1859
Brown, Jane to William Longworth 8-12-1854 (8-16-1854)
Brown, Julia A. to Edward N. Hill 9-24-1844
Brown, L. A. [Lucy A.] to Wm. Shaw 4-23-1853 (4-26-1853) *
Brown, L. J. to M. W. Love 9-3-1857
Brown, Martha to William Chadwell 6-8-1868 B
Brown, Martha to William Wiers 11-17-1856
Brown, Mary J. to Bishop Nevels 9-16-1865 (9-21-1865)
Brown, Matilda to Thomas Sutton 12-21-1855 (12-25-1855)
Browning, Maoma to Nathaniel Watson 4-10-1865
Brownlow, Franky to Edward Black 12-18-1839 (12-22-1839)
Brownlow, Sarah to Wilson Jackson 8-22-1854
Bruce, Trifany? to John M. Leach? 9-30-1842 (10-2-1842)
Bruer?, Silvey to Arthur Collins 1-17-1848
Brummet, Elith to Jacob Massa 10-29-1850 (10-31-1850)
Brummit, Sarah to Wm. Sowder 4-6-1846 (4-9-1846)
Bruor, Elizabeth to John Maples 11-28-1854 (11-30-1854)
Brusten, Emaley to William N. McWilliams 5-11-1849 (5-24-1849)
Bruster, E. to John Eastridge 11-9-1852 (11-11-1852)
Bruster, Martha J. to Martin Cadle 2-19-1838
Bryant, Rebecca to George W. Sharp 8-29-1851
Buchanan, Adeline to William H. Sowder 1-2-1868
Buchanan, Hester A. to Benjamin F. Haskins 1-7-1851
Buchanan, Jane to Calvin Teague 7-21-1858
Buchanan, Julia A. to Richard Knight 11-28-1867
Buchanan, Mary A.? to Landon C. Minter 1-15-1867 (1-30-1867)

Buchanan, Nancy to J. B. S. Leforce 6-11-1868
Buchanan, Sarah Ann to Ed Jackson 1-23-1866 B
Buchanan, Sarah to Matthew Goin 3-12-1868 B
Buchanan, Tilda to Toney Buchanan 1-25-1866 B
Buckanan, H. A. to Henry Davis 6-16-1852 (6-18-1852)
Buckhanan, Sarah to John A. Davis 8-8-1843
Buice?, E. to E. King 2-9-1846 (2-12-1846)
Bulb, Sarah C. to John Smith 4-22-1855 (not exec.)
Bull, Jane to Miland Hopson 1-26-1856 (1-27-1856)
Bull, S. C. to R. Houston 1-4-1858
Bull, S. C. to R. Howerton 1-4-1858
Bull, Susan to Martain Burchfield 4-2-1842
Bullard, Elizabeth Jane to Elias Cerrel 1-15-1868 (1-16-1868)
Bullard, Elizabeth to J. W. Lane 1-21-1864
Bullard, Elizabeth to James S. Killion 1-23-1867 (1-24-1867)
Bullard, Martha J. to Thomas J. Niel 1-27-1857
Bullard, Nancy to John Denny 2-20-1847 (2-21-1847)
Bullard, Polly Ann to James Williams 1-20-1846
Bullard, Rebecca to J. Jarnigain 1-20-1855 (1-21-1855)
Bullard, S. S. to John O. Neal 2-22-1853
Bunch, Adaline to John Bunch 10-5-1866 (10-4?-1866)
Bunch, Elizabeth to William Gains 8-25-1843 (8-27-1843)
Bunch, Jane to Henley Hurst 5-10-1855
Bunch, L. to Robet Hurst 11-24-1857 (11-26-1857)
Bunch, Loisa to Robert Hurst 11-24-1857
Bunch, Malissa to George W. Carpenter 7-7-1857
Bunch, Morning to Green B. Bunch 5-23-1855
Bunch, Sarah A. to Harid? Hopson 4-7-1847 (4-8-1847)
Bunch, Sindney to Joshua Moyers 9-3-1850 (9-4-1850)
Bunch, Tabitha to Harry Nunn 8-5-1848 (8-6-1848)
Bunch, Winna to James M. Carter 10-11-1865 (10-13-1865)
Bundon, Sarah to Elisha Clark 11-14-1858
Bundren, Arrena to Jno. Sanders 12-24-1838 (12-25-1838)
Bundren, Elizabeth to Anderon Malicoat? 2-9-1844
Bundren, Elizabeth to Michal Cole 4-1-1851 (4-17-1851)
Bundren, Martha to William N. Waller 1-1-1856 (1-27-1856)
Bundren, Mary to Pryor Davault 3-28-1868
Bundren, Patsy to William Deans 1-12-1848 (2-2-1848)
Burch, Eliza J. to F. H. Vickery 9-27-1852
Burch, Elizabeth J. to Isom Gibson 1-1-1844 (1-2-1844)
Burch, Mary A. to Stephen Gase 9-17-1853 (9-18-1853)
Burch, Mary to Henry Warick 6-5-1847 (6-6-1847)
Burchet, Silvena to John Cunningham 8-30-1855
Burchett, Mary to Isaac Litterall 2-7-1859
Burchett, Sarah to Henry Fritts 11-3-1845 (11-19-1845)
Burchfield, Angeline to Calaway Greer 2-13-1867 (2-14-1867)
Burchfield, Florintha J. to Joseph K. Hansard 6-15-1866 (6-21-1866)
Burchfield, Mary A. to Robert M. Thompson 1-10-1867
Burgin, Belenda to William Blankinship 10-7-1842
Burk, Elisabeth B. to George Redman 11-1-1855 (11-3-1855)
Burk, Eliza to Lafayette Graham 1-16-1855 (1-17-1855)
Burk, Margret to Isaac Gentry 4-4-1859
Burk, Mary A. to Burton McBee 1-1-1848 (1-3-1848)
Burk, Sarah to John Haley 1-8-1857
Burket, Mary A. to Tilman H. Moor 12-29-1849 (12-25?-1849)
Burkhart, Jane to Thos. C. Pane 6-2-1854 (6-6-1854)
Burns, Nancy Jane to William Barren 8-18-1847 (8-20-1847)
Burns, Polly to Wm. Upton? 6-13-1849 (6-15-1849)
Burns, Sarah to Eli Hawkins 7-1-1854
Burton, Polla to Anderson Carpentr? 9-3-1844
Bush, Avda to James Bush 11-13-1856
Bussel, Mary E. to Robert A. Abs 2-20-1854
Bussel, Sarah to James Forgerson 10-15-1853 (10-16-1853)
Bussell, Elizabeth to Enoch Hill 11-12-1851 (11-16-1851)
Bussle, M. to J. Garland 11-10-1852 (11-12-1852)
Butcher, Eliza to Samuel Kibert 6-6-1853 (6-7-1853)
Butcher, Louiza to James Bussell 5-1-1867 (5-3-1867)
Butcher, Mary E. to B. H. M. Cole 7-23-1849
Butcher, Mary to Shadrick Cosley 10-30-1858
Butcher, Millia to Brownlow Murphey 6-24-1867 B
Butcher, Minerva to John B. Crabtree 9-21-1855 (9-23-1855)
Cadel, Mariah to William Jones 10-5-1844 (10-6-1844)
Cadle, A. J. to G. W. Rose 12-17-1852 (12-22-1852)
Cadle, Elizabeth to James Higgins 7-27-1853 (7-28-1853)
Cadle, Elvira to Henry Carrell 9-1-1851 (9-4-1851)
Cadle, Emly J. to Timothy G. Sivil 1-1-1867 (1-3-1867)
Cadle, Frances A. to William R. Otey 11-12-1866 (11-15-1866)
Cadle, Julia Ann to George Hamelton 7-23-1848 (7-27-1848)
Cadle, L. to F. M. Hosford 12-17-1852 (12-22-1852)
Cadle, May Ann to Henry P. Luster? 4-30-1840 (5-1-1840)
Cadle, N. to L. Parton 11-6-1859
Cadle, Sarah R. to Wm. M. Bruister 2-5-1857
Cailor, Elizabeth to David Cardwell 3-26-1850 (3-20?-1850)
Cain, Perlina to James F. Fernay? 1-21-1844
Cain, Serrena to Jesse Graves 11-26-1867 (11-28-1867)
Cain, Tempy? A. to Ezekiel Gooden 9-18-1842
Calar?, Sarah to John A. Buchanan 10-18-1842 (10-23-1842)

Calestane?, Jane to Elisha Butcher 11-28-1843 (12-1-1843)
Callaham?, L. to Jesse Seafield? 3-28-1846 (4-4-1846)
Calline, Salla to John Sufrage 9-19-1844
Callor, Polly to Moses Jones 1-1-1851 (1-2-1851)
Calon, Jane A. to Elias Presley? 9-19-1849 (9-20-1845?)
Calone, Vina to Henry Poore 3-10-1849 (3-11-1849)
Caly, Elizabeth to John Fugate 7-3-1865 (7-6-1865)
Camier?, Eliza to Brison Collins 2-2-1843
Camin?, E. J. to Wm. P. Harris 1-27-1846 (1-28-1846)
Campbell, Adaline to John Cloud 4-5-1850 (4-7-1850)
Campbell, Darkey to Morris P.? Rowatt? 9-26-1843 (9-27-1843)
Campbell, E. to M. Roolin 8-6-1858
Campbell, Elisabeth to Hugh G. Bray 1-19-1856
Campbell, Emily A. to Levi Brooks 7-1-1848 (7-5-1848)
Campbell, Emily to Edward Bray 8-10-1850 (8-11-1850)
Campbell, Laverta to John G. Williams 7-19-1852
Campbell, Levisa? to A. Campbell 10-2-1844 (11-2-1844)
Campbell, Louisa to James R. Jennings 2-20-1840
Campbell, Lucretia to John W. Walker 7-21-1850
Campbell, Lucy Ann to Preston Brooks 6-15-1857
Campbell, Lucy to Abraham Lewis 11-8-1859
Campbell, M. to S. Chadwell 1-26-1853 (1-27-1853)
Campbell, M. to Thos. Campbell 2-18-1853
Campbell, Mary Ann to James Walker 7-2-1849
Campbell, Mary Ann to James Walker 7-20-1849
Campbell, Sally to Enoch Carmack 12-17-1858
Cane?, Mary to William Hornis? 7-11-1844
Cannon, Malinda to William E. Berry 2-22-1868 (2-25-1868)
Capps, Leor? to Isaac Shelvy? 4-27-1847 (4-29-1847)
Capps, Mary to M. C. Collins 12-19-1865 (12-25-1865)
Cardwell, Catharine to J. T. Snider 10-8-1866 (10-9-1866)
Cardwell, Lucinda to Nicolis Slatton 5-2-1856 (5-7-1856)
Cardwell, M. to George W. Beelor 1-18-1853 (1-19-1853)
Cardwell, Martha to Williaml Lovelace 1-3-1867
Cardwell, Nancy to J. Cunningham 12-23-1844
Carmack, Elizabeth to James Longworth 3-15-1854 (3-19-1854)
Carmack, Mary ann to David Redman 9-5-1841
Carnard?, Elisabeth? to William A. Standsbery? 7-20-1846 (8-21-1846)
Carnell, Sarah to William Ellison 8-28-1866 (9-30-1866)
Caroll, Sarah to Robert Quay 1-7-1838
Carpenter, Jane to Adam Summermon 6-29-1839 (6-30-1839)
Carpenter, Jane to William Young 7-18-1839
Carpenter, Lotty to Jeremiah Singleton 11-30-1838 (1-22-1838)
Carpenter, Louisa to Lenard G. Harper 11-5-1848
Carpenter, Louiza to Henry C. Davault 8-10-1868 (8-13-1868)
Carpenter, Mahulda to W. H. Jones 12-29-1865 (12-29-1865)
Carpenter, Malisa to William Burton 10-3-1844
Carpenter, Mary to William Spradling 10-31-1850
Carpenter, Nancy O. to Eldrage? Mullens 3-17-1848
Carpenter, Nancy O. to Geo. W. West 1-9-1864
Carpenter, Susanah to Stokley Alton 10-7-1844 (10-8-1844)
Carpentur?, Arminda to John Myers 10-9-1843 (10-19-1843)
Carr, Manerva to Mathew Sharp 12-4-1849 (12-6-1849)
Carr, Martha J. to Thos. Redmon 1-4-1850 (1-6-1850)
Carr, Mary A. to Marion Moyers 2-7-1856
Carr, Rhoda to Moses Retter 1-5-1842 (1-6-1842)
Carrell, Amilia A. to Isaiah C. Poor 7-25-1868 (7-26-1868)
Carrell, Cathrine to Hyram Ford 4-15-1860
Carrell, L. to Boston Clap 2-21-1853 (3-?-1853)
Carrell, Nancy to Wiley Ellison 8-21-1867 (8-24-1867)
Carroll, Sarah to William Lock 4-5-1844
Carter, C. to Daniel Hopson 3-25-1853 (3-26-1853)
Carter, Lavina to Greenberry Lawson 4-12-1844 (4-16-1844)
Carter, Mary C. to Rubin R. Sanders 3-23-1865 (3-24-1865)
Carter, Nancy L. to William McNeil 12-22-1849 (12-27-1849)
Carter, Nancy to Benjamin S.? Carter 10-22-1843 (10-23-1843)
Carter, Sarah to Jessee Aries 8-1-1859
Carter?, Eliza Jane to Georg Cartar? 1-28-1845 (1-29-1845)
Carter?, Sarah to John Pillian 10-30-1845 (11-2-1845)
Casady, Nancy to Madison Burchfield 9-9-1852
Catterell?, Mary to William R. Gibson 3-18-1843 (3-21-1843)
Cauk?, Margret to William Dickinson 9-16-1845
Cawood, Rhoda Jane to J. H. Cogar 10-30-1854 (11-1-1854)
Caywood, Anna to Henderson Rogers 9-13-1848 (9-28-1848)
Caywood, Barbara to Hugh L. W. Rogers ?-10-1010 (10-10-1010)
Caywood, Rachael to Henry H. Sharp 8-12-1854 (8-21-1854)
Cemor, Sarah to William Hurst 1-27-1842
Chadwell, E. to Armstrong Brooks 6-14-1858
Chadwell, Elizabeth to Andrew Brooks 4-1-1856 (4-10-1856)
Chadwell, Elizabeth to William Taylor 2-15-1867 (2-17-1867)
Chadwell, Lucyann to H. Lane 12-19-1857
Chadwell, Mary Ann to John Campbell 5-15-1850 (5-16-1850)
Chadwell, Mary to James D. McKeehan 6-12-1866 (6-14-1866)
Chadwell, Nancy N. to Arthur Jones 6-2-1856
Chadwell, Sallie A. to Roland Hurst 8-8-1866 (8-9-1866)
Chadwell, Sarah to Isaac Southern 11-7-1843 (10?-8-1843)
Chadwell, Susan to Jas. W. Taylor 1-9-1839 (1-10-1839)

Chadwell, Susanah to John Chapman 5-29-1845 (6-8-1845)
Chadwich?, Charaty? to John M. White 10-22-1846
Chance, Nancy to Jacob Manawy 1-20-1854
Cheek, Ann to George Hale 12-24-1855 (12-25-1855)
Cheek, Catharin to Henry A. Brown 5-6-1840
Chick, Elizabeth to James Brown 11-11-1848
Chick, Jane to Doctor H. Owens 1-22-1850 (1-23-1850)
Childers, Eliza J. to Abraham Cadle 2-24-1851 (2-26-1851)
Childers, Susan to Wm. Ely 5-29-1851 (5-20-1851)
Christa, Cathrine to Jno. Grimes 5-4-1852 (5-6-1852)
Chumbley, Elender to George W. Jones 10-14-1850
Chumbley, Elizabeth to Crage Salyers 4-5-1854
Chumbley, Milley to Watesel Lay 4-9-1850
Chumbley, Moholey? to Joseph McWilliams 5-28-1844 (5-29-1844)
Chumbly, Emily to Riley Clark 1-1-1850
Chumbly, Molinda? to John Slatton 9-6-1845
Chumbly, Sarah to John Lingar 1-27-1838 (2-13-1838)
Chumley, Elizebeth to E. S. Grant? 12-6-1858
Chumley, Margret to Thomas Grubb 11-23-1859
Chumley, Sarah to Thos. Cairdny? 11-5-1855
Chumley, Sarah to Thos. Condrey 11-5-1855
Clapp, Anna to W. A. Gray 1-26-1859
Clapp, Elisabeth? to Alexander Tanny? 8-22-1848
Clapp, Sarah to Josiah Presley 11-15-1865 (11-17-1865)
Clark, M. (Martha) to Martin (Marcus) Cadle 2-10-1858 (2-11-1858)
Clark, Margaret to Wm. Graham 5-21-1855
Clark, Sallie M. to Richard B. Parsons 5-7-1867 (5-9-1867)
Clarkson, Angeline to Adam Y. Snavely 2-20-1867
Clarkson, Martha to William Clarkson 7-30-1843
Clause, Nancy to Wm. Ramsey 12-10-1839 (12-11-1838)
Clemings, Manerva to Thomas Norton 3-25-1868 (3-26-1868)
Clemmens, Martha to Hiram Ellison 8-5-1857 (8-6-1857)
Cline, Jane to John D. Belamy 10-2-1855
Cloud, Charlota J. to James Carr 7-10-1848 (7-13-1848)
Cloud, Eliza to James H. Taylor 9-2-1854 (9-3-1854)
Cloud, Louisa to Isaac Miller 6-17-1845
Cloud, Mariah to Stephen Armstrong 12-20-1867 B
Cloud, Mariah to Wm. Hodge 10-8-1844 (10-10-1844)
Cloud, Martha E. to Wm. L. Harmon 7-19-1855
Cloud, Nancy to John McMakan 12-2-1838 (12-6-1838)
Cloud, Orleana to Pleasant M. Hodges 12-30-1848
Cloud?, Polley to Russel Brewor? 11-4-1844 (11-7-1844)
Cocks, Nancy to William Carmack 9-23-1847 (9-7?-1847)
Code, Sarah to Samuel D. Code 12-21-1841
Cole, Margret to Sterling B. Carter 1-18-1847 (1-19-1847)
Coleman, Catharine to Wiley Fugate 2-12-1867 B
Coleson, Jane to Wm. Cox 1-15-1859
Collens, Nila to Rial Ramsy 1-6-1854 (1-7-1854)
Collens, Sarah E. to Jacob M. Drummons 2-23-1867 (2-24-1867)
Collensworth, Elizabeth J. to Jacob Washington Ayers 1-4-1853 (1-5-1853)
Collensworth, Elzera to Joshua Hamelton 10-27-1838 (10-29-1838)
Collensworth, Louiza M. to James L. Smith 8-20-1867 (8-21-1867)
Collilns, Catharine to Stewart Collins 3-8-1845 (3-9-1845)
Collins, Ann to Caloway Collins 6-16-1857 (6-17-1857)
Collins, Barbery to Zoe Harvey 7-2-1856
Collins, F. to Wiat Collins 4-20-1853 (4-21-1853)
Collins, Fama to Howard King 12-24-1850
Collins, Frances J. to Aham Cupp 1-14-1868
Collins, L. to Wm. Capps 11-10-1858 (11-13-1857?)
Collins, Louiza M. to Leroy Collins 11-8-1867
Collins, Lucinda to William Capps 11-10-1857 (11-?-1857)
Collins, Margaret to Alexr. Collins 5-13-1840
Collins, Martha to David Brader 5-13-1865
Collins, Mary A. to Mc. Sulfradge 8-14-1867 (8-15-1867) B
Collins, Mary A. to William Scrichfield 6-3-1856 (6-5-1856)
Collins, Mary Ann to James T.? McCard? 2-18-1844
Collins, Mary to Ephraim Northern 8-26-1867 (8-29-1867)
Collins, N. to Elisha Eastes 7-1-1853 (8-1-1853)
Collins, Prudy? to Crispin Collins 1-19-1843 (1-22-1843)
Collins, R. to Peter Wolfenbarger 9-4-1850 (9-9-1850)
Collins, Sarah to Isaac Massingale 4-15-1851 (4-16-1851)
Collins, Susannah to Mathew Ousley 8-17-1857 (8-19-1857)
Collinsworth, S. to D. Roland 2-22-1856 (2-24-1856)
Colman, Sarah to John Jackson 4-6-1843 (4-15-1843)
Colston, Ellender to John T. Ball 8-17-1866 (8-20-1866)
Condry, Mary to Docker Willis 9-14-1854
Conner, Elizabeth to Thomas T. Shumate 12-31-1866 (1-1-1867)
Cook, Ann Jane to Daniel Jones 9-1-1847 (no return)
Cook, Eliza F. to Ervin Brack 8-22-1856
Cook, Emanda to John Sulfrage 3-29-1856 (3-30-1856)
Cook, Emely E. to Claiborne Cook 3-31-1866 (4-1-1866)
Cook, M. E. to Elijah Jones 12-23-1858
Cook, Mahala to Spencer Edwards 7-19-1866 (7-22-1866)
Cook, Margaret to Andrew Sulfrage 9-17-1851 (9-18-1851)
Cook, N. L. to P. Cook 12-24-1851 (12-25-1851)
Cookard?, Polly to James M. Hurst 6-22-1842
Corban, H. A. to Ricahrd T. Evans 6-18-1857

Cormeny, Martha to Claiborne Johnson 11-6-1867 (11-7-1867)
Cornell, Lidda to Boston Clapp 11-4-1854
Coterell, S. J. to H. Sewell 4-22-1858
Cottrell, V. A. to William F. Ball 3-11-1850 (3-19-1850)
Covy, Mary to Mark Cadle 8-6-1838 (8-9-1838)
Cowan, Jane to R. F. Harris 10-6-1857
Coward, Elizabeth to Joseph D. Sharp 3-18-1854 (3-23-1854)
Cox, Mahala J. to Wiley Cox 5-9-1868 (5-10-1868)
Cox, Mary to James Chick 6-6-1856
Cox, Mary to William Chick 2-5-1845 (2-6-1845)
Cox, Matilda to Thomas Coffer 7-24-1854
Cox, Peggy to Robert Cheek 9-22-1849
Cox, Polly to Enan Carmach 8-26-1853
Cox, Priscilla to Joseph Eastes 5-24-1849
Cox, Sarah J. to James Hale 9-25-1853
Crabtree, Elizabeth to John W. Pridemore 3-4-1868
Crabtree, Elizabeth to William Lastly? 12-25-1839
Crabtree, Fereby to John ____ 1-22-1842
Crage, Sarah to James M. Stout 6-28-1846 (11-29-1846)
Crank?, Deborah to Jesse Bruice? 5-21-1842 (5-22-1842)
Cress, Elizabeth to William Wells 4-5-1851 (4-6-1851)
Crigger, B. to James Rollens 1-26-1859
Crigor, Rachel to Franklin Gallion 4-27-1854 (5-7-1854)
Crockett, Elizabeth J. to Newton A. Evans 3-7-1848
Crockett, Sarah A. to Jonathan Bales 9-4-1855 (9-27-1855)
Cross, Catherine to Thomas Marlom 9-9-1849 (9-12-1849)
Cross, Emly to Robert Vanforkis 5-1-1865 (5-4-1865)
Croxdale, Sarah to Peter Parkey 12-14-1850
Croxdale?, Nancy to Henry Doiel 2-24-1846 (2-26-1846)
Crumbley, F. to Joel Venany? 1-18-1845
Crumbley, Polley? to Calvin Ramsey 10-12-1846 (10-14-1846)
Crumbly, Belenda to James H. Davis 11-2-1838 (11-4-1838)
Crumpley, Marium to Skelton Willis 2-15-1868 (2-16-1868)
Crutchfield, Alzira to William Carmon 3-12-1867 (3-14-1867)
Crutchfield, Susan to Thomas McClane 2-21-1838 (2-22-1838)
Cuff, Feba to Georg Daniel 10-15-1864 (10-16-1864)
Culberson, J. to H. Malone 8-28-1852 (9-2-1852)
Culbyhouse, Louvania C. to William Clouse 2-1-1868 (2-2-1868)
Culeyhouse, Susana E.? to William Clouse 7-31-1867
Culm, Nancy Rosan to Hyram Avonin 8-30-1865 (9-3-1865)
Cumber?, Rachael to Richard Singleton 10-20-1839
Cuningham, Alley to John Hodges 3-26-184 (3-28-1849)
Cunningham, Eliza to Anderson W. Herrell 6-26-1847 (6-26-1847)
Cunningham, Nancy E. to James C. Carter 2-24-1868 (2-25-1868)
Cupp, A. to J. Bransom 12-9-1852
Cupp, Elizabeth to Calvin Watson 2-3-1865 (2-4-1865)
Cupp, Polly to Stephen Drummond 3-24-1842
Curry, Elizabeth to Samuel Chance 1-30-1858
Cyraus, Frances to Wm. Whiteted? 6-1-1842 (6-21-1842)
Daey?, Olley? to George R. Word 2-7-1848
Danahoo, Mary Ann to Moses J. Renfro 1-28-1843
Daniel, Abagil S. to Wm. J. Paul 9-24-1866 (9-27-1866)
Daniel, Mary Jane to Isaac Cupp 4-5-1858 (4-11-1858)
Daniel, Mourning E. to Jacob W. Estep 11-6-1866 (11-8-1866)
Daniel, Nancy M. to John L. Daniel 2-7-1855 (2-8-1855)
Daniels, Catherine to Wm. B. Lawson 9-4-1851 (9--24-1851)
Daniels, Louiza to Bartholomew Combs 4-24-1867 (4-25-1867)
Daniels, Nelly Ann to Joseph Paul 12-3-1865 (12-7-1865)
Dannel, Rachel J. to Henry Yearry 5-14-1854 (5-28-1854)
Datsan?, Sarah to William Chumley 10-6-1846 (9-5-1846?)
Davault, Catharine to John T. Bridine!? 2-6-1854
Davault, Emeline to Anderson Cope 1-11-1867 (1-13-1867)
Davault, Mary M. to Thompson H. Cash 8-16-1859
Davenport, Jemima to John D. Garrett 7-29-1852
Davis, B. to J. M. Lenvar? 10-13-1852
Davis, Caroline to H. Haynes 7-31-1852 (8-1-1852)
Davis, Cristeena to Thos. M. Grayson 1-23-1857
Davis, Elen to Lewis C. Pridda 4-28-1850
Davis, Elizabeth to Daunt Hamblin 11-11-1856 (11-16-1856)
Davis, Elizabeth to James C. Hodge 10-3-1857
Davis, Elizabeth to Joseph Harp 4-29-1858
Davis, Elizabeth to Sterling Person? 12-8-1849 (12-9-1849)
Davis, Elza to Mark Shoemate 10-8-1866 (10-11-1866)
Davis, Emily to Henry Hatfield 11-13-1841 (11-21-1841)
Davis, Emily to John Ray 2-1-1844 (2-3-1844)
Davis, Leuisey to D. Jinnings 8-19-1858
Davis, Loisa to Jeptha Lynch 11-4-1846 (11-5-1846)
Davis, Lucindy to John Sulivan 10-19-1842 (10-20-1842)
Davis, M. to Jacob Walker 11-9-1846
Davis, Margaret R. to John F. Saville 5-23-18687
Davis, Martha to Mitchel A. Wilson 4-10-1867 (4-11-1867)
Davis, Martha to Pleasant H. Person 9-23-1848
Davis, Martha to Robert Beard 7-20-1850
Davis, Martha to Rowen Elrod 1-18-1847 (1-21-1847)
Davis, Mary L. to John Richardson 2-13-1868
Davis, Mary to Absalom G. Smith 2-5-1857 (2-22-1857)
Davis, Mary to Adam Hatfield 10-7-1839 (10-13-1839)

Davis, Parkey to Preston Wiloby 11-9-1857
Davis, Patey? to Enoch C. Simmions? 9-4-1847 (9-5-1847)
Davis, Sarah J. to Wm. H. Croushorn 9-9-1856
Davis, Sarah to Henry Hatfield 1-7-1867 (2-24-1867)
Davis, Sodnia? to Frank H. Wylie 3-6-1852 (3-11-1852)
Davis, Tempy? to Vincen Roley 8-21-1844
Davis?, Elizabeth? to D. W. Jones 5-4-1844 (5-5-1844)
Davis?, M. to S. McCankey? 11-15-1845 (11-23-1845)
Davisson, Emeline to Alexander Chadwell 9-22-1866 (9-23-1866)
Davy, Lewisa to John Barnard 11-21-1858
Davy, Margaret to William Keck 12-19-1866 (12-23-1866)
Day, Catharine to William S. Hurst 5-18-1859?
Day, Eliza to George Evans 1-30-1844 (2-1-1844)
Day, Elizabeth to Tennessee Bruden? 7-4-1839
Day, Hoday? M. to Nelson Harp 11-25-1858
Day, Iselee to Wm. Killeren 10-25-1864 (10-25-1864)
Day, Louisa to Mariel Hill 1-11-1847
Day, M. to James A. Kibert 3-8-1853
Day, Martha A. to James C. Hamilton 9-9-1867 (11-7-1867)
Day, Mary to Henry Colston 12-24-1853
Day, Mary to Isaac Ford 1-5-1863 (1-6-1863)
Day, Nancy to Thomas Evans 4-20-1850 (4-21-1850)
Day, Sarah A. to Luke Wright 1-14-1868 (1-19-1868)
Day, Sarah J. to Hugh L. Freeman 10-4-1866
Day, Sarah to Andrew J. Brock 12-13-1841 (12-16-1841)
Day, Sarah to Elisha Fortner 12-4-1858
Day, Sarah to Russel Breeden? 5-13-1847 (5-14-1847)
Debusk, Ann to J. M. Ryans 10-3-1865 (10-5-1865)
Debusk, Mary J. to John H. Logans 8-20-1868
Debusk, Ulinney to Benjamin J. Roe 2-12-1868 (2-13-1868)
Dees, Rhoda to Paschal Tucker 2-24-1844 (2-29-1844)
Denham, Mildred to Lee Fugate 1-31-1867 B
Denham, Nancy V. to Paschal Collins 9-26-1866 (9-27-1866) B
Denham, Sarah A. to Hamilton Cadle 12-23-1858
Denney, Sarah J. to James F. Neely 3-5-1868
Devault, Adaline to William R. Hayse 2-5-1849 (2-22-1849)
Devault, Huldy to Wiley Jone 1-13-1866 (1-14-1866)
Devault, Manervy to Henry C. Hodges 8-23-1849
Devault, Margret to Henry Wilborne 11-21-1850
Devenport, M. J. to William Garrett 5-22-1853
Devenport, Martha to J. H. Edmonston 4-5-1854 (4-6-1854)
Dickinson, E. C. to Leander Miller 8-26-1851
Dickinson, Matilda to William Epps 2-2-1859
Dickinson, Neppy to Lewis Fawbush 9-5-1867 B
Dinkins, Mahala to Ephraim Dobbs 4-20-1850 (4-21-1850)
Dinsmore, Mary I. to Russel Breeding 2-3-1849
Divault, Elizabeth to Bartley Willis 8-28-1858
Dobbs, Louisa to Thos. L. Sawyers 7-30-1839
Dobbs, Pheoba to John Gibson 4-30-1852 (no return)
Dobins, Mary to Arthur L. Jones 11-28-1849
Dobkins, Barthina to Jno. C. Dodson 10-19-1839
Dobkins, Lucinda to Nathaniel Brooks 7-27-1850 (7-28-1850)
Dobkins, M. A. to Prior Cuningham 6-29-1844
Dobkins, Manery? to Joseph H. Bullard 7-20-1848
Dobkins, Nancy to James Belvin 1-30-1839
Dobkins, Phibi to William Latham 8-24-1839
Dodson, Jane to Lynch Hatfield 2-24-1840 (2-27-1840)
Doke, Mary to Hiram Messer 3-4-1848
Doolen, Ann to Henry Sumpter 4-12-1839
Doolin, Susannah to Thomas Clarrick? 11-26-1842
Dorethy, E. to M. Jene? 3-28-1846 (4-4-1846)
Doset, Elizabeth to Andrew Mynett 1-29-1838 (2-1-1838)
Dotson, Elisabeth to William A. Cook 1-15-1856 (1-16-1856)
Doty, Elizabeth to John Wyatt 9-30-1842
Dougherty, B. to Wm. Dosset 1-12-1853 (1-13-1853)
Dougherty, Lucenda to Henry Walker 7-20-1839 (7-21-1839)
Dougherty, Martha J. to D. B. Tackitt 2-27-1855
Dougherty, Nancy to Enas Day 1-29-1845 (1-30-1845)
Dougherty, Rhoda to Martin Harris 8-303-1839 (8-20-1839)
Dowys?, Rebecca to Peter Balloo 9-10-1838 (9-15-1838)
Drummons, F. to Stephen Croft 5-30-1853 (5-31-1853)
Duff?, Nancy Ann to John Eversal? 9-30-1846
Dulin, Elender to James Upton? 11-27-1853
Dulin, Elizabeth to Simpson Casey 5-21-1850
Dulin, Malvina to David Callahan 1-18-1854 (1-19-1854)
Dulin?, Mary A. to Mark? Mannon 2-15-1847
Duncan, Nancy to James Guy 9-1-1866 (9-2-1866)
Dunn, Anna to Adam Sowder 10-9-1855 (10-15-1855)
Dunn, Catherine to Eli Keck 2-8-1866 (2-8-1866)
Dunn, Delila? A. to Abraham Carmack 10-21-1848 (10-22-1848)
Dunn, Elizabeth to James K. P. Mayes 7-31-1866 (8-5-1866)
Dunn, Malinda to David Hopper 9-26-1855 (9-30-1855)
Dunn, Rachel to Joseph Branscome 12-15-1849 (12-20-1849)
Dunsmore, Amanda to Jobe C. Standefer 7-16-1866
Dunsmore, Margret V. to Martin V. Shultz 11-13-1850
Dutton, Elizabeth to William F. Gibson 4-1-1844
Dykes, Martha J. to Franklin Brogan 3-4-1857

Eads, Elizabeth to Jackson Berry 9-18-1849 (9-19-1849)
Eads?, Mary to Thos. Crafford 1-15-1847 (1-17-1847)
Earles, Elizabeth to Willialm Holland 8-30-1854 (8-31-1854)
Easley, Frances to Pleasant B. Jackson 8-31-1854
Eastes, Lucida to Peter Owens 12-10-1849 (12-12-1849)
Eastes, Nancy F. to Francis Cunningham 11-12-1856
Eastis, M. M. to S. Stanaford 6-3-1858
Eastis, Mary to William Hurst 1-2-1851
Eastrage, Lucy Ann to Zackariah Sutton 10-24-1844
Eastrage, Malinda to A. I. Pridemore 8-5-1844 (8-18-1844)
Eastrage, Milla to Daniel Killian 7-14-1854 (7-16-1854)
Eastrage, Nancy to George Campbell 2-10-1842
Eastridge, Louisa to Benjamin Campbell 9-28-1842 (9-29-1842)
Eastridge, Susanah to A. J. Thompson 9-3-1866 (9-14-1866)
Eastridge?, Temperance to Adam Clouse 4-18-1840 (4-25-1840)
Eastus, Jane to Charles W. Runnyans 8-27-1839
Eastus, Nancy to William Rutledge 11-23-1839
Edmonson, Mary to James K. Ousley 10-5-1867 (10-10-1867)
Edny, Nancy A. to J. H. Smith 6-27-1865 (7-1-1865)
Edwards, Anna to Benjamin F. Hopper 3-8-1867 (3-30-1867)
Edwards, Elizabeth to Henry Keck 5-17-1839 (5-19-1839)
Edwards, Malvina to Thos. Gilbert 11-24-1847
Edwards, Mary Jane to James W. Plank 9-28-1848
Edwards, Polly to Thos. Parkey 3-34?-1848
Edwards, Rachel to Eli Goins 8-8-1849 (8-9-1849)
Edwards, Sarah to Jordan Hunter 8-26-1859
Eldrage?, Tabitha to Archable? Owens 8-24-1844 (8-29-1844)
Elerson, Nancy to Joseph Lambert 12-27-1855
Eley?, Mary to Preston Sparks 1-24-1849
Ellerson, Elizabeth to M. B. Nunn 10-17-1853 (10-20-1853)
Ellerson, Louisa to Henry Berry 11-20-1855
Ellerson, Margaret to Richard G. Sherp? 6-8-1854 (6-10-1854)
Ellerson, Sarah to Benj. Berry 10-3-1853 (2-24-1854)
Ellis, Elizabeth to John Lorton? 10-14-1843 (10-17-1843)
Ellis, Margarett to Joshua H. Chapman 2-8-1844
Ellis, Mary to Hiram Sivan [sic] 9-4-1851
Ellison, Catharine to Marcillis Yoakum 7-30-1859
Ellison, Nancy E. to James A. Smith 10-30-1846
Ellison, Nancy to John Clemmons 7-22-1854 (7-24-1854)
Ellison, Susan to George Ellison 12-6-1854 (12-7-1854)
Ely, Belinda to Wm. E. Watts 11-28-1863 (12-1-1863)
Ely, M. D. to Thomas Sparks 12-5-1859
Ely, Martha Virginia to Benjamin F. Conner 11-3-1866
Ely, Mary D. to Elisha A. Presnell 8-16-1853
England, Elizabeth to Thompson Sherman 1-8-1844 (1-9-1844)
England, Febe C. to J. Fudington 3-31-1857
England, Martha E. to John Lambert 1-24-1843 (1-25-1843)
England, Martha to Joseph Simmons 8-5-1865 (8-24-1865)
England, Mary to B. F. Norvell 9-19-1851 (9-23-1851)
England, Mary to Robert Sanders 1-20-1844 (1-21-1844)
England, Mary to William Dikson 9-4-1865 (9-7-1865)
England, Melvina to Geoge W. Mattox 6-9-1865 (6-11-1865)
England, Melvina to George W. Maddox 6-9-1865
England, Nancy to Parker D. Reynolds 9-19-1865 (9-28-1865)
England, Pheoba to Hu L. Freeman 3-1-1852
England, Sarah to John W. Davis 8-22-1865 (8-24-1865)
England, Thursy to Isaac A. Grimes 9-5-1838
England?, Caroline to Isaac W. Poor 7-25-1867 (8-1-1867)
Englant, Mary to Henry Carroll 9-1-1849 (8?-3-1849)
Englebarger, Lucinda to Calvin Sullivan 10-6-1866 (10-7-1866)
Englent, Martha to George Sutton 2-25-1851 (8-12-1851)
Eperson, Sidney to Richard Kindred 9-19-1865
Epperon?, Nancy L. to William C. Epperson 10-16-1863
Epperson, Ann to James Hodges 4-5-1855
Epperson, Martha E. to Gabriel H. Moles 1-16-1867 (1-17-1867)
Eppes, Margret to Preston Hodges 11-25-1866 B
Epps, Sarah to James A. Day 7-30-1867
Estep, Martha J. to Andrew Mannon 10-4-1866 (10-10-1866)
Estep, Nancy E. to Jas. P. Campbell 10-30-1865 (11-2-1865)
Estept, Matilda J. to Adam C.? Yeary 1-9-1856 (1-13-1856)
Estice, Judah E. L.? to Calvin Brooks 11-7-1843 (11-8-1843)
Estice, Sarah Ann to Matthew Whiteaker 6-6-1843
Etten, Deaner to Washington Holden 1-2-1846
Etter, D. to W. Holden 2-2-1848 (2-3-1848)
Evans, ~~illegible~~
Evans, Emily C. to James Fordy? 8-22-1844
Evans, Hetty Ann to John Killion 6-24-1868 (6-25-1868)
Evans, Louisa A. to Wm. R. Sevier 12-26-1864
Evans, Louisa to William Kirkpatrick 11-18-1841
Evans, Lucenta to W. B. Jonns 9-23-1865 (9-26-1865)
Evans, Lucy Janes? to William Epps 5-2-1843
Evans, Mary to Andrew Hurst 10-23-1853
Evans, N. to Alexander Givens 5-22-1853
Evans, Nancy to Woodbery Robinson 10-18-1849 (10-26-1849)
Evans, Polly to Lewis Day 1-11-1842 (1-23-1842)
Evans, Prissilla to Jesse J. Geabolf? 7-24-1839 (7-28-1839)
Evans, Sarah to Samuel Breeding 9-6-1852 (9-7-1852)

Evans, Thursa Ann to Robert Greer 10-18-1845 (10-12?-1845)
Eve, Elisabeth? E. to John L. Swann? 7-23-1846 (8-2-1846)
Fairchilds, Elizabeth to Samuel McCullough 1-24-1843 (1-26-1843)
Falkner, Licha? to Ezekiel Goodin 3-26-1848
Falkner, Mary A. to Jacob Cupp 12-22-1848
Farmer, Elisabeth M. to James D. Hurst 11-25-1848 (11-26-1848)
Farmer, P. to F. Arwine 8-6-1858 (8-8-1858)
Fauche?, Hanah to John Ellis 4-12-1846 (4-13-1846)
Felps, Catherine to Prior L. Vance 2-19-1850 (2-22-1850)
Fergerson, Rachel to Thomas England 9-9-1859
Fernell, Eliza to John F. Woodson 2-8-1848 (2-9-1848)
Fernell, Catharin to Greenberry Short 7-13-1842 (7-14-1842)
Ferrel, Amanda to Rodden F. Owens 5-25-1848
Ferrell, Sally to George Givin 2-16-1839 (2-17-1839)
Ferrile, Emily to Silas D. Woods 3-3-1840
Field?, Effy to Preston Morgan 4-13-1839
Fielos?, Elender to William Dulin 7-25-1844
Fisher, Elisabeth to John T. Jones 9-6-1856
Flemings, Sarah to John Hopson 4-27-1855 (4-29-1855)
Fletcher, Lena? to Jonas Snavely 8-3-1850 (8-4-1850)
Fletcher, Nancy J. to William H. McNeil 8-14-1867 (8-22-1867)
Fletcher, Sally to John Clouse 10-17-1839
Fletchere, Mary Ann to Jirriael? Smith 12-25-1843 (12-27-1843)
Flinchum, Nancy to Boston Clapp 7-23-1855 (7-26-1855)
Flinchum, Sarah to Jesse Hopper 1-24-1867
Fly, Matilda to Edmand Napeer 10-21-1843
Ford, Lavina to Jesse Lynch 6-15-1839 (6-18-1839)
Ford, Lucinda to J. W. Smith 11-7-1848 (11-9-1848)
Ford, Martha to L. L. Minton 4-26-1866
Ford, Rhoda to George Day 11-29-1854 (11-30-1854)
Forgerson, Elisabeth? to M. B. Nunn 11-26-1845 (11-28-1845)
Forgerson, Louisa J. to John Richerson 12-24-1852 (12-26-1852)
Fortiner, Sarah to William Johnson 3-1-1841
Fortner (was Evans), Mary E. to Reason M. Fortner no dates (before 1869)
Fortner, E. J. to Lawson Doriant 1-14-1853 (1-166-1853)
Fortner, Louiza M. E. to John B. Goin 10-21-1867 (10-24-1867)
Fortner, Martha M. to James C. Runions 2-5-1856
Fortner, Mary to Christopher Turner 10-12-1859
Fortner, Sarah to William Johnson 2-23-1842 (3-1-1842)
Fowler, Jincy C. to John C. Collins 2-25-1856 (2-28-1856)
Fox, M. to A. Fox 5-1-1858
Fox, M. to W. J. Houston 9-16-1857
Fox, Matilda to William J. Venoy 10-15-1853
Fox, Rachal to John Painter 12-27-1852 (1-4-1853)
Frasher, Zilpha J. to William Baylay? 6-25-1849 (6-26-1849)
Freeman, Jane to Ransam? Hose 11-25-1845
Freeman, Rebecca to Lasarus Dodson 6-21-1839 (6-29-1839)
Freemana, Catherine J. to Isaac Shumate 10-8-1851 (10-9-1851)
Freemon, Cela to Henry Sharp 7-5-1838 (7-6-1838)
Freyor, Sarah to James Roark 7-28-1855 (7-29-1855)
Friar, Rebecca to John J. F. Eastes 8-15-1849 (8-16-1849)
Frier, Abigal to Roman Owens 1-17-1848 (1-18-1848)
Frith, Elizabeth to Thomas J. Goin 7-17-1868 (7-25-1868)
Frith, Nancy to C. Q. Sulfrig 2-5-1862 (2-7-1862)
Fugate, Catharine L. to Edward E. Eppes 11-22-1866
Fugate, Elisabeth A. to Hugh Parkey 11-11-1856 (11-20-1856)
Fugate, Lizzie R. to Tipton Evans 2-4-1857
Fugate, Lucy Jane to Robert C. Woodson 10-3-1849 (10-4-1849)
Fugate, Mary Ann to Albert D. Overton 9-24-1866 (9-2?-1866)
Fugate, R. to M. G. Parkey 4-16-1859
Fugate, Rachel to Wm. L. Overton 6-8-1840
Fulkerson, Martha to Mathis Kelley 10-27-1866 B
Fulks, Priscella to Jefferson Chick 4-19-1843 (4-20-1843)
Fullington, Elizabeth to James C Whitaker 12-16-1858
Fullington, Jane to John Peck 7-3-1855
Fullington, Margart to John Guy 1-22-1856
Fullington, Rhoda to James D. Fields 2-21-1852
Fullington, Sarah V. to James Jones 8-7-1856
Fulp, E. to A. Fulp 7-30-1852 (8-1-1852)
Fulp, Jane to Vincent Moyer 3-19-1842 (4-14-1842)
Fulps, Abigail? to Jeremiah Hopper 5-22-1839 (5-24-1839)
Fulps, Cyntha to George M.? Lewis 9-16-1848 (9-17-1848)
Fulps, Rebecca to Ganeum McBee 7-16-1849
Fults, ~~illegible~~ J. to John Owens 12-4-1846
Fults, Sarah J. to Jacob Carmack 2-4-1851
Fultz, Sarah to James F. Brooks 11-1-1866 (11-4-1866)
Fultz, Sarah to Rice Hayse 4-7-1854
Furgason, Lucy J. to Timothy Eastrage 11-23-1850
Furgerson, Nancy to Robert A. Brooks 3-27-1867 (3-31-1867)
Furgerson, S. to B. Lambert 7-16-1854 (7-18-1855?)
Furgerson, Sarah to Benjamin Lambert 7-16-1854
Furgeson, Sarah to M. B. Nunn 4-7-1849
Furgeson, Tabitha to Newton Myers 12-18-1854 (12-24-1854)
Furry, Margaret to J. H. Ellis 2-21-1840 (12-23-39)[sic]
Furry, Margaret to James H. Ellis 12-21-1839
Furry, Mary to Ezekiel Dougherty 8-30-1838 (9-4-1838)
Furry, Sarah to Abraham Jones 9-1-1838

Fusan, Adaline to Wm. Kesterson 9-20-1854
Fusian, Elizabeth to Benajah Peace? 10-1-1839? (10-7-1838)
Gains, Perlina to George W. Pridda 12-17-1853
Garland, Malinda to Lewis Kibert 6-28-1852 (6-30-1852)
Garnett, Matilda to Benjamin Dickinson 6-21-1849
Garrett, Mary to Henry H. J. T. Graham 2-27-1868 B
Garull, Martha A. to Wm. Richardson 9-19-1853
Geasley, Polly to David Sanders 8-5-1850 (8-7-1850)
Gentry, Elizabeth to Josiah Russell 8-13-1839
Geoge, Sela to Samuel Harris 9-27-1850
George, Ellis to Joseph Carter 1-23-1848 (1-27-1848)
George, Nancy to J. M. Marcum 4-6-1851 (4-7-1851)
German?, Mary T. to Jasper Keck 9-4-1861 (9-15-1861)
Gibert, Polly to Claborne Welbourn 4-13-1839 (4-14-1839)
Gibert?, Susannah to James M. Martain 3-27-1842 (3-30-1842)
Gibson, B. A. to B. P.? Bullard 4-7-1858
Gibson, C. to W. S. Bell 8-9-1853
Gibson, Caroline to Wm. S. Bell 7-9-1853 B
Gibson, Cathrine to Danl. W. Ellis 12-22-1851
Gibson, Lina to Alexander Robinson 12-26-1867 (1-10-1868) B
Gibson, Nancy to Wayde Collins 10-11-1856
Gibson, Rebeca Perlina to Isaac Bullars 5-13-1854
Gideans, Martha to John Allen 3-31-1838 (4-1-1838)
Gilbert, Nancy to Elijah Marian? 1-16-1845 (1-19-1845)
Gilbert, Nancy to William McNeal 12-6-1839
Gillasie, Mary A. to Bolivar Bannum 10-28-1865 (10-29-1865)
Gilpin, Matilda J. to David Chadwell 10-23-1857
Gilpson, Luiza to James Cheek 1-30-1865
Glenn, Mary A. to James T.? Shields 5-11-1848
Goforth, N. R. to W. R. Cox 10-20-1864 (10-23-1864)
Goforth, Sarah Matilda to Jeptha? Edwards 4-23-1842 (5-16-1842)
Goin, Elizabeth to James Mooney 12-13-1858
Goin, Marlenia to James P. Johnson 6-18-1868 (6-20-1868)
Goin, Martha J. to Andrew J. Goin 5-4-1867
Goin, Mary A. to William Hacker 2-23-1865 (2-26-1865)
Goin, Mary to John McQuary 12-29-1865 (12-30-1865)
Goin, S. E. to Thomas Burch 10-12-1857
Goin, Tempey A. to John W. Cheatham 10-30-1866 (10-31-1866)
Goinbral, Druciler to Harvy Smith 9-23-1844
Going, Cass? Ann to John L. Going 7-27-1843 (7-30-1843)
Goins, Elender E. to Joseph P. Johnson 1-29-1850
Goins, Elinor to Andrew Phillips 4-25-1857 (4-26-1857)
Goins, Elizabeth to John Goins 4-4-1851 (4-30-1851)
Goins, Jane to Elisha Hall 9-29-1847
Goins, L. to J. M. Yaden 8-11-1853 (8-12-1853)
Goins, Lucinda to J. M. Yaden 7-11-1853 (8-12?-1853)
Goins, Malinda to William J. Raney 10-30-1856 (11-3-1856)
Goins, Mary A. to Wm. H. Mays 5-23-1853 (5-24-1853)
Goins, Minerva A. to W. P. Brooks 4-25-1857 (4-26-1857)
Goins, Mirah to Wm. H. Sparks 10-8-1851
Goins, Mohaby? to John Green 4-14-1845 (4-4?-1845)
Goins, Nancy to Jas. Fortner 9-1-1852 (9-2-1852)
Gollehorn, Nancy to John Houston 5-11-1868 (5-14-1868) *
Gons, Omey to Ezekiel Raney 2-1-1853
Good, Mary A. to John Bush 7-27-1867 (7-29-1867)
Goodman, Mary A. to Ralph Gowns 5-11-1854
Goodman, Rebeca to Uriah Gowens 4-7-1854 (4-13-1854)
Gooman, Mary A. to John Fulp 11-10-1864 (11-29-1864)
Gowin, Martha J. to Andrew Phellps 12-5-1837
Gowins, Nancy to Urior? Gowins? 9-26-1846 (9-27-1846)
Grace, Elisabeth to John Cowen 1-19-1856 (1-22-1856)
Grace, R.? to Wm. Barnes 5-9-1846 (5-17-1846)
Grace, Rosemial? to John Barns? 1-14-1842
Grace, Soperia? to ----- Liford 6-12-1843
Grace, William to Druciller Cadle 1-18-1845
Graceclose, Catharin to Hubbard Bralock 12-10-1842 (12-12-1842)
Graceclose, S. J. to James M. Pugh 1-15-1853 (1-23-1853)
Graham, C. H. to Wm. H. Patterson 9-1-1859
Graham, Eliza J. to Thos. J. Johnston 4-17-1839
Graham, Jane to E. V. Wallon 12-30-1846
Graham, Jane to H. Burchfield 7-2-1846
Graham, Lucy A. to J. M. England 1-31-1866
Graham, Margaret E. to William Neil 2-11-1840
Graham, Martha A. to Edward Jackson 11-27-1867 B
Graham, Mary Louisa to Theophilus Rogan 12-14-1853
Graham, Sarah A. to W. A. L. Blackburn 9-1-1857
Grantham, Harriet to Benjamin D. Miles? 9-25-1841 (9-26-1841)
Grantham, Rebeca to John T. Mongomry 4-28-1865 (4-31?-1865)
Grantum, Virginia A. to William G. Davis 3-16-1858
Graves, Elizabeth to Levi Sharp 1-18-1840 (6-30-1840)
Graves, Sally to Michael Maser 4-18-1840 (5-3-1840)
Graves, Sarah A. to A. McConnel 3-19-1840 (3-13?-1840)
Gray, Elizabeth to Samuel Jennings 4-7-1866 (4-9-1866)
Gray, Polly to James McCullum? 3-15-1847 (3-22-1847)
Grazy?, Sarah F. to B. L. Kelly 9-27-1852
Green, Elisabeth to John Wells 6-14-1856 (6-16-1856)
Green, Eliza to Thos. J. Lanham 7-25-1838

Green, Elizabeth to Andrew J. Hamilton 12-29-1866 (1-1-1867)
Green, Lewisa to Gainford Upton 3-23-1859
Green, Louisanna to James Doyle 10-10-1849
Green, Lucy to James M. Hicks 7-4-1849 (7-10-1849)
Green, M. A. to Robert Simmons 7-1-1853
Green, Mary to Samuel E. Rowlan 2-22-1867 (2-24-1867)
Green, Nancy E. to Noah Harrel 3-14-1850 (3-17-1850)
Green, Nancy to A. M. Beard 2-26-1852
Green, Ruth to David A. Samuel 9-14-1852
Green, T. to James W. Norton? 6-12-1848 (6-15-1848)
Greenlee, Gemmima E. to Wm. McKee 12-21-1855
Greenlee, M. W. to Isaac Poore 7-3-1865 (7-19-1865)
Greenlee, Patsy L. to Jacob Vaughn 11-15-1851 (11-18-1851)
Greer, Elizabeth A. to Robt. Lingar 11-12-1865 (11-13-18650)
Greer, Manervy to Joseph Moore 1-19-1843
Greer, Nancy Rebecca to Elijah Thomas 11-21-1867 (11-24-1867)
Greer, Permelia to William C. McBee 12-10-1839 (12-15-1839)
Greer, V. M. to Isaac Presnell 8-5-1858 (8-12-1858)
Gresly?, Rebecca to Alfed Tredaway 11-3-1849
Griffen, Almiry to Wm. T. Larance 11-17-1859
Griger, Martha Ann to Joseph Shelton 4-27-1868
Grigery, Susan to William Wyatt 11-18-1846 (11-8?-1846)
Grimes, Betsy Ann to Richard Crabtree 8-16-1849 (8-17-1849)
Grimes, Cathrine to G. Tailor 2-21-1853
Grimes, Elizabeth to John W. Wright 7-6-1868 (7-9-1868)
Grimes, Malissa to Daniel Sutteen 7-28-1856
Grimes, Margret J. to Thomas Chadwell 12-25-1858
Grimes, Martha to Presley G. Burk 8-23-1854 (8-24-1854)
Grimes, Mary to Camador Rogers 3-25-1849 (3-26-1849)
Grimes, Sarah to Moses Hatfield 6-17-1847 (6-20-1847)
Grimes?, Polly to Richard Carder 10-4-1841 (12-22-1841)
Grocecloce?, Anny to Esom Loves 3-29-1844
Grosse, Jane to Daniel Criger 12-24-1866 (12-27-1866)
Grows, Mildred to Wm. Munday 12-13-1853 (12-?-1853)
Grubb, Nancy to John Bruster 6-2-1851
Grubb, Permela C. to Jesse Childers 2-26-1855
Guinn?, Martha F. to G. W. Myers 9-26-1850
Guthery, Hannah to Charley M. Day 12-15-1843 (12-17-1843)
Guthrie, Mary Ann to Hillary Gibson 2-25-1856 (2-28-1856)
Guy, Emeline to Samuel Arnold 8-15-1868 (8-16-1868)
Guy, Jane to James Rose 1-8-1866 (1-26-1866)
Guy, Martha to Wm. jr. Greer 12-22-1863 (12-24-1863)
Gwin, R. to Thomas Color 7-29-1858
Hacker, Rebecca to Henry Sourd? 11-3-1851 (11-4-1851)
Hail, Camfred to Isaac Carmac 3-14-1838 (3-27-1838)
Hail, Sarah to William Cox 9-16-1867 (9-17-1867)
Hale, Elizabeth to George A. Dickson 7-1-1853
Hale, Ester to Dolin Lake 5-1-1854 (5-2-1854)
Hale, Mary to Isaac Bush 10-2-1867 (10-3-1867)
Hall, Elizabeth E. to John Z. Kivit 8-24-1857
Hall, Emeliza to Scott Atkins 11-8-1854
Hall, Mary to Arnal Hipsher 10-18-1854 (10-19-18540
Hall, Nancy to Oliven Tackett 12-12-1839
Hall, S. to A. Marion? 11-18-1845
Hall, Susan to Ambrose Arthur 9-19-1838
Hall, Susan to Elijah Hedrick 4-12-1855 (4-13-1855)
Halton, Eliza to John Lorton 12-2-1850 (2-20-1851)
Hamach, N. to Edmon Maples 3-26-1853
Hamblin, Emaline to Spencer King 10-11-1848 (10-12-1848)
Hamblin, Juda to Leroy Hamblin 4-21-1845? (4-23-1846)
Hamblin, Sarah to John A. Littrell 9-25-1856
Hamelton, Elizabeth to Morwrixes? Cook 1-5-1854 (1-6-1854)
Hamelton, Julia to Robert C. Luster? 1-18-1850 (marr, no date)
Hamelton, Martha to Joel Southerland 4-14-1842
Hamelton, Nancy to Wm. Hamelton 4-26-1839 (4-30-1839)
Hamelton, Polly to William Carroll 10-24-1839 (10-31-1839)
Hamelton, Sarah to Isaac Vanbebber 7-23-1839 (7-30-1839)
Hamilton, Sarah to William A. Cook 2-15-1855
Hamlin, Jane to Evan Ball 11-17-1866 (11-25-1866)
Hamlin, Manda M. to John Combs 9-7-1867 (9-8-1867)
Hamllan?, Ledna A. to Richard D. Crabtree 4-18-1854 (4-21-1854)
Hammack, Becky to Latan Rannins? 7-18-1846 (7-19-1846)
Hammock, Betsy to Wm. Maples 9-25-1841 (9-30-1841)
Hamons, Elender to William Hamons 1-8-1850
Hamons, Sally to David Cape? 6-15-1846
Hampton, Martha to Hiram Callep 10-18-1855
Harda, E. C. to F. S. White 5-21-1851 (6-20-1851)
Hardy, Emly to J. S. White 6-21-1851
Hardy, Mary to John Bright 1-9-1850 (1-10-1850)
Hardy, Susan M. to John Owens 11-22-1847 (11-25-1847)
Hargis, Nancy to Franklin Jackson 4-1-1855
Haris, Sarah Ann to Alfred Busick 11-1-1858
Harison?, Rachel to Hesakiah Moyers 3-1-1849 (3-4-1849)
Harkins, Fany to Marshal Woodson 7-16-1852
Harkins, N. to A. Sebolt 1-31-1852 (2-1-1852)
Harman, Mary to Isaac Davis 12-13-1854 (no return)
Harmon, Harriet M. to Sterling Keck 10-11-1866 (10-18-1866)

Harmon, Sarah to F. H. Wiley 10-5-1865
Harp, Mariah to W. D. Williams 9-5-1865 (9-21-1865)
Harp, Nancy to Joshua Teague 10-31-1856
Harp, Rebecca to Andrew H. Parker 9-10-1856
Harpa, Abby to John Simmons 7-31-1857 (8-11-1857)
Harper, Jane to Wornick Butcher 5-17-1867 (5-18-1867) B
Harper, Mary J. to Flemon Willis 11-13-1849
Harral, Wilmirth? to Joseph Bunch 7-28-1842
Harrel, Lousa to John Hickle 6-25-1853 (7-7-1853)
Harrell, Elizabeth to Robert J. Gourley 7-10-1858
Harrell, Margart to Abner Nunn 12-15-1838
Harrell, Pheeby to Reubin Burch 7-2-1845 (7-3-1845)
Harrell, Rhoda J. to James T. Hurst 9-21-1867 (10-9-1867)
Harrell, Sarah M. to James McGinnes 10-30-1867 (10-31-1867)
Harris, E. J. to Georg? Cartor 1-28-1845
Harris, Martha to Ransom Eldridge 9-5-1857
Harris, Melley? to John F. Thompson 10-7-1842 (10-8-1842)
Harris, Susan to John Loc? 2-21-1865
Harris, Susan to John Loe 2-21-1865
Harris?, Anny to Henry Baker 7-16-1842 (7-19-1842)
Harrison, Betsey Ann to Fidello Dykes 10-8-1855 (10-11-1855)
Harrison, Manervy Jane to James F. D. S. Smith 4-25-1853 (4-28-1853)
Hart, Rachel to William Camran 11-5-1849 (11-10-1849)
Haskins, Nancy to George W. Ball 3-24-1858
Hatfield, Bisa to Nathaniel Erles 3-21-1851 (3-22-1851)
Hatfield, Catharine to William Ramsey 2-6-1868
Hatfield, Cathrine to Greenberry Hatfield 8-31-1852 (9-1-1852)
Hatfield, E. to John Grimes 6-4-1845 (6-5-1845)
Hatfield, Elizabeth to Allen Ketron 2-8-1865
Hatfield, Elizabeth to James Leforce 7-3-1865 (7-6-1865)
Hatfield, Ellander to Henry Cole 8-31-1859
Hatfield, Frances to Preston Davis 9-19-1867 (9-26-1867)
Hatfield, Frankey to Preston Davis 9-19-1867
Hatfield, Hella to Lynch Hatfield 9-10-1852
Hatfield, Jeminia to William Ayers 4-22-1843 (4-23-1843)
Hatfield, Levina to James Simmons 7-14-1854
Hatfield, Manervy to James N. Lifard? 4-29-1843 (4-30-1843)
Hatfield, Mary to Jas. Louthr? 5-9-1846
Hatfield, Mary to Wm. Whitaker 10-8-1851 (10-9-1851)
Hatfield, Matilda to Robert Deen 3-1-1856 (4-4-1856)
Hatfield, S. to F. Longworth 4-29-1858
Hatfield, Sarah to Lewis Wilburn 10-7-1867 (10-12-1867)
Havely?, Mary? to John W. Crisp 7-4-1845 (7-8-1845)
Hawkins, Luhamy to John W. Ayers 11-17-1859
Hawley?, M. B. to John B. Parker 9-21-1845? (9-6-1846?)
Hawthorne, Bartheny to Alford Hynes 9-11-1865 (9-18-1865)
Haynes, Celia to Henry Bullard 9-26-1853
Haynes, Mary Jane to Robert G. Parks 5-5-1857 (5-19-1857)
Haynes, Melvina J. to J. W. Alston 11-4-1865 (11-5-1865)
Hays?, Elizabeth to Wm. Owens 10-11-1843 (10-12-1843)
Hayse, Nancy to Daniel Morrison 6-23-1865
Hazelwood, Elisebeth to Allen Thomas 3-3-1855 (3-26-1855)
Hazelwood?, Emaley to E. Campbell 6-24-1845 (6-4?-1845)
Heath, E. to D. Sharp 1-1-1852 (1-8-1852)
Hedrick, Susan to James Russell 6-11-1866
Heil, Elizabeth to Henry Buis 8-16-1866 B
Heller, Jane to John Keites 9-20-1865 (9-21-1865)
Helms, Elisebeth to William C. Wallace 12-28-1854 (1-2-1855)
Helms, Mary J. to Joseph January 2-9-1852 (2-12-1852)
Helton, Carolinle to Alson? Hetton 1-25-1843 (1-26-1843)
Helton, Louza to S. B. Kirby 9-29-1865 (10-1-1865)
Helton?, Emaline to Peter Hellon? 1-14-1849 (1-18-1849)
Henderon, E. M. to Nelson Robinson 2-24-1853
Henderson, Adaline? to Reubin Kesterson? 8-26-1845
Henderson, Caroline to Stokely R. Lanham 6-2-1842
Henderson, Clementin N. to Caleb N. Thompson 8-10-1848 (8-11-1848)
Henderson, Margaret to James Hoskins 4-20-1856 (4-21-1856)
Henderson, Martha Ann to Robert Southern 5-31-1849
Henderson, Perlina to Eldrage? H. Lanham 9-10-1845 (11-11-1845)
Henderson, Polly to Hiram Hoskins 6-8-1844 (6-10-1844)
Henderson, Sarah to Hawkins Campbell 8-16-1854
Hendrix, Molinda to George Washington Wallace 10-16-1841 (10-17-1841)
Herell?, M. E. to B. Poor 6-14-1845
Herral, Elizabeth to William Hopson 7-5-1843 (7-6-1843)
Herrall, Rachel to James C. Herrall 1-28-1843 (1-29-1843) *
Herrel, M. to Augustus Carrel 7-4-1853
Herrell, Matida? to Wm. Owsley 2-25-1845
Herrell, Elender to James Minton 9-30-1847 (10-?-1847)
Herrell, Elvira? M. to Jas. Carell 10-27-1845
Herrell, Levica to Silvester Nunn 11-12-1845 (11-13-1845)
Herrell, Levisa to Silvester? Num? 11-12-1845
Herrell, Mariah J. to Sterling Nunn 10-4-1850 (10-5-1850)
Herrell, Mariah to Sterling Nunn 4-19-1850
Herrell, Mary to Augustus Carrell 7-4-1853
Herrell, Mary to William Edens 11-11-1855
Herrell, N. A. [Nancy] to Wm. McNeelance 3-18-1853 (3-20-1853)
Herrell, R. C. to D. C. Cline 12-18-1852 (12-28-1852)
Herrell, R. S. to A. Carrell 12-18-1851
Herron, Nancy to Hiram Heller 10-9-1866 (10-19-1866)
Hicks, Jane to Judan? Hunter? 11-15-1844 (11-18-1844)
Hicks, Martha to William Cunningham 12-18-1843 (12-22-1843)
Hicks, Pheby to James Price 2-1-1849 (2-8-1849)
Higginbottom, Elizabeth J. to Calvin Stamper 9-1-1857
Hill, Barthena to Thomas Cox 1-10-1840 (1-12-1840)
Hill, Boni to Wilson Guy 9-12-1865
Hill, Clary to Johnathan Barnard 2-22-1846 (2-27-1846)
Hill, Elizabeth to Canady Peck 4-27-1857
Hill, Mahaley to Henry Mills 2-1-1847
Hill, Mary A. to James T. Martin 2-28-1865 (3-1-1865)
Hill, Mary to Edwin Pace 10-7-1853
Hill, Nairvsty? to David Brooks 4-23-1858 (5-25-1858)
Hill, S. to D. Lawson 6-2-1845 (6-5-1845)
Hill, Susan C. to Zachariah T. Hill 8-13-1868
Hill, Susan to William Lambert 12-30-1854 (1-4-1855)
Hinton?, Nancy A. to Daniel Littrell 6-28-1850
Hix, Becky to Thos. Young 9-5-1857
Hix, Rebeckey to Jos. M. Johnson 1-10-1846
Hix, Sarah A. to Green B. Rite 3-8-1855
Hix?, Orlena to Edwards Fields 9-11-1849 (9-17-1849)
Hobbs, Ann to Andrew B. Smith 8-27-1847 (8-29-1847)
Hobbs, Elisabeth Jane to Sterling G. Coleman 7-10-1845 (7-13-1845)
Hobbs, Elsebeth to Randolph Noe 1-9-1855
Hobbs, R. to John White 12-14-1847
Hobbs, Rutha M. to Clinton Brooks 7-6-1866 (7-8-1866)
Hockins, Ruthy to E. C. Admes? 12-4-1858
Hodge, Jane to James M. Carr 4-12-1844 (4-14-1844)
Hodge, Rebecca to C. B. Bullard 11-10-1838
Hodge, Sarah to A. M. Jennings 5-17-1858 (5-23-1858)
Hodges, Beste A. to Preston Dunsmore 2-2-1850
Hodges, Elisabeth to Elijah Hodges 12-16-1847
Hodges, Louisa to L. B. Shomate? 4-4-1846 (4-5-1846)
Hodges, Louisa to William B. Alexander 10-2-1847 (10-7-1847)
Hodges, Louiza to John Harvey 7-25-1867 (7-28-1867)
Hodges, Lucy J. to Prior L. Hurst 5-24-1856 (5-25-1856)
Hodges, Mahala to Samuel Shoemaker 1-4-1851
Hodges, Martha A. to Fredrick H. Austin 5-15-1867
Hodges, Mary to Royal Neil 3-1-1843
Hodges, Rachel M. to Philip Minton 10-4-1849 (10-5-1849)
Hodges, Sarah to John T. Leffue 9-21-1867 (10-16-1867)
Hollan, Lucinda to John Falkner 1-10-1849 (1-14-1849)
Hollan, Mary A. to Levi Willis 12-1-1856
Hollansworth, Eliza J. to J. C. Large 9-5-1859
Holley, Eliza W. to Henley C. Brians 12-25-1866
Hollin, Barbra to William Ritter 11-27-1846
Hollins, Martha to Danil Rader 5-13-1865 (5-14-1865)
Hollinsworth, Nancy M. to Isah M. Fortner 9-17-1858 (9-21-1858)
Hollon, Nancy to Wiley Cazort 2-27-1848 (2-29-1848)
Hollon?, Nancy to Wiley Cazort? 2-27-1848 (2-29-1848)
Holt, Lavesa to Thos. P. Bray 7-22-1843 (7-24-1843)
Holt, Matilda to James A. Willis 2-24-1856 (3-4-1856)
Holton, Mary to James Dikes 1-14-1850 (1-17-1850)
Holton, Melvina to Wesley Fonel 4-28-1865 (5-1-1865)
Holton, O. to S. Fortner 8-11-1853 (8-14-1853)
Holton, O. to Solomon Fortner 7-11-1853
Holton?, Lewrittey? to Ryley Dykes 2-17-1845
Honeycutt, Elizabeth to Henderson Knuckels 9-27-1866
Honeycutt, Elizabeth to James Robinson 8-26-1839 (8-27-1839)
Honeycutt, Elizabeth to Wm. Houston 10-11-1841 (10-14-1841)
Honeycutt, H. R. to S. A. Woods 11-3-1852 (11-4-1852)
Hooper, Malinda to William Marteal 1-20-1844 (1-21-1844)
Hopkins, Bilenda? to John Molana? 12-16-1843 (12-17-1843)
Hopkins, Catharin J. to Joseph Farris? 5-16-1842 (5-17-1842)
Hopkins, Elisa? to J. R. Hopkins 9-27-1845
Hopkins, Elisabeth? to David Farby? 8-14-1846 (8-16-1846)
Hopkins, Mary Ann to Stuphin? Hopkins 6-7-1843
Hopkins, Polly to Josiah? _____ 6-20-1846
Hopkins, Sarah E. to Jacob S. Slauter 12-15-1866 (12-20-1866)
Hoposon, Unica to Henry Ritter 12-17-1853 (12-18-1853)
Hopper, Ann to Elvis Hill 12-9-1847 (12-14-1847)
Hopper, Charity to Isaac Hammack 6-11-1856 (6-14-1856)
Hopper, Frankey to Richard H. Harper 5-19-1849 (5-24-1849)
Hopper, Loucinda to George Powell 11-22-1839 (11-23-1839)
Hopper, Lousa to Abram Cupp 4-12-1852
Hopper, M. J. to M. Brewer 2-14-1853 (2-17-1853)
Hopper, Manerva to Johnson Mayse 6-29-1857 (7-2-1857)
Hopper, Mary A. to D. A. Carr 2-8-1866 (2-9-1866)
Hopper, Nancy to J. S. Cassel? 8-28-1845
Hopper, Rachel to Hugh Graham 12-9-1847
Hopper, Sarah? Jane to Greenberry Right 11-23-1841 (11-25-1841)
Hopper, Serena to M. L. Odel 10-22-1856
Hopper, Susan to J. C. Hooker 8-30-1865
Hopper, Susannah to William McFarland 9-2-1847
Hopper, Viny to David Reen 11-17-1865 (11-24-1865)
Hopson, M. J. to M. V. Bunch 1-2-1856 (2-7-1856)

Hopson, Mary J. to M. V. Bunch 2-2-1856
Hopson, Nancy J. to George P. Rosenbalm 4-9-1857
Hopson, Nancy L. to Wm. C. Epperson 10-14-1853 (10-16-1853)
Hopson, Syntha A. to Anderson Carpenter 5-12-1843 (5-18-1843)
Hosford, Elisebeth J. to James O. Childs 1-8-1855 (1-9-1855)
Hoskins, E. to Wm. Cox 2-18-1846
Hoskins, Elisabeth? to William Cox 2-18-1846 (3-5-1846)
Hoskins, Elizabeth to William Bailey 2-1-1844
Hoskins, Esther to John Ball 2-11-1867 (2-14-1867)
Hoskins, Esther? to Jo Hiram? Pridmore 6-11-1840
Hoskins, Lucy A. to William Woodson 5-20-1868 (5-23-1868)
Hoskins, Mary to James Johnson 10-10-1866 (10-11-1866)
Hoskins, Ruth to Isaac A. Campbell 12-25-1854 (no return)
Hoult, Lucy to Geo. Sumpter 7-26-1838
Householder, Mary to David Estice 1-2-1844
Houston, Louisa to Marshal Seals 9-4-1850
Houston, Mary L. to Robert E. Patterson 10-8-1857
Houston, Russilla Ann to Wm. P. Bales 6-4-1850
Howard, Elizabeth to Bowling Lee 7-2-1852 (7-2-1852)
Howel, Elizabeth to William Louis 4-2-1850 (4-2-1859)
Howel?, Neoma to Felix Brachett? 8-13-1846
Howell, Maranda to Dunkin Hash 10-29-1858
Howerton, Allsey to John Lacock 9-9-1856 (9-11-1856)
Howerton, Catharine to James Lea 11-4-1843 (11-9-1843)
Howerton, Reeny to Wm. Rogers 11-10-1865
Hubbard, Rhoda J. to Martin Stuard 9-30-1867
Huddleston, Anna to Wilborn Pendleton 10-2-1849 (10-4-1849)
Huddleston, Effa to Allen Marlor 8-12-1851 (8-28-1851)
Huddleston?, Effy to Elisha Nunn 8-1-1838
Huff, Lundy to Monroe Curtis 12-24-1850
Huff, Margaret to John W. Kincaid 8-19-1857
Huff, Sarah to Lafayette Evans 11-11-1848
Huffaker, Sally to Wm. McHenry 2-25-1839 (2-28-1839)
Hughes, Nancy to Thomas Clapp 11-21-1854 (11-22-1854)
Hughs, Elizabeth to John W. Clapp 11-11-1851
Humphria, Fanna to David Chadwell 5-15-1853 (5-17-1853)
Hunacutt, Elizabeth to George Braden 5-12-1853 (5-28-1853)
Hunnacott, Malvina to Philip Roth 2-20-1855
Hunsford, Catherine to Thos. A. Harmon 1-3-1866 (1-4-1866)
Hunter, Barbara to Robert Henson 10-19-1851
Hunter, Barbry to Benjamin Ausmus 5-20-1863 (5-22-1863)
Hunter, Cathrine to Madison Dun 5-6-1867 (5-7-1867)
Hunter, Elizabeth to Wm. F. Leach 7-10-1857 (7-16-1857)
Hunter, Eve to Benjamin A. Yaden 3-27-1843 (4-2-1843)
Hunter, Nancy to Thomas Robinson 1-18-1842 (1-23-1842)
Hunter, Polly to Linneius? Billingsley 12-26-1845 (1-4-1846)
Hunter, Rachel to Daniel Hooper 9-25-1850 (9-26-1850)
Hunter, Sarah to William W. Lynch 8-17-1847 (exe, no date)
Hunter, Sinda to James Edwards 8-27-1856
Hunter, Sinda to Sterling W. Lynch 12-12-1854
Hunter, Souson to Caloway Graves 9-6-1858
Hunucutt?, Malinda? to Preston C. Goforth 7-23-1845 (7-24-1845)
Hurley, L. J. to John Wilson 10-7-1853 (10-9-1853)
Hurley?, Vina to William Legeor? 8-27-1842 (8-28-1842)
Hurst, Angeline to Wm. Nave 12-12-1854 (12-12-1855?)
Hurst, Catharine B. to John A. Kelley 12-27-1866
Hurst, Cerena to George W. Wilson 1-26-1850 (1-27-1850)
Hurst, Elisa to Granville? A. Cheek 11-20-1839 (11-21-1839)
Hurst, Elisabeth? to Nelson Evans 11-7-1845 (11-9-1845)
Hurst, Eliza to Harper Rice 12-30-1848 (12-31-1848)
Hurst, Eliza to James C. Harrell 3-17-1859 (3-23-1859)
Hurst, Emly to Harrell Rosenbalm 3-29-1859
Hurst, Emly to Thos. Henderson 4-11-1854
Hurst, Faney B. to E. D. Willis 4-13-1868
Hurst, Fanny to James H. Cimen 3-29-1854 (3-24?-1854)
Hurst, Hester to Archa T. York 10-18-1859
Hurst, Lerinda? to John Robinson 12-17-1847 (12-23-1847)
Hurst, Louisa to Jno. McNew? 4-11-1840
Hurst, Lucindy to John Graves 5-23-1840
Hurst, Mahala to Robert Harrell 1-5-1850 (1-6-1850)
Hurst, Mahala to William Hodges 3-27-1868
Hurst, Malasha to John Evans 7-15-1849
Hurst, Manday to Richard Harrell 8-25-1859
Hurst, Mariah to John M. Baker 12-5-1855
Hurst, Martha to Daniel Vance 9-25-1856 (10-2-1856)
Hurst, Martha to Zachariah Whicker? 7-18-1849 (7-11?-1849)
Hurst, Mary A. to James Nice 1-21-1857 (1-27-1857)
Hurst, Mary to Anderson Shelton 11-12-1859
Hurst, Mary to Bartlett Willis 3-20-1855
Hurst, Matilda to James A. Persifall 9-19-1853
Hurst, Nancy to Clinton Y. Rice 7-25-1854 (7-26-1854)
Hurst, Nancy to David B. Capps 3-17-1842
Hurst, Nuvena to Lemuel Waters 7-26-1858 (7-27-1858)
Hurst, Polly to Walter? Hatfield? 4-10-1845
Hurst, Rebecca to Neil Breeding 4-23-1850 (4-28-1850)
Hurst, Sarah A. to George Smith 5-12-1852
Hurst, Sarah E. to John H. Shelton 10-14-1867 (10-17-1867)

Hurst, Sarah E. to Wiley Garlin 6-2-1859
Hurst, Sarah to Isaac Stuart 6-24-1849
Hurst, Sarah to Jacob Garrison 1-20-1851 (1-23-1851)
Hurst, Sementha to Claiborne McBee 2-25-1840
Hurst, Syntha to John Ritter 7-24-1839
Hurst, V. to W. Willis 6-18-1852 (6-24-1852)
Hurst, Virginia to John M. Brent 1-14-1856 (no return)
Hurst, Winney to Gideon Brocks 8-19-1841
Hutcherson, Ann M. to Mathew Young 7-3-1854 (7-4-1854)
Hyden, Susan E. to Joseph Marsee 1-1-1868
Hyden, Susan E. to Joseph S. Marsee 1-1-1868
Hyslep, Sarah to Allen Parrett 12-6-1854 (12-10-1854)
Hysyes?, B. A. to P. Dunsmore 4-2-1850 (3?-3-1850)
Idle, Nancy to John Biggs 5-23-1859
Ingram, Josephin to James Collins 4-5-1858
Ingram, L. to A. Collins 10-14-1857
Inklebarger, A. to R. Killion 9-17-1856
Inklebarger, N. A. to Robert Killion 9-17-1856
Inklebarger, N. A. to Robert Killion 9-17-1856 (9-21-1856)
Isaacks, Elizabeth to Jesse Fortner 1-29-1839
Isral, Nancy to Evean Chance 12-3-1859
Jackson, America to Smith Overbey 10-27-1857
Jackson, Geminia to Dawson Lamb 7-15-1850
Jackson, Jane to James Parten 2-21-1844 (2-22-1844)
Jackson, Mary Ann to William Gibert? 3-26-1842
Jackson, Matilda to George Barton 7-25-1848
Jackson, Ruth to Jas. Butcher 5-19-1838
Jackson, Ruthy to Joseph Butcher 5-19-1838
Jackson, Sarah Ann to Henry Goin 9-8-1868 (9-10-1868) B
James, Eliza to Lisay? Hurst 4-12-1843
James, Pheba to Elisha Clark 10-29-1846 (11-1-1846)
Janeway, Nancy to Larkin? D. Sharp 6-19-1847 (6-20-1847)
Jenkins, Elmeda A. to Brazeal Burch 4-7-1851
Jennings, Catharine to Wesley Porrott? 9-7-1844 (9-8-1844)
Jennings, Eliza A. to William M. Clevelan 4-17-1850
Jennings, Louisa to Bartley Willis 6-6-1857
Jennings, Lucinda to Robert Yoakum 6-19-1856 (6-20-1856)
Jennings, M. E. to George T. Wells 9-1-1853
Jennings, Malinda to Nathaniel Dunn 4-26-1845 (4-27-1845)
Jennings, Manervy to Philip Bully 1-22-1845
Jennings, Margaret to Granville Hodges 7-31-1857
Jennings, Nancy to Lewis Jones 6-28-1851 (7-17-1851)
Jinkins, Mary to Thomas Sprowls 2-12-1868 (2-14-1868)
Jinnings, Lucy to Wm. C. Inkelbary 8-9-1858
Johnson, Cinthy M. to James D. Burchett 9-6-1845 (9-11-1845)
Johnson, E. to Ellis Owens 1-28-1854 (1-29-1854)
Johnson, Elizabeth to Elias Owens 7-28-1854
Johnson, Elizabeth to J. B. Millis 12-22-1844
Johnson, Elizabeth to W. M. W. Anderson 10-12-1850 (10-13-1850)
Johnson, Ellender to John S. Jennings 5-21-1867
Johnson, Louisa to John C. Jones 9-13-1854 (9-14-1854)
Johnson, Lucinda to John Mays 10-30-1843 (11-7-1843)
Johnson, Margaret to Thos. W. Breeding 2-13-1852 (2-15-1852)
Johnson, Martha J. to Thomas Goin 2-9-1859
Johnson, Martha to Lafayett Good 10-7-1867 (10-8-1867)
Johnson, Mary to John D. Keck 5-30-1868 (5-31-1868)
Johnson, Nancy to Calvin Dowel 7-15-1847 (7-15-1847)
Johnson, Nancy to Dowel Collins 8-4-1856 (8-28-1856)
Johnson, Nancy to Richmon Cavit 8-21-1856 (8-24-1856)
Johnson, Orleany to William F. Toney? 5-5-1849
Johnson, Rachael to Preston Fostnez? 8-16-1841
Johnson, Sarah E. to Newton Keck 3-16-1868 (3-25-1868)
Johnson, Sarah to Thos. Brooks 3-12-1856
Johnston, Sally to Levi Brewer 3-6-1838
Johnston, Sarah to W. W. Greer 11-10-1854 (11-12-1854)
Joihnstan, Lurana to Matthew Bussel 5-24-1838
Jones, Achsah J. to James Debusk 12-15-1856
Jones, Ackey? to Edmon Davis 4-15-1845
Jones, Barthene to Jacob Pike 10-29-1846 (11-1-1846)
Jones, D. L. to M. A. Cook 11-23-1846
Jones, Darcas to Carter Thomas 9-21-1866 (10-7-1866) B
Jones, Elisabeth to William Standafer 3-5-1847
Jones, Eliza to James Mayes 11-3-1865
Jones, Elizabeth to Ambrose Sawyers 5-27-1848 (5-30-1848)
Jones, Hester A. to Wm. S. Culvyhouse 8-18-1855
Jones, Jane to Josiah Wyatt 5-28-1849 (5-31-1849)
Jones, Linda Ann to William T. Epperson 9-30-1854
Jones, Louisa E. to Wm. Capps 9-4-1859
Jones, Louisa to Jesse B. Rowlett 2-20-1856
Jones, Louiza to Matthew Richie 3-30-1867 (4-7-1867) B
Jones, Maiah to Calvin Short 6-21-1854 (6-26-1854)
Jones, Malinda to N. Hopkins 8-28-1846
Jones, Margaret to Stephen Chance 2-13-1856
Jones, Mariah to Elisha Estice 10-17-1843 (10-18-1843)
Jones, Martha J. to John Roark 3-6-1854 (3-10-1854)
Jones, Mary J. to James H. Hughs 12-29-1863
Jones, Mary M. to Alexander Cornelson 12-2-1853 (12-3-1853)

Jones, Mary to John Jennings 3-23-1855 (3-25-1855)
Jones, Mary to Overton Mopin 9-20-1853 (10-?-1853)
Jones, Matilda E. to H. M. Sharp 3-15-1850 (3-19-1850)
Jones, Milla to John Sumpter 5-8-1855
Jones, Nancy W. to Chastin? S. Moore 11-27-1841
Jones, Nancy to Arthor? Hopkins 5-9-1844 (5-11-1844)
Jones, Nancy to Jacob Humfleet 1-27-1851
Jones, Nancy to Richard Powel 1-12-1847
Jones, Orlena to Thomas Simmons 1-28-1851
Jones, Sarah E. to John Elison 4-3-1854 (4-7-1854)
Jones, Sarah Jane to James Goforth 9-15-1842
Jones, Sarah to John H. Martin 1-3?-1859
Jones, Sidney Ann to Charles Bussle? 11-16-1843 (11-17-1843)
Jones, V. E. to J. Miller 8-1-1853
Jones, V. E. to Jurean Miller 7-1-1853
Jones?, Eliza to Nathaniel Presnell 2-10-1842 (2-11-1842)
Jones?, Jane to Coventan Collensworth 1-30-1839 (1-31-1839)
Jourden, Mary to Sterling Hammock 10-26-1843
Kawin, Kisicror? to Daniel Theirs 9-23-1847 (9-24-1847)
Keck, Jane to John Goin 6-30-1863
Keck, Mary J. to Francis Cox 12-6-1854
Keck, Mary to John Houston 2-12-1866 (2-15-1866)
Keck, Mary to Sturling Gowin 10-2-1839
Keck, Mary to William Whiteted 8-14-1848 (8-16-1848)
Keck, Monerva to C. J. Hopper 9-4-1865 (9-5-1865)
Keith, Sarah to Samuel Lane 12-27-1849
Kellams, Minerva to Nutan Sampson 10-18-1855
Kelley, Amada to Ensley Posey 7-30-1868 B
Kelley, Maria to Wm. G. Fulp 11-20-1851
Kelley, N. to L. R. Carr 6-19-1852 (12-16-1852)
Kelley, Sarah A. to James K. Greer 6-6-1868 (6-7-1868)
Kellons?, N. I. to Thos. B. Taff? 10-4-1845 (10-5-1845)
Kelly, Margaret M. to Shermon W. Ousley 12-19-1856
Kelly, Rachael to Robert Vandeventer 6-19-1859
Kerby, Nancy to Royal Jennings 4-6-1866 (4-8-1866)
Kerby, Perlina to John Bunnels 1-29-1866
Kesterson, Caroline to James C. Hunt 12-29-1852 (12-30-1852)
Kesterson, Eliza to McKenna Dulin 4-17-1850
Kesterson, Elizabeth to John Lynch 8-8-1850
Kesterson, Elizabeth to John Michel 11-20-1855 (11-22-1855)
Kesterson, Jane to Barnet? Campbell 3-26-1840
Kesterson, Martha Jane to Melburn Overton 1-29-1868 (1-30-1868)
Kesterson, N. to Joseph Buise 6-16-1853
Kesterson, Polly to Moses Smith 3-24-1849 (3-26-1849)
Kestrson, Lucinda to Francis M. Hatfield 9-23-1854 (9-27-1854)
Kid, Harrett to John Berry 12-27-1837 (12-29-1837)
Kilbert, Emily to William M. Carr 1-20-1855 (1-25-1855)
Killian, Mandy to Nelson Rutledge 3-14-1857
Killin, Lucy to James H. Sands 12-12-1867
Killion, Ann to Abel Lanham 2-15-1846
Killion, Mildred to Wilson Goins 1-15-1857
Kincaid, Darcus to Walter R. Buchanan 7-23-1855 (7-27-1855)
Kincaid, Manervia J. to John M. Vanbebber 4-12-1843 (4-?-1843)
Kincaid, Mary to Jerry Kincaid 3-8-1866 (3-16-1866) B
Kincaid, N. to J. F. Cain 10-26-1853 (11-3-1853)
Kincaid, Permila? to Wm. Wilson 12-3-1839
King, E. to Isaac Lewis 2-24-1858
King, Elixna? to William C. Willis 1-20-1842 (1-21-1842)
King, Lucy to George W. Miller 5-9-1840
King, M. J. to Robert Ruha? 3-24-1846 (4-1-1846)
King, Mary Ann to Wm. Bowman 10-2-1846 (10-7-1846)
King, Nancy to John Houston 12-23-1846 (12-27-1846)
King, Sarah A. to Joel Payne 11-5-1853
King, Susannah to Mathias C. Roach 7-25-1855 (7-29-1855)
Kinser, A. E. to D. F. Payne 6-29-1865
Kirk, Milly to John Thomas 10-22-1846 (10-24-1846)
Kirk, Sarah Ann to Joseph Thomas 5-7-1846 (5-?-1846)
Kirkpatrick, Ann to Thomas McDermott 4-19-1865
Kitinger, Dasha to F. B. Phillips 5-12-1856 (5-18-1856)
Knight, Claricey? to Drury D. Gibson 1-28-1847
Knuckles?, Ann to B. F. Young 6-3-1843
Koiner?, Ollie to Elisha Nun 2-9-1861 (2-11-1861)
Kulley?, Mary J. to William Dotson 12-19-1848 (12-25-1848)
Lambdge, Elisebeth to Joshua Rossan? 1-17-1844 (1-18-1844)
Laffoon, Sally to Mark Jones 1-7-1847
Laffoon, Sarah to James L. Harper 7-1-1853
Laffoon, Sarah to James L. Harper 8-1-1853 (8-2-1853)
Lajasce?, Eliza to James K. Rogers 6-17-1842
Lake, E. to J. Williams 2-3-1852
Lake, Mary to Benjamin F. Gowin 11-28-1853
Lakins, Mary E. to James H. Sims 1-3-1868
Lakins, Matilda to Thomas Harvy 7-26-1856
Lambert, Elisabeth? to G. W. Hamelton 12-3-1845
Lambert, Lydia Ann to William England 10-11-1843 (10-14-1843)
Lambert, Mary M. to John Simmons 3-3-1851 (3-5-1851)
Lambert, Mollie to Seabord Bussell 4-7-1867 (4-28-1867)
Lambert, Nancy to Patrick Lenard 11-22-1867 (11-28-1867)

Lambert, Polly to Stephen Southern 8-13-1839
Lambert, Sousan to Jeramiah Ellison 11-23-1859
Lamone?, Cleressey? to Eli D. Cane 7-31-1846
Lane, E. [Elizabeth] to Wm. B. Hansard 4-30-1853 (5-1-1853)
Lane, Emily Ann to Isaac? Yoakum 6-26-1848 (7-1-1858)
Lane, Lidaey? to William Strevels? 1-3-1846 (1-3-1845?)
Lane, Margaret to G. W. Lane 9-1-1865
Lane, Margaret to G. W. Sane 9-1-1865 (9-3-1865)
Lane, Matilda to G. W. Smith 1-7-1839 (1-13-1839)
Lane, Mollie to Jac Turner 12-30-1865 (12-31-1865)
Lane, Roda V. to Thos. C. White 2-5-1851
Lane, Syntha Ann to Henry P. Moyers 2-8-1868 (2-9-1868)
Lane, Thurisa Ann to Timothy Eastrage 11-4-1856 (11-6-1856)
Lane?, Nancy to William Strevle 5-11-1842 (5-15-1842)
Lanham, Elisabeth to William Willis 1-14-1851 (1-15-1851)
Lanham, Elizabeth J. to Benjamin F. Campbell 11-20-1866
Lanham, Ivey Ann to John Flecher? 12-21-1846 (12-24-1846)
Lanham, Lucy Ann to James D. Green 12-2-1843 (12-3-1843)
Lanham, Lurina to John Jones 8-4-1854
Lanham, Mary Jane to William Green 8-14-1838 (8-16-1838)
Lanham, Matilda to John Killion 5-29-1846
Lanham, Mildred to Boyer Bullard 1-25-1848 (1-?-1848)
Lanham, Orleany to E. D. Willis 1-18-1845
Lanham, Samiramiss? to Andrew Killion 2-15-1846
Lankford, Emaline to John Nelson 4-14-1856
Large, Deby to William Price 9-11-1845
Large, Mary Ann to William H. Carman 10-20-1858
Large, Pheby to John Thomas 2-15-1846
Large, Sally to John Hicks 8-3-1846
Lassey, Rachael to Alexander Carter 11-16-1841 (11-21-1841)
Latan?, Margarett to Lewis? Rhea? 11-14-1842 (11-22-1842)
Late?, Venila to John Marlow 5-16-1842 (5-25-1842)
Lathan?, Emaley? to Aquillah? Farmer 6-29-1846
Laws, Franky to Jesse Wilson 2-23-1857
Lawsan?, Malissa to Wiley Barnard 6-19-1847
Lawson, E. to Thos. Mays 2-21-1846
Lawson, Elizabeth to Wm. A. Pace 10-20-1854 (11-6-1854)
Lawson, H. (Hanah) to Samuel Harris 7-12-1853 (7-13-1853)
Lawson, Mary Ann to George Parks 11-25-1858
Lawson, Nancy to Leander Taylor 3-25-1868 (3-26-1868)
Lawson, Rhoda to William Mills 12-19-1839
Lawson, Sarah to James Mills 12-21-1839
Lawson, Sarah to Thos. Lawson 1-27-1846 (1-30-1846)
Lay, Deliza to Preston Townzeen 3-31-1855
Lay, Elizabeth to Cleveland McCrary 11-?-1849 (12-16-1849)
Lay, Elizabeth to Silas Helton 12-22-1865 (12-24-1865)
Lay, Sarah to Enas Allin 1-23-1850 (1-24-1850)
Lea, Mandy to Michael Sowder 9-28-1843
Lea, Peggy to Larkin Webb 2-26-1839 (2-28-1839)
Lea, Sally to Elijah Jones? 2-9-1844
Leach, July A. to Daniel Bomon 6-10-1865 (6-22-1865)
Leach, July A. to Daniel Bowman 6-10-1865
Leach, Martha to Anderson Bowman 1-16-1855 (1-21-1855)
Leach, Minerva H. to Wm. T. White 12-2-1854 (no return)
Leake, ____ to John Barnett 3-30-1865 (3-31-1865)
Leath, Martha J. to Thos. Hall 7-30-1856
Leavis?, Selina to John M. Smith 3-29-1851 (4-4-1851)
Lee, Calvina to Lewis Lucker? 12-17-1849
Lee, Delila to Samuel Wiat 5-1-1851 (5-6-1851)
Lee, Dicy to Iredale Webb 5-19-1840
Lee, Eliza to Andrew C. Jones 9-14-1847
Lee, Emaley to Johnson Davis 2-9-1847
Lee, Jane to James Owens 9-1-1853 (no return)
Lee, Lidda Green to James Burket 5-18-1850
Lee, Louisa to A. Vanbebber 2-25-1848
Lee, Martha Jane to James Jackson 12-5-1853 (12-6-1853)
Lee, Orlena to Ralph Burket 5-2-1850
Lee, Rebecka to Gabril Lee 9-23-1858
Lee, Sarah to Samuel Reed 12-7-1846
Leforce, Milia J. to Daniel Marlar 8-23-1867 (8-12-1867)
Leford, Matilda to James Grimes 9-29-1841 (9-30-1841)
Legeer?, Polly to Wm. Wheelus 4-1-1839 (4-11-1839)
Lemon, Nancy to Daniel D. _____ ?-??-1848
Lemara, Mary to William K. Sharp 9-15-1849 (9-20-1849)
Lenard, Cathrine to Ewing Bales 8-21-1853 (9-8-1853)
Lenard?, Elisabeth? to James Canner? 1-27-1849 (1-28-1849)
Leonard, Margaret to Parks Lock 1-19-1855
Letterrell, J. to Jacob Redmon 12-26-1866 (12-27-1866)
Lewis, Bethena to Prior McBee 9-18-1851
Lewis, Catherine E. to Benjamin F. Davis 8-24-1853 (8-25-1853)
Lewis, Eliza A. to John Gregery 8-24-1859
Lewis, Louisa to Jacob Walker 11-26-1846
Lewis, Lucinda to Heston Davis 12-2-1845 (12-4-1845)
Lewis, Lucresa to Willson Morgan 7-15-1853 (7-16-1853)
Lewis, M. A. to C. Goin 1-20-1862 (1-24-1862)
Lewis, M. to Joseph Waymires 9-28-1858
Lewis, Martha to R. S. Seals 10-6-1855 (10-7-1855)

Lewis, Mary Ann to Drury Lawson? 1-19-1846 (1-20-1846)
Lewis, Nancy I. to Samuel McBee 11-6-1849
Lewis, Orlena to David W. Carr? 11-4-1857
Lewis, Pasefy Timey? to Carey Myers 1-29-1849 (2-1-1849)
Lewis, Phebe E. to Isaac W. Arnwine 12-14-1867 (12-19-1867)
Lewis, Rebecca to Bowyer Beeler 2-2-1850 (2-21-1850)
Lewis, Sarah to Oliver Campbell 2-9-1854
Lickliter, Rebecca to William Guthry 5-18-1839 (5-19-1839)
Liford, Livisa? to James Waller 12-5-1843 (12-10-1843)
Liford, Mary to William Daniel 1-11-1847 (1-12-1847)
Liford, Sophia to Elemuel H. Ares 9-18-1851 (9-20-1851)
Like, M. to Nathaniel Marr 3-7-1853
Lin?, Sidney to Richd. Sowder 2-17-1840 (5-17-1840)
Linch, Mary to William M. Rite 6-5-1849 (6-6-1849)
Linsa, Margaret to Alexander Chadwell 2-24-1855 (2-25-1855)
Linsey, Margaret to Enos Day 3-1-1858
Litrell, Abagil to D. M. Burchett 3-5-1858
Litrell, Abigale to D. N. Burchett 3-5-1858
Litterall, Rachel to James Willson 7-21-1859
Litterele, Sarah to Lewis Lingar 12-4-1867 (1-12-1867?)
Little, Susanah to Charles Blankinship 7-21-1838 (7-22-1838)
Littral, Sarah E. to John W. Grammer? 7-22-1847 (7-25-1847)
Lock, Levina to James M. Prideman? 10-30-1847 (10-31-1847)
Lock, Rachel E. to John Ball 5-11-1843 (5-14-1843)
Locke, Kissash to Heram Hoskins 1-3-1838 (1-4-1838)
Locke, Martha J. to Briant Baker 2-9-1838 (2-14-1838)
Locke, Nancy to Vardamon Minton 8-25-1838
Lockmillor?, M. J. to S. Bales 5-16-1846 (5-17-1846)
Lockoral?, Rebecker? to Lewis Garland? 9-16-1844
Lockwood, Julia A. to Peter Fips 4-29-1846 (4-30-1846)
Lolson?, Rebecca to Bales Shomate 3-4-1850 (3-7-1850)
Longworth, Matilda to John H. Brooks 1-11-1848
Longworth, Sarah to John Brock? 12-22-1849 (12-23-1849)
Lorton, Mary E. to N. H. Moore 8-13-1857
Lorton, Sarah to Perry Monsy 3-3-1856 (3-4-1856)
Loson, Rachel to Andrew Hatfield 9-2-1850 (9-5-1850)
Louden, Frances Jane to Isreal Cole 10-17-1848
Lovel, Elizabeth to Charles Flemming 3-31-1855 (4-7-1855)
Lunday, Elizabeth to Even Carmack 12-8-1858
Lynch, B. to Wm. Graves 5-26-1858
Lynch, Barberry to John S. Cain 2-8-1850 (2-12-1850)
Lynch, Dicy M. to Martin J. Edwards 12-4-1867 (12-5-1867)
Lynch, Lucinda to Elijah Braden 2-5-1850 (2-10-1850)
Lynch, Manervy to McKindry Elleron 9-15-1849 (10-2-1849)
Lynch, Margret Elviny? to Jonathan Sharp 1-5-1846 (1-8-1846)
Lynch, Mary to William Hurst 5-24-1856 (5-25-1856)
Lynch, Nancy to A. Russel 12-12-1855 (12-16-1855)
Lynch, Nancy to David Lynch 12-28-1843
Lynch, Nancy to Green B. W. Ford 6-15-1839 (6-?-1839)
Lynch, Phebe to Jas. Dosset 2-11?-1840
Lynch, Respy to Jno. Braden 12-11-1838
Lynch, Sarah to Hiram A. Rivett 10-15-1856
Lynch, Sarah to Ransam Cupp 7-8-1839 (7-14-1839)
Lyncy, Evaline to John Minton 5-15-1850
Lyncy, Sarah to Wiley Hubbard 12-6-1854 (12-2-1854)
Lyons, Minervy to Jeremiah Ellerson 9-17-1856
Maddy, Mahala to Madison Hollensworth 9-12-1838 (9-18-1838)
Maden, Anjaline to Hemelton Sanders 7-30-1850 (8-1-1850)
Maden, Nancy to Eleane? Reed 1-25-1847 (1-26-1847)
Maden, Nella to George Hurst 10-4-1856
Madux, R. to James B. Gibbs 4-26-1859
Magard, Elender to Wiley Carmack 12-2-1856
Magard, Martha to Job B. Crabtree 6-18-1867 (6-20-1867)
Mahane?, Susan to James Harlis 6-15-1847 (6-17-1847)
Maiden, Malinda to James Howerton 5-31-1855 (6-3-1855)
Main, Martha A. to George M. Thomas 4-1-1868 (4-9-1868)
Malacott, Nancy Jane to Seth Atkins 3-21-1859
Malicoat, Mary to John Bratcher 10-16-1852
Mallicoat, Emaline to Asa Rosan? 3-23-1849 (3-25-1849)
Maloney, Elizabeth to Wm. Erls 5-23-1866
Maniak, ----- to Stephen Hopkins 11-15-1839
Mannan, Minta to Thomas Pillian 10-18-1851 (11-6-1851)
Mannon?, Nancy to Henry Claxton 2-21-1843
Manon, Mary Jane to David Hill 5-26-1855
Mapels, Olley to William R. Barns 8-1-1866 (8-13-1866)
Maples, Betsy to David Ray 2-9-1839
Maples, Susan M. to Hiram D. Massengale 11-19-1857
Maples, Susan to J. W. Black 7-14-1855
Maples, Susan to Wm. King 8-5-1852
Marcu, Nancy to Matthias? Hinshilder? 11-23-1843 (6-10-1844)
Marcum, Abigail to Davis Tolbert 4-25-1868 (5-7-1868)
Marcum, Eliza to Nicholas S. Pugh 10-25-1856 (11-26-1856)
Marcum, Elizabeth Jane to James H. Osborn? 12-31-1844 (1-1-1845)
Marcum, Lack G. to Henry Ayers 11-20-1848 (11-24-1848)
Marcum, Mary A. H. to Abner C. Hansard 10-11-1842
Marcum, Merica to Wm. Bailey 12-30-1858
Marcum, Roday? H. to Wm. G. Payne 7-23-1845

Marcum, Selina to Solomon D. Hobbs 2-5-1851 (2-7-1851)
Marcus, M. C. to A. J. Housholder 9-24-1844 (9-24-1844)
Marcy, M. to Ledford Parrot 3-7-1853 (3-10-1853)
Margraes, Mary to Arthur Speer? 4-13-1842 (4-14-1842)
Margraves, L. J. to J. M. Cass 2-24-1853
Margraves, Margaret to Joseph Neal 11-?-1849 (11-29-1849)
Marion, Fannie to Ezekiel Rainey 7-11-1868 (7-26-1868)
Marlar, Catharine to William H. Taylor 1-21-1867 (1-25-1867)
Marler, Mary to Major Brewer 1-22-1845 (1-26-1845)
Marsh, Elizabeth to Samuel Kibert 1-28-1867 (1-31-1867)
Martain, Lucinda to Martain Fugate 11-25-1856 (11-27-1856)
Martain, Viney to Allen Burnet 5-9-1840
Martin, Manilia to James Cassel 12-28-1867 (12-29-1867)
Martin, Marian J. E. to John M. Sawyers 4-3-1849
Martin, Martha Ann to William Parkey 2-15-1846
Masan, Caroline to Ellerlley? Neil 4-18-1847 (4-1?-1847)
Masan, Delpha to William Wilborne 7-29-1846
Masengale, Elisabeth to William P. Campbell 1-5-1856 (1-6-1856)
Masingil?, K. to John Roarks 3-2-1846 (3-5-1846)
Mason, C. J. to S. W. Stone 6-19-1865
Mason, Elizabeth to John Evans 2-5-1852
Mason, Elizabeth to Wm. C. Sharp 9-27-1851 (10-2-1851)
Mason, Elvisy? to Nathan Lawson 6-8-1844 (6-9-1844)
Mason, Lucy A. to Harvey Ritchie 6-11-1867 (6-20-1867)
Mason, Lucy to Christian Cox 9-18-1854 (9-19-1854)
Mason, M. J. to R. F. Overton 6-9-1865 (6-11-1865)
Mason, Martha Jane to R. F. Overton 6-9-1865 (6-11-1865)
Mason, Mary Ann to Jno. D. Mathes 3-26-1839
Mason, Mary to William E. Cline 3-28-1854 (3-30-1854)
Mason, Nancy to Sterling? J. Barnard 1-25-1845 (1-27-1845)
Mason, Nevesta to Leander Miller 7-10-1854 (7-11-1854)
Mason, Sarah to Wm. White 12-15-1841 (12-26-1841)
Massa, Susan to John Lamdon 7-29-1854 (8-2-1854)
Massengale, E. to D. Cosby 10-4-1852 (10-12-1852)
Massingale, Sarah to John Cosby 7-4-1859
Mathis, E. L. to James F. Redmond 7-24-1858
Mathis, Emaline to Jas. Barnard 3-30-1858
Maticks, Julia A. to Fidelio Rossan 3-10-1857
Mattocks, M. to L. H. Wilcoks 11-10-1857 (11-15-1857)
Mattocks, Margarett to L. H. Wilcocks 11-10-1857 (11-15-1857)
Mattox, Nancy to Jonathan C. _____ 11-18-1841 (11-19-1841)
Maurae, Levisa to Hiram Furry 8-17-1842
Mayabb, Emaline to John M. Shaw 3-7-1854
Mayer, Olive to Thomas Sutton 11-2-1859
Mayers, Nancy W. to Eligah Forgerson 5-25-1858 (5-31-1858)
Mayers, Presellar to Alexander Perce 9-19-1857
Mayes, Elizabeth to Benjamin Parker 8-29-1865 (8-31-1865)
Mayes, Lucinda to G. G. Seals 10-15-1856 (11-19-1856)
Mayes, Nancy to Daniel Morris 6-23-1865
Mayes?, Ann to David Williams 7-8-1848 (7-13-1848)
Mays, Jemima? to Nathan Collins 3-7-1843
Mays, Martha Jane to George B. Needham 9-3-1842 (9-11-1842)
Mays, Susanah to Alexander England 2-22-1847 (3-4-1847)
Mays?, Nancy to James Burk 10-22-1842
McAnalla?, Manila to John L. Sensabagh? 6-7-1847 (6-9-1847)
McAnnaly?, S. to Jos. Hazs 2-15-1845
McBee, Elizabeth A. to Alferd Hopper 3-22-1853 (3-24-1853)
McBee, Emeline to Calvin McBee 11-27-1846 (1-10-1847)
McBee, L. J. to William W. Jones 1-13-1853
McBee, Mohaley to John Killion 5-10-1865
McBee, Polly A. to James Blancit 7-16-1859
McBee, Sallie to James H. Snider 1-31-1867 (1-31-1867)
McBee, Susan to Sanford Ciseroe Lynch 1-25-1868 (1-27-1868)
McClary, Mary E. to Rufus N. Lay 2-24-1852 (2-29-1852)
McClary, Sidna to Wm. Martin 1-25-1853 (1-6-1853)
McClellan, Martha to William Lynch 12-4-1850
McClellan, Marthena to W. F. Parks 12-20-1851 (12-28-1851)
McClelland, S. to Elias Blansett 9-30-1853 (10-2-1853)
McCollum, Margaret to Adam Olinger 8-24-1857
McConkuy?, Mary to A. I. Mulhohs 7-27-1844 (8-1-1844)
McCrary, Jane to Anneas Ely 5-27-1843 (5-28-1843)
McCrary, Louisa to James Venable 7-23-1846
McCrary, Sarah Ann to C. M. Day 4-22-1856
McCulla, Jane to John Ristan 2-1-1856 (2-4-1856)
McDaniels, J. to A. Lee 8-12-1852 (8-13-1852)
McFarlin, Margaret to James McCarty 1-20-1842 (1-21-1842)
McGee, Luckrisha? to C. Baker 11-24-1845 (11-27-1845)
McGee, Mary to James Carter 9-2-1865 (10-?-1865)
McGeorge, A. to Wm. Taillor 2-26-1858
McGeorge, Agness to Wm. Tailor 2-26-1858
McHenry, Frances J. to Thomas J. Wheeler 9-20-1839 (10-8-1839)
McHenry, Mary to Joseph White 6-28-1847 (7-1-1847)
McKeehan, A. E. to James F. Wallin 1-7-1856
McKehan, Nancy to F. Perkins 1-17-1839 (1-9?-1839)
McKehan?, Nancy to Felix Pirkins 1-17-1839
McMahan, Margaret to Gustavis Carral 8-1-1865
McMahan, Permealy? to John Moor 6-26-1846

McMahon, Margret to Alexander Ellis 1-31-1857
McMillion?, Lidia? to William Burket? 2-1-1847
McNealance, Candus to Bazebel Burch 10-11-1851 (10-17-1851)
McNeelence?, Fanny to William Cannon 8-9-1848
McNeil, Ann to Martain Barlet? 1-7-1843 (1-8-1843)
McNeil, Jane to Wm. Venable 2-1-1846
McNeil, Malenda to James F. Edwards 2-10-1842
McNeil, Margret to Thomas Gibson 1-5-1859
McNeil, Matilda J. to J. F. McNeel 11-3-1865 (11-9-1865)
McNew, Catharine to Albert Williamson 5-19-1854 (5-21-1854)
McNew, Martha Jane to Robt. B. Lane? 2-20-1840 (2-27-1840)
McNew, Sarah to Alfred Evans 6-23-1847 (6-22?-1847)
McNiel, Mary to Christian Plank 3-8-1852 (3-11-1852)
McNielin?, Margaret to Lee? White 6-16-1842
McVay, Elizabeth A. to Caleb Goin 1-28-1864
McVay, Elizabeth A. to James K. Goin 12-6-1865 (12-7-1865)
McVay, Mary to Hugh Hanes 7-28-1854
McVay, Milley to Richard Harper 4-7-1848
McVay, Minervy J. to Henry H. Friar 1-19-1867 (1-20-1867)
McVay, Nancy to Ira Scalf 1-27-1854 (2-2-1854)
McVay, Polley to George M. Qualls 2-14-1854
McVay, R. to Henry Plank 4-7-1853
McVey?, Thirsa to James Hunter 10-10-1849 (10-12-1849)
McWilliams, S. to R. E. Crockett 8-31-1852 (9-4-1852)
Mcbee, Sally to Harvy Powell 5-3-1838 (5-6-1838)
Mealer, Susan to Thomas J. Davis 3-18-1868 (3-19-1868)
Meeler, Surrena to Charles Bussell 10-9-1838
Meyers, Rachel M. to Wm. B. McDaniel 10-5-1866 (10-11-1866)
Meyers, Sarah to John B. Nelson 3-24-1858
Meyers, Suphronia C. to Prior L. McBee 12-14-1867 (12-15-1867)
Michel, Malissa to James Barnard 1-21-1851 (1-3?-1851)
Middleton, Nancy to B. F. Cloud 5-10-1850 (5-14-1850)
Miller, Angelina to Henry Hepsher 2-7-1851 (2-27-1851)
Miller, B. to J. S. Wilson 9-6-1852
Miller, Emaley to Milton Hurst 1-20-1847 (1-21-1847)
Miller, L. B. to Marshall L. Kincaid 9-30-1857
Miller, M. J. to J. L. Collins 3-31-1857
Miller, M. J. to J. L. Collons 3-21-1857 (3-23-1857)
Miller, Margaret E. to Zack S. Gibson 11-2-1851
Miller, Martha to James M. Miller 1-30-1868 (2-3-1868)
Miller, Minerva to George R. Johnson 10-5-1856
Miller, Polly to Sampson Taylor 7-27-1839
Miller, S. J. to Benj. Dunn 10-11-1852
Miller, S. to L. Hurst 3-24-1846 (3-36-1846)
Miller, Thursey to Sturling C. Kincaid 3-17-1858
Mills, Elizabeth to James McKenny 8-31-1850 (8-12-1852)
Mills, Frankey I.? to William Baker 9-26-1849
Mink, Sarah to King Eldrige 11-21-1848
Minton, Catharine to E. W. Hatfield 7-13-1865 (7-12-1865)
Minton, Elizabeth to James F. Griffin 7-11-1868 (7-15-1868)
Minton, Elizabeth to James McAfee? 8-29-1845 (8-30-1845)
Minton, Jemima to Jove Baley 3-16-1867 (3-17-1867)
Minton, Mary to Jobe Baley 1-28-1857
Minton, Mary to Joseph Lay 12-20-1865 12-21-1865
Minton?, Catharine to William Beaty 12-26-1842
Mise, Elander to Joseph Collins 10-12-1854 (10-14-1854)
Mise, Narcissa to William Mise 12-18-1854 (12-21-1854)
Mitchel, Manila to James McAnelly 1-22-1842 (1-26-1842)
Mitchel, Mary Ann to Wm. H. Wallie 9-19-1844 (9-22-1844)
Mitchell, Eliza to Thomas Jones 11-6-1867
Mize, Dithula to Alexander Wilson 1-3-1867 (1-4-1867) B
Mize, Julian to Nathan Cotton 9-2-11867 B
Mize, Margaret to Houston Yearey 12-24-1866 (1-25-1866) B
Mize, Mary to Calvin Mize 11-15-1856 (11-25-1856)
Mize, T. A. to B. T. Bell 12-14-1852 (12-19-1852)
Monday, Hariet E. to Andrew J. Lynch 5-16-1851 (5-18-1851)
Monday, Nancy E. to George Frior 2-3-1851 (2-5-1851)
Monday, Rachel M. to James Fletcher 7-25-1868
Montgomery, Rebecca to Samuel Lamar? 7-5-1842
Montgumary?, Mary to Landax? C. Minter? 4-4-1842 (4-5-1842)
Moody, Margret K. to James T. Ford 1-10-1848 (1-13-1848)
Moody, Rebecca R. to John Corman 4-24-1851
Moody, Wineford M. J. to D. T. Cline 10-12-1857
Moor, Eliza Jane to Owen Willson 7-9-1846
Moor, Hetty to Thos. Lawson 8-7-1846
Moor, Lucy to William Rogers 1-5-1839
Moor, Lucy to Wm. Rogers 1-5-1839 (1-6-1839)
Moor, M. A. to D. B. Sweet 12-31-1852
Moor, Mary to Constantin? Smith 2-6-1847 (2-11-1847)
Moor, Nancy A. to Reubin Norris 9-1-1845
Moore, Caroline to Granville McBee 9-13-1847 (9-16-1847)
Moore, Catherine to Geo. J. Upton 10-1-1851 (10-3-1851)
Moore, D. M. to Wm. Ousley 5-7-1852
Moore, Elisabeth J. to Green B. Cadle 5-9-1848
Moore, Franky to Solomon Fulps 7-31-1852 (8-2-1852)
Moore, Jane to Moses Willis 1-17-1852 (1-18-1852)
Moore, Louiza C. to William H. Lovel 7-4-1868 (7-5-1868)

Moore, Lutissia to Thomas Gilbert 2-21-1865
Moore, M. L. to John M. Jones 10-28-1858
Moore, Martha to James P. jr. Brooks 8-5-1858
Moore, Mary to Jno. Jennings 7-23-1838
Moore, Mary to William E. Dean 3-7-1843
Moppin, Thursa M. to John M. Michel 3-11-1857
Morgan, Sallie to William Hatfield 5-16-1868
Morison, M. A. to James Roarkes 5-1-1865 (5-4-1865)
Morris, Delila to J. M. Lowe 9-9-1844
Morris, Julia to Abner Fields 1-31-1846
Morris, Mary to Edward Poor 4-5-1856 (4-10-1856)
Morris, S. to H. Stewarts 11-30-1852
Morrison, Nervesta to Joseph Clark 3-16-1867 (3-17-1867)
Moser?, Mahaley? to Eli Shelton 4-3-1847 (4-4-1847)
Moses, Susan A. to John F. Berry 2-14-1850
Moshy?, Sarah to Jas. Woods 5-16-1846 (5-17-1846)
Mosley, Elizabeth to Caleb Overcash 4-16-1867 (4-5?-1867)
Moss, M. A. to Wm. C. Kincaid 7-18-1858
Moss, Mary L. to John C. Moyers 9-21-1867 (9-22-1867)
Moss, Olivia P. to James M. Kincaid 3-3-1856
Moss, Olivia to Joseph White 10-10-1855 (10-11-1855)
Moss, Sophiah W. to William R. Yoakum 3-1-1859
Mountain, Catharine M. to Isaac N. Ford 11-28-1853 (12-1-1854?)
Mountain, Elizabeth R. to Richard B. Forde 9-24-1855
Moyers, H.? to William N. Moyers 5-14-1840
Moyers, Mary to Sebastian Graves 3-17-1851 (3-18-1851)
Moyers, Sarah F. to J. W. Smith 6-12-1865 (6-15-1865
Mullens, Mary E. to Green B. Howerton 2-5-1868 (2-6-1868)
Muncy, Lucy to Robert Sutten 9-30-1838
Munday, Malissa to William Chittum 8-5-1848 (8-8-1848)
Mundy, Mary E. to William Carroll 7-7-1851 (7-17-1851)
Murphey, Almira A. to Wm. H. Deaton 1-18-1868 (1-19-1868)
Murphey, Elizabeth to C. H. Cowan 3-3-1866 (3-6-1866)
Murphey, Emily to Madison Morgan 6-19-1867
Murphey, Malinda to Francis M. Fulta 10-2-1856 (10-3-1856)
Murphey, Malissa to George Chadwell 10-11-1856
Murphey, Malissa to John Fults 11-15-1846
Murphey, Martha J. to Newton A. Cox 1-8-1868 (1-9-1868)
Murphey, Turressy to John Roark 11-10-1857
Murphy, Leeby Ann? to Michel? Powers 1-26-1846 (2-6-1846)
Murry, Anna? to Franklin Redmon 1-7-1846 (1-15-1846)
Mustart, Elizabeth to Leander Snavely 9-9-1865
Myers, Caroline to Ezekial E. England 7-25-1854 (7-27-1854)
Myers, Louiza to Robert Pierce 4-29-1867
Myers, Mary J. to James Lane 12-28-1864 (12-27-1864)
Myes, Mary to Hugh Myes 1-11-1854 (1-12-1854)
Nance, Polly to David Nicely 2-8-1848 (2-17-1848)
Nash, Amanda to John F. Berry 11-23-1846 (11-24-1846)
Nash, Caroline to Daniel Sharp 12-27-1852
Nash, Elizabeth to Jacob Sharp 3-13-1840
Nash, Elizabeth to Thomas B. Walker 9-15-1842
Nash, Manda to Wm. Nash 5-9-1846
Nave, Margaret to Mark Hurst 12-22-1854 (1-12-1855)
Nave, Mary to M. D. Southern 1-29-1856
Neal, Lucy Jane to James H. Rigsbee 7-21-1868 (7-26-1868)
Nealley, Polly to Andrew Messer 8-10-1859
Needham, Martha M. to Isom L. Meyers 2-24-1866 (3-1-1866)
Needham, Monday to Wm. Harden 9-10-1855 (9-27-1855)
Neil, Edney I. to A. S. Russel 1-11-1845 (1-16-1845)
Neil, Eliza to H. C. King 2-18-1852
Neil, Malinda to Wesley Chittam 3-26-1850
Neil, Mary Ann to Alexe Dobkins 3-18-1839 (4-2-1839)
Neil, P. A. to Fidelio Bales 2-15-1853
Neil, Sarah to Robert Hurst 9-29-1842
Nelson, E. to Jas. Cumming 5-24-1858 (5-25-1858)
Nevels, Sarah to James P. Taylor 4-8-1867 (4-14-1867)
Newlee, Ada M. to John W. Divine 4-17-1865 (4-17-1865)
Nicely, Melvina to John Brock 6-1-1839 (6-3-1839)
Niel, M. to Joseph G. Scott 2-3-1853
Niel, Nancy to Jacob G. Owens 11-29-1853
Nisbert?, Jane to James Whitemore 10-15-1864 (10-31-1864)
No?, Susan to Joel Barker 2-14-1845
Noel, Adalade B. to Joseph Carden 5-2-1849
Norman, Lurinn to Emanuel Blanch 2-16-1859
Norris, Agness to Henry McGonigal 5-15-1843 (5-26-1843)
Norvell, L.? to I.? England 1-16-1852
Norvell, Margret R. to William L. Monday 8-22-1850
Norvell, Margret M. to William L. Munday 2-14-1850
Norvell, Rebecca J. to Elijah Hudson 12-19-1843
Nove?, L. T. to Simpson Parks 8-20-1845 (8-21-1845)
Nuckles, Sarah to Harmon Tuder 5-18-1854
Nunn, Bartheny to James S.? Rice 6-20-1842
Nunn, Delpha to William Nunn 8-25-1846 (8-27-1846)
Nunn, Eliza to Hugh Hall 11-14-1857
Nunn, Flurrender to Russel Nunn 11-24-1841 (11-25-1841)
Nunn, Louisa to Nelson Taylor 9-10-1838
Nunn, Lugana to Sylvester Harrell 7-20-1848

Nunn, Margaret to Silvester Nunn 7-28-1852 (7-29-1852)
Nunn, Mary to Phaskil B. Nunn 2-21-1856
Nunn, Vineny to Philip Veatch 3-20-1842 (6-20-1842)
Nunn?, Emaley to Fredrick Fults 7-25-1846
Oaks, Elender? to Wm. H. Sharp 4-18-1845 (4-20-1845)
Oaks, Eliziabeth to Jas. Cox 10-5-1865 (10-27-1865)
Oaks, Mary to Mathew Tucker 1-27-1846 (1-28-1846)
Odel, Elizabeth M. to Henry Ellison 10-10-1851
Odel, Louisa to Lindsa Nelson 3-22-1856 (3-23-1856)
Odell, Antamasa to Spencer? Edwards 10-28-1841
Odle, Mahala to Fannister Sulfrage 5-5-1866 (5-6-1866)
Oliver, Eliza to Elisha Hollan 9-26-1848 (9-27-1848)
Oneil, Polly Ann to Shadrick Moor 4-7-1845 (4-12-1845)
Ousley, Elizabeth to John B. Malone 2-18-1852
Ousley, Martha E. to Isaac M. Jessee 10-19-1867 (10-24-1867)
Ousley, Mary to Marquirus Cook 5-23-1852
Ousley, Nancy to W. W. Greer 2-22-1867 (2-23-1867)
Ousley, Polly A. to William Minton 11-1-1848
Overbay, Martha to Daniel Tapp 6-9-1866 (6-10-1866)
Overholt, Julyann to Joel Johnson 7-27-1859
Overlay?, Sarah A. to Wm. L. Odle 8-28-1854
Overton, Mary E. to John Fugate 2-5-1851 (2-6-1851)
Overton, Matilda to Albert Dougherty 10-4-1847 (10-7-1847)
Owen, Louisa to John J. Moncy? 5-29-1847
Owens, Elisabeth? to Presley Cottral 8-24-1844 (8-25-1844)
Owens, Lilly J. to Wm. McBee 9-29-1849 (10-5-1849)
Owens, Lucinda to Houston McBee 2-28-1848 (3-9-1848)
Owens, M. to G. Massingale 3-3-1852 (3-6-1852)
Owens, Martha to Carroll Gibbs 12-21-1845 (12-23-1845)
Owens, Mary to George Powell 9-12-1843
Owens, Mary to J. W. Baxter 8-20-1865 (8-30-1865)
Owens, Nancy to Wesley Simmons 8-2-1849 (8-3-1849)
Owens, Patia to Elijah Edmonson 8-20-1868 (8-21-1868)
Owin, Ruthy to Wm. Eldridge 1-23-1844 (1-25-1844)
Owsley, Charity to W. B. Pheleps 11-12-1837
Owsley, Mary to Marcus Flemming? 9-1-1843 (10-2-1843)
Pain, Joannes? to Nelson Berry 6-20-1843
Painter, Rachal to Wm. S. Willson 2-23-1857
Pall, Jane to Jessee Hooper 2-15-1838
Parker, Elizabeth to Franklin Pridda 1-20-1854 (1-21-1854)
Parker, Mary to Enas? Day 4-22-1842
Parker, Nancy to Daniel Cupp 12-4-1845 (12-6-1845)
Parker?, Louisa to Charles H. Havely? 8-11-1846
Parkey, Barbary to James Ritchie 7-7-1840
Parkey, Elisabeth S. to Milbern Overton 10-26-1846 (10-28-1846)
Parkey, Mary A. to Robert R. Overton 9-18-1866 (9-2?-1866)
Parkey, Matilda to Henry F. Coleman 2-15-1867
Parkey, Rebecco to Hendly? Fugate 4-18-1843 (4-20-1843)
Parks, Barberry to Elihue Walker 10-4-1856 (10-5-1856)
Parks, Louisa to Samuel Walker 3-13-1848 (3-16-1848)
Parks, Martha J. to James P. Bolton 3-15-1867 (3-21-1867)
Parks, Nevesta to Abraham Collinsworth 2-25-1855 (2-26-1855)
Parm, Elizabeth to Calvin Bull 9-21-1857
Parratt, Judy? to H. A. Johnson 12-18-1846 (12-18-1845?)
Parrott, M. A. to M. Marson 2-12-1855 (2-15-1855)
Parrott, Martha J. to John R. Parrott 2-18-1857 (2-19-1857)
Parrott, Mourning to Henry Beach 11-14-1846 (11-23-1846)
Parrott?, Mar to W. S. Gillenwater 2-21-1846
Parry, Susan to William E. Cline 11-17-1855 (11-18-1855)
Parsen, Mary C. to J. Minton 11-7-1864 (11-8-1864)
Parton, China to Joseph Owens 1-27-1853 (1-30-1853)
Parton, Emelia to Christian Henderson 1-17-1839 (2-9-1839)
Parton, Mary to Samuel Hubbrt? 1-22-1845 (3-22-1845)
Patten, S. J. to John Haynes 10-29-1852
Patterson, Ellen to Wm. Moore 6-5-1852 (6-6-1852)
Patterson, Laura to Alexander Allen 4-18-1868 (4-22-1868)
Patterson, Margaret to John White 9-26-1851 (9-27-1851)
Patterson, Margaret to Timothy Whiteaker 4-15-1867 (4-16-1867)
Patterson, Margret to Wm. H. Ketrom 1-13-1866 (1-18-1866)
Patterson, Mary A. to John T. Roark 7-8-1867 (7-11-1867)
Patterson, Melvina to Randolph Jones 8-26-1867 (9-5-1867) B
Patterson, Tabitha to Henry Dotson 12-12-1865 (12-27-1865) B
Paul?, Susan to Wm. M. Rogers 2-26-1840
Pearson, Catharin to Walter Davis 12-20-1842 (12-22-1842)
Peck, M. to W. Croxdale 9-24-1852
Peck, Mary to John Dobbs 3-9-1852 (no return)
Peck, Nancy to James Chittan 9-13-1848 (9-16-1848)
Peck, Pheba to Samuel Garland 2-20-1862 (2-24-1862)
Peck, Sarah A. to Isral Coles 6-13-1849 (6-14-1849)
Perman, S. M to Stephen Arnold 11-2-1853 (11-3-1853)
Perry, Elizabeth to G. W. Rogers 4-22-1859
Perry, Jane to Richard Scalf 3-1-1852 (3-2-1852)
Perry, Jane to Silas T. Kelton 3-9-1865
Perry, Mary E. to Fidelio White 3-15-1851 (3-18-1851)
Persifield, Malinda to James J. Gibson 3-9-1867 (3-10-1867)
Person, Emaley to Wiley Rowe 1-5-1847 (1-6-1847)
Pew, Nancy Ann to Isaac Hopkins 4-22-1843 (4-30-1843)

Pew, Sarah to Wm. P. Liford 8-23-1851 (8-24-1851)
Phelips, Polly A. to Henry A. Burchfield 4-15-1843 (4-16-1843)
Phelps, Eliza A. to Hamilton Rosenbalm 9-1-1866 (9-2-1866)
Phillips, Mariah to Frankllin Kyle 5-13-1867 B
Pike, Nancy Jane to John Ford 4-29-1867
Pitman, Elizabeth Ann to Patrick Willis 12-13-1845 (12-14-1845)
Pitman, Emaline to George Allen 8-3-1850 (8-7-1850)
Pitman, Mary to Andrew J. Breeding 5-19-1847
Pitman, Nancy to James True? 12-15-1841 (12-17-1841)
Pittman, Louisa to T. L. Hurst 2-11-1852 (2-12-1852)
Poff, Nancy to William? W. Yoakum 9-26-1850 (12-30-1850)
Poindexter, Sarah M. to Nathaniel S. Havlaen? 4-18-1849
Ponder, Nancy to William Baker 1-20-1851
Poor, E. to Isham Moyers 11-7-1859
Poor, L. J. to Robert Hicks 2-15-1858 (3-11-1858)
Poor, Lucy to John Clark 1-13-1868 (1-14-1868)
Poor, Margaret E. to Francis M. Wyatt 7-27-1868
Poor, Mary Jane to James A. Robert 2-19-1856
Poor, Mary to James Carroll 2-7-1855 (2-8-1855)
Poor, Nancy M. to Parrish Dobbs 10-10-1860
Poore, L. J. to R. Hicks 2-15-1858 (3-11-1858)
Poore, Melvina to J. W. Poore 3-13-1858 (3-15-1858)
Poore, Sarah A. to John Sands 12-14-1858 (12-18-1858)
Posey, Bethena to Aaron Ritter 9-13-1853
Posey, Elizabeth to Daniel C. Cline 10-7-1855 (10-30-1855)
Posey, Susanah to Joseph Anderson West 1-6-1848
Posey?, Malinda Jane to Matin? H. West? 5-29-1846 (5-31-1846)
Powell, Elmirah to Elihu Jones 5-2-1840
Powell, Polla? to John Owsley 8-29-1844 (9-22-1844)
Powell, Rosa A. to John E. Laffoon 2-1-1851 (2-2-1851)
Powers, Ann Eliza to Lemuel Ball 1-18-1849
Powers, Magret to Hugh G. White 9-17-1850
Powers, Martha? C. to John Woods 6-26-1845 (6-25?-1845)
Powers, Noomy? to Isaac Eastrage 12-29-1841
Powers, Virginia A. to Jas. Newby 8-3-1852
Preday, Chaniy? to Henry Renolos? 10-13-1844
Presby, Elisabt? to David? Wetherford? 6-8-1846
Preslee?, Martha to Alvis Hunnacutt 7-18-1849 (7-19-1849)
Presley, Berthena? to Thos. Collins 1-29-1847 (1-31-1847)
Presley, Nancy to Geoge Hill 11-22-1855
Presley, Temprance to Josiah Chadwich? 1-13-1847 (1-14-1847)
Presly, Lidda to Alexander Harrell 5-20-1846 (5-21-1846)
Presly, Polly to William Romines 10-12-1839 (10-13-1839)
Pressley, Elizabeth to Abraham Balis 11-28-1849 (11-29-1849)
Prestley, Rebecca to Binson? Sweet 11-27-1848
Price, Phebe to John Carmon 10-3-1849 (10-4-1849)
Pridda, Elen to Jacob Davis 5-7-1850
Priddy, M. J. to John Hood 7-27-1852
Priddy, Sarah to Andrew J. Davis 3-12-1852 (3-14?-1852)
Pridemoore?, Rachel to Wm. H. Litrell 12-19-1842 (12-25-1842)
Pridemore, Charlotta to Samuel Pearmon 9-1-1868 (9-3-1868)
Pridemore, Jane to James Lee 11-10-1866 (6-16-1867)
Pridemore, Mary to James Grimes 10-31-1844 (11-3-1844)
Pridemore, Millay to Noah Eastrage? 12-30-1845 (1-4-1846)
Pridemore, Sarah to John Sutton 12-4-1844 (12-16-1844)
Prisley?, Jane to John Hicks 8-3-1844 (8-5-1844)
Proff, Susan to John Parker 1-8-1852
Proffet, Malinda to David Brooks 5-10-1854 (1?-11-1854)
Proffett, Telitha to Abraham Wright 8-8-1863 (8-10-1863)
Proffit, Cathrine to David Leach 11-30-1850
Proffit, Elizabeth to Benjamin Ausmus 8-24-1857
Province, Hannah to Hiram C. Wereman? 2-1-1844 (2-22-1844)
Province, Mary to James Gibson 9-23-1847
Pruett, Lucinda to Daniel B. Bales 6-22-1867 (6-27-1867)
Putchard?, Polly to Nelson Gowin 10-8-1839 (10-10-1839)
Qualls, Julia to Daniel Spillars 4-18-1850
Qualls, Martha E. to Miles J. Scalf 7-10-1854 (no return)
Qualls, Meala E. to Samwell P. Ellis 6-10-1854
Qualls?, E.J. to James Spillers? 7-8-1847
Quarles, Martha to Pleasant England 7-12-1855
Quarles, Olly to David Willis 11-10-1859
Raby, Mary to James Turnbull 12-4-1845
Radner, S. to H. C. Simons 11-10-1864
Ragan, Nancy to Elijah Gregory 8-1-1848 (8-18-1848)
Ragan?, Nancy to Zephaniah Dunn 7-28-1848 (8-6-1848)
Raider, Sarah to Joel Johnson 1-2-1854 (no return)
Ramsey, Elizabeth to Morgan J. Woodson 9-28-1849
Ramsey, Luritta to William Welch 4-16-1839 (8-18-1839)
Ramsey, Mary to Martin Wilkerson 3-16-1868 (3-18-1868)
Ramsey, Polly to John Baker 9-15-1850
Raney, Fanny to John Goin 10-27-1859
Ray, Louisa to Wyley Laycock 8-1-1838 (8-12-1838)
Ray?, Elisabeth? Ann to Benjamin Burchett 12-26-1845 (12-30-1845)
Read, Marcynann to Elihugh Baker 3-10-1838 (4-7-1838)
Readman, Sarah to John Owens 2-10-1855 (2-13-1855)
Reason, Jane to Silas Hopper 12-13-1865 (12-14-1865)
Rector, Anna to Jesse Eads 1-23-1851 (1-24-1851)

Rector, Elizabeth to William Cox 12-4-1839
Rector, Mary A. V. to Saml. O. Mink 11-8-1865 (11-20-1866?)
Rector, Susannah to Jesse Rector 9-2-1839 (9-3-1839)
Redmon, Catharine to A. M. Cadle 12-31-1867
Redmon, Jane to Johnson Burk 2-10-1855 (9-8-1855)
Redrick, Elizabeth to Watesel Hargraves 5-20-1868 (5-22-1868)
Reece, Mary E. to Montgumry Harrell 11-28-1859
Reed, Frances to Ewing Gibson 9-2-1856
Reed, S.? to Thomas Earls 5-3-1858
Reed, Sary to John Minton 7-11-1843
Rennels, Nancy to David Chadwell 3-26-1850 (3-28-1850)
Renolos, Margret to John Chany? 7-20-1845
Renols, Elizabeth to Hugh H. Graves 12-14-1850 (12-31-1850)
Reyers, Elizabeth to Jason Russell 6-15-1858
Rhea, Mary to Stephen Allen 4-5-1838
Rhey, Milly? to Wm. Shanon? 12-7-1844 (12-8-1844)
Rice, Alyra? to Isaac Walker 3-8-1848 (3-9-1848)
Rice, Cintha A. to Thos. N. Lay 3-28-1856
Rice, Lucinda to Elisha Kirby 11-2-849 (11-3-1849)
Rice, Nancy Ann to D. I. Gilbert 1-15-1845 (1-17-1845)
Richardson, Elizabeth to H. Condry 1-10-1852
Richardson, Mary A. to Calvin Cunningham 8-19-1859
Richardson, S. J. to J. C. Large 11-28-1851 (11-24-1851)
Richardson, Sarah J. to Solomon? Wesley 11-28-1849
Richerson, M. to David Mayse 10-6-1855
Richie, Lucinda to Ephriam Davis 12-14-1866 (12-16-1866) B
Riggs, Matilda A. to Solomon L. Woodward 4-26-1851 (5-1-1851)
Right, Elizabeth to Isaac Bolinger 1-13-1842 (1-22-1842)
Riley, C. to M. Overton 1-27-1846 (1-28-1846)
Riley, L. M. to Alvis P. Coleman 10-18-1853
Riley, Nancy to Columbus Ely 5-22-1865 (5-25-1865)
Rite, Martha C. to Jacob Wilson 6-17-1868 (6-28-1868)
Ritter, Catharine to Andrew Williams 6-20-1846 (6-21-1846)
Ritter, Charlotta to Isham Myres? 4-21-1846 (4-22-1846)
Ritter, Elizabeth M. to Harrod Hopson 12-23-1847
Ritter, Elmira to Aaron Hurst 1-27-1840
Ritter, J. to Wm. Y. Hopson 3-2-1853 (3-3-1853)
Ritter, Orlina? to Hugh Cane? 12-24-1839
Ritter, Polly to Elnathan Cloud 1-30-1847 (1-?-1847)
Ritter, Sary? Ann to Joel Taylor 1-15-1847
Ritter, Susannah to Anderson Drummonds 3-13-1848 (3-19-1848)
Ritter?, Hanner? to Richard Hopson 7-15-1845
Rittere, Amanda to John Overholser 1-25-1859
Roark, Elizabeth to Wm. Dearnal 8-20-1838 (8-21-1838)
Roark, Louisa to Calvin Massengle 1-27-1849
Roarks?, Sintha to William Williams 7-2-1845 (7-3-1845)
Roberts, Celia to Thomas Gibson 7-21-1856 (7-22-1856)
Roberts, Elisabeth J. to James R. Simmons 4-7-1856 (4-8-1856)
Roberts, Harriet to Z. Friar 8-21-1859
Roberts, Martha C. to Andrew T. Cash 2-28-1865 (3-1-1865)
Roberts, Martha to John W. Hall 9-23-1847
Roberts, Mary L. to George W. Campbell 1-14-1868 (12?-16-1868)
Roberts, Susan to Elijah Smith 2-17-1854 (11-5-1854)
Robertson, Caroline to Isaac R. Lynch 1-1-1867 (1-3-1867)
Robertson, Lizzie to Joseph B. Niel 7-24-1856
Robertson, Mary J. to Alexander Jones 6-8-1867 (6-20-1867)
Robinson, Cornelia to George F. Chadwell 9-12-1867
Robinson, Eliza to William J. Canter 2-28-1842
Robinson, Labitha to Wm. Lamare 2-24-1838 (2-27-1838)
Robinson, Louisa to William P. Collens 2-22-1854
Robinson, Rebecca to Austin Honeycut 5-14-1839
Roddy, Mary C. to John E. Day 12-23-1855
Roden, M. to Emanuel Collins 3-31-1853 (4-3-1853)
Roger, Mary H. to Squire Marcum 10-1-1867 (10-3-1867)
Rogers, Amy to James L. Mayers 12-7-1867 (12-12-1867)
Rogers, Caroline M. to Wm. J. McNew 4-26-1845 (5-1-1845)
Rogers, Dicey? M. to C. F.? Rice 1-28-1847
Rogers, Emily b. to Henry Nash 12-6-1848 (12-14-1848)
Rogers, Harriett L. to John F. McNew 12-28-1867 (12-29-1867)
Rogers, Martha L. to Nelson C. Bowman 12-23-1847
Rogers, Mary A. to David C. Maupin 8-20-1867 (8-22-1867)
Rogers, Mary Emily (Polly) to Thos. Ausmus 3-4-1853
Rogers, Mary to John Upton 7-7-1851 (7-9-1851)
Rogers, Sarah A. to Albert G. Williamson 8-25-1866
Rogers, Selia C. to Asa M. Ellison 3-19-1867 (3-20-1867)
Rogers?, E. to Jacob Wolfenbargor 8-27-1845 (8-28-1845)
Rogers?, Rebecca to Wm. Robinson 9-10-1839 (9-17-1839)
Roland, Elizabeth to Jonathan Prideman 12-30-1852 (1-1-1853)
Roland, Louisa to Wm. F. Collinsworth 11-2-1850
Roland, Mary to Albert Simmons 12-30-1852
Roland, Mary to Washington Greer 12-29-1855 (1-1-1856)
Roland, Ruth to Jefferson Jackson 8-7-1856 (8-10-1856)
Rolin, Elizabeth to William Norvell 7-30-1850 (8-4-1850)
Rolin, Rachal to Samuel Arnel 11-24-1846 (11-25-1846)
Rollins, Mary to Levi Carmack 9-15-1847 (9-20-1847)
Root, Olive to John Alexander 3-5-1842 (3-10-1842)
Rosan, Eliza A. to Werley Harrison 3-5-1856 (3-9-1856)

Rosan, S. to D. Goins 1-10-1852 (1-1?-1852)
Rosanbalm, Elizabeth to James A. Williams 7-13-1867 (7-18-1867)
Rose, C. to E. L. Scott 5-2-1853 (5-3-1853)
Rose, Cornelia to Robert Neal 12-18-1854
Rose, Deborah to George W. Thomas 3-1-1856
Rose, Emily to John M. Grimes 9-11-1847
Rose, Lucinda to James P. Cadle 6-25-1853 (6-26-1853)
Rose, Mary E. to Jeremiah Penington 8-3-1867 (8-4-1867) B
Rosebalm, Eliza to David R. Hopson 5-17-1851 (6-1-1851)
Rosenbalm, Mary K. to John A. West 2-2-1857 (2-5-1857)
Rosenbalm, Rinda to James Bullen 10-8-1853
Roson, Jane to Stephen Craft 12-28-1867
Rossan?, Mary to Thomas C. Killion 6-11-1842 (6-12-1842)
Rossin, Phebe Jane to Wm. R. Dykes 10-1-1851 (10-5-1851)
Roward, Polly Ann to James J. Lambert 10-11-1843 (10-14-1843)
Rowe, Elizabeth to Thos. Epison 1-31-1840 (2-6-1840)
Rowland, Ruthy S. to John Lankford 1-25-1844 (1-26-1844)
Rowlet, Lucy A. to Farwick Collinsworth 3-10-1851 (3-11-1851)
Rowlett, Virginia to Henry Brown 9-28-1853
Rowlette, M. S. E. to B. Brooks 9-28-1839
Rows, Jane to Alvis Brogan 4-27-1853 (4-30-1853)
Rowson, E. A. to V. Harrison 12-7-1857
Rowwlet, Masora to James Eldrige 2-5-1853
Runion, Lucy J. to George B. Owens 11-20-1854
Runions, Emly to John Fultze 3-5-1865
Runions, Mary M. to David F. Carr 11-5-1866 (11-25-1866)
Runnalds, Winney to Pleasant Miller 1-14-1840 (1-23-1840)
Runnions, Martha J. to Thos. Friar 2-3-1848 (2-4-1848)
Runolds?, Ann to David Miller? 11-13-1841 (11-28-1841)
Russel, Rachael to Alvis Whitted 1-24-1852 (1-30-1852)
Russel, S. to J. M. Lewis 11-27-1852 (11-28-1852)
Russell, Elizabeth to Williamson Laycock 11-13-1839 (12-13-1839)
Russell, Nancy to Isaac Grabill 10-25-1848 (10-26-1848)
Russell, Serena? to Wm. Provance 2-20-1846 (2-22-1846)
Ruth, Sarah to Wiley Bartlet no date (Dec 1859?)
Rutledge, Nancy to Wilbourne Hooper 5-2-1850
Ryan, M. J. to John M. Shaw 11-15-1853
Saler, Malinda to Edward Upton 7-22-1859
Salyers, Cathrine to Wm. .D. Lynch 2-4-1856 (2-14-1856)
Salyers, Elizabeth to Joseph Sephis 3-24-1859 (no executed)
Salyers, Rachel to William P. Dean 1-15-1850
Sanders, Angelina to James Rosan 12-4-1848 (12-10-1848)
Sanders, Lavina to Samuel W. Pleming 12-19-1839
Sanders, Lurinda to Thomas Wallis 10-6-1848 (10-8-1848)
Sanders, Luritta to Reuben Cardwell 10-29-1844 (10-31-1844)
Sanders, Mary Jane to William W. Corbin 10-9-1855 (10-10-1855)
Sanders, Melvina to George C. Corrbin 9-3-1859
Sanders, Minda to William E. Pearson 4-18-1867
Sanders, Rawsy? to Royal Lebow 10-23-1839 (12-15-1839)
Sauls, C. to M. B. Cadle 4-17-1859
Sawyers, Mary J. to John J. Carrol 7-17-1848 (7-19-1848)
Scalf, Christiana to John Woods 7-24-1851
Scalf, Mailda to Jacob Shilby 8-14-1851
Scalf, Tebitha to Cornelus Trent 1-6-1854
Scelf?, Matilda to Zackariah Trent 2-12-1850
Schrichfield, Orlena to David Young 2-4-1856 (2-5-1856)
Scivofield?, Clarkis to William Welch 3-29-1843
Scofield?, M. A. to A. F. Cromwell? 11-19-1844 (11-21-1844)
Scott, Anny to Samuel Woodson 9-15-1866 B
Scott, Catharine R. to Tilmon A. Hamilton 10-20-1866 (10-28-1866)
Scott, Dosha to Mastin Gipson 12-23-1846 (12-24-1846)
Scott, Isabella F. to Wm. J. L. C. Miller 12-11-1863 (12-29-1863)
Scrichfield, Barthena to G. W. Pridemore 10-9-1854 (10-10-1854)
Scrichfield, Susan to A. Ham Cupp 8-2-1854
Scritchfield, B. to George W. Pridemoore 7-4-1853
Scritchfield, Elizabeth to Henry Cole 10-13-1851 (10-17-1851)
Scritchfield, Sarah to Stephen Lea 3-12-1851 (3-13-1851)
Seal, Elizabeth to Moab? Hammon 5-5-1842 (7-10-1842)
Seals, Annice to James Shelly 10-23-1847 (11-4-1847)
Seals, Josephen to Henry Hopper 7-3-1868 (7-4-1868)
Seals, Mahala to John H. Carr 4-24-1850 (4-26-1850)
Seals, Manervy to William Wilbern 1-24-1843 (1-29-1843)
Seals, Patcy to John Purkeyfile? 1-10-1846
Seals, Peggy to David Huddleston 10-16-1839 (10-17-1839)
Seebolt?, Martha to William Sulfridge 3-30-1850
Self, Catherine to Miles Scalf 9-14-1854
Semmonds, Lavina to John Forgerson 9-12-1839
Sensabaugh, Manila to James Montgomery 4-11-1858
Serber, Rachel to Andrew J. Green 4-15-1857
Sevord, Mary A. to John McBee 1-18-1853 (1-19-1853)
Sewell, Ann Jane to John H. Kelley 7-11-1849
Sewell, Julia to D. A. Jennings 10-20-1865 B
Sewell, M. V. to J. L. Evans 6-16-1852 (6-17-1852)
Sexton, Mary to Thomas Rite 9-8-1849 (9-15-1849)
Sharp, C. J. to Wm. Mason 12-11-1851
Sharp, Catherin L. to James L. Russel 12-20-1845 (12-25-1845)
Sharp, E. C. to Wm. A. Wilson 9-22-1851

Sharp, Eliza to James H. Lyngar? 9-6-1856 (9-7-1856)
Sharp, Elizabeth Ann to William L. Smith 2-19-1856
Sharp, Emaline to John Burnett 1-8-1856 (1-10-1856)
Sharp, L. G. to G. B. Consley 6-30-1865
Sharp, Leta to Asa Brogan 2-4-1850 (2-7-1850)
Sharp, Louisa to John Robinson 9-21-1839 (9-22-1839)
Sharp, Mary to Joel Turner 11-14-1845 (11-19-1845)
Sharp, Mary to Nathaniel D. Cain 2-25-1843
Sharp, Nancy to Wm. B. Dunn 11-30-1844 (12-4-1844)
Sharp, Neely to John Cox 12-21-1846 (12-22-1846)
Sharp, Neely to Squire C. Hurst 2-24-1840 (2-27-1840)
Sharp, Permelia? to Haisel? Hill 8-16-1847 (8-26-1847)
Sharp, Polly Ann to James Caymard? 12-9-1846
Sharp, Ruthy J. to Wm. H. Cawood 9-18-1858
Sharp, Sarah C. to Benj. F. Carr 11-28-1863 (12-6-1863)
Sharp, Sarah to Jesse Green Palmer 1-14-1843 (1-?-1843)
Sharp, Sarah to John Malone 2-1-1844 (2-8-1844)
Sharp, Sela to Lewis C. Grimes 12-4-1854 (12-5-1854)
Sharp, Winna R. to M. C. Goin 9-3-1855
Sheare, Cathrine to Reuben Bremmer 10-17-1853 (10-19-1853)
Sheckels?, Nancy to John Shelby 10-23-1844 (10-27-1844)
Shelby, Malissa J. to Anderson Fergerson 2-1-1868 (2-2-1868)
Shelby, Sarah to Jesse Lay 9-6-1845 (7-3-1846)
Shelby, Susannah to John Green 1-17-1844 (1-18-1844)
Shelton, Elizabeth to Green Berry Hayes 10-19-1867 (10-20-1867)
Shelton, Letia to Jas. Carpenter 6-6-1852 (6-8-1852)
Shelton, Teney? to Fielding Hodges 1-1-1848 (1-5-1848)
Shelvy, M. to John W. Deane 8-18-1859
Sherac?, Mary Ann to John Strevels 10-19-1849 (10-21-1849)
Shipmon, Nancy to Hezekiah Jones 12-5-1866
Shoemaker, Elisabeth to John Bellema 1-20-1851 (1-21-1851)
Shoemaker, Mary to Leftrage Clark 3-12-1844
Shoemate, Elizabeth to William Sawyers 11-24-1854
Shoemate, Leta S. to William F. Retherford 4-7-1859
Shoemate, Lucy to Wm. B. Hodges 7-15-1856
Shoemate, Menervy J. to Mathew C. McDonal 12-9-1846 (12-17-1846)
Shofner, Cathrine to A. Keck 1-17-1855 (12-18-1855)
Shofner, Mary to Fredrick Keck 12-21-1854 (12-28-1854)
Shofner, Sally to Josiah Crawford 7-21-1849 (7-22-1849)
Shofney?, Elisabeth to Ambris? Sharp 12-15-1847 (12-16-1847)
Shofny?, Margret to John Nelson 5-26-1846
Shoftner, Sally to Noah Lamb 7-30-1855 (8-1-1855)
Shomate?, Nancy L. to Robert S. Bains? 9-6-1845 (9-7-1845)
Short, Harriet D. to Samuel M. Carson 8-15-1853
Short, Martha to Henry Grimes 9-13-1852 (9-14-1852)
Short, Martha to John Brown 3-15-1867 (3-17-1867)
Shransbule, Sarah A. to Wiley F. Garland 3-12-1855 (3-13-1855)
Shultz?, Elisabeth? M. to B. F. Cloud 12-29-1845
Shumate, Ann to Samuel Litrell 12-30-1838 (12-31-1838)
Shumate, Eliza to George M. Billingly 8-9-1842
Sierben, Margaret to John Eastrage 10-16-1856
Siler, Mary to Alvin King 7-19-1853 (7-22-1853)
Simmerman, Elizabeth to Henderson Jones 3-21-1853
Simmons, Arah J. to Wm. M. Duncan 8-1-1867 (8-4-1867)
Simmons, Catharine to Dulany P. Harmon 5-2-1867 (5-3-1867)
Simmons, Elizabeth to James H. Burnett 4-25-1868 (4-26-1868)
Simmons, Manda to Joseph Wallen 12-2-1858
Simmons, Nancy to Daniel Tyar 9-20-1865
Simmons, Nancy to Jas. P. Sands 12-2-1856
Simmons, Phebywathy Altemere to Abraham Meyers 3-11-1853 (3-13-1853)
Simmons, Rebecca A. to John Marcum 1-13-1852
Simmons, Winny to Hamelton McAnelly 2-5-1842 (2-6-1842)
Simons, Mary H. to H. W. Fulth 12-5-1864 (12-6-1864)
Simons, Nancy A. to J. M. Harmon 7-18-1865 (7-20-1865)
Simpson, Mary E. to M. P. Morseless 5-10-1865
Simpson, Mary to Lewis Tass 1-12-1865 (12-12-1865)
Sims, Elizabeth to Josiah Ramsey 2-23-1845 (3-2-1845)
Singleton, Mary A. to Anderson Barnard 7-9-1847 (7-10-1847)
Singletree, Charlottee to C. J. Dalton 11-14-1856
Skaggs, Susan to Spencer Ousley 10-17-1849 (10-21-1849)
Slatten?, Polly to William Carroll 2-8-1839 (2-21-1839)
Slaven?, Ony? to Larkan Vandevarter? 4-5-1842 (4-7-1842)
Slone, Martha to Robert McGinis 12-11-1854 (12-14-1854)
Slotton, Ally to William Meotor? 8-24-1842 (10-25-1842)
Smith, Anna to William King 9-8-1856 (9-8-1856)
Smith, Catharin to John C. Colson 11-20-1843 (12-25-1843)
Smith, Cintha to Jesse Collins 8-17-1838 (8-18-1838)
Smith, Eleana? to Thomas Warrin? 12-9-1844 (12-12-1844)
Smith, Eliza A. to Hamilton Collins 1-29-1868
Smith, Elizabeth to Elbert Jinkins 1-15-1868
Smith, Emaline to Creed Rowland 12-17-1842 (12-22-1842)
Smith, Emiline to John Beason 8-15-1866 (8-16-1866)
Smith, Fanny to Owin Edwards 9-13-1843 (12-11-1843)
Smith, Lety to John Hacker 9-22-1849 (10-5-1849)
Smith, Louiza to Andrew Cantwell 5-24-1867 (5-26-1867)
Smith, Manervy to John Vanderpool 3-18-1843
Smith, Manirvy? to Hugh Nighbert 1-29-1839 (1-30-1839)
Smith, Margaret to Washington Rowe 1-9-1840 (1-10-1840)
Smith, Margret J. to John W. Davis 3-16-1868 (3-28-1868)
Smith, Martha A. to Joseph Moody 1-10-1856 (1-24-1856)
Smith, Mary A. to Collin? Bailey? 11-1-1842 (11-2-1842)
Smith, Mary to Hiram Messer 8-28-1848 (8-29-1848)
Smith, Mary to Robert Smith 2-13-1867 (2-15-1867)
Smith, Nim? to C. Korly 11-10-1864
Smith, Polly to Abadiah Collins 12-20-1839
Smith, Polly to Michail T. Brown 7-21-1858 (7-25-1858)
Smith, Polly to Russell Miller? 3-10-1840
Smith, Rachael to Wm. Rutherford 10-9-1841 (10-10-1841)
Smith, Rebecca to Richard Stephens 8-25-1852
Smith, Sarah J. to Isaac Johnson 8-8-1852
Smith, Sarah to Cany Moyers 7-15-1846
Smith, Sarah to Joab Cook 8-30-1855
Smith, Tennessee R. to William H. Townsley 4-15-1868 (4-16-1868)
Smith, Timpa? to Joshua Adams 10-3-1843 (11-2-1843)
Smith, W. to William Dowell 10-22-1853
Smith, ____ to William B. Ford 12-16-1847 (12-19-1847)
Smithe, S. to William Pearson 5-12-1858
Snaveley, Sarah A. to John S. Cress 9-8-1867
Snavely, Rachel to John Lunday 12-20-1843 (12-21-1843)
Snavely, Sophia to Adam Groseclose? 4-6-1840 (4-8-1840)
Snitchfield, Sarah J. to Volentine Moyers 10-19-1852
Snow, Nancy to Samuel Thomas 2-9-1847 (2-11-1847)
Snuffer, Charity to Roblins? Jones 5-18-1844 (5-20-1844)
Snuffer, Elizabeth to James Vanbebber 12-30-1839 (2-14-1841?)
Soard, Minerva to Jas. C. England 9-20-1865 (9-21-1865)
Soullivan, Amelia to J. D. Moritz 6-8-1866 (6-9-1866)
Sourd, Rebecca to John Runnolds 11-26-1867
Southern, Loucy to George Forber 11-15-1839
Southern, Margaret to George Epps 11-20-1855 (11-22-1855)
Southern, Mary to Ambrous Johnson 12-1-1841 (12-2-1841)
Southern, Mary to Andrew J. Johnson 8-1-1867
Southern, Matilda to Charles Goin 3-12-1868 B
Southern, Mary to Wayman Lambert 2-12-1839 (2-19-1839)
Southern, Sarah to Timothy Whitaker 11-30-1841 (12-1-1841)
Southers, Elizabeth to Noel Seals 4-25-1866 (5-10-1866)
Sowder, A. to Wm. Thomas 5-8-1858?
Sowder, Amanda to Sasival? Jones 9-25-1852 (9-26-1852)
Sowder, Cathrine to Henry Sharp 12-22-1849 (1-1-1850)
Sowder, Elisabeth to Russel Davis 2-18-1856 (2-22-1856)
Sowder, Elizabeth to Benager Harpe 4-18-1848 (4-19-1848)
Sowder, Elizabeth to John L. Lane 10-4-1838 (10-14-1838)
Sowder, Mary Jane to Joseph Sharp 11-7-1851 (11-11-1851)
Sowders, Anah to Madison Keck 2-3-1866 (2-8-1866)
Soweler, Mary J. to Wm. Goin 11-6-1865
Spark, Pheba to David Janes 10-23-1855
Sparks, Phoebe to Joseph Edwards 3-13-1848 (3-14-1848)
Speak, R. M. to James Painter 9-19-1853 (9-22-1853)
Spiers, Elejiceia to John Brink? 6-7-1845
Sprinkles, Margret Ann to George Cadle 6-5-1859
Spurlock, Nancy to Robert Garrett 9-18-1850
Standerfe?, Hannah to Jno. J. Baker 6-11-1840
Standsford, Elizabeth to Joseph Hatfield 1-1-1868
Staneford, Lucind to Hubberd Moore 2-21-1865
Stanerford, Martha to Eldridge Hurst 8-1-1867 (8-9-1867)
Stansbery, Rachel to Isaac Bainman 1-31-1859
Stansbery, Sarah to Saml. J. Greenlee 11-13-1865 (11-27-1865)
Stansbury, Cathrine to Daniel King 10-6-1857
Stansbury, Margaret to Thomas B. Hopson 2-12-1856 (2-14-1856)
Stansbury, Polly to John Howerton 9-24-1856 (9-25-1856)
Stephens, Matilda to Isaac Eastridge 4-23-1867 (5-19-1867)
Stillwell, Emeline to Jackson Hester 10-25-1866 (10-25-1866)
Stine, Emely J. to Hiram A. Kivett 12-14-1867 (12-29-1867)
Stinner, Nancy J. to Jacob Willson 5-5-1865
Stone, Amanda to Wiley Dunsmore 10-18-1859
Stone, Emaly? to John Simmons 1-1-1849 (1-22-1849)
Stone, Fanny B. to Isaac M. Hurst 6-7-1855
Stone, Manervey to Drewrey Laffoon 12-19-1850
Stone, Margret N. to John L. Saunders 11-20-1865 (11-22-1865)
Stone, Nancy J. to John A. Snider 12-26-1863 (12-31-1863)
Stone, Perlina to Riley H. Lynch 10-30-1856
Stone, S. to H. Hurst 3-6-1846 (3-8-1846)
Stowers, Sarah to Andrew Hubbard 7-14-1843 (7-18-1843)
Strevels, Mary A. to James Maples 9-28-1850
Strevels?, Polly to Nicalis? Monor? 4-13-1847 (4-15-1847)
Strifle?, Jane to William Sexton 4-20-1839 (3-?-1838?)
Stuart, Nancy to James Joice 11-21-1855 (11-22-1855)
Stubblefield, Alemida? to Samuel McBee 7-21-1849
Stublefield, Mahaly I.? to James Laughmiller 1-30-1848 (2-10-1848)
Subar, Mary to Moses B. Mullins 3-3-1865 (4-6-1865)
Sulfrage, Mary to George F. Rider 1-14-1867
Sullivan, Minerva to Thos. Lankford 6-26-1856 (6-29-1856)
Sullivan, Nancy to William Cox 10-21-1867 (10-23-1867)
Sullivan, Polly to William Itson 8-7-1850 (8-8-1850)
Sumpter, Manirva to Isaac Wallar 12-2-1844

Sumpter, Polley? to Kindruk? Holt 2-15-1845 (2-20-1845)
Sumpton, Elizabeth to Thomas Baker no date (summer 1859?)
Sumptre, Ann to Thomas J. Baker 8-7-1858
Surber, Tempe A. to James D. Crawford 12-22-1854 (12-24-1854)
Susong, Ceseer? to Samuel L. Minton 9-13-1850 (10-3-1850)
Susong, Jane to R. Vanbebber 1-19-1858 (1-20-1858)
Susong, Margaret J. to Robert Vanbebber 1-19-1858 (1-20-1858)
Susong, Margha to John Chance 2-22-1853 (2-24-1853)
Susong, Mary to J. M. Wheelar 11-8-1856 (11-9-1856)
Suthern, Nervesty M. to Isaac M. Johnson 2-26-1859
Sutton, Abigail to John Marcum 11-9-1850
Sutton, Barbery to Wm. Gibbs 8-10-1844 (8-12-1844)
Sutton, Miscelany to Enos Seal 3-11-1867 (3-19-1867)
Sutton, Susan to James W. Yeary 1-25-1848
Sutton?, Nancy to Nelson Cheek 12-12-1847 (12-13-1847)
Sweet, Emiline? to Jno. Grubb 4-10-1845
Sweet, Polly to William Graham 12-4-1847 (12-5-1847)
Sword, B. to A. Harral 10-20-1857
Taker, Emily L. to Elbert Rice? 2-14-1850
Tate, Nancy to James Harp 7-15-1850
Tate, Susan to Joshua Crabtree 2-11-1853 (2-12-1853)
Tate, Susan to Joshway Crabtree 2-11-1854 (2-12-1854)
Taylor, Elizabeth J. to Hiram Crouch 9-7-1857
Taylor, Juicy to William Arber 1-22-1842 (1-23-1842)
Taylor, Nancy to Shelton Stanter 12-21-1863
Teague, Martha to George W. Williams 8-26-1867 (8-29-1867)
Thacker, Cacey? to Thos. Zicks 2-24-1849 (2-25-1849)
Thacker, Nancy to Mathew A. Helton? 11-18-1846 (11-26-1846)
Thacker, S. A. to F. Hendricks 7-19-1853
Thacker, S. A. to Fealix Hendrick 7-19-1853
Thomas, A. to Daniel McKamy 9-25-1865
Thomas, Alendor P. to Jesse Harp 10-31-1856 (11-6-1856)
Thomas, Alpha Ann to Elisha Lake 3-8-1853
Thomas, Catharine to Joseph Wadkins 1-9-1838
Thomas, Eliza to Benjamin Parrott 1-18-1867 (1-28-1867)
Thomas, Elizabeth A. to Samuel P. McKinney 9-25-1865 (9-28-1865)
Thomas, I.? to John Powers 2-9-1847 (2-11-1847)
Thomas, Levina? R. to Alford Marcum? 11-7-1845 (11-9-1845)
Thomas, Martha to Nicholas M. Roberts 9-10-1848 (9-20-1848)
Thomas, Mary to Wm. A. Marcum 3-15-1851 (3-16-1851)
Thomas, Syntha to Samuel Lewis 8-16-1867 (8-22-1867) B
Thomopson, Eliza A. to George W. Lewis 6-24-1848 (6-25-1848)
Thompson, Catharine to Greenberry Ford 1-14-1838
Thompson, Cathrine S. to James Snodgrass 1-7-1856 (1-8-1856)
Thompson, E. A. to James Simmons 10-8-1845 (10-9-1845)
Thompson, Frances C. to Cyrus A. Snow 11-22-1867 (11-23-1867)
Thompson, L. J. to F. J. Jessee 9-22-1857
Thompson, Luhany to William Cox 12-31-1839 (1-1-1840)
Thompson, Margarett to Andrew Leicey 8-3-1867 (8-4-1867) B
Thompson, Margret to Robert Stone 9-9-1859
Thompson, Martha L. to Obediah Cardwell 3-8-1842
Thompson, Nancy A. to Thos. M. Carter 8-19-1855 (8-21-1855)
Thompson, Sarah Ann to Nathan H. Moore 7-25-1844
Toin, E. to M. Keck 1-30-1846 (1-31-1846)
Toliver, Tabitha? L. to Esaw Sharp 3-1-1842 (3-6-1842)
Tomlinson, Watstill to T. A. H. Ousley 5-7-1852 (5-9-1852)
Toney, Eliza to Christopher Deans 6-12-1847 (6-16-1847)
Toney, Elizabeth M. to John Thacker 6-28-1854
Toney?, Nancy to Bluford? Woodall 1-11-1845 (1-12-1845)
Tony, Mary to A. I.? W. Parker 11-7-1846 (11-8-1846)
Totten?, Rachel to James Drake 9-4-1842
Townsel, Eliza T. to John R. Wilmer 11-9-1859
Townsley, Abagal to S. A. Cowen 11-18-1862 (11-20-1862)
Townsley, Mahaley to Campbell? Brummit 6-19-1847 (6-22-1847)
Townsley, Polly to David Fullington 3-1-1856 (3-2-1856)
Townsly, Lucinda to W. Murry 5-20-1858
Trease, Minervy to Jackson Holt 9-22-1857
Treece, Olivia to John Moss 11-27-1867 (11-28-1867)
Treese, E. (Elvereen) to Noah Day 9-1-1853
Treese, Emily A. to Prior L. Cloud 8-26-1856 (8-28-1856)
Treese?, Carolina to Jerrice? B. Mays 1-21-1842 (1-30-1842)
Tresley, Franky J. to J. W. A. Collings 11-24-1860
True, Eliza to J. Hopson 6-12-1852
Tucker, Cynthia M. to John Mussey? 10-10-1850
Tucker, J. to P. Louder 7-12-1860 (7-14-1860)
Tucker, Mary to Bezeet? Burch 6-11-1842 (6-14-1842)
Tucker, Sarah Jane to Elbert S. Hodges 4-9-1851 (4-10-1841)
Tulnies?, Aatt? M. to J. L. Ledbetter 8-25-1861 (8-25-1862)
Turnbull, Nancy? to Arnold? Hellon? 6-3-1844 (6-20-1844)
Turner, Elizabeth to William Sowder 5-9-1857
Turner, Martha M. to Joseph Griffin 12-3-1867
Tussey?, Amanda J. to Jonathan T.? Walker 12-23-1843 (12-25-1843)
Upton, Nancy J. to Thomas Hatfield 7-4-1850 (7-6-1850)
Vanaver, Sarah to James H. Taylor 11-1-1855 (11-4-1855)
Vanbebber, Eliza to John Wagby? 8-19-1850 (8-15?-1850)
Vanbebber, Marlena to John Cawood 7-12-1843
Vanbebber, Martha to Ewing Yoakum 3-15-1845 (3-27-1845)

Vanbebber, Mary to Taylor Parrott 11-10-1867 B
Vanbeber, Murica Jane to Samuel King 6-1-1865
Vanbeber?, Nancy Malinda to Canada Rogers 10-2-1846
Vanbibber, Healen to R. F. Mason 9-27-1851 (10-1-1851)
Vance, Agga to Enoch Bush 11-19-1838 (11-20-1838)
Vance, Anna to Wiley Keribey 11-23-1859
Vance, C. to Ransom Cupp 3-7-1853 (3-8-1853)
Vance, Martha A. to William D. Jennings 10-31-1867
Vance, Martha to Martin V. Davault 4-9-1868 (4-10-1868)
Vance, Mary to John Lambert 9-1-1854
Vance, Pricila? to William Janeway 11-6-1845 (11-9-1845)
Vandergriff, Winney to Ezekiel Robinson 11-15-1849
Vanderpool, Nancy to Nathaniel Cress 1-25-1851 (2-2-1851)
Vanderpool, Sarah to Benjamin L. Huddleston 5-19-1845 (5-24-1849)
Vanderpool, Telitha? to David Huddleston 10-23-1849 (10-24-1849)
Vane, Sarah to William Owens 8-5-1844 (8-6-1844)
Vannoy, Winna to J. M. Massengle 12-28-1855
Vanoy, Elizabeth to Lazarous Estes 2-6-1867
Vanoy, Mary to Isaac Gowin 12-19-1839 (12-22-1839)
Vanoy, Permdy to John Baker 2-21-1838 (2-22-1838)
Vaughn, Jane to Matthew Cadle 9-1-1866 (9-6-1866)
Vaughn, M. J. to Wm. J. Lea 3-2-1858 (3-4-1858)
Vaughn, Martha Jane to Elonza D. Butcher 6-11-1849 (6-12-1849)
Vaughn, Matilda J. to Wm. A. Lea 3-2-1858
Vaughn, Susan to James Hermen? 2-17-1847 (2-18-1847)
Venable, Elender to George McCrary 11-17-1849 (11-18-1849)
Venable, Louisa to A. V. B. Moody 12-28-1854
Venable, Mary to Andrew J. Dunkin? 6-26-1847 (5?-27-1847)
Venable, N. to Peter McCrary 2-12-1853 (2-13-1853)
Venable, Nancy to John H. Carr 6-7-1866
Vennoy, Angeline to Sterling Nunn 12-25-1848 (1-4-1849)
Venoy, Levinda to William L. Vannoy 12-10-1847
Venoy, Lucy S. to William L. Venoy 11-29-1849 (12-1-1849)
Vermillion, Elizabeth to William Parker 3-21-1848
Vermillion, Nancy to Calvin Hayse 1-10-1853 (1-11-1853)
Vermillion, Patsy to Rice Whitaker 2-1-1853
Vidtoe, Martha to Anderson Kerby 3-25-1865
Vigger?, Rhoda Burnt to Johnston Jones 2-27-1839
Vitatoe, Malinda to Reuben Bean 3-13-1867 (3-14-1867)
Vitetoe, Martha E. to William H.. Johnson 11-26-1868 (11-29-1866)
Waddy, Sarah to James Braden 10-13-1838
Wagener, S. to Spenser Hooper 8-9-1858
Walker, Ann to John Lewis 1-24-1853
Walker, Lucy Jane to John W. Loop 3-5-1867
Walker, Mahala to Samuel Janeway 10-19-1867 (10-20-1867)
Walker, Malinda to Alvis Brogan 9-21-1847 (9-23-1847)
Walker, Martha A. to William H. Norton 3-1-1848 (3-5-1848)
Walker, Mary M. to John A. Casada 1-2-1867 (1-3-1867)
Walker, Sarah to Eldridge Campbell 8-31-1842 (9-1-1842)
Walker, Sidna to John Grub 2-10-1857
Walland, Sarah to Martin Gambral 8-20-1851
Wallen, China to Moses McAfee 11-22-1844
Wallen, E. to William Collinsworth 10-4-1853 (10-5-1853)
Wallen, Mary A. to William Chumbly 6-21-1851
Waller, Ellender to George W. Jennings 3-2-1844 (3-3-1844)
Waller, Mary M. to Calloway Nunn 8-13-1857
Wamiers?, Mary to John Lynch 6-28-1846 (7-3-1846)
Wanocott, Emily J. to _____ S.? White 7-24-1843 (8-3-1843)
Ward, Amanda M. L. to Joab January 11-23-1843
Ward, Elisabeth? to Frustan Nunn 2-17-1848
Ward, Letty to William Warnicutt 12-21-1842 (12-23-1842)
Ward, Marry to Pryor Davault 9-16-1858
Ward, Mary to Jas. R. Carpenter 1-12-1864
Warf, Elizabeth to Scott Standley 8-27-1868
Warnacutt, Letta to John M. T. Shishen 5-31-1848
Waters, Manerva J. to John M. Shaw? 8-1-1865 (8-2-1865)
Weaver, Lucinda to John A. Collins 2-6-1854 (2-14-1854)
Webb, Elizabeth to Riley Stansbury 1-15-1848
Webb, M. to J. McCrary 8-30-1852 (8-31-1852)
Webb, Milly to Jacob Reed 12-31-1846
Webb, Polly to Abejah? Bray 1-4-1838 (1-10-1839?)
Webb, Sophia Jane to Madison Goins 2-19-1855 (2-22-1855)
Weever?, Sarah to Thos. Eads? 8-17-1846 (8-18-1846)
Weir, Margaret to Robert Gibbs 10-26-1843
Weir, Matilda? to A. A. McAmis 1-8-1840 (1-9-1840)
Weir, Polly to Spencer Chaden 11-17-1842 (11-20-1842)
Welch, Eliza A. to Wm. C. Wireman 4-23-1852
Welch, Martha to Jesse L. Jones 6-30-1838 (7-3-1838)
Welch, Mary to Randolph Furry 4-6-1838 (4-7-1838)
Welch, Perlina to John A. Horvell 4-4-1868 (4-9-1868)
Welch, Polly to Edmund Murry 8-2-1850 (8-1?-1850)
Welch, S. to J. M. Welch 3-7-1846 (3-8-1846)
Welch, Sarah to Jeremiah Burchfield 2-21-1849
Wellman, Marthy to William Goss 5-19-1865
Wells, Eliza to Jesse Hopper? 8-2-1845 (8-3-1845)
Wells, Elizabeth to Benjamin Pike 12-15-1848 (12-17-1848)
Wells, H. to Wm. H. Harper 9-17-1853 (9-18-1853)

Wells, Jane to Sylvester Whited 10-11-1853
Wells, N. to L. W. Frasher 10-8-1857
Wells, Sarah to J. Cress 4-12-1858
Wells, Sarah to James M. Blancit 3-3-1859
West, Eliza to David Howerton 10-17-1866 (11-2-1866)
West, Elizabeth to George Johnson 6-7-1855
West, Mary to George W. Williams 7-20-1867 (7-21-1867)
West, Sarah to D. W.? Bunch 4-7-1858
West, Sarah to John Berry 8-26-1858
Western, Polly to John Doye 12-18-1846 (12-20-1846)
Wheelor, Polly to Jacob Susong 11-29-1854 (11-30-1854)
Whitaker, E. to A. Brooks 11-15-1852 (11-18-1852)
Whitaker, E. to James R. Owens 1-25-1853
Whitaker, Eliza to William Cosbey 3-18-1865 (3-22-1865)
Whitaker, Melvina to James Campbell 8-14-1843 (8-15-1843)
Whitaker, Milla to Joseph Lambert 8-5-1854 (8-6-1854)
Whitaker, Nancy N. to James L. Rice 1-10-1859
Whitaker, Nancy N. to Reuben M. Cook 1-18-1848 (1-19-1848)
Whitaker, Nancy to J. Ellerson 4-14-1857
Whitaker, Sarah to Zachariah Brooks 10-19-1853 (10-20-1853)
White, Anna to Thos. Brewer 9-20-1844 (9-21-1844)
White, E. E. to Peter Graves 12-6-1851 (12-28-1851)
White, Elizabeth to Flemman? Huddleston 10-26-1843 (10-26-1843)
White, Helen G. to Beverly P. White 11-24-1867
White, Jane to Isaac Yoakum 6-18-1859
White, Jucy to Francis Graham 7-16-1855 (7-19-1855)
White, Malvina to John Y.? Chadwich 7-26-1847 (7-29-1847)
White, Mary J. to J. T. Ellis 11-9-1864
White, Mary to M. M. Rogers 11-16-1846
White, Nancey E. to Isaac H. Sharp 3-5-1866 (3-15-1866)
White, Nancy to John Lynch 8-19-1865 (8-20-1865)
Whiteaker, Mary to Timothy Friar 8-3-1843
Whitecar, Elizabeth to Traves? Brooks 2-8-1843
Whited?, Cementha to Danl. Keck 7-16-1839 (7-18-1839)
Whiteted, P. to D. B. Badwor? 9-20-1852 (9-23-1852)
Wien?, Nancey? to William Brown 2-2-1849
Wilborne?, Dicey? to James Perkeyfile? 10-17-1845 (11-10-1845)
Wilbourne?, Martha to Thos. Baldridge 8-16-1850 (8-17-1850)
Wilburn?, Suanah? to Jacob Smiley 3-27-1844
Wilcock, Jane to Ire Rawson 10-29-1857 (11-1-1857)
Wilcocks, Jane to Ire Rowson 10-29-1857 (11-1-1857)
Wilder, Amy to William Maville 6-10-1865
Willcox, Margret to John Eapps 11-24-1860
Williaims, Mary E. to Jackson Landers 6-27-1842 (6-30-1842)
Williams, A. J. to J. G. Wilcox 12-19-1865 (ret. no ctf.)
Williams, Anna to John B. Lynch 12-20-1854
Williams, Eliza to George W. Williams 7-24-1867 (7-28-1867)
Williams, Elizabet? to Pleasant C. Munday 10-9-1841 (10-17-1841)
Williams, Haner? to E. J Odell 1-8-1848 (1-13-1848)
Williams, Louiza to George Hall 11-11-1867
Williams, Louiza to William Sutton 10-16-1867 (10-20-1867)
Williams, Luticia to J. Calvin Massingille 11-9-1851
Williams, Martha to Isaac A. Campbell 12-8-1866 (12-25-1866)
Williams, Mary Ann to Amariah Hurst 12-19-1839
Williams, Nancy to Calvin C. Woodward 8-18-1842 (8-20-1842)
Williams, Nancy to James A. England 12-9-1867 (12-11-1867)
Williams, Polly to Timothy Roarks 3-12-1840
Williams, Polly to Wiatt J. Robinson 10-12-1839
Williams, Rachael to John E. R. Gray 1-13-1849
Williams, Sarah to Henry? Edwards 11-8-1844 (11-10-1844)
Williams, Sarah to Silas Glanden 9-7-1839 (9-8-1839)
Williamson, Sinda to Nelson Baker 5-7-1854
Willing, Margaret to S. P. Ely 6-5-1865 (6-6-1865)
Willis, Elizabeth to Garett Southern 6-26-1850
Willis, Elizabeth to Garrett Southern 7-16-1850 (7-17-1850)
Willis, Levisa? to Silas Williams 1-14-1843
Willis, Louisa to John Rose 9-7-1865
Willis, Lousa Marie? to Isaac Guim? 1-21-1849 (1-23-1849)
Willis, Lucinda to William Oaks 9-26-1851 (9-28-1851)
Willis, Luritta to Henry Evans 9-24-1854
Willis, Mary to John Barnes 10-24-1851 (10-26-1851)
Willis, Mary to John Burch 12-30-1841 (1-2-1842)
Willis, Milley to Saviour? Gibson? 12-29-1842
Willis, Nancey to Mageror Holland 1-25-1859
Willis, Nancy to Daniel F. Sowder 1-16-1847 (2-21-1847)
Willis, Polly to George Fields? 11-2-1846 (12-20-1846)
Willis, Rosanah to Matthew Whiteaker 6-12-1866 (6-14-1866)
Willis, Sarah to John W. Ales 11-8-1866
Willis, Thersa Ann to William B. Lane 8-4-1849 (8-5-1849)
Wills, Martha to James Hopson 10-26-1844
Willson, Cathrine to Caswell Redmon 10-11-1856
Willson, Jane to Nelson Riley 5-29-1851
Willson, Martha to James C. Royston 1-15-1859
Willson, Mary to Joseph Stuart 11-6-1859
Willson, Norciss to N. McCrary 4-29-1844 (4-30-1844)
Willson, S. M. to John S. Jackson 7-17-1858
Willson, ____ to John Graves 10-7-1844 (10-13-1844)

Wilson, Catharin to George W. Cup 12-7-1841
Wilson, Cristiniy? to Jefferson Trese 2-19-1842
Wilson, Elisabeth to John McMahon? 5-19-1849
Wilson, Elizabeth to Littleton Mize 2-16-1851 (2-27-1851)
Wilson, Emily to P. P. Duygns? 4-13-1844
Wilson, Harriet to Elihu Wilson 1-19-1867 B
Wilson, Hessie S. to John T. Mason 8-18-1866 (8-19-1866)
Wilson, Malinda to Hiram Overton 1-17-1867 (1-18-1867) B
Wilson, Margaret to Wm. Tramel 1-21-1852 (1-22-1852)
Wilson, Melvinia to Doctor Brooks 1-21-1868 (1-22-1868) B
Wilson, Nancy to Solomon King 8-16-1853 (8-18-1853)
Wilson, Rachel S. to William Clouse 7-9-1845 (7-11-1845)
Wilson, Sarah E. to Robert H. Hall 7-18-1857 (7-22-1857)
Wilson, T. N. to Nelson Bowman 8-26-1847
Wilson, Tabitha to Albert Williams 12-5-1867
Wilsono, M. A. to J. Rose 9-13-1854
Winn, E. to Wm. H. Blackomone? 3-9-1846 (3-18-1846)
Wircick, Margret to George Devault 10-6-1847
Wirich, Catharine to Joseph Thomas 5-28-1839 (5-8?-1839)
Woatan?, Nancy to David Fulks 10-17-1843 (10-18-1843)
Wolf, Elizabeth to Britton Bull 10-31-1866
Wolf, Francis to John A. Hobbs 8-9-1857
Wolfenbarger, E. to James Slone 12-9-1845
Wolven, Lelitha to Eli Fugate 1-31-1842 (2-1-1842)
Wombels, Polly to Pharo Parton 4-10-1856 (4-12-1856)
Wood, Matilda to Wiley Sharp 10-22-1851 (9-20-1849)
Wood, Polly to Gamon McBee 10-14-1851 (10-16-1851)
Woodard, Ledia to Stokley Doyby 4-13-1847 (4-15-1847)
Woodard, Margrett to David Painter 4-7-1856 (4-10-1856)
Wooderd, Louisa E. to Malin Goodman 2-5-1856 (2-14-1856)
Woods, Sarah to Jos. Mize 7-28-1853 (no return)
Woodson, Eliza to James Lay 8-26-1856 (8-28-1856)
Woodson, Elizabeth Jane to John Meelor 2-18-1848 (3-19-1848)
Woodson, Ester to Caswell Inman 11-4-1865 (11-19-1865)
Woodson, Mary to Moses Cottrell 2-15-1856
Woodson, Rebecca to Samuel Feaburs 3-18-1868 (3-19-1868) B
Woodson, Sarah to Sterling C. Kincaid 9-15-1847 (not executed)
Woodward, Nancy to James M. Honeycutt 3-4-1850
Woollem, Catharine to Nelson Carrons 4-13-1854 (4-14-1854)
Worley, Margaret to William Taff? 6-14-1842 (6-15-1842)
Worrick, Elizabeth Ann to Ralph Hatfield 1-25-1843 (1-26-1843)
Worwick, Tempia Catharine to Isaac Bullard 9-17-1866
Woshawm, Jane to Levi Willis 11-18-1859
Wright, Judy Ann to John R. Cassle 2-15-1840 (2-18-1840)
Wright, Mary to William A. Hatchell 2-19-1868 (2-20-1868)
Wright, Nancy to James Bruce 12-25-1864 (12-28-1864)
Wright, Sarah A. to James A. Smith 3-31-1868 (4-2-1868)
Write, Nancy to Elijah Taylor 9-10-1844
Wyeman, Mary Jane to George W. Ritchards 3-7-1859
Yaden, Ann to John Raney 5-31-1854 (6-1-1854)
Yaden, Elizabeth J. to E. E. Janes 10-24-1855 (10-25-1855)
Yaden, Rebecca to John Keck 4-14-1843
Yaunce?, Elizabeth? to Nathaniel M. Scott 11-24-1845 (12-4-1845)
Yeaden, R. C. to J. Mayse 8-6-1857
Year?, Martha? to James Snavely 7-11-1845 (7-17-1845)
Yearry, Mary to David Winegar? 12-4-1843 (12-7-1843)
Yeary, M. B. to S. E. Harris 12-5-1851
Yeary, Nancy M. to Martin Early 2-15-1867 (2-17-1867)
Yerra, Rebecca to Luther R. Rowlett 8-26-1856
Yoakeem, Hina M. to J. M. Vanbebber 12-1-1851 (12-14-1851)
Yoakum, M. to D. D. Burk 5-17-1858 (5-23-1858)
Yoakum, Martha J. to Lafayett M. Carr 11-21-1859
Yoakum, Mary T. to Joseph Russell 10-25-1859
York, Amelia to Samuel Colwell 4-19-1849
York, Elizabeth to Israel K. Woollum 7-4-1867
York, Martha to Thomas Rigsby 7-30-1866
Young, M. A. to Joseph Greenlee 9-2-1859
Young, Margret to James Wells 3-30-1856
Young, Missouri A. to Wm. S. Miller 12-1-1866 (12-5-1866)
Young, Vesty to James Morrison 7-21-1857
Zeck, Eliza to Jno. Connor 10-5-1838 (10-7-1838)
Zick, Mary to Leander Young 4-8-1851 (4-13-1851)
Zicks, Cathrine to Geo. W. Brooks 4-3-1848

Claiborne County, Tennessee

Marriages

1868 – 1891

Byron and Barbara Sistler

Byron Sistler & Associates, Inc.
1984

Claiborne County, Tennessee, Marriages 1868-1891

Copyright © 1984 by Byron Sistler
All rights reserved.

Originally printed, Nashville, 1984
Byron Sistler and Associates, Inc.

Janaway Publishing, Inc.
2412 Nicklaus Dr.
Santa Maria, California 93455
(805) 925-1038
www.JanawayPublishing.com

2007

ISBN 10: 1-59641-078-7
ISBN 13: 978-1-59641-078-7

Made in the United States of America

CLAIBORNE COUNTY, TN MARRIAGES

1868-91

Where two dates appear on an entry, the first one is the date license was issued, the second (in parentheses) the date marriage was solemnized. If only one date, either the marriage did not take place or at least there was no return to the courthouse.

We transcribed these marriage records directly from a microfilmed copy of the original county marriage books, so error, where it occurs, will usually be our own responsibility. However, it should be remembered that entries in the books themselves were copied from the licenses by clerks, and it is obvious from examining the pages that many of them were not prepared with great care.

In most cases the original licenses and bonds are not available, having been lost or destroyed.

Byron Sistler
Barbara Sistler

Nashville, TN
November, 1984

Claiborne County Grooms

Adams, James to Elizabeth Hatfield 12-17-1880 (12-19-1880)
Adams, William to Racheal Bowman 12-15-1877 (12-16-1877)
Adkins, Joe A. to Mary L. Evans 6-12-1889
Adkins, John to Sarah J. Davidson 1-11-1872 (1-12-1872)
Agee, Mathew to Sarah F. Gulley 7-15-1871 (8-9-1871)
Ailes, James to Elisabeth Standfer 2-22-1890
Ailes, John W. to Mary Earls 9-2-1889 (9-3-1889)
Ales, Samuel to Mary J. Dinkins 10-17-1869
Ales, Wm. P. to Nancy M. Fergerson 3-26-1870 (3-27-1870)
Alexander, D. B. to Barbara Cawood 10-29-1873 (11-2-1873)
Alexander, D. B. to Esther C Carr 8-8-1889 (8-11-1889)
Allen, Andrew to Lucinda Cloud 11-11-1869 B
Altum, John R. to Sarah Maney 9-7-1877 (9-9-1877)
Anderson, E. M. to Maranda Carter 11-18-1873 (11-19-1873)
Anderson, Jeramiah to Sary Shelbun 1-27-1872
Anderson, Jerry to Sarah Peters 1-6-1883 (no return)
Arnold, J. C. to Katey Wyrick 2-9-1884 (2-10-1884)
Arnold, John C. to Nancy Massingill 8-23-1869 (8-26-1869)
Arnwine, Wm. to Matild P. L. J. Mason 10-19-1881 (10-20-1881)
Asburn, John to Sarah J. Willson 6-13-1875
Atkins, A. S. to S. A. Hodges 1-29-1879 (1-30-1879)
Atkins, John H. to Laura Breeding 3-8-1890 (3-12-1890)
Ausburn, A. C. to Ollie McNeil 5-12-1877 (5-13-1877)
Ausburn, Thos. D. to Martha G. Estes 4-17-1884
Ausburn, Thos. to Lora Munn 11-22-1888 (11-23-1888)
Ausmus, B. F. to M. A. Rogers 10-15-1879 (1-5-1880)
Ausmus, B. to China Odell 8-1-1881 (8-8-1881)
Ausmus, Charley to Martha Owens 3-23-1888
Ausmus, David to A. C. Wright 12-31-1878
Ausmus, Hiram M. to Salley N. Bolingly 4-?-1879 (4-17-1879)
Ausmus, Jesse L. to Mary L. Cawood 12-19-1875 (12-23-1875)
Ausmus, W. H. to Sarah A. Russell 11-11-1881 (11-14-1881)
Ausmus, Wm. jr. to Mary J. Carr 6-23-1887 (6-25-1887)
Ayers, J. T. to Rachel E. Thomas 4-4-1882 (no return)
Ayers, Joe Wesley to Nancy Marcum 12-8-1882 (12-10-1882)
Bailey, Charley to Docia Bolton 11-8-1890
Bailey, Winsbee to Casa Miller 10-31-1888
Baker, Arch to Cora Wilson 2-7-1891 (2-8-1891)
Baker, Archilas to Lousana Pearson 9-22-1879 (10-19-1879)
Baker, Daniel B. to Louisa Pearson 12-8-1876 (12-12-1876)
Baker, Elija to Meda Powers 2-11-1875
Baker, George W. to Margret J. Liford 10-26-1877 (no return)
Baker, Henry to Nancy Sulfridg 5-7-1881 (5-8-1881)
Baker, John to Elizebth Jones 9-16?-1882 (no return)
Baker, Joseph to Louisa Mason 12-8-1876
Balden, William B. to Mary Jane Burchfield 7-25-1877 (7-26-1877)
Baldwin, J. W. to Sary C. Bellamy 6-1-1884? (1-1-1884)
Baldwin, John M. to M. J. Burchfield 11-25-1879 (no return)
Baldwin, T. B. to Sallie Howard 2-14-1881 (2-17-1881)
Baldwin, W. M. to Emily Belemy 6-9-1886 (6-10-1886)
Bales, Abe to Mint Hopson 3-8-1886
Balins, Plesant to Mary J. Briton 10-4-1883 (10-12-1883)
Ball, Thos. to Sarah A. Woodson 10-16-1886 (10-17-1886)
Ball, Wm. S. to Mary Jane Pridemore 12-18-1868 (12-24-1868)
Ball?, John to Elizabeth Cox 8-6-1870 (8-7-1870)
Balton, J. F. to R. A. Mayers 6-10-1883
Bamman, James M. to Clory B. Moyers 2-21-1875
Bandin, J. H. to A. Ritter 1-21-1880 (1-22-1880)
Bane, Thomas T. to Elisbeth Roberts 9-10-1870 (9-16-1870)
Banes, William A. to China A. Dunsmore 12-12-1874 (12-14-1874)
Bare, B. F. to M. E. Lane 4-19-1887
Barett, Thomas J. to Mary Huckes? 3-17-1879
Barlow, J. M. to Mary Mize 12-27-1888
Barnard, Anderson to E. V. Smith 10-18-1882 (10-19-1882)
Barnard, George to Clifford Chambers 8-6-1877
Barnard, Henderson to Anjaline Willis 1-27-1881 (1-30-1881)
Barnard, Jerry to Elizabeth Meigs 2-18-1875 (2-21-1875)
Barnard, John to Allie Seals 5-16-1888 (5-19-1888)
Barnard, Robbert to Martha Acuff 12-17-1884 (12-21-1884)
Barnard, STerling to Catherine Howerton 12-12-1876 (12-21-1876)
Barnard, Samuel to Emaline Barnard 2-15-1882? (no return)
Barnard, W. H. to Mary A. E. Barnard 10-3-1878 (10-6-1878)
Barnard, Wm. to Rebeca Grubb 10-24-1881 (10-27-1881)
Barnes, Elbert to Mary Sulfrage 2-6-1891 (2-8-1891)
Barnes, Henry to Minie Rollens 10-15-1890 (10-16-1890)
Barnes, William F. to Susan Cavane? 5-29-1882
Barnet, Andrew to Nancy Campbell 1-10-1880
Barnet, James to Sally Jones 7-4-1887 (7-10-1887)
Barnett, Grant to Nancy A. Parton 1-14-1891 (no return)
Barns, James W. to Elizabeth J. Criger 11-22-1869 (11-28-1869)
Barns, Sterling to C. A. Hatfield 2-11-1880
Bartlett, Claiborne to Amanda Brock 12-8-1879
Bartlett, James to Allace Bolton 11-27-1880 (11-28-1880)
Bartlett, Wiley to Ollie Walker 2-5-1882
Bassell, Joseph to Martha Fultz 4-1-1871
Bateman, C. H. to Alice M. Atkins 5-10-1886 (5-16-1886)
Batey, Henry G. to Alice Patterson 10-2-1871 (no return)

Batey, Heny to Millie Hodges 1-31-1882
Bawn, James T. to Lowese E. Northan 6-3-1878 (no return)
Baylor, Henry D. to Mary E. Hodges 9-29-1874
Bean, Benjamin to Elisabeth A. Cupp 8-7-1888 (8-9-1888)
Bean, Robt. to Salley Ann Bruce 6-25-1888 (6-28-1888)
Beason, George W. to E. J. Dosset 12-13-1880 (no return)
Beeler, David F. to Lucinda M. Maupin 1-19-1869 (1-21-1869)
Beeler, Isaac M. to J. B. Sharp 5-16-1872
Beeler, Jesse to Cova? Blackburn 11-26-1881
Beeler, Marshal to Ollie Rogers 12-10-1883 (no return)
Beeler, William H. H. to Talitha C. Wright 2-14-1869
Been, Isaac to Mary Patterson 5-8-1885 (no return)
Been, Ruben to Mary A. Roch 6-17-1882
Beese, Wm. H. to Elizabeth Daulton 8-?-1879 (no return)
Beeson, Preston to Mary Edwards 12-16-1888 (12-17-1888)
Belcher, Orvel to Sarah Sailer 2-4-1880 (no return)
Bell, Chas. to India Poor 12-25-1888 (12-26-1888)
Bell, R. H. to L. J. Sharp 10-12-1886 (10-13-1886)
Bennett, G. W. to Joanah Walker 5-30-1880
Bentley, W. S. to M. E. Hill 9-11-1889
Bently, William to Heti? A. Hill 10-12-1874
Berry, J. H. to Jennie Knuthank? 11-15-1884
Berry, William to Elizabeth Wills 5-9-1877 (5-10-1877)
Bery, Dock to Rebeca Jones 8-1-1878
Beson, John to Caroline Johnson 3-12-1883 (3-14-1883)
Bible, P. L. to L. C. Richardson 3-7-1891 (3-16-1891)
Bickerson, Timothy Robt. to Lillay May Ales 3-10-1888 (3-11-1888)
Billingsley, John W. to Martha A. Watson 10-29-1870 (11-2-1870)
Billingsley, Robert W. to Emly Collinesworth 1-17-1883 (1-18-1883)
Billingsly, G. M. to Celie Pearce 9-1-1882 (9-7-1882)
Billingsly, Joseph to Isabel Bolinger 2-17-1870 (2-20-1870)
Billingsly, Wm. to Rachael Balinger 11-4-1871 (11-5-1871)
Binir, Waymen L. to Mary A. Green 9-18-1881
Bird, James to Catharine McDaniel 9-21-1868
Bird, William to Elizabeth Morgan 7-9-1877
Birk, James to Martha C. Birk 2-26-1880 (no return)
Bishop, John to Molley Susong 9-24-188? (9-26-1886)
Bishop, W. H. to Hester A. Cupp 3-9-1888 (3-11-1888)
Black, John to Melvina Watson 4-21-1885 (4-23-1885)
Blackben, Leon to Lucinda Bull 8-7-1880 (8-8-1880)
Blackburn, J. H. to Manda J. Meyers 11-7-1884? (11-12-1884)
Blake, Wm. to Nancy J. Harvey 3-1-1884
Blancett, Arch. to Angaline Collins 12-25-1884 (1-12-1885)
Blancett, T. H. to L. Parsom 2-24-1880 (2-29-1880)
Blansett, Archibald E. to Sarah Rosanah Lynch 5-8-1869 (5-9-1869)
Blaylock, Joseph to Margaret Lock 9-14-1868 (9-16-1868)
Blevens, Isaac to Angeline Loop 12-31-1877 (no return)
Boens, John W. to Susan Farmer 10-5-1868 (10-6-1868)
Boling, William to Lutisia A. Davis 6-11-1874
Bolinger, Benjamin to Sallie Ann Yoakum 11-26-1869 (11-28-1869)
Bolinger, P. M. to Nancy C. Wylie 7-24-1890
Bolltrip, G. W. to Mary A. Hurst 6-27-1888 (7-1-1888)
Bolton, Daniel M. to Zilvena Jones 8-1-1870 (8-7-1870)
Bolton, G. S. to Vina More 4-7-1887 (not executed)
Bolton, J. A. to Judie L. Owens 2-28-1891 (3-1-1891)
Bolton, J. J. to Mary Owen 12-21-1886 (12-26-1886)
Bolton, Joseph to Jane Bartlett 2-5-1888
Bolton, Winston to Helen Smith 3-11-1890 (3-12-1890)
Bomar, B. F. to Lucy B. Neal 12-23-1890
Bosteck, Wm. R. to Martha T. Bowman 2-13-1883 (2-15-1883)
Bostic, J. V. to S. J. Brewman 12-25-1885
Bosworth, Joe F. to Lizzie Vial 8-28-1890
Bowlin, J. W. to Nancy Mayes 7-12-1882 (7-13-1882)
Bowling, H. L. to Mary Jane Carroll 4-4-1889 (4-6-1889)
Bowman, C. W. to Elizabeth Jackson 11-13-1884 (11-21-1884)
Bowman, J. S. to Hanah Blake 7-17-1882
Bowman, James A. to Martha Leach 2-18-1869 (2-19-1869)
Bradley, George to Suzy Burns 5-30-1889
Brafford, S. F. to Laura Newlee 8-12-1875 (not returned)
Branscom, A. F. to Dicey Davis 5-6-1885 (5-7-1885)
Branscom, Phillip to Dolly Rogers 5-31-1873
Branscom, Thomas to Annah Mayes 10-11-1872 (10-13?-1872)
Branscom, Wm. to Ann Smith 2-15-1874 (2-22-1874)
Branson, Daniel A. to Mary I. England 7-29-1875 (8-1-1875)
Branson, Isaac to Norra Owens 8-21-1889 (no return)
Branson, John H. to Martha M. Cupp 7-17-1884
Brantly, J. R. to R. J. Dunn 10-6-1883
Branum, James to Elisabeth Wallis 8-22-1874? (8-22-1875)
Bray, Beaugard to Ludie Campbell 12-22-1882
Bray, J. P. to Ollie Clarxten 9-?-1882 (9-24-1882)
Bray, Jame to Sarah Wyatt 2-7-1881
Breeden, Joseph to Matilda Peeters 4-8-1871 (4-9-1871)
Breeding, Edward to Amanda Cheatham 11-9-1890
Breeding, George W. to Lucy (Mrs.) Fletcher 6-17-1881
Breeding, J. N. to N. O. Epperson 3-?-1879 (3-20-1879)
Breeding, James M. to Matilda Harrell 1-27-1870
Breeding, John to Mary Ausmus 3-15-1884

Breeding, Perry C. to Susan A. Hurst 8-3-1876 (8-6-1876)
Breeding, Wiley C. to Ellen O. Eperson no date (late 1877?)
Brewer, Arthur to Mary Cabbage 12-20-1809 (with 1890)
Brewer, James to Martha Doyel 2-2-1881 (3-6-1881)
Briant, Sidney B. to Mary J. Kock 12-21-1890 (no return)
Brice?, John to Jane Evans 1-25-1873 (1-26-1873) B
Briens?, Wm. to Linda Rall 8-28-1880
Brim, Wm. to S. E. Carroll 3-13-1889 (3-14-1889)
Brit?, George W. to Pheba C. Peck 3-1-1878 (3-3-1878)
Brittain, Chadwell to Mary Chadwell 7-14-1870 (7-17-1870)
Britton, William to Elalia Ball 12-19-1874 (12-20-1874)
Brock, Elisha to Mary Haskins 12-6-1886
Brogan, Asa to Jane Mountain 3-29-1883 (4-3-1883)
Brogan, Charley to Ellen Fugate 4-19-1890 (no return)
Brogan, G. L. to R. E. Goin 4-7-1881 (4-28-1881)
Brogan, James M. to Susan E. Sharp 11-25-1872 (11-28-1872)
Brogan, John F. to P. C. N. Jones 10-9-1876 (10-12-1876)
Brogan, N. A. to Emily J. Jones 10-7-1873 (10-9-1873)
Brogans, James to Louisa Fugate 12-27-1889 (12-29-1889)
Brogans, James to Mary J. Ogan 11-9-1883 (11-11-1883)
Brooks, Abraham to Lucy Estep 8-22-1873 (8-24-1873)
Brooks, Alexander to M. J. Chadwell 3-18-1881 (no return)
Brooks, Allen to Margret J. Minton 10-10-1870 (10-13-1870)
Brooks, Allen to Serelda J. Sutton 12-10-1874 (12-11-1874)
Brooks, B. H. to Allie Claxton 7-23-1884 (7-24-1884)
Brooks, Boston to Malinda Goin 11-21-1868 (11-22-1868) B
Brooks, Boston to Orlenia Wilson 7-3-1871 (7-6-1871)
Brooks, Clinton C. to Louisa Brooks 2-21-1877 (no return)
Brooks, Dock to Allice Rogers 11-25-1884
Brooks, Elbert N. to Elizabeth Brooks 9-18-1876 (no return)
Brooks, Eldridg C. to Mary A. Moore 1-3-1882 (1-5-1882)
Brooks, Ewin to Rossie A. Welch 10-24-1890 (10-26-1890)
Brooks, Ewing to Martha Ann Brooks 8-31-1876 (9-3-1876)
Brooks, F. T. to Mary Smith 12-26-1870 (12-27-1870)
Brooks, G. A. to Mary J. Jones 3-10-1883? (no return)
Brooks, G. A. to Perlina Brooks 9-12-1883
Brooks, G. C. to Marthey J. Montgomery 8-8-1887 (8-11-1887)
Brooks, G. W. to Kesey J. Adams 2-28-1882 (3-5-1882)
Brooks, G. W. to Nancy Chadwell 1-4-1873 (no return)
Brooks, George to Mary E. Wilson 1-9-1874
Brooks, H. C. to Esther Monday 12-6-1881 (12-13-1881)
Brooks, Humphrey to Caroline Wilson 4-7-1882 (no return)
Brooks, I.? A. to Liza G. Willson 6-12-1882 (6-13-1882)
Brooks, J. A. to Frances Richardson 12-28-1878 (12-29-1878)
Brooks, J. C. to Matilda Longworth 1-14-1880 (1-15-1880)
Brooks, J. T. to Lucy Amos 9-22-1890
Brooks, James M. to L. S. A. Pace 3-19-1880 (3-20-1880)
Brooks, James to Ann Hopson 12-15-1875 (12-16-1875)
Brooks, Jasper to Margart Brooks 9-18-1879
Brooks, Jermiah to E. J. Bolton 12-23-1872 (12-24-1872)
Brooks, Jery to Rhoda Estes 7-12-1879 (7-13-1879)
Brooks, John H. to Malissa Welch 9-12-1877 (no return)
Brooks, John L. to Rebeca A. Brown 11-14-1876 (no return)
Brooks, John to Sarelda Smith 12-9-1886 (no return)
Brooks, Joseph to Arrena Brooks 11-12-1868 (11-13-1868)
Brooks, Levi to Cornelia Williams 4-4-1885 (4-5-1885)
Brooks, Levi to Ettie Johnson 11-5-1888 (11-11-1888)
Brooks, Lewis C. to Martha E. Bales 2-12-1878 (no return)
Brooks, Lewis to Malissa Ramsey 6-10-1876 (no return)
Brooks, Lewis to Martha A. Wilson 12-27-1880 (1-1-1881)
Brooks, Lewis to Mary McDaniel 10-23-1872 (no return)
Brooks, Lewis to Matilda Huffeld 8-16-1890 (no return)
Brooks, Montie to John Townsley 12-3-1887 (12-4-1887)
Brooks, Morrison to Lucinda Mise 10-9-1874 (10-8?-1874)
Brooks, Moses C. to Nancy E. (Mrs.) Yeary 9-5-1881 (11-17-1881)
Brooks, Nelson P. H. to Mary E. Esteps 5-9-1884 (5-10-1884)
Brooks, Newton to Martha Brooks 8-31-1870 (9-4-1870)
Brooks, Newton to Mary Rose 11-16-1875 (11-17-1875)
Brooks, Robert to M. E. Smith 7-31-1882 (8-6-1882)
Brooks, Robin to Angeline Whitaker 4-3-1874 (no return)
Brooks, Robt. to Manda J. Brooks 1-12-1889 (1-13-1889)
Brooks, Sterling to Alice J. Williams 1-15-1884 (1-15-1884)
Brooks, T. A. to Theressa Brooks 1-11-1889 (1-13-1889)
Brooks, Taylor to Lucinda Mize 6-12-1874 (not executed)
Brooks, Taylor to Martha Denham 1-29-1876 (no return)
Brooks, Taylor to Martha Houston 3-24-1883
Brooks, Tip to Barbery Ballou 8-7-1890 (8-13-1890)
Brooks, Travis to Rache Raney 10-30-1887
Brooks, W. F. to Mary C. Nevels 12-21-1888 (12-23-1888)
Brooks, W. M. to Martha Parks 11-3-1888 (11-4-1888)
Brooks, W. N. to Sarah J. Bales 6-9-1883 (6-10-1883)
Brooks, W. W. to Amanda Estep no date (Oct 1884?)
Brooks, William F. to Elizabeth Smith 3-4-1869 (3-11-1869)
Brooks, Wm. J. to Elizabeth Campbell 11-17-1877 (no return)
Brooks, Wm. to Mary Causbey 7-26-1887 (7-28-1887)
Brooks, Woodson to Elizabeth Brooks 3-6-1876 (3-7-1876)
Brooks, Z.? C. to Eliza Brooks 8-29-1871 (9-3-1871)

Brooks, Zachariah C. to Emeline Scott 2-9-1870 (2-12-1870)
Browing, H. B. to Nancy Maricle 9-24-1879
Brown, Abriham to Mary Martin 2-8-1886 (2-14-1886)
Brown, Calvin to Matilda Woolf 8-17-1889 (8-18-1889)
Brown, Columbus to Lizzie Baley 6-13-1882
Brown, Harvey to Liccie Haynes 5-25-1888
Brown, James to Eliza Campbell 2-11-1885 (2-12-1885)
Brown, Jefferson to Susie Dixie 6-8-1887
Brown, John to M. Edwards 6-16-1880 (no return)
Brown, John to Martha J. Northan 3-25-1880 (no return)
Brown, John to Mary Crofford 8-22-1888
Brown, Moses to Jane Campbell 4-12-1872 (4-21-1872)
Brown, Nelson to Jane Petree 2-10-1876 (2-13-1876)
Brown, T. G. to Mattie R. White 4-2-1884
Brown, Thomas to S. E. Snavley 10-8-1879 (10-9-1879)
Brown, William to Martha J. Maricle 8-5-1879
Brown, William to Mary Estep 12-6-1869 (12-9-1869)
Browning, Wesley to Orlena Greenlee 2-10-1880 (2-12-1880)
Brownlow, J. Fauster to Rutha Fugate 5-28-1870 (5-29-1870)
Bruce, Airs M. to Lucretia McCrary 9-29-1873 (10-6-1873)
Bruce, Marion J. to Sallie A. Sparks 1-15-1883 (1-16-1883)
Bruce, William H. to Nelley Carr 12-7-1890 (12-9-1890)
Bruer, David to Martha Burk 3-11-1874 (3-12-1874)
Bruer, Jesse to Martha Rosson 4-2-1873 (4-3-1873)
Brunton, James M. to A. M. Stoute 12-15-1883
Bryan, Octava L. to Lumll? Robertson 6-15-1885 (6-16-1885)
Bryant, D. C. to M. A. Freeman 1-18-1887 (11-20-1887)
Bryant, Daniel to Virginia E. Newbey 7-22-1873 (7-24-1873)
Bryant, D. N. to Martha Greer 10-25-1884 (10-26-1884)
Bryant, G. W. to _____ Southern 9-6-1890
Bryant, J. G.? to Loo Rogers 1-4-1887 (1-6-1887)
Bryant, Saml. to Mary Ann Cox 2-11-1889 (2-17-1889)
Buchanan, James M. to Mary E. Smith 10-23-1874 (no return)
Buckanan, James L. to Ellen Jackson no dates
Buckhart, L. C. to Fannie Duff 10-27-1887
Buis, Green to Lizzie Robertson 9-12-1888 (12-18-1888)
Buis, Henly to M. E. Overton 10-6-1879 (10-9-1879)
Buis, Henry to Rittey Ramsey 9-13-1877 (9-14-1877) B
Buis, Nelson to Elizabeth Fulkerson 9-25-1876
Buis, Reubin (Rev. Esq.) to Milly Fugate 7-6-1885 (7-22-1885)
Bull, James to Sally N. Keck 11-14-1878
Bull, Joseph to Louise Moyers 12-2-1881 (12-4-1881)
Bullar, William to Sarah Rogers 12-6-1872 (12-7-1872)
Bullard, Joseph to Reetha Serler? 12-27-1878
Bullin, D. A. to A. L. Hurst 12-20-1883
Bumgardner, John H. to Bell Birk 9-23-1879 (no return)
Bunch, John W. to Sarah Hurst 4-12-1888
Bunch, Richard E. to Martha C. Hurst 9-28-1881 (9-29-1881)
Bunch?, James to S. J. West 6-1-1884 (6-3-1884)
Bundren, James H. to Jane Cole 8-17-1889 (no return)
Bundren, Wm. to Harriet Jennings 4-21-1877 (4-22-1877)
Burch, G. W. to Amanda J. Grubbs 6-14-1882
Burch, Thomas to Loucinda Cassall 11-2-1874 (no return)
Burch, W. H. to Sarah M. Heaath 11-21-1883 (no return)
Burch, Wiley P. to Clementine Walker 10-23-1871 (10-27-1871)
Burchell, Daniel N. to Marjorie Sproles 2-6-1884 (no return)
Burchett, George B. to Eliza A. Littrell 4-6-1869 (4-8-1869)
Burchett, H. L. to Mary Clark 8-10-1880
Burchett, James M. to Louisa Brooks 8-26-1871 (8-27-1871)
Burchett, Larkin L. to Mary A. Littrell 1-5-1869 (1-7-1869)
Burchett, William to Elizabeth Hill 3-20-1879
Burchfield, J. M. to Roda Shiflet 1-12-1889 (1-20-1889)
Burchfield, Jas. to Alice Snodgrass 2-21-1886 (no return)
Burding, L. G. to Pertina Simmons 8-21-1872 (no return)
Burford, Robt. to Mag Buis 12-12-1888
Burk, Daniel to Sarah M. Moyers 4-12-1874
Burk, James T. to M. E. Hooper 10-16-1879
Burk, James T. to M. E. Hopson 10-16-1879 (no return)
Burk, James to Jaley Campbell 8-1-1877 (no return)
Burk, John S. to Mary Overbay 2-17-1889
Burk, Lafayett J. to Loucinda K. Henegar 2-7-1885
Burk, William A. to E. B. Hicks 8-13-1877
Burks, Richard to Sarah E. Williams 1-6-1886 (1-28-1886)
Burnett, Burchett W. to Jane Kesterson 10-4-1868 (10-5-1868)
Burnett, Dairden? W. to Lucy Asberry 9-3-1875
Burnett, J. S. to A. Medaris 10-8-1874
Burnett, Joab E. to Sintha Ann Finar 10-2-1868 (10-5-1868)
Bush, Elisha to Melbina McCarrol 9-26-1881
Bush, Roboert to Sarah Felps 5-18-1786 (8-27-1876)
Bush, William to Sarah E. Liler 10-4-1879 (10-5-1879)
Busick, E. C. to Mary Johns 12-20-1878 (no return)
Busk, Joseph K. to Rida M. Boneamar 1-5-1879
Bussell, Andrew to Emily Hill 9-2-1882 (9-3-1882)
Bussell, James to Pheby Cloud 1-11-1883
Bussell, John F. to Martha Jane Gwin 9-8-1888 (9-9-1888)
Bussell, Joseph to Sarah Crawford 9-20-1881
Bussell, Joseph to Sarah Hatfield 1-29-1876 (no return)

Bussell, Samuel to Mary J. Hatfield 9-25-188? (10-2-1886)
Bussell, Thos. to Rebeca Rice 12-24-1889 (no return)
Butcher, Elvin to Cordelia E. Brogan 9-16-1871 (9-21-1871)
Butcher, Jackson to Nancy McNeil 6-17-1889
Butcher, Nathan to M. C. Brogan 11-10-1877 (11-15-1877)
Butcher, Nathan to Mary Jane Sharp 8-7-1869 (8-8-1869)
Butcher, Warrack to Mary Stergeon 4-11-1871
Butcher, Warrick to Manda Coleton 4-1-1869 (4-3-1869) B
Butler, Allen to Celea Mullens 6-26-1878 (6-27-1878)
Butler, Allen to Cena Mullens 6-26-1878 (no return)
Butler, James Robt. to Mollie Glenn Snodgrass 3-18-1873 (no return)
Butly, Richard S. to Eliza Robinson 1-21-1885 (1-22-1885)
Cadle, A. G. to Augusta Hawley 12-18-1871 (12-24-1871)
Cadle, James M. to Maggie B. Logans 2-19-1890 (2-20-1890)
Cadle, Mathew to Mary J. Van 10-15-1877
Cadle, W. F. to Martha O. King 11-30-1883 (no return)
Cain, H. M. to Rachal A.? Rogers 1-24-1883 (no return)
Cain, W. J. to Florence Lyons 3-4-1874 (3-5-1874)
Caler, John to Alice Ellison 7-22-1885 (7-26-1885)
Caler, M. F. to Fanney Welch 4-13-1871 (not executed)
Caler, Thomas to Sarah Roark 8-17-1878 (no return)
Call, J. W. D. to M. T. M. Gray 1-11-1889
Callaway, Charles to Marry Howard 8-10-1881
Calor, James W. to Mary V. Sutton 6-29-1886 (7-8-1886)
Calor, Thomas to Sarah Roark 8-17-1878
Caman, J. N. to Rebeca Burk 8-15-1877
Campbell, A. to M. E. Chadwell 6-2-1879 (no return)
Campbell, Alexander to Sarah C. Campbell 4-7-1880 (4-8-1880)
Campbell, B. F. to Sane Tuggle 4-3-1881
Campbell, Barnett to Annie Gibson 2-9-1878 (no return)
Campbell, Benj. to Feebee Bartlett 10-2?-1872 (no return)
Campbell, C. B. to D. B. Essor 6-31?-1884 (7-31-1884)
Campbell, C. Y. to M. E. Ensor 2-10-1881
Campbell, David H. to Mary Jane Grimes 3-26-1869 (3-29-1869)
Campbell, David to Missouri Williams 9-15-1874 (no return)
Campbell, Elbert to Catherin Brown 3-20-1880 (3-21-1880)
Campbell, G. M. to Maggie Payne 10-10-1888 (10-11-1888)
Campbell, George to M. Longmoyers 12-5-1877 (no return)
Campbell, George to Matilda Clarkston 9-23-1869
Campbell, George to Virdy Robarts 5-8-1890
Campbell, Isaac H. to Allace Nunn 1-20-1890 (1-23-1890)
Campbell, Isaac to Florence Debusk 3-25-1872 (4-28-1872)
Campbell, Jacob C. to Manerva (Mis) Danuels 9-1-1881 (9-2-1881)
Campbell, James B. to Martha J. Massingill 3-26-1878 (3-28-1878)
Campbell, James to Lindey Hurst 11-28-1880
Campbell, James to Louisa Davis 12-21-1871
Campbell, Levi to Nancy Roark 6-15-1879
Campbell, Manda to John Loop 8-21-1889 (8-22-1889)
Campbell, Mucillan? J. to Salley M. Hall 4-5-1887
Campbell, N. J. to Lucy Williams 1-17-1885 (10-18-1885)
Campbell, Nelson to Martha J. Lewis 3-15-1883
Campbell, Oliver to Eliza A. Brown 11-8-1872
Campbell, Peter H. to Lettia Gibson 11-26-1869 (11-27-1869)
Campbell, S. M. to Ida B. Mayes 7-19-1890 (7-20-1890)
Campbell, Sterling to Barbary Yeary 10-27-1869 (no return)
Campbell, Tilmon to Mossie Brooks 9-10-1909 (with 1890)
Campbell, W. A. to Matilda Turner 11-16-1882
Campell, J. J. to A. T. Jones 2-24-1881
Candry, Angeline to William Woodson 12-15-1878
Canell, Benj. F. to Sarah S. Lambert 2-18-1874 (2-22-1874)
Canell, Wm. to Catharine Moyers 3-4-1874 (3-26-1874)
Capper, H. N. to S. A. Branson 4-1-1880
Capps, G. W. to ----- England 12-31-1889 (1-1-1890)
Capps, Jacob to Rachel? Calwell 6-18-1870 (6-19-1870)
Cardwell, Anderson to Margaret M. Robinson 3-20-1870
Cardwell, C. C. to Martha Smith 10-14-1873 (10-22-1873)
Cardwell, E. W. to Mary J. Smith 1-29-1878 (no return)
Cardwell, James F. to Sarah J. Parsons 12-14-1870 (12-15-1870) B
Cardwell, John W. to Millie McDaniel 10-28-1868 (10-29-1868)
Cardwell, Obediah to Sarah Hurst 11-3-1890
Cardwell, R. F. to ----- ----- 9-21-1885
Cardwell, Wm. to Martha L. Hellems 8-24-1871
Cardwell, Z. G. to M. L. Young 1-3-1881 (no return)
Carell, Daniel to Almeda Johnson 9-23-1890
Carmack, Abram to Martha J. Snaveley 10-22-1877 (no return)
Carmack, H. H. to Ella Morrison 1-26-1882 (1-31-1882)
Carmack, Isaac to Mary Burchett 11-19-1883 (no return)
Carmack, John A. to Martha J. Wright 10-25-1877
Carmack, John O. to Angline Carmack 3-5-1881 (3-6-1881)
Carmack, John to Angeline Brown 5-31-1880
Carmack, Joseph to Sarah E. Dunn 12-14-1888 (12-16-1888)
Carmon, J. R. to Ida B. Clark 1-29-1890 (2-3-1890)
Carmon, Nathan E. to Rachal Ayers 12-8-1882 (12-10-1882)
Carmony, James L. to Mary Hatfield 7-22-1870 (7-24-1870)
Carpenter, Charley to Tishey Fullington 4-10-1890
Carpenter, Geo. to Lucy J. Harvey 10-26-1886 (10-28-1886)
Carpenter, J. H. to Ollie Hodges 1-10-1888

Carpenter, James M. to Melvina Willis 2-19-1874 (2-25-1874)
Carpenter, James R. to Mary Willis 9-22-1868 (7?-23-1868)
Carpenter, James to Betha Bones 11-13-1889 (11-14-1889)
Carpenter, Jesse to July Cloud 2-25-1871 (2-26-1871)
Carpenter, John H. to Mary Hodges 8-6-1877 (no return)
Carpenter, John H. to Sarrah Willis 8-31-1870 (9-1-1870)
Carpenter, W. H. to Nancy Cheek 11-1-1879 (11-5-1879)
Carpenter, William C. to Elizabeth M. Hurst 5-3-1878 (no return)
Carpenter, Wm. H. to Anjaline Harvey 4-13-1882 (7-4-1882)
Carr, A. C. to Allice King 7-13-1887 (7-14-1887)
Carr, A. C. to Hettie Edds 9-23-1889
Carr, David to Sarah Collinsworth 5-24-1886 (5-6?-1886)
Carr, G. S. to Sallie E. Johnson 2-25-1890 (2-26-1890)
Carr, J. W. to Loucinda Lawson 5-25-1884
Carr, James C. to Janie Macky 11-5-1881
Carr, James M. to Mary E. Sharp 9-3-1870
Carr, James P. to Josephine Simmons 3-18-1874 (4-23-1874)
Carr, John C. to Amanda S. Scott 9-23-1874 (no return)
Carr, L. R. to Comfort Brogan 1-17-1874 (1-20-1874)
Carr, R. F. to Sally K. Fulkerson 3-1-1880
Carr, S. J. to Angie Mountain 10-4-1881 (10-23-1881)
Carr, W. S. to Hester S. (Miss) Treece 5-24-1874 (5-31-1874)
Carr, W. S. to Mary E. Love 5-15-1879
Carrel, Burgan to Mary Jones 6-29-1879
Carrell, E. B. to Emley M. Poor 8-2-1872 (no return)
Carrell, Thomas to Anny Gillis 2-14-1889 (2-15-1889)
Carrell, William to Leaty Retherford 3-28-1869
Carter, Henry to Mary E. Weaver 2-3-1887 (2-4-1887)
Carter, John to Susan Jesse 4-17-1880
Carter, Malinda to Josiah Presly 1-9-1885 (no return)
Cartwright, William A. to Nancy A. Thompson 8-21-1874
Cary, Thomas J. to Margaret O. Sparks 9-29-1877 (9-30-1877)
Casey, Daniel to Margret Siler 5-6-1875
Cassell, Wm. N. to Catharine Meyers 3-17-1874 (no return)
Cassid, Wm. F. to Maulis? Owens 2-9-1877
Causby, Hiam to Sarah A. Suthern 5-13-1871 (5-16-1871)
Causby, Wm. jr. to Mary Brooks 12-26-1878 (12-27-1878)
Cavin, M. F. to Molley Cadle 9-27-1887 (no return)
Cawood, D. A. to Mary Wyman 1-6-1881
Cawood, I. J. to Esther Sharp 7-26-1880
Cawood, J. C. to M. J. Yokum 2-2-1885 (2-8-1885)
Cawood, John to Eliza Yoakum 7-20-1880 (8-1-1880)
Cawood, John to Mary Jane Johnson 7-22-1870 (7-24-1870)
Cawood, Stephen H. to Louiza A. Rogers 5-19-1869
Cawood, Stephen to Mary Jane Moss 3-18-1872 (3-21-1872)
Chadwell, A. J. to Corney G. Rutledge 4-29-1876 (4-30-1876)
Chadwell, A. J. to H. L. Bowman 12-7-1880 (no return)
Chadwell, Alexander to Caroline Campbell 9-30-1874 (10-4-1874)
Chadwell, Alexander to Elizabeth Crabtree 9-2-1869 (9-9-1869)
Chadwell, E. C. to China Chadwell 5-13-1884 (5-18-1884)
Chadwell, Ewin to Jennie Serber 12-18-1889 (12-19-1889)
Chadwell, G.? F. to Lucinda Cockram 12-31-1879
Chadwell, Galvin to A. E. Jackson 12-15-1878
Chadwell, Harmon to Malinda Brown 12-24-1869 (12-26-1869)
Chadwell, Henry to Ellin Channon 2-17-1881
Chadwell, Isaac to Mary C. Parks 11-18-1882 (no return)
Chadwell, James F. to Martha Estes 3-4-1888
Chadwell, Pleasant M. to Martha E. Brooks 11-24-1870
Chadwell, Thomas to Vina Webb 2-18-1887 (2-20-1887)
Chadwell, William to Alice Thomas 2-26-1885 (2-27-1885)
Chadwell, Wm. T. to Mary J. Parker 1-19-1879
Chadwick, Lewis to Provey Smith 12-24-1874
Chadwick, Tandy to Anjaline Hayes 2-23-1877 (2-26-1877)
Chance, L. C. to Ollie Seal 6-9-1884 (6-22-1884)
Chapbell, A. A. to Carnie May Rose 12-4-1890
Cheatham, Benjamin F. to Dicey M. Harrell 2-8-1869 (no return)
Cheatham, J. D. to Cora B. Shipley 10-6-1888
Cheatham, Thos. N. to Margret Keck 12-18-1883 (no return)
Cheatham, Tobi to Ama Lenar 3-28-1885 (no return)
Cheatham, W. L. to Jennie Steward 2-14-1889 (2-23-1889)
Cheek, George W. to Amanda Sandifer 9-24-1883 (no return)
Cheek, J. K. to Jane Hopson 10-8-1883
Cheek, Jame to Mary Marsh 12-12-1880
Cheek, Robert to Elizabeth Petree 8-14-1872 (no return)
Cheetham, Fate to Eliza Guarling? 4-14-1873 (no return)
Chick, James M. to Nancy Cox 1-3-1870 (1-9-1870)
Christian, William to Ollie Hurst 9-16-1886 (no return)
Christian, Wm. to Eliza Duncan 12-18-1890 (12-21-1890)
Chumbley, James F. to Sally B. Cline 2-18-1880 (2-19-1880)
Chumbly, John to Eliza Gruthan 2-12-1869 (2-14-1869)
Chumbly, William H. to Emily Runions 9-11-1869 (9-12-1869)
Chumley, James F. to Mary Phillips 10-9-1869 (10-10-1869)
Cinniman, Henry to Janey Rider 8-10-1882 (8-13-1882)
Claiborn, B. F. to R. H. Rogers 10-29-1874
Claiborne, B. F. to R. C. Rogers 10-29-1874 (no return)
Clamant, Wm. F. to Louisa J. Rowe 9-2-1878 (9-3-1878)
Clark, Aaron to Sallie Noe 6-18-1870 (6-19-1870)

Clark, Hen. to Lucy McAfee 2-13-1885
Clark, John to Sarah Elrod 11-6-1878 (1-2-1879)
Clark, Joseph C. to Sarah J. Carr 4-12-1875 (4-29-1875)
Clark, William R. to Matilda Emeline Poor 4-11-1888 (no return)
Clarkson, Albert to Margret Crutchfield 11-5-1874 (no return)
Clarkston, Wm. to Liza Jane Manning 8-17-1888 (8-19-1888)
Clarxtin, John to Julia Longworth 5-29-1882 (6-4-1882)
Clary, J. T. to Mary Smith 2-11-1877
Clary, John to J. J. Gibbs 11-19-1885
Claud, Andy to Matilda Woodson 8-21-1873
Clause, J. M. to Nancy J. Mansey 5-15-1875
Clauson, Thomas J. to Sarah M. Cain 8-4-1869 (8-5-1869)
Clawson, James to Sarah A. Ausmus 11-20-1877
Clay, Wm. J. to Melvina Meyers 11-9-1877 (no return)
Cleaveland, John A. to Amanda Carroll 10-1-1875 (10-20-1875)
Clement, John J. to Eliza Collins 7-18-1872 (7-21-1872)
Clement, Nathan C. to Louisa Davis 12-12-1874 (1-14-1875)
Cline, C. R. to M. A. Pressnell 12-30-1889 (1-2-1890)
Cline, James to Mary Carman 5-29-1889 (no return)
Cline, Jefferson to Luda Marcomb 7-2-1882
Cline, R. S. to Sarah Minton 12-29-1886 (12-30-1886)
Cline, R. T. to S. S. O. Goin 7-10-1886 (7-24-1886)
Cloud, A. M. to Mary A. Johnson 6-3-1875
Cloud, Fredrick to Jane Hurst 2-6-1869 (2-10-1869) B
Cloud, H. P. to Matilda Graham 1-8-1880? (1-8-1881)
Cloud, John to Tarica Robinson 1-19-1882
Cloud, Jordan to Matilda Day 3-6-1874 (3-7-1874)
Cloud, Morgan to Sarah Murry 2-8-1879 (2-9-1879)
Cloud, W. H. to Salley Richardson 9-13-1887 (9-14-1887)
Clouse, Alexander to Martha Hopkins 1-21-1883 (2-4-1883)
Cockerell, Robt. L. to Maggie Terrell 2-1-1891
Cockrum, A. H. to Delila Mayes 10-24-1883 (10-28-1883)
Coffee, George to Martha Cain 2-20-1871 (2-23-1871)
Cole, Campbell to Liddy A. Loop 1-18-1873 (1-23-1873)
Cole, Isaac R. to S. Gast 7-19-1879 (7-2?-1879)
Cole, John to N. E. Pillian 2-4-1881 (no return)
Cole, John to Pulina? Loosen? 1-19-1878
Cole, Josiah to Hesther A. Harman 10-1-1879 (10-2-1879)
Cole, Josiah to Nancy E. Painter 1-20-1872 (1-21-1872)
Cole, Wm. H. to Margaretth Jones 3-5-1883 (no return)
Cole, Wm. M. to M. J. Loope 6-19-1873
Cole, Wm. M. to Martha Lynes 9-8-1888 (9-16-1888)
Coleman, Geo. to Susan Hughes 8-2-1882
Coleman, Geo. to Susey Hughes 12-5-1887
Colens, Wm. S. to Margrett Owens 11-16-1878
Colinsworth, Wm. J. to China Cottrell 12-25-1881
Collett, G. N. to Mary Kincaid 7-26-1887 (8-14-1887)
Collingsworth, Wm. to Jane Baley 2-5-1885
Collins, Anderson to Martha Allen 2-8-1869 (2-22-1869)
Collins, Andrew N. to Martha E. Collins 3-17-1869 (3-18-1869)
Collins, D. J. M. to Elizabeth Presley 8-4-1889
Collins, Eldredge to Elizabeth Biggs 6-8-1878
Collins, Eldridg to Elizabeth Biggs 6-8-1878 (no return)
Collins, Emanuel to Marry E. Devault 8-17-1881 (8-18-1881)
Collins, Emmanuel to Maria Zeaks 4-22-1871 (4-23-1871)
Collins, Garrett to Sarah Elizabeth Jennings 10-?-1872 (no return)
Collins, Henderson to Margret Biggs 11-28-1877 (no return)
Collins, Henry to Delila Shockley 9-8-1887
Collins, J. M. to Sarah M. Wilson 2-4-1878 (no return)
Collins, J. Vann? to Mary Ann Epperson 2-16-1870
Collins, James H. to Nancy M. Hipsher 10-13-1888 (10-14-1888)
Collins, James M. to Mary Doyle 3-10-1880 (3-11-1880)
Collins, James to Sarah Hendrickson 7-17-1881
Collins, Javun? to Nancy Lane 4-4-1887
Collins, Joel to Loucinda Collins 8-28-1882
Collins, John to Margrett Willis 11-7-1890 (no return)
Collins, Joseph Y. to Orlenie C. Denham 2-21-1882 (2-31?-1882)
Collins, Joshua M. to Jane Simmons 9-28-1872 (no return)
Collins, Noble to Loucinda Gibson 2-6-1878 (2-7-1878)
Collins, Obediah to Angeline Hipsher 2-29-1884 (3-1-1884)
Collins, Sterling to Lourena Collins 7-3-1880 (6?-29-1880)
Collins, Thomas to Rhoda Owens 3-26-1881
Collins, William H. to Rachel C. Keck 2-28-1887 (3-3-1887)
Collins, William S. to Nancy E. Collins 2-10-1882 (2-11-1882)
Collins, Wm. to Jane Raden 1-19-1871
Collinsworth, A. M. to Rachel Maples 10-6-1888 (no return)
Collinsworth, Abraham to Mollie Bailey 6-5-1889 (6-6-1889)
Collinsworth, George to Matailda Ausben 10-14-1880
Collinsworth, J. F. to Orlina Briant 12-23-1884
Collinsworth, John J. to Frances A. Corbin 9-25-1869 (9-26-1869)
Collinsworth, Thomas to Sarah Watson 12-23-1868 (12-25-1868)
Colson, John C. to Susan Catterell 5-12-1875 (5-13-1875)
Colson, Nelson to Martha D. Hoskins 1-28-1873 (no return)
Combs, Geo. to Alice Baker 6-15-1885
Combs, John to Marry Surber 11-24-1880 (no return)
Compliman, Wm. to Tisha Fuson 12-24-1890 (12-26-1890)
Conaray, James H. to Vina E. Fultz 6-8-1889 (6-9-1889)

Conatser, Reuben to Mahala Farmer 5-13-1871
Condry, James H. to R. H. Murrisson 3-23-1878 (3-28-1878)
Cook, Allen to Lyddia Meyers 7-31-1885 (8-2-1885)
Cook, Claiborne to Martha A. Bolton 3-11-1878 (no return)
Cook, E. B. to M. J. Bolton 7-1-1889 (7-7-1889)
Cook, John D. to Mary Ann Estes 12-20-1883 (no return)
Cook, John to Loucinda Collins 6-21-1886 (6-25-1886)
Cook, Robert F. to Elizabeth R. Clouse 4-21-1882 (4-23-1882)
Cook, S. B. to Jane Thacker 2-16-1887 (2-17-1887)
Cook, Simon to George Williams 9-16-1890
Cook, William to Mary J. Martin 3-23-1877 (no return)
Cook, Wm. to Eliza M. Cunningham 7-15-1871 (7-16-1871)
Cooks, Rufus to Sarah Wilkenson 7-3-1884
Corban, A. C. to Sarah A. Breeding 10-16-1875 (10-17-1875)
Cosbey, James to Nancy J. Snaveley 12-13-1876 (no return)
Cosbey, John to Ingbo Hatfield 5-31-1878
Cosbey, Thomas to Nancy L. Southern 1-26-1869 (1-28-1869)
Cosby, David to Hanner Cosby 8-6-1883 (no return)
Cosby, G. W. to Mandy Whitaker 12-18-1884 (no return)
Cosby, W. P. to America Ellison 10-25-1890 (no return)
Cottrell, A. W. to M. M. Beyers 5-11-1878 (5-12-1878)
Cottrell, C. B. to Martha Kincaid 9-1-1874 (9-3-1874)
Cottrell, G. G. to Sarah Woolfenbarger 9-3-1881 (9-4-1881)
Cottrell, John S. to Lela R. Harbison 12-27-1884
Cottrell, S. E. to Mary J. Monday 9-18-1878
Cousley, Hiram to Rachel Hill 8-12-1876 (8-13-1876)
Cowan, James J. to Frances M. Clap? 11-20-1877
Cowan, William to Nancy Jane Cox 11-12-1868 (11-1?-1868)
Cox, George M. to Lucy J. Burchfield 8-13-1874
Cox, John to Martha Check 3-29-1871
Cox, Johnson to Eliza Spangler 11-23-1889 (11-24-1889)
Cox, Joseph W. to Mary C. McNeel 10-24-1871 (no return)
Cox, P. L. to Mary R. Mayes 12-24-1876 (12-25-1876)
Cox, T. G. to Caty J. Keck 1-8-1888
Cox, Thos. to Mary Mason 2-16-1889 (no return)
Cranshanul, Thomas W. to C. F. Shoumate 12-6-1879 (12-11-1879)
Crawford, John H. to Mabrey Crawford 11-30-1877 (no return)
Crawford, Samuel to Eliza Lambert 3-6-1876
Crawford, Samuel to Martha Crawford 10-1-1870 (10-2-1871?)
Creger, George to Martha J. Laws 12-23-1868 (1-14-1869)
Crichfield, Prier? L. S. to Caroline Stanifer 2-10-1872 (2-15-1872)
Crockett, John M. to Alis V. Litterell 9-3-1877
Crockett, Scy to Elizabeth Colston 8-2-1882
Crofferd, John C. to C. D. Mayers 7-12-1880 (7-16-1880)
Crook, Bishop to M. J. Pearson 2-22-1872
Cross, Thomas to Charity Percival 7-29-1871 (7-30-1871)
Cross, H. to E. J. Shumate 9-14-1878
Croxdale, Isom to Nancy Jennings 12-24-1872 (12-25-1872)
Cruchfield, T. A. to E. J. Samford 11-5-1879 (11-27-1879)
Crutchfield, Amos to Louisa J. Ingleton 2-24-1872 (2-25-1872)
Crutchfield, James A. to Tempy Chadwick 9-3-1873 (9-4-1873)
Crutchfield, John T. to Margaret M. Mayes 12-23-1869
Crutchfield, John to Catherine Owens 8-11-1871 (8-12-1871)
Crutchfield, Thomas to Mary Chick 1-4-1869 (1-10-1869)
Cuningham, A. J. to Allice Crutchfield 4-18-1888 (no return)
Cuningham, C. L. to Ollie Sulfridge 11-7-1887 (11-10-1887)
Cuningham, John B. to Martha J. Whitacre 10-25-1878
Cunningham, Homer? to Betty Evans 8-26-1873 (8-28-1873)
Cunningham, J. B. to M. L. Whiteaker 10-24-1877 (no return)
Cunningham, J. F. to Mattie Musser 1-17-1891
Cunningham, James L. to Mary E. Jones 2-28-1870 (3-3-1870)
Cunningham, Jas. M. to Arminta Greer 7-14-1883 (no return)
Cunningham, Martin to Mary Ann Matilda Bolton 5-5-1877 (5-6-1877)
Cunningham, Wm. F. to Dora Davis 12-24-1887 (12-25-1887)
Cunningham, Wm. N. to Phebe Howerton 7-29-1874 (7-30-1874)
Cupp, George W. to Mariah E. Goin 1-24-1871 (1-27-1871)
Cupp, George W. to Mary E. Moyers 6-23-1877 (6-2-1877)
Cupp, J. N. to M. C. Moyers 7-19-1880 (7-22-1880)
Cupp, James to Fanney E. Snider 4-8-1887 (4-7?-188?)
Cupp, John to Sarah E. England 7-14-1874 (no return)
Cupp, Joseph to Catherine Ales 12-10-1870 (12-11-1870)
Cupp, Maynard to C. E. Robinson 2-1-1887 (2-3-1887)
Cupp, Nathan P. to S. A. Tague 4-17-1884 (4-18-1884)
Cupp, Prier to Sarah E. Smith 1-13-1891 (1-18-1891)
Cupp, Tennessee C. to Ellen F. Ford 4-10-1872 (4-14-1872)
Cupp, Valentine to Elizabeth Jane Ford 10-30-1885 (11-1-1885)
Dalton, Isaac H. to Eliza Littrell 10-25-1881 (10-30-1881)
Dandridge, Solomon to Lovey Smith 3-31-1890 (no return) B
Daniel, G. W. to Luesa Lambert 6-22-1888 (6-24-1888)
Daniel, James C. to Eliza Causbey 3-30-1888
Daniel, Robert to Mary J. Hatfield 2-26-1872
Daniel, W. M. to Elisabeth Green 11-18-1890 (no return)
Daniel, Wm. J. to Louisa J. Poor 11-14-1873 (11-15-1873)
Daniel, Wm. to Mary L. Shelton 12-6-1890 (no return)
Dannel, Washington to Mary Poor 10-6-1884 (10-12-1884)
Dantton?, John to Lucey Sandifer 2-18-1882 (no return)
Darit?, Henry to Francis Longar 3-23-1878

Darris, King to Harriet Lean Weaver 6-18-1876
Daulton, H. P. to Sarah E. Waller 4-12-1888 (4-15-1888)
Davidson, Anderson to Eliza Jones 8-29-1879
Davidson, Wm. to Margret Smith 3-16-1880 (3-27-1880)
Davis, Bradford to Luticia Ann Brown 4-19-1869
Davis, F. M. to Bell Burch 12-30-1889 (1-1-1890)
Davis, Isaieh to Margaret Bray 6-29-1872 (6-30-1872)
Davis, J. E. to Margaret Fox 1-8-1888? (1-10-1889)
Davis, J. H. to Lamsa Crutchfield 4-20-1872 (4-21-1872)
Davis, J. H. to O. M. Pearson 7-27-1880 (8-8-1880)
Davis, J. S. to J. P. Peck 1-14-1878 (no return)
Davis, Joel C. to Mary Sanders 3-22-1871
Davis, John C. to Mary E. A. Huster 6-10-1889 (6-11-1889)
Davis, John F. to Cornelia A. Cook 3-27-1869 (3-29-1869)
Davis, John J. to S. L. Johnson 2-16-1884 (2-18-1884)
Davis, John to F. C. Turner 12-11-1880
Davis, L. T. to Amanda Alexander 8-28-1886 (no return)
Davis, Mart to Jance? Leabow? 7-13-1888 (7-14-1888)
Davis, Pror to Sarah Realey 10-26-1880 (no return)
Davis, Richard to Souzanah Bryant 3-24-1871
Davis, S. D. to Sarah J. Ainslow? 4-29-1890
Davis, Sterling N. to Nervesta A. Harrell 2-19-1876 (2-20-1876)
Davis, Sterling to Ida Rosson 2-7-1887 (2-13-1887)
Davis, Thomas J. to Nancy A. Shoemate 4-18-1882 (no return)
Davis, Thos. J. to Nancy A. Shoemate 4-16-1882
Davis, Wm. E. C. to Martha J. Lawson 10-13-1877 (no return)
Davis, Wm. H. to Milley A. Sowder 1-30-1879
Davy, William to N. A. Robinson 1-6-1882 (no return)
Davy, Wm. J. to M. P. Neeley 8-?-1880 (no return)
Dawken, Harvy to Jane Brown 6-28-1879
Day, Burton to Perylee Sharp 8-8-1875
Day, Charles to Melvina Cloud 12-27-1872
Day, Frank to Elizabeth E. (Mrs.) Brooks 7-11-1881 (no return)
Day, Gilbert to Phebe Cloud 8-29-1874 (8-30-1874) B
Day, J. M. to Elizabeth Neeley 8-11-1880 (8-12-1880)
Day, W. P. to Sarah J. Sands 11-23-1889 (11-24-1889)
Day, Wiley to Mary Widner 2-21-1890 (2-23-1890)
Day, William T. to Sarah Greer 12-17-1873 (12-18-1874)
Day, Wm. A. to Hattie C. Ritchie 12-12-1888
Day, Wm. F. to S. A. Harman 5-1-1885 (5-3-1885)
Day, Wm. M. to Rosie Farmer 6-21-1887
Dean, Henderson to Surrellay J. Brooks 2-1-1878
Dean, William to Rachal Cole 1-19-1882
Dean, Wm. Prior to Sarilda Brooks 10-20-1888 (10-24-1888)
Deatherage, G. B. to Mary Tallian 3-2-1879
Deaton, I. L. to Rhoda Morrisson 11-30-1886 (2-22-1887)
Debusk, Campbell to Eliza E. Thomas 1-26-1882
Debusk, Jno? to Betty Drummon 9-7-1889 (6?-8-1889)
Debusk, T. J. J. to Salley C. Harmon 11-2-1886 (11-7-1886)
Deen, Henly R. to Malisey a. Lauson 9-25-1878 (no return)
Demarcus, F. E. to May Hodges 9-2-1886 (9-4-1886)
Demarcus, J. to America Hooks 1-22-1887 (1-23-1887)
Denham, James D. to Clara Browning 10-11-1871 (10-12-1871)
Denny, Wm. to Malind Bayley 8-22-1880 (8-23-1880)
Dickinson, John P. A. to Carrie Dishman 6-12-1877
Dingus, Rolley to Martha Ann Lambert 4-23-1882 (no return)
Disney, D. E. to H. E. Hart 9-?-1881
Dizman?, Eli to Mary Evans 8-1-1872
Dobbs, James to Sarah Elizabeth Ales 9-28-1869
Dobbs, William to Adaline Cook 2-17-1869 (2-21-1869)
Dobson, H. M. to Orlena Carr 2-21-1887 (3-2-1887)
Dodson, Anderson to Eady Smalls 2-13-1869 B
Dooley, Jacob to Margaret Edens? 11-6-1888
Dooley, William A. to Sarah F. Longworth 2-27-1869 (3-4-1869)
Dotson, Wm. M. to L. O. West 2-24-1883
Doyel, Wm. to Sarah Sparks 10-13-1871 (10-15-1871)
Doyl, J. W. to Loucinda Burchfield 10-25-1884 (no return)
Doyl, W. T. to Minda Medlock 1-17-1876 (8-17-1876)
Doyle, John to Sarah E. Pike 6-30-1874 (7-1-1874)
Drommons, A.B. to Sarah S. Lynch 11-12-1882 (11-16-1882)
Drummons, A. B. to Eliza Mink 9-30-1875
Drummons, Marion M. to E. E. Thompson 2-10-1886
Drummons, Tandy J. to T. J. Treece 2-1-1886
Drummons, Wm. A. to Sibby Ford 6-5-1871
Duff, Andrew to Catharine Ledington 5-5-1888
Duncan, A. J. to Emely M. Carroll 11-18-1874 (11-22-1874)
Duncan, B. F. to Harrett M. Mathis 12-23-1874
Duncan, James M. to Martha Macline 4-8-1881
Duncan, John to M. C. Baldwin 11-21-1882 (11-22-1882)
Duncan, Samson to Syrrener J. Gilbert 10-18-1874 (no return)
Duncan, Wm. H. to Rebecca J. Ferguson 3-29-1876
Duncan, Wm. H. to Sarey J. Brooks 5-6-1871
Dunmore, Preston to Ellen T. Wells 1-14-1878 (1-15-1878)
Dunn, Henry A. jr. to Rebeck J. Hill 2-6-1880 (2-11-1880)
Dunn, Joseph to Salley Morgan 3-11-1890
Dunn, Joseph to Sarah A. Hopper 2-7-1878
Dunsmore, M. to Emeline Cook 2-23-1880 (3-7-1880)

Dunsmore, Nathan to Catharine G. Stone 9-21-1886 (9-23-1886)
Dunsmore, T. N. to Mollie Payne 1-16-1890 (1-25-1890)
Dunsmore, W. L. to Mary E. Thomas 7-28-1884 (7-30-1884)
Dykes, V. A. to Carna Greer 9-6-1888 (no return)
Dyre, C. P. L. to Sarah M. Lewis 11-11-1887 (11-20-1887)
Eagle, James to Allie Collins 5-28-1886 (5-29-1886)
Ealy, Benjamin to Nancy E. Parrot 5-4-1879
Ealy, Daniel to Lithy Willis 6-4-1880
Earl, D. C. to Eliza Snider 10-30-1882 (10-22-1882)
Earl, D. C. to Melley England 1-2-1877 (1-7-1877)
Earle, Perry to Mary Hix 5-5-1875
Earles, Nathaniel to Liddy Hicks 9-7-1871
Earles, William to Sarah J. Pratt 3-25-1885
Earley, Thos. to Martha J. Roe 11-29-1888
Earls, A. J. to Susan Snider 9-11-1880 (9-12-1880)
Earls, Pery to Cornelia Morgan 1-14-1882 (1-15-1882)
Earls, Thomas to S. C. Newport 7-5-1882 (7-17-1882)
Earls, Wm. J. to Eliza Jennings 4-8-1889
Earls, Wm. to Emiline Collins 11-22-1890
Earls, Wm. to Linda Bullin 10-1-1887 (10-2-1887)
Easles, J. C. to Mary Ellisson 2-7-1884
Eason, Timothy to Margret Bazel 10-30-1878 (10-31-1878)
Eastes, John to Mary Jane Casey 5-10-1869 (5-13-1869)
Eastridge, E. D. to Ollie Cunningham 10-16-1888 (10-18-1888)
Eastridge, Geo. to Nancy J. Brook 10-2-1873 (10-5-1873)
Eastridge, George to Mary J. Brooks 10-2-1873 (10-5-1873)
Eastridge, I. S. P. to Mary Lucus 7-13-1887 (no return)
Eastridge, Pleasant to Elizabeth Lambert 3-23-1872 (3-24-1872)
Edds, Anderson to Melia Cloud 11-16-1880 (4-8-1880?)
Edds, Andy to Liza Cole 7-27-1887 (7-28-1887)
Edem, Hiram to Elizabeth McVay 11-19-1883 (11-20-1883)
Edens, Wm. to Clementine McVay 3-3-1884 (3-6-1884)
Edington, F. M. to Mary Bell Lambert 10-27-1887 (no return)
Edmondson, R. L. to Mary Goin 11-13-1889 (11-14-1889)
Edmondson, W. T. to M. J. Seal 7-1-1889 (7-4-1889)
Edmonson, D. C. to M. S. Lyons 6-22-1886 (6-24-1886)
Edmonson, George W. to Virginia Cole 6-14-1877 (no return)
Edmonson, W. L. to Catherine Goins 1-1-1884
Edward, R. M. to Clarra A. Huffaker 2-18-1879 (no return)
Edwards, Houston to Nancy A. Keck 6-4-1889 (6-8-1889)
Edwards, Jefferson D. to Charloty J. Goin 12-9-1879
Edwards, Jefferson to Jane Ausmus 1-3-1890 (1-23-1890)
Edwards, Jeptha to Lucynda Haley 1-27-1883 (1-28-1883)
Edwards, John to Lidey Key 12-17-1878
Edwards, Joseph H. to Sarah Guy 2-7-1887 (2-9-1887)
Edwards, Leonadus to Salyann Leasley 8-26-1878 (9-19-1878)
Edwards, Mantain to Anna Goin 1-23-1875
Edwards, Wm. P. to Nancy Beesom 10-11-1872 (10-13-1872)
Eggers, G. W. to Rutha Hicks 3-20-1890
Eley, J. D. to S. A. Minter 3-26-1882
Elison, Bery to Adeline Edwards 4-26-1883 (4-27-1883)
Elison, Joseph to Ellen Dunn 5-18-1883 (5-24-1883)
Elison, Thomas to Elizabeth Hatfield 3-31-1881 (4-3-1881)
Ellis, J. G. to Emley Cawood 6-14-1880 (6-17-1880)
Ellis, J. L. to L. E. Bauman 3-15-1881 (3-17-1881)
Ellis, James L. to Runce? Gibson 7-23-1885
Ellis, O. H. to Millie M. Cawood 3-1-1883
Ellis, Solimon to Sarah E. Lambert 11-29-1877 (no return)
Ellison, A. L. to Rachel Edwards 9-14-1892 (9-16-1882)
Ellison, Bery to Malinda J. Taylor 3-5-1883 (3-6-1883)
Ellison, D. M. to Susan Edwards 11-21-1888 (11-22-1888)
Ellison, Irre? S. to Tlara? E. Lingar 6-23-1888 (no return)
Ellison, Jermiah to Eliza Sandifer 3-4-1872
Ellison, Joseph to Elizabeth Lambert 2-6-1880 (2-7-1880)
Ellison, Lilbourn W. to Mary Jane Snavely 3-17-1869 (no return)
Ellison, Thomas to Mary Elizabeth Kibert 7-8-1869 (7-15-1869)
Ellison, Thos. to Molley Remon 10-2-1886 (10-3-1886)
Ellison, Wm. H. to Mary M. Owens 8-24-1882 (8-25-1882)
Ellison, Wm. M. to Katie Ausmus 12-29-1885 (12-31-1885)
Ely, B. F. to Nancy M. Carman 2-20-1877 (2-22-1877)
Ely, Isaac to Annah C. Hammock 11-30-1877 B?
Ely, J. D. to Maggie A. Shell 4-21-1888 (4-22-1888)
Ely, John to Rebecca Eads 5-17-1870 (5-18-1870)
Ely, Joseph Marion to Elizabeth Jane Hartgroves 4-21-1869 (no return)
Ely, Morris to Eliza Carr 5-26-1873 (6-1-1873)
Ely, T. J. to Nancy M. Billingsley 1-27-1876 (1-30-1876)
Ely, W. P. to Harriet Sharp 12-22-1884
Elye, James M. to Lucy E. Hansard 1-11-1869 (1-12-1869)
England, Benj. D. to Martha J. Collins 3-14-1888
England, F. H. to Sterling Houston 9-25-1880 (8?-25-1880)
England, Hire to Surelda Cox 12-20-1877
England, Isaac R. to Martha A. Fortner 11-6-1872 (11-7-1872)
England, James to Mary J. Whitaker 11-10-1880 (no return)
England, John to Margret Gibbs 12-18-1870 (12-20-1870)
England, Joseph to Sarah Conner 1-6-1880
England, Lafayett to Rhoda M. Whitaker 11-22-1883 (11-23-1883)
England, R. F. to Mary Bell Haynes 9-7-1886 (9-9-1886)

England, Samuel H. to Margaret Johnson 8-27-1873 (8-28-1873)
England, Thomas to Mary Cox 12-23-1878 (3-14-1879)
England, Thomas to Nancy Carrell 11-7-1882 (no return)
England, Valentine to Rhoda E. Ford 9-18-1885 (9-22-1885)
England, William Mc. to Sarah A. Simmons 12-29-1869 (1-2-1870)
England, William to Fanney Carroll 7-21-1877 (no return)
England, William to Nancy Canell 7-17-1878 (no return)
England, Wm. to Elizabeth Brooks 9-30-1873
Epperson, Ancil to Margaret R. West 12-15-1888 (12-16-1888)
Epperson, George to Cornelia Hurst 3-24-1884
Epperson, John to Eliza Waagonar Fanny Lee 3-3-1880 (3-7-1880)
Epperson, Ruben to Fannie Hurst 1-1-1883 (1-7-1883)
Epperson, Wm. to Sarah Jane Hurst 12-13-1888 (12-18-1888)
Eppes, Charles to A. R. Gibeson 3-26-1879 (3-27-1879)
Esessary, Elbert S. to Martha J. Hurst 10-7-1869
Essary, Columbus to Docia Henderson 12-23-1886 (12-24-1886)
Essary, D. A. to Lizzy Coatney 11-1-1888
Essary, E. H. to Dora Robinson 12-31-1885
Essary, G. H. to China A. McCray 10-27-1885 (10-28-1885)
Essary, George W. to Sarah Hurgton? 2-19-1873 (2-20-1873)
Essary, Joseph F. to Elizabeth McIfee 2-17-1879 (2-20-1879)
Essary, Robert to Ellen Welsh 12-24-1890 (12-25-1890)
Essary, T. A. to Sa Pain 11-?-1878 (11-23-1878)
Essary, T. E. to Fanney Bulcher 11-21-1888 (11-22-1888)
Essary, T. S. (Rev.) to M. E. Campbell 9-10-1885
Essary, Thomas J. to Matilda F. Lester 12-20-1882 (12-21-1882)
Essary, Wm. M. to Rhoda Hall 1-4-1888
Estep, James to Jane Jones 8-16-1884 (8-31-1884)
Estep, John T. to Minervia Clarkson 3-5-1890
Estep, John to Matilda Brown 4-24-1880 (4-25-1880)
Estep, Samuel to Matilda Nevels 9-26-1868 (10-1-1868)
Estepp, William to Josephine Brown 1-20-1877 (no return)
Estept, John to Nancy Edens 8-20-1886 (8-22-1886)
Estes, Fielding to Amanda Carmack 5-16-1885 (5-17-1885)
Estes, Joe to Sarah Hayes 1-24-1889
Estis, Wm. to Mary J. Osborn 4-10-1875 (no return)
Estridg, John to P. A. Mathus 10-18-1879
Estridge, Isaac to Sarah Bogal 10-1-1883 (no return)
Estridge, Isom to Sarah Jane Haynes 12-5-1868 (12-6-1868)
Estridge, Robert to Marth Lambert 9-19-1878
Evans, Andrew to Malinda Lions 12-?-1879 (12-23-1879)
Evans, Britton to Margarett Cloud 4-9-1882
Evans, D. L. to Mollie Jennings 1-1-1879
Evans, David to Angeline Buchanon 1-19-1871
Evans, J. B. to A. O. Epperson 8-7-1882
Evans, Jesse to Eliza Hurst 11-30-1870
Evans, John O. to Marticia McCrary 10-3-1870 (10-9-1870)
Evans, John to Martha McCany 4-30-1881 (5-7-1881)
Evans, Lafayett to Elizabeth Guinn 1-6-1883 (1-7-1883)
Evans, Samuel to Lowsanna P. Pearson 7-28-1887 (8-9-1887)
Evans, Silas W. to Maggie Lane 7-30-1875 (no return)
Ewing, Alfred to Marry Jones 10-10-1880 (10-14-1880)
Fane, Fidance to Mary J. Mayer 7-24-1880
Farer, Bartley to Rutha Chadwell 2-1-1879 (2-5-1879)
Farley, Henry C. to Elisabeth Casewell 9-27-1889 (10-1-1889)
Farmer, A. J. to Orlenia Niceley 4-6-1872 (4-11-1872)
Farmer, C. M. to M. C. M. Poor 10-8-1884 (10-12-1884)
Farmer, Hugh to Sally Robertson 12-28-1886 (12-30-1886)
Farmer, James P. to Allas Johnsonton 8-24-1878 (8-25-1878)
Farmer, John to Lary Williams 9-4-1880 (9-5-1880)
Farmer, William to Racheal Bray 11-30-1877 (no return)
Farmer, Wm. to Melvina Collins 6-29-1876 (7-2-1876)
Farrall?, Robert to Mary Standifer 11-6-1874 (11-15-1874)
Farris, William to Vesty Neal 10-16-1875 (10-17-1875)
Faulkner, William to Sarah E. Day 7-14-1874 (no return)
Fawhugh, Lewis to Sharlet Kinningham 4-8-1871 (4-25-1871)
Felps, Joseph to Vandelle Carr 3-8-1878 (no return)
Fergerson, Robert to Eliza Guinn 1-15-1883 (no return)
Fergerson, Wm. M. to Catherin E. Lynch 11-29-1882 (11-30-1882)
Ferrell, Joseph to Maggie Wytt 11-27-1884
Fields, Richard F. to Emely Eastus 12-20-1873 (12-21-1873)
Fields, Elbert H. to E. C. Sulfridg 9-2-1879
Fields, George to Martha J. Nance 5-1-1878 (no return)
Fields, Obediah to Charity M. England 2-21-1890 (2-23-1890)
Fields, Obediah to Elizabeth Lynch 4-11-1877 (4-14-1877)
Fields, Robt. to Gusly Lee Robertson 8-28-1888 (8-30-1888)
Fields, Wm. H. to Jane Rogers 1-31-1874
Finnel, Wesley to Rhoda Coward 1-11-1882
Fisher, Samuel to Susan Tutter 12-13-1890
Flaman, John W. to Alice Hopkins 8-28-1881
Fleacher, Thomas to Sarah J. Bray 6-14-1875
Fleeman, Joseph to Mary Luster 3-18-1871 (3-21-1871)
Fleming, Baley to Jemima Brewer 8-26-1869
Fletcher, Alferd to Elizabeth Harpp 11-16-1878
Fletcher, B. M. to Mary J. Ellison 6-14-1883 (6-17-1883)
Fletcher, David J. to Manerva T. Maney 8-8-1877 (8-12-1877)
Fletcher, William to Georgia Cowan 7-22-1887

Foard, A. L. to H. E. Minton 8-28-1879 (8-31-1879)
Foddis, Henry to Mary Eastridge 11-14-1888 (11-18-1888)
Ford, C. W. to N. A. McBee 7-25-1888 (7-29-1888)
Ford, G. C. to M. C. Russell 9-2-1880 (no return)
Ford, G. F. to Matilda Keck 3-26-1881 (3-31-1881)
Ford, G. W. to M. O. Drummons 12-10-1879 (12-23-1879)
Ford, Jamaes to Salley Robinson 1-11-1888 (1-12-1888)
Ford, James R. to Martha J. Carmon 8-9-1873 (8-14-1873)
Ford, P. L. to E. J. Ford 12-6-1880 (12-9-1880)
Ford, T. F. to Suda Edmonson 10-29-1890 (10-30-1890)
Ford, Wm. L. to Sarah E. Russell 12-3-1881 (12-4-1881)
Forgerson, James K. to Loweza E. Patterson 8-31-1870 (no return)
Forkner, Ellen to Marien Hickey 5-4-1885 (5-6-1885)
Fortner, J. T. to E. Bolinger 4-12-1890 (4-13-1890)
Fortner, S. E. to S. J. Erving 7-5-1888
Fortune, J.? P. to Morning Hill 11-14-1890 (no return)
Fosneeker, John to Joaner M. C. Jones 1-21-1876
Fourkner, T. F. to Eliza Brooks 6-5-1880 (6-6-1880)
Fox, Abraham to Mary Medowley 2-3-1871 (2-22-1871)
Fox, Madison to Arebell Roberts 5-7-1888
Fraley, C. H. to Nancy C. Suil 6-1-1888 (6-2-1888)
Francisco, A. J. to Sarah E. Goin 3-2-1872 (3-5?-1872)
Francisco, I. P. to Atarsiet? Moyers 11-24-1881 (no return)
Francisco, J. I. to Pheebee E. Keck 9-23-1871 (sol.)
Francisco, J. W. to Louisa M. Shoemate 11-7-1888 (11-8-1888)
Frazier, Joseph to C. M. Beeler 12-23-1889
Frazier, Samuel to Elizabeth Russesll 4-7-1877
Freeman, A. J. to C. J. Debusk 10-30-1879 (11-2-1879)
Freeman, M. D. to Mary A. Sharp 2-14-1872 (2-18-1872)
Freeman, R. C. to A. M. Pearce 1-12-1885
Freeman, William G. to Sarah Ely 1-9-1869 (1-10-1869)
Friar, Elisha to Nancy J. Large 8-1-1878 (no return)
Friar, S. S. to Mary Reece 7-2-1890 (7-27-1890)
Friar, W. .T. to Lucy J. Lambert 7-28-1877 (7-29-1877)
Frier, Isaac B. to Emly Curler 11-4-1877
Frierson?, I. T. to Susan Debusk 3-3-1884
Frith, William to Susan Rose 3-7-1877 (no return)
Frith, Wm. to Molley Hendricks 3-12-1887
Frost, Faris to Marinda Childers 8-5-1884
Fry, James R. to Mary M. Harrell 3-3-1876 (3-12-1876)
Fry, Wm. J. to Roda Hatfield 2-25-1878 (no return)
Fuegate, David to Sarah Colson 10-2-1871 (10-5-1871)
Fuetz, Damirel B. to Mandy E. (Mis) Abshier 6-24-1881
Fugate, David to Jane Pates 4-28-1879 (no return)
Fugate, James H. to Elvarena Smith 3-27-1869 (3-28-1869)
Fugate, R. E. to R. Suits? 3-1-1883
Fugate, Sterling to Lucinda Sturgeon 10-16-1869 (10-21-1869)
Fugate, Wm. to Martha J. Walker 5-27-1878 (no return)
Fulington, Carter to Mary Wright 11-5-1884 (11-6-1884)
Fulkerson, A. H. to Ida Fulkerson 3-8-1880
Fulkerson, Dal to Emaline Margraves 1-31-1882
Fulkerson, Dallis to Emley M. Graves 7-27-1878
Fulkerson, Daniel to Ada Evans 3-18-1871
Fulkerson, P. G. to Emma V. Glenn 7-14-1869
Fulkerson, P. G. to Jane E. Treece 12-20-1882 (12-25-1882)
Fulkerson, Thos. G. to Hallie Evans 10-9-1883 (10-10-1883)
Fulkerson, W. W. to Eleanor? Patterson? 9-17-1877
Fullington, J. J. to Rebecca J. Duncan 6-5-1886 (6-6-1886)
Fulton, James to S. J. Brooks 2-2-1880 (2-8-1880)
Fults, John to Catharine Absher 12-26-1874 (no return)
Fultz, A. e. to Ann P. Shaw 8-11-1883 (8-12-1883)
Fultz, Frederick to Eliza J. Ramsey 5-18-1871
Fultz, Fredrick to Elizabeth Owens 7-2-1877
Fultz, Jackson to Elizabeth Hurst 9-1-1884 (9-4-1884)
Fultz, James to Eliza Campbell 12-2-1881 (12-4-1881)
Fultz, James to Frances Poor 3-21-1883
Fultz, John to Jane Friar 4-16-1886 (4-18-1886)
Fultz, John to Martha Jane Fields 4-23-1877
Fultz, John to Martha M. Taylor 9-1-1873 (9-3-1873)
Fultz, Lewis to Margrett Whitaker 9-17-1880 (9-18-1880)
Fultz, John to Caroline Johnson 6-1-1888 (no return)
Fultz, Robert N. to Catharine North 7-30-1875
Fultz, Thos. to Priscilla Cheek 10-7-1889
Furgerson, J. J. to B. A. Fultz 11-28-1879
Furgerson, Joel to Allace Jones 11-26-1883 (11-28-1883)
Furgerson, John to Mary E. Essary 12-24-1873 (12-25-1873)
Furgerson, Thomas to Mary A. Cunningham 2-12-1880 (no return)
Furgurson, J. N. to Virginia Brashiers 8-18-1885 (8-20-1885)
Furguson, A. J. to B. N. Phillips 1-18-1886
Furguson, Thomas to Margret Owens 6-2-1877 (6-3-1877)
Fussel?, J. R. to Elizabeth Branscom 6-2-1882 (no return)
Gaffner, R. S. to Melvina Shap 11-29-1890 (11-30-1890)
Galden, John E. to Sarah F. Fleaman 5-12-1876 (5-14-1876)
Galden, John to Sela A. Gibson 1-19-1871
Garford, F. G. to M. J. Brown 1-29-1891 (no return)
Garland, Hiram to Elizabeth (Mis) Trent 7-23-1881 (7-24-1881)
Garlin, Samuel to Rutha Bussell 1-27-1881

Garrett, Britton to Susan Bowman 8-6-1869
Garrett, Charles D. to Sarah A. Conner? 9-5-1879 (9-7-1879)
Garrett, John A. to S. A. Doughty 8-26-1880
Gaylor, John to Malinda Pike 3-17-1871
George, Barnett to Amanda Houston 3-9-1869 (3-12-1869) B
Ghose, James to M. J. Stump 1-3-1880
Gib, Lewis to Cola Catharine Wilson 2-11-1891 (2-12-1891)
Gibbs, Andrew to Martha J. Maddox 11-8-1883 (no return)
Gibbs, F. A. to Manervey England 3-12-1869 (3-17-1869)
Gibbs, James B. to Perlina Hopper 10-3-1882
Gibbs, James M. to Elizabeth Jackson 5-5-1869 (no return)
Gibbs, Joseph M. to Elizabeth Jackson 5-24-1869
Gibbs, Z. to Mary Maddux 8-20-1885 (8-22-1885)
Gibbs?, David N. to Liza Ann Mattox 5-11-1872 (5-12-1872)
Gibson, David C. to Louisa Wester 2-14-1872 (2-15-1872)
Gibson, Dudley to Elisabeth Thomas 5-17-1889 (5-19-1889)
Gibson, Isreal C. to Winney Yoakum 3-14-1873
Gibson, James K. to Helan Sumate 6-19-1880 (6-20-1880)
Gibson, James to Mary Fugate 12-12-1871 (12-14-1871)
Gibson, John C. to Mary Justice 12-25-1889 (no return)
Gibson, Lee to Mary Hoskin 4-10-1875 (no return)
Gibson, William G. to Amanda S. Scott 9-24-1874
Gibson, Willis to Nsly? (Mrs.) Collins 6-2-1881 (6-3-1881)
Gibson, Wm. R. to Marry Ridings 6-22-1880 (6-23-1880)
Gibson, Yarnon to Mary Ann Persell 7-29-1882
Gilbert, A. E. to Sarah Overbay 7-26-1879 (7-29-1879)
Gilbert, Arch to Sally Lynch 12-27-1886 (12-28-1886)
Gilbert, James to Mary A. Welch? 10-20-1887 (10-30-1887)
Gilbert, Reuben to Sarah Luckadoo 6-8-1872
Gilbert, Thos. to Martha Lookeydos 5-31-1881 (6-4-1881)
Gilpin, Johna? to Elizabeth Fultz 5-19-1870 (5-22-1870)
Gipson, James to Martha West 6-20-1876 (6-25-1876)
Goforth, Jesse to Mary J. Vanbebber 11-1-1873 (11-2-1873)
Goin, A. B. to Narcis Killion 6-28-1880 (6-27?-1880)
Goin, Edward to Elvira Goin 11-21-1868 (11-22-1868) B
Goin, Elihugh to Rinda McDaniel 1-9-1881 (1-16-1881)
Goin, Gorg to Cela Odel 9-6-1878 (9-7-1878)
Goin, James C. to Cornelia A. Goforth 9-13-1873 (9-14-1873)
Goin, James P. to Elizabeth Dobbs 8-7-1877
Goin, Jasper to Racheal Hunter 11-16-1872 (11-17-1872)
Goin, John L. to Libbi Smith 12-19-1870 (12-22-1870)
Goin, P. L. to M. B. Carman 11-20-1878 (11-21-1878)
Goin, Pleasant to Harriet Soard 12-23-1876 (12-24-1876)
Goin, R. E. to G. F. Thomas 8-14-1885 (8-15-1885)
Goin, Sterling to Dicy M. Davis 9-24-1870 (9-26-1870)
Goin, W. W., esq. to Sarah C. McDavid 11-5-1885
Goin, Wm. H. to Louiza J. Mayes 11-23-1872 (11-28-1872)
Goin, Wm. J. to Susana C. Minton 5-9-1878
Goin, Wm. T. to Maggie Hendricks 4-7-1887 (4-8-1887)
Goin, Wm. W. to Manday J. Cowan 3-15-1873 (3-20-1873)
Golden, David C. to Ollie A. Cassada 9-22-1890 (9-25-1890)
Golden, Richard to Louiza Crousham 1-1-1869 (1-3-1869)
Golden, W. P. to Sary J. Right 4-6-1879
Golden, W. T., esq. to Marth L. McCauds 11-28-1885 (11-29-1885)
Good, J. L. to Dora Hopkins 10-22-1882
Goodrum, J. M. to Malinda Canon 3-8-1878 (3-10-1878)
Gorden, Wm. to Nancy Poor 5-6-1871 (5-7-1871)
Gordon, James to Mary Sutton 5-18-1889
Gordon, Robert to Lucy Lions 8-15-1879 (8-17-1879)
Gorleinee?, Lemuel to Martha Bussell 10-22-1886 (no return)
Gose, George to Sarah R. King 8-2-1875
Gose, John to M. A. Smith 11-30-1889 (12-1-1889)
Gose, Stephen to Susan Lawse 4-2-1888 (4-17-1888)
Gose?, James W. to R. H. Cole 1-27-1876
Graham, J. P. to Sarah A. Cawood 1-4-1871 (1-12-1871)
Graham, Jamie to Catherine Kile 1-31-1878 (no return)
Graham, John J. to Polley E. Ausmus 5-21-1890 (5-22-1890)
Graham, Lewis to Harriet Jackson 8-13-1874
Grant, Granville to Elizabeth K. Ford 10-23-1873 (no return)
Grantham, B. F. to V. A. Golden 4-18-1872 (4-21-1872)
Grantham, J. R. to M. M. Briant 5-19-1878
Granthum, B. F. to Va? Golden 4-18-1872 (no return)
Grasen, Cread to Lewsindey Tyne 12-25-1879
Gray, B. B. to Sarah Beramen 2-15-1884 (2-17-1884)
Gray, Elisha to Martha Jane Willis 8-7-1869 (8-15-1869)
Gray, G. B. to Virginia R. McManaway 1-17-1872 (1-21-1872)
Gray, Hop to Jennie Wyley 1-29-189? (1-30-1891)
Gray, James to Harret Green 6-4-1882
Gray, James to Mary Goin 11-2-1879
Gray, James to Sarah L. Blancet 8-26-1879 (8-28-1879)
Gray, John to Martha Overbey 10-22-1875 (10-23-1875)
Gray, John to Sofier Eastridge 4-22-1871
Gray, Nathan to Eliz. Coleman 1-29-1872 (2-2-1873?)
Gray, Nathan to Elizabeth Coalman 1-29-1872 (4-16-1873)
Gray, Price to Abney Curbey 2-12-1886 (2-15-1886)
Gray, Prince to Sarah Fortner 3-6-1883 (4-11-1883)
Gray, Wm. Y. to S. L. Soard 7-21-1879

Green, Amos to Martha Bray 10-8-1887 (10-9-1887)
Green, David B. to Nancy Jane Rowald 5-20-1878 (6-2-1878)
Green, G. W. to Martha Grilley 12-3-1881
Green, George to Susan Reimer 11-27-1880 (no return)
Green, John C. to Matilda Row 2-2-1880 (2-15-1880)
Greenlee, Alexander to Nancy J. Paul 5-5-1871 (5-7-1871)
Greenlee, Jesse M. to Martha Margarett Wells 5-22-1869 (5-23-1869)
Greer, David to America Whitaker 11-9-1888 (11-11-1888)
Greer, James P. to Mary Meyers 7-3-1874
Greer, John to Josephine Mullins 11-27-1885
Greer, Martin to Melvina Moyers 2-2-1876 (no return)
Greer, Preston to Sarah A. Bryant 12-12-1884 (12-14-1884)
Greer, Thomas to Sarah L. Briant 5-21-1874
Greer, Thos. G. to Sarah J. Johnson 3-9-1874 (no return)
Greer, Wm. to Nancy Hopson 8-19-1875 (8-18?-1875)
Gregory, Geo. A. to Susan M. Goodon 7-1-1885
Griffen, James to Mary H. Cline 10-24-1882 (10-26-1882)
Griffen, John R. to Matilda Brogan (Jones Ads?) 5-27-1881 (5-29-1881)
Griffen, Mat to Lo. Young 3-30-1880 (4-1-1880)
Griffin, Joseph to Mary Parry 1-15-1890
Grimes, James W. to Delilia J. Muncey 1-7-1869 (1-10-1869)
Grimes, James to Rutha Rolin 9-3-1888 (9-12-1888)
Grubb, Jasper to Nancy A. Monsey 4-12-1879 (no return)
Grubb, Milton M. to Rebecca A. Arwine 10-3-1870 (10-13-1870)
Grubb, S. F. to Elizabeth Wolf 11-3-1883 (11-8-1883)
Grubb, Samuel E. to R. E. Odle 9-27-1880 (9-30-1880)
Grubb, William to Susan Scaggs 4-18-1878
Grubb, Wm. to Elizabeth Williams 12-23-1881 (12-24-1881)
Guarlen, Ruben to Mary M. Marsh 8-23-1873 (8-24-1873)
Guin, John A. to A. Cox 4-1-1879 (4-13-1879)
Gulin, Richard to Nancy E. Wallace 4-20-1888
Gulley, B. F. to Barthina Kibert 12-23-1873 (12-24-1873)
Gulley, Wm. to Easter Cimesbery? 11-20-1886 (11-28-1886)
Gunn, Stephen to Crese Thomas 10-26-1882 (9?-26-1882)
Guthery, G. M. to Caroline M. Howard 2-23-1891 (2-24-1891)
Guy, John to Sarah M. Berry 1-15-1882
Guy, William H. to N. V. Simmons 9-8-1874 (no return)
Guy, Wm. W. to Annie Robertson 9-18-1888 (9-20-1888)
Guyn, William H. to Elizabeth Burk 2-11-1869
Gwin, Isaac to Martha Burk 10-18-1888
Hailey, Samuel to Mary Goin 11-11-1876 (11-12-1876)
Hale, William to Jane Ball 2-2-1877 (no return)
Halebraten, George to Luvernia Poor 7-22-1882 (7-25-1882)
Haley, John R. to M. H. Otey 9-25-1879
Halfield, Elihu to Elizabeth Deen 3-24-1885 (4-7-1885)
Hall, James F. to Marry (Mrs.) Tate 3-8-1881 (3-20-1881)
Hall, James to Nety Willmouth 4-13-1880
Hall, Jas. to Margret Johnson 11-15-1873
Hall, Jessee L. to Sarah A. Ausmus 11-12-1887 (11-17-1887)
Hall, John C. to Eliza F. Carter 9-19-1868
Hall, Thommas to Jane Bartlett 1-25-1881 (1-26-1881)
Hall, W. B. to Martha J. Harrigan 4-3-1871
Hall, Wm. A. to E. C. Harris 2-16-1879
Hambin, S. to N. J. Taylor 10-23-1890
Hamblen, F. M. to Polley Sawder 8-5-1875
Hamblin, John M. to Polly Sauner? 8-5-1875
Hamby, Joseph to Tulitha Widner 12-10-1880
Hamilton, J. B. to Maggie Snavely 2-26-1888
Hamlet, Jas. to Ollie Rayner 1-12-1885
Hamlet, Samuel to Medea J. Phillips 9-6-1886 (9-10-1886)
Hamlett, James E. to Manervia Moyers 12-28-1874 (12-31-1874)
Hamlin, John to Sopha Wilson 10-9-1884
Hamlin, Semblen to Rebaca Cook 11-4-1879
Hammock, I. J. to Manervy (Mrs.) Ellison 7-10-1881
Hamner, E. N. to Serena J. Williams 1-26-1887 (1-27-1887)
Hamock, A. J. to L. J. Rose 3-5-1885 (3-8-1885)
Hampton?, Samuel to Elizabeth Napper 6-7-1880 (6-10-1880)
Hanlin, F. O. to L. E. Lisk 12-23-1880 (12-26-1880)
Hanrey, Peter to Manervy Rich 8-4-1880 (no return)
Hansard, S. F. to Ninnie Wyley 12-29-1885 (12-30-1885)
Hansard, S. F. to Numie? Wryly 12-29-1885 (12-30-1885)
Hansard, Wm. R. to Marry Harman 4-2-1881 (4-20-1881)
Hansard, Wm. R. to Orlena C. Yodon 2-25-1886
Hansord, Abner C. to Sarah Short 12-25-1872 (12-29-1872)
Hansord, Peter to Nancy Lester 10-8-1873
Hansward, Isaac J. to Louisa C. Gipson 7-23-1870 (7-24-1870)
Hargraves, James to Sarah Cunningham 8-19-1877 (8-20-1877)
Hargraves, John F. to Susan Miller 12-2-1879
Hargraves, Robert to G. W. Ferbort? 7-11-1878
Haris, J. H. to Sarah J. Sawyers 1-2-1879
Harison, George W. to Hulda E. Waric 6-6-1883 (6-7-1883)
Harmon, J. L. to M. A. Dunn 3-12-1890 (4-17-1890)
Harmon, James H. to Frances E. Travies 3-3-1884 (3-6-1884)
Harmon, L. G. to Ida R. Roop 7-2-1884
Harp, L. S. to Susan F. Peace 7-4-1880
Harp, Levi to M. J. Marsee 5-10-1882 (no return)
Harp, Nelson to Sarah M. Chumley 9-20-1872 (9-22-1872)

Harpe, Levi to Nancy J. Morser? 5-10-1882
Harper, Azariah to Nancy Ann Stansberry 6-22-1874
Harper, John S.? to Mary Blancett 1-24-1882 (1-26-1882)
Harper, Louis B. to L. B. Carter 5-31-1883
Harper, T. B. to Liza McDaniel 11-25-1882 (no return)
Harper, William N. to Sarah Lane 6-20-1876 (6-21-1876)
Harper, William to Mary C. Stansberry 5-7-1874
Harrel, William P. to Mary C. Ritter 3-16-1872 (3-27-1872)
Harrell, D. H. to Mary C. West 8-7-1883 (8-9-1883)
Harrell, D. H. to Mary M. Hurst 2-22-1890
Harrell, D. H. to Thursa A. Janeway 11-4-1871 (11-5-1871)
Harrell, Floid to Gelana A. Tate 8-22-1881 (8-26-1881)
Harrell, Ham to Delce Nunn 6-15-1878 (6-16-1878)
Harrell, Harrie? to Delie Neems? 6-15-1878 (no return)
Harrell, J. B. to Mary Jane Roark 4-13-1889
Harrell, J. S. to Sallie D. Hodges 8-26-1886 (8-27-1886)
Harrell, J. S. to Tina Breeding 8-31-1883 (9-2-1883)
Harrell, James E. to Persiller Harrell 12-9-1882 (12-24-1882)
Harrell, James L. to Oley Moyers 2-1-1873 (2-2-1873)
Harrell, John J. to Martha Brooks 1-17-1872 (1-19-1872)
Harrell, N. J. to Mary C. Hodges 8-12-1890 (8-23-1890)
Harrell, Richard to Maggie D. Fulton 6-7-1879 (6-8-1879)
Harrell, Thomas to Martha Hurst 7-?-1883? (7-26-1883)
Harrell, W. D. to Nancy J. Herrell 1-6-1888
Harrell, Wm. D. to Siller West 11-22-1878 (11-23-1878)
Harris, Araham (Abraham?) to Mary C. Blancett 8-23-1881 (8-25-1881)
Harris, Madison M. to Louisa Cattrell 7-4-1871
Harrison, John to Nancy Tinnell 8-3-1887 (8-7-1887)
Harrison, Sheldon E. to Mary E. Cunningham 1-31-1870 (2-3-1870)
Hart, Elbert to Martha G. Williams 10-17-1871
Haskins, James M. to Manda Brooks 9-21-1886 (9-23-1886)
Haskins, R. F. to K. J. Sewsang 9-7-1889? (9-18-1879)
Hatfied?, Riley to Mimey Lawsen 10-3-1870 (10-9-1870)
Hatfield, Alvis to S. L. Pratt 2-16-1882 (no return)
Hatfield, Burel to Nancy J. Cole 6-13-1878 (no return)
Hatfield, Cephus to Lucy Bussell 11-23-1889 (11-24-1889)
Hatfield, Elihu to Elizabeth Deen 4-7-1885 (no return)
Hatfield, G. B. to Francy Price 11-19-1886 (11-20-1886)
Hatfield, G. W. to Emolin Shuler 2-19-1879 (no return)
Hatfield, G. W. to Sarah J. Frier 3-?-1879 (3-13-1879)
Hatfield, James to Elizabeth Woolf 12-16-1881 (12-28-1881)
Hatfield, James to Jane Northern 8-11-1875 (8-12-1875)
Hatfield, John to Martha Hatfield 2-29-1884
Hatfield, Moses to Emaline Shulan 3-6-1882 (3-7-1882)
Hatfield, Wm. H. to Cissy Marsee 3-12-1882
Hatfield, Wm. L. to Mary Jane Hayes 4-15-1871 (4-16-1871)
Hatfield, Wm. P. to Jane Longworth 8-11-1870 (8-13-1870)
Hatfields, Wm. to Susan Fields 12-10-1881 (12-11-1882?)
Hawskins, Thomas H. to Nancy J. Arnet 5-1-1871
Hayens, D. M. to M. J. Sharp 11-6-1878 (11-14-1878)
Hayes, James H. to Matilda E. Fish 10-5-1869
Hayes, James to Quillin ----- 10-22-1886 (10-24-1886)
Haynes, John to Susan Davis 4-19-1884 (4-4?-1884)
Hayse, C. W. to Mary Row 5-7-1888 (5-27-1888)
Hayslwood, B. F. to Margret Luster 9-17-1870 (9-18-1870)
Hazelwood, Daniel to Mary A. Crabtree 7-12-1873 (7-13-1873)
Hazelwood, Lewis to Fannie Bruster 5-26-1883
Heath, G. W. to S. E. (Miss) Keck 2-27-1890 (3-2-1890)
Heath, J. L. to L. B. Gray 2-24-1887
Heck, William to Nancy J. Bussell 11-14-1888 (11-18-1888)
Helms, F. B. to Nevesta Baker 11-9-1875 (no return)
Hembree, John M. to Corline King 10-14-1883
Hemphill, Andrew Mc. to America E. Hembree 8-17-1869
Henderson, Calvin A. to Manerva E. Reed 2-25-1871 (2-26-1871)
Henderson, Dock to Maggie Hurst 12-27-1886
Henderson, Riley to Adaline Hatfield 12-17-1880 (no return)
Hendrickson, E. M. to Alis Davis 1-23-1877 (2-1-1877)
Heninger, M. E. to M. M. Sanders 4-18-1882 (4-20-1882)
Henry, Andrew to Emaline Smith 10-9-1877 (10-11-1877)
Henry, W. F. to Montana Allen 12-25-1888
Henry, William to Louisa Simmons 3-9-1878
Hensley, James to Louisa Howard 5-10-1890 (5-11-1890)
Hensley, Jessey to Martha Robert 11-14-1874 (no return)
Herd, Eldridg to Polley A. Harris 3-27-1881
Herrell, George to Mary Carter 10-9-1880 (no return)
Hickey, Marien to Ellen Forkner 5-4-1885 (5-6-1885)
Hickey, Thomas J. to Rachal Goin 1-8-1881
Hickman, Andrew to Sarah Cadle 2-18-1883
Hickman, G. W. to Mary Phillips 5-16-1887 (5-19-1887)
Hicks, B. F. to Manervia Goin 8-18-1877
Hicks, H. M. to Nelley Rol 11-24-1890 (no return)
Hicks, John to Mary Hammons 4-18-1888
Hicks, John to Susan Lumpkins 4-27-1888
Hicks, Thomas to Martha Ann Gibbs 9-28-1869 (9-30-1869)
Hicman, J. A. J. to Susan Hall 11-17-1884 (11-18-1884)
Hill, Elijah to Sarah Catharine Bruce 12-19-1868 (12-24-1868)
Hill, F. H. to Lizzie Neel 10-29-1877 (11-1-1877)

Hill, Finley to Mary Newby 8-2-1882
Hill, G. C. to Mina Green 7-10-1890
Hill, G. W. to Sarah Brooks 6-?-1882
Hill, Henry to Vicey Hawl 9-6-1870
Hill, Hiram to Lucy Lambert 5-31-1888 (6-2-1888)
Hill, Hiram to Nancy Sandifer 12-29-1875 (no return)
Hill, Hugh to Aggie Kiltz 11-20-1872 (11-21-1872)
Hill, I. N. to L. J. Baker 10-24-1880 (10-30-1880)
Hill, Jackson to Lizzy Steel 8-25-1888
Hill, James W. to Malinda Daniel 7-18-1873 (7-20-1873)
Hill, John to Elizabeth Calton 10-8-1881
Hill, John to Martha M. Brooks 11-21-1873 (no return)
Hill, M. E. to Wm. S. Bentley 9-11-1889
Hill, Merril to Cornelia Ann Needham 11-25-1872 (12-3-1872)
Hill, T. T. to Mariah Treece 12-11-1883 (no return)
Hill, W. W. to Sarah E. Southern 12-14-1876
Hill, William J. to Elizabeth Pace 7-19-1869 (no return)
Hill, William R. to Jane Jones 1-6-1877
Hipsher, Henry to Judy Easley 2-9-1870 (2-13-1870) B
Hipsher, W. C. to Matilda Barnard 7-25-1887 (no return)
Hitaker, Wm. R. to Delila Grelly 12-2-1881
Hix, John to Hariet Smith 2-13-1878 (no return)
Hix, Joshua F. to Mary Carrell 8-4-1873
Hix, Wm. H. to Martha Goin 8-3-1877
Hixen, J. D. to Sarah L. Blanset 8-31-1887
Hock, Jesse J. to Sarah L. Shipman 1-26-1878 (no return)
Hocks?, John to Vest Morrison 7-21-1870
Hodges, George R. to Mary A. Hurst 11-30-1868 (12-3-1868)
Hodges, Granville to Mary C. Guy 12-10-1890 (12-11-1890)
Hodges, J. A. to M. C. Lewis 9-8-1883 (9-13-1883)
Hodges, J. E. to Temperance Nants 10-30-1878
Hodges, J. W. to Eliza Jane Neeham 8-24-1877 (8-30-1877)
Hodges, John W. to Mary E. Peeters 3-24-1871 (3-26-1871)
Hodges, John to Barthener Anderson 9-25-1878
Hodges, L. T. to Mary Ann Cowan 5-5-1885
Hodges, Preston to Lucy Ann Rogers 1-25-1883 (no return)
Hodges, R. H. to Zelpha Jennings 7-9-1892 (no return)
Hodges, William to Sarah McColough 10-22-1888 (10-25-1888)
Hodges, Wm. B. to Malisa A. Leabow 7-13-1878 (7-14-1878)
Hodges, Zackariah to Anne White 11-22-1871 (11-23-1871)
Holaway, John to Mary B. Thomas 12-24-1888
Hollen, C. M. to Mary Goin 4-8-1882 (no return)
Hollen, Calvin to Martha Rose 12-7-1872 (12-8-1872)
Hollingsworth, Franklin to Rhoda J. King 8-9-1875 (8-12-1875)
Hollingsworth, R. W. to Sarah A. Yoakum 12-3-1873 (11-28-1873?)
Hollinsworth, L. E. to Eliza J. Chadwick 9-15-1874 (no return)
Holt, N. L. to S. E. Mayes 12-17-1883 (12-18-1883)
Holt, S. M. to Nancie A. Mayes 8-17-1885 (8-19-1885)
Honby, A. B. to Jansey Collins 11-4-1886 (no return)
Honeycut, Henry P. to Hester J. Russell 4-22-1882 (4-23-1882)
Honeycutt, A. G. to Sarah E. Robertson 10-22-1887 (10-23-1887)
Honeycutt, Peter S. to Chrisleener Moyers 10-4-1879
Hook?, Silas to Mary J. England 10-19-1872 (10-20-1872)
Hooper, W. H. to Sarah J. Welch 8-17-1889 (8-18-1889)
Hoopper, William F. to Sarah Owens 1-4-1870 (1-6-1870)
Hopkins, J. H. to Sarah Sowder 1-12-1883 (1-13-1883)
Hopper, Daniel D. to Elizabeth Edwards 1-18-1870 (1-24-1870)
Hopper, David M. to Elizabeth A. Dunn 7-18-1882 (7-23-1882)
Hopper, George W. to Malinda Mayes 7-11-1874 (7-26-1874)
Hopper, George to Martha L. Rollins 8-8-1874 (8-9-1874)
Hopper, Hesekah to Bethina Stansberry 1-12-1881 (no return)
Hopper, John to Mary A. Dunn 1-3-1881 (1-6-1881)
Hopper, John to Tennessee Smith 9-5-1878 (9-22-1878)
Hopper, Newton J. to Melvinia Seal 8-17-1872 (8-18-1872)
Hopper, S. B. to Rachel Hunter 2-26-1883 (3-1-1883)
Hopper, William to Jane McDaniel 6-12-1882
Hopson, A. J. to M. J. Hurst 10-29-1879 (no return)
Hopson, C. M. to Hattie C. Sterns 5-5-1878 (4?-5-1878)
Hopson, Danel to Margrett Wright 2-10-1883 (2-11-1883)
Hopson, J. B. to Elida? Overholster 10-2-1880 (10-31-1880)
Hopson, Jesse H. to July Ritter 4-29-1874 (4-30-1874)
Hopson, Jesse to Elizabeth Johnson 4-21-1875 (4-25-1875)
Hopson, John C. to R. M. Collinsworth 1-14-1880 (no return)
Hopson, John to Mahulda J. Lovelace 9-23-1875
Hopson, Russell to Mary M. Hopson 9-2-1872
Hopson, Wm. to Louisa Hurst 12-29-1872
Horn, John T. to Mary? R. Golden 4-2-1872
Horrace?, R. F. to Emily Jones 7-21-1886
Hoskins, Henry to Celia Webb 4-26-1888 (no return)
Hoskins, J. G. to Marry G. (Miss) Brown 7-25-1881
Houston, Benjaman F. to Sariah Jane Redmond 8-30-1870 (9-8-1870)
Houston, Berry F. to Martha L. Ridings 4-5-1873 (no return)
Houston, J. P. to Sarah N. Lynch 5-26-1882? (5-28-1882)
Houston, James to Tissue Kelley 7-12-1888
Houston, Sterling to F. H. England 9-25-1880 (8?-25-1880)
Houston, W. S. to Sara Keck 2-26-1879
Houston, William to Barthena Robinson 10-15-1877 (10-18-1877)

Houston, William to Louease Jennings 3-16-1882 (3-22-1882)
Houston, Wm. H. to Anna Keck 4-22-1871 (sol., no date)
Howard, Elihu to Mary Shell 3-24-1885
Howard, John E. to Mary Vanbebber 1-4-1869
Howard, M. D. to Mary E. McBee 9-12-1879
Howard, Madison W. to Addie Evans 9-24-1889 (9-29-1889)
Howard, Reece to Fanny Ramsey 7-15-1876 (no return)
Howard, W. H. to M. A. Simmons 12-28-1881 (12-29-1881)
Howard, Wilkeson to Jennie Dunkin 2-11-1886 (2-4?-1886)
Howerton, Thos. J. to Lucy M. Clement 2-19-1884
Howerton, Wm. B. to L. V. Mayers 2-16-1881 (no return)
Hubard, W. P. to Ollie S. Yoakum 3-8-1884 (2?-17-1884)
Huffker, O. C. to M. A. Cawood 12-30-1880 (no return)
Hufsedler, G. W. P. to Catharine Pearson 2-14-1874 (2-26-1874)
Hufsutter, G. W. P. to Catharine Pearson 2-14-1874 (2-26-1874)
Hughes, James to Florance A. Kincaid 8-10-1885 (8-13-1885)
Hughes, Patrick to Willie Ann Cline 11-6-1887
Hughes, S. F. to E. P. Hughes 5-10-1886
Hughs, Andrew C. to Elizabeth Hurst 8-13-1873
Hughs, Idel to Martha Rosenbalm 1-3-1870 (1-6-1870)
Humfleet, Arthur to Manerva Sprinkles 2-19-1869
Hummers, T. B. to Sarah J. Clark 1-15-1878 (no return)
Hunley, John to Jane Lingar 1-30-1870
Hunley, P. L. to Lucinda Gibbs 4-11-1883 (no return)
Hunt, Ross to Sarah England 4-26-1873 (4-27-1873)
Hunter, Henry to Mary A. Graves 1-24-1887 (1-26-1887)
Hunter, Henry to Sarah E. Ausmus 8-21-1869 (8-24-1869)
Hunter, Jefferson to Martha Davis 8-4-1871 (8-6-1871)
Hunter, Jefferson to Rinda Hopper 9-17-1890 (10-7-1890)
Hunter, Joseph to Nancy Bowman 12-26-1881
Hurst, A. G. to Mary E. Barlow 5-24-1880 (5-27-1880)
Hurst, Alaxander to Martha Hurst 10-19-1870 (10-20-1870)
Hurst, Alexander to Sarah E. Willis 10-19-1868
Hurst, Allen to Jane Parker 3-4-1880 (no return)
Hurst, Alvis C. to Louiza E. Hurst 5-4-1887 (5-5-1887)
Hurst, Andrew to Emeline Barnes 3-15-1870 (no return) B
Hurst, E. A. to Ollie Carr 7-26-1882 (7-27-1882)
Hurst, Elbert to Elisa Richmon 12-5-1877 (12-6-1877)
Hurst, Eldridge to Elizabeth Eastridge 11-1-1875
Hurst, Franklin to Nancy Parker 1-8-1876
Hurst, Geo. W. to Mary Bunch 6-14-1888
Hurst, George to Allis Fawbush 12-5-1877 (no return)
Hurst, George to Emly Mason 6-11-1877
Hurst, Henery to Jane Bunch 6-11-1874
Hurst, Henly S. to Nancy L. Parker 9-20-1875 (no return)
Hurst, Henly to Louiza Simmons 1-15-1879 (1-16-1879)
Hurst, Isaac C. to Sarah Hurst 8-21-1873
Hurst, James B. to Louiza Harrell 2-5-1869 (2-7-1869)
Hurst, James B. to Mary Cheetam 11-30-1870 (no return)
Hurst, James T. to Marisa A. Hurst 4-15-1878 (4-18-1878)
Hurst, James to Phebe Simmons 7-22-1876 (7-23-1876)
Hurst, Jesse to Sarah Hodges 10-19-1868
Hurst, John R. to Louisa Green 12-8-1877 (no return)
Hurst, John to Mollie Penelton 10-6-1890 (no return)
Hurst, Leander to Annie Robertson 3-5-1890
Hurst, Lee to Sarah Houston 3-24-1877 (no return)
Hurst, Lewis to Dollie Robinson 8-17-1882
Hurst, Nathan to Lucy A. Goin 12-12-1885 (12-18-1885)
Hurst, Neil to Carna Jones 5-5-1890 (5-11-1890)
Hurst, Nelson to Faney Hurst 9-25-1880 (9-26-1880)
Hurst, Nelson to Nancy J. Hayes 7-9-1879 (7-10-1879)
Hurst, Perry to Sarah F. Barlow 2-18-1884 (2-21-1884)
Hurst, Pleasant W. to Mary A. West 8-21-1873
Hurst, Prior to Lidda Rogers 11-11-1887 (11-12-1887)
Hurst, Robt. to Minna B. Carpenter 4-7-1888
Hurst, Rodman to Matild Bunch 5-3-1880 (5-6-1880)
Hurst, Rolin to Cornie Buchanan 1-31-1882
Hurst, Samuel F. to Mary J. Hurst 10-22-1881
Hurst, Samuel to L. C. Barlow 11-17-1884 (11-18-1884)
Hurst, W. A. to Sarah A. Hopson 10-3-1877 (10-4-1877)
Hurst, W. B. to Emley E. Harrell 9-4-1884 (9-7-1884)
Hurst, W. D. to Udoxie Colson 10-30-1890 (no return)
Hurst, W. H. to Sarah C. Ritter 3-28-1890 (no return)
Hurst, W. M. to Matilda Lawson 7-20-1887 (no return)
Hurst, Wesley to Louisa Houston 10-9-1871 (10-10-1871)
Hurst, Wesley to Mary Hughes 10-4-1887 (10-6-1887)
Hurst, William to Matilda Asberry 5-6-1877
Hurstard?, Rufus F. to Catharine Roland 9-26-1870
Hutson, Henry J. to Lusaney M. Mitchel 4-24-1876 (4-25-1876)
Hyatt, George to Lucy Thomas 12-23-1870
Hyatt, Joseph to Lidda J. Munk 8-4-1889 (no return)
Hyden, J. D. M. to Marry Baker 2-17-1881
Hyett, James to Mary J. Speeks 5-26-1871
Idle, Banil R. to Nancy Liveley 12-20-1875
Irvin, I. A. to Letitia Johnson 8-23-1881 (8-25-1881)
Irvin, John B. to M. L. McClure 9-26-1884 (9-28-1884)
Jackson, Andrew to Anne Jennings 6-16-1884
Jackson, Henry to Fanny Knight 11-21-1889
Jackson, Luk to Allace Hurst 2-13-1882 (no return)
Jackson, Luther to Mary Esley 12-20-1883 (no return)
Jainaway, Thomas to R. J. Fulph 1-30-1879 (1-31-1879)
Janeway, James N. to Louiza Rosenbalm 1-31-1870 (2-10-1870)
Janeway, Prior L. to Marth J. Meyers 12-2-1882 (12-3-1882)
Janeway, Wm. to Luretta Wells 1-31-1873 (2-2-1873)
Jarvis, Ambrewis? to Sallie G. Herd 7-6-1882
Jayne, Hilry B. to Eliza A. Henderson 2-16-1878 (2-21-1878)
Jenins?, Robt. to Louisa Davis 9-23-1873 (no return)
Jenkins, Jessee to Elizabeth George 8-23-1870 (8-25-1870)
Jennings, Alexander to Cornelia J. Lanham 2-17-1869 (2-18-1869)
Jennings, Alexander to Elizabeth Langham 5-9-1878 (no return)
Jennings, Barney to Viny Ausburn 11-23-1875
Jennings, Frank to Eliza A. Payne 11-3-1890 (11-10-1890)
Jennings, Guss to Larrie? Wells 7-26-1882 (no return)
Jennings, Henly to Josefine Osburn 10-22-1886 (no return)
Jennings, James to Frances R. Hurst 4-8-1878
Jennings, John to Lucinda Clementine Chadwell 1-13-1876 (1-15-1876)
Jennings, Neel to Lucinda Hoskins 7-6-1874 (5?-9-1874)
Jennings, Neil to Lucinda Campbell 3-14-1889 (3-17-1889)
Jennings, W. M. to F. A. Stone 2-2-1880 (no return)
Jennings, William to Adilid? Perry 8-24-1876
Jennings, William to Jula Buchanan 12-26-1884
Jesse, Ballard to Jemima O. Mountain 2-2-1874 (no return)
Jesse, Lee to Sarah Gamble 9-10-1877 (no return)
Jessee, J. D. to Jennie Snodgrass 9-22-1890 (9-24-1890)
Jessee, William G. to Martha E. Walker 6-20-1874 (6-21-1874)
Jessee, Wm. L. to Lucy J. Cruchfield 1-6-1880 (1-15-1880)
Johnson, A. J. to Martha J. Ausmus 12-20-1873 (7-19-1874)
Johnson, A. J. to P. B. Cox 4-29-1883
Johnson, Andrew to Martha M. Meelor 3-12-1883
Johnson, Daniel to Mary J. Hembree 8-17-1869
Johnson, Elijah to Elizabeth A. Keck 1-15-1871 (1-24-1871)
Johnson, George D. to Elizabeth Reece 1-30-1869 (1-31-1869)
Johnson, George to Matilda Smith 1-3-1876 (1-6-1876)
Johnson, I. J. to Carnela Davis 9-1-1879 (9-7-1879)
Johnson, Isaac B. to Celia C. Watson 8-1-1874 (no return)
Johnson, J. B. to M. E. Monk 12-18-1889 (12-19-1889)
Johnson, J. S. to Lucy Tiller 1-7-1881
Johnson, Jacob? to Nancy A. Beeson 1-21-1887 (1-23-1887)
Johnson, James to Emeline Harvey 1-13-1873 (1-16-1873)
Johnson, James to R. A. Grason 12-8-1882
Johnson, Joseph to Susan L. C. Robinson 9-11-1868 (9-17-1868)
Johnson, Lilburn to Louiza J. Hopper 12-18-1868 (12-20-1868)
Johnson, Pleasant to Emiline Davis 8-4-1876 (8-6-1876)
Johnson, Pleasant to Sarah Hayse 10-19-1888 (10-23-1888)
Johnson, Robert to Delainia Cox 5-15-1880 (5-16-1880)
Johnson, William J. to Nancy M. Fugate 3-2-1869 (3-4-1869)
Johnson, William to Jinsey Nervesta King 2-10-1869 (no return)
Johnson, William to Mary Johnson 11-29-1875
Johnson, Wm. to Dacie? Collilns 11-18-1879 (no return)
Johnston, Wm. W. to Martha J. Cox 7-20-1887 (7-31-1887)
Jon?, Brick? to Martha Collins 1-27-1872 (1-28-1872)
Jones, Calven to Martha Thompson 8-31-1878
Jones, Elihu E. to Nancy Tenn Vanbebber 3-1-1882 (3-4-1882)
Jones, G. H. to M. K. Cottrell 11-1-1884 (11-11-1884)
Jones, G. W. to M. J. Brotherton 12-9-1890
Jones, George to Mary Swillivan 9-22-1870
Jones, Isaac M. to Margaret J. Cook 11-18-1871 (11-19-1871)
Jones, Jasper to Frances Gray 9-5-1877
Jones, Jasper to Sarah E. Roark 6-15-1879
Jones, John to Livina Neeley 5-24-1883 (5-25-1883)
Jones, John to Mary J. Lawson 12-30-1872
Jones, John to Sarah Hurst 7-3-1889 (7-4-1889)
Jones, Peter to America Willis 9-17-1885 (9-19-1885)
Jones, R. H. to Gussey Compton 1-6-1889
Jones, Randolph to Sarah Neel 1-13-1873 (1-14-1873)
Jones, Richard to Henrietta Shipley 12-27-1869 (12-28-1869)
Jones, Samuel to Lucy Bussell 2-11-1878 (2-12-1878)
Jones, Thomas to Elizabeth Rogers 6-28-1871 (6-30-1871)
Jones, Thomas to Mary McCrary 11-13-1888 (no return)
Jones, Thomas to Pheby Lawson 11-8-1881 (3-5-1882)
Jones, Wiley to Caroline Davis 3-19-1874
Jones, Wiley to Hasey Nelson 1-20-1874 (no return)
Jones, William to Anna E. Harvein 10-18-1873 (10-30-1873)
Jones, Wily to Elizabeth Nelson 7-13-1882 (7-23-1882)
Jones, Wm. L. to Mary Jane Taylor 8-29-1870
Jones, Wm. to Anna E. Havrin? 10-18-1873 (no return)
Jones, Wm. to Sarah Collins 11-18-1879 (11-19-1879)
Jons, John to W. K. Colenworth 12-24-1878
Jonson, D. to A. E. Wade 1-18-1879 (1-19-1879)
Jordan, Jackson to Sufinild Daniel 11-1-1876 (11-2-1876)
Jordan, James C. to Mary Collins 10-7-1880 (10-8-1880)
Jorden, Joseph to Elizabeth Whitaker 8-2-1884 (no return)
Justice, John W. to Larinda Collinsworth 8-30-1871 (9-6-1871)
Keck, A. C. to Parley Cox 4-29-1887 (5-1-1887)

Keck, Elijah to Racheal E. Dunn 4-20-1872 (4-28-1872)
Keck, Henry to Louiza J. Lynch 7-24-1869 (7-29-1869)
Keck, John to Caty Keck 9-23-1889 (9-27-1889)
Keck, Mathew C. to Matilda Goin 9-17-1870 (9-18-1870)
Keck, N. L. to L. E. Monly? 6-9-1888 (no return)
Keck, Phillip F. to Sarah J. Sanders? 10-22-1871 (10-23-1871)
Keck, Phillip to Loucinda Pike 8-2-1880 (8-5-1880)
Keck, Phillip to Maggy Rosson 9-18-1888 (9-20-1888)
Keck, Phillip to Malinda Dunn? 4-15-1874 (no return)
Keck, T. C. to C. J. Hopper 6-16-1888 (6-17-1888)
Keck, Thomas C. to Malinda A. Francisco 3-22-1882 (3-26-1882)
Keck, W. C. to E. Hodges 9-?-1886 (9-30-1886)
Keck, William to Sarah E. Beeson 11-11-1870 (11-13-1870)
Keck?, Josiah L. to Rach. C. Dunn 3-13-1875 (3-21-1875)
Keizer, Wm. to Sarah Smith 1-3-1885
Kelley, James M. to Laura J. Anderson 8-25-1874 (8-27-1874)
Kelley, John W. to Mandy J. Harrell 1-25-1871 (1-26-1871)
Kelley, M. R. to M. L. Burchfield 1-20-1873 (1-23-1873)
Kelley, Right to Sarah Marjors 9-?-1878 (9-20-1878)
Kelley, William to Liza D. Buchanan 5-25-1882 (no return)
Kellian, David to Margret Adams 1-14-1880 (1-15-1880)
Kellion, Thomas to Sarah Crutchfield 10-1-1884 (10-9-1884)
Kerr, Alexander to S. E. Right 6-29-1889 (not exec.)
Kesterson, Garrett H. to Cornelia Overton 9-19-1877 (9-20-1877)
Kesterson, Newton E. to E. T. Knoblin 10-20-1882 (10-22-1882)
Kesterson, Newton E. to Sarah C. Deck 11-19-1884 (11-20-1884)
Kesterson, Samuel to Benena V. Lambert 1-25-1873 (1-26-1873)
Keton, James to Phoeba Rice 1-16-1889 (1-17-1889)
Keton, Joseph to Derushia Odelle 9-21-1882 (9-24-1882)
Ketron, William H. to Frances O. Jones 10-5-1868 (10-6-1868)
Kibert, Henry to Elizebeth Cadle 6-18-1879
Kibert, James A. to Calas R. King 1-5-1872 (1-11-1872)
Kibert, James H. to Emely Fultz 5-29-1874 (5-20?-1874)
Kibert, Wiley to Cornelia Bussell? 8-12-1882 (no return)
Kibert?, Samuel to Sarah Bussell 5-23-1871
Killian, Danuel to Margarett Adams? 1-14-1881 (no return)
Killian, Joseph to Loucinda Crutchfield 4-17-1878 (4-18-1878)
Killian, Levi to Sarrah Rector 11-7-1870 (11-9-1870)
Killian, William to Jerusia Cole 9-24-1874 (no return)
Killian, Wm. to Lavina Lynch 5-2-1872 (5-3-1872)
Killion, Hugh to Alice J. Doris 7-21-1884
Killion, Wm. to Matilda Beason 11-29-1879
Kincaid, Black to Alice White 3-5-1885 (no return)
Kincaid, Creed to Sarah E. Crockett 1-1-1875 (1-2-1875)
Kincaid, Emond? to Roxey Stokley? 11-25-1890 (no return)
Kincaid, John to Tennessee Kincaid 12-22-1884 (12-25-1884)
Kincaid, Lewis to Alis Calston 10-23-1874
Kincaid, Lewis to Elizabeth Day 8-4-1884 (8-5-1884)
Kincaid, Nicos? to Mary Jennings 3-13-1873 (3-14-1873)
Kincaid, Paul to Dianer Huse 9-18-1870 (9-19-1870)
Kincaid, Preston to Margret White 4-29-1879
Kincaid, Preston to Mary E. Mount 4-2-1869 (4-4-1869) B
Kincaid, Scott to Caldana Turner 12-25-1879 (1-2-1879?)
Kincaid, Stepen to Lucie Williams 12-27-1873 (12-28-1873)
Kincaid, W. H. S. to Sallie E. Payne 8-9-1873 (no return)
Kincaid, Wm. to Elizabeth Cloud 11-29-1877 (no return)
Kinder, Hiram to Emley Reece 8-13-1881 (8-16-1881)
King, Danuel to E. S. Fugate? 3-18-1881 (3-19-1881)
King, Henry to Catherine Debusk 1-14-1875
King, J. W. to Maggie R. King 9-19-1888 (9-20-1888)
King, James F. to Mary Leach 10-4-1880 (no return)
King, James to Mary E. Minton 8-28-1879 (8-31-1879)
King, John to Sary Osben 11-22-1870
King, Melvin to Corra Bell Bolinger 8-3-1888 (8-9-1888)
King, Nathan H. to E. C. Gamble 11-27-1874 (11-29-1874)
King, Robt. to Eliza Caylor 6-27-1887
King, T. R. to Elbarrie? Baldwin 5-6-1889 (5-9-1889)
King, W. A. to Maggie Hayes 11-9-1887 (11-10-1887)
King, W. F. to Sarah E. King 11-2-1889 (11-3-1889)
King, Wesley to Elizabeth Harrell 11-11-1870 (11-13-1870)
King, Wm. F. to Orpha Siler 1-15-1869
King, Wm. P. to Martha E. Lainies 9-15-1887 (9-16-1887)
Kirbey, H. C. to M. J. Harper 6-9-1880
Kirby, E. to Rosana Asbery 7-10-1880 (7-11-1880)
Kirby, Henry to Martha Luverna Mathis 5-10-1873 (5-11-1873)
Kivit, W. F. to Juliam Overbay 10-2-1882 (10-8-1882)
Knight, James to Ellen Raney 6-1-1889
Knontt, J. C. to Ellen S. Higgins 1-12-1871
Kyle, Jackson to Malinda Overton 7-31-1884
Lafard, Hiram to Sarah Sulffurdg 10-30-1879 (11-2-1879)
Lagin?, John to Sary M. Mays 3-24-1871
Laikin, William to Rutha Headrick 10-25-1870
Laine, Joseph to L. C. Young 2-22-1879 (no return)
Lamb, Wm. G. to Melsina Gibbs 10-22-1880 (10-23-1880)
Lambdin, Andrew to Amy Bowman 8-11-1869 (8-12-1869)
Lambdin, Siler to Eliza Standfield 10-6-1868
Lambdin, William to Martha Chadwell 5-26-1883

Lambert, Andrew to Jennie Luster 12-5-1884 (12-7-1884)
Lambert, Benjerman to Elizabeth Ledwod? 1-1-1879 (1-2-1879)
Lambert, E. H. to Mary Berk 9-15-1887 (no return)
Lambert, George to Mahaley Hatfield 6-4-1879 (6-9-1879)
Lambert, James to Elizabeth Hayes 8-20-1874 (no return)
Lambert, James to Leeby? Irvin 1-27-1889
Lambert, Jefferson to Jane Crawford 1-2-1873 (1-5-1873)
Lambert, John F. to Martha Lamber 1-10-1880 (2-11-1880)
Lambert, John to Nancy Fletcher 12-3-1880
Lambert, Joseph to J. Cosbey 12-11-1875 (12-26-1876?)
Lambert, Joseph to Matilda E. Casey 5-9-1870 (5-12-1870)
Lambert, Samuel to E. A. Shoemate 12-24-1881 (12-25-1881)
Lambert, W. T. to Rebecca J. Richardson 2-3-1890 (2-9-1890)
Lampkins, Thos. to Maggie Tullington 4-17-1889 (4-18-1889)
Lane, Geo. to Nancy Singleton 1-17-1888
Lane, H. C. to Nancy Wisp? 11-13-1886 (11-14-1886)
Lane, James to Nancy Goodin 11-4-1873
Lane, John M. to Selah Bullard 5-30-1875
Lane, Sterling to Jane Rose 6-5-1876
Langham, M. G. to L. C. Lambert 12-11-1886 (12-12-1886)
Lanham, E. A. to Dosia Riley 12-31-1884 (no return)
Lanham, Joseph C. to Marry (Mrs.) Jennings 6-21-1881 (6-23-1881?)
Lanham, Nelson P. to Amanda Jones 3-16-1869 (3-18-1869)
Lanham, Robert to Minee Patterson 9-1-1880 (9-12-1880)
Lanham, W. H. to Sally Gilliwaters 10-22-1873 (11-23-1873)
Lankford, Hilton? to Mary Heck 9-4-1879
Large, Joseph S. to Lucinda Carmon 12-15-1869 (no return)
Large, T. F. to T. M. Gibson 11-2-1888 (11-4-1888)
Large, W. B. to Daisy? Ann McClure 11-3-1875 (11-4-1875)
Large, W. S. to L. J. Yoakum 9-5-1884 (no return)
Law, Thos. to Nancy Mayse 10-1-1873 (no return)
Laws, John to Lucy Carter 4-30-1886 (5-1-1886)
Laws, W. C. to Mary E. Edmondson 7-25-1885? (7-26-1885)
Lawsom, H. F. to Nancy J. Rice 6-28-1880 (no return)
Lawson, Allen to Mary Carmack 11-17-1881 (no return)
Lawson, Drewey to Racheal A. Dean 3-4-1878 (3-6-1878)
Lawson, Isom to Sarah E. Massingill 1-13-1873 (1-16-1873)
Lawson, J. W. to Susan Fin? West 4-22-1875 (4-24-1875)
Lawson, James to Mary E. Hopson 1-14-1880 (1-15-1880)
Lawson, Lee to Sweet Lucy ___ 8-15-1885 (7?-15-1885)
Lawson, Milam to Mahulda Welch 7-11-1873 (7-13-1873)
Lawson, Milum to Mahulda Welch 7-11-1873 (no return)
Lawson, Percy G. to Emely Thomas 12-23-1874 (12-24-1874)
Laxten, Balis to Eliza Vaughn 7-28-1879
Laykins, W. N. to Nancey J. Barnard 2-17-1874 (2-19-1874)
Leabolt, John to Elisabeth Messer 3-2-1887 (3-3-1887)
Leabow, Isham G. to Rachal Rogers 10-18-1885
Leabow, Sterling L. to Sarah Elizabeth Ann Loop 4-10-1869 (4-11-1869)
Leach, Eliakum to Margaret Holliway 2-28-1870
Leach, Jefferson to Betty Graves 2-3-1882 (no return)
Leach, John C. to Eleyan Brooks 8-2-1889 (8-4-1889)
Leach, W. C. to Mary King 12-25-1881
Lebolt, Alexander to A. C. Mising? 2-23-1874
Lebow, Calaway to Lourina M. Blansett 1-19-1877 (1-21-1877)
Lebow, Nelson to Malinda Day 10-1-1869 (10-3-1869) B
Lee, Bowl to Manervia Young 2-22-1877
Lee, Calvin to Syntha Graham 12-23-1872 (12-26-1872)
Lee, Henry to Mary McDaniel 11-19-1888 (11-20-1888)
Lee, Pearse to Liza Forgason 5-27-1882 (5-28-1882)
Lee, Stephen to S. E. Dannel 8-29-1884
Leebow, Robert to Elviry Nite 10-7-1872
Leemare, James F. to Sary J. McCarty 9-1-1881 (8?-4-1881)
Leffler, R. W. to Elizabeth York 2-8-1891
Lelio?, Nelson to Teritha Ritchey 5-13-1876
Lemar, Danil F. to Elizabeth O. Davis 2-13-1883 (2-27-1883)
Lemons, William to Martha Harris 10-13-1868 (no return)
Lenard, Patrick to Lucy L. Brooks 7-8-1876 (7-13-1876)
Lenard, Robert to Manda Dalton 12-17-1886 (12-23-1886)
Lesly, Jasper to Hanna J. McGlothen 5-20-1872
Lester, Green B. to Eliza Ann Fleamon 1-20-1870 (1-25-1870)
Lester, J. A. to Jennie Brooks 12-6-1891 (S/B 1890?)
Leusher?, Samuel to Sarah J. Leach 12-?-1879 (12-15-1879)
Lewis, Charley to Jane Chadwell 11-7-1868 (11-12-1868) B
Lewis, Daniell to Celia Colston 12-23-1879
Lewis, G. M. to M. C. Harrell 6-13-1880 (no return)
Lewis, J. N. to Mary J. Walker 11-21-1876 (11-23-1876)
Lewis, John M. to Louisa Garison 4-27-1883
Lewis, Joseph to Luanny Pearson 4-14-1877 (4-26-1877)
Lewis, T. G. to Dualla Lewis 6-27-1879
Lewis, William to Mary A. Shumate 2-19-1890 (2-23-1890)
Liford, Elias to Annie Minton 11-3-1869 (11-12-1869)
Liford, G. W. to Elizabeth Campbell 10-31-1872
Liford, Hiram to Elizabeth Robinson 8-22-1883 (no return)
Liford, James to Elizabeth Campbell 11-17-1877
Lingar, John to Melvinea Collensworth 4-23-1870 (4-24-1870)
Lingar, Robt. to Mattie Lambert 1-14-1888 (1-15-1888)
Lingnar, Harvey to Elizabeth Luster 3-7-1871 (3-12-1871)

Lisk, John A. to Louisa Sanders 8-11-1883 (8-12-1883)
Lister, R. C. to Elizabeth Flemon 10-17-1880
Litterell, John A. to S. M. Freeman 5-11-1888
Litterell, Wm. to Mary Jane Daniels 10-12-1888 (10-14-1888)
Little, Joseph C. to Salle E. Longmiers 1-24-1883 (1-25-1883)
Littrell, Isaac to Mary Liford 8-18-1882 (8-20-1882)
Littrell, John A. to Clemetine Chadwell 2-25-1871 (2-26-1871)
Littrell, L.B. to Eliza? J. Williams 12-1-1877 (12-2-1877)
Lively, William to Mary Hopson 1-26-1875 (2-7-1875)
Livingston, George to Ensihel? Collins 11-8-1881 (11-9-1881)
Lockely, George W. to Margret E. Thomas 9-29-1875 (no return)
Loftice, R. W. to D. A. Crockett 8-27-1882
Loftice, William D. to Rhoda Jones 9-12-1878
Loftis, Herod to Mary Crocket 2-23-1873 (2-24-1873)
Logan, Fred to Mary Poor 10-11-1890 (10-12-1890)
Logan, Fred to Rachel Robinson 2-24-1889
Long, Henry to Sarah J. Lewis 2-7-1870 (3-7-1870)
Long, James to Lucinda M. Brown 12-12-1875 (12-13-1875)
Longman, Fillmore to Mary Wheeler 10-8-1878 (10-12-1878)
Longwood, George W. to Mary E. Brooks 2-8-1876 (2-10-1876)
Longworth, Elbert to Mary E. Montgomery 12-7-1888 (12-9-1888)
Longworth, J. M. to Eliz M. Brooks 2-14-1882 (2-16-1882)
Longworth, John to Elisabeth Daniel 9-15-1875 (9-16-1875)
Longworth, William to Margret Daniel 9-15-1875 (9-16-1875)
Longworth, Wm. to L. J. Baker 3-3-1881 (3-4-1881)
Lood, Samuel M. to Ollie M. McVey 4-28-1888 (4-29-1888)
Loop, A. to Amanda Horman 5-30-1874 (5-31-1874)
Loop, J. P. to ___ Welch 4-27-1888 (no return)
Loop, J. R. to Jane Crutchfield 11-9-1872
Loop, John to Manda Campbell 8-21-1889 (8-22-1889)
Loop, Joseph L. to Manila S. Farmer 4-8-1878 (no return)
Loop, Lewis to Catharine Edmonson 10-4-1877 (no return)
Loskeydoo, John W. to Frances Good 1-5-1881 (1-6-1881)
Losson, Perygram to Manda J. Willright 7-31-1882 (no return)
Love(lace?), John to Mahulda Barnard 1-27-1872 (1-28-1872)
Love, R. T. to Virginia Willson 2-23-1890
Loyad, J. J. to Lucy C. Sharp 1-8-1879
Luford, Duff to Nancy J. Muncy 12-16-1870 (12-18-1870)
Lundy, John to Mary Houston 9-4-1883 (9-6-1883)
Lundy, Thomas to Rachel Houstin 7-25-1890 (8-10-1890)
Lundy, William to Elizabeth Shipley 8-19-1884
Lynch, Alex to Katie McBee 3-3-1886 (3-4-1886)
Lynch, Alfred C. to Rachal L. Bishop 1-3-1883 (1-4-1883)
Lynch, G. W. to Nancy Day 10-30-1885 (11-1-1885)
Lynch, George C. to Emely Ford 2-4-1891
Lynch, Greenbery F. to Elizabeth England 12-26-1871 (12-28-1871)
Lynch, Henry to M. E. Margraves 4-8-1880
Lynch, J. R. to M. V. Killion 2-6-1891 (2-8-1891)
Lynch, J. T. to Florance V. Green 12-24-1890
Lynch, James M. to Rachel Bryant 2-10-1887 (3-20-1887)
Lynch, Jesse W. to R. M. McClewer 10-22-1880 (10-23-1880)
Lynch, John A. to Margret L. Daniel 5-15-1883
Lynch, John to Marth Duncan 6-14-1884 (6-15-1884)
Lynch, R. D. to Mary Bowlinger 1-13-1885 (no return)
Lynch, Samuel to Matilda Marsee 8-6-1879 (8-7-1879)
Lynch, Sanferd to M. H. E. Danel 7-28-1879
Lynch, Wm. E. to Lucinda McBee 12-5-1868 (12-6-1868)
Lynd?, Thos. to Mary Chadwell 10-3-1885
Lyttle, Dale C. to Virginia McPherson 12-12-1868 (no return)
M?, Lewis G. to M. J. Muncey 2-15-1879 (6-20-1880!)
MacNeal, B. F. to Lucretia Wolf 4-25-1874 (4-26-1874)
Maddox, John W. to Sally A. Collins 10-23-1885 (10-25-1885)
Mainvill?, Stephen G. to Lucinda M. Goin 2-19-1871 (2-23-1871)
Major, John to Lucey Sharp 12-26-1887 (no return)
Major, John to Lucy Sharp 12-25-1888 (12-27-1888)
Malicote, P. L. to Ann C. Carter 10-22-1881 (10-23-1881)
Malone, Haris to Matilda Huff 2-22-1882 (2-24-1882)
Malone, John to Susan Kincaid 4-10-1882 (4-14-1882) B
Manion, Andrew to Annie M. Mason 1-8-1889
Manis, Dalsey L. to Susan Reace? 1-21-1891 (1-25-1891)
Manis, W. E. to Caley Warrick 4-16-1889 (5-25-1889)
Manis, William to Laura Bartlett 9-6-1890 (9-7-1890)
Manning, Andrew to Martha S. Cook ?-?-1880 (?-?-1880?)
Manning, J. C. to Margaret McDaniel 8-10-1889 (no return)
Maples, Leroy to Martha Hollingsworth 8-2-1888 (8-10-1888)
Maples, Levander to Sarah J. Maples 9-23-1871 (9-28-1871)
Marcum, Robert O. to Canda Hunt 10-14-1880
Marcum, Thomas to Mary E. Litterell 9-8-1877 (9-9-1877)
Marcum, WM. to Elizabeth Roark 10-9-1876 (10?-11-1876)
Margraves, William to M. J. Longworth 8-22-1884 (8-23-1884)
Maricle, P. W. to Mary Goins 12-27-1887
Mark, John to Sarah M. Barton 3-30-1874
Marsee, Jacob M. to Cinda Hunter 10-11-1881 (no return)
Marsee, Jacob to Sinda Hunter 10-11-1881 (10-13-1881)
Marsee, John A. to Sely A. McKinibee? 3-25-1886
Marsee, John to C. T. Smith 11-7-1884
Marsee, Joseph to Martha Denne 1-30-1881 (1-31-1881)

Marsee, William H. to Mary Jane Hopper 11-7-1874 (no return)
Marsh, James to Eliza A. Allenen 11-12-1873 (11-14-1873)
Martin, A. J. to Elizabeth Snoveley 11-12-1877 (no return)
Martin, Jeff to Polley Burrell 8-25-1888
Martin, Marshell to Amanda Deen 5-30-1883 (6-2-1883)
Marton, Marchal to Adaline Hatfield 2-18-1881 (2-20-1881)
Masengill, John to Elizabeth Cosbey 10-30-1880
Mason, E. T. to Lowenda Hall 10-25-1871 (10-26-1871)
Mason, George to Harret Yoakum 4-27-1874 (5-3-1874)
Mason, George to Margret Mitheal 12-24-1870 (12-25-1870)
Mason, Gordy to Mary Eley 9-18-1885
Mason, James K. to Engline Gooden 11-10-1870
Mason, John E. to P. Yoakum 3-7-1881 (3-10-1881)
Mason, Larkin B. to America E. Smith 4-18-1887 (5-9-1887)
Mason, Plesant R. to Eneline Mason 7-27-1882
Mason, Reubin to Nancy Hickman 2-2-1881 (2-3-1881)
Mason, William to Elen Golden 11-?-1890 (11-3-1890)
Mason, William to Jane Buchanon 1-21-1882
Mason, Wm. T. to Sarah Patterson 2-28-1871
Massengal, John to Nancy Brooks 2-18-1887 (2-24-1887)
Massengill, Benjamine to Elizabeth Brooks 5-5-1877 (no return)
Massengill, Calaway to Mary Elison 1-17-1884 (no return)
Massengill, Levli to Sarah Ramsey 4-9-1877
Massengill, Nelson to Lizie Skidmore 10-21-1882 (10-22-1882)
Massengill, Reuben to Eliza J. Crage 3-28-1870
Massengill, Walter E. to Catherine L. England 11-24-1876
Massey, R. G. to Catherine Jones 7-27-1877
Massingal, R. H. to L. M. Riddle 10-6-1887
Mathews, Lynch to Harriett M. Beeson 1-12-1887 (1-13-1887)
Mathis, Henry to Eliza Neil 12-30-1882
Mathis, Nelson to Martha Eastridge 12-17-1874
Mathis, William M. to Christena Poor 6-29-1875
Mathis, Wm. N. to E. M. Duncan 1-28-1881
Mattox, Charles to Nancy Capps 6-4-1870 (6-5-1870)
Maupin, F. to Maggie Lane 11-26-1881 (11-27-1881)
Mayer, Johnson to Mary Ann Rogers 8-18-1884 (8-19-1884)
Mayer, W. E. C. to Anna Baylor 6-26-1885 (6-30-1885)
Mayers, James T. to Mary A. Breeding 7-15-1882 (7-30-1882)
Mayers, Robert to Martha A. Watson 11-23-1882
Mayers, Wm. M. to Luvenda Hopper 1-27-1871 (1-28-1871)
Mayes, Daniel H. to Manerva E. Campbell 8-30-1871 (8-31-1871)
Mayes, George W. to Angeline Branscomb 4-1-1871 (4-2-1871)
Mayes, N. T. to Rebeck Keck 10-27-1889
Mayes, P. H. to Moley E. Stump 10-19-1878 (no return)
Mayes?, Thomas J. to Emly Menroy? 12-2-1876 (12-7-1876)
Maynard, B. G. to Mary L. Evans 6-20-1878
Mayse, David H. to Lizzie B. Thompson 2-5-1889 (no return)
Mayse, John M. to Malinia Waymoreson 3-6-1872 (3-7-1872)
Maze, Padric to Rachel Moore 9-10-1878
McAfee, James to Nancy Brock 2-16-1886 (2-18-1886)
McBary, J. F. to Lumbera A. Cadle 1-5-1887 (1-6-1887)
McBee, J. E. to N. A. Celley 9-26-1878
McBee, J. L. to Virginia C. Larmer 2-13-1883 (no return)
McBee, John to Mary (Mrs.) Brown 6-3-1881
McBee, Robert to Mary Welch 9-11-1878 (9-12-1878)
McBee, Vincent D. to Martha M. Monk 9-4-1889 (9-8-1889)
McBee, W. E. to Mary McVay 2-17-1874 (2-19-1874)
McBee?, John M. to Sarah C. Killian 10-9-1874 (no return)
McCauley, D. A. to Minerva Chesley 8-31-1887
McCery, John to J. A. Harman 12-30-1878
McClain, W. J. to Martha J. Pratt 5-12-1883 (5-13-1883)
McClure, M. L. to John B. Irvin 9-26-1884 (9-28-1884)
McCollough, A. A. to Martha Breeding 11-22-1889 (11-24-1889)
McCollough, S. F. to Mary Sanders 9-3-1888 (9-8-1888)
McConnell, R. F. to P. C. Quillenin 6-20-1884
McCoy, Francis J. to Carnie Jennings 2-23-1891
McCrank, Sam to Effie B. Clark 6-21-1884 (6-24-1884)
McCrary, G. W. to D. S. Sharp 12-17-1881 (12-22-1881)
McCrary, Patton to America Wyley 9-6-1888 (9-9-1888)
McCrary, Peter to Mary C. Indman 6-14-1879
McCrary, Tipton to Darcus Branscom 11-27-1885 (11-29-1885)
McCulley, Ham to Sarah A. Davis 7-18-1878 (7-21-1878)
McDaniel, ? to Nancy ? Bunniam 4-6-1876
McDonald, Wm. D. to Chiney Odle 1-3-1881 (no return)
McDonell, William to Addy Barnard 1-16-1890 (1-19-1890)
McEwen, R. E. to Mary A. Patterson 11-16-1870 (11-17-1870)
McFall, William to Mary J. Gibson 7-27-1882
McHenry, A. to Mary M. Ausmus 4-3-1876 (4-6-1876)
McIntosh, John Ross to Dora Bell Cottrell 1-7-1890
McKey, Elias to Rebeca C. Hart 3-7-1881
McKinzie, H. W. to Lizzie Casada 4-30-1890 (no return)
McMahan, Anderson to N. J. Reader 12-16-1880
McMahan, Joseph to Annie Rogers 8-19-1886
McManaway, Wm. T. to Jennie Greer 9-9-1872 (no return)
McNeal, John to Mariam Hazelwood 1-29-1870 (no return)
McNealy, Elwood to Maggie Hill 1-15-1891 (no return)
McNeeley, Samuel to Mary L. Furgerson 3-12-1888 (3-15-1888)

McNeely, W. H. to Mary A. Mayers 2-14-1881 (2-17-1881)
McNeil, Benjamin to Josefine Baker 12-20-1871 (12-21-1871)
McNew, David H. to Martha Brather 3-15-1873 (3-16-1873)
McNew, James to Docia Owens 12-4-1889 (12-8-1889)
McNew, W. J. to M. J. Bratcher 4-25-1874
McNiel, Geo. to Nowesta Estes 5-10-1884
McNiel, John A. to Eliza Southern 11-4-1869
McNiel, V. H. to Emily Fultz 1-13-1884
McPhetridg, B. to N. L. E. Lewis 8-24-1886 (8-26-1886)
McStewart, Wm. to Martha Percival 1-30-1871
McVay, F. L. to Mary E. Scott 8-30-1878 (9-1-1878)
McVay, J. F. to S. E. Lewis 1-5-1881 (1-6-1881)
McVay, James to Margaret Hall 8-27-1869 (8-29-1869)
McWilliams, J. W. to Levesta Davy 5-1-1881
Medley, John W. to Sarah A. Calwell 12-26-1874
Meeley, J. N. to N. A. Keehan? 9-10-1878 (9-12-1878)
Melton, Sephen to Dollie Arnold 9-14-1878
Mercer, James F. to Jemima F. Calger 11-4-1874
Messer, W. S. to Martha Lambert 2-4-1888 (no return)
Meyers, B. L. to Sarah Walker 11-3-1873 (no return)
Meyers, Elisha to Mary Smith 2-7-1891 (2-8-1891)
Meyers, H. B. to Mary A. Brylls 12-13-1884 (12-14-1884)
Meyers, H. E. to H. A. Snodgrass 9-1-1866 (no return)
Meyers, I. L. to Martha Ellison 1-20-1886
Meyers, Isaac to Sarah Eldridge 12-5-1884? (12-11-1884)
Meyers, Isaac to Sarah J. Folkner 8-24-1881 (8-25-1881)
Meyers, Isom to Mary J. Cupp 9-4-1869 (9-5-1869)
Meyers, J. C. to M. A. Doset 12-2-1884 (12-4-1884)
Meyers, J. L. to Martha Elison 4-2-1884 (no return)
Meyers, J. L. to Maryan Francisco 8-8-1879
Meyers, Jacob to Eliza Killian 10-20-1870
Meyers, James L. to P. E. Williams 12-27-1884 (no return)
Meyers, Jefferson to S. J. Mink 8-2-1879 (8-10-1879)
Meyers, John M. to Loo B. Rogers 12-3-1887 (12-4-1887)
Meyers, John to Hester A. Cox 3-6-1882 (3-29-1882)
Meyers, John to R. S. Tramel 12-12-1878 (12-15-1878)
Miller, Charles C. to Sarah Rymer 3-15-1870 (3-17-1870)
Miller, David E. to Orlena Mayes 2-2-1882 (2-6-1882)
Miller, E. D. to M. A. McBee 3-5-1881 (no return)
Miller, F. L. to Betsey Creg 3-4-1889 (3-5-1889)
Miller, G. W. to Margret Bruce 5-21-1883 (5-27-1883)
Miller, George to Anna Carr 7-29-1882 (8-6-1882)
Miller, John P. to Racha Rose 10-15-1880 (10-19-1880)
Miller, John to Kitty Slusher 9-10-1874 (no return)
Miller, John to Mandy Harper 10-15-1873
Miller, M. V. to Martha Davis 7-27-1886 (7-29-1886)
Miller, Thomas J. to Cornelis Breeding 3-9-1882 (3-19-1882)
Miller, Wm. to Miry Lewis? 10-31-1872 (11-2-1872)
Milligana, Wm. to Martha Pults 2-17-1890 (no return)
Mink, Calvin M. to Jane Testament 11-27-1871 (12-30-1871)
Mink, J. E. to Matilda Taylor 2-?-1880 (2-12-1880)
Mink, J. K. to L. L. Linch 10-26-1886 (10-28-1886)
Mink, J. R. to Jane Addams 3-23-1871
Mink, James O. to Sarah A. Ford 6-27-1882 (6-29-1882)
Mink, John H. to Mary J. Drummons 1-27-1874 (1-29-1874)
Mink, Samuel O. to Frances A. Neeley 3-28-1878 (3-29-1878)
Mink, W. S. to W. A. Lynch 11-7-1888 (11-8-1888)
Mink, Wm. B. to A. B. Drummons 8-19-1880
Mintar, Thomas to D. Wells 1-10-1880 (1-3-1880)
Minten, John to Vergena A. Moody 9-4-1883 (9-6-1883)
Minter, Jas. to Margaret J. Neely 10-20-1885 (11-1-1885)
Minter, Thos. to Jane Trent 6-5-1885? (no return)
Minton, B. F. to Sarah Venerable 5-27-1876
Minton, D. C. to Magnoley Jennings 4-20-1889 (4-21-1889)
Minton, Frankliln B. to Josephine McVay 12-28-1881 (12-29-1881)
Minton, G. W. to America Peters 10-13-1876
Minton, George to Frances Smith 3-15-1887 (no return)
Minton, J. A. to Orlenia Cupp 2-17-1874 (2-18-1874)
Minton, James to Amanda Thompson 12-10-1890
Minton, John to Nancy Longworth 2-15-1872
Minton, John to Sarah Golden 9-10-1887 (9-11-1887)
Minton, Joseph to Jane Minton 7-12-179 (11-13-1880)
Minton, Lewis to Susan Jessee 1-31-1877 (no return)
Minton, Lewis to Wady Elizabeth Howsley 10-2-1877 (No return)
Minton, Mitcheal to Martha Green 4-11-1872 (no return)
Minton, Robert to M. McBee 1-13-1878 (No return)
Minton, Samuel to Delamey Goin 3-4-1884 (3-6-1884)
Minton, Taylor to Amanda Killion 2-22-1887
Minton, W. E. to H. E. Griffin 7-9-1879
Minton, William C. to Marry E. Snider 8-24-1876 (8-27-1876)
Mintun, James A. to Ruth Lunda 3-11-1886
Miracle, Calvin to Manerva J. Webb 3-18-1870 (3-17-1870?)
Miracle, Daniel E. to Elizabeth Goin 2-2-1871
Miricle, Fredrick D. to Mary M. Cillums 7-17-1877 (7-18-1877)
Mitchel, John H. to L. J. Sanders 8-12-1871 (8-13-1871)
Mitchell, Calvin to Kessiah Day 1-14-1871 (1-15-1871)
Mize, Alwane to Orlena Wilson 8-9-1887 (8-10-1887) B

Mize, Claiborne M. to Lucinda Brooks 11-22-1883 (no return)
Mize, John T. to Nancy Parkey 2-28-1881 (3-30-1881)
Mize, Thos. to Malisa Mriz? 8-11-1873 (no return)
Moncy, Edward to Isabella Niceley 2-15-1878 (no return)
Moncy, Franklin F. to Sarah E. Davis 8-25-1874 (8-27-1874)
Monday, James W. to Vicy Williams 12-10-1888 (12-11-1888)
Monday, Samuel C. to Rachel C. Marsee 9-6-1883 (9-16-1883)
Monk, John A. to Manervia M. Kindrick 10-20-1875 (no return)
Monrowe, Marten to Nancy Deyer 12-2-1882 (12-3-1882)
Montgomery, G. W. to Eugenia N. Arnold 6-2-1883 (6-3-1883)
Montgomery, William to Lucy A. Brooks 2-17-1882 (2-19-1882)
Moody, J. F. to Nancy O. Cline 10-23-1882 (10-26-1882)
Moody, John M. to Sarah J. Lynch 4-11-1883 (no return)
Moody, M. V. to Mariah C. Smith 11-15-1877 (no return)
Mooer?, Henry to Annie Riley 11-11-1884
Moony, J. M. to L. E. Ford 9-29-1885 (10-8-1885?)
Mor, William N. to M. J. Honeycutt 11-20-1880
Morakle, James M. to N. J. Crawford 8-20-1875 (8-23-1875)
More, Calvin to Narcissa Davis 3-25-1870
More, David to Eliza Jackson 3-13-1879
More, Wm. Nelson to Lucinda Toliver 8-?-1888 (8-8-1888)
Morgan, Isaac to Belle Brewer 9-29-1890 (9-30-1890)
Morgan, Preston to Sarah Brackins 2-7-1883
Morgan, William T. to Martha Jane Gibson 4-5-1869 (4-8-1869)
Morison, J. L. to Louisey Johnston 7-?-1879 (7-7-1879)
Morrison, J. L. to L. E. Pearson 2-2-1885 (2-10-1885)
Morrison, Richard to Amanda Brooks 10-12-1869 (10-13-1869)
Morten, Ale to Eliz. Brown 3-23-1886 (3-4?-1886)
Mosley, William to Gemima Jones 6-4-1877
Moss, James F. to Louiza C. White 3-16-1869 (3-21-1869)
Moss, M. J. to S. J. Treece 11-21-1877 (no return)
Mountain, J. W. to S. V. Simmons 11-29-1889
Mountain, Samuel K. to Nancy J. Janeway 10-18-1872 (10-20-1872)
Mountain, W. E. to S. E. Carman 4-7-1884 (4-12-1884)
Mountgomery, Hugh T. to Matilda Sutten 12-?-1870 (no return)
Mounts, C. S. to Lula M. Neil 7-13-1888 (7-15-1888)
Moyers, A. L. to Sarah V. McDaniel 2-17-1874 (2-19-1874)
Moyers, Benjamine L. to Rinela Harper 2-2-1876 (2-3-1876)
Moyers, Cornelius to Orph E. Clark 3-14-1880
Moyers, H. B. to P. A. Heck 9-27-1882 (9-28-1882)
Moyers, Henry M. to Mary E. Cheatham 9-22-1869 (9-23-1869)
Moyers, Horace M. to Harriet M. Ousley 5-20-1874 (5-21-1874)
Moyers, Isaac to Loucreecy Blackburn 4-2-1880 (4-3-1880)
Moyers, J. M. to T. C. Ridens 12-27-1888 (no return)
Moyers, James L. to P. E. Williams 12-27-1884
Moyers, Martin to M. O. Cline 12-7-1881 (12-8-1882?)
Moyers, Newton to Sarah Treece 10-1-1879 (10-5-1879)
Moyers, Peter to Hester A. Hayes 7-4-1883 (7-13-1883)
Moyers, Philip N. to Eliz. C. Hickel 3-4-1873 (4-5-1873)
Moyers, Vincent to Rachel A. Treece 10-30-1883 (11-1-1883)
Moyers, William A. to Netty M. Branscom 12-3-1883 (no return)
Moyers, Wm. H. to Elizabeth Mattox 8-26-1871 (8-27-1871)
Moyers, Wm. H. to Mary Raney 6-14-1882
Mozingo, G. W. to Adaline Ellis 11-2-1888 (11-4-1888)
Mullins, H. H. to Mary J. Hill 1-31-1874
Mullins, John to Luverne Noe 12-4-1888
Munch, Edward to Malissa Brown 6-23-1878 (6-24-1878)
Muncy, John to R. L. D. Smith 9-1-1882 (9-14-1882)
Muncy, M. to L. D. Smith 10-11-1882 (10-12-1882)
Muncy, Peter to Melvina Wells 2-12-1875 (2-13-1875)
Muncy, Samuel to Isabel Nicly 1-31-1879 (2?-2-1879)
Munsey, John to Evaline Drumons 4-3-1888 (4-4-1888)
Munsey, Taylor to Adaline Niceley 6-18-1876 (6-20-1876)
Murphrey, Richard to Elizabeth Sowell 1-17-1883 (1-18-1883)
Murphy, Willson to Mandy Miller 8-18-1877
Musgraves, Tennessee to Anna Miller 11-13-1872 (no return)
Mustard, Isaac to Nancy Jane Ball 1-3-1876
Mustard, John F. to Sarah F. Daniel 9-25-1877
Musterd, Jobe to Emly Fultz 1-15-1881 (1-16-1881)
Myers, James S. to Mary Elizabeth Mink 5-8-1877 (5-10-1877)
Myers, Millerd to A. H. E. Woodard 7-22-1884 (7-27-1884)
Myers, Robert to Martha A. Watson 11-23-1882 (no return)
Myers, Silas to Mary Jane Underwood 1-10-1889? (1-12-1890)
Myers, William H. to Louisa L. Yoakum 8-25-1879 (8-28-1879)
Nance, Gorg to Martha Hopson 3-22-1879 (no return)
Nash, Charles W. to Mary V. Wierman 1-19-1870 (1-20-1870)
Nash, R. N. to Caroline Sulfridge 8-29-1888 (9-2-1888)
Nathen, Nancy to Jacob Willis 2-7-1886
Needham, G. B. to Nancy Debusk 8-10-1888 (8-17-1888)
Needham, M. F. to Sarah J. Carr 10-9-1875 (10-21-1875)
Neeham, J. M. to M. J. McCrary 10-26-1883 (10-28-1883)
Neeley, Wm. J. to Racheal L. Chance 10-8-1874 (no return)
Neely, Charles to Celia Meyers 4-25-1871
Neil, D. A. to M. A. Pain 2-26-1880
Neil, John P. to Sarah Mullins 12-25-1886 (no return)
Neil, Joseph to Jane Lynch 10-7-1880 (10-8-1880)
Nelems, G. M. to R. A. Taylor 11-29-1890

Nelms, Williams to Fannie Noe 12-27-1889
Nelson, George to Margarett Hatfield 7-29-1882 (7-30-1882)
Nelson, John to Mary A. Wilkerson 12-6-1886 (12-9-1886)
Nelson, William to Loisa J. Anderson 3-4-1872 (3-9-1872)
Nevels, George to Emeline Busick 11-30-1871 (no return)
Nevels, George to Louisa Baker 2-7-1872 (2-11-1872)
Newbey, Wm. to Margret Burk 2-23-1879
Newby, B. F. to Mariah Hurt 3-30-1872 (no return)
Newly, M. M. to Sarah J. Hopkins 5-24-1873 (5-28-1873)
Nicholds, Alfred to Crotia Ann Fendry 2-8-1876
Nicly, James to Sarah L. Blancet 8-28-1879 (no return)
Nicols, Benjamin to Susan Bowls 11-7-1872
Niel, J. F. to Melvina E. Carr 6-18-1870 (6-19-1870)
Nix, John to Mary Powers 2-11-1875
Noak, George to Louisa Hill 2-4-1876
Noblen, W. T. to M. L. Epperson 6-9-1879 (6-10-1879)
Noe, Daniel to Racheal Harrell 3-28-1871 (4-2-1871)
Noe, J. N. to Martha J. Turner 8-10-1879
Noe, Nathaniel to Sarah Penington 2-26-1884 (no return)
Noe, Rufus N. to Margret Hill 11-13-1877 (11-15-1877)
Noe, Woodson to Martha Thompson 12-25-1871
Norel, W. A. to Mary A. Welch 5-9-1878
Northen, Nelson to Pollie Lawson 12-6-1882 (no return)
Northern, Salem to Nancy S. Chance 2-8-1877
Northern, Solomon to Mary Johnson 10-1-1868 (no return)
Northern?, James N. to Elizabeth Crutchfield 12-17-1873 (12-18-1873)
Norvell, Elias J. to Vesta Ritter 8-29-1871 (8-31-1871)
Oaks, D. L. to Sallie Evans 10-25-1884 (12-4-1884)
Oaks, Isaac to Rainey Hensley 6-20-1874
Odell, John to Elisabeth Barnard 6-26-1875 (6-27-1875)
Odell, Johnathan to Elizabeth Keck 10-14-1877 (10-20-1877)
Odell, Marshal L. to Sarah M. Edwards 5-26-1869 (5-27-1869)
Oell?, Thomas H. to Animack Fugate 4-1-1881
Oley, C. H. to M. J. Sharp 11-19-1885 (12-28-1885)
Ollis, Thomas to Tulisha B. Hudleston 3-20-1883
Orath, John to Lucinda Hodges 4-23-1890
Orick, J. P. to R. E. Owens 10-7-1882 (10-8-1882)
Orick, John P. to Rachal E. Owens 10-7-1882 (no return)
Orourke, R. E. to Dora Por 9-12-1890 (10-5-1890)
Orsick, William H. to Elizabeth M. Hipsher 5-4-1877
Osborn, C. F. to Sarah Parker 12-14-1881
Osborn, Wm. T. to Rachal Debusk 10-1-1881
Otey, James T. to Nancy J. Sharp 4-9-1870 (4-10-1870)
Ousley, G. M. D. to Anna Edmonson 1-24-1874 (1-29-1874)
Ousley, John H. to Susan Edmondson 3-20-1880 (3-21-1880)
Overbay, James W. to Elizabeth Lumpkins 8-17-1874
Overholder, N. F. to Sarah Epperson 11-16-1888 (11-18-1888)
Overholser, L. C. to Lucy A. Hurst 2-14-1879 (2-16-1879)
Overholster, H. H. to Matilda West 11-14-1884 (11-17-1884)
Overley, Herrod to Elizabeth E. McCarty 8-17-1877 (10-7-1877)
Overton, Boid to Mariah Smith 5-2-1873 (no return)
Overton, Hamlet to Jane Easley 1-17-1872 (1-20-1872)
Overton, Henry to Matin Eastly 2-14-1885 (2-15-1885)
Overton, James to Rhoda Lanham 12-23-1885 (12-24-1885)
Overton, John to Mary F. Baley 1-3-1870 (1-10-1870) B
Overton, M. to Carnie Overton 12-3-1890 (no return) B
Overton, Warren D. to Almeta P. Riley 10-3-1881 (10-4-1881)
Overton, Wilburn to Mary F. Gillinwaters 5-18-1880 (5-19-1880)
Owen, James to Rebecca Lambert 1-4-1887 (1-9-1887)
Owens, A. J. to Margrett Richardson 6-2-1883 (6-3-1883)
Owens, Alfred to Rhoda Cupp 9-10-1874 (9-13-1874)
Owens, D. F. to R. J. Burchett 12-1-1876 (2-3-1876)
Owens, D. S. to G. B. (Mrs.) Douthe 12-9-1888
Owens, D. S. to Martha C. Goss 11-22-1878 (11-23-1878)
Owens, David N. to Mary J. Cheek 3-10-1877 (3-11-1877)
Owens, David to Matilda J. Pearson 10-23-1884 (11-2-1884)
Owens, Esawlandium to Rachal Sharp 10-4-1880 (10-8-1880)
Owens, F. M. to Hannah M. Briant 5-1-1876 (no return)
Owens, George P. to B. A. Crabtree 11-26-1881 (11-27-1881)
Owens, George P. to Lucy A. Cook 6-26-1877 (7-1-1877)
Owens, George W. to Sarah Fields 8-22-1876 (8-23-1876)
Owens, Jame to H. L. Cook 2-3-1881 (no return)
Owens, James M. to Sarah F. Sandifer 9-30-1881 (2-3-1882?)
Owens, James to Fanney B. Robertson 11-17-1888 (no return)
Owens, James to Sarah J. Kelleron 3-17-1883 (3-22-1883)
Owens, James to Sarah Walker 4-2-1881
Owens, John T. to Elizabeth Lanham 12-19-1870 (12-25-1870)
Owens, John to Mary E. Cosby 9-11-1881 (9-12-1881)
Owens, Joshua to Elizebeth Ausban 5-22-1879 (5-29-1879)
Owens, M. to Elizabeth Lovel 3-3-1879 (3-5-1879)
Owens, Rayman to Margret Fugate 8-14-1879 (8-16-1879)
Owens, Raymond to Rebecca Absher 12-21-1887 (12-21-1888?)
Owens, Robert to Eliza Longworth 9-15-1882 (9-24-1882)
Owens, Thomas to Martha Mannon 12-5-1879 (no return)
Owens, Thos. J. to Catharine Lewis 2-24-1890 (2-25-1890)
Owens, W. B. to Lucy Campbell 12-22-1877 (12-23-1877)
Owens, William W. S. to Elizabeth Doyel 8-23-1869 (8-29-1869)

Owens, Wm. B. to Aby Masingill 8-30-1880 (9-2-1880)
Owens, Wm. H. to Martha A. Furgerson 1-2-1869 (1-3-1869)
Owens, Wm. P. to Margaret Wilson 5-17-1871 (no return)
Oxford, Wm. to Maggie Jones 12-3-1887? (12-4-1887)
Pace, George W. to Rachel Elizabeth Brooks 1-27-1877 (1-28-1877)
Painter, William to Margaret A. Hall 2-19-1869 (2-21-1869)
Palmer, J. G. to Arminda Needham 10-28-1868 (10-29-1868)
Pane, George W. to Sarah J. Wilson 12-18-1873 (no return)
Panes?, Landrum to Nancy Turner 3-9-1885 (3-10-1885)
Paness, Wesley to Nancy Mury 5-18-1871
Panter, Clint to Mollie Brock 12-16-1885 (12-17-1885)
Panter, Winton to Mary Manis 9-1-1886 (9-2-1886)
Paris, John to Cornely Waler 11-1-1879 (11-3-1879)
Paris, Wm to Martha Lundy 8-18-1871 (8-20-1871)
Paris, Wm. to Mathawsen Bemer 7-26-1886 (crossed out)
Parker, J. D. to Elisabeth Heath 10-6-1888 (10-11-1888)
Parker, James T. to Nancy C. Harrell 5-2-1874 (5-4-1874)
Parker, Jerry R. to Mallie Harrell 10-20-1877 (10-21-1877)
Parker, Jobe to Susan Turner 12-31-1879
Parker, Robert to Lucy Parker 3-28-1871
Parker, Thomas to Catherin Lane 10-23-1879
Parkey, H. G. to Lou A. Kincaid 1-5-1885
Parkey, Hardy to Mandy Rolen 5-6-1873 (no return)
Parkey, Israel to Susan Coleman 4-5-1876 (4-7-1876)
Parkey, Jasper to Jane (Miss) Hithhorne 7-14-1890 (7-16-1890) B
Parkey, Thomas to Elizabeth Coleman 4-13-1874 (4-14-1874)
Parkey, Thos. to Elizabeth Coleman 4-13-1874 (no return)
Parkey, William to Emelinle Davault 12-4-1869 (12-5-1869) B
Parks, R. M. to Julia Chadwell 1-13-1882? (1-13-1882)
Parks, Tennessee M. to Olley Stone 10-15-1870 (10-16-1870)
Parks, Wm. to M. A. Sanders 11-?-1879? (11-14-1879)
Parky, James to Rucia Overton 2-9-1878 (no return)
Parr, Smith to Martha J. Woods 8-2-1871 (8-3-1871)
Parratt, Taylor to Rachael Robinson 2-10-1872
Parsifield, David W. to Martha Sprinkle 9-6-1870 (no return)
Partin, William to Nancy Partin 12-29-1879 (12-26?-1879)
Parton, J. W. to M. J. Webe? 12-31-1880
Parton, William to Mary Jane Ingrum 5-7-1870 (6-7-1870)
Pate, W. L. to Mary E. Degord? 4-1-1886
Patrick, Henry to Sarah Bowman 12-20-1874 (12-3?-1874)
Patterson, Elbert to Sarah Lanham 12-4-1883 (no return)
Patterson, George W. to Elizabeth Bedsaw 11-22-1879 (11-23-1879)
Patterson, H. M. to Maggie Marcrum 11-12-1884 (11-13-1884)
Patterson, Houston to Emma B. Campbell 8-20-1873
Patterson, James to Margret Lanham 6-14-1884 (6-15-1884)
Patterson, Robert to Catherine Lambert 9-13-1876 (9-21-1876)
Patterson, Robt. L. to Emma E. Snavely 12-6-1888 (12-12-1888)
Patterson, Wm. to Hester S. Treece 1-7-1888
Patterson?, Hamey to Nancy Estridge 10-19-1881 (10-20-1881)
Paul, David to Nancy J. Greenlee 3-31-1877
Paul, James to Millie Honeycut 2-26-1886 (2-28-1886)
Paul, John to J. L. Keck 11-5-1879 (no return)
Paul, Moses to Elizabeth McFarler 1-3-1884
Paul, Richard to Sarah M. Collins 12-29-1882 (12-31-1882)
Paul, Thomas to Mary Williams 10-1-1887
Paul, Wm. J. to Sarah Moor 12-8-1884
Payn, James to Priscila Williams 8-28-1878?
Payne, R. B. to Martha J. Wiley 3-11-1871 (3-16-1871)
Payne, W. L. to Mollie Greer 12-22-1878 (12-24-1878)
Pearce, A. M. to R. C. Freeman 1-12-1885
Pearce?, J. H. to Margette Harris 10-31-1878 (1-9-1879)
Pearson, J. B. to M. L. Johnson 7-24-1879 (10-19-1879)
Pearson, Lewis T. to Allice Cloud 2-3-1870
Pearson, W. R. to V. M. Barnard 11-23-1887 (12-1-1887)
Pearson, William to Elizabeth Rowe 10-9-1877 (no return)
Pearson, Wm. to Nanney State 2-18-1888 (2-20-1888)
Peck, Charly to Malinda Brooks 7-20-1877
Peerce, Isaac to Margret M. Tumel 1-30-1880 (1-31-1880)
Pendegrass, D. C. to M. Bolton 9-8-1879
Pennington, Wm. to Nancy J. King 5-20-1883
Perce, A. T. to O. T. McCarty 8-6-1880
Perkins, Peter to Manirva Buckhanon 1-5-1871
Perkins, S. F. to Elizibeth Sitser 7-20-1882 (7-23-1882?)
Perman, Waldegrave to Mary H. Cottereil 4-24-1889
Perry, J. N. to Vera C. McBee 10-20-1878 (no return)
Perry, R. H. to M. L. Wilson 3-30-1882 (4-1-1882)
Peter, James J. to Analin Hanson 11-1-1879 (no return)
Peters, Elias to Mary E. Watson 11-27-1888
Petree, Robert to Nancy Cluck? 10-21-1873 (10-26-1873)
Phelps, David to Nancy S. Mitchell 12-25-1888 (12-26-1888)
Phelps, Green to Lizzie McDaniel 5-15-1885 (5-16-1885)
Phelps, John to Nancy Jane Taner 1-29-1876 (1-30-1876)
Phillipps, J. B. to Margaret Lunda 10-9-1887
Phillips, Henry to Josephine Gray 12-14-1876 (12-16-1876)
Phillips, Herkles to Jane Bruce 3-1-1879
Phillips, J. W. to Margret S. Felps 1-11-1878 (no return)
Phillips, John to Mary Saylor 9-8-1886

Phillips, Lewis W. to D. C. Gibson 1-7-1881 (no return)
Pickrell, Charles W. to Cornelie A. Graham 12-21-1882
Pierce, Isaac A. to Mary A. Smith 1-10-1883 (no return)
Pierce, J. W. to Margret W. N. Alexander 2-3-1872 (2-8-1872)
Pierce, John H. to Louisa M. Peters 2-20-1881
Pike, Benjamin F. to Tilda E. Shofner 7-3-1888 (7-4-1888)
Pike, James to Vienna Maler 9-30-1879
Plank, Robt. to Martha (Miss) Jones 6-14-1885
Plank, Robt. to Martha E. Jones 6-11-1885 (no return)
Poor, A. J. to Susan B. Cline 12-24-1886 (12-25-1886)
Poor, B. M. to Martha L. Mathis 11-16-1874 (11-21-1874)
Poor, Baxter to E. O. Mathis 3-15-1881 (3-16-1881)
Poor, Baxter to Easter Orlena Mathis 3-15-1881 (no return)
Poor, D. M. to Margaret L. Lunch 6-18-1872
Poor, Ed. to Ollie Lease? 10-5-1885?
Poor, Grant to Mary Jane Carroll 10-23-1890
Poor, H. G. to Lucy J. Carmon 7-30-1877 (8-5-1877)
Poor, Huffman to Dora Russell 10-26-1889 (no return)
Poor, James to Elizabeth J. Cupp 10-9-1875 (10-10-1875)
Poor, N. W. to Melvina Cupp 5-31-1889
Poor, Prior E. to Saraha L. Daniel 5-31-1878 (no return)
Poor, Prior to Elizabeth Mathus 10-30-1883
Poor, R. M. to Sarah A. Cupp 8-4-1884
Poor, Richard W. to Sibba A. Drummond 12-21-1868 (12-24-1868)
Poor, S. C. to Mary A. Sands 11-6-1882 (11-7-1882)
Poor, T. Wm. to Elvira Whitman 5-3-1886 (5-4-1886)
Poor, Thos. C. to Nancy M. Cline 7-27-1872
Poor, W. T. to Mary H. Waters 4-10-1877 (1-27-1878)
Porness?, G. B. to M. B. Mackey 6-10-1883
Posoey, B. M. to Loucinda Cunnningham 4-30-1875
Posoey, Ensley to Cornelia Buckanan 5-12-1877
Posoey, Jubilee to Mary A. Lee 5-13-1871 (5-14-1871)
Posoey, William F. to Margaret Soliver 1-11-1870 (1-19-1870)
Potees, E. B. to Lawry An Gibson 6-14-1879
Powel, Houston to Cleapatra Ousley 12-28-1874 (no return)
Powell, F. M. to Ollie J. Jones 4-1-1876 (4-4-1876)
Powell, Isaac to Calie J. Freman 1-5-1883 (1-7-1883)
Powell, James to Elizabeth Chumbley 7-12-1872 (no return)
Powell, N. H. to Martha J. C. Stone 11-22-1876 (11-23-1876)
Powell, P. F. to Mary Carnell 4-17-1880 (4-19-1880)
Powell, Pleasant F. to Lucinda L. Cross 1-19-1876 (1-20-1876)
Powers, G. B. to Sarah Pearce 8-10-1879
Powers, George to Lesca Marsee 7-28-1881
Powers, Wm. N. to P. J. Powers 9-26-1881
Prater?, Georg to Elizabeth King 9-6-1878 (9-7-1878)
Prator, A. C. to Martha Cosby 11-?-1886 (no return)
Prator, Alfred C. to Mary V. Fletcher 2-28-1883
Prator, John F. to Nancy Crutchfield 1-21-1878
Pratt, J. K. to Catharine Goin 11-18-1890
Pratt, Wm. to Jane Hodges 6-21-1890 (6-22-1890)
Pratutt?, George to Lilia Baker 9-4-1890
Presenell, Shade to Martha L. Owens 5-24-1890 (5-25-1890)
Presley, Elizabeth to D. J. M. Collins 8-4-1889
Presley, Josiah to Elizabeth Jackson 6-10-1884 (no return)
Presley, W. J. to Elizabeth Eastus 12-20-1873 (12-21-1873)
Presly, Josiah to Malinda Carter 1-9-1885 (no return)
Pressley, John to Mary C. Carter 9-23-1886 (no return)
Pressnell, Joseph to M. C. Cox 8-?-1890 (8-31-1890)
Price, D. B. to Mary Ann Carroll 12-20-1888 (12-25-1888)
Price, Henry to Allace Carrell 9-23-1889 (12-13-1889)
Price, Jamee to Fany Parson 12-19-1877 (12-20-1877)
Price, John to Mary M. Carell 3-17-1883 (3-14?-1883)
Pridemore, George to Bella Carmon 12-18-1886 (12-19-1886)
Pridemore, Hiram to Susa Ann Sorton 2-25-1874 (2-26-1874)
Pridmore, Chad to Elizabeth Johnson 3-4-1871 (3-5-1871)
Priffit, Wm. to Manerva Shelton 3-28-1885
Profett, John to Esther Love (Mis) Rogers 7-29-1881
Proffit, Granvill S. to Jesy M. Smith 10-9-1877
Provence, Samuel to Nancy Pridemore 12-20-1873 (1-4-1874)
Provene, Jeramiah to Mary Jane Johnson 11-30-1874 (12-17-1874)
Purky, James A. to Emaline Pearson 12-21-1882 (12-24-1882)
Pursifal, M. J. to Orpha Hurst 3-13-1878 (3-14-1878)
Quarland?, Prier to Sarah Simmons 12-24-1878
Quimer, G. W. to Martha B. Carr 11-24-1886
Quisenberry, Andrew to M. E. Ares 4-26-1886 (4-27-1886)
Raines, James to Loucind King 8-30-1883
Raines, W. H. to Polly E. King 5-28-1882
Rains, Jefferson to Phaney Turner 6-15-1872 (no return)
Ramsey, Mc. to Eliza Williaimls 11-7-1868 (11-8-1868)
Ramsey, Solomon to Marry J. Williams 8-20-1879
Ranes, B. F. to Fanny Morsee 12-14-1877
Ranes, Henry to Sofa A. Hamblin 2-3-1869
Ranes, J. P. to Nany Yoakum 9-5-1884 (no return)
Raney, D. S. to Elizabeth Bullis 3-26-1885 (3-28-1885)
Raney, Elijah W. to Martha Edwards 9-2-1871 *
Rater, T. C. to Mary Ote 10-21-1878
Ray, Samuel to Jane Pridemore 8-4-1871

Read, Jas. to Martha E. Simmons 4-1-1884
Readmon, Hosey to Mary Ely 9-27-1877
Rector, G. W. to Victory A. Debusk 10-1-1883 (10-4-1883)
Redman, Danul to Parrott Freeman 5-1-1889
Redmon, E. S. to Harriet Seals 2-16-1886 (2-6?-1886)
Redmond, Jobe C. to Mery E. Nelson 5-8-1883 (5-9-1883)
Redmond, Levi to M. Jackson 12-23-1872 (12-25-1872)
Redmond, W. H. to Jane Farmer 11-14-1890 (11-15-1890)
Reece, Daniel to Matilda J. Estis 8-27-1870 (9-27-1870)
Reece, Isaac to Jane Smith 8-21-1875 (8-22-1875)
Reece, Jacob M. to Sarah E. Powers 12-20-1886 (12-30-1886)
Reece, Jacob to Sarah E. Dunsmore 12-12-1874 (12-17-1874)
Reece, W. M. to Mella Hall 11-26-1890
Reed, Andrew to M. J. Wilaford 10-19-1882
Reed, Bellenvin to Mary Lane 8-18-173 (8-21-1873)
Reed, James M. to Margrett M. Tennels 4-24-1882
Reed, James to Hariett C. Lawson 4-2-1879 (4-22-1879)
Reede, Wm. to Mary Wilford 9-6-1879 (9-8-1879)
Reedy, J. L. to Mary Stone 10-8-1884 (10-11-1884)
Reese, A. J. to M. Robinson 8-30-1879 (8-31-1879)
Reese, Wm. M. to Catherine Wolf 7-25-1870 (7-28-1870)
Reice, James to Margaret Northern 11-27-1886 (no return)
Retter, J. R. to Mary Hurst 10-29-1878 (10-31-1878)
Reynolds, Charley to Harriett Harvey 12-24-1889 (no return)
Reynolds, James E. to Sarah E. Hurst 2-5-1887 (2-6-1887)
Rhea, G. W. to M. R. Shipley 7-7-1890 (7-8-1890)
Rice, Clinton to Jane Martan 7-?-1879 (7-8-1879)
Rice, David to Nancy Clark 10-24-1871
Rice, Franklin to Orlenia Houston 8-6-1869 B
Rice, J. B. to M. C. Dooly 12-28-1876
Rice, Marshel M. to Margaret Bowls 8-17-1887 (no return)
Rice, Stephen to Margertee Ford 4-22-1880 (4-23-1880)
Rich, Charles to Mary Cain 10-5-1871
Richardson, D. to M. C. Henniger 4-17-1890 (4-14?-1890)
Richardson, G. W. to N. E. Runion 12-14-1878
Richardson, J. A. to Juluy? Roark 9-27-1889 (no return)
Richardson, James to M. F. Lambert 8-13-1878
Richardson, James to Margrett Roark 10-2-1880 (10-3-1880)
Richardson, M. B. to W. T. Vansel 1-5-1885 (no return)
Richman, M. D. to Saluda J. Sewell 2-9-1875 (2-11-1875)
Richman, Nathaniel E. to Mary E. Morison 8-8-1883
Riddle, Murphrea H. to Juda Lake 8-24-1875
Riddle, Thos. A. to Margret Johnson 12-25-1884 (12-27-1884)
Ridens, John to Elizabeth Sparks 11-24-1874 (12-24-1874)
Ridens, John to Julia A. Tennel 6-23-1883 (no return)
Rider, H. V. to Hattie C. Sanders 8-14-1889 (8-15-1889)
Rider, Richard to Frances A. Carter 9-2-1869
Ridings, William to M. A. England 11-5?-1880 (11-7-1880)
Ridings, Williams to Margrett A. Linnals 5-28-1881 (5-29-1881)
Right, James to Sarah Chamberlain 9-29-1876 (10-1-1876)
Rigsbee, Andrew to Susan A. Mathis 4-29-1880
Rigsbey, G. W. to N. A. Poor 1-19-1879 (1-20-1879)
Riley, Evan to Elizabeth Davis 9-24-1870 (9-25-1870)
Riley, Floid to Martha Kyle 11-24-1883 (no return)
Riley, Hiram to A. J. Brooks 1-1-1879 (no return)
Riley, Nelson to Amendy Enser 6-10-1879 (no return)
Riley, Thomas to Elizabeth Lasley 4-5-1869 (4-8-1869)
Riley, Thos. to Martha J. Fugate 1-14-1874 (1-15-1874)
Riley, Wm. to Nervesta Parkey 10-5-1882 (no return)
Riley, Zachariah to Martha Jane Parkey 4-19-1876 (no return)
Rillens, David to Elmiriy Tolliver 10-7-1871 (10-8-1871)
Rine, Henry J. to Sarah E. Gibson 12-1-1881 (12-2-1881)
Ritchardson, James to Mary F. Lambert 8-13-1878 (no return)
Rite, William to Margrett Thomas 12-21-1880
Ritter, H. H. to Elisabeth Yoakum 12-7-1874 (12-13-1874)
Ritter, Nathan S. to Malinda E. Poor 5-4-1872 (no return)
Roark, B. F. to Mary J. Lambert 11-23-1877 (no return)
Roark, Fredrick to Margret J. Banen 11-17-1877
Roark, James to Nancy Cunningham 9-6-1869
Roark, Jermiah to Nancy E. Patterson 11-24-1871 (11-28-1871)
Roark, Joseph to Eliza E. Friar 11-2-1868 (11-3-1868)
Roark, Timothy to Elizabeth Vaun 8-24-1877
Roark, Timothy to Margret Eastridge 5-4-1878 (5-12-1878)
Roark, Timothy to Ollie Carman 1-6-1886 (1-7-1886)
Roark, Wm. to Sarah J. Sutton 5-16-1871
Robatare, Elias P. to A. L. Age 11-23-1878
Roberds, Absolem to Nancy Reece 8-25-1886 (no return)
Roberson, Benjamin to Angeline Cautton 8-28-1878 (no return)
Roberson, Henly to M. A. Lusen 9-28-1878 (9-30-1878)
Robert, Josiiah to Sarah C. Daniel 12-7-1872 (12-8-1872)
Roberts, Thos. to Laura Vaughn 9-23-1886
Roberts, Z. S. to Emlie McQuister 4-4-1871
Robertson, James A. to M. M. Standifer 4-14-1881 (4-19-1881)
Robertson, James D. to Sarah N. Powell 1-10-1874
Robertson, Lemuel to C. S. Lane 5-31-1887
Robertson, Lumll? to Octava L. Bryant 6-15-1885 (6-16-1885)
Robertson, Thomas to Tobitha J. England 3-11-1878 (no return)

Robertson, Toliver to Marth (Mrs.) England 6-10-1881 (6-19-1881)
Robertson, W. D. to Carma Debusk 10-17-1889 (10-27-1889)
Robertson, William to Mary Drummons 1-28-1891 (2-8-1891)
Robin, J. to Mary Hurst 7-10-1880
Robins, James B. to Eliza Hurst 8-19-1874
Robinson, Benjamine to Mary Murphy 1-6-1876
Robinson, H. H. to Lettie J. Baylor 5-7-1873 (5-8-1873)
Robinson, Harvey to Mary Morgan 8-6-1873 (9-6-1873)
Robinson, J. B. to Mollie Simmons 9-18-1886 (no return)
Robinson, J. N. to Florah Robinson 11-3-1875 (11-4-1875)
Robinson, J. W. to Nancy Widener 9-30-1885 (10-3-1885)
Robinson, R. L. to Rachial L. Davies 9-17-1884
Robinson, Reuben R. to Lucinda J. Burch 10-7-1869
Robinson, Richard T. to Martha McBee 11-18-1869 (11-21-1869)
Robinson, Robert H. to Manervia J. McBee 10-6-1877 (no return)
Robinson, Thos. to Elizabeth George 7-17-1884
Robinson, Warren? to Lizza Siggar 9-1-1890 (no return)
Robinson, Winton to Beceyann Furry 2-19-1881 (2-10-1881)
Robinson, Wm. T. to Sarah Russell 8-31-1877 (no return)
Roe, Benj. J. to Pulaski A. J. Simmons 10-28-1868 (10-29-1868)
Roe, William to Verny Bremer 7-21-1890 (7-22-1890)
Rogers, C. C. to Anna Ausmus 12-29-1888 (12-30-1888)
Rogers, C. H. to Mollie Cotterell 1-25-1888
Rogers, F. G. to M. M. Neil 11-5-1883 (11-8-1883)
Rogers, Felix G. to Juda J. Yoakum 11-2-1877 (11-4-1877)
Rogers, George B. to Rattie L. Markham 12-8-1890 (no return)
Rogers, H. M. to Amanda Bamman 11-18-1875
Rogers, J. A. to A. B. Rogers 1-20-1887
Rogers, J. M. to Melvina Bolinger 4-25-1890 (5-4-1890)
Rogers, Jesse L. to Annie M. Fetridge 10-24-1877
Rogers, John A. to M. V. Rogers 12-21-1878
Rogers, John F. to C. Hopper 1-19-1881 (1-20-1881)
Rogers, John F. to Lucinda Cawood 8-10-1869 (8-12-1869)
Rogers, John F. to Melviny M. Cawood 11-22-1880 (no return)
Rogers, John N. to Catherine Welch 11-22-1872 (11-23-1872)
Rogers, M. A. to B. F. Ausmus 10-15-1879 (1-5-1880)
Rogers, R. B. to Aly Rogers 12-7-1876
Rogers, Rice to Mary Bowman 7-31-1879 (no return)
Rogers, Timothy S. to Marlenia McBee 12-17-1868 (12-20-1868)
Rogers, W. B. to Mary A. Ausmus 10-11-1886 (10-27-1886)
Rogers, Wm. F. to Susan E. Rogers 4-24-1889 (8?-24-1889)
Rogers, Wm. J. W. to Susan R. Bullard 9-8-1872
Rogers, Wm. Riley to Sarah J. Rowat? 2-9-1875 (2-11-1875)
Rolan, Wm. H. to N. J. Margraves 12-19-1879 (12-21-1879)
Rolin, James to Rutha Brooks 3-2-1882 (3-5-1882)
Rolins, Smith to Mary Bull 11-13-1879
Rollin, Elbert to Matilda Anderson 12-22-1880 (12-24-1880)
Rolling, George W. to Phebe Jones 4-18-1869
Rollins, James to Amanda Arnett 5-22-1871
Rollins, William to S. J. Right 8-1-1882 (8-2-1882)
Rook?, James to Nancy Steel 3-5-1883
Roop, E. L. to M. E. Leabow 8-30-1884 (9-4-1884)
Rose, George to Malinda Pearce 8-10-1879
Rose, James to Martha J. Lanksford 4-4-1890 (7-28-1890)
Rose, John to Nancy Harper 11-10-1876
Rose, Tillman H. to Florance R. Halls 5-28-1872 (5-30-1872)
Rose, Wm. to Mollie Samuel 7-22-1883
Rosenbalm, David to Louisa Hurst 10-31-1874 (11-1-1874)
Rosenbalm, Henry to Mary Warric 5-17-1883
Rosenbalm, Isaac to Docia A. Brown 5-28-1881
Rosenbalm, John P. to Nancy J. Evans 2-10-1870 (2-13-1870)
Rosenbalm, W. L. to Nancy J. Parris 9-15-1886 (9-16-1886)
Rosenbalm, Wm. to Cordelia Neil 5-23-1885 (no return)
Rosenbam, Frank to Rachel Goin 1-13-1880 (no return)
Rosier, Hampton to Sibire E. Jones 12-23-1871 (12-24-1871)
Ross, Wm. H. to Matilda Collins 10-18-1870 (10-10-1871)
Rouse, Harriel to Mary M. Goforth 11-10-1869 (11-14-1869)
Rouse, J. M. to S. T. Johnson 8-2-1889
Rouse, Preston E. to Mary J. Dockery 2-6-1889 (2-7-1889)
Rowe, J. F. to Mary Smith 12-7-1885 (12-10-1885)
Rowland, George to Mary Yeary 1-19-1883 (12-2-1883)
Rowlen, Peter to E. Estept 1-15-1884 (no return)
Rowlend, Peter H. to Martha Campbell 2-20-1869 (2-25-1869)
Rowlet, L. R. to Mollie Connor 1-19-1888 (1-26-1888)
Rowlett, Levi to Martha B. Campbell 6-9-1888 (no return)
Rowlett, W. F. to Amanda Carmack 5-1-1880 (5-2-1880)
Rucker, George to Martha M. England 12-24-1882
Runnions, A. W. to C. Owen 12-25-1876
Runnions, Ewing to Rhoda Cook 3-27-1877 (3-29-1877)
Runnions, G. W. to Lucy Ann Painter 2-7-1874 (2-8-1874)
Rush, R. C. to M. S. Pearson 1-28-1885
Russ, Wm. to Mary A. Parks 1-2-1871
Russ?, Robert R. to Mary C. Lawson 3-4-1869
Russell, A. L. to Martha M. Forkner 12-14-1880 (12-16-1880)
Russell, G. W. to S. J. Robertson 4-10-1888 (4-15-1888)
Russell, J. H. to Elisabeth Smith 4-24-1888 (4-26-1888)
Russell, J. T. to Martha Treece 4-10-1888 (4-15-1888)
Russell, Jackson to Mary Lee 8-10-1889 (8-11-1889)
Russell, James to Amanda Kincaid 1-14-1881? (1-30-1881)
Russell, Jessie to Emiley Ausmus 12-24-1885
Russell, Lewis to America E. Evans 10-11-1890 (no return)
Russell, Robert F. to Mary Teague 10-29-1869 (11-4-1869)
Russell, T. J. to M. Lundy 10-10-1873 (10-12-1873)
Russell, W. H. to Elizabeth Treece 5-31-1889 (no return)
Russell, W. S. to Nancy Carr 9-13-1890 (9-14-1890)
Russell, Wm. B. to Sarah A. Goforth 1-7-1871 (1-8-1871)
Russell, Wm. F. to Emiley M. Ford 5-19-1877 (5-21-1877)
Russell, Wm. M. to Nancey Moyers 6-19-1880 (6-27-1880)
Rutherford, Bruce H. to Mary E. Farmer 12-3-1889 (12-4-1890?)
Rutherford, J. H. to Ophal Hurst 3-19-1878
Rymor, William to Lucy Prydemore 3-29-1876 (no return)
Sailor, Albert to Milli? J. Sailor 11-11-1878
Samfor, John to Sally Green 7-4-1890 (7-5-1890)
Samler, John to Elizabeth Whiteaker 8-25-1871 (8-27-1871)
Samlo, Jack (Jacob?) to Marry Howard 1-31-1881
Sample, John A. to Elizabeth Gamrell 1-19-1872
Sampson, Samuel to Arrenia Martin 11-25-1872
Sander, Garrett to Elizabeth Turner 10-21-1882
Sanders, Alexander to Sallie Shoemate 10-27-1882 (no return)
Sanders, George W. to Sarah F. Agey 10-21-1869 (10-24-1869)
Sanders, George to Elisabeth Cloud 8-30-1888
Sanders, Harvey to N. S. Cross 5-25-1885
Sandford, Teb to Lucy England 11-20-1888 (11-22-1888)
Sandifer, Floyd to Lucy Jane Jones 3-26-1877 (3-29-1877)
Sandifer, John to Sarah Williams 10-9-1886
Sandifer, Samuel to Alis Marcum 3-13-1877
Sands, Layfett to Ollie Ramey 3-4-1881 (3-6-1881)
Santifer, Wm. H. to Mary A. Hill 10-18-1872 (no return)
Saterfield, James to Elizabeth Bunch 8-16-1882 (8-17-1882)
Satterfield, John W. to Cordelia Hurst 5-2-1877 (5-3-1877)
Sawyers, Charley to Sarrah A. Cupp 11-9-1878
Saylor, Jerry to L. M. Saylor 2-19-1881
Saylor, Levi to Nancy Upton 6-23-1881
Scarborough, John H. to Mary F. Fulkerson 11-8-1876 (11-9-1876)
Schott, Nathaniel to E. F. A. Brills 5-8-1878
Schott, Nathaniel to E. T. A. Bailey 5-8-1878
Scots?, James to Laney H. Sulfridge 5-20-1886
Scott, Boston to Sarah Shultz 7-23-1872
Scott, Charles W. to Margret King 3-22-1879
Scott, J. S. to Nancy A. Colvord 7-29-1885? (8-2-1886)
Scott?, Richard to Mary E. Mason 5-23-1871 (no return)
Seabolt, Lewis to Susanah King 5-26-1869 (5-27-1869)
Seal, L. F. to Hallie Pearson 5-7-1889 (5-19-1889)
Seal, W. P. C. to Savana Lawson? 1-6-1890 (no return)
Seal, Wm. to Sudie Hodges 12-12-1882 (12-17-1882)
Seale, E. W. to Mary L. McNiel 5-6-1884 (no return)
Seals, Zack to Sarah Collin 1-7-1888 (1-8-1888)
Sebolt, J. L. to Isabel Settum 4-11-1885 (no return)
Sebolt, John to Sarah J. Ares 12-15-1881 (12-22-1881)
Sebolt?, John to Mary Sulfridg 9-25-1880 (10-3-1880)
Semore, Wm. H. to A. Chadwick 12-14-1881
Senseney, J. R. to Orleana Hughes 12-5-1887
Serber, A. J. to Rachel Maples 4-11-1889 (no return)
Sergent, Ephram to Sarah Griffiths 10-5-1881
Sewell, J. J. to N. E. Owens 7-7-1878
Sewell, J. J. to N. E. Sewell 4-17-1890
Sexton, John to Demarius Aleree? 12-26-1881
Sexton, Morgan to Malinday Ingle 7-28-1872 (no return)
Shade, Augustas to Jennie Huff 3-21-1883 (3-22-1883)
Sharp, A. J. to Mary A. Greer 3-14-1888 (3-15-1888)
Sharp, Calven to Matilda Brogan 11-13-1879 (11-27-1879)
Sharp, Frankling to Polley E. Needham 10-30-1879
Sharp, H. F. to Mary F. Rogers 2-18-1871 (2-19-1871)
Sharp, Harrison to Pollyanna Caul 3-?-1875 (3-18-1875)
Sharp, James M. K. to Sarah E. Schooler 7-3-1869 (7-4-1869)
Sharp, James to Sarah A. Hopper 12-23-1882 (12-24-1882)
Sharp, John G. to Mary A. Carr 1-4-1875 (1-12-1875)
Sharp, Johnathan to Amanda Parrott 11-5-1881
Sharp, W. H. to Sarah McCary 9-6-1880 (9-9-1880)
Sharp, W. L. to M. B. Alexander 11-6-1888 (11-7-1888)
Sharp, Wesley to Rosa Collinsworth 2-17-1875
Sharpsher, Jas. S. to Rutha Row 6-21-1880 (6-21-1880)
Shaufner, Calaway to Elizabeth Simmons 10-11-1877
Shell, H. D. to Victory Wheeler 12-4-1879 (no return)
Shell, James to Virginia Hurst 2-9-1888
Shelton, Christopher D. to Polly A. Barnard 3-9-1869 (3-11-1869)
Shelton, Fielding to Vashti Taylor no date (Jan 1885?)
Shelton, Fielding to Vesta Tylor 2-14-1885
Shelton, Henry to Louisa Vance 2-4-1882 (2-5-1882)
Shelton, Henry to Rebeca Mason 6-28-1883
Shelton, N. J. to Eliza Breeding 11-16-1887 (11-17-1887)
Shelton, William to Nancy Maddix 11-11-1880
Shepard, Robt. D. to Frances M. Russell 8-25-1889
Shepley, Edward P. to America Houghes 4-8-1878 (4-3?-1878)

Sheton, William to Nancy C. Mattox 7-6-1889
Shipley, E. P. to America Hughes 2-6-1885
Shipley, W. S. to Sarah E. Chadwick 8-4-1873
Shipley, William to Margaret Buiser 9-17-1868 (9-18-1868)
Shipman, Frank to Mary Willis 9-4-1882 (9-7-1882)
Shoemaker, B. R. to M. M. Harmon 8-7-1875 (8-11-1875)
Shoemaker, Thos. R. to Malinda Epps 6-3-1874 (6-4-1874)
Shofner, Caliway to Ellin J. Howard 6-11-1882
Shopsher, Henry to Martha Davis 5-18-1886 (5-19-1886)
Shultz, B. F. to Eliza J. Johnson 4-30-1872
Shultz, Thomas to Marry Fullington 3-19-1881 (3-24-1881)
Shultz, W. F. to A. Breeding 8-20-1881 (8-21-1881)
Shumate, Henry to Lardy Gulley 2-10-1889
Shumate, Thomas A. to Elisabeth Provene 11-30-1874 (no return)
Shupe, William to Manerva Russell 11-15-1890 (no return)
Sikes, Henry to Rebecca Widby 6-23-1887
Siler, Geo. M. to Harriett Bilingley 12-12-1887
Siler, H. V. B. to Matilda Terry 1-4-1890
Siler, Maynard to Ella Sharp 2-10-1888 (no return)
Simes, J. H. to Marry Epperson 10-6-1879
Simmon, David to Martha A. Weaver 11-3-1890 (11-4-1890)
Simmons, A. D. to H. M. Yoakum 12-2-1873 (12-4-1873)
Simmons, G. S. M. to L. C. Simmons 4-29-1874
Simmons, James C. to Annie Loaness 10-26-1887
Simmons, Joseph to Catherine Johnson 10-25-1879 (no return)
Simmons, S. M. to Nellie Colwell 8-19-1888 (no return)
Simpson, John to Basia Colston 6-8-1887
Sims, Benjamin to Mary Farlor 10-19-1868 (10-22-1868) B
Sims, James to Hellen Cole 6-6-1889 (6-9-1889)
Singleton, George C. to Mary E. Freman 4-23-1883 (4-29-1883)
Singleton, Hamilton to Julia Ann Epperson 4-25-1873 (4-26-1874?)
Sitner, Henry to Mina Perkins 1-22-1883 (2-2-1883)
Sivills, T. G. to R. M. Green 12-26-1880
Sivils, Wm. to Tiliva? Lewis 2-5-1891 (no return)
Skaggs, D. M. to Marry E. Jessee 5-21-1881 (5-28-1881)
Skaggs, Elbrig to Sarah B. Harmon 14-4-1882 (12-7-1882)
Smith, Alex to Ellie Brown? 4-4-1885 (no return)
Smith, Alexander to Eliza Davidson 6-14-1879 (6-15-1879)
Smith, Benj. to Mary Jane Norvill 1-14-1871 (1-18-1871)
Smith, Campbell to Martha A. Miller 12-28-1871
Smith, D. C. to E. A. Dunsmore 3-9-1879
Smith, David to Susan Cook 3-4-1877 (no return)
Smith, Elijah to Sarah ___ 4-6-1877 (no return)
Smith, F. H. to Cordelin Carr 10-16-1886 (10-17-1886)
Smith, George to Elizabeth Cox 11-29-1883
Smith, H. M. to E. A. Cawood 12-11-1882 (12-14-1882)
Smith, J. M. to Manila A. Walker 9-6-1877 (9-9-1877)
Smith, J. P. to C. J. Carney 10-20-1882 (10-22-1882)
Smith, J. W. to Louiza D. Collins 1-4-1890 (1-5-1890)
Smith, J. W. to Minervia Lakins 3-11-1876 (3-12-1876)
Smith, James H. to Martha J. Washam 1-26-1872 (1-28-1872)
Smith, James H. to Poley Barnard 2-24-1879 (2-27-1879)
Smith, James to Eliza J. Newby 9-13-1879
Smith, John K. L. to Martha J. Kesterson 1-21-1871 (1-26-1871)
Smith, John W. to Anne M. Honeycutt 2-13-1872 (2-15-1872)
Smith, John W. to Melvina Muncy 10-10-1885
Smith, John to Margaret Cupp 6-29-1885 (7-5-1885)
Smith, Nathaniel to Ester Hunter 2-23-1877 (2-24-1877)
Smith, Richard to Elizebeth Standiford 5-21-1879 (5-22-1879)
Smith, Solaman to Martha Jerdan 10-7-1879 (10-24-1879)
Smith, Sterliing to Margret Rutherford 12-21-1876
Smith, Thomas to Nancey Meiher 9-31?-1880 (9-10-1880)
Smith, Thos. to Martha Noah 12-26-1888 (12-27-1888)
Smith, W. H. to Florance Maddox 5-3-1886
Smith, W. H. to Rebecca Mason 2-28-1887 (3-2-1887)
Smith, William to Mary Louiza Laycock 12-29-1868
Smith, Wm. to Sarah Toliver 1-2-1888
Snavely, J. G. to Martha E. Nevels 10-24-1884 (10-25-1885)
Snavely, Jacob to Sarah Holladay 12-12-1878
Snavely, Leander to Mary E. Estept 9-21-1888 (9-24-1888)
Sneed, John S. to Susan A. Hill 12-26-1868 (12-27-1868)
Snider, Frank to Jennie Mink 6-22-1889 (6-23-1889)
Snider, James to Tennessee Keck 10-9-1884
Snider, Lafay W. to Sarah F. Debusk 3-8-1888
Snider, Wm. to L. C. Sans 7-31-1880
Snoddy, Thos. A. to Susan L. Shiply 4-8-1886
Soard, Isaac to Mary Jennings 7-24-1877 (no return)
Soard, John to Melvina Moyers 8-5-1880 (no return)
Solliver, John to Mary Kelly 3-29-1884 (3-30-1884)
Southern, Garrett to Margaret Lambert no dates (mid-1885?)
Southern, H. B. to Mary E. Parker 8-20-1887 (8-21-1887)
Southern, Henry B. to Martha S. Bolton 12-15-1876 (no return)
Southern, John B. to N. A. Brown 1-2-1889
Southern, Leander to Lucy J. Brooks 1-16-1877
Southern, Leander to Nancy Amicks 10-11-1882 (no return)
Southern, Nelson to Louisey Whitaker 4-23-1879 (4-4?-1879)
Southers, Garrett? to Margaret Lambert 6-10-1885 (6-11-1885)

Sowder, J. H. to Mollie Hasp 2-19-1884 (1?-29-1884)
Sowder, M. J. to Harriett E. Cox 12-28-1886
Sowder, William D. to Nancy A. Collins 9-14-1890 (9-18-1890)
Spangler, A. G. to Ann Bolinger 12-4-1880 (12-12-1880)
Sparks, Calvin to Sackey Collins 2-24-1875 (no return)
Sparks, Jefferson to Minervy Redmon 12-2-1880 (12-4-1880)
Sparks, John to Margret Ridings 1-12-1876
Sparks, Taylor to Mary E. Bingem 8-29-1882
Spartis, Jeff to Martha Francisco 6-21-1885
Spence, Benjamine F. to Nancy Elizabeth Reece 2-3-1877
Spence, Clark to Manervia Harvey 10-27-1876
Spence, Jas. H. to Marth J. Nance 11-28-1885 (11-29-1885)
Spradling, Franklin to Rutha Odell 9-22-1890 (9-28-1890)
Spradling, Jas. E. to Martha E. Barnard 1-2-1886 (1-5-1888)
Spradling, John R. to Sarah Carpenter 12-14-1878 (12-19-1878)
Spradlins, Wesley A. to Mollie E. Tucker 10-29-1877 (10-30-1877)
Sprales, R. C. to Matilda J. Dalton 10-25-1881 (10-30-1881)
Stafford, James A. to Jane Vaughn 3-29-1882 (no return)
Stagall, James to Liza Singleton 11-15-1882 (no return)
Standerfer, Claiborne to Eliza Robinson 1-1-1870
Standerfer, James R. to Manda Hurst 9-11-1874
Standfield, Emley to Sarah A. Hamblin 5-17-1877
Standifer, David to Dora Blansit 5-25-1878 (5-26-1878)
Standifer, David to Laura Standifer 11-24-1888 (11-25-1888)
Standifer, Isaac to Nervesta Smith 1-24-1874
Standifer, J. T. to Sarah Neil 12-24-1876 (no return)
Standifer, Kinard to Eliza (Miss) Manis 5-17-1888 (5-18-1888)
Stanifer, John to Mary Lenard 12-23-1870 (12-25-1870)
Stansbery, Thomas Lafayette to Artiemis Johnson 4-24-1873 (3-19-73)[sic]
Stevens, William F. to Susan M. Cornett 9-17-1880
Steward, Lewis H. to C. Jones 1-21-1880
Stewart, W. M. C. to Elizabeth Pursifal 12-12-1875
Stewart, Wm. to Ellen Keel 11-21-1875
Stivers, J. W. to Lucy T. Ford 9-16-1878
Stokeley, Jackson to Tempy J. Vanbebber 11-12-1868 (11-27-1868) B
Stone, James L. to S. A. Bussell 3-12-1881
Stone, Robert to Virginia S. Bowns 8-20-1874
Stone, Thomas W. to Harriet Hurst 8-4-1877
Stone, William N. to Louisa Breeding 5-2-1874 (5-3-1874)
Stone, Willis H. to Martha J. Hodges 10-26-1871
Strake?, John R. to Sarah J. Readmon 11-5-1873 (11-6-1873)
Straugh, J. B. to M. E. Mink 2-19-1885
Strump, James T. to Cordelia J. Jannings 12-23-1886 (12-27-1886)
Stump?, Hugh to Lucy Fultz 5-12-1890 (5-14-1890)
Suffrage, Daniel to Laura J. Shultz 12-24-1874 (no return)
Suits, R. to R. E. Fugate 3-1-1883
Sulferage, Clinton to Elizabeth Baines? 11-27-1870 (11-28-1870)
Sulfrage, Wm. to Louisa Hicks 9-27-1887 (9-28-1887)
Sulfredg, John to Emoline Mullins 2-17-1881 (no return)
Sulfridg, William to Mary J. Waters 10-23-1884
Sulfridge, Green P. to Louisa Dunsmore 1-4-1876 (1-25-1876)
Sulfrige, Robert to Elizabeth Smith 4-5-1873
Sullivan, Caliway to Nancy Carrell 10-13-1884
Sullivan, J. H. to Rachael Neel 1-13-1873 (1-30-1873)
Sullivan, Nelson to Mary J. Moseley 10-24-1890
Sullivan, Wm. to Mary L. Wallace 12-22-1890 (12-23-1890)
Sumate, W. F. C. to Mary J. Colenworth 12-26-1878
Sumpt, Henderson to Nancy Owens 7-?-1879 (7-22-1879)
Sumpter, Barnett to Sarah Southern 2-15-1877 (no return)
Sumpter, Elbert to Angeline Suthers 1-31-1874
Sumpter, Elbert to Sarah Brooks 4-7-1877 (4-8-1877)
Sumpter, Walter to Elizabeth Hopkins 7-23-1878 (no return)
Sumptor, William to Mandy L. E. Tesnay 2-19-1872
Sumter, T. S. to Lucy A. Davis 4-16-1874
Sumter, T. S. to Susa A. Davis 4-16-1874 (no return)
Surber, Andrew to Mary P. Lenard 8-7-1883 (no return)
Surber, Andy to Sarah E. Baker 3-28-1882 (no return)
Surber, D. J. to Emly Woolf 5-25-1872
Surber, Joseph to Milley Wolfenbarger 1-18-1870 (1-19-1870)
Susong, Jacob to Nancy Brooks 11-14-1883 (11-24-1883)
Suthern, Pleasant to L. Henderson 1-28-1873 (2-22-1873)
Suttan, Andrew to Marthia E. Williams 3-6-1872 (3-7-1872)
Sutton, Doctor John to Mary E. Brooks 7-23-1881 (7-24-1881)
Sutton, Harrison to Elizabeth Brown 7-31-1877 (no return)
Sutton, Henry to Melinda Sutton 2-25-1885 (2-27-1885)
Sutton, Jackson to Matilda T. Parks 1-29-1880 (1-28?-1880)
Sutton, James to Elisabeth Snavely 7-22-1875 (7-25-1875)
Sutton, James to Elizabeth Lambert 12-18-1885 (12-20-1885?)
Sutton, John to Mathuleen Breeden 2-27-1875 (2-28-1875)
Sutton, Thomas to M. J. Thompson 10-4-1882 (10-5-1882)
Sutton, Washington to Rachel Ball 8-7-1874 (8-9-1874)
Sutton, Wm. F. to Nancy A. Estes 7-22-1880 (7-25-1880)
Sweat, Clint to Edwina Malone 12-28-1886
Sweet, Brownlow to Alice Sauls? 11-9-1888 (11-11-1888)
Sweet, G. S. to Martha C. Western 5-7-1888 (5-20-1888)
Sweet, John to Sallie Wesley 10-24-1883 (no return)
Sword, Pinkney J. to Nancy E. Simpson 2-29-1872

Tague, C. G. to M. E. Landmo? 2-15-1880
Tague, Thomas to Nancy J. Owens 10-4-1880 (10-10-1880)
Tandion?, John to Martha Wilbern 7-24-1881
Taylor, C. W. to Jane Harris 2-12-1881 (2-15-1881)
Taylor, J. M. to Sarah L. Denton 9-4-1879
Taylor, James to Martha Jane Hatfield 4-27-1876
Taylor, John A.? to Martha Nevels 2-18-1871 (2-19-1871)
Taylor, John to Hannah Ray 1-28-1877
Taylor, Joseph G. to Mary Loser 4-30-1881 (5-1-1881)
Taylor, Samuel to Lucy J. Hill 1-23-1872 (1-24-1872)
Teague, George to Angeline Spanldon 12-8-1870
Tenaure?, John? to Mary Tanner 6-18-1870
Tennison, James to Salley Mink 11-15-1890 (no return)
Tenson, W. P. to Frances England 1-8-1873
Tesney, James to Sarah Ellison 7-6-1870 (7-7-1870)
Teury?, John to Mary Ellis 11-10-1873
Thacker, B. A. to Mary J. Burch 11-10-1877 (11-11-1877)
Thacker, G. R. to C. M. Lyons 2-19-1884 (2-21-1884)
Thacker, G. R. to E. P. Larmer 7-29-1876 (7-30-1876)
Thacker, Peter to Martha Webb 12-1-1881
Thacker, R. B. to Pulasky T. Carr 10-9-1877
Thacker, Samuel to Manerva Sulfridg 5-5-1883 (5-6-1883)
Thacker, William T. to Orlena E. Owens 6-19-1877 (6-21-1877)
Thomas, David to Lucy Grimes 9-17-1871
Thomas, Frank W. to Mary E. Emmett 12-18-1890 (no return)
Thomas, G. F. to S. E. Goin 8-14-1885 (8-15-1885)
Thomas, Harmon to Thursey Tate 1-23-1871
Thomas, James H. to Phily E. Lingar 3-10-1877 (3-11-1877)
Thomas, James to Mary Campbell 4-22-1875
Thomas, John R. to Addie H. Clark 12-11-1888 (12-13-1888)
Thomas, John to Matildy White 8-21-1870
Thomas, Joseph to Molly Lingar 12-21-1888 (12-23-1888)
Thomas, Lee to Frances Williams 3-7-1876 (3-9-1876)
Thomas, William to Madora Harbison 9-15-1880 (9-16-1880)
Thomas?, Hiram to Thursa Tate 12-?-1870 (12-10-1870)
Thompson, Andrew J. to Anna J. Perkins 12-15-1868 (12-16-1868)
Thompson, Elbert to Martha Bayley 1-26-1871
Thompson, Frank to Julia McNeell 12-30-1886 (no return)
Thompson, J. N. to Sallie Mannon 11-4-1881 (11-6-1881)
Thompson, James A. to Nancy Emeline Rigsbee 4-17-1869 (4-18-1869)
Thompson, John N. to M. J. Countice 9-22-1880
Thompson, John to Serena Marical 2-24-1881
Thompson, Lewis to Nancy Welch 10-24-1888 (10-27-1888)
Thompson, Robert to Fanny McMannyway 5-6-1874 (5-7-1874)
Thomsan, James A. to Lucy J. Taylor 11-30-1874 (12-2-1874)
Tillason, Ewin to Lucinda C. Hall 2-25-1871 (3-24-1871)
Tiner, Elisha to Nancy J. Large 8-1-1878? (8-4-1878)
Tinnel, P. A. to Elizabeth Capps 12-31-1889 (1-4-1890)
Tinnel, Thomas M. to S. C. Wilson 11-3-1888 (no return)
Tinsley, James to Emely Mark 12-4-1869
Tolaver, A. R. to Emma Lasley 3-1-1888 (3-4-1888)
Tolaver, Azeriah to Martha Mattax 4-20-1869 (4-25-1869)
Tolaver, J. B. to N. J. Shelton 11-7-1888
Tolliver, A. J. to Loucinda Smith 11-3-1883 (11-4-1883)
Tolliver, Josiah to Nancy Bidins 11-23-1870 (11-24-1870)
Tolliver, William H. to Milley Ann Parten 11-28-1869
Tolliver, William to Matilda Collins 10-23-1869 (10-31-1869)
Toneur, James to Celia Wilson 8-14-1887
Townsley, J. D. to Nanie McCrary 8-6-1881 (9-1-1881)
Townsley, James J.? to Luticia Russell 5-6-1871
Townsley, John to Mintie Brooks 12-3-1887 (12-4-1887?)
Travis?, J. D. to Manda J. Wilder 9-19-1871
Treece, J. N. to Jane Fugate 6-27-1872
Treece, Jefferson to Narcissus Day 12-9-1876 (12-10-1876)
Treece, Jesse to Elizabeth Bruce 10-8-1869 (10-10-1869)
Treece, S. J. to M. L. Reid 1-10-1884
Treece, Squire to Elizabeth Venerable 1-29-1876 (1-30-1876)
Treece, Wm. to Martha? Bishop 8-16-1873 (8-21-1873)
Trent, G. R. to Melvina England 4-16-1885
Trent, John E. to Jennie E. Jenings 8-27-1888 (9-12-1888)
Trury, Thomas to Eliza Canon 4-29-1870 (5-5-1870)
Try, John to Lucy Ann Chadwell 11-2-1886
Tullington, Robert to Martha Moro 5-13-1887 (no return)
Tully, Caswell to Nancy A. Barnard 10-17-1887
Tunmire, John N. to Martha A. Phillips 3-6-1869 (3-7-1869)
Turner, Andrew to Mary Evans 6-7-1880 (no return)
Turner, Gilbert to Frannie Raines 3-27-1880
Turner, Henry to Hannah Green 1-16-1873 (1-22-1873)
Turner, Hiram to Susan Jennings 4-11-1871 (4-8?-1871)
Turner, John W. to Polley Davis 2-17-1872
Turner, Levi to Rolley Massey 11-16-1886 (11-18-1886)
Turner, Robert to Elisabeth Ealley 1-10-1879
Turner, S. C. to Martha Rose 1-16-1881
Turner, Speedwell to Elizabeth Canell? 11-25-1877
Underwood, John to M. J. Owens 10-22-1887 (10-23-1887)
Underwood, John to Mary Yoakum 10-14-1874
Upton, J. J. to Frances Hurt 8-23-1882 (9-1-1882)
Upton, James E. to Elizabeth Jones 10-22-1881 (no return)
Vanable, Jefferson to Mary Owens 12-29-1880 (12-30-1880)
Vananoy, W. G. to Elizabeth Estes 9-10-1870 (9-11-1870)
Vanay, James H. to Matilda J. Venable 4-1-1876 (4-2-1876)
Vanay, John C. to Louisia Hoskins 10-15-1874 (10-19-1874)
Vanbebber, Andrew E. to Martha M. (Mrs.) Beason 7-8-1881 (7-10-1881)
Vanbebber, David to Martha E. Blackbern 8-26-1886
Vanbebber, Ewan to Lucy Blackburn 9-24-1888
Vanbebber, G. W. to M. M. Vanbebber 1-26-1879 (2-9-1879)
Vanbebber, H. M. to Dora Hill 12-7-1889 (12-9-1889)
Vanbebber, J. L. to Sarah J. Kincaid 1-3-1873
Vanbebber, Riley to Frances Jane Eads 8-18-1877 (8-22-1877)
Vanbebber, William M. to Mary A. Jones 2-18-1871 (2-22-1871)
Vanbeben, Georg to Elizabeth Jones 2-26-1881
Vance, George to Marthey Hopson 3-22-1879
Vance, John T. to Letty Lambert 1-6-1873 (1-7-1873)
Vann, James to Sarah Cadle 4-22-1881
Vann, R. T. to L. J. Wilson 7-26-1890 (7-27-1890)
Vanoy, James H. to Martha A. Lewis 4-18-1888 (4-19-1888)
Vansel, W. T. to M. B. Richardson 1-5-1885 (no return)
Varner, John to Maggie Varner 12-6-1888
Vaughn, John to Mary Roads 1-20-1879 (no return)
Venable, J. N. to Nancy E. Vanoy 1-26-1884
Venable, Rufus to O. Hopper 2-8-1880
Venerable, Moses to Sarah J. Hopper 11-29-1877
Venerable, Wm. to Mary E. Bartlett 1-2-1872 (1-21-1872)
Wagoner, W. M. to Leona Cadle 9-21-1888 (9-22-1888)
Walker, Daniel to Jane Brown 7-1-1876 (7-2-1876)
Walker, Daniel to Mary Mountain 5-5-1871 (5-8-1871)
Walker, Ewens? to Matilda E. Swift? 10-27-1877 (11-1-1877)
Walker, H. H. to Sarah Ousley 4-27-1873 (5-2-1873)
Walker, J. T. to Laura V. Sermer? 3-25-1872 (4-28-1872)
Walker, James A. to Sallie E. Hansard 9-20-1882 (9-21-1882)
Walker, John to Margaret A. Houston 10-6-1873 (10-16-1873)
Walker, Joseph A. to Cata Ellen Hansard 12-1-1890 (12-4-1890)
Walker, M. G. to M. E. Johnston 12-28-1881 (12-29-1881)
Walker, S. H. to L. J. Davis 6-2-1875 (6-3-1875)
Walker, Selmon to Malinda Bellamy 1-11-1872
Walker, Sterling to Ellen Pearson 4-30-1870 (5-5-1870)
Walker, Sterling to Margaret E. Hamlet 7-1-1882 (7-6-1882)
Walker, T. G. to Mary E. Stewart 3-6-1888 (3-8-1888)
Walker, Thos. to Franky Luss 12-24-1890
Walker, W. G. to Nanna E. Mountain 12-5-1885 (12-6-1885)
Walker, Wm. to Mary J. Liford 3-16-1871 (3-18-1871)
Walker, Wm. to Susan McCollough 8-22-1889
Wall, W. A. to Ella Clapp 9-30-1886
Wallace, Thomas J. to Nancy Duncan 2-10-1869
Wallace, Thomas to Pheby Clingsworth 8-17-1871 (8-19-1871)
Wallace, Wm. to Ginnia Duncan 1-14-1873 (1-17-1873)
Wallace, Wm. to Marry L. Linch 10-10-1881 (10-13-1881)
Waller, W. A. to Margaret A. McDaniel 12-23-1889 (12-24-1889)
Walp?, Sterling to Racheal Walker 4-7-1873 (4-10-1873)
Ward, Bartley to Sofrona Pearson 9-26-1884 (no return)
Ward, Bartly to Safronea Pearson 9-26-1884 (10-19-1884)
Ward, John P. to Kate M. Evans 12-27-1877
Ward, William B. to Louisa E. Barnard 3-11-1875 (3-14-1875)
Watson, George W. to Sarah J. Day 12-13-1873 (12-19-1873)
Watson, J. W. to Molley Smith 10-19-1886 (10-23-1886)
Watson, Robert B. to Mary M. Cole 11-2-1883 (11-4-1883)
Watson, Wm. to Mary J. Turner 2-5-1885? (2-5-1885)
Weatherford, David to Faney Wheeler 12-8-1873
Weaver, L. to Elisabeth Shofner 4-5-1887 (4-11-1887)
Weaver?, Wm. to M. A. Buis 5-1-1879 (no return)
Webb, J. H. to Linda Stone 12-23-1885
Webb, James M. to Mary E. Longmire 11-15-1873 (11-19?-1873)
Weever, Wm. W. to Sarah E. Haney 11-16-1872 (11-18-1873?)
Welch, A. D. to Verna Carr 3-17-1888 (3-18-1888)
Welch, Andrew to Martha McBee 10-21-1890 (10-22-1890)
Welch, George to Mary J. Gibson 10-13-1883 (10-14-1883)
Welch, James to Eliza E. Essary 12-24-1884 (no return)
Welch, Jasper to Luvernia Parker 9-9-1887 (9-10-1887)
Welch, John T. to Matilda Burchfield 8-16-1877
Welch, Joseph C. to Mary A. Robinson 1-7-1882
Welch, Joseph to Melvina Owens 6-16-1877 (6-17-1877)
Welch, Jourdon P. to Mandy Lesley 5-22-1872
Welch, M. T. to Luda Campbell 12-22-1888 (12-23-1888)
Welch, W. H. to M. T. Carr 10-4-1886 (10-10-1886)
Wells, Jeremiah to Vandellea Phelps 2-28-1890 (3-2-1890)
Wells, Thos. to Lucey J. Janeway 12-28-1872 (1-1-1873)
Wells, Walter to Mary J. Hopson 10-8-1889 (10-10-1889)
Wells, William to Mary Jennings 6-6-1869
Weres, Jasper to Rusha Rowlen 11-16-1884
West, David N. to Rebeca Hurst 5-4-1877 (5-6-1877)
West, George W. to Helen Southern 4-22-1869 (4-25-1869)
West, J. F. to Manerva E. Janeway 8-10-1874 (8-12-1874)
West, James to Margaret Collins 7-6-1887 (7-24-1887)
West, Marion to Susan M. Mullins 6-9-1883 (6-10-1883)

West, Philip to Martha J. Allen 7-31-1871 (8-2-1871)
West, William to Jane Singleton 2-13-1877 (2-15-1877)
West, Wm. N. to Louisa Oliver 12-31-1880 (1-4-1881)
Westen, James to Mary E. Brogan 9-19-1885 (9-20-1885)
Wheeler, D. A. to Jenney Ann Bruce 10-4-1886 (10-6-1886)
Wheeler, Henry to Margret Elizbeth Chadwick 9-12-1871
Wheeler, James to Temprance Chadwick 12-2-1880
Wheeler, Mack to Marica J. Parrott 4-21-1883 (4-29-1883)
Whitacre, J. W. to Ester Parker 1-19-1887 (1-20-1887)
Whitaker, Alen to Martha Cook 9-29-1887 (10-2-1887)
Whitaker, B. F. to Ms? A. Whitaker 12-31-1878 (1-1-1879)
Whitaker, Clinton to Jannina Whitaker 1-5-1882 (1-8-1881)
Whitaker, John to Mary Cook 8-2-1888 (8-5-1888)
White, C. B. to Jennie Gibson 7-22-1879 (7-24-1879)
White, Lewis to Margret Herel? 8-14-1872 (no return)
Whiteaker, Calvin to Elizabeth Whiteaker 6-16-1870 (6-19-1870)
Whiteaker, G. G. to Martha Greer 1-27-1876 (no return)
Whiteaker, Geo. to Elizabeth Whiteaker 1-1-1885 (1-4-1885)
Whiteaker, George W. to Sarah Rourk 12-17-1869 (12-19-1869)
Whiteaker, Giles to July Lenard 4-17-1890 (4-21-1890)
Whiteaker, John G. to Orphey Harkraider 11-9-1869 (11-14-1869)
Whiteaker, John to Elizabeth Roark 9-20-1873 (9-21-1873)
Whiteaker, Joseph to Marth J. Cunningham 12-27-1877 (12-28-1877)
Whiteaker, Rice to Sarah Brooks 12-30-1868 (12-31-1868)
Whiteaker, Samuel to Cornela Whiteaker 2-4-1891 (2-5-1891)
Whiteaker, William F. to Martha Ann Gilbert 9-21-1869 (9-26-1869)
Whiteaker, William P. to Louisa Roark 12-21-1874 (12-22-1874)
Whiteaker, Wm. to Laura Ann Bussell 5-15-1890 (5-18-1890)
Whiteaker, ___ to Winey Dungin? 6-27-1878
Whitelock, J. W. to Allice Lambert 1-21-1891
Whitlock, S. M. to Salley J. Byers 12-19-188? (12-18-1886)
Whitmore, Scott to Fannie McManaway 11-22-1889 (11-24-1889)
Whitson, Daniel to Mary J. Mathis 12-23-1874 (12-24-1874)
Whitson, Vincent to M. A. Inkelbarger 12-26-1878
Widmar, David M. to R. L. Moyers 1-6-1890 (no return)
Widner, Andrew to Maggy Cole 11-24-1890
Widner, J. W. to Sintha A. Smith 10-19-1886 (10-24-1886)
Widner, John to Bettie Poor 8-12-1888
Widner, W. R. to P. E. Goin 1-17-1889 (no return)
Wilcox, Lilbern to Phieby Honley 3-20-1881 (4-3-1881)
Wilder, D. N. to Caroline Bisner 9-2-1887 (no return)
Wilder, G. B. to Ann Goin 10-17-1879
Wilder, Scott to I. S. Goin 4-26-1881 (4-16-1881)
Wilder, William A. to Mary J. Moody 2-2-1882
Wilder, Wm. J. to Elviry Goin 11-23-1871
Wilder, Wm. to Mary Goin 4-23-1881 (no return)
Wiley, John C. to Malinda C. Kibert 9-16-1877
Wiley, R. F. to Mary Payne 9-3-1877
Wiley, Robert G. to Sarah Butler 8-30-1875 (9-2-1875)
Will, Jasper T. to Dora P. Hurst 10-3-1887 (no return)
Willas, Wm. to Mandy C. Parton 8-22-1871
William, Williams to Eliza Cadle 1-20-1885
William, Zimry to Martha Turner 8-10-1887 (8-11-1887)
Williams, Alexander to Sarah Massengill 2-12-1877 (no return)
Williams, Andrew J. to Sarah E. Calor 6-30-1883 (6-15?-1883)
Williams, Elbert to Mary Roarks 1-15-1875
Williams, F. M. to Martha Littrell 5-22-1880 (5-23-1880)
Williams, Geo. W. to Winie Gibbs 2-2-1890
Williams, Hark to Louisa Johnson 1-21-1886 (1-26-1886)
Williams, Henly to Mary J. Hopper 11-5-1885
Williams, Henry to Bettima Greenlee 10-27-1887
Williams, J. G. to Malissa Nevels 8-9-1887
Williams, J. H. to Matilda Cheatham 10-29-1877
Williams, James A. to Nancy A. Cunningham 4-14-1878
Williams, Jasper to Hannah Cosby 9-14-1876 (no return)
Williams, Jeramiah to Jane Goin 5-20-1871 (5-21-1871)
Williams, Jeremiah to Margret Va? McWilliams 6-8-1877
Williams, John F. to Martha Williams 2-7-1891
Williams, John R. to Frances Goin 4-4-1875
Williams, John T. to Minerva Fletcher 8-23-1890 (8-24-1890)
Williams, John to Mary E. Hamilton 3-26-1877
Williams, Lewis to Margret Stigall 3-27-1878
Williams, M. P. to Orlena Summers 1-15-1886 (1-6?-1886)
Williams, Moses to Amey Goin 5-1-1885 (no return)
Williams, T. M. to Eliza J. Conner 4-15-1883 (no return)
Williams, Timothy to Ritta Kesterson 10-24-1890 (10-26-1890)
Williams, Timothy to Susan Ousley 6-13-1874 (6-14-1874)
Williams, Vinson to Martha Goin 12-12-1881 (12-22-1881)
Williams, W. H. to P. A. Littrell 10-10-1877 (no return)
Williams, William C. to Matilda Hopper 5-12-1878
Williams, William to Mattie Evans 6-4-1883 (6-21-1883?)
Williams, Wm. H. to Mary A. Poor 5-3-1875
Williams, Wm. to Lucy Ann Cosby 9-3-1875 (9-5-1875)
Williams, Wm. to Marth S. Wagoner 2-26-1885
Williams, Zinni to Racheal Parker 6-2-1873 (6-3-1873)
Willimony?, James to Nancy Condry 1-3-1871 (no return)
Willis, D. G. to Martha Willmot 10-7-1868 (10-8-1868)

Willis, David R. to Rebecca J. Robinson 1-10-1870
Willis, Hen. to Marg. Collins 3-16-1886 (3-23-1886)
Willis, Jacob to Nancy Nathen 2-7-1886
Willis, John W. to Lucy J. Gulley 4-8-1876 (4-9-1876)
Willis, William A. to Nancy Coward 4-12-1869 (4-16-1869)
Willis, William to Nancy Ales 12-16-1881
Willis, Wm. to Margart Lawson 9-25-1879 (9-27-1879)
Willmouth, Joseph to Nettie Hodges 6-24-1880 (no return)
Willson, Bud to S. A. Devault 5-5-1879 (5-6-1879)
Willson, Dan? R. to Laviny Ramsey 4-18-1872
Willson, Jefferson to Matilda Jones 8-23-1879 (8-24-1879)
Willson, Sherman to S. E. Kock 2-5-1890
Willson, Steward to Mary Pridemore 8-19-1882
Wilmont, William to C. Hurst 7-23-1879 (7-24-1879)
Wilmot, Charlie to Thersa Willis 9-2-1875
Wilson, Benj. to Martha Ramsey 11-17-1884 (11-18-1884)
Wilson, David M. to Clary L. Moyers 9-22-1869 (9-23-1869)
Wilson, Floid to Mary E. Boner 12-25-1883 (no return)
Wilson, J. L. to Louisa Moyers 9-1-1871 (not executed)
Wilson, J. L. to Margaret Ann Trey? 1-28-1874 (no return)
Wilson, James to Margaret Ellison 6-2-1887
Wilson, Jesse L. to Mary Rason 10-19-1872 (10-20-1872)
Wilson, Jordon to Elizabeth Riley 3-18-1881 (3-19-1880?)
Wilson, Nathaniel to S. E. Davis 8-23-1873 (no return)
Wilson, Thos. S. to Kittie Gibson 10-13-1873
Wilson, William C. to Mary A. Havens 11-27-1869 (11-28-1869)
Wilson, William to Emily Cawood 7-8-1870 (7-9-1870)
Wilson, Wm. to Mary Townsley 10-20-1888
Winkler, Mark to Elizabeth McCollugh 4-4-1881 (4-10-1881)
Wires, John to Elizabeth Longworth 11-15-1882 (11-16-1882)
Wise, William H. to Louisa C. Harrell 8-20-1877 (8-26-1877)
Wolf, Andrew to Margret Liford no date (before 1879?)
Wolf, Arch. to Allace Grubb 10-8-1884 (10-9-1884)
Wolf, William to Elizabeth Brooks 10-17-1884 (no return)
Wolfe, Arch to Jennie Colson 8-19-1882 (8-12-1882)
Wolfenberger, Wm. to Lourinda J. Hopson 11-15-1889 (11-17-1889)
Wood, William to Margret J Taylor 3-1-1878
Wood, Wm. to Sarah A. Jones 10-15-1885
Woodard, Elbert to M. E. Carmack 1-15-1879 (1-19?-1879)
Woodard, James to Mary Williams 10-7-1872 (10-11-1872)
Woodard, William to Matilda Morgan 11-18-1880 (11-21-1880)
Woods, John T. to Dory J. Robinson 5-29-1884
Woods, John to Sarrah Parry 5-16-1872 (no return)
Woodson, Aaron to Pheba O. Brooks 12-28-1877 (no return)
Woodson, Clint to Margret Dennison 4-8-1871 (4-15-1871)
Woodson, G. W. to M. E. Yoakum 2-7-1880
Woodson, Georg to Sarah Parkey 4-25-1879 (4-26-1879)
Woodson, Jerome to Martha J. Painter 12-28-1875
Woodson, Smith T. to Margret Louisa Smith 2-21-1876 (no return)
Woodson, Thomas to Marth Good 5-22-1884
Woodson, Thomas to Mary Percifield 6-28-1879
Woodson, William to Angeline Candry 12-15-1878
Word, Bartly A. to Catharine Reece 7-14-1874
Woulf, D. F. to Mary Yoakum 8-30-1879 (8-31-1879)
Wright, James to Mary A. Francisco 3-13-1890
Wright, William to Marinda Patterson 7-13-1884 (no return)
Wurman, Jerry P. to Mary C. Hobbs 3-21-1888 (3-22-1888)
Wyatt, W. S. to C. J. Runions 11-9-1887
Wyerman, James to Martha Cadle 9-28-1869
Wyley, F. H. to A. P. Mountain 3-16-1889 (3-17-1889)
Wyley, T. M. to ___ Brooks 12-29-1888 (no return)
Wyley, William to Rachel Cole 10-8-1890 (10-7?-1890)
Yadan, Joseph H. to Esther B. Vanbebber 11-29-1879
Yeary, Benedick to Adaline Hatfield 11-2-1868 (11-11-1868)
Yeary, James W. to Amand Yeary 3-2-1883 (3-11-1883)
Yeary, W. T. to Cornelia Dennam 1-14-1886 (1-18-1886)
Yeary, William E. to Parthena Baker 2-18-1875 (2-21-1875)
Yeary, Wm. M. to Manda J. Estep 12-24-1885 (1-3-1886)
Yoakum, B. S. to Mollie Gaynor 1-13-1886 (1-14-1886)
Yoakum, Ewing F. to Liza V. Mountin 9-18-1881 (9-20-1881)
Yoakum, Frank to Frances Wheeler 3-10-1881 (3-12-1881)
Yoakum, George to Louise Welch 2-24-1870 (2-27-1870)
Yoakum, James R. to Mary Hodges 2-9-1869 (2-11-1869)
Yoakum, James to L. J. Yoakum 8-21-1880 (9-16-1880)
Yoakum, John to Eliza Richardson 11-5-1872
Yoakum, John to Louisa Burchfield 8-6-1877 (8-12-1877)
Yoakum, Marcillus to Eliza Welch 8-12-1872 (no return)
Yoakum, Moses to Jane Shipley 8-26-1887 (8-28-1887)
Yoakum, R. H. to Minie Stansberry 1-27-1881 (1-30-1881)
Yoakum, Scott to Margaret C. Campbell 10-26-1889
Yoakum, Scott to Marry Smith 6-23-1881
Yoakum, T. B. to Elizabeth Lynch 12-25-1877 (1-2-1878)
Yoakum, Tayler J. to Martha Pierman 11-28-1871 (12-3-1871)
Yoakum, W. G. to Martha J. Birdine 2-13-1883 (2-15-1883)
Yoakum, William H. F. H. to Mariah Burchfield 10-12-1874 (10-15-1874)
Yokum, J. M. to Cordelia Cawood 9-29-1885 (10-1-1885)
Yorke, John P. to Martha Harpe 4-?-1884 (2?-20-1884)

Young, Frank to Mary M. Collins 9-25-1879 (no return)
Young, James to Lucretia L. Upton 6-22-1889 (6-23-1889)
Young, Pleasant to Catherine Lee 1-27-1872 (1-28-1872)
Young, William to Elizabeth Hopkins 7-23-1878
Younge, Calvin to Sarah J. Spurlock 2-12-1878 (2-13-1878)
Younge, William F. to Margret Lee 4-24-1878
Younts, Richard to Delany Pridmore 11-20-1872 (12-1-1872)
Zapp, Daniel to Lidian Edmonson 9-30-1875
Zecks, Thos. to Martha Rugens 9-15-1888 (2-16-1888)
____, Davies to Hannah Day 4-4-1879

-----, ----- to R. F. Cardwell 9-21-1885
-----, Quillin to James Hayes 10-22-1886 (10-24-1886)
Absher, Catharine to John Fults 12-26-1874 (no return)
Absher, Rebecca to Raymond Owens 12-21-1887 (12-21-1888?)
Abshier, Mandy E. (Mis) to Damirel B. Fuetz 6-24-1881
Acuff, Martha to Robbert Barnard 12-17-1884 (12-21-1884)
Adams, Kesey J. to G. W. Brooks 2-28-1882 (3-5-1882)
Adams, Margret to David Kellian 1-14-1880 (1-15-1880)
Adams?, Margarett to Danuel Killian 1-14-1881 (no return)
Addams, Jane to J. R. Mink 3-23-1871
Age, A. L. to Elias P. Robatare 11-23-1878
Agey, Sarah F. to George W. Sanders 10-21-1869 (10-24-1869)
Ainslow?, Sarah J. to S. D. Davis 4-29-1890
Aleree?, Demarius to John Sexton 12-26-1881
Ales, Catherine to Joseph Cupp 12-10-1870 (12-11-1870)
Ales, Lillay May to Timothy Robt. Bickerson 3-10-1888 (3-11-1888)
Ales, Nancy to William Willis 12-16-1881
Ales, Sarah Elizabeth to James Dobbs 9-28-1869
Alexander, Amanda to L. T. Davis 8-28-1886 (no return)
Alexander, M. B. to W. L. Sharp 11-6-1888 (11-7-1888)
Alexander, Margret W. N. to J. W. Pierce 2-3-1872 (2-8-1872)
Allen, Martha J. to Philip West 7-31-1871 (8-2-1871)
Allen, Martha to Anderson Collins 2-8-1869 (2-22-1869)
Allen, Montana to W. F. Henry 12-25-1888
Allenen, Eliza A. to James Marsh 11-12-1873 (11-14-1873)
Amicks, Nancy to Leander Southern 10-11-1882 (no return)
Amos, Lucy to J. T. Brooks 9-22-1890
Anderson, Barthener to John Hodges 9-25-1878
Anderson, Laura J. to James M. Kelley 8-25-1874 (8-27-1874)
Anderson, Loisa J. to William Nelson 3-4-1872 (3-9-1872)
Anderson, Matilda to Elbert Rollin 12-22-1880 (12-24-1880)
Ares, M. E. to Andrew Quisenberry 4-26-1886 (4-27-1886)
Ares, Sarah E. to John Sebolt 12-15-1881 (12-22-1881)
Arnet, Nancy J. to Thomas H. Hawskins 5-1-1871
Arnett, Amanda to James Rollins 5-22-1871
Arnold, Dollie to Sephen Melton 9-14-1878
Arnold, Eugenia N. to G. W. Montgomery 6-2-1883 (6-3-1883)
Arwine, Rebecca A. to Milton M. Grubb 10-3-1870 (10-13-1870)
Asberry, Lucy to Dairden? W. Burnett 9-3-1875
Asberry, Matilda to William Hurst 5-6-1877
Asbery, Rosana to E. Kirby 7-10-1880 (7-11-1880)
Atkins, Alice M. to C. H. Bateman 5-10-1886 (5-16-1886)
Ausban, Elizebeth to Joshua Owens 5-22-1879 (5-29-1879)
Ausben, Mataiilda to George Collinsworth 10-14-1880
Ausburn, Viny to Barney Jennings 11-23-1875
Ausmus, Anna to C. C. Rogers 12-29-1888 (12-30-1888)
Ausmus, B. F. to M. A. Rogers 10-15-1879 (1-5-1880)
Ausmus, Emiley to Jessie Russell 12-24-1885
Ausmus, Jane to Jefferson Edwards 1-3-1890 (1-23-1890)
Ausmus, Katie to Wm. M. Ellison 12-29-1885 (12-31-1885)
Ausmus, Martha J. to A. J. Johnson 12-20-1873 (7-19-1874)
Ausmus, Mary A. to W. B. Rogers 10-11-1886 (10-27-1886)
Ausmus, Mary M. to A. McHenry 4-3-1876 (4-6-1876)
Ausmus, Mary to John Breeding 3-15-1884
Ausmus, Polley E. to John J. Graham 5-21-1890 (5-22-1890)
Ausmus, Sarah A. to James Clawson 11-20-1877
Ausmus, Sarah A. to Jessee L. Hall 11-12-1887 (11-17-1887)
Ausmus, Sarah E. to Henry Hunter 8-21-1869 (8-24-1869)
Ayers, Rachal to Nathan E. Carmon 12-8-1882 (12-10-1882)
Bailey, E. T. A. to Nathaniel Schott 5-8-1878
Bailey, Mollie to Abraham Collinsworth 6-5-1889 (6-6-1889)
Baines?, Elizabeth to Clinton Sulferage 11-27-1870 (11-28-1870)
Baker, Alice to Geo. Combs 6-15-1885
Baker, Josefine to Benjamin McNeil 12-20-1871 (12-21-1871)
Baker, L. J. to I. N. Hill 10-24-1880 (10-30-1880)
Baker, L. J. to Wm. Longworth 3-3-1881 (3-4-1881)
Baker, Lilia to George Pratutt? 9-4-1890
Baker, Louisa to George Nevels 2-7-1872 (2-11-1872)
Baker, Marry to J. M. Hyden 2-17-1881
Baker, Nevesta to F. B. Helms 11-9-1875 (no return)
Baker, Parthena to William E. Yeary 2-18-1875 (2-21-1875)
Baker, Sarah E. to Andy Surber 3-28-1882 (no return)
Baldwin, Elbarrie? to T. R. King 5-6-1889 (5-9-1889)
Baldwin, M. C. to John Duncan 11-21-1882 (11-22-1882)
Bales, Martha E. to Lewis C. Brooks 2-12-1878 (4-13-1890)
Bales, Sarah E. to W. N. Brooks 6-9-1883 (6-10-1883)
Baley, Jane to Wm. Collingsworth 2-5-1885
Baley, Lizzie to Columbus Brown 6-13-1882
Baley, Mary F. to John Overton 1-3-1870 (1-10-1870) B
Balinger, Rachael to Wm. Billingsly 11-4-1871 (11-5-1871)
Ball, Elalia to William Britton 12-19-1874 (12-20-1874)
Ball, Jane to William Hale 2-2-1877 (no return)
Ball, Nancy Jane to Isaac Mustard 1-3-1876
Ball, Rachel to Washington Sutton 8-7-1874 (8-9-1874)
Ballou, Barbery to Tip Brooks 8-7-1890 (8-13-1890)
Bamman, Amanda to H. M. Rogers 11-18-1875
Banen, Margret J. to Fredrick D. Roark 11-17-1877

Barlow, L. C. to Samuel Hurst 11-17-1884 (11-18-1884)
Barlow, Mary E. to A. G. Hurst 5-24-1880 (5-27-1880)
Barlow, Sarah F. to Perry Hurst 2-18-1884 (2-21-1884)
Barnard, Addy to William McDonell 1-16-1890 (1-19-1890)
Barnard, Elisabeth to John Odell 6-26-1875 (6-27-1875)
Barnard, Emaline to Samuel Barnard 2-15-1882? (no return)
Barnard, Louisa E. to William B. Ward 3-11-1875 (3-14-1875)
Barnard, Mahulda to John Love(lace?) 1-27-1872 (1-28-1872)
Barnard, Martha E. to Jas. E. Spradling 1-2-1886 (1-5-1888)
Barnard, Mary A. E. to W. H. Barnard 10-3-1878 (10-6-1878)
Barnard, Matilda to W. C. Hipsher 7-25-1887 (no return)
Barnard, Nancey J. to W. N. Laykins 2-17-1874 (2-19-1874)
Barnard, Nancy A. to Caswell Tully 10-17-1887
Barnard, Poley to James H. Smith 2-24-1879 (2-27-1879)
Barnard, Polly A. to Christopher B. Shelton 3-9-1869 (3-11-1869)
Barnard, V. M. to W. R. Pearson 11-23-1887 (12-1-1887)
Barnes, Emeline to Andrew Hurst 3-15-1870 (no return) B
Bartlett, Feebee to Benj. Campbell 10-2?-1872 (no return)
Bartlett, Jane to Joseph Bolton 2-5-1888
Bartlett, Jane to Thommas Hall 1-25-1881 (1-26-1881)
Bartlett, Laura to William Manis 9-6-1890 (9-7-1890)
Bartlett, Mary E. to Wm. Venerable 1-2-1872 (1-21-1872)
Barton, Sarah M. to John Mark 3-30-1874
Bauman, L. E. to J. L. Ellis 3-15-1881 (3-17-1881)
Bayley, Malind to Wm. Denny 8-22-1880 (8-23-1880)
Bayley, Martha to Elbert Thompson 1-26-1871
Baylor, Anna to W. E. C. Mayer 6-26-1885 (6-30-1885)
Baylor, Lettie J. to H. H. Robinson 5-7-1873 (5-8-1873)
Bazel, Margret to Timothy Eason 10-30-1878 (10-31-1878)
Beason, Martha M. (Mrs.) to Andrew E. Vanbebber 7-8-1881 (7-10-1881)
Beason, Matilda to Wm. Killion 11-29-1879
Bedsaw, Elizabeth to George W. Patterson 11-22-1879 (11-23-1879)
Beeler, C. M. to Douglas Frazier 12-23-1889
Beesom, Nancy to Wm. P. Edwards 10-11-1872 (10-13-1872)
Beeson, Harriett M. to Lynch Mathews 1-12-1887 (1-13-1887)
Beeson, Nancy A. to Jacob? Johnson 1-21-1887 (1-23-1887)
Beeson, Sarah E. to William Keck 11-11-1870 (11-13-1870)
Belemy, Emily to W. M. Baldwin 6-9-1886 (6-10-1886)
Bellamy, Malinda to Selmon Walker 1-11-1872
Bellamy, Sary C. to J. W. Baldwin 6-1-1884? (1-1-1884)
Bemer, Mathawsen to Wm. Paris 7-26-1886 (crossed out)
Bentley, Wm. S. to M. E. Hill 9-11-1889
Beramen, Sarah to B. B. Gray 2-15-1884 (2-17-1884)
Berk, Mary to E. H. Lambert 9-15-1887 (no return)
Berry, Sarah M. to John Guy 1-15-1882
Beyers, M. M. to A. W. Cottrell 5-11-1878 (5-12-1878)
Bidins, Nancy to Josiah Tolliver 11-23-1870 (11-24-1870)
Biggs, Elizabeth to Eldredge Collins 6-8-1878
Biggs, Elizabeth to Eldridg Collins 6-8-1878 (no return)
Biggs, Margret to Henderson Collins 11-28-1877 (no return)
Bilingley, Harriett to Geo. M. Siler 12-12-1887
Billingsley, Nancy M. to T. J. Ely 1-27-1876 (1-30-1876)
Bingem, Mary E. to Taylor Sparks 8-29-1882
Birdine, Martha J. to W. G. Yoakum 2-13-1883 (2-15-1883)
Birk, Bell to John H. Bumgardner 9-23-1879 (no return)
Birk, Martha C. to James Birk 2-26-1880 (no return)
Bishop, Martha? to Wm. Treece 8-16-1873 (8-21-1873)
Bishop, Rachal L. to Alfred C. Lynch 1-3-1883 (1-4-1883)
Bisner, Caroline to D. N. Wilder 9-2-1887 (no return)
Blackbern, Martha E. to David Vanbebber 8-26-1886
Blackburn, Cova? to Jesse Beeler 11-26-1881
Blackburn, Loucreecy to Isaac Moyers 4-2-1880 (4-3-1880)
Blackburn, Lucy to Ewan Vanbebber 9-24-1888
Blake, Hanah to J. S. Bowman 7-17-1882
Blancet, Sarah L. to James Gray 8-26-1879 (8-28-1879)
Blancet, Sarah L. to James Nicly 8-28-1879 (no return)
Blancett, Mary C. to Araham (Abraham?) Harris 8-23-1881 (8-25-1881)
Blancett, Mary to John S.? Harper 1-24-1882 (1-26-1882)
Blanset, Sarah L. to J. D. Hixen 8-31-1887
Blansett, Lourina M. to Calaway Lebow 1-19-1877 (1-21-1877)
Blansit, Dora to David Standifer 5-25-1878 (5-26-1878)
Bogal, Sarah to Isaac Estridge 10-1-1883 (no return)
Bolinger, Ann to A. G. Spangler 12-4-1880 (12-12-1880)
Bolinger, Corra Bell to Melvin King 8-3-1888 (8-9-1888)
Bolinger, E. to J. T. Fortner 4-12-1890 (4-13-1890)
Bolinger, Isabel to Joseph Billingsly 2-17-1870 (2-20-1870)
Bolinger, Melvina to J. M. Rogers 4-25-1890 (5-4-1890)
Bolingly, Salley N. to Hiram M. Ausmus 4-?-1879 (4-17-1879)
Bolton, Allace to James Bartlett 11-27-1880 (11-28-1880)
Bolton, Docia to Charley Bailey 11-8-1890
Bolton, E. J. to Jermiah Brooks 12-23-1872 (12-24-1872)
Bolton, M. J. to E. B. Cook 7-1-1889 (7-7-1889)
Bolton, M. to D. C. Pendegrass 9-8-1879
Bolton, Martha A. to Claiborne Cook 3-11-1878 (no return)
Bolton, Martha S. to Henry B. Southern 12-15-1876 (no return)
Bolton, Mary Ann Matilda to Martin Cunningham 5-5-1877 (5-6-1877)
Boneamar, Rida M. to Joseph K. Busk 1-5-1879

Boner, Mary E. to Floid Wilson 12-25-1883 (no return)
Bones, Betha to James Carpenter 11-13-1889 (11-14-1889)
Bowlinger, Mary to R. D. Lynch 1-13-1885 (no return)
Bowls, Margaret to Marshel M. Rice 8-17-1887 (no return)
Bowls, Susan to Benjamin Nicols 11-7-1872
Bowman, Amy to Andrew Lambdin 8-11-1869 (8-12-1869)
Bowman, H. L. to A. J. Chadwell 12-7-1880 (no return)
Bowman, Martha T. to Wm. R. Bosteck 2-13-1883 (2-15-1883)
Bowman, Mary to Rice Rogers 7-31-1879 (no return)
Bowman, Nancy to Joseph Hunter 12-26-1881
Bowman, Racheal to William Adams 12-15-1877 (12-16-1877)
Bowman, Sarah to Henry Patrick 12-20-1874 (12-3?-1874)
Bowman, Susan to Britton Garrett 8-6-1869
Bowns, Virginia S. to Robert Stone 8-20-1874
Brackins, Sarah to Preston Morgan 2-7-1883
Branscom, Darcus to Tipton McCray 11-27-1885 (11-29-1885)
Branscom, Elizabeth to J. R. Fussel? 6-2-1882 (no return)
Branscom, Netty M. to William A. Moyers 12-3-1883 (no return)
Branscomb, Angeline to George W. Mayes 4-1-1871 (4-2-1871)
Branson, S. A. to H. N. Capper 4-1-1880
Brashiers, Virginia to J. N. Furgurson 8-18-1885 (8-20-1885)
Bratcher, M. J. to W. J. McNew 4-25-1874
Brather, Martha to David H. McNew 3-15-1873 (3-16-1873)
Bray, Margaret to Isiaeh Davis 6-29-1872 (6-30-1872)
Bray, Martha to Amos Green 10-8-1887 (10-9-1887)
Bray, Racheal to William Farmer 11-30-1877 (no return)
Bray, Sarah J. to Thomas Fleacher 6-14-1875
Breeden, Mathuleen to John Sutton 2-27-1875 (2-28-1875)
Breeding, A. to W. F. Shultz 8-20-1881 (8-21-1881)
Breeding, Cornelis to Thomas J. Miller 3-9-1882 (3-19-1882)
Breeding, Eliza to N. J. Shelton 11-16-1887 (11-17-1887)
Breeding, Laura to John H. Atkins 3-8-1890 (3-12-1890)
Breeding, Louisa to William N. Stone 5-2-1874 (5-3-1874)
Breeding, Martha to A. A. McCollough 11-22-1889 (11-24-1889)
Breeding, Mary A. to James T. Mayers 7-15-1882 (7-30-1882)
Breeding, Sarah A. to A. C. Corban 10-16-1875 (10-17-1875)
Breeding, Tina to J. S. Harrell 8-31-1883 (9-2-1883)
Bremer, Verny to William Roe 7-21-1890 (7-22-1890)
Brewer, Belle to Isaac Morgan 9-29-1890 (9-30-1890)
Brewer, Jemima to Baley Fleming 8-26-1869
Brewman, S. J. to J. V. Bostic 12-25-1885
Briant, Hannah J. to F. M. Owens 5-1-1876 (no return)
Briant, M. M. to J. R. Grantham 5-19-1878
Briant, Orlina to J. F. Collinsworth 12-23-1884
Briant, Sarah L. to Thomas Greer 5-21-1874
Brills, E. F. A. to Nathaniel Schott 5-8-1878
Briton, Mary J. to Plesant Balins 10-4-1883 (10-12-1883)
Brock, Amanda to Claiborne Bartlett 12-8-1879
Brock, Mollie to Clint Panter 12-16-1885 (12-17-1885)
Brock, Nancy to James McAfee 2-16-1886 (2-18-1886)
Brogan (Jones Ads?), Matilda to John R. Griffen 5-27-1881 (5-29-1881)
Brogan, Comfort to L. R. Carr 1-17-1874 (1-20-1874)
Brogan, Cordelia E. to Elvin Butcher 9-16-1871 (9-21-1871)
Brogan, M. C. to Nathan Butcher 11-10-1877 (11-15-1877)
Brogan, Mary E. to James Westen 9-19-1885 (9-20-1885)
Brogan, Matilda to Calven Sharp 11-13-1879 (11-27-1879)
Brook, Nancy J. to Geo. Eastridge 10-2-1873 (10-5-1873)
Brooks, A. J. to Hiram Riley 1-1-1879 (no return)
Brooks, Amanda to Richard Morrison 10-12-1869 (10-13-1869)
Brooks, Arrena to Joseph Brooks 11-12-1868 (11-13-1868)
Brooks, Eleyan to John C. Leach 8-2-1889 (8-4-1889)
Brooks, Eliz M. to J. M. Longworth 2-14-1882 (2-16-1882)
Brooks, Eliza to T. F. Fourkner 6-5-1880 (6-6-1880)
Brooks, Eliza to Z.? C. Brooks 8-29-1871 (9-3-1871)
Brooks, Elizabeth E. (Mrs.) to Frank Day 7-11-1881 (no return)
Brooks, Elizabeth to Benjamine Massengill 5-5-1877 (no return)
Brooks, Elizabeth to Elbert N. Brooks 9-18-1876 (no return)
Brooks, Elizabeth to William Wolf 10-17-1884 (no return)
Brooks, Elizabeth to Wm. England 9-30-1873
Brooks, Elizabeth to Woodson Brooks 3-6-1876 (3-7-1876)
Brooks, Jennie to J. A. Lester 12-6-1891 (S/B 1890?)
Brooks, Louisa to Clinton C. Brooks 2-21-1877 (no return)
Brooks, Louisa to James M. Randall 9-26-1871 (9-27-1871)
Brooks, Lucinda to Claiborne M. Mize 11-22-1883 (11-29-1883)
Brooks, Lucy A. to William Montgomery 2-17-1882 (2-19-1882)
Brooks, Lucy J. to Leander Southern 1-16-1877
Brooks, Lucy L. to Patrick Lenard 7-8-1876 (7-13-1876)
Brooks, Malinda to Charly Peck 7-20-1877
Brooks, Manda J. to Robt. Brooks 1-12-1889 (1-13-1889)
Brooks, Manda to James M. Haskins 9-21-1886 (9-23-1886)
Brooks, Margart to Jasper Brooks 9-18-1879
Brooks, Martha Ann to Ewing Brooks 8-31-1876 (9-3-1876)
Brooks, Martha E. to Pleasant M. Chadwell 11-24-1870
Brooks, Martha M. to John Hill 11-21-1873 (no return)
Brooks, Martha to John J. Harrell 1-17-1872 (1-19-1872)
Brooks, Martha to Newton Brooks 8-31-1870 (9-4-1870)
Brooks, Mary E. to Doctor John Sutton 7-23-1881 (7-24-1881)

Brooks, Mary E. to George W. Longwood 2-8-1876 (2-10-1876)
Brooks, Mary J. to George Eastridge 10-2-1873 (10-5-1873)
Brooks, Mary to Wm. jr. Causby 12-26-1878 (12-27-1878)
Brooks, Mintie to John Townsley 12-3-1887 (12-4-1887?)
Brooks, Mossie to Tilmon Campbell 9-10-1909 (with 1890)
Brooks, Nancy to Jacob Susong 11-14-1883 (11-24-1883)
Brooks, Nancy to John Massengal 2-18-1887 (2-24-1887)
Brooks, Perlina to G. A. Brooks 9-12-1883
Brooks, Pheba O. to Aaron Woodson 12-28-1877 (no return)
Brooks, Rachel Elizabeth to George W. Pace 1-27-1877 (1-28-1877)
Brooks, Rutha to James Rolin 3-2-1882 (3-5-1882)
Brooks, S. J. to James Fulton 2-2-1880 (2-8-1880)
Brooks, Sarah to Elbert Sumpter 4-7-1877 (4-8-1877)
Brooks, Sarah to G. W. Hill 6-?-1882
Brooks, Sarah to Rice Whiteaker 12-30-1868 (12-31-1868)
Brooks, Sarey J. to Wm. H. Duncan 5-6-1871
Brooks, Sarilda to Wm. Prior Dean 10-20-1888 (10-24-1888)
Brooks, Surrellay J. to Henderson Dean 2-1-1878
Brooks, Theressa to T. A. Brooks 1-11-1889 (1-13-1889)
Brooks, ____ to T. M. Wyley 12-29-1888 (no return)
Brotherton, M. J. to G. W. Jones 12-9-1890
Brown, Angeline to John Carmack 5-31-1880
Brown, Catherin to Elbert Campbell 3-20-1880 (3-21-1880)
Brown, Docia A. to Isaac Rosenbalm 5-28-1881
Brown, Eliz. to Ale Morten 3-23-1886 (3-4?-1886)
Brown, Eliza A. to Oliver Campbell 11-8-1872
Brown, Elizabeth to Harrison Sutton 7-31-1877 (no return)
Brown, Jane to Daniel Walker 7-1-1876 (7-2-1876)
Brown, Jane to Harvy Dawken 6-28-1879
Brown, Josephine to William Estepp 1-20-1877 (no return)
Brown, Lucinda M. to James Long 12-12-1875 (12-13-1875)
Brown, Luticia Ann to Bradford Davis 4-19-1869
Brown, M. J. to F. G. Garford 1-29-1891 (no return)
Brown, Malinda to Harmon Chadwell 12-24-1869 (12-26-1869)
Brown, Malissa to Edward Munch 6-23-1878 (6-24-1878)
Brown, Marry G. (Miss) to J. G. Hoskins 7-25-1881
Brown, Mary (Mrs.) to John McBee 6-3-1881
Brown, Matilda to John Estep 4-24-1880 (4-25-1880)
Brown, N. A. to John B. Southern 1-2-1889
Brown, Rebeca A. to John L. Brooks 11-14-1876 (no return)
Brown?, Ellie to Alex Smith 4-4-1885 (no return)
Browning, Clara to James D. Denham 10-11-1871 (10-12-1871)
Bruce, Elizabeth to Jesse Treece 10-8-1869 (10-10-1869)
Bruce, Jane to Herkles Phillips 3-1-1879
Bruce, Jenney Ann to D. A. Wheeler 10-4-1886 (10-6-1886)
Bruce, Margret to G. W. Miller 5-21-1883 (5-27-1883)
Bruce, Salley Ann to Robt. Bean 6-25-1888 (6-28-1888)
Bruce, Sarah Catharine to Elijah Hill 12-19-1868 (12-24-1868)
Bruster, Fannie to Lewis Hazelwood 5-26-1883
Bryant, Octava L. to Luml? Robertson 6-15-1885 (6-16-1885)
Bryant, Rachel to James M. Lynch 2-10-1887 (3-20-1887)
Bryant, Sarah A. to Preston Greer 12-12-1884 (12-14-1884)
Bryant, Souzanah to Richard Davis 3-24-1871
Brylls, Mary A. to H. B. Meyers 12-13-1884 (12-14-1884)
Buchanan, Cornie to Rolin Hurst 1-31-1882
Buchanan, Jula to William Jennings 12-26-1884
Buchanan, Liza D. to William Kelley 5-25-1882 (no return)
Buchanon, Angeline to David Evans 1-19-1871
Buchanon, Jane to William Mason 1-21-1882
Buckanan, Cornelia to Ensley Posoey 5-12-1877
Buckhanon, Manirva to Peter Perkins 1-5-1871
Buis, M. A. to Wm. Weaver? 5-1-1879 (no return)
Buis, Mag to Robt. Burford 12-12-1888
Buiser, Margaret to William Shipley 9-17-1868 (9-18-1868)
Bulcher, Fanney to T. E. Essary 11-21-1888 (11-22-1888)
Bull, Lucinda to Leon Blackben 8-7-1880 (8-8-1880)
Bull, Mary to Smith Rolins 11-13-1879
Bullard, Selah to John M. Lane 5-30-1875
Bullard, Susan R. to Wm. J. W. Rogers 9-8-1872
Bullin, Linda to Wm. Earls 10-1-1887 (10-2-1887)
Bullis, Elizabeth to D. S. Raney 3-26-1885 (3-28-1885)
Bunch, Elizabeth to James Saterfield 8-16-1882 (8-17-1882)
Bunch, Jane to Henery Hurst 6-11-1874
Bunch, Mary to Geo. W. Hurst 6-14-1888
Bunch, Matild to Rodman Hurst 5-3-1880 (5-6-1880)
Burch, Bell to F. M. Davis 12-30-1889 (1-1-1890)
Burch, Lucinda J. to Reuben R. Robinson 10-7-1869
Burch, Mary J. to B. A. Thacker 11-10-1877 (11-11-1877)
Burchett, Mary to Isaac Carmack 11-19-1883 (no return)
Burchett, R. J. to D. F. Owens 12-1-1876 (2-3-1876)
Burchfield, Loucinda to J. W. Doyl 10-25-1884 (no return)
Burchfield, Louisa to John Yoakum 8-6-1877 (8-12-1877)
Burchfield, Lucy J. to George M. Cox 8-13-1874
Burchfield, M. J. to John M. Baldwin 11-25-1879 (no return)
Burchfield, M. L. to M. R. Kelley 1-20-1873 (1-23-1873)
Burchfield, Mariah to William H. F. H. Yoakum 10-12-1874 (10-15-1874)
Burchfield, Mary Jane to William B. Balden 7-25-1877 (7-26-1877)

Burchfield, Matilda to John T. Welch 8-16-1877
Burk, Elizabeth to William H. Guyn 2-11-1869
Burk, Margret to Wm. Newbey 2-23-1879
Burk, Martha to David Bruer 3-11-1874 (3-12-1874)
Burk, Martha to Isaac Gwin 10-18-1888
Burk, Rebeca to J. N. Caman 8-15-1877
Burns, Suzy to George Bradley 5-30-1889
Burrell, Polley to Jeff Martin 8-25-1888
Busick, Emeline to George Nevels 11-30-1871 (no return)
Bussell, Laura Ann to Wm. Whiteaker 5-15-1890 (5-18-1890)
Bussell, Lucy to Cephus Hatfield 11-23-1889 (11-24-1889)
Bussell, Lucy to Samuel Jones 2-11-1878 (2-12-1878)
Bussell, Martha to Lemuel Gorleinee? 10-22-1886 (no return)
Bussell, Nancy J. to William Heck 11-14-1888 (11-18-1888)
Bussell, Rutha to Samuel Garlin 1-27-1881
Bussell, S. A. to James L. Stone 3-12-1881
Bussell, Sarah to Samuel Kibert 5-23-1871
Bussell?, Cornelia to Wiley Kibert 8-12-1882 (no return)
Butler, Sarah to Robert G. Wiley 8-30-1875 (9-2-1875)
Byers, Salley J. to S. M. Whitlock 12-19-188? (12-18-1886)
Cabbage, Mary to Arthur Brewer 12-20-1809 (with 1890)
Cadle, Eliza to Williams William 1-20-1885
Cadle, Elizabeth to Henry Kibert 6-18-1879
Cadle, Leona to W. M. Wagoner 9-21-1888 (9-22-1888)
Cadle, Lumbera A. to J. F. McBary 1-5-1887 (1-6-1887)
Cadle, Martha to James Wyerman 9-28-1869
Cadle, Molley to M. F. Cavin 9-27-1887 (no return)
Cadle, Sarah to Andrew Hickman 2-18-1883
Cadle, Sarah to James Vann 4-22-1881
Cain, Martha to George Coffee 2-20-1871 (2-23-1871)
Cain, Mary to Charles Rich 10-5-1871
Cain, Sarah M. to Thomas J. Clauson 8-4-1869 (8-5-1869)
Calger, Jemima F. to James F. Mercer 11-4-1874
Calor, Sarah E. to Andrew J. Williams 6-30-1883 (6-15?-1883)
Calston, Alis to Lewis Kincaid 10-23-1874
Calton, Elizabeth to John Hill 10-8-1881
Calwell, Rachel? to Jacob Capps 6-18-1870 (6-19-1870)
Calwell, Sarah A. to John W. Medley 12-26-1874
Campbell, Caroline to Alexander Chadwell 9-30-1874 (10-4-1874)
Campbell, Eliza to James Brooks 2-11-1885 (2-12-1885)
Campbell, Eliza to James Fultz 12-2-1881 (12-4-1881)
Campbell, Elizabeth to G. W. Liford 10-31-1872
Campbell, Elizabeth to James Liford 11-17-1877
Campbell, Elizabeth to Wm. J. Brooks 11-17-1877 (no return)
Campbell, Emma B. to Houston Patterson 8-20-1873
Campbell, Jaley to James Burk 8-1-1877 (no return)
Campbell, Jane to Moses Brown 4-12-1872 (4-21-1872)
Campbell, Lucinda to Neil Jennings 3-14-1889 (3-17-1889)
Campbell, Lucy to W. B. Owens 12-22-1877 (12-23-1877)
Campbell, Luda to M. T. Welch 12-22-1888 (12-23-1888)
Campbell, Ludie to Beaugard Bray 12-22-1882
Campbell, M. E. to T. S. (Rev.) Essary 9-10-1885
Campbell, Manda to John Loop 8-21-1889 (8-22-1889)
Campbell, Manerva E. to Daniel H. Mayes 8-30-1871 (8-31-1871)
Campbell, Margaret C. to Scott Yoakum 10-26-1889
Campbell, Martha B. to Levi Rowlett 6-9-1888 (no return)
Campbell, Martha to Peter H. Rowlend 2-20-1869 (2-25-1869)
Campbell, Mary to James Thomas 4-22-1875
Campbell, Nancy to Andrew Barnet 1-10-1880
Campbell, Sarah C. to Alexander Campbell 4-7-1880 (4-8-1880)
Candry, Angeline to William Woodson 12-15-1878
Canell, Nancy to William England 7-17-1878 (no return)
Canell?, Elizabeth to Speedwell Turner 11-25-1877
Canon, Eliza to Thomas Trury 4-29-1870 (5-5-1870)
Canon, Malinda to J. M. Goodrum 3-8-1878 (3-10-1878)
Capps, Elizabeth to P. A. Tinnel 12-31-1889 (1-4-1890)
Capps, Nancy to Charles Mattox 6-4-1870 (6-5-1870)
Carell, Mary M. to John Price 3-17-1883 (3-14?-1883)
Carmack, Amanda to Fielding Estes 5-16-1885 (5-17-1885)
Carmack, Amanda to W. F. Rowlett 5-1-1880 (5-2-1880)
Carmack, Angline to John O. Carmack 3-5-1881 (3-6-1881)
Carmack, M. E. to Elbert Woodard 1-15-1879 (1-19?-1879)
Carmack, Mary to Allen Lawson 11-17-1881 (no return)
Carman, M. B. to P. L. Goin 11-20-1878 (11-21-1878)
Carman, Mary to James Cline 5-29-1889 (no return)
Carman, Nancy M. to B. F. Ely 2-20-1877 (2-22-1877)
Carman, Ollie to Timothy Roark 1-6-1886 (1-7-1886)
Carman, S. E. to W. E. Mountain 4-7-1884 (4-12-1884)
Carmon, Bella to George Pridemore 12-18-1886 (12-19-1886)
Carmon, Lucinda to Joseph S. Large 12-15-1869 (no return)
Carmon, Lucy J. to H. G. Poor 7-30-1877 (8-5-1877)
Carmon, Martha J. to James R. Ford 8-9-1873 (8-14-1873)
Carnell, Mary to P. F. Powell 4-17-1880 (4-19-1880)
Carney, C. J. to J. P. Smith 10-20-1882 (10-22-1882)
Carpenter, Minna B. to Robt. Hurst 4-7-1888
Carpenter, Sarah to John R. Spradling 12-14-1878 (12-19-1878)
Carr, Anna to George Miller 7-29-1882 (8-6-1882)

Carr, Cordelin to F. H. Smith 10-16-1886 (10-17-1886)
Carr, Eliza to Morris Ely 5-26-1873 (6-1-1873)
Carr, Esther C to D. B. Alexander 8-8-1889 (8-11-1889)
Carr, M. T. to W. H. Welch 10-4-1886 (10-10-1886)
Carr, Martha B. to G. W. Quimer 11-24-1886
Carr, Mary A. to John G. Sharp 1-4-1875 (1-12-1875)
Carr, Mary J. to Wm. jr. Ausmus 6-23-1887 (6-25-1887)
Carr, Melvina E. to J. F. Niel 6-18-1870 (6-19-1870)
Carr, Nancy to W. S. Russell 9-13-1890 (9-14-1890)
Carr, Nelley to William H. Bruce 12-7-1890 (12-9-1890)
Carr, Ollie to E. A. Hurst 7-26-1882 (7-27-1882)
Carr, Orlena to H. M. Dobson 2-21-1887 (3-2-1887)
Carr, Pulasky T. to R. B. Thacker 10-9-1877
Carr, Sarah J. to Joseph C. Clark 4-12-1875 (4-29-1875)
Carr, Sarah J. to M. F. Needham 10-9-1875 (10-21-1875)
Carr, Vandelle to Joseph Felps 3-8-1878 (no return)
Carr, Verna to A. D. Welch 3-17-1888 (3-18-1888)
Carrell, Allace to Henry Price 9-23-1889 (12-13-1889)
Carrell, Mary to Joshua F. Hix 8-4-1873
Carrell, Nancy to Caliway Sullivan 10-13-1884
Carrell, Nancy to Thomas England 11-7-1882 (no return)
Carroll, Amanda to John A. Cleaveland 10-1-1875 (10-20-1875)
Carroll, Emely M. to A. J. Duncan 11-18-1874 (11-22-1874)
Carroll, Fanney to William England 7-21-1877 (no return)
Carroll, Mary Ann to D. B. Price 12-20-1888 (12-25-1888)
Carroll, Mary Jane to Grant Poor 10-23-1890
Carroll, Mary Jane to H. L. Bowling 4-4-1889 (4-6-1889)
Carroll, S. E. to Wm. Brim 3-13-1889 (3-14-1889)
Carter, Ann C. to P. L. Malicote 10-22-1881 (10-23-1881)
Carter, Eliza F. to John C. Hall 9-19-1868
Carter, Frances A. to Richard Rider 9-2-1869
Carter, L. B. to Louis B. Harper 5-31-1883
Carter, Lucy to John Laws 4-30-1886 (5-1-1886)
Carter, Malinda to Josiah Presly 1-9-1885 (no return)
Carter, Maranda to E. M. Anderson 11-18-1873 (11-19-1873)
Carter, Mary C. to John Pressley 9-23-1886 (no return)
Carter, Mary to George Herrell 10-9-1880 (no return)
Casada, Lizzie to H. W. McKinzie 4-30-1890 (no return)
Casewell, Elisabeth to Henry C. Farley 9-27-1889 (10-1-1889)
Casey, Mary Jane to John Eastes 5-10-1875 (5-13-1869)
Casey, Matilda E. to Joseph Lambert 5-9-1870 (5-12-1870)
Cassada, Ollie A. to David C. Golden 9-22-1890 (9-25-1890)
Cassall, Loucinda to Thomas Burch 11-2-1874 (no return)
Catterell, Susan to John C. Colson 5-12-1875 (5-13-1875)
Cattrell, Louisa to Madison M. Harris 7-4-1871
Caul, Pollyanna to Harrison Sharp 3-?-1875 (3-18-1875)
Causbey, Eliza to James C. Daniel 3-30-1888
Causbey, Mary to Wm. Brooks 7-26-1887 (7-28-1887)
Cautton, Angeline to Benjamin Roberson 8-28-1878 (no return)
Cavane?, Susan to William F. Barnes 5-29-1882
Cawood, Barbara to D. B. Alexander 10-29-1873 (11-2-1873)
Cawood, Cordelia to J. M. Yokum 9-29-1885 (10-1-1885)
Cawood, E. A. to H. M. Smith 12-11-1882 (12-14-1882)
Cawood, Emily to William Wilson 7-8-1870 (7-9-1870)
Cawood, Emley to J. G. Ellis 6-14-1880 (6-17-1880)
Cawood, Lucinda to John F. Rogers 8-10-1869 (8-12-1869)
Cawood, M. A. to O. C. Huffker 12-30-1880 (no return)
Cawood, Mary L. to Jesse L. Ausmus 12-19-1875 (12-23-1875)
Cawood, Melviny M. to John F. Rogers 11-22-1880 (no return)
Cawood, Millie M. to O. H. Ellis 3-1-1883
Cawood, Sarah A. to J. P. Graham 1-4-1871 (1-12-1871)
Caylor, Eliza to Robt. King 6-27-1887
Celley, N. A. to J. E. McBee 9-26-1878
Chadwell, China to E. C. Chadwell 5-13-1884 (5-18-1884)
Chadwell, Clemetine to John A. Littrell 2-25-1871 (2-26-1871)
Chadwell, Jane to Charley Lewis 11-7-1868 (11-12-1868) B
Chadwell, Julia to R. M. Parks 1-13-1882? (1-13-1882)
Chadwell, Lucinda Clementine to John Jennings 1-13-1876 (1-15-1876)
Chadwell, Lucy Ann to John Try 11-2-1886
Chadwell, M. E. to A. Campbell 6-2-1879 (no return)
Chadwell, M. J. to Alexander Brooks 3-18-1881 (no return)
Chadwell, Martha to William Lambdin 5-26-1883
Chadwell, Mary to Chadwell Brittain 7-14-1870 (7-17-1870)
Chadwell, Mary to Thos. Lynd? 10-3-1885
Chadwell, Nancy to G. W. Brooks 1-4-1873 (no return)
Chadwell, Rutha to Bartley Farer 2-1-1879 (2-5-1879)
Chadwick, A. to Wm. H. Semore 12-14-1881
Chadwick, Eliza J. to L. E. Hollinsworth 9-15-1874 (no return)
Chadwick, Margret Elizbeth to Henry Wheeler 9-12-1871
Chadwick, Sarah E. to W. S. Shipley 8-4-1873
Chadwick, Temprance to James Wheeler 12-2-1880
Chadwick, Tempy to James A. Crutchfield 9-3-1873 (9-4-1873)
Chamberlain, Sarah to James Right 9-29-1876 (10-1-1876)
Chambers, Clifford to George Barnard 8-6-1877
Chance, Nancy S. to Salem Northern 2-8-1877
Chance, Racheal L. to Wm. J. Neeley 10-8-1874 (no return)
Channon, Ellin to Henry Chadwell 2-17-1881

Cheatham, Amanda to Edward Breeding 11-9-1890
Cheatham, Mary E. to Henry M. Moyers 9-22-1869 (9-23-1869)
Cheatham, Matilda to J. H. Williams 10-29-1877
Check, Martha to John Cox 3-29-1871
Cheek, Mary J. to David N. Owens 3-10-1877 (3-11-1877)
Cheek, Nancy to W. H. Carpenter 11-1-1879 (11-5-1879)
Cheek, Priscilla to Thos. Fultz 10-7-1889
Cheetam, Mary to James B. Hurst 11-30-1870 (no return)
Chesley, Minerva to D. A. McCauley 8-31-1887
Chick, Mary to Thomas Crutchfield 1-4-1869 (1-10-1869)
Childers, Marinda to Faris Frost 8-5-1884
Chumbley, Elizabeth to James Powell 7-12-1872 (no return)
Chumley, Sarah M. to Nelson Harp 9-20-1872 (9-22-1872)
Cillums, Sarah M. to Fredrick D. Miricle 7-17-1877 (7-18-1877)
Cimesbery?, Easter to Wm. Gulley 11-20-1886 (11-28-1886)
Clap?, Frances M. to James J. Cowan 11-20-1877
Clapp, Ella to W. A. Wall 9-30-1886
Clark, Addie H. to John R. Thomas 12-11-1888 (12-13-1888)
Clark, Effie B. to Sam McCrank 6-21-1884 (6-24-1884)
Clark, Ida B. to J. R. Carmon 1-29-1890 (2-3-1890)
Clark, Mary to H. L. Burchett 8-10-1880
Clark, Nancy to David Rice 10-24-1871
Clark, Orph E. to Cornelius Moyers 3-14-1880
Clark, Sarah J. to T. B. Hummers 1-15-1878 (no return)
Clarkson, Minervia to John T. Estep 3-5-1890
Clarkston, Matilda to George Campbell 9-23-1869
Clarxten, Ollie to J. P. Bray 9-?-1882 (9-24-1882)
Claxton, Allie to B. H. Brooks 7-23-1884 (7-24-1884)
Clement, Lucy M. to Thos. J. Howerton 2-19-1884
Cline, M. O. to Martin Moyers 12-7-1881 (12-8-1882?)
Cline, Mary H. to James Griffen 10-24-1882 (10-26-1882)
Cline, Nancy M. to Thos. C. Poor 7-27-1872
Cline, Nancy O. to L. F. Moody 10-23-1882 (10-26-1882)
Cline, Sally B. to James F. Chumbley 2-18-1880 (2-19-1880)
Cline, Susan B. to A. J. Poor 12-24-1886 (12-25-1886)
Cline, Willie Ann to Patrick Hughes 11-6-1887
Clingsworth, Pheby to Thomas Wallace 8-17-1871 (8-19-1871)
Cloud, Allice to Lewis T. Pearson 2-3-1870
Cloud, Elisabeth to George Sanders 8-30-1888
Cloud, Elizabeth to Wm. Kincaid 11-29-1877 (no return)
Cloud, July to Jesse Carpenter 2-25-1871 (2-26-1871)
Cloud, Lucinda to Andrew Allen 11-11-1869 B
Cloud, Margarett to Britton Evans 4-9-1882
Cloud, Melia to Anderson Edds 11-16-1880 (4-8-1880?)
Cloud, Melvina to Charles Day 12-27-1872
Cloud, Phebe to Gilbert Day 8-29-1874 (8-30-1874) B
Cloud, Pheby to James Bussell 1-11-1883
Clouse, Elizabeth R. to Robert F. Cook 4-21-1882 (4-23-1882)
Cluck?, Nancy to Robert Petree 10-21-1873 (10-26-1873)
Coalman, Elizabeth to Nathan Gray 1-29-1872 (4-16-1873)
Coatney, Lizzy to D. A. Essary 11-1-1888
Cockram, Lucinda to G.? F. Chadwell 12-31-1879
Cole, Hellen to James Sims 6-6-1889 (6-9-1889)
Cole, Jane to James H. Bundren 8-17-1889 (no return)
Cole, Jerusia to William Killian 9-24-1874 (no return)
Cole, Liza to Andy Edds 7-27-1887 (7-28-1887)
Cole, Maggy to Andrew Widner 11-24-1890
Cole, Mary M. to Robert B. Watson 11-2-1883 (11-4-1883)
Cole, Nancy J. to Burel Hatfield 6-13-1878 (no return)
Cole, R. H. to James W. Gose? 1-27-1876
Cole, Rachal to William Dean 1-19-1882
Cole, Rachel to William Wyley 10-8-1890 (10-7?-1890)
Cole, Virginia to George W. Edmonson 6-14-1877 (no return)
Coleman, Eliz. to Nathan Gray 1-29-1872 (2-2-1873?)
Coleman, Elizabeth to Thomas Parkey 4-13-1874 (4-14-1874)
Coleman, Elizabeth to Thos. Parkey 4-13-1874 (no return)
Coleman, Susan to Israel Parkey 4-5-1876 (4-7-1876)
Colenworth, Mary J. to W. F. C. Sumate 12-26-1878
Colenworth, W. K. to John Jons 12-24-1878
Coleton, Manda to Warrick Butcher 4-1-1869 (4-3-1869) B
Collensworth, Melvinea to John Lingar 4-23-1870 (4-24-1870)
Colllins, Dacie? to Wm. Johnson 11-18-1879 (no return)
Collin, Sarah to Zack Seals 1-7-1888 (1-8-1888)
Collinesworth, Emly to Robert W. Billingsley 1-17-1883 (1-18-1883)
Collins, Allie to James Eagle 5-28-1886 (5-29-1886)
Collins, Angaline to Arch. Blancett 12-25-1884 (1-12-1885)
Collins, D. J. M. to Elizabeth Presley 8-4-1889
Collins, Eliza to John J. Clement 7-18-1872 (7-21-1872)
Collins, Emiline to Wm. Earls 11-22-1890
Collins, Ensihel? to George Livingston 11-8-1881 (11-9-1881)
Collins, Jansey to A. B. Honby 11-4-1886 (no return)
Collins, Loucinda to Joel Collins 8-28-1882
Collins, Louciana to John Cook 6-21-1886 (6-25-1886)
Collins, Louiza D. to J. W. Smith 1-4-1890 (1-5-1890)
Collins, Lourena to Sterling Collins 7-3-1880 (6?-29-1880)
Collins, Marg. to Hen. Willis 3-16-1886 (3-23-1886)
Collins, Margaret to James West 7-6-1887 (7-24-1887)

Collins, Martha E. to Andrew N. Collins 3-17-1869 (3-18-1869)
Collins, Martha J. to Benj. D. England 3-14-1888
Collins, Martha to Brick? Jon? 1-27-1872 (1-28-1872)
Collins, Mary M. to Frank Young 9-25-1879 (no return)
Collins, Mary to James C. Jordan 10-7-1880 (10-8-1880)
Collins, Matilda to William Tolliver 10-23-1869 (10-31-1869)
Collins, Matilda to Wm. H. Ross 10-18-1870 (10-10-1871)
Collins, Melvina to Wm. Farmer 6-29-1876 (7-2-1876)
Collins, Nancy A. to William D. Sowder 9-14-1890 (9-18-1890)
Collins, Nancy E. to William S. Collins 2-10-1882 (2-11-1882)
Collins, Nsly? (Mrs.) to Willis Gibson 6-2-1881 (6-3-1881)
Collins, Sackey to Calvin Sparks 2-24-1875 (no return)
Collins, Sally A. to John W. Maddox 10-23-1885 (10-25-1885)
Collins, Sarah M. to Richard Paul 12-29-1882 (12-31-1882)
Collins, Sarah to Wm. Jones 11-18-1879 (11-19-1879)
Collinsworth, Larinda to John W. Justice 8-30-1871 (9-6-1871)
Collinsworth, R. M. to John C. Hopson 1-14-1880 (no return)
Collinsworth, Rosa to Wesley Sharp 2-17-1875
Collinsworth, Sarah to David Carr 5-24-1886 (5-6?-1886)
Colson, Jennie to Arch Wolfe 8-19-1882 (8-12-1882)
Colson, Sarah to David Fuegate 10-2-1871 (10-5-1871)
Colson, Udoxie to W. D. Hurst 10-30-1890 (no return)
Colston, Basia to John Simpson 6-8-1887
Colston, Celia to Daniell Lewis 12-23-1879
Colston, Elizabeth to Scy Crockett 8-2-1882
Colvord, Nancy A. to J. S. Scott 7-29-1885? (8-2-1886)
Colwell, Nellie to S. M. Simmons 8-19-1888 (no return)
Compton, Gussey to R. H. Jones 1-6-1889
Condry, Nancy to James Willimoy? 1-3-1871 (no return)
Conner, Eliza J. to T. M. Williams 4-15-1889 (no return)
Conner, Sarah to Joseph England 1-6-1880
Conner?, Sarah A. to Charles D. Garrett 9-5-1879 (9-7-1879)
Connor, Mollie to L. R. Rowlet 1-19-1888 (1-26-1888)
Cook, Adaline to William Dobbs 2-17-1869 (2-21-1869)
Cook, Cornelia A. to John F. Davis 3-27-1869 (3-29-1869)
Cook, Emeline to M. Dunsmore 2-23-1880 (3-7-1880)
Cook, H. L. to Jame Owens 2-3-1881 (no return)
Cook, Lucy A. to George P. Owens 6-26-1877 (7-1-1877)
Cook, Margaret J. to Isaac M. Jones 11-18-1871 (11-19-1871)
Cook, Martha S. to Andrew Manning 7-31-1885 (8-20-1885?)
Cook, Martha to Alen Whitaker 9-29-1887 (10-2-1887)
Cook, Mary to John Whitaker 8-2-1888 (8-5-1888)
Cook, Rebaca to Semblen Hamllin 11-4-1879
Cook, Rhoda to Ewing Runnions 3-27-1877 (3-29-1877)
Cook, Susan to David Smith 3-4-1877 (no return)
Corbin, Frances A. to John J. Collinsworth 9-25-1869 (9-26-1869)
Cornett, Susan M. to William F. Stevens 9-17-1880
Cosbey, Elizabeth to John Masengill 10-30-1880
Cosbey, J. to Joseph Lambert 12-11-1875 (12-26-1876?)
Cosby, Hannah to Jasper Williams 9-14-1876 (no return)
Cosby, Hanner to David Cosby 8-6-1883 (no return)
Cosby, Lucy Ann to Wm. Williams 9-3-1875 (9-5-1875)
Cosby, Martha to A. C. Prator 11-?-1886 (no return)
Cosby, Mary E. to John Owens 9-11-1881 (9-12-1881)
Cotterell, Mary H. to Waldegrave Perman 4-24-1889
Cotterell, Mollie to C. H. Rogers 1-25-1888
Cottrell, China to Wm. J. Colinsworth 12-25-1881
Cottrell, Dora Bell to John Ross McIntosh 1-7-1890
Cottrell, M. K. to G. H. Jones 11-1-1884 (11-11-1884)
Countice, M. J. to John N. Thompson 9-22-1880
Cowan, Georgia to William Fletcher 7-22-1887
Cowan, Manday J. to Wm. W. Goin 3-15-1873 (3-20-1873)
Cowan, Mary Ann to L. T. Hodges 5-5-1885
Coward, Nancy to William A. Willis 4-12-1869 (4-16-1869)
Coward, Rhoda to Wesley Finnel 1-11-1882
Cox, A. to John A. Guin 4-1-1879 (4-13-1879)
Cox, Delainia to Robert Johnson 5-15-1880 (5-16-1880)
Cox, Elizabeth to George Smith 11-29-1883
Cox, Elizabeth to John Ball? 8-6-1870 (8-7-1870)
Cox, Harriett E. to M. J. Sowder 12-28-1886
Cox, Hester A. to John Meyers 3-6-1882 (3-29-1882)
Cox, M. C. to Joseph Pressnell 8-?-1890 (8-31-1890)
Cox, Martha J. to Wm. W. Johnston 7-20-1887 (7-31-1887)
Cox, Mary Ann to Saml. Bryant 2-11-1889 (2-17-1889)
Cox, Mary to Thomas England 12-23-1878 (3-14-1879)
Cox, Nancy Jane to William Cowan 11-12-1868 (11-1?-1868)
Cox, Nancy to James M. Chick 1-3-1870 (1-9-1870)
Cox, P. B. to A. J. Johnson 4-29-1883
Cox, Parley to A. C. Keck 4-29-1887 (5-1-1887)
Cox, Surelda to Hire England 12-20-1877
Crabtree, B. A. to George P. Owens 11-26-1881 (11-27-1881)
Crabtree, Elizabeth to Alexander Chadwell 9-2-1869 (9-9-1869)
Crabtree, Mary A. to Daniel Hazelwood 7-12-1873 (7-13-1873)
Crage, Eliza J. to Reuben Massengill 3-28-1870
Crawford, Jane to Jefferson Lambert 1-2-1873 (1-5-1873)
Crawford, Mabrey to John H. Crawford 11-30-1877 (no return)
Crawford, Martha to Samuel Crawford 10-1-1870 (10-2-1871?)

Crawford, N. J. to James M. Morakle 8-20-1875 (8-23-1875)
Crawford, Sarah to Joseph Bussell 9-20-1881
Creg, Betsey to F. L. Miller 3-4-1889 (3-5-1889)
Criger, Elizabeth J. to James W. Barns 11-22-1869 (11-28-1869)
Crocket, Mary to Herod Loftis 2-23-1873 (2-24-1873)
Crockett, D. A. to R. W. Loftice 8-27-1882
Crockett, Sarah E. to Creed Kincaid 1-1-1875 (1-2-1875)
Crofford, Mary to John Brown 8-22-1888
Cross, Lucinda L. to Pleasant F. Powell 1-19-1876 (1-20-1876)
Cross, N. S. to Harvey Sanders 5-25-1885
Crousham, Louiza to Richard Golden 1-1-1869 (1-3-1869)
Cruchfield, Lucy J. to Wm. L. Jessee 1-6-1880 (1-15-1880)
Crutchfield, Allice to A. J. Cuningham 4-18-1888 (no return)
Crutchfield, Elizabeth to James N. Northern? 12-17-1873 (12-18-1873)
Crutchfield, Jane to J. R. Loop 11-9-1872
Crutchfield, Lamsa to J. H. Davis 4-20-1872 (4-21-1872)
Crutchfield, Loucinda to Joseph Killian 4-17-1878 (4-18-1878)
Crutchfield, Margret to Albert Clarkson 11-5-1874 (no return)
Crutchfield, Nancy to John F. Prator 1-21-1878
Crutchfield, Sarah to Thomas Kellion 10-1-1884 (10-9-1884)
Cunningham, Eliza M. to Wm. Cook 7-15-1871 (7-16-1871)
Cunningham, Marth J. to Joseph Whiteaker 12-27-1877 (12-28-1877)
Cunningham, Mary A. to Thomas Furgerson 2-12-1880 (no return)
Cunningham, Mary E. to Sheldon E. Harrison 1-31-1870 (2-3-1870)
Cunningham, Nancy A. to James A. Williams 4-14-1878
Cunningham, Nancy to James Roark 9-6-1869
Cunningham, Ollie to E. D. Eastridge 10-16-1888 (10-18-1888)
Cunningham, Sarah to James Hargraves 8-19-1877 (8-20-1877)
Cunnningham, Loucinda to B. M. Posoey 4-30-1875
Cupp, Elisabeth A. to Benjamin Bean 8-7-1888 (8-9-1888)
Cupp, Elizabeth J. to James Poor 10-9-1875 (10-10-1875)
Cupp, Hester A. to W. H. Bishop 3-9-1888 (3-11-1888)
Cupp, Margaret to John Smith 6-29-1885 (7-5-1885)
Cupp, Martha M. to John H. Branson 7-17-1884
Cupp, Mary J. to Isom Meyers 9-4-1869 (9-5-1869)
Cupp, Melvina to N. W. Poor 5-31-1889
Cupp, Orlenia to J. A. Minton 2-17-1874 (2-18-1874)
Cupp, Rhoda to Alfred Owens 9-10-1874 (9-13-1874)
Cupp, Sarah A. to R. M. Poor 8-4-1884
Cupp, Sarrah A. to Charley Sawyers 11-9-1878
Curbey, Abney to Price Gray 2-12-1886 (2-15-1886)
Curler, Emly to Isaac B. Frier 11-4-1877
Dalton, Manda to Robert Lenard 12-17-1886 (12-23-1886)
Dalton, Matilda J. to R. C. Sprales 10-25-1881 (10-30-1881)
Danel, M. H. E. to Sanferd Lynch 7-28-1879
Daniel, Elisabeth to John Longworth 9-15-1875 (9-16-1875)
Daniel, Malinda to James W. Hill 7-18-1873 (7-20-1873)
Daniel, Margret L. to John A. Lynch 5-15-1883
Daniel, Margret to William Longworth 9-15-1875 (9-16-1875)
Daniel, Sarah C. to Josiiah Robert 12-7-1872 (12-8-1872)
Daniel, Sarah F. to John F. Mustard 9-25-1877
Daniel, Saraha L. to Prior E. Poor 5-31-1878 (no return)
Daniel, Sufinild to Jackson Jordan 11-1-1876 (11-2-1876)
Daniels, Mary Jane to Wm. Litterell 10-12-1888 (10-14-1888)
Dannel, S. E. to Stephen Lee 8-29-1884
Danuels, Manerva (Mis) to Jacob C. Campbell 9-1-1881 (9-2-1881)
Daulton, Elizabeth to Wm. H. Beese 8-?-1879 (no return)
Davault, Emelinle to William Parkey 12-4-1869 (12-5-1869) B
Davidson, Eliza to Alexander Smith 6-14-1879 (6-15-1879)
Davidson, Sarah J. to John Adkins 1-11-1872 (1-12-1872)
Davies, Rachial L. to R. L. Robinson 9-17-1884
Davis, Alis to E. M. Hendrickson 1-23-1877 (2-1-1877)
Davis, Carnela to I. J. Johnson 9-1-1879 (9-7-1879)
Davis, Caroline to Wiley Jones 3-19-1874
Davis, Dicey to A. F. Branscom 5-6-1885 (5-7-1885)
Davis, Dicy M. to Sterling Goin 9-24-1870 (9-26-1870)
Davis, Dora to Wm. F. Cunningham 12-24-1887 (12-25-1887)
Davis, Elizabeth O. to Danil F. Lemar 2-13-1883 (2-27-1883)
Davis, Elizabeth to Evan Riley 9-24-1870 (9-25-1870)
Davis, Emiline to Pleasant Johnson 8-4-1876 (8-6-1876)
Davis, L. J. to S. H. Walker 6-2-1875 (6-3-1875)
Davis, Louisa to James Campbell 12-21-1871
Davis, Louisa to Nathan C. Clement 12-12-1874 (1-14-1875)
Davis, Louisa to Robt. Jenins? 9-23-1873 (no return)
Davis, Lucy A. to T. S. Sumter 4-16-1874
Davis, Lutisia A. to William Boling 6-11-1874
Davis, Martha to Henry Shopsher 5-18-1886 (5-19-1886)
Davis, Martha to Jefferson Hunter 8-4-1871 (8-6-1871)
Davis, Martha to M. V. Miller 7-27-1886 (7-29-1886)
Davis, Narcissa to Calvin More 3-25-1870
Davis, Polley to John W. Turner 2-17-1872
Davis, S. E. to Nathaniel Wilson 8-23-1873 (no return)
Davis, Sarah A. to Ham McCulley 7-18-1878 (7-21-1878)
Davis, Sarah E. to Franklin F. Moncy 8-25-1874 (8-27-1874)
Davis, Susa A. to T. S. Sumter 4-16-1874 (no return)
Davis, Susan to John Haynes 4-19-1884 (4-4?-1884)
Davy, Levesta to J. W. McWilliams 5-1-1881

Day, Elizabeth to Lewis Kincaid 8-4-1884 (8-5-1884)
Day, Hannah to Davies 4-4-1879
Day, Kessiah to Calvin Mitchell 1-14-1871 (1-15-1871)
Day, Malinda to Nelson Lebow 10-1-1869 (10-3-1869) B
Day, Matilda to Jordan Cloud 3-6-1874 (3-7-1874)
Day, Nancy to G. W. Lynch 10-30-1885 (11-1-1885)
Day, Narcissus to Jefferson Treece 12-9-1876 (12-10-1876)
Day, Sarah E. to William Faulkner 7-14-1874 (no return)
Day, Sarah J. to George W. Watson 12-13-1873 (12-19-1873)
Dean, Racheal A. to Drewey Lawson 3-4-1878 (3-6-1878)
Debusk, C. J. to A. J. Freeman 10-30-1879 (11-2-1879)
Debusk, Carma to W. D. Robertson 10-17-1889 (10-27-1889)
Debusk, Catherine to Henry King 1-14-1875
Debusk, Florence to Isaac Campbell 3-25-1872 (4-28-1872)
Debusk, Nancy to G. B. Needham 8-10-1888 (8-17-1888)
Debusk, Rachal to Wm. T. Osborn 10-1-1881
Debusk, Sarah F. to Lafay W. Snider 3-8-1888
Debusk, Susan to I. T. Frierson? 3-3-1884
Debusk, Victory A. to G. W. Rector 10-1-1883 (10-4-1883)
Deck, Sarah C. to Newton E. Kesterson 11-19-1884 (11-20-1884)
Deen, Amanda to Marshell Martin 5-30-1883 (6-2-1883)
Deen, Elizabeth to Elihu Halfield 3-24-1885 (4-7-1885)
Deen, Elizabeth to Elihu Hatfield 4-7-1885 (no return)
Degord?, Mary E. to W. L. Pate 4-1-1886
Denham, Martha to Taylor Brooks 1-29-1876 (no return)
Denham, Orlenie C. to Joseph Y. Collins 2-21-1882 (2-31?-1882)
Dennam, Cornelia to W. T. Yeary 1-14-1886 (1-18-1886)
Denne, Martha to Joseph Marsee 1-30-1881 (1-31-1881)
Dennison, Margret to Clint Woodson 4-8-1871 (4-15-1871)
Denton, Sarah L. to J. M. Taylor 9-4-1879
Devault, Marry E. to Emanuel Collins 8-17-1881 (8-18-1881)
Devault, S. A. to Bud Willson 5-5-1879 (5-6-1879)
Deyer, Nancy to Marten Monrowe 12-2-1882 (12-3-1882)
Dinkins, Mary J. to Samuel Ales 10-17-1869
Dishman, Carrie to John P. A. Dickinson 6-12-1877
Dixie, Susie to Jefferson Brown 6-8-1887
Dobbs, Elizabeth to James P. Goin 8-7-1877
Dockery, Mary J. to Preston E. Rouse 2-6-1889 (2-7-1889)
Dooly, M. C. to J. B. Rice 12-28-1876
Doris, Alice J. to Hugh Killion 7-21-1884
Doset, M. A. to J. C. Meyers 12-2-1884 (12-4-1884)
Dosset, E. J. to George W. Beason 12-13-1880 (no return)
Doughty, S. A. to John A. Garrett 8-26-1880
Douthe, G. B. (Mrs.) to D. S. Owens 12-9-1888
Doyel, Elizabeth to William W. S. Owens 8-23-1869 (8-29-1869)
Doyel, Martha to James Brewer 2-2-1881 (3-6-1881)
Doyle, Mary to James M. Collins 3-10-1880 (3-11-1880)
Drummon, Betty to Jno? Debusk 9-7-1889 (6?-8-1889)
Drummond, Sibba A. to Richard W. Poor 12-21-1868 (12-24-1868)
Drummons, A. B. to Wm. B. Mink 8-19-1880
Drummons, M. O. to G. W. Ford 12-10-1879 (12-23-1879)
Drummons, Mary J. to John H. Mink 1-27-1874 (1-29-1874)
Drummons, Mary to William Robertson 1-28-1891 (2-8-1891)
Drumons, Evaline to John Munsey 4-3-1888 (4-4-1888)
Duff, Fannie to L. C. Buckhart 10-27-1887
Duncan, E. M. to Wm. N. Mathis 1-28-1881
Duncan, Eliza to Wm. Christian 12-18-1890 (12-21-1890)
Duncan, Ginnia to Wm. Wallace 1-14-1873 (1-17-1873)
Duncan, Marth to John Lynch 6-14-1884 (6-15-1884)
Duncan, Nancy to Thomas J. Wallace 2-10-1869
Duncan, Rebecca J. to J. J. Fullington 6-5-1886 (6-6-1886)
Dungin?, Winey to ____ Whiteaker 6-27-1878
Dunkin, Jennie to Wilkeson Howard 2-11-1886 (2-4?-1886)
Dunn, Elizabeth A. to David M. Hopper 7-18-1882 (7-23-1882)
Dunn, Ellen to Joseph Elison 5-18-1883 (5-24-1883)
Dunn, M. A. to J. L. Harmon 3-12-1890 (4-17-1890)
Dunn, Mary A. to John Hopper 1-3-1881 (1-6-1881)
Dunn, R. J. to J. R. Brantly 10-6-1883
Dunn, Rach. C. to Josiah L. Keck? 3-13-1875 (3-21-1875)
Dunn, Racheal E. to Elijah Keck 4-20-1872 (4-28-1872)
Dunn, Sarah E. to Joseph Carmack 12-14-1888 (12-16-1888)
Dunn?, Malinda to Phillip Keck 4-15-1874 (no return)
Dunsmore, China A. to William A. Banes 12-12-1874 (12-14-1874)
Dunsmore, E. A. to D. C. Smith 3-9-1879
Dunsmore, Louisa to Green P. Sulfridge 1-4-1876 (1-25-1876)
Dunsmore, Sarah E. to Jacob Reece 12-12-1874 (12-17-1874)
Eads, Frances Jane to Riley Vanbebber 8-18-1877 (8-22-1877)
Eads, Rebecca to John Ely 5-17-1870 (5-18-1870)
Ealley, Elisabeth to Robert Turner 1-10-1879
Earls, Mary to John W. Ailes 9-2-1889 (9-3-1889)
Easley, Jane to Hamlet Overton 1-17-1872 (1-20-1872)
Easley, Judy to Henry Hipsher 2-9-1870 (2-13-1870) B
Eastly, Matin to Henry Overton 2-14-1885 (2-15-1885)
Eastridge, Elizabeth to Eldridge Hurst 11-1-1875
Eastridge, Margret to Timothy Roark 5-4-1878 (5-12-1878)
Eastridge, Martha to Nelson Mathis 12-17-1874
Eastridge, Mary to Henry Foddis 11-14-1888 (11-18-1888)

Eastridge, Sofier to John Gray 4-22-1871
Eastus, Elizabeth to W. J. Presley 12-20-1873 (12-21-1873)
Eastus, Emely to Elbert F. Fields 12-20-1873 (12-21-1873)
Edds, Hettie to A. C. Carr 9-23-1889
Edens, Nancy to John Estept 8-20-1886 (8-22-1886)
Edens?, Margaret to Jacob Dooley 11-6-1888
Edmondson, Mary E. to W. C. Laws 7-25-1885? (7-26-1885)
Edmondson, Susan to John H. Ousley 3-20-1880 (3-21-1880)
Edmonson, Anna to G. M. D. Ousley 1-24-1874 (1-29-1874)
Edmonson, Catharine to Lewis Loop 10-4-1877 (no return)
Edmonson, Lidian to Daniel Zapp 9-30-1875
Edmonson, Suda to T. F. Ford 10-29-1890 (10-30-1890)
Edwards, Adeline to Bery Elison 4-26-1883 (4-27-1883)
Edwards, Elizabeth to Daniel D. Hopper 1-18-1870 (1-24-1870)
Edwards, M. to John Brown 6-16-1880 (no return)
Edwards, Martha to Elijah W. Raney 9-2-1871 *
Edwards, Mary to Preston Beeson 12-16-1888 (12-17-1888)
Edwards, Rachel to A. L. Ellison 9-14-1892 (9-16-1882)
Edwards, Sarah M. to Marshal L. Odell 5-26-1869 (5-27-1869)
Edwards, Susan to D. M. Ellison 11-21-1888 (11-22-1888)
Eldridge, Sarah to Isaac Meyers 12-5-1884? (12-11-1884)
Eley, Mary to Gordy Mason 9-18-1885
Elison, Martha to J. L. Meyers 4-2-1884 (no return)
Elison, Mary to Calaway Massengill 1-17-1884 (no return)
Ellis, Adaline to G. W. Mozingo 11-2-1888 (11-4-1888)
Ellis, Mary to John Teury? 11-10-1873
Ellison, Alice to John Caler 7-22-1885 (7-26-1885)
Ellison, America to W. P. Cosby 10-25-1890 (no return)
Ellison, Manervy (Mrs.) to I. J. Hammock 7-10-1881
Ellison, Margaret to James Wilson 6-2-1887
Ellison, Martha to I. L. Meyers 1-20-1886
Ellison, Mary J. to B. M. Fletcher 6-14-1883 (6-17-1883)
Ellison, Sarah to James Tesney 7-6-1870 (7-7-1870)
Ellisson, Mary to J. C. Easles 2-7-1884
Elrod, Sarah to John Clark 11-6-1878 (1-2-1879)
Ely, Mary to Hosey Readmon 9-27-1877
Ely, Sarah to William G. Freeman 1-9-1869 (1-10-1869)
Emmett, Mary E. to Frank W. Thomas 12-18-1890 (no return)
England, ----- to G. W. Capps 12-31-1889 (1-1-1890)
England, Catherine L. to Walter E. Massengill 11-24-1876
England, Charity M. to Obediah Fields 2-21-1890 (2-23-1890)
England, Elizabeth to Greenbery F. Lynch 12-26-1871 (12-28-1871)
England, F. H. to Sterling Houston 9-25-1880 (8?-25-1880)
England, Frances to W. P. Tenson 1-8-1873
England, Lucy to Teb Sandford 11-21-1888 (11-22-1888)
England, M. A. to William Ridings 11-5?-1880 (11-7-1880)
England, Manervey to F. A. Gibbs 3-12-1869 (3-17-1869)
England, Marth (Mrs.) to Toliver Robertson 6-10-1881 (6-19-1881)
England, Martha M. to George Rucker 12-24-1882
England, Mary J. to Silas Hook? 10-19-1872 (10-20-1872)
England, Mary L. to Daniel A. Branson 7-29-1875 (8-1-1875)
England, Melley to D. C. Earl 1-2-1877 (1-7-1877)
England, Melvina to G. R. Trent 4-16-1885
England, Sarah E. to John Cupp 7-14-1874 (no return)
England, Sarah to Ross Hunt 4-26-1873 (4-27-1873)
England, Tobitha J. to Thomas Robertson 3-11-1878 (no return)
Enser, Amey to Nelson Riley 6-10-1879 (no return)
Ensor, M. E. to C. Y. Campbell 2-10-1881
Eperson, Ellen O. to Wiley C. Breeding no date (late 1877?)
Epperson, A. O. to J. B. Evans 8-7-1882
Epperson, Julia Ann to Hamilton Singleton 4-25-1873 (4-26-1874?)
Epperson, M. L. to W. T. Noblen 6-9-1879 (6-10-1879)
Epperson, Marty to J. H. Simes 10-6-1879
Epperson, Mary Ann to J. Vann? Collins 2-16-1870
Epperson, N. O. to J. N. Breeding 3-?-1879 (3-20-1879)
Epperson, Sarah to N. F. Overholder 11-16-1888 (11-18-1888)
Epps, Malinda to Thos. R. Shoemaker 6-3-1874 (6-4-1874)
Erving, S. J. to S. E. Fortner 7-5-1888
Esley, Mary to Luther Jackson 12-20-1883 (no return)
Essary, Eliza E. to James Welch 12-24-1884 (no return)
Essary, Mary E. to John Furgerson 12-24-1873 (12-25-1873)
Essor, D. B. to C. B. Campbell 6-31?-1884 (7-31-1884)
Estep, Amanda to W. W. Brooks no date (Oct 1884?)
Estep, Lucy to Abraham Brooks 8-22-1873 (8-24-1873)
Estep, Manda J. to Wm. M. Yeary 12-24-1885 (1-3-1886)
Estep, Mary to William Brown 12-6-1869 (12-9-1869)
Esteps, Mary E. to Nelson P. H. Brooks 5-9-1884 (5-10-1884)
Estept, E. to Peter Rowlen 1-15-1884 (no return)
Estept, Mary E. to Leander Snavely 9-21-1888 (9-24-1888)
Estes, Elizabeth to W. G. Vananoy 9-10-1870 (9-11-1870)
Estes, Martha G. to Thos. D. Ausburn 4-17-1884
Estes, Martha to James F. Chadwell 3-4-1888
Estes, Mary Ann to John D. Cook 12-20-1883 (no return)
Estes, Nancy A. to Wm. F. Sutton 7-22-1880 (7-25-1880)
Estes, Nowesta to Geo. McNiel 5-10-1884
Estes, Rhoda to Jery Brooks 7-12-1879 (7-13-1879)
Estis, Matilda J. to Daniel Reece 8-27-1870 (9-27-1870)

Estridge, Nancy to Hamey Patterson? 10-19-1881 (10-20-1881)
Evans, Ada to Daniel Fulkerson 3-18-1871
Evans, Addie to Madison Howard 9-24-1889 (9-29-1889)
Evans, America E. to Lewis Russell 10-11-1890 (no return)
Evans, Betty to Homer? Cunningham 8-26-1873 (8-28-1873)
Evans, Hallie to Thos. G. Fulkerson 10-9-1883 (10-10-1883)
Evans, Jane to John Brice? 1-25-1873 (1-26-1873) B
Evans, Kate M. to John P. Ward 12-27-1877
Evans, Mary L. to B. G. Maynard 6-20-1878
Evans, Mary L. to Joe A. Adkins 6-12-1889
Evans, Mary to Andrew Turner 6-7-1880 (no return)
Evans, Mary to Eli Dizman? 8-1-1872
Evans, Mattie to William Williams 6-4-1883 (6-21-1883?)
Evans, Nancy J. to John P. Rosenbalm 2-10-1870 (2-13-1870)
Evans, Sallie to D. L. Oaks 10-25-1884 (12-4-1884)
Farlor, Mary to Benjamin Sims 10-19-1868 (10-22-1868) B
Farmer, Jane to W. H. Redmond 11-14-1890 (11-15-1890)
Farmer, Mahala to Reuben Conatser 5-13-1871
Farmer, Manila S. to Joseph L. Loop 4-8-1878 (no return)
Farmer, Mary E. to Bruce H. Rutherford 12-3-1889 (12-4-1890?)
Farmer, Rosie to Wm. M. Day 6-21-1887
Farmer, Susan to John W. Boens 10-5-1868 (10-6-1868)
Fawbush, Allis to George Hurst 12-5-1877 (no return)
Felps, Margret S. to J. W. Phillips 1-11-1878 (no return)
Felps, Sarah to Roboert Bush 5-18-1786 (8-27-1876)
Fendry, Crotia Ann to Alfred Nicholds 2-8-1876
Ferbort?, G. W. to Robert Hargraves 7-11-1878
Fergerson, Nancy M. to Wm. P. Ales 3-26-1870 (3-27-1870)
Ferguson, Rebecca J. to Wm. H. Duncan 3-29-1876
Fetridge, Annie M. to Jesse L. Rogers 10-24-1877
Fields, Martha Jane to John Fultz 4-23-1877
Fields, Sarah to George W. Owens 8-22-1876 (8-23-1876)
Fields, Susan to Wm. Hatfields 12-10-1881 (12-11-1882?)
Finar, Sintha Ann to Joab E. Burnett 10-2-1868 (10-5-1868)
Fish, Matilda E. to James H. Hayes 10-5-1869
Fleaman, Sarah F. to John E. Galden 5-12-1876 (5-14-1876)
Fleamon, Eliza Ann to Green B. Lester 1-20-1870 (1-25-1870)
Flemon, Elizabeth to R. C. Lister 10-17-1880
Fletcher, Lucy (Mrs.) to George W. Breeding 6-17-1881
Fletcher, Mary V. to Alfred C. Prator 2-28-1883
Fletcher, Minerva to John T. Williams 8-23-1890 (8-24-1890)
Fletcher, Nancey to John Lambert 12-3-1880
Folkner, Sarah J. to Isaac Meyers 8-24-1881 (8-25-1881)
Ford, E. J. to P. L. Ford 12-6-1880 (12-9-1880)
Ford, Elizabeth Jane to Valentine Cupp 10-30-1885 (11-1-1885)
Ford, Elizabeth K. to Granville Grant 10-23-1873 (no return)
Ford, Ellen F. to Tennessee C. Cupp 4-10-1872 (4-14-1872)
Ford, Emely to George C. Lynch 2-4-1891
Ford, Emiley M. to Wm. F. Russell 5-19-1877 (5-21-1877)
Ford, L. E. to J. M. Moony 9-29-1885 (10-8-1885?)
Ford, Lucy T. to J. W. Stivers 9-16-1878
Ford, Margertee to Stephen Rice 4-22-1880 (4-23-1880)
Ford, Rhoda E. to Valentine England 9-18-1885 (9-22-1885)
Ford, Sarah A. to James O. Mink 6-27-1882 (6-29-1882)
Ford, Sibby to Wm. A. Drummons 6-5-1871
Forgason, Liza to Pearse Lee 5-27-1882 (5-28-1882)
Forkner, Ellen to Marien Hickey 5-4-1885 (5-6-1885)
Forkner, Martha M. to A. L. Russell 12-14-1880 (12-16-1880)
Fortner, Martha A. to Near R. England 11-6-1872 (11-7-1872)
Fortner, Sarah to Prince Gray 3-6-1883 (4-11-1883)
Fox, Margaret to J. E. Davis 1-8-1888? (1-10-1889)
Francisco, Malinda A. to Thomas C. Keck 3-22-1882 (3-26-1882)
Francisco, Martha to Jeff Spartis 6-21-1885
Francisco, Mary A. to James Wright 3-13-1890
Francisco, Maryan to J. L. Meyers 8-8-1879
Freeman, M. A. to D. C. Bryant 1-18-1887 (11-20-1887)
Freeman, Parrott to Danul Redman 5-1-1889
Freeman, R. C. to A. M. Pearce 1-12-1885
Freeman, S. M. to John A. Litterell 5-11-1888
Freman, Calie J. to Isaac Powell 1-5-1883 (1-7-1883)
Freman, Mary E. to George C. Singleton 4-23-1883 (4-29-1883)
Friar, Eliza E. to Joseph Roark 11-2-1868 (11-3-1868)
Friar, Jane to John Fultz 4-16-1886 (4-18-1886)
Frier, Sarah J. to G. W. Hatfield 3-?-1879 (3-13-1879)
Fugate, Animack to Thomas H. Oell? 4-1-1881
Fugate, Ellen to Charley Brogan 4-19-1890 (no return)
Fugate, Jane to J. N. Treece 6-27-1872
Fugate, Louisa to James Brogans 12-27-1889 (12-29-1889)
Fugate, Margret to Rayman Owens 8-14-1879 (8-16-1879)
Fugate, Martha J. to Thos. Riley 1-14-1874 (1-15-1874)
Fugate, Mary to James Gibson 12-12-1871 (12-14-1871)
Fugate, Milly to Reubin (Rev. Esq.) Buis 7-6-1885 (7-22-1885)
Fugate, Nancy M. to William J. Johnson 3-2-1869 (3-4-1869)
Fugate, R. E. to R. Suits 3-1-1883
Fugate, Rutha to J. Fauster Brownlow 5-28-1870 (5-29-1870)
Fugate?, E. S. to Danuel King 3-18-1881 (3-19-1881)
Fulkerson, Elizabeth to Nelson Buis 9-25-1876

Fulkerson, Ida to A. H. Fulkerson 3-8-1880
Fulkerson, Mary F. to John H. Scarborough 11-8-1876 (11-9-1876)
Fulkerson, Sally K. to R. F. Carr 3-1-1880
Fullington, Marry to Thomas Shultz 3-19-1881 (3-24-1881)
Fullington, Tishey to Charley Carpenter 4-10-1890
Fulph, R. J. to Thomas Jainaway 1-30-1879 (1-31-1879)
Fulton, Maggie D. to Richard Harrell 6-7-1879 (6-8-1879)
Fultz, B. A. to J. J. Furgerson 11-28-1879
Fultz, Elizabeth to Johna? Gilpin 5-19-1870 (5-22-1870)
Fultz, Emely to James H. Kibert 5-29-1874 (5-20?-1874)
Fultz, Emily to V. H. McNiel 1-13-1884
Fultz, Emly to Jobe Musterd 1-15-1881 (1-16-1881)
Fultz, Lucy to Hugh Stump? 5-12-1890 (5-14-1890)
Fultz, Martha to Joseph Bassell 4-1-1871
Fultz, Vina E. to James H. Conaray 6-8-1889 (6-9-1889)
Furgerson, Martha A. to Wm. H. Owens 1-2-1869 (1-3-1869)
Furgerson, Mary L. to Samuel McNeeley 3-12-1888 (3-15-1888)
Furry, Beceyann to Winton Robinson 2-19-1881 (2-10-1881)
Fuson, Tisha to Wm. Compliman 12-24-1890 (12-26-1890)
Gamble, E. C. to Nathan H. King 11-27-1874 (11-29-1874)
Gamble, Sarah to Lee Jesse 9-10-1877 (no return)
Gamrell, Elizabeth to John A. Sample 1-19-1872
Garison, Louisa to John M. Lewis 4-27-1883
Gast, S. to Isaac R. Cole 7-19-1879 (7-2?-1879)
Gaynor, Mollie to B. S. Yoakum 1-13-1886 (1-14-1886)
George, Elizabeth to Jessee Jenkins 8-23-1870 (8-25-1870)
George, Elizabeth to Thos. Robinson 7-17-1884
Gibbs, J. J. to John Clary 11-19-1885
Gibbs, Lucinda to P. L. Hunley 4-11-1883 (no return)
Gibbs, Margret to John England 12-18-1870 (12-20-1870)
Gibbs, Martha Ann to Thomas Hicks 9-28-1869 (9-30-1869)
Gibbs, Melsina to Wm. G. Lamb 10-22-1880 (10-23-1880)
Gibbs, Winie to Geo. W. Williams 2-2-1890
Gibeson, A. R. to Charles Eppes 3-26-1879 (3-27-1879)
Gibson, Annie to Barnett Campbell 2-9-1878 (no return)
Gibson, D. C. to Lewis W. Phillips 1-7-1881 (no return)
Gibson, Jennie to C. B. White 7-22-1879 (7-24-1879)
Gibson, Kittie to Thos. S. Wilson 10-13-1873
Gibson, Lawry An to E. B. Potees 6-14-1879
Gibson, Lettia to Peter H. Campbell 11-26-1869 (11-27-1869)
Gibson, Loucinda to Noble Collins 2-6-1878 (2-7-1878)
Gibson, Martha Jane to William T. Morgan 4-5-1869 (4-8-1869)
Gibson, Mary J. to George Welch 10-13-1883 (10-14-1883)
Gibson, Mary J. to William McFall 7-27-1882
Gibson, Runce? to James L. Ellis 7-23-1885
Gibson, Sarah E. to Henry J. Rine 12-1-1881 (12-2-1881)
Gibson, Sela A. to John Galden 1-19-1871
Gibson, T. M. to T. F. Large 11-2-1888 (11-4-1888)
Gilbert, Martha Ann to William F. Whiteaker 9-21-1869 (9-26-1869)
Gilbert, Syrrener J. to Samson Duncan 10-18-1874 (no return)
Gillinwaters, Mary F. to Wilburn Overton 5-18-1880 (5-19-1880)
Gillis, Anny to Thomas Carrell 2-14-1889 (2-15-1889)
Gilliwaters, Sally to W. H. Lanham 10-22-1873 (11-23-1873)
Gipson, Louisa C. to Isaac J. Hansward 7-23-1870 (7-24-1870)
Glenn, Emma V. to P. G. Fulkerson 7-14-1869
Goforth, Cornelia A. to James C. Goin 9-13-1873 (9-14-1873)
Goforth, Mary M. to Hazel Rouse 11-10-1869 (11-14-1869)
Goforth, Sarah A. to Wm. B. Russell 1-7-1871 (1-8-1871)
Goin, Amey to Moses Williams 5-1-1885 (no return)
Goin, Ann to G. B. Wilder 10-17-1879
Goin, Anna to Mantain Edwards 1-23-1875
Goin, Catharine to J. K. Pratt 11-18-1890
Goin, Charloty J. to Jefferson D. Edwards 12-9-1879
Goin, Delamey to Samuel Minton 3-4-1884 (3-6-1884)
Goin, Elizabeth to Daniel E. Miracle 2-2-1871
Goin, Elvira to Edward Goin 11-21-1868 (11-22-1868) B
Goin, Elviry to Wm. J. Wilder 11-23-1871
Goin, Frances to John R. Williams 4-4-1875
Goin, I. S. to Scott Wilder 4-26-1881 (4-16-1881)
Goin, Jane to Jeramiah Williams 5-20-1871 (5-21-1871)
Goin, Lucinda M. to Stephen G. Mainvill? 2-19-1871 (2-23-1871)
Goin, Lucy A. to Nathan Hurst 12-12-1885 (12-18-1885)
Goin, Malinda to Boston Brooks 11-21-1868 (11-22-1868) B
Goin, Manervia to B. F. Hicks 8-18-1877
Goin, Mariah E. to George W. Cupp 1-24-1871 (1-27-1871)
Goin, Martha to Vinson Williams 12-12-1881 (12-22-1881)
Goin, Martha to Wm. H. Hix 8-3-1877
Goin, Mary to C. M. Hollen 4-8-1882 (no return)
Goin, Mary to James Gray 11-2-1879
Goin, Mary to R. L. Edmondson 11-13-1889 (11-14-1889)
Goin, Mary to Samuel Hailey 11-11-1876 (11-12-1876)
Goin, Mary to Wm. Wilder 4-23-1881 (no return)
Goin, Matilda to Mathew C. Keck 9-17-1870 (9-18-1870)
Goin, P. E. to W. R. Widner 1-17-1889 (no return)
Goin, R. E. to G. L. Brogan 4-7-1881 (4-28-1881)
Goin, Rachal to Thomas J. Hickey 1-8-1881
Goin, Rachel to Frank Rosenbam 1-13-1880 (no return)

Goin, S. E. to G. F. Thomas 8-14-1885 (8-15-1885)
Goin, S. S. O. to R. T. Cline 7-10-1886 (7-24-1886)
Goin, Sarah E. to A. J. Francisco 3-2-1872 (3-5?-1872)
Goins, Catherine to W. L. Edmonson 1-1-1884
Goins, Mary to P. W. Maricle 12-27-1887
Golden, Elen to William Mason 11-?-1890 (11-3-1890)
Golden, Mary? R. to John T. Horn 4-2-1872
Golden, Sarah to John Minton 9-10-1887 (9-11-1887)
Golden, V. A. to B. F. Grantham 4-18-1872 (4-21-1872)
Golden, Va? to B. F. Grantham 4-18-1872 (no return)
Good, Frances to John W. Loskeydoo 1-5-1881 (1-6-1881)
Good, Marth to Thomas Woodson 5-22-1884
Gooden, Engline to James K. Mason 11-10-1870
Goodin, Nancy to James Lane 11-4-1873
Goodon, Susan M. to Geo. A. Gregory 7-1-1885
Goss, Martha C. to D. S. Owens 11-22-1878 (11-23-1878)
Graham, Cornelie A. to Charles W. Pickrell 12-21-1882
Graham, Matilda to H. P. Cloud 1-8-1880? (1-8-1881)
Graham, Syntha to Calvin Lee 12-23-1872 (12-26-1872)
Grason, R. A. to James Johnson 12-8-1882
Graves, Betty to Jefferson Leach 2-3-1882 (no return)
Graves, Emley M. to Dallis Fulkerson 7-27-1878
Graves, Mary A. to Henry Hunter 1-24-1887 (1-26-1887)
Gray, Frances to Jasper Jones 9-5-1877
Gray, Josephine to Henry Phillips 12-14-1876 (12-16-1876)
Gray, L. B. to J. L. Heath 2-24-1887
Gray, M. T. M. to J. W. D. Call 1-11-1889
Green, Elisabeth to W. M. Daniel 11-18-1890 (no return)
Green, Florance V. to J. T. Lynch 12-24-1890
Green, Hannah to Henry Turner 1-16-1873 (1-22-1873)
Green, Harret to James Gray 6-4-1882
Green, Louisa to John R. Hurst 12-8-1877 (no return)
Green, Martha to Mitcheal Minton 4-11-1872 (no return)
Green, Mary A. to Waymen L. Binir 9-18-1881
Green, Mina to G. C. Hill 7-10-1890
Green, R. M. to T. G. Sivills 12-26-1880
Green, Sally to John Samfor 7-4-1890 (7-5-1890)
Greenlee, Bettima to Henry Williams 10-27-1887
Greenlee, Nancy J. to David Paul 3-31-1877
Greenlee, Orlena to Wesley Browning 2-10-1880 (2-12-1880)
Greer, Arminta to Jas. M. Cunningham 7-14-1883 (no return)
Greer, Carna to V. A. Dykes 9-6-1888 (no return)
Greer, Jennie to Wm. T. McManaway 9-9-1872 (no return)
Greer, Martha to G. G. Whiteaker 1-27-1876 (no return)
Greer, Martha to G. N. Bryant 10-25-1884 (10-26-1884)
Greer, Mary A. to A. J. Sharp 3-14-1888 (3-15-1888)
Greer, Mollie to W. L. Payne 12-22-1878 (12-24-1878)
Greer, Sarah to William T. Day 12-17-1873 (12-18-1874)
Grelly, Delila to Wm. R. Hitaker 12-2-1881
Griffin, H. E. to W. E. Minton 7-9-1879
Griffiths, Sarah to Ephram Sergent 10-5-1881
Grilley, Martha to G. W. Green 12-3-1881
Grimes, Lucy to David Thomas 9-17-1871
Grimes, Mary Jane to David H. Campbell 3-26-1869 (3-29-1869)
Grubb, Allace to Arch. Wolf 10-8-1884 (10-9-1884)
Grubb, Rebeca to Wm. Barnard 10-24-1881 (10-27-1881)
Grubbs, Amanda J. to G. W. Burch 6-14-1882
Gruthan, Eliza to John Chumbly 2-12-1869 (2-14-1869)
Guarling?, Eliza to Fate Cheetham 4-14-1873 (no return)
Guinn, Eliza to Robert Fergerson 1-15-1883 (no return)
Guinn, Elizabeth to Lafayett Evans 1-6-1883 (1-7-1883)
Gulley, Lardy to Henry Shumate 2-10-1889
Gulley, Lucy J. to John W. Willis 4-8-1876 (4-9-1876)
Gulley, Sarah F. to Mathew Agee 7-15-1871 (8-9-1871)
Guy, Mary C. to Granville Hodges 12-10-1890 (12-11-1890)
Guy, Sarah to Joseph H. Edwards 2-7-1887 (2-9-1887)
Gwin, Martha Jane to John F. Bussell 9-8-1888 (9-9-1888)
Haley, Lucynda to Jeptha Edwards 1-27-1883 (1-28-1883)
Hall, Lowenda to E. T. Mason 10-25-1871 (10-26-1871)
Hall, Lucinda C. to Ewin Tillason 2-25-1871 (3-24-1871)
Hall, Margaret A. to William Painter 2-19-1869 (2-21-1869)
Hall, Margaret to James McVay 8-27-1869 (8-29-1869)
Hall, Mella to W. M. Reece 11-26-1890
Hall, Rhoda to Wm. M. Essary 1-4-1888
Hall, Salley M. to Mucillan? J. Campbell 4-5-1887
Hall, Susan to J. A. J. Hicman 11-17-1884 (11-18-1884)
Halls, Florance R. to Tillman H. Rose 5-28-1872 (5-30-1872)
Hamblin, Sarah A. to Emley Standfield 5-17-1877
Hamblin, Sofa M. to Henry Ranes 2-3-1869
Hamilton, Mary E. to John Williams 3-26-1877
Hamlet, Margarett E. to Sterling Walker 7-1-1882 (7-6-1882)
Hammock, Annah C. to Isaac Ely 11-30-1877 B?
Hammons, Mary to John Hicks 4-18-1888
Haney, Sarah E. to Wm. W. Weever 11-16-1872 (11-18-1873?)
Hansard, Cata Ellen to Joseph A. Walker 12-1-1890 (12-4-1890)
Hansard, Lucy E. to James M. Elye 1-11-1869 (1-12-1869)
Hansard, Sallie E. to James A. Walker 9-20-1882 (9-21-1882)

Hanson, Analin to James J. Peter 11-1-1879 (no return)
Harbison, Lela R. to John S. Cottrell 12-27-1884
Harbison, Madora to William Thomas 9-15-1880 (9-16-1880)
Harkraider, Orphey to John G. Whiteaker 11-9-1869 (11-14-1869)
Harman, Hesther A. to Josiah Cole 10-1-1879 (10-2-1879)
Harman, J. A. to John McCery 12-30-1878
Harman, Marry to Wm. R. Hansard 4-2-1881 (4-20-1881)
Harman, S. A. to Wm. F. Day 5-1-1885 (5-3-1885)
Harmon, M. M. to B. R. Shoemaker 8-7-1875 (8-11-1875)
Harmon, Salley C. to T. J. J. Debusk 11-2-1886 (11-7-1886)
Harmon, Sarah B. to Elbrig Skaggs 14-4-1882 (12-7-1882)
Harpe, Martha to John P. Yorke 4-?-1884 (2?-20-1884)
Harper, M. J. to H. C. Kirbey 6-9-1880
Harper, Mandy to John Miller 10-15-1873
Harper, Nancy to John Rose 11-10-1876
Harper, Rinela to Benjamine L. Moyers 2-2-1876 (2-3-1876)
Harpp, Elizabeth to Alferd Fletcher 11-16-1878
Harrell, Dicey M. to Benjamin F. Cheatham 2-8-1869 (no return)
Harrell, Elizabeth to Wesley King 11-11-1870 (11-13-1870)
Harrell, Emley E. to W. B. Hurst 9-4-1884 (9-7-1884)
Harrell, Louisa to William H. Wise 8-20-1877 (8-26-1877)
Harrell, Louiza to James B. Hurst 2-5-1869 (2-7-1869)
Harrell, M. C. to G. M. Lewis 6-13-1880 (no return)
Harrell, Mallie to Jerry R. Parker 10-20-1877 (10-21-1877)
Harrell, Mandy J. to John W. Kelley 1-25-1871 (1-26-1871)
Harrell, Mary M. to James R. Fry 3-3-1876 (3-12-1876)
Harrell, Matilda to James M. Breeding 1-27-1870
Harrell, Nancy C. to James T. Parker 5-2-1874 (5-4-1874)
Harrell, Nervesta A. to Sterling N. Davis 2-19-1876 (2-20-1876)
Harrell, Persiller to James E. Harrell 12-9-1882 (12-24-1882)
Harrell, Racheal to Daniel Noe 3-28-1871 (4-2-1871)
Harrigan, Martha J. to W. B. Hall 4-3-1871
Harris, E. C. to Wm. A. Hall 2-16-1879
Harris, Jane to C. W. Taylor 2-12-1881 (2-15-1881)
Harris, Margette to J. H. Pearce? 10-31-1878 (1-9-1879)
Harris, Martha to William Lemons 10-13-1868 (no return)
Harris, Polley A. to Eldridg Herd 3-27-1881
Hart, H. E. to D. E. Disney 9-?-1881
Hart, Rebeca C. to Elias McKey 3-7-1881
Hartgroves, Elizabeth Jane to Joseph Marion Ely 4-21-1869 (no return)
Harvein, Anna E. to William Jones 10-18-1873 (10-30-1873)
Harvey, Anjaline to Wm. H. Carpenter 4-13-1882 (7-4-1882)
Harvey, Emeline to James Johnson 1-13-1873 (1-16-1873)
Harvey, Harriett to Charley Reynolds 12-24-1889 (no return)
Harvey, Lucy J. to Geo. Carpenter 10-26-1886 (10-28-1886)
Harvey, Manervia to Clark Spence 10-27-1876
Harvey, Nancy J. to Wm. Blake 3-1-1884
Haskins, Mary to Elisha Brock 12-6-1886
Hasp, Mollie to J. H. Sowder 2-19-1884 (1?-29-1884)
Hatfield, Adaline to Benedick Yeary 11-2-1868 (11-11-1868)
Hatfield, Adaline to Marchal Marton 2-18-1881 (2-20-1881)
Hatfield, Adaline to Riley Henderson 12-17-1880 (12-19-1880)
Hatfield, C. A. to Sterling Barns 2-11-1880
Hatfield, Elizabeth to James Adams 12-17-1880 (12-19-1880)
Hatfield, Elizabeth to Thomas Elison 3-31-1881 (4-3-1881)
Hatfield, Ingbo to John Cosbey 5-31-1878
Hatfield, Mahaley to George Lambert 6-4-1879 (6-9-1879)
Hatfield, Margarett to George Nelson 7-29-1882 (7-30-1882)
Hatfield, Martha Jane to James Taylor 4-27-1876
Hatfield, Martha to John Hatfield 2-29-1884
Hatfield, Mary J. to Robert Daniel 2-26-1872
Hatfield, Mary J. to Samuel Bussell 9-25-188? (10-2-1886)
Hatfield, Mary to James L. Carmony 7-22-1870 (7-24-1870)
Hatfield, Roda to Wm. J. Fry 2-25-1878 (no return)
Hatfield, Sarah to Joseph Bussell 1-29-1876 (no return)
Havens, Mary A. to William C. Wilson 11-27-1869 (11-28-1869)
Havrin?, Anna E. to Wm. Jones 10-18-1873 (no return)
Hawl, Vicey to Henry Hill 9-6-1870
Hawley, Augusta to A. G. Cadle 12-18-1871 (12-24-1871)
Hayes, Anjaline to Tandy Chadwick 2-23-1877 (2-26-1877)
Hayes, Elizabeth to James Lambert 8-20-1874 (no return)
Hayes, Hester A. to Peter Moyers 7-4-1883 (7-13-1883)
Hayes, Maggie to W. A. King 11-9-1887 (11-10-1887)
Hayes, Mary Jane to Wm. L. Hatfield 4-15-1871 (4-16-1871)
Hayes, Nancy J. to Nelson Hurst 7-9-1879 (7-10-1879)
Hayes, Sarah to Joe Estes 1-24-1889
Haynes, Liccie to Harvey Brown 5-25-1888
Haynes, Mary Bell to R. F. England 9-7-1886 (9-9-1886)
Haynes, Sarah Jane to Isom Estridge 12-5-1868 (12-6-1868)
Hayse, Sarah to Pleasant Johnson 10-19-1888 (10-23-1888)
Hazelwood, Mariam to John McNeal 1-29-1870 (no return)
Heaath, Sarah M. to W. H. Burch 11-21-1883 (no return)
Headrick, Rutha to William Laikin 10-25-1870
Heath, Elisabeth to J. D. Parker 10-6-1888 (10-11-1888)
Heck, Mary to Hilton? Lankford 9-4-1879
Heck, P. A. to H. B. Moyers 9-27-1882 (9-28-1882)
Hellems, Martha L. to Wm. Cardwell 8-24-1871

Hembree, America E. to Andrew Mc. Hemphill 8-17-1869
Hembree, Mary J. to Daniel Johnson 8-17-1869
Henderson, Docia to Columbus Essary 12-23-1886 (12-24-1886)
Henderson, Eliza A. to Hilry B. Jayne 2-16-1878 (2-21-1878)
Henderson, L. to Pleasant Suthern 1-28-1873 (2-22-1873)
Hendricks, Maggie to Wm. T. Goin 4-7-1887 (4-8-1887)
Hendricks, Molley to Wm. Frith 3-12-1887
Hendrickson, Sarah to James Collins 7-17-1881
Henegar, Loucinda K. to Lafayett J. Burk 2-7-1885
Hennigier, Nancy J. to W. D. Richardson 4-17-1890 (4-14?-1890)
Hensley, Rainey to Isaac Oaks 6-20-1874
Herd, Sallie G. to Ambrewis? Jarvis 7-6-1882
Herel?, Margret to Lewis White 8-14-1872 (no return)
Herrell, Nancy J. to W. D. Harrell 1-6-1888
Hickel, Eliz. C. to Philip N. Moyers 3-4-1873 (4-5-1873)
Hickey, Marien to Ellen Forkner 5-4-1885 (5-6-1885)
Hickman, Nancy to Reubin Mason 2-2-1881 (2-3-1881)
Hicks, E. B. to William A. Burk 8-13-1877
Hicks, Liddy to Nathaniel Earles 9-7-1871
Hicks, Louisa to Wm. Sulfrage 9-27-1887 (9-28-1887)
Hicks, Rutha to G. W. Eggers 3-20-1890
Higgins, Ellen S. to J. C. Knontt 12-13-1871
Hill, Dora to H. M. Vanbebber 12-7-1889 (12-9-1889)
Hill, Elizabeth to William Burchett 3-20-1879
Hill, Emily to Andrew Bussell 9-2-1882 (9-3-1882)
Hill, Heti? A. to William Bently 10-12-1874
Hill, Louisa to George Noak 2-4-1876
Hill, Lucy J. to Samuel Taylor 1-23-1872 (1-24-1872)
Hill, M. E. to Wm. S. Bentley 9-11-1889
Hill, Maggie to Elwood McNealy 1-15-1891 (no return)
Hill, Margret to Rufus N. Noe 11-13-1877 (11-15-1877)
Hill, Mary A. to Wm. H. Santifer 10-18-1872 (no return)
Hill, Mary J. to H. H. Mullins 1-31-1874
Hill, Morning to J.? P. Fortune 11-14-1890 (no return)
Hill, Rachel to Hiram Cousley 8-12-1876 (8-13-1876)
Hill, Rebeck J. to Henry A. jr. Dunn 2-6-1880 (2-11-1880)
Hill, Susan A. to John S. Sneed 12-26-1868 (12-27-1868)
Hipsher, Angeline to Obediah Collins 2-29-1884 (3-1-1884)
Hipsher, Elizabeth M. to William H. Orsick 5-4-1877
Hipsher, Nancy M. to James H. Collins 10-13-1888 (10-14-1888)
Hithhorne, Jane (Miss) to Jasper Parkey 7-14-1890 (7-16-1890) B
Hix, Mary to Perry Earle 5-5-1875
Hobbs, Mary C. to Jerry P. Wurman 3-21-1888 (3-22-1888)
Hodges, E. to W. C. Keck 9-?-1886 (9-30-1886)
Hodges, Jane to Wm. Pratt 6-21-1890 (6-22-1890)
Hodges, Lucinda to John Orath 4-23-1890
Hodges, Martha J. to Willis H. Stone 10-26-1871
Hodges, Mary C. to N. J. Harrell 8-12-1890 (8-23-1890)
Hodges, Mary E. to Henry D. Baylor 9-29-1874
Hodges, Mary to James R. Yoakum 2-9-1869 (2-11-1869)
Hodges, Mary to John H. Carpenter 8-6-1877 (no return)
Hodges, May to F. E. Demarcus 9-2-1886 (9-4-1886)
Hodges, Millie to Heny Batey 1-31-1882
Hodges, Nettie to Joseph Willmouth 6-24-1880 (no return)
Hodges, Ollie to J. H. Carpenter 1-10-1888
Hodges, S. A. to A. S. Atkins 1-29-1879 (1-30-1879)
Hodges, Sallie D. to J. S. Harrell 8-26-1886 (8-27-1886)
Hodges, Sarah to Jesse Hurst 10-19-1868
Hodges, Sudie to Wm. Seal 12-12-1882 (12-17-1882)
Holladay, Martha to Jacob Snavely 12-12-1878
Hollingsworth, Martha to Leroy Maples 8-2-1888 (8-10-1888)
Holliway, Margaret to Eliakum Leach 2-28-1870
Honeycut, Millie to James Paul 2-26-1886 (2-28-1886)
Honeycutt, Anne M. to John W. Smith 2-13-1872 (2-15-1872)
Honeycutt, M. J. to William N. Mor 11-20-1880
Honley, Phieby to Lilbern Wilcox 3-20-1881 (4-3-1881)
Hooks, America to J. Demarcus 1-22-1887 (1-23-1887)
Hooper, M. E. to James T. Burk 10-16-1879
Hopkins, Alice to John W. Flaman 8-28-1881
Hopkins, Dora to J. L. Good 10-22-1882
Hopkins, Elizabeth to Walter Sumpter 7-23-1878 (no return)
Hopkins, Elizabeth to William Young 7-23-1878
Hopkins, Martha to Alexander Clouse 1-21-1883 (2-4-1883)
Hopkins, Sarah J. to M. M. Newly 5-24-1873 (5-28-1873)
Hopper, C. J. to T. C. Keck 6-16-1888 (6-17-1888)
Hopper, C. to John F. Rogers 1-19-1881 (1-20-1881)
Hopper, Louiza J. to Lilburn Johnson 12-18-1868 (12-20-1868)
Hopper, Luvenda to Wm. M. Mayers 1-27-1871 (1-28-1871)
Hopper, Mary J. to Henly Williams 11-5-1885
Hopper, Mary Jane to William H. Marsee 11-7-1874 (no return)
Hopper, Matilda to William C. Williams 5-12-1878
Hopper, O. to Rufus Venable 2-8-1880
Hopper, Perlina to James B. Gibbs 10-3-1882
Hopper, Rinda to Jefferson Hunter 9-17-1890 (10-7-1890)
Hopper, Sarah A. to James Sharp 12-23-1882 (12-24-1882)
Hopper, Sarah A. to Joseph Dunn 2-7-1878
Hopper, Sarah J. to Moses Venerable 11-29-1877

Hopson, Ann to James Brooks 12-15-1875 (12-16-1875)
Hopson, Jane to J. K. Cheek 10-8-1883
Hopson, Lourinda J. to Wm. Wolfenberger 11-15-1889 (11-17-1889)
Hopson, M. E. to James T. Burk 10-16-1879 (no return)
Hopson, Martha to Gorg Nance 3-22-1879 (no return)
Hopson, Marthey to George Vance 3-22-1879
Hopson, Mary E. to James Lawson 1-14-1880 (1-15-1880)
Hopson, Mary J. to Walter Wells 10-8-1889 (10-10-1889)
Hopson, Mary M. to Russell Hopson 9-2-1872
Hopson, Mary to William Lively 1-26-1875 (2-7-1875)
Hopson, Mint to Abe Bales 3-8-1886
Hopson, Nancy to Wm. Greer 8-19-1875 (8-18?-1875)
Hopson, Sarah A. to W. A. Hurst 10-3-1877 (10-4-1877)
Horman, Amanda to A. Loop 5-30-1874 (5-31-1874)
Hoskin, Mary to Lee Gibson 4-10-1875 (no return)
Hoskins, Louisia to John C. Vanay 10-15-1874 (10-19-1874)
Hoskins, Lucinda to Neel Jennings 7-6-1874 (5?-9-1874)
Hoskins, Martha D. to Nelson Colson 1-28-1873 (no return)
Houghes, America to Edward P. Shepley 4-8-1878 (4-3?-1878)
Houstin, Rachel to Thomas Lundy 7-25-1890 (8-10-1890)
Houston, Amanda to Barnett George 3-9-1869 (3-12-1869) B
Houston, Louisa to Wesley Hurst 10-9-1871 (10-10-1871)
Houston, Margaret A. to John Walker 10-6-1873 (10-16-1873)
Houston, Martha to Taylor Brooks 3-24-1883
Houston, Mary to John Lundy 9-4-1883 (9-6-1883)
Houston, Orlenia to Franklin Rice 8-6-1869 B
Houston, Sarah to Lee Hurst 3-24-1877 (no return)
Houston, Sterling to F. H. England 9-25-1880 (8?-25-1880)
Howard, Caroline M. to G. M. Guthery 2-23-1891 (2-24-1891)
Howard, Ellin J. to Caliway Shofner 6-11-1882
Howard, Louisa to James Hensley 5-10-1890 (5-11-1890)
Howard, Marry to Charles Callaway 8-10-1881
Howard, Marry to Jack (Jacob?) Samio 1-31-1881
Howard, Sallie to T. B. Baldwin 2-14-1881 (2-17-1881)
Howerton, Catherine to STerling Barnard 12-12-1876 (12-21-1876)
Howerton, Phebe to Wm. N. Cunningham 7-29-1874 (7-30-1874)
Howsley, Wady Elizabeth to Lewis Minton 10-2-1877 (No return)
Huckes?, Mary to Thomas J. Barett 3-17-1879
Hudleston, Tulisha B. to Thomas Ollis 3-20-1883
Huff, Jennie to Augustas Shade 3-21-1883 (3-22-1883)
Huff, Matilda to Haris Malone 2-22-1882 (2-24-1882)
Huffaker, Clarra A. to R. M. Edward 2-18-1879 (no return)
Huffeld, Matilda to Lewis Brooks 8-16-1890 (no return)
Hughes, America to E. P. Shipley 2-6-1885
Hughes, E. P. to S. F. Hughes 5-10-1886
Hughes, Mary to Wesley Hurst 10-4-1887 (10-6-1887)
Hughes, Orleana to J. R. Senseney 12-5-1887
Hughes, Susan to Geo. Coleman 12-5-1887
Hughes, Susey to Geo. Coleman 12-5-1887
Hunt, Canda to Robert O. Marcum 10-14-1880
Hunter, Cinda to Jacob M. Marsee 10-11-1881 (no return)
Hunter, Ester to Nathaniel Smith 2-23-1877 (2-24-1877)
Hunter, Racheal to Jasper Goin 11-16-1872 (11-17-1872)
Hunter, Rachel to S. B. Hopper 2-26-1883 (3-1-1883)
Hunter, Sinda to Jacob Marsee 10-11-1881 (10-13-1881)
Hurgton?, Sarah to George W. Essary 2-19-1873 (2-20-1873)
Hurst, A. L. to D. A. Bullin 12-20-1883
Hurst, Allace to Luk Jackson 2-13-1882 (no return)
Hurst, C. to William Wilmont 7-23-1879 (7-24-1879)
Hurst, Cordelia to John W. Satterfield 5-2-1877 (5-3-1877)
Hurst, Cornelia to George Epperson 3-24-1884
Hurst, Dora P. to Jasper T. Will 10-3-1887 (10-5-1887)
Hurst, Eliza to James B. Robins 8-19-1874
Hurst, Eliza to Jesse Evans 11-30-1870
Hurst, Elizabeth M. to William C. Carpenter 5-3-1878 (no return)
Hurst, Elizabeth to Andrew C. Hughs 8-13-1873
Hurst, Elizabeth to Jackson Fultz 9-1-1884 (9-4-1884)
Hurst, Faney to Nelson Hurst 9-25-1880 (9-26-1880)
Hurst, Fannie to Ruben Epperson 1-1-1883 (1-7-1883)
Hurst, Frances R. to James Jennings 4-8-1878
Hurst, Harriet to Thomas W. Stone 8-4-1877
Hurst, Jane to Fredrick Cloud 2-6-1869 (2-10-1869) B
Hurst, Lindey to James Campbell 11-28-1880
Hurst, Louisa to David Rosenbalm 10-31-1874 (11-1-1874)
Hurst, Louisa to Wm. Hopson 12-29-1872
Hurst, Louiza E. to Alvis C. Hurst 5-4-1887 (5-5-1887)
Hurst, Lucy A. to L. C. Overholser 2-14-1879 (2-16-1879)
Hurst, M. J. to A. J. Hopson 10-29-1879 (no return)
Hurst, Maggie to Dock Henderson 12-27-1886
Hurst, Manda to James R. Standerfer 9-11-1874
Hurst, Marisa A. to James T. Hurst 4-15-1878 (4-18-1878)
Hurst, Martha C. to Richard E. Bunch 9-28-1881 (9-29-1881)
Hurst, Martha J. to Elbert B. Esessary 10-7-1869
Hurst, Martha to Alexander Hurst 10-19-1870 (10-20-1870)
Hurst, Martha to Thomas Harrell 7-?-1883? (7-26-1883)
Hurst, Mary A. to G. W. Boltrip 6-27-1888 (7-1-1888)
Hurst, Mary A. to George R. Hodges 11-30-1868 (12-3-1868)

Hurst, Mary J. to Samuel F. Hurst 10-22-1881
Hurst, Mary M. to D. H. Harrell 2-22-1890
Hurst, Mary to J. R. Retter 10-29-1878 (10-31-1878)
Hurst, Mary to J. Robin 7-10-1880
Hurst, Ollie to William Christian 9-16-1886 (no return)
Hurst, Ophal to J. H. Rutherford 3-19-1878
Hurst, Orpha to M. J. Pursifal 3-13-1878 (3-14-1878)
Hurst, Rebeca to David N. West 5-4-1877 (5-6-1877)
Hurst, Sarah E. to James E. Reynolds 2-5-1887 (2-6-1887)
Hurst, Sarah Jane to Wm. Epperson 12-13-1888 (12-18-1888)
Hurst, Sarah to Isaac C. Hurst 8-21-1873
Hurst, Sarah to John Jones 7-3-1889 (7-4-1889)
Hurst, Sarah to John W. Bunch 4-12-1888
Hurst, Sarah to Obediah Cardwell 11-3-1890
Hurst, Susan A. to Perry C. Breeding 8-3-1876 (8-6-1876)
Hurst, Virginia to James Shell 2-9-1888
Hurt, Frances to J. J. Upton 8-23-1882 (9-1-1882)
Hurt, Mariah to B. F. Newby 3-30-1872 (no return)
Huse, Dianer to Paul Kincaid 9-18-1870 (9-19-1870)
Huster, Mary E. A. to John C. Davis 6-10-1889 (6-11-1889)
Indman, Mary C. to Peter McCrary 6-14-1879
Ingle, Malinday to Morgan Sexton 7-28-1872 (no return)
Ingleton, Louisa J. to Amos Crutchfield 2-24-1872 (2-25-1872)
Ingrum, Mary Jane to William Parton 5-7-1870 (6-7-1870)
Inkelbarger, M. A. to Vincent Whitson 12-26-1878
Irvin, John B. to M. L. McClure 9-26-1884 (9-28-1884)
Irvin, Leeby? to James Lambert 1-27-1889
Jackson, A. E. to Galvin Chadwell 12-15-1878
Jackson, Eliza to David More 3-13-1879
Jackson, Elizabeth to C. W. Bowman 11-13-1884 (11-21-1884)
Jackson, Elizabeth to James M. Gibbs 5-5-1869 (no return)
Jackson, Elizabeth to Joseph M. Gibbs 5-24-1869
Jackson, Elizabeth to Josiah Presley 6-10-1884 (no return)
Jackson, Ellen to James L. Buckanan no dates
Jackson, Harriet to Lewis Graham 8-13-1874
Jackson, M. to Levi Redmond 12-23-1872 (12-25-1872)
Janeway, Lucey J. to Thos. Wells 12-28-1872 (1-1-1873)
Janeway, Manerva E. to J. F. West 8-10-1874 (8-12-1874)
Janeway, Nancy J. to Samuel K. Mountain 10-18-1872 (10-20-1872)
Janeway, Thursa A. to D. H. Harrell 11-4-1871 (11-5-1871)
Jannings, Cordelia J. to James T. Strump 12-23-1886 (12-27-1886)
Jenings, Jennie E. to John E. Trent 8-27-1888 (9-12-1888)
Jennings, Anne to Andrew Jackson 6-16-1884
Jennings, Carnie to Francis J. McCoy 2-23-1891
Jennings, Eliza to Wm. J. Earls 4-8-1889
Jennings, Harriet to Wm. Bundren 4-21-1877 (4-22-1877)
Jennings, Louease to William Houston 3-16-1882 (3-22-1882)
Jennings, Magnoley to D. C. Minton 4-20-1889 (4-21-1889)
Jennings, Marry (Mrs.) to Joseph C. Lanham 6-21-1881 (6-23-1881?)
Jennings, Mary to Isaac Soard 7-24-1877 (no return)
Jennings, Mary to Nicos? Kincaid 3-13-1873 (3-14-1873)
Jennings, Mary to William Wells 6-6-1869
Jennings, Mollie to D. L. Evans 1-1-1879
Jennings, Nancy to Isom Croxdale 12-24-1872 (12-25-1872)
Jennings, Sarah Elizabeth to Garrett Collins 10-?-1872 (no return)
Jennings, Susan to Hiram Turner 4-11-1871 (4-8?-1871)
Jennings, Zelpha to R. H. Hodges 7-9-1892 (no return)
Jerdan, Martha to Solaman Smith 10-7-1879 (10-24-1879)
Jesse, Susan to John Carter 4-17-1880
Jessee, Marry E. to D. M. Skaggs 5-21-1881 (5-28-1881)
Jessee, Susan to Lewis Minton 1-31-1877 (no return)
Johns, Mary to E. C. Busick 12-20-1878 (no return)
Johnson, Almeda to Daniel Carell 9-23-1890
Johnson, Artiemis to Thomas Lafayette Stansbery 4-24-1873 (3-19-73)[sic]
Johnson, Caroline to John Beson 3-12-1883 (3-14-1883)
Johnson, Caroline to Richard Fultz 6-1-1888 (no return)
Johnson, Catherine to Joseph Simmons 10-25-1879 (no return)
Johnson, Eliza J. to B. F. Shultz 4-30-1872
Johnson, Elizabeth to Chad Pridmore 3-4-1871 (3-5-1871)
Johnson, Elizabeth to Jesse Hopson 4-21-1875 (4-25-1875)
Johnson, Ettie to Levi Brooks 11-5-1888 (11-11-1888)
Johnson, Letitia to I. A. Irvin 8-23-1881 (8-25-1881)
Johnson, Louisa to Hark Williams 1-21-1886 (1-26-1886)
Johnson, M. L. to J. B. Pearson 7-24-1879 (10-19-1879)
Johnson, Margaret to Samuel H. England 8-27-1873 (8-28-1873)
Johnson, Margret to Jas. Hall 11-15-1873
Johnson, Margret to Thos. A. Riddle 12-25-1884 (12-27-1884)
Johnson, Mary A. to A. M. Cloud 6-3-1875
Johnson, Mary Jane to Jeramiah Provene 11-30-1874 (12-17-1874)
Johnson, Mary Jane to John Cawood 7-22-1870 (7-24-1870)
Johnson, Mary to Solomon Northern 10-1-1868 (no return)
Johnson, Mary to William Johnson 11-29-1875
Johnson, S. L. to John J. Davis 2-16-1884 (2-18-1884)
Johnson, S. T. to J. M. Rouse 8-2-1889
Johnson, Sallie E. to G. B. Carr 2-25-1890 (2-26-1890)
Johnson, Sarah J. to Thos. G. Greer 3-9-1874 (no return)
Johnsonton, Allas to James P. Farmer 8-24-1878 (8-25-1878)

Johnston, Louisey to J. L. Morison 7-?-1879 (7-7-1879)
Johnston, M. E. to M. G. Walker 12-28-1881 (12-29-1881)
Jones, A. T. to J. J. Campell 2-24-1881
Jones, Allace to Joel Furgerson 11-26-1883 (11-28-1883)
Jones, Amanda to Nelson P. Lanham 3-16-1869 (3-18-1869)
Jones, C. to Lewis H. Steward 1-21-1880
Jones, Carna to Neil Hurst 5-5-1890 (5-11-1890)
Jones, Catherine to R. G. Massey 7-27-1877
Jones, Eliza to Anderson Davidson 8-29-1879
Jones, Elizabeth to Georg Vanbeben 2-26-1881
Jones, Elizabeth to James E. Upton 10-22-1881 (no return)
Jones, Elizabeth to John Baker 9-16?-1882 (no return)
Jones, Emily J. to N. A. Brogan 10-7-1873 (10-9-1873)
Jones, Emily to R. F. Horrace? 7-21-1886
Jones, Frances O. to William H. Ketron 10-5-1868 (10-6-1868)
Jones, Gemima to William Mosley 6-4-1877
Jones, Jane to James Estep 8-16-1884 (8-31-1884)
Jones, Jane to William R. Hill 1-6-1877
Jones, Joaner M. C. to John Fosneeker 1-21-1876
Jones, Lucy Jane to Floyd Sandifer 3-26-1877 (3-29-1877)
Jones, Maggie to Wm. Oxford 12-3-1887? (12-4-1887)
Jones, Margarett to Wm. H. Cole 3-5-1883 (no return)
Jones, Marry to Alfred Ewing 10-10-1880 (10-14-1880)
Jones, Martha (Miss) to Robt. Plank 6-14-1885
Jones, Martha E. to Robt. Plank 6-11-1885 (no return)
Jones, Mary A. to William M. Vanbebber 2-18-1871 (2-22-1871)
Jones, Mary E. to James L. Cunningham 2-28-1870 (3-3-1870)
Jones, Mary J. to G. A. Brooks 3-10-1883? (no return)
Jones, Mary to Burgan Carrel 6-29-1879
Jones, Matilda to Jefferson Willson 8-23-1879 (8-24-1879)
Jones, Ollie J. to F. M. Powell 4-1-1876 (4-4-1876)
Jones, P. C. N. to John F. Brogan 10-9-1876 (10-12-1876)
Jones, Phebe to George W. Rolling 4-18-1869
Jones, Rebeca to Dock Bery 8-1-1878
Jones, Rhoda to William D. Loftice 9-12-1878
Jones, Sally to James Barnet 7-4-1887 (7-10-1887)
Jones, Sarah A. to Wm. Wood 10-15-1885
Jones, Sibire E. to Hampton Rosier 12-23-1871 (12-24-1871)
Jones, Zilvena to Daniel M. Bolton 8-1-1870 (8-7-1870)
Justice, Mary to John C. Gibson 12-25-1889 (no return)
Keck, Anna to Wm. H. Houston 4-22-1871 (sol., no date)
Keck, Caty J. to T. G. Cox 1-8-1888
Keck, Caty to John Keck 9-23-1889 (9-27-1889)
Keck, Elizabeth A. to Elijah Johnson 1-15-1871 (1-24-1871)
Keck, Elizabeth to Johnathan Odell 10-14-1877 (10-20-1877)
Keck, J. L. to John Paul 11-5-1879 (no return)
Keck, Margret to Thos. N. Cheatham 12-18-1883 (no return)
Keck, Matilda to G. F. Ford 3-26-1881 (3-31-1881)
Keck, Nancy A. to Houston J. Edwards 6-4-1889 (6-8-1889)
Keck, Pheebee E. to J. I. Francisco 9-23-1871 (sol.)
Keck, Rachel C. to William H. Collins 2-28-1887 (3-3-1887)
Keck, Rebeck to N. T. Mayes 10-27-1889
Keck, S. E. (Miss) to G. W. Heath 2-27-1890 (3-2-1890)
Keck, Sally N. to James Bull 11-14-1878
Keck, Sara to W. S. Houston 2-26-1879
Keck, Tennessee to James Snider 10-9-1884
Keehan?, N. A. to J. N. Meeley 9-10-1878 (9-12-1878)
Keel, Ellen to Wm. Stewart 11-21-1875
Kelleron, Sarah J. to James Owens 3-17-1883 (3-22-1883)
Kelley, Tissue to James Houston 7-12-1888
Kelly, Mary to John Solliver 3-29-1884 (3-30-1884)
Kesterson, Jane to Burchett W. Burnett 10-4-1868 (10-5-1868)
Kesterson, Martha J. to John K. L. Smith 1-21-1871 (1-26-1871)
Kesterson, Ritta to Timothy Williams 10-24-1890 (10-26-1890)
Key, Lidey to John Edwards 12-17-1878
Kibert, Barthina to B. F. Gulley 12-23-1873 (12-24-1873)
Kibert, Malinda C. to John C. Wiley 9-16-1877
Kibert, Mary Elizabeth to Thomas Ellison 7-8-1869 (7-15-1869)
Kile, Catherine to Jamie Graham 1-31-1878 (no return)
Killian, Eliza to Jacob Meyers 10-20-1870
Killian, Sarah C. to John M. McBee? 10-9-1874 (no return)
Killion, Amanda to Taylor Minton 3-22-1887
Killion, M. V. to J. R. Lynch 2-6-1891 (2-8-1891)
Killion, Narcis to A. B. Goin 6-28-1880 (6-27?-1880)
Kiltz, Aggie to Hugh Hill 11-20-1872 (11-21-1872)
Kincaid, Amanda to James Russell 1-14-1881? (1-30-1881)
Kincaid, Florance A. to James Hughes 8-10-1885 (8-13-1885)
Kincaid, Lou A. to H. G. Parkey 1-5-1885
Kincaid, Martha to C. B. Cottrell 9-1-1874 (9-3-1874)
Kincaid, Mary to G. N. Collett 7-26-1887 (8-14-1887)
Kincaid, Sarah J. to J. L. Vanbebber 1-3-1873
Kincaid, Susan to John Malone 4-10-1882 (4-14-1882) B
Kincaid, Tennessee to John Kincaid 12-22-1884 (12-25-1884)
Kindrick, Manervia M. to John A. Monk 10-20-1875 (no return)
King, Allice to A. C. Carr 7-13-1887 (7-14-1887)
King, Calas R. to James A. Kibert 1-5-1872 (1-11-1872)
King, Corline to John M. Hembree 10-14-1883

King, Elizabeth to Georg Prater? 9-6-1878 (9-7-1878)
King, Jinsey Nervesta to William Johnson 2-10-1869 (no return)
King, Loucind to James Raines 8-30-1883
King, Maggie R. to J. W. King 9-19-1888 (9-20-1888)
King, Margret to Charles W. Scott 3-22-1879
King, Martha O. to W. F. Cadle 11-30-1883 (no return)
King, Mary to W. C. Leach 12-25-1881
King, Nancy J. to Wm. Pennington 5-20-1883
King, Polly E. to W. H. Raines 5-28-1882
King, Rhoda J. to Franklin Hollingsworth 8-9-1875 (8-12-1875)
King, Sarah E. to W. F. King 11-2-1889 (11-3-1889)
King, Sarah R. to George Gose 8-2-1875
King, Susanah to Lewis Seabolt 5-26-1869 (5-27-1869)
Kinningham, Sharlet to Lewis Fawhugh 4-8-1871 (4-25-1871)
Knight, Fanny to Henry Jackson 11-21-1889
Knoblin, E. T. to Newton E. Kesterson 10-20-1882 (10-22-1882)
Knuthank?, Jennie to J. H. Berry 11-15-1884
Kock, Mary J. to Sidney B. Briant 12-21-1890 (no return)
Kock, S. E. to Sherman Willson 2-5-1890
Kyle, Martha to Floid Riley 11-24-1883 (no return)
Lainies, Martha E. to Wm. P. King 9-15-1887 (9-16-1887)
Lake, Juda to Murphrea H. Riddle 8-24-1875
Lakins, Minervia to J. W. Smith 3-11-1876 (3-12-1876)
Lamber, Martha to John F. Lambert 1-10-1880 (2-11-1880)
Lambert, Allice to J. W. Whitelock 1-21-1891
Lambert, Benena V. to Samuel Kesterson 1-25-1873 (1-26-1873)
Lambert, Catherine to Robert Patterson 9-13-1876 (9-21-1876)
Lambert, Eliza to Samuel Crawford 3-6-1876
Lambert, Elizabeth to James Sutton 12-18-1885 (12-20-1885?)
Lambert, Elizabeth to Joseph Ellison 2-6-1880 (2-7-1880)
Lambert, Elizabeth to Pleasant Eastridge 3-23-1872 (3-24-1872)
Lambert, L. C. to M. G. Langham 12-11-1886 (12-12-1886)
Lambert, Letty to John T. Vance 1-6-1873 (1-7-1873)
Lambert, Lucy J. to W. .T. Friar 7-28-1877 (7-29-1877)
Lambert, Lucy to Hiram Hill 5-31-1888 (6-2-1888)
Lambert, Luesa to G. W. Daniel 6-22-1888 (6-24-1888)
Lambert, M. F. to James Richardson 8-13-1878
Lambert, Margaret to Garrett Southern no dates (mid-1885?)
Lambert, Margaret to Garrett? Southers 6-10-1885 (6-11-1885)
Lambert, Marth to Robert Estridge 9-19-1878
Lambert, Martha Ann to Rolley Dingus 4-23-1882 (no return)
Lambert, Martha to W. S. Messer 2-4-1888 (no return)
Lambert, Mary Bell to F. M. Edington 10-27-1887 (no return)
Lambert, Mary F. to James Ritchardson 8-13-1878 (no return)
Lambert, Mary J. to B. F. Roark 11-23-1877 (no return)
Lambert, Mattie to Robt. Lingar 1-14-1888 (1-15-1888)
Lambert, Rebecca to James Owen 1-4-1887 (1-9-1887)
Lambert, Sarah E. to Solimon Ellis 11-29-1877 (no return)
Lambert, Sarah S. to Benj. F. Canell 2-18-1874 (2-22-1874)
Landmo?, M. E. to C. G. Tague 2-15-1880
Lane, C. S. to Lemuel Robertson 5-31-1887
Lane, Catherine to Thomas Parker 10-23-1879
Lane, M. E. to B. F. Bare 4-19-1887
Lane, Maggie to F. Maupin 11-26-1881 (11-27-1881)
Lane, Maggie to Silas W. Evans 7-30-1875 (no return)
Lane, Mary to Bellenvin Reed 8-18-173 (8-21-1873)
Lane, Nancy to Javun? Collins 4-4-1887
Lane, Sarah to William N. Harper 6-20-1876 (6-21-1876)
Langham, Elizabeth to Alexander Jennings 5-9-1878 (no return)
Lanham, Cornelia J. to Alexander Jennings 2-17-1869 (2-18-1869)
Lanham, Elizabeth to John T. Owens 12-19-1870 (12-25-1870)
Lanham, Margret to James Patterson 6-14-1884 (6-15-1884)
Lanham, Rhoda to James Overton 12-23-1885 (12-24-1885)
Lanham, Sarah to Elbert Patterson 12-4-1883 (no return)
Lanksford, Martha J. to James Rose 4-4-1890 (7-28-1890)
Large, Nancy J. to Elisha Friar 8-1-1878 (no return)
Large, Nancy J. to Elisha Tiner 8-1-1878? (8-4-1878)
Larmer, E. P. to G. R. Thacker 7-29-1876 (7-30-1876)
Larmer, Virginia C. to J. L. McBee 2-13-1883 (no return)
Lasley, Elizabeth to Thomas Riley 4-5-1869 (4-8-1869)
Lasley, Emma to A. R. Tolaver 3-1-1888 (3-4-1888)
Lauson, Malisey a. to Henly R. Deen 9-25-1878 (no return)
Laws, Martha J. to George Creger 12-23-1868 (1-14-1869)
Lawse, Susan to Stephen Gose 4-2-1888 (4-17-1888)
Lawsen, Mimey to Riley Hatfied? 10-3-1870 (10-9-1870)
Lawson, Hariett C. to James Reed 4-2-1879 (4-22-1879)
Lawson, Loucinda to J. W. Carr 5-25-1884
Lawson, Margart to Wm. Willis 9-25-1879 (9-27-1879)
Lawson, Martha J. to Wm. E. C. Davis 10-13-1877 (no return)
Lawson, Mary C. to Robert R. Russ? 3-4-1869
Lawson, Mary J. to John Jones 12-30-1872
Lawson, Matilda to W. M. Hurst 7-20-1887 (no return)
Lawson, Pheby to Thomas Jones 11-8-1881 (3-5-1882)
Lawson, Pollie to Nelson Northen 12-6-1882 (no return)
Lawson?, Savana to W. P. C. Seal 1-6-1890 (no return)
Laycock, Mary Louiza to William Smith 12-29-1868
Leabow, M. E. to E. L. Roop 8-30-1884 (9-4-1884)

Leabow, Malisa A. to Wm. B. Hodges 7-13-1878 (7-14-1878)
Leabow?, Jance? to Mart Davis 7-13-1888 (7-14-1888)
Leach, Martha to James A. Bowman 2-18-1869 (2-19-1869)
Leach, Mary to James F. King 10-4-1880 (no return)
Leach, Sarah J. to Samuel Leusher? 12-?-1879 (12-15-1879)
Lease?, Ollie to Ed. Poor 10-5-1885?
Leasley, Salyann to Leonadus Edwards 8-26-1878 (9-19-1878)
Ledington, Catharine to Andrew Duff 5-5-1888
Ledwod?, Elizabeth to Benjerman Lambert 1-1-1879 (1-2-1879)
Lee, Catherine to Pleasant Young 1-27-1872 (1-28-1872)
Lee, Eliza Waagonar Fanny to John Epperson 3-3-1880 (3-7-1880)
Lee, Margret to William F. Younge 4-24-1878
Lee, Mary A. to Jubilee Posoey 5-13-1871 (5-14-1871)
Lee, Mary to Jackson Russell 8-10-1889 (8-11-1889)
Lenar, Ama to Tobi Cheatham 3-28-1885 (no return)
Lenard, July to Giles Whiteaker 4-17-1890 (4-21-1890)
Lenard, Mary P. to Andrew Surber 8-7-1883 (no return)
Lenard, Mary to John Stanifer 12-23-1870 (12-25-1870)
Lesley, Mandy to Jourdon P. Welch 5-22-1872
Lester, Matilda F. to Thomas J. Essary 12-20-1882 (12-21-1882)
Lester, Nancy to Peter Hansord 10-8-1873
Lewis, Catharine to Thos. J. Owens 2-24-1890 (2-25-1890)
Lewis, Dualla to T. G. Lewis 6-27-1879
Lewis, M. C. to J. A. Hodges 9-8-1883 (9-13-1883)
Lewis, Martha A. to James H. Vanoy 4-18-1888 (4-19-1888)
Lewis, Martha J. to Nelson Campbell 3-15-1883
Lewis, N. L. E. to B. McPhetridg 8-24-1886 (8-26-1886)
Lewis, S. E. to J. F. McVay 1-5-1881 (1-6-1881)
Lewis, Sarah J. to Henry Long 2-7-1870 (3-7-1870)
Lewis, Sarah M. to C. P. L. Dyre 11-11-1887 (11-20-1887)
Lewis, Tiliva? to Wm. Sivils 2-5-1891 (no return)
Lewis?, Miry to Wm. Miller 10-31-1872 (11-2-1872)
Liford, Margret J. to George W. Baker 10-26-1877 (no return)
Liford, Margret to Andrew Wolf no date (before 1879?)
Liford, Mary J. to Wm. Walker 3-16-1871 (3-18-1871)
Liford, Mary to Isaac Littrell 8-18-1882 (8-20-1882)
Liler, Sarah E. to William Bush 10-4-1879 (10-5-1879)
Linch, L. L. to J. K. Mink 10-26-1886 (10-28-1886)
Linch, Marry L. to Wm. Wallace 10-10-1881 (10-13-1881)
Lingar, Jane to John Hunley 1-30-1870
Lingar, Molly to Joseph Thomas 12-21-1888 (12-23-1888)
Lingar, Phily E. to James H. Thomas 3-10-1877 (3-11-1877)
Lingar, Tiara? E. to Irre? S. Ellison 6-23-1888 (no return)
Linnals, Margrett A. to Williams Ridings 5-28-1881 (5-29-1881)
Lions, Lucy to Robert Gordon 8-15-1879 (8-17-1879)
Lions, Malinda to Andrew Evans 12-?-1879 (12-23-1879)
Lisk, L. E. to F. O. Hanlin 12-23-1880 (12-26-1880)
Litterell, Alis V. to John M. Crockett 9-3-1877
Litterell, Mary E. to Thomas Marcum 9-8-1877 (9-9-1877)
Littrell, Eliza A. to George B. Burchett 4-6-1869 (4-8-1869)
Littrell, Eliza to Isaac H. Dalton 10-25-1881 (10-30-1881)
Littrell, Martha to F. M. Williams 5-22-1880 (5-23-1880)
Littrell, Mary A. to Larkin L. Burchett 1-5-1869 (1-7-1869)
Littrell, P. A. to W. M. Williams 10-10-1879 (no return)
Liveley, Nancy to Banil R. Idle 12-20-1875
Loaness, Annie to James C. Simmons 10-26-1887
Lock, Margaret to Joseph Blaylock 9-14-1868 (9-16-1868)
Logans, Maggie B. to James M. Cadle 2-19-1890 (2-20-1890)
Longar, Prancis to Henry Darit? 3-23-1878
Longmiers, Salle E. to Joseph C. Little 1-24-1883 (1-25-1883)
Longmire, Mary E. to James M. Webb 11-15-1873 (11-19?-1873)
Longmoyers, M. to George Campbell 12-5-1877 (no return)
Longworth, Eliza to Robert Owens 9-15-1882 (9-24-1882)
Longworth, Elizabeth to John Wires 11-15-1882 (11-16-1882)
Longworth, Jane to Wm. P. Hatfield 8-11-1870 (8-13-1870)
Longworth, Julia to John Clarxtin 5-29-1882 (6-4-1882)
Longworth, M. J. to William Margraves 8-22-1884 (8-23-1884)
Longworth, Matilda to J. C. Brooks 1-14-1880 (1-15-1880)
Longworth, Nancy to John Minton 2-15-1872
Longworth, Sarah F. to William A. Dooley 2-27-1869 (3-4-1869)
Lookeydos, Martha to Thos. Gilbert 5-31-1881 (6-4-1881)
Loop, Angeline to Isaac Blevens 12-31-1877 (no return)
Loop, John to Manda Campbell 8-21-1889 (8-22-1889)
Loop, Liddy A. to Campbell Cole 1-18-1873 (1-23-1873)
Loop, Sarah Elizabeth Ann to Sterling L. Leabow 4-10-1869 (4-11-1869)
Loope, M. J. to Wm. M. Cole 6-19-1873
Loosen?, Pulina? to John Cole 1-19-1878
Loser, Mary to Joseph G. Taylor 4-30-1881 (5-1-1881)
Love, Mary E. to W. S. Carr 5-19-1879
Lovel, Elizabeth to M. Owens 3-3-1879 (3-5-1879)
Lovelace, Mahulda J. to John Hopson 9-23-1875
Luckadoo, Sarah to Reuben Gilbert 6-8-1872
Lucus, Mary to I. S. P. Eastridge 7-13-1887 (no return)
Lumpkins, Elizabeth to James W. Overbay 8-17-1874
Lumpkins, Susan to John Hicks 4-27-1888
Lunch, Margaret L. to D. M. Poor 6-18-1872
Lunda, Margaret to J. B. Phillipps 10-9-1887

Lunda, Ruth to James A. Mintun 3-11-1886
Lundy, M. to T. J. Russell 10-10-1873 (10-12-1873)
Lundy, Martha to Wm. Paris 8-18-1871 (8-20-1871)
Lusen, M. A. to Henly Roberson 9-28-1878 (9-30-1878)
Luss, Franky to Thos. Walker 12-24-1890
Luster, Elizabeth to Harvey Lingnar 3-7-1871 (3-12-1871)
Luster, Jennie to Andrew Lambert 12-5-1884 (12-7-1884)
Luster, Margret to B. F. Hayslwood 9-17-1870 (9-18-1870)
Luster, Mary to Joseph Fleeman 3-18-1871 (3-21-1871)
Lynch, Catherin E. to Wm. M. Fergerson 11-29-1882 (11-30-1882)
Lynch, Elizabeth to Obediah Fields 4-11-1877 (4-14-1877)
Lynch, Elizabeth to T. B. Yoakum 12-25-1877 (1-2-1878)
Lynch, Jane to Joseph Neil 10-7-1880 (10-8-1880)
Lynch, Lavina to Wm. Killian 5-2-1872 (5-3-1872)
Lynch, Louiza J. to Henry Keck 7-24-1869 (7-29-1869)
Lynch, Sally to Arch Gilbert 12-27-1886 (12-28-1886)
Lynch, Sarah J. to John M. Moody 4-11-1883 (no return)
Lynch, Sarah N. to J. P. Houston 5-26-1882? (5-28-1882)
Lynch, Sarah Rosanah to Archibald E. Blansett 5-8-1869 (5-9-1869)
Lynch, Sarah S. to A.B. Drommons 11-12-1882 (11-16-1882)
Lynch, W. A. to W. S. Mink 11-7-1888 (11-8-1888)
Lynes, Martha to Wm. M. Cole 9-8-1888 (9-16-1888)
Lyons, C. M. to G. R. Thacker 2-19-1884 (2-21-1884)
Lyons, Florence to W. J. Cain 3-4-1874 (3-5-1874)
Lyons, M. S. to D. C. Edmonson 6-22-1886 (6-24-1886)
Mackey, M. B. to G. B. Porness? 6-10-1883
Macky, Janie to James C. Carr 11-5-1881
Macline, Martha to James M. Duncan 4-8-1881
Maddix, Nancy to William Shelton 11-11-1880
Maddox, Florance to W. H. Smith 5-3-1886
Maddox, Martha J. to Andrew Gibbs 11-8-1883 (no return)
Maddux, Mary to Z. Gibbs 8-20-1885 (8-22-1885)
Maler, Vienna to James Pike 9-30-1879
Malone, Edwina to Clint Sweat 12-28-1886
Maney, Manerva T. to David J. Fletcher 8-8-1877 (8-12-1877)
Maney, Sarah to John R. Altum 9-7-1877 (9-9-1877)
Manis, Eliza (Miss) to Kinard Standifer 5-17-1888 (5-18-1888)
Manis, Mary to Winton Panter 9-1-1886 (9-2-1886)
Manning, Liza Jane to Wm. Clarkston 8-17-1888 (8-19-1888)
Mannon, Martha to Thomas Owens 12-5-1879 (no return)
Mannon, Sallie to J. N. Thompson 11-4-1881 (11-6-1881)
Mansey, Nancy J. to J. M. Clause 5-15-1875
Maples, Rachel to A. J. Serber 4-11-1889 (no return)
Maples, Rachel to A. M. Collinsworth 10-6-1888 (no return)
Maples, Sarah J. to Levander Maples 9-23-1871 (9-28-1871)
Marcomb, Luda to Jefferson Cline 7-2-1882
Marcrum, Maggie to H. M. Patterson 11-12-1884 (11-13-1884)
Marcum, Alis to Samuel Sandifer 3-13-1877
Marcum, Nancy to Joe Wesley Ayers 12-8-1882 (12-10-1882)
Margraves, Emaline to Dal Fulkerson 1-31-1882
Margraves, M. E. to Henry Lynch 4-8-1880
Margraves, Sarah to Wm. H. Rolan 12-20-1879 (12-21-1879)
Marical, Serena to John Thompson 2-24-1881
Maricle, Martha J. to William Brown 8-5-1879
Maricle, Nancy to H. B. Browing 9-24-1879
Marjors, Sarah to Right Kelley 9-?-1878 (9-20-1878)
Mark, Emely to James Tinsley 12-4-1869
Markham, Rattie L. to George B. Rogers 12-8-1890 (no return)
Marsee, Cissy to Wm. H. Hatfield 3-12-1882
Marsee, Lesca to George Powers 7-28-1881
Marsee, M. J. to Levi Harp 5-10-1882 (no return)
Marsee, Matilda to Samuel Lynch 8-6-1879 (8-7-1879)
Marsee, Rachel C. to Samuel C. Monday 9-6-1883 (9-16-1883)
Marsh, Mary M. to Ruben Guarlen 8-23-1873 (8-24-1873)
Marsh, Mary to Jame Cheek 12-12-1880
Martan, Jane to Clinton Rice 7-?-1879 (7-8-1879)
Martin, Arrenia to Samuel Sampson 11-25-1872
Martin, Mary J. to William Cook 3-23-1877 (no return)
Martin, Mary to Abriham Brown 2-8-1886 (2-14-1886)
Masingill, Aby to Wm. B. Owens 8-30-1880 (9-2-1880)
Mason, Annie M. to Andrew Manion 1-8-1889
Mason, Emily to George Hurst 6-11-1877
Mason, Eneline to Plesant R. Mason 7-27-1882
Mason, Louisa to Joseph Baker 12-8-1876
Mason, Mary E. to Richard Scott? 5-23-1871 (no return)
Mason, Mary to Thos. Cox 2-16-1889 (no return)
Mason, Matild P. L. J. to Wm. Arnwine 10-19-1881 (10-20-1881)
Mason, Rebeca to Henry Shelton 6-28-1883
Mason, Rebecca to W. H. Smith 2-28-1887 (3-2-1887)
Massengill, Sarah to Alexander Williams 2-12-1877 (no return)
Massey, Rolley to Levi Turner 11-16-1886 (11-18-1886)
Massingill, Martha J. to James B. Campbell 3-26-1878 (3-28-1878)
Massingill, Nancy to John C. Arnold 8-23-1869 (8-26-1869)
Massingill, Sarah E. to Isom Lawson 1-13-1873 (1-16-1873)
Mathis, E. O. to Baxter Poor 3-15-1881 (3-16-1881)
Mathis, Easter Orlena to Baxter Poor 3-15-1881 (no return)
Mathis, Harrett M. to B. F. Duncan 12-23-1874

Mathis, Martha L. to B. M. Poor 11-16-1874 (11-21-1874)
Mathis, Martha Luverna to Henry Kirby 5-10-1873 (5-11-1873)
Mathis, Mary J. to Daniel Whitson 12-23-1874 (12-24-1874)
Mathis, Susan A. to Andrew Rigsbee 4-29-1880
Mathus, Elizabeth to Prior Poor 10-30-1883
Mathus, P. A. to John Estridg 10-18-1879
Mattax, Martha to Azeriah Tolaver 4-20-1869 (4-25-1869)
Mattox, Elizabeth to Wm. H. Moyers 8-26-1871 (8-27-1871)
Mattox, Liza Ann to David N. Gibbs? 5-11-1872 (5-12-1872)
Mattox, Nancy C. to William Sheton 7-6-1889
Maupin, Lucinda M. to David F. Beeler 1-19-1869 (1-21-1869)
Mayer, Mary J. to Fidance Fane 7-24-1880
Mayers, C. D. to John C. Crofferd 7-12-1880 (7-16-1880)
Mayers, L. V. to Wm. B. Howerton 2-16-1881 (no return)
Mayers, Mary A. to W. H. McNeely 2-14-1881 (2-17-1881)
Mayers, R. A. to J. F. Balton 6-10-1883
Mayes, Annah to Thomas Branscom 10-11-1872 (10-13?-1872)
Mayes, Delila to A. H. Cockrum 10-24-1883 (10-28-1883)
Mayes, Ida B. to S. M. Campbell 7-19-1890 (7-20-1890)
Mayes, Louiza J. to Wm. H. Goin 11-23-1872 (11-28-1872)
Mayes, Malinda to George W. Hopper 7-11-1874 (7-26-1874)
Mayes, Margaret M. to John T. Crutchfield 12-23-1869
Mayes, Mary R. to P. L. Cox 12-24-1876 (12-25-1876)
Mayes, Nancie A. to S. M. Holt 8-17-1885 (8-19-1885)
Mayes, Nancy to J. W. Bowlin 7-12-1882 (7-13-1882)
Mayes, Orlena to David E. Miller 2-2-1882 (2-6-1882)
Mayes, S. E. to N. L. Holt 12-17-1883 (12-18-1883)
Mays, Sary M. to John Lagin? 3-24-1871
Mayse, Nancy to Thos. Law 10-1-1873 (no return)
McAfee, Lucy to Hen. Clark 2-13-1885
McBee, Katie to Alex Lynch 3-3-1886 (3-4-1886)
McBee, Lucinda to Wm. E. Lynch 12-5-1868 (12-6-1868)
McBee, M. A. to E. D. Miller 3-5-1881 (no return)
McBee, M. to Robert Minton 1-13-1878 (No return)
McBee, Manervia J. to Robert H. Robinson 10-6-1877 (no return)
McBee, Marlenia to Timothy S. Rogers 12-17-1868 (12-20-1868)
McBee, Martha to Andrew Welch 10-21-1890 (10-22-1890)
McBee, Martha to Richard T. Robinson 11-18-1869 (11-21-1869)
McBee, Mary E. to M. D. Howard 9-12-1879
McBee, N. A. to C. W. Ford 7-25-1888 (7-29-1888)
McBee, Vera C. to J. N. Perry 10-20-1878 (no return)
McCany, Martha to John Evans 4-30-1881 (5-7-1881)
McCarrol, Melbina to Elisha Bush 9-26-1881
McCarty, Elizabeth E. to Herrod Overley 8-17-1877 (10-7-1877)
McCarty, O. T. to A. T. Perce 8-6-1880
McCarty, Sary J. to James F. Leemare 9-1-1881 (8?-4-1881)
McCary, Sarah to W. H. Sharp 9-6-1880 (9-9-1880)
McCauds, Marth L. to W. T., esq. Golden 11-28-1885 (11-29-1885)
McClewer, R. M. to Jesse W. Lynch 10-22-1880 (10-23-1880)
McClure, Daisy? Ann to W. B. Large 11-3-1875 (11-4-1875)
McClure, M. L. to John B. Irvin 9-26-1884 (9-28-1884)
McCollough, Susan to Wm. Walker 8-22-1889
McCollugh, Elizabeth to Mark Winkler 4-4-1881 (4-10-1881)
McColough, Sarah to William Hodges 10-22-1888 (10-25-1888)
McCrary, Lucretia to Airs M. Bruce 9-29-1873 (10-6-1873)
McCrary, M. J. to J. M. Neeham 10-26-1883 (10-28-1883)
McCrary, Marticia to John O. Evans 10-3-1870 (10-9-1870)
McCrary, Mary to Thomas Jones 11-13-1888 (no return)
McCrary, Nanie to J. D. Townsley 8-6-1881 (9-1-1881)
McCray, China A. to G. H. Essary 10-27-1885 (10-28-1885)
McDaniel, Catharine to James Bird 9-21-1868
McDaniel, Jane to William Hopper 6-12-1882
McDaniel, Liza to T. B. Harper 11-25-1882 (no return)
McDaniel, Lizzie to Green Phelps 5-15-1885 (5-16-1885)
McDaniel, Margaret A. to W. A. Waller 12-23-1889 (12-24-1889)
McDaniel, Margaret to J. C. Manning 8-10-1889 (no return)
McDaniel, Mary to Henry Lee 11-19-1888 (11-20-1888)
McDaniel, Mary to Lewis Brooks 10-23-1872 (no return)
McDaniel, Millie to John W. Cardwell 10-28-1868 (10-29-1868)
McDaniel, Rinda to Elihugh Goin 1-9-1881 (1-16-1881)
McDaniel, Sarah V. to A. L. Moyers 2-17-1874 (2-19-1874)
McDavid, Sarah C. to W. W., esq. Goin 11-5-1885
McFarler, Elizabeth to Moses Paul 1-3-1884
McGlothen, Hanna J. to Jasper Lesly 5-20-1872
McIfee, Elizabeth to Joseph F. Essary 2-17-1879 (2-20-1879)
McKinibee?, Sely A. to John A. Marsee 3-25-1886
McManaway, Fannie to Scott Whitmore 11-22-1889 (11-24-1889)
McManaway, Virginia C. to G. B. Gray 1-17-1872 (1-21-1872)
McMannyway, Fanny to Robert Thompson 5-6-1874 (5-7-1874)
McNeel, Mary C. to Joseph W. Cox 10-24-1871 (no return)
McNeell, Julia to Frank Thompson 12-30-1886 (no return)
McNeil, Nancy to Jackson Butcher 6-17-1889
McNeil, Ollie to A. C. Ausburn 5-12-1877 (5-13-1877)
McNiel, Mary L. to E. W. Seale 5-6-1884 (no return)
McPherson, Virginia to Dale C. Lyttle 12-12-1868 (no return)
McQuister, Emlie to Z. S. Roberts 4-4-1871
McVay, Clementine to Wm. Edens 3-3-1884 (3-6-1884)

McVay, Elizabeth to Hiram Edem 11-19-1883 (11-20-1883)
McVay, Josephine to Franklin B. Minton 12-28-1881 (12-29-1881)
McVay, Mary to W. E. McBee 2-17-1874 (2-19-1874)
McVey, Ollie M. to Samuel M. Lood 4-28-1888 (4-29-1888)
McWilliams, Margaret Va? to Jeremiah Williams 6-8-1877
Medaris, A. to J. S. Burnett 10-8-1874
Medlock, Minda to W. T. Doyl 1-17-1876 (8-17-1876)
Medowley, Mary to Abraham Fox 2-3-1871 (2-22-1871)
Meelor, Mary M. to Andrew Johnson 3-12-1883
Meigs, Elizabeth to Jerry Barnard 2-18-1875 (2-21-1875)
Meiher, Nancey to Thomas Smith 9-31?-1880 (9-10-1880)
Menroy?, Emly to Thomas J. Mayes? 12-2-1876 (12-7-1876)
Messer, Elisabeth to John Leabolt 3-2-1887 (3-3-1887)
Meyers, Catharine to Wm. N. Cassell 3-17-1874 (no return)
Meyers, Celia to Charles Neely 4-25-1871
Meyers, Lyddia to Allen Cook 7-31-1885 (8-2-1885)
Meyers, Manda J. to J. H. Blackburn 11-7-1884? (11-12-1884)
Meyers, Marth J. to Prior L. Janeway 12-2-1882 (12-3-1882)
Meyers, Mary to James P. Greer 7-3-1874
Meyers, Melvina to Wm. J. Clay 11-9-1877 (no return)
Miller, Anna to Tennessee Musgraves 11-13-1872 (no return)
Miller, Casa to Winsbee Bailey 10-31-1888
Miller, Mandy to Willson Murphy 8-18-1877
Miller, Martha A. to Campbell Smith 12-28-1871
Miller, Susan to John F. Hargraves 12-2-1879
Mink, Eliza to A. B. Drummons 9-30-1875
Mink, Jennie to Frank Snider 6-22-1889 (6-23-1889)
Mink, M. E. to J. B. Straugh 2-19-1885
Mink, Mary Elizabeth to James S. Myers 5-8-1877 (5-10-1877)
Mink, S. J. to Jefferson Meyers 8-2-1879 (8-10-1879)
Mink, Salley to James Tennison 11-15-1890 (no return)
Minter, S. A. to J. D. Eley 3-26-1882
Minton, Annie to Elias Liford 11-3-1869 (11-12-1869)
Minton, H. E. to A. L. Foard 8-28-1879 (8-31-1879)
Minton, Jane to Joseph Minton 7-12-179 (11-13-1880)
Minton, Margret J. to Allen Brooks 10-10-1870 (10-13-1870)
Minton, Mary E. to James King 8-28-1879 (8-31-1879)
Minton, Sarah to R. S. Cline 12-29-1886 (12-30-1886)
Minton, Susana C. to Wm. J. Goin 5-9-1878
Mise, Lucinda to Morrison Brooks 10-9-1874 (10-8?-1874)
Mising?, A. C. to Alexander Lebolt 2-23-1874
Mitchel, Lusaney M. to Henry J. Hutson 4-24-1876 (4-25-1876)
Mitchell, Nancy S. to David Phelps 12-25-1888 (12-26-1888)
Mitheal, Margret to George Mason 12-24-1870 (12-25-1870)
Mize, Lucinda to Taylor Brooks 6-12-1874 (not executed)
Mize, Mary J. to J. M. Barlow 12-27-1888
Monday, Esther to H. C. Brooks 12-6-1881 (12-13-1881)
Monday, Martha to S. E. Cottrell 9-18-1878
Monk, M. E. to J. B. Johnson 12-18-1889 (12-19-1889)
Monk, Martha M. to Vincent D. McBee 9-4-1889 (9-8-1889)
Monly?, L. E. to N. L. Keck 6-9-1888 (no return)
Monsey, Nancy A. to Jasper Grubb 4-12-1879 (no return)
Montgomery, Marthey J. to G. C. Brooks 8-8-1887 (8-11-1887)
Montgomery, Mary E. to Elbert Longworth 12-7-1888 (12-9-1888)
Moody, Mary J. to William A. Wilder 2-2-1882
Moody, Vergena A. to John Minten 9-4-1883 (9-6-1883)
Moor, Sarah to Wm. J. Paul 12-8-1884
Moore, Mary A. to Eldridg C. Brooks 1-3-1882 (1-5-1882)
Moore, Rachel to Padric Maze 9-10-1878
More, Martha to Robert Tullington 3-23-1887 (no return)
More, Vina to G. S. Bolton 4-7-1887 (not executed)
Morgan, Cornelia to Pery Earls 1-14-1882 (1-15-1882)
Morgan, Elizabeth to William Bird 7-9-1877
Morgan, Mary to Harvey Robinson 8-6-1873 (9-6-1873)
Morgan, Matilda to William Woodard 11-18-1880 (11-21-1880)
Morgan, Salley to Joseph Dunn 3-11-1890
Morison, Mary E. to Nathaniel E. Richman 8-8-1883
Morrison, Ella to H. H. Carmack 1-26-1882 (1-31-1882)
Morrison, Vest to John Hocks? 7-21-1870
Morrisson, Rhoda to I. L. Deaton 11-30-1886 (2-22-1887)
Morsee, Fanny to B. F. Ranes 12-14-1877
Morser?, Nancy J. to Levi Harpe 5-10-1882
Moseley, Mary L. to Nelson Sullivan 10-24-1890
Moss, Mary Jane to Stephen Cawood 3-18-1872 (3-21-1872)
Mount, Mary E. to Preston Kincaid 4-2-1869 (4-4-1869) B
Mountain, A. P. to F. H. Wyley 3-16-1889 (3-17-1889)
Mountain, Angie to S. J. Carr 10-4-1881 (10-23-1881)
Mountain, Jane to Asa Brogan 3-29-1883 (4-3-1883)
Mountain, Jemima O. to Ballard Jesse 2-2-1874 (no return)
Mountain, Mary to Daniel Walker 5-5-1871 (5-8-1871)
Mountain, Nanna E. to W. G. Walker 12-5-1885 (12-6-1885)
Mountin, Liza V. to Ewing F. Yoakum 9-18-1881 (9-20-1881)
Moyers, Atarsiet? to I. P. Francisco 11-24-1881 (no return)
Moyers, Catharine to Wm. Canell 3-4-1874 (3-26-1874)
Moyers, Chrisleener to Peter S. Honeycutt 10-4-1879
Moyers, Clary L. to David M. Wilson 9-22-1869 (9-23-1869)
Moyers, Clory B. to James M. Bamman 2-21-1875

Moyers, Louisa to J. L. Wilson 9-1-1871 (not executed)
Moyers, Louise to Joseph Bull 12-2-1881 (12-4-1881)
Moyers, M. C. to J. N. Cupp 7-19-1880 (7-22-1880)
Moyers, Manervia to James E. Hamlett 12-28-1874 (12-31-1874)
Moyers, Mary E. to George W. Cupp 6-23-1877 (6-2-1877)
Moyers, Melvina to John Soard 8-5-1880 (no return)
Moyers, Melvina to Martin Greer 2-2-1876 (no return)
Moyers, Nancey to Wm. M. Russell 6-19-1880 (6-27-1880)
Moyers, Oley to James L. Harrell 2-1-1873 (2-2-1873)
Moyers, R. L. to David M. Widmar 1-6-1890 (no return)
Moyers, Sarah M. to Daniel Burk 4-12-1874
Mriz?, Malisa to Thos. Mize 8-11-1873 (no return)
Mullens, Celea to Allen Butler 6-26-1878 (6-27-1878)
Mullens, Cena to Allen Butler 6-26-1878 (no return)
Mullins, Emoline to John Sulfredg 2-17-1881 (no return)
Mullins, Josephine to John Greer 11-27-1885
Mullins, Sarah to John P. Neil 12-25-1886 (no return)
Mullins, Susan M. to Marion West 6-9-1883 (6-10-1883)
Muncey, Delilia J. to James W. Grimes 1-7-1869 (1-10-1869)
Muncey, M. J. to Lewis G. M? 2-15-1879 (6-20-1880!)
Muncy, Melvina to John W. Smith 10-10-1885
Muncy, Nancy J. to Duff Luford 12-16-1870 (12-18-1870)
Munk, Lidda J. to Joseph Hyatt 8-4-1889 (no return)
Munn, Lora to Thos. Ausburn 11-22-1888 (11-23-1888)
Murphy, Mary to Benjamine Robinson 1-6-1876
Murrisson, R. H. to James H. Condry 3-23-1878 (3-28-1878)
Murry, Sarah to Morgan Cloud 2-8-1879 (2-9-1879)
Mury, Nancy to Wesley Paness 5-18-1871
Musser, Mattie to J. F. Cunningham 1-17-1891
Nance, Marth J. to Jas. H. Spence 11-28-1885 (11-29-1885)
Nance, Martha J. to George Fields 5-1-1878 (no return)
Nants, Temperance to J. E. Hodges 10-30-1878
Napper, Elizabeth to Samuel Hampton? 6-7-1880 (no return)
Nathen, Nancy to Jacob Willis 2-7-1886
Neal, Lucy B. to B. F. Bomar 12-23-1890
Neal, Vesty to William Farris 10-16-1875 (10-17-1875)
Needham, Arminda to J. G. Palmer 10-28-1868 (10-29-1868)
Needham, Cornelia Ann to Merril Hill 11-25-1872 (12-3-1872)
Needham, Polley E. to Frankling Sharp 10-30-1879
Neeham, Eliza Jane to J. W. Hodges 8-24-1877 (8-30-1877)
Neel, Lizzie to F. H. Hill 10-29-1877 (11-1-1877)
Neel, Rachael to J. H. Sullivan 1-13-1873 (1-30-1873)
Neel, Sarah to Randolph Jones 1-13-1873 (1-14-1873)
Neeley, Elizabeth to J. M. Day 8-11-1880 (8-12-1880)
Neeley, Frances A. to Samuel O. Mink 3-28-1878 (3-29-1878)
Neeley, Livina to John Jones 5-24-1883 (5-25-1883)
Neeley, M. P. to Wm. J. Davy 8-?-1880 (no return)
Neely, Margaret J. to Jas. Minter 10-20-1885 (11-1-1885)
Neems?, Delie to Harrie? Harrell 6-15-1878 (no return)
Neil, Cordelia to Wm. Rosenbalm 5-23-1885 (no return)
Neil, Eliza to Henry Mathis 12-30-1882
Neil, Lula M. to C. S. Mounts 7-13-1888 (7-15-1888)
Neil, M. M. to F. G. Rogers 11-5-1883 (11-8-1883)
Neil, Sarah to J. T. Standifer 12-24-1876 (no return)
Nelson, Elizabeth to Wily Jones 7-13-1882 (7-23-1882)
Nelson, Hasey to Wiley Jones 1-20-1874 (no return)
Nelson, Mery E. to Jobe C. Redmond 5-8-1883 (5-9-1883)
Nevels, Malissa to J. G. Williams 8-9-1887
Nevels, Martha E. to J. G. Snavely 10-24-1884 (10-25-1885)
Nevels, Martha to John A.? Taylor 2-18-1871 (2-19-1871)
Nevels, Mary C. to W. F. Brooks 12-21-1888 (12-23-1888)
Nevels, Matilda to Samuel Estep 9-26-1868 (10-1-1868)
Newbey, Virginia E. to Daniel Bryant 7-22-1873 (7-24-1873)
Newby, Eliza J. to James Smith 9-13-1879
Newby, Mary to Finley Hill 8-2-1882
Newlee, Laura to S. F. Brafford 8-12-1875 (not returned)
Newport, S. C. to Thomas Earls 7-5-1882 (7-17-1882)
Niceley, Adaline to Taylor Munsey 6-18-1876 (6-20-1876)
Niceley, Isabella to Edward Moncy 2-15-1878 (no return)
Niceley, Orlenia to A. J. Farmer 4-6-1872 (4-11-1872)
Nicly, Isabel to Samuel Muncy 1-31-1879 (2?-2-1879)
Nite, Elviry to Robert Leebow 10-7-1872
Noah, Martha to Thos. Smith 12-26-1888 (12-27-1888)
Noe, Fannie to Williams Nelms 12-27-1889
Noe, Luverne to John Mullins 12-4-1888
Noe, Sallie to Aaron Clark 6-18-1870 (6-19-1870)
North, Catharine to Robert N. Fultz 7-30-1875
Northan, Lowese E. to James T. Bawn 6-3-1878 (no return)
Northan, Martha J. to John Brown 3-25-1880 (no return)
Northern, Jane to James Hatfield 8-11-1875 (8-12-1875)
Northern, Margaret to James Reice 11-27-1886 (no return)
Norvill, Mary Jane to Benj. Smith 1-14-1871 (1-18-1871)
Nunn, Allace to Isaac H. Campbell 1-20-1890 (1-23-1890)
Nunn, Delce to Ham Harrell 6-15-1878 (6-16-1878)
Odel, Cela to Gorg Goin 9-6-1878 (9-7-1878)
Odell, China to B. Ausmus 8-1-1881 (8-8-1881)
Odell, Rutha to Franklin Spradling 9-22-1890 (9-28-1890)

Odelle, Derushia to Joseph Keton 9-21-1882 (9-24-1882)
Odle, Chiney to Wm. D. McDonald 1-3-1881 (no return)
Odle, R. E. to Samuel E. Grubb 9-27-1880 (9-30-1880)
Ogan, Mary J. to James Brogans 11-9-1883 (11-11-1883)
Oliver, Louisa to Wm. N. West 12-31-1880 (1-4-1881)
Osben, Sary to John King 11-22-1870
Osborn, Mary J. to Wm. Estis 4-10-1875 (no return)
Osburn, Josefine to Henly Jennings 10-22-1886 (no return)
Ote, Mary to T. C. Rater 10-21-1878
Otey, M. H. to R. E. Haley 9-25-1879
Ousley, Cleapatra to Houston Powel 12-28-1874 (no return)
Ousley, Harriet M. to Horace M. Moyers 5-20-1874 (5-21-1874)
Ousley, Sarah to H. H. Walker 4-27-1873 (5-2-1873)
Ousley, Susan to Timothy Williams 6-13-1874 (6-14-1874)
Overbay, Juliam to W. F. Kivit 10-2-1882 (10-8-1882)
Overbay, Mary to John S. Burk 2-17-1889
Overbay, Sarah to A. E. Gilbert 7-26-1879 (7-29-1879)
Overbey, Martha to John Gray 10-22-1875 (10-23-1875)
Overholster, Elida? to J. B. Hopson 10-2-1880 (10-31-1880)
Overton, Carnie to M. Overton 12-3-1890 (no return) B
Overton, Cornelia to Garrett H. Kesterson 9-19-1877 (9-20-1877)
Overton, M. E. to Henly Buis 10-6-1879 (10-9-1879)
Overton, Malinda to Jackson Kyle 7-31-1884
Overton, Rucia to James Parky 2-9-1878 (no return)
Owen, C. to A. W. Runnions 12-25-1876
Owen, Mary to J. J. Bolton 12-21-1886 (12-26-1886)
Owens, Catherine to John Crutchfield 8-11-1871 (8-12-1871)
Owens, Docia to James McNew 12-4-1889 (12-8-1889)
Owens, Elizabeth to Fredrick Fultz 7-2-1877
Owens, Judie L. to J. A. Bolton 2-28-1891 (3-1-1891)
Owens, M. J. to John Underwood 10-22-1887 (10-23-1887)
Owens, Margret to Thomas Furguson 6-2-1877 (6-3-1877)
Owens, Margrett to Wm. S. Colens 11-16-1878
Owens, Martha L. to Shade Presenell 5-24-1890 (5-25-1890)
Owens, Martha to Charley Ausmus 3-23-1888
Owens, Mary M. to Wm. H. Ellison 8-24-1882 (8-25-1882)
Owens, Mary to Jefferson Vanable 12-29-1880 (12-30-1880)
Owens, Maulis? to Wm. F. Cassid 2-9-1877
Owens, Melvina to Joseph Welch 6-16-1877 (6-17-1877)
Owens, N. E. to J. J. Sewell 7-7-1878
Owens, Nancy J. to Thomas Tague 10-4-1880 (10-10-1880)
Owens, Nancy to Henderson Sumpt 7-?-1879 (7-22-1879)
Owens, Norra to Isaac Branson 8-21-1889 (no return)
Owens, Orlena E. to William T. Thacker 6-19-1877 (6-21-1877)
Owens, R. E. to J. P. Orick 10-7-1882 (10-8-1882)
Owens, Rachal E. to John P. Orick 10-7-1882 (no return)
Owens, Rhoda to Thomas Collins 3-26-1881
Owens, Nancy with William F. Hoopper 1-4-1870 (1-6-1870)
Pace, Elizabeth to William J. Hill 7-19-1869 (no return)
Pace, L. S. A. to James M. Brooks 3-19-1880 (3-20-1880)
Pain, M. A. to D. A. Neil 2-26-1880
Pain, Sa to T. A. Essary 11-?-1878 (11-23-1878)
Painter, Lucy Ann to G. W. Runnions 2-7-1874 (2-8-1874)
Painter, Martha J. to Jerome Woodson 12-28-1875
Painter, Nancy E. to Josiah Cole 1-20-1872 (1-21-1872)
Parker, Ester to J. W. Whitacre 1-19-1887 (1-20-1887)
Parker, Jane to Allen Hurst 3-4-1880 (no return)
Parker, Lucy to Robert Parker 3-28-1871
Parker, Luvernia to Jasper Welch 9-9-1887 (9-10-1887)
Parker, Mary E. to H. B. Southern 8-20-1887 (8-21-1887)
Parker, Mary J. to Wm. T. Chadwell 1-19-1879
Parker, Nancy L. to Henly S. Hurst 9-20-1875 (no return)
Parker, Nancy to Franklin Hurst 1-8-1876
Parker, Racheal to Zinni Williams 6-2-1873 (6-3-1873)
Parker, Sarah to C. F. Osborn 12-14-1881
Parkey, Martha Jane to Zachariah Riley 4-19-1876 (no return)
Parkey, Nancy to John T. Mize 2-28-1881 (3-30-1881)
Parkey, Nervesta to Wm. Riley 10-5-1882 (no return)
Parkey, Sarah to Georg Woodson 4-25-1879 (4-26-1879)
Parks, Martha to W. M. Brooks 11-3-1888 (11-4-1888)
Parks, Mary A. to Wm. Russ 1-2-1871
Parks, Mary C. to Isaac Chadwell 11-18-1882 (no return)
Parks, Matilda T. to Jackson Sutton 1-29-1880 (1-28?-1880)
Parris, Nancy J. to W. L. Rosenbalm 9-15-1886 (9-16-1886)
Parrot, Nancy E. to Benjamin Ealy 5-4-1879
Parrott, Amanda to Johnathan Sharp 11-5-1881
Parrott, Marica J. to Mack Wheeler 4-21-1883 (4-29-1883)
Parry, Mary to Joseph Griffin 1-15-1890
Parry, Sarrah to John Woods 5-16-1872 (no return)
Parsom, L. to T. H. Blancett 2-24-1880 (2-29-1880)
Parson, Fany to Jamee Price 12-19-1877 (12-20-1877)
Parsons, Sarah J. to James F. Cardwell 12-14-1870 (12-15-1870) B
Parten, Milley Ann to William H. Tolliver 11-28-1869
Partin, Nancy to William Partin 12-29-1879 (12-26?-1879)
Parton, Mandy C. to Wm. Willas 8-22-1871
Parton, Nancy A. to Grant Barnett 1-14-1891 (no return)
Pates, Jane to Danel Fugate 4-28-1879 (no return)

Patterson, Alice to Henry G. Batey 10-2-1871 (no return)
Patterson, Loweza E. to James K. Forgerson 8-31-1870 (no return)
Patterson, Marinda to William Wright 7-13-1884 (no return)
Patterson, Mary A. to R. E. McEwen 11-16-1870 (11-17-1870)
Patterson, Mary to Isaac Been 5-8-1885 (no return)
Patterson, Minee to Robert Lanham 9-1-1880 (9-12-1880)
Patterson, Nancy E. to Jermiah Roark 11-24-1871 (11-28-1871)
Patterson, Sarah to Wm. T. Mason 2-28-1871
Patterson?, Eleanor? to W. W. Fulkerson 9-17-1877
Paul, Nancy J. to Alexander Greenlee 5-5-1871 (5-7-1871)
Payne, Eliza A. to Frank Jennings 11-3-1890 (11-10-1890)
Payne, Maggie to G. M. Campbell 10-10-1888 (10-11-1888)
Payne, Mary to R. F. Wiley 9-3-1877
Payne, Mollie to T. N. Dunsmore 1-16-1890 (1-25-1890)
Payne, Sallie E. to W. H. S. Kincaid 8-9-1873 (no return)
Peace, Susan F. to L. S. Harp 7-4-1880
Pearce, A. M. to R. C. Freeman 1-12-1885
Pearce, Celie to G. M. Billingsly 9-1-1882 (9-7-1882)
Pearce, Malinda to George Rose 8-10-1879
Pearce, Sarah to G. B. Powers 8-10-1879
Pearson, Catharine to G. W. P. Hufsedler 2-14-1874 (2-26-1874)
Pearson, Catharine to G. W. P. Hufsutter 2-14-1874 (2-26-1874)
Pearson, Ellen to Sterling Walker 4-30-1870 (5-5-1870)
Pearson, Emaline to James A. Purky 12-21-1882 (12-24-1882)
Pearson, Hallie to L. F. Seal 5-7-1889 (5-19-1889)
Pearson, L. E. to J. L. Morrison 2-2-1885 (2-10-1885)
Pearson, Louisa to Daniel B. Baker 12-8-1876 (12-12-1876)
Pearson, Lousana to Archilas Baker 9-22-1879 (10-19-1879)
Pearson, Lowsanna P. to Samuel Evans 7-28-1887 (8-9-1887)
Pearson, Luanny to Joseph Lewis 4-14-1877 (4-26-1877)
Pearson, M. J. to Bishop Crook 2-22-1872
Pearson, M. S. to R. C. Rush 1-28-1885
Pearson, Matilda J. to David Owens 10-23-1884 (11-2-1884)
Pearson, O. M. to J. H. Davis 7-27-1880 (8-8-1880)
Pearson, Safronea to Bartly Ward 9-26-1884 (10-19-1884)
Pearson, Sofrona to Bartley Ward 9-26-1884 (no return)
Peck, J. P. to J. S. Davis 1-14-1878 (no return)
Peck, Pheba C. to George W. Brit? 3-1-1878 (3-3-1878)
Peeters, Mary E. to John W. Hodges 3-24-1871 (3-26-1871)
Peeters, Matilda to Joseph Breeden 4-8-1871 (4-9-1871)
Penelton, Mollie to John Hurst 10-6-1890 (no return)
Penington, Sarah to Nathaniel Noe 2-26-1884 (no return)
Percifield, Mary to Thomas Woodson 6-28-1879
Percival, Charity to Thomas Cross 7-29-1871 (7-30-1871)
Percival, Martha to Wm. McStewart 1-30-1871
Perkins, Anna J. to Andrew J. Thompson 12-15-1868 (12-16-1868)
Perkins, Mina to Henry Sitner 1-22-1883 (2-2-1883)
Perry, Adilid? to William Jennings 8-24-1876
Persell, Mary Ann to Yarnon Gibson 7-29-1882
Peters, America to G. W. Minton 10-13-1876
Peters, Louisa M. to John H. Pierce 2-20-1881
Peters, Sarah to Jerry Anderson 1-6-1883 (no return)
Petree, Elizabeth to Robert Cheek 8-14-1872 (no return)
Petree, Jane to Nelson Brown 2-10-1876 (2-13-1876)
Phelps, Vandellea to Jeremiah Wells 2-28-1890 (3-2-1890)
Phillips, B. N. to A. J. Furguson 1-18-1886
Phillips, Martha A. to John N. Tunmire 3-6-1869 (3-7-1869)
Phillips, Mary to G. W. Hickman 5-16-1887 (5-19-1887)
Phillips, Mary to James F. Chumley 10-9-1869 (10-10-1869)
Phillips, Medea L. to Samuel Hamlet 9-6-1886 (9-10-1886)
Pierman, Martha to Tayler J. Yoakum 11-28-1871 (12-3-1871)
Pike, Loucinda to Phillip Keck 8-2-1880 (8-5-1880)
Pike, Malinda to John Gaylor 3-17-1871
Pike, Sarah E. to John Doyle 6-30-1874 (7-1-1874)
Pillian, N. E. to John Cole 2-4-1881 (no return)
Poor, Bettie to John Widner 8-12-1888
Poor, Christena to William M. Mathis 6-29-1875
Poor, Emley M. to E. B. Carrell 8-2-1872 (no return)
Poor, Frances to James Fultz 3-21-1883
Poor, India to Chas. Bell 12-25-1888 (12-26-1888)
Poor, Louiza J. to Wm. J. Daniel 11-14-1873 (11-15-1873)
Poor, Luvernia to George Halebraten ?-11-1881 (?-21-1880)
Poor, M. C. M. to C. M. Farmer 10-8-1884 (10-12-1884)
Poor, Malinda E. to Nathan S. Ritter 5-4-1872 (no return)
Poor, Mary A. to Wm. H. Williams 5-3-1875
Poor, Mary to Fred Logan 10-11-1890 (10-12-1890)
Poor, Mary to Washington Dannel 10-6-1884 (10-12-1884)
Poor, Matilda Emeline to William R. Clark 4-11-1888 (no return)
Poor, N. A. to G. W. Rigsbey 1-19-1879 (1-20-1879)
Poor, Nancy to Wm. Gorden 5-6-1871 (5-7-1871)
Por, Dora to R. E. Orourke 9-12-1890 (10-5-1890)
Powell, Sarah N. to James D. Robertson 1-10-1874
Powers, Mary to John Nix 2-11-1875
Powers, Meda to Elija Baker 2-11-1875
Powers, P. J. to Wm. N. Powers 9-26-1881
Powers, Sarah E. to Jacob M. Reece 12-20-1886 (12-30-1886)
Pratt, Martha J. to W. J. McClain 5-12-1883 (5-13-1883)

Pratt, S. L. to Alvis Hatfield 2-16-1882 (no return)
Pratt, Sarah J. to William Earles 3-25-1885
Presley, Elizabeth to D. J. M. Collins 8-4-1889
Presly, Josiah to Malinda Carter 1-9-1885 (no return)
Pressnell, M. A. to C. R. Cline 12-30-1889 (1-2-1890)
Price, Francy to G. B. Hatfield 11-19-1886 (11-20-1886)
Pridemore, Jane to Samuel Ray 8-4-1871
Pridemore, Mary Jane to Wm. S. Ball 12-18-1868 (12-24-1868)
Pridemore, Mary to Steward Willson 8-19-1882
Pridemore, Nancy to Samuel Provence 12-20-1873 (1-4-1874)
Pridmore, Delany to Richard Younts 11-20-1872 (12-1-1872)
Provene, Elisabeth to Thomas A. Shumate 11-30-1874 (no return)
Prydemore, Lucy to William Rymor 3-29-1876 (no return)
Pults, Martha to Wm. Milligana 2-17-1890 (no return)
Pursifal, Elizabeth to W. M. C. Stewart 12-12-1875
Quillein, P. C. to R. F. McConnell 6-20-1884
Raden, Jane to Wm. Collins 1-19-1871
Raines, Frannie to Gilbert Turner 3-27-1880
Rall, Linda to Wm. Briens? 8-28-1880
Ramey, Ollie to Layfett Sands 3-4-1881 (3-6-1881)
Ramsey, Eliza J. to Frederick Fultz 5-18-1871
Ramsey, Fanny to Reece Howard 7-15-1876 (no return)
Ramsey, Laviny to Dan? R. Willson 4-18-1872
Ramsey, Malissa to Lewis Brooks 6-10-1876 (no return)
Ramsey, Martha to Benj. Wilson 11-17-1884 (11-18-1884)
Ramsey, Rittey to Henry Buis 9-13-1877 (9-14-1877) B
Ramsey, Sarah to Levli Massengill 4-9-1877
Raney, Ellen to James Knight 6-1-1889
Raney, Mary to Wm. H. Moyers 6-14-1882
Raney, Rache to Travis Brooks 10-30-1887
Rason, Mary to Jesse L. Wilson 10-19-1872 (10-20-1872)
Ray, Hannah to John Taylor 1-28-1877
Rayner, Ollie to Jas. Hamlet 1-12-1885
Reace?, Susan to Dalsey L. Manis 1-21-1891 (1-25-1891)
Reader, N. J. to Anderson McMahan 12-16-1880
Readmon, Sarah J. to John R. Strake? 11-5-1873 (11-6-1873)
Realey, Sarah to Pror Davis 10-26-1880 (no return)
Rector, Sarrah to Levi Killian 11-7-1870 (11-9-1870)
Redmon, Minervy to Jefferson Sparks 12-2-1880 (12-4-1880)
Redmond, Sariah Jane to Benjaman F. Houston 8-30-1870 (9-8-1870)
Reece, Catharine to Bartly A. Word 7-14-1874
Reece, Elizabeth to George D. Johnson 1-30-1869 (1-31-1869)
Reece, Emley to Hiram Kinder 8-13-1881 (8-16-1881)
Reece, Mary to S. S. Friar 7-2-1890 (7-27-1890)
Reece, Nancy Elizabeth to Benjamine F. Spence 2-3-1877
Reece, Nancy to Absolem Roberds 8-25-1886 (no return)
Reed, Manerva E. to Calvin A. Henderson 2-25-1871 (2-26-1871)
Reid, M. L. to S. J. Treece 1-10-1884
Reimer, Susan to George Green 11-27-1880 (no return)
Remon, Molley to Thos. Ellison 10-2-1886 (10-3-1886)
Retherford, Leaty to William Carrell 3-28-1869
Rice, Nancy J. to H. F. Lawsom 6-28-1880 (no return)
Rice, Phoeba to James Keton 1-16-1889 (1-17-1889)
Rice, Rebeca to Thos. Bussell 12-24-1889 (no return)
Rich, Manervy to Peter Hanrey 8-4-1880 (no return)
Richardson, Eliza to John Yoakum 11-5-1883 (no return)
Richardson, Frances to J. A. Brooks 12-28-1878 (12-29-1878)
Richardson, L. C. to P. L. Bible 3-7-1891 (3-16-1891)
Richardson, M. B. to W. T. Vansel 1-5-1885 (no return)
Richardson, Margrett to A. J. Owens 6-2-1883 (6-3-1883)
Richardson, Rebecca J. to W. T. Lambert 2-3-1890 (2-9-1890)
Richardson, Salley to W. H. Cloud 9-13-1887 (9-14-1887)
Richmon, Elisa to Elbert Hurst 12-5-1877 (12-6-1877)
Riddle, L. M. to R. H. Massingal 10-6-1887
Ridens, T. C. to J. M. Moyers 12-27-1888 (no return)
Rider, Janey to Henry Cinniman 8-10-1882 (8-13-1882)
Ridings, Margret to John Sparks 1-12-1876
Ridings, Marry to Wm. R. Gibson 6-22-1880 (6-23-1880)
Ridings, Martha L. to Berry F. Houston 4-5-1873 (no return)
Right, S. E. to Alexander Kerr 6-29-1889 (not exec.)
Right, S. J. to William Rollins 8-1-1882 (8-2-1882)
Right, Sary J. to W. P. Golden 4-6-1879
Rigsbee, Nancy Emaline to James A. Thompson 4-17-1869 (4-18-1869)
Riley, Almeta P. to Warren D. Overton 10-3-1881 (10-4-1881)
Riley, Annie to Henry Mooer? 11-11-1884
Riley, Dosia to E. A. Lanham 12-31-1884 (no return)
Riley, Elizabeth to Jordon Wilson 3-18-1881 (3-19-1880?)
Ritchey, Teritha to Nelson Lelio? 5-13-1876
Ritchie, Hattie C. to Wm. A. Day 12-12-1888
Ritter, A. to J. H. Bandin 1-21-1880 (1-22-1880)
Ritter, July to Jesse H. Hopson 4-29-1874 (4-30-1874)
Ritter, Mary C. to William P. Harrel 3-16-1872 (3-27-1872)
Ritter, Sarah C. to W. H. Hurst 3-28-1890 (no return)
Ritter, Vesta to Elias J. Norvell 8-29-1871 (8-31-1871)
Roads, Mary to John Vaughn 1-20-1879 (no return)
Roark, Elizabeth to John Whiteaker 9-20-1873 (9-21-1873)
Roark, Elizabeth to WM. Marcum 10-9-1876 (10?-11-1876)

Roark, Juluy? to J. A. Richardson 9-27-1889 (no return)
Roark, Louisa to William P. Whiteaker 12-21-1874 (12-22-1874)
Roark, Margrett to James Richardson 10-2-1880 (10-3-1880)
Roark, Mary Jane to J. B. Harrell 4-13-1889
Roark, Nancy to Levi Campbell 6-15-1879
Roark, Sarah E. to Jasper Jones 6-15-1879
Roark, Sarah to Thomas Caler 8-17-1878 (no return)
Roark, Sarah to Thomas Calor 8-17-1878
Roarks, Mary to Elbert Williams 1-15-1875
Robarts, Virdy to George Campbell 5-8-1890
Robert, Martha to Jessey Hensley 11-14-1874 (no return)
Roberts, Arebell to Madison Fox 5-7-1888
Roberts, Elisbeth to Thomas T. Bane 9-10-1870 (9-16-1870)
Robertson, Annie to Leander Hurst 3-5-1890
Robertson, Annie to Wm. W. Guy 9-18-1888 (9-20-1888)
Robertson, Fanney B. to James Owens 11-17-1888 (no return)
Robertson, Gusly Lee to Robt. Fields 8-28-1888 (8-30-1888)
Robertson, Lizzie to Green Buis 12-12-1888 (12-18-1888)
Robertson, Lumll? to Octava L. Bryan 6-15-1885 (6-16-1885)
Robertson, S. J. to G. W. Russell 4-10-1888 (4-15-1888)
Robertson, Sally to Hugh Farmer 12-28-1886 (12-30-1886)
Robertson, Sarah E. to A. G. Honeycutt 10-22-1887 (10-23-1887)
Robinson, Barthena to William Houston 10-15-1877 (10-18-1877)
Robinson, C. E. to Maynard Cupp 2-1-1887 (2-3-1887)
Robinson, Dollie to Lewis Hurst 8-17-1882
Robinson, Dora to E. H. Essary 12-31-1885
Robinson, Dory J. to John T. Woods 5-29-1884
Robinson, Eliza to Claiborne Standerfer 1-1-1870
Robinson, Eliza to Richard S. Butly 1-21-1885 (1-22-1885)
Robinson, Elizabeth to Hiram Liford 8-22-1883 (no return)
Robinson, Florah to J. N. Robinson 11-3-1875 (11-4-1875)
Robinson, M. to A. J. Reese 8-30-1879 (8-31-1879)
Robinson, Margaret M. to Anderson Cardwell 3-20-1870
Robinson, Mary A. to Joseph C. Welch 1-7-1882
Robinson, N. A. to William Davy 1-6-1882 (no return)
Robinson, Rachael to Taylor Parratt 2-10-1872
Robinson, Rachel to Fred Logan 2-24-1889
Robinson, Rebecca J. to David R. Willis 1-10-1870
Robinson, Salley to Jamaes Ford 1-11-1888 (1-12-1888)
Robinson, Susan L. C. to Joseph Johnson 9-11-1868 (9-17-1868)
Robinson, Tarica to John Cloud 1-19-1882
Roch, Mary A. to Ruben Been 6-17-1882
Roe, Martha J. to Thos. Earley 11-29-1888
Rogers, A. B. to J. A. Rogers 1-20-1887
Rogers, Allice to Dock Brooks 11-25-1886
Rogers, Aly to R. B. Rogers 12-7-1876
Rogers, Annie to Joseph McMahan 8-19-1886 (no return)
Rogers, Dolly to Phillip Branscom 5-31-1873
Rogers, Elizabeth to Thomas Jones 6-28-1871 (6-30-1871)
Rogers, Esther Love (Mis) to John Profett 7-29-1881
Rogers, Jane to Wm. H. Fields 1-31-1874
Rogers, Lidda to Prior Hurst 11-11-1887 (11-12-1887)
Rogers, Loo B. to John M. Meyers 12-3-1887 (12-4-1887)
Rogers, Loo to J. G.? Bryant 1-4-1887 (1-6-1887)
Rogers, Louiza A. to Stephen H. Cawood 5-19-1869
Rogers, Lucy Ann to Preston Hodges 1-25-1883 (no return)
Rogers, M. A. to B. F. Ausmus 10-15-1879 (1-5-1880)
Rogers, M. V. to John A. Rogers 12-21-1878
Rogers, Mary Ann to Johnson Mayer 8-18-1884 (8-19-1884)
Rogers, Mary F. to H. F. Sharp 2-18-1871 (2-19-1871)
Rogers, Ollie to Marshal Beeler 12-10-1883 (no return)
Rogers, R. C. to B. F. Claiborne 10-29-1874 (no return)
Rogers, R. H. to B. F. Claiborn 10-29-1874
Rogers, Rachal A.? to H. M. Cain 1-24-1883 (no return)
Rogers, Rachal to Isham G. Leabow 10-18-1885
Rogers, Sarah to William Bullar 12-6-1872 (12-7-1872)
Rogers, Susan E. to Wm. F. Rogers 4-24-1889 (8?-24-1889)
Rol, Nelley to H. M. Hicks 11-24-1890 (no return)
Roland, Catharine to Rufus F. Hurstard? 9-26-1870
Rolen, Mandy to Hardy Parkey 5-6-1873 (no return)
Rolin, Rutha to James Grimes 9-3-1888 (9-12-1888)
Rollens, Minie to Henry Barnes 10-15-1890 (10-16-1890)
Rollins, Martha L. to George Hopper 8-8-1874 (8-9-1874)
Roop, Ida R. to L. G. Harmon 7-2-1884
Rose, Carnie May to A. A. Chapbell 12-4-1890
Rose, Jane to Sterling Lane 6-5-1876
Rose, L. J. to A. J. Hamock 3-5-1885 (3-8-1885)
Rose, Martha to Calvin Hollen 12-7-1872 (12-8-1872)
Rose, Martha to S. C. Turner 1-16-1881
Rose, Mary to Newton Brooks 11-16-1875 (11-17-1875)
Rose, Racha to John P. Miller 10-15-1880 (10-19-1880)
Rose, Susan to William Frith 3-7-1877 (no return)
Rosenbalm, Louiza to James N. Janeway 1-31-1870 (2-10-1870)
Rosenbalm, Martha to Idel Hughs 1-3-1870 (1-6-1870)
Rosson, Ida to Sterling Davis 2-7-1887 (2-13-1887)
Rosson, Maggy to Phillip Keck 9-18-1888 (9-20-1888)
Rosson, Martha to Jesse Bruer 4-2-1873 (4-3-1873)

Rourk, Sarah to George W. Whiteaker 12-17-1869 (12-19-1869)
Row, Mary to C. W. Hayse 5-7-1888 (5-27-1888)
Row, Matilda to John C. Green 2-2-1880 (2-15-1880)
Row, Rutha to Jas. S. Sharpsher 6-21-1880 (6-21-1880)
Rowald, Nancy Jane to David B. Green 5-20-1878 (6-2-1878)
Rowat?, Sarah J. to Wm. Riley Rogers 2-9-1875 (2-11-1875)
Rowe, Elizabeth to William Pearson 10-9-1877 (no return)
Rowe, Louisa J. to Wm. F. Clamant 9-2-1878 (9-3-1878)
Rowlen, Rusha to Jasper Weres 11-16-1884
Rugens, Martha to Thos. Zecks 9-15-1888 (2-16-1888)
Runion, N. E. to G. W. Richardson 12-14-1878
Runions, C. J. to W. S. Wyatt 11-9-1887
Runions, Emily to William H. Chumbly 9-11-1869 (9-12-1869)
Runnions, Nancy A. to George McDaniel 4-6-1876
Russell, Dora to Huffman Poor 10-26-1889 (no return)
Russell, Frances M. to Robt. D. Shepard 8-25-1889
Russell, Hester J. to Henry P. Honeycut 4-22-1882 (4-23-1882)
Russell, Luticia to James J.? Townsley 5-6-1871
Russell, M. C. to G. C. Ford 9-2-1880 (no return)
Russell, Manerva to William Shupe 11-15-1890 (no return)
Russell, Sarah A. to W. H. Ausmus 11-11-1881 (11-14-1881)
Russell, Sarah E. to Wm. L. Ford 12-3-1881 (12-4-1881)
Russell, Sarah to Wm. T. Robinson 8-31-1877 (no return)
Russesll, Elizabeth to Samuel Frazier 4-7-1877
Rutherford, Margret to Sterliing Smith 12-21-1876
Rutledge, Corney G. to A. J. Chadwell 4-29-1876 (4-30-1876)
Rymer, Sarah to Charles C. Miller 3-15-1870 (3-17-1870)
Sailer, Sarah to Orvel Belcher 2-4-1880 (no return)
Sailor, Milli? J. to Albert Sailor 11-11-1878
Samford, E. J. to T. A. Cruchfield 11-5-1879 (11-27-1879)
Samuel, Mollie to Wm. Rose 7-22-1883
Sanders, Hattie C. to H. V. Rider 8-14-1889 (8-15-1889)
Sanders, L. J. to John H. Mitchel 8-12-1871 (8-13-1871)
Sanders, Louisa to John A. Lisk 8-11-1883 (8-12-1883)
Sanders, M. A. to Wm. Parks 11-?-1879? (11-14-1879)
Sanders, M. M. to M. E. Heninger 4-18-1882 (4-20-1882)
Sanders, Mary to Joel C. Davis 3-22-1871
Sanders, Mary to S. F. McCollough 9-3-1888 (9-8-1888)
Sanders?, Sarah J. to Phillip F. Keck 10-22-1871 (10-23-1871)
Sandifer, Amanda to George W. Cheek 9-24-1883 (no return)
Sandifer, Eliza to Jermiah Ellison 3-4-1872
Sandifer, Lucey to John Dantton? 2-18-1882 (no return)
Sandifer, Nancy to Hiram Hill 12-29-1875 (no return)
Sandifer, Sarah F. to James M. Owens 9-30-1881 (2-3-1882?)
Sands, Mary A. to S. C. Poor 11-6-1882 (11-7-1882)
Sands, Sarah J. to W. P. Day 11-23-1889 (11-24-1889)
Sans, L. C. to Wm. Snider 7-31-1880
Sauls?, Alice to Brownlow Sweet 11-9-1888 (11-11-1888)
Sauner?, Polly to John M. Hamblin 8-5-1875
Sawder, Polley to J. M. Hamblen 8-5-1875
Sawyers, Sarah J. to J. H. Haris 1-2-1879
Saylor, L. M. to Jerry Saylor 2-19-1881
Saylor, Mary to John Phillips 9-8-1886
Scaggs, Susan to William Grubb 4-18-1878
Schooler, Sarah E. to James M. K. Sharp 7-3-1869 (7-4-1869)
Scott, Amanda S. to John C. Carr 9-23-1874 (no return)
Scott, Amanda S. to William G. Gibson 9-24-1874
Scott, Emeline to Zachariah C. Brooks 2-9-1870 (2-12-1870)
Scott, Mary E. to F. L. McVay 8-30-1878 (9-1-1878)
Seal, M. J. to W. T. Edmondson 7-1-1889 (7-4-1889)
Seal, Melvinia to Newton J. Hopper 8-17-1872 (8-18-1872)
Seal, Ollie to L. C. Chance 6-9-1884 (6-22-1884)
Seals, Allie to John Barnard 5-16-1888 (5-19-1888)
Seals, Harriet E. S. Redmon 2-16-1886 (2-6?-1886)
Serber, Jennie to Ewin Chadwell 12-18-1889 (12-19-1889)
Serler?, Reetha to Joseph Bullard 12-27-1878
Sermer?, Laura V. to J. T. Walker 3-25-1872 (4-28-1872)
Settum, Isabel to J. L. Sebolt 4-11-1885 (no return)
Sewell, N. E. to J. J. Sewell 4-17-1890
Sewell, Saluda J. to M. D. Richman 2-9-1875 (2-11-1875)
Sewsang, K. J. to R. F. Haskins 9-7-1889? (9-18-1879)
Shap, Melvina to R. S. Gaffner 11-29-1890 (11-30-1890)
Sharp, D. S. to G. W. McCrary 12-17-1881 (12-22-1881)
Sharp, Ella to Maynard Siler 2-10-1888 (no return)
Sharp, Esther to I. J. Cawood 7-26-1880
Sharp, Harriet to W. P. Ely 12-22-1884
Sharp, J. B. to Isaac M. Beeler 5-16-1872
Sharp, L. J. to R. H. Bell 10-12-1886 (10-13-1886)
Sharp, Lucey to John Major 12-26-1881 (no return)
Sharp, Lucy C. to J. J. Loyad 1-8-1879
Sharp, Lucy to John Major 12-25-1888 (12-27-1888)
Sharp, M. J. to C. H. Oley 11-19-1885 (12-28-1885)
Sharp, M. J. to D. M. Hayens 11-6-1878 (11-14-1878)
Sharp, Mary A. to M. D. Freeman 2-14-1872 (2-18-1872)
Sharp, Mary E. to James M. Carr 9-3-1870
Sharp, Mary Jane to Nathan Butcher 8-7-1869 (8-8-1869)
Sharp, Nancy J. to James T. Otey 4-9-1870 (4-10-1870)

Sharp, Perylee to Burton Day 8-8-1875
Sharp, Rachal to Esawlandium Owens 10-4-1880 (10-8-1880)
Sharp, Susan E. to James M. Brogan 11-25-1872 (11-28-1872)
Shaw, Ann P. to A. e. Fultz 8-11-1883 (8-12-1883)
Shelbun, Sary to Jeramiah Anderson 1-27-1872
Shell, Maggie A. to J. D. Ely 4-21-1888 (4-22-1888)
Shell, Mary to Elihu Howard 3-24-1885
Shelton, Manerva to Wm. Priffit 3-28-1885
Shelton, Mary L. to Wm. Daniel 12-6-1890 (no return)
Shelton, N. J. to J. B. Tolaver 11-7-1888
Shiflet, Roda to J. M. Burchfield 1-12-1889 (1-20-1889)
Shipley, Cora B. to J. D. Cheatham 10-6-1888
Shipley, Elizabeth to William Lundy 8-19-1884
Shipley, Henrietta to Richard Jones 12-27-1869 (12-28-1869)
Shipley, Jane to Moses Yoakum 8-26-1887 (8-28-1887)
Shipley, M. R. to G. W. Rhea 7-7-1890 (7-8-1890)
Shiply, Susan L. to Thos. A. Snoddy 4-8-1886
Shipman, Sarah L. to Jesse J. Hock 1-26-1878 (no return)
Shockley, Delila to Henry Collins 9-8-1887
Shoemate, E. A. to Samuel Lambert 12-24-1881 (12-25-1881)
Shoemate, Louisa M. to J. W. Francisco 11-7-1888 (11-8-1888)
Shoemate, Nancy A. to Thomas J. Davis 4-18-1882 (no return)
Shoemate, Nancy A. to Thos. J. Davis 4-16-1882
Shoemate, Sallie to Alexander Sanders 10-27-1882 (no return)
Shofner, Elisabeth to L. Weaver 4-5-1887 (4-11-1887)
Shofner, Tilda E. to Benjamin F. Pike 7-3-1888 (7-4-1888)
Short, Sarah to Abner C. Hansord 12-25-1872 (12-29-1872)
Shoumate, C. F. to Thomas W. Cranshanul 12-6-1879 (12-11-1879)
Shulan, Emaline to Moses Hatfield 3-6-1882 (3-7-1882)
Shuler, Emolin to G. W. Hatfield 2-19-1879 (no return)
Shultz, Laura J. to Daniel Suffrage 12-24-1874 (no return)
Shultz, Sarah to Boston Scott 7-23-1872
Shumate, E. J. to W. H. Cross 9-14-1878
Shumate, Mary A. to William Lewis 2-19-1890 (2-23-1890)
Siggar, Lizza to Warren? Robinson 9-1-1890 (no return)
Siler, Margret to Daniel Casey 5-6-1875
Siler, Orpha to Wm. F. King 1-15-1869
Simmons, Elizabeth to Calaway Shaufner 10-11-1877
Simmons, Jane to Joshua M. Collins 9-28-1872 (no return)
Simmons, Josephine to James P. Carr 3-18-1874 (4-23-1874)
Simmons, L. C. to G. S. M. Simmons 4-29-1874
Simmons, Louisa to William Henry 3-9-1878
Simmons, Louiza to Henly Hurst 1-15-1879 (1-16-1879)
Simmons, M. A. to W. H. Howard 12-28-1881 (12-29-1881)
Simmons, Martha E. to Jas. Read 4-1-1884
Simmons, Mollie to J. B. Robinson 9-18-1886 (no return)
Simmons, N. V. to William H. Guy 9-8-1874 (no return)
Simmons, Pertina to L. G. Burding 8-21-1872 (no return)
Simmons, Phebe to James Hurst 7-22-1876 (7-23-1876)
Simmons, Pulaski A. J. to Benj. J. Roe 10-28-1868 (10-29-1868)
Simmons, S. V. to J. W. Mountain 11-29-1889
Simmons, Sarah A. to William Mc. England 12-29-1869 (1-2-1870)
Simmons, Sarah to Prier Quarland? 12-24-1878
Simpson, Nancy E. to Pinkney J. Sword 2-29-1872
Singleton, Jane to William West 2-13-1877 (2-15-1877)
Singleton, Liza to James Stagall 11-15-1882 (no return)
Singleton, Nancy to Geo. Lane 1-17-1888
Sitser, Elizibeth to S. F. Perkins 7-20-1882 (7-23-1882)
Skidmore, Lizie to Nelson Massengill 10-21-1882 (10-22-1882)
Slusher, Kitty to John Miller 9-10-1874 (no return)
Smalls, Eady to Anderson Dodson 2-13-1869 B
Smith, America E. to Larkin B. Mason 4-18-1887 (5-9-1887)
Smith, Ann to Wm. Branscom 2-15-1874 (2-22-1874)
Smith, C. T. to John Marsee 11-7-1884
Smith, E. V. to Anderson Barnard 10-18-1882 (10-19-1882)
Smith, Elisabeth to J. H. Russell 4-24-1888 (4-26-1888)
Smith, Elizabeth to Robert Sulfrige 4-5-1873
Smith, Elizabeth to William F. Brooks 3-4-1869 (3-11-1869)
Smith, Elvarena to James H. Fugate 3-27-1869 (3-28-1869)
Smith, Emaline to Andrew Henry 10-9-1877 (10-11-1877)
Smith, Frances to George Minton 3-15-1887 (no return)
Smith, Harriet to John Tux 2-13-1878 (no return)
Smith, Helen to Winston Bolton 3-11-1890 (3-12-1890)
Smith, Jane to Isaac Reece 8-21-1875 (8-22-1875)
Smith, Jesy M. to Granvill S. Proffit 10-9-1877
Smith, L. D. to M. Muncy 10-11-1882 (10-12-1882)
Smith, Libbi to John L. Goin 12-19-1870 (12-22-1870)
Smith, Loucinda to A. J. Tolliver 11-3-1883 (11-4-1883)
Smith, Lovey to Solomon Dandridge 3-31-1890 (no return) B
Smith, M. A. to John Gose 11-30-1889 (12-1-1889)
Smith, M. E. to Robert Brooks 7-31-1882 (8-6-1882)
Smith, Margret Louisa to Smith T. Woodson 2-21-1876 (no return)
Smith, Margret to Wm. Davidson 3-16-1880 (3-27-1880)
Smith, Mariah C. to M. V. Moody 11-15-1877 (no return)
Smith, Mariah to Boid Overton 5-2-1873 (no return)
Smith, Marry to Scott Yoakum 6-23-1881
Smith, Martha to C. C. Cardwell 10-14-1873 (10-22-1873)

Smith, Mary A. to Isaac A. Pierce 1-10-1883 (no return)
Smith, Mary E. to James M. Buchanan 10-23-1874 (no return)
Smith, Mary J. to E. W. Cardwell 1-29-1878 (no return)
Smith, Mary to Elisha Meyers 2-7-1891 (2-8-1891)
Smith, Mary to F. T. Brooks 12-26-1870 (12-27-1870)
Smith, Mary to J. F. Rowe 12-7-1885 (12-10-1885)
Smith, Mary to J. T. Clary 2-11-1877
Smith, Matilda to George Johnson 1-3-1876 (1-6-1876)
Smith, Molley to J. W. Watson 10-19-1886 (10-23-1886)
Smith, Nervesta to Isaac Standifer 1-24-1874
Smith, Provey to Lewis Chadwick 12-24-1874
Smith, R. L. D. to John Muncy 9-1-1882 (9-14-1882)
Smith, Sarah E. to Prier Cupp 1-13-1891 (1-18-1891)
Smith, Sarah to Wm. Keizer 1-3-1885
Smith, Sarelda to John Brooks 12-9-1886 (no return)
Smith, Sintha A. to J. W. Widner 10-19-1886 (10-24-1886)
Smith, Tennessee to John Hopper 9-5-1878 (9-22-1878)
Snaveley, Martha J. to Abram Carmack 10-22-1877 (no return)
Snaveley, Nancy J. to James Cosbey 12-13-1876 (no return)
Snavely, Elisabeth to James Sutton 7-22-1875 (7-25-1875)
Snavely, Emma E. to Robt. L. Patterson 12-6-1888 (12-12-1888)
Snavely, Maggie to J. B. Hamilton 2-26-1888
Snavely, Mary Jane to Lilbourn W. Ellison 3-17-1869 (no return)
Snavley, S. E. to Thomas Brown 10-8-1879 (10-9-1879)
Snider, Eliza to D. C. Earl 10-30-1882 (10-22-1882)
Snider, Fanney E. to James Cupp 4-8-1887 (4-7?-188?)
Snider, Marry E. to William C. Minton 8-24-1876 (8-27-1876)
Snider, Susan to A. J. Earls 9-11-1880 (9-12-1880)
Snodgrass, Alice to Jas. Burchfield 2-21-1886 (no return)
Snodgrass, H. A. to H. E. Meyers 9-1-1866 (no return)
Snodgrass, Jennie to J. D. Jessee 9-22-1890 (9-24-1890)
Snodgrass, Mollie Glenn to James Robt. Butler 3-18-1873 (no return)
Snoveley, Elizabeth to A. J. Martin 11-12-1877 (no return)
Soard, Harriet to Pleasant Goin 12-23-1876 (12-24-1876)
Soard, S. L. to Wm. Y. Gray 7-21-1879
Soliver, Margaret to William F. Posoey 1-11-1870 (1-19-1870)
Sorton, Susa Ann to Hiram Pridemore 2-25-1874 (2-26-1874)
Southern, Eliza to John A. McNiel 11-4-1869
Southern, Helen to George W. West 4-22-1869 (4-25-1869)
Southern, Nancy L. to Thomas Cosbey 1-26-1869 (1-28-1869)
Southern, Sarah E. to W. W. Hill 12-14-1876
Southern, Sarah to Barnett Sumpter 2-15-1877 (no return)
Southern, ___ to G. W. Bryant 9-6-1890
Sowder, Milley A. to Wm. H. Davis 1-30-1879
Sowder, Sarah to J. H. Hopkins 1-12-1883 (1-13-1883)
Sowell, Elizabeth to Richard Murphrey 1-17-1883 (1-18-1883)
Spangler, Eliza to Johnson Cox 11-23-1889 (11-24-1889)
Spanldon, Angeline to George Teague 12-8-1870
Sparks, Elizabeth to John Ridens 11-24-1874 (12-24-1874)
Sparks, Margaret O. to Thomas J. Cary 9-29-1877 (9-30-1877)
Sparks, Sallie A. to Marion J. Bruce 1-15-1883 (1-16-1883)
Sparks, Sarah to Wm. Doyel 10-13-1871 (10-15-1871)
Speeks, Mary J. to James Hyett 5-26-1871
Sprinkle, Martha to David W. Parsifield 9-6-1870 (no return)
Sprinkles, Manerva to Arthur Humfleet 2-19-1869
Sproles, Marjorie to Daniel N. Burchell 2-6-1884 (no return)
Spurlock, Sarah J. to Calvin Younge 2-12-1878 (2-13-1878)
Standfer, Elisabeth to James Ailes 2-22-1890
Standfield, Eliza to Siler Lambdin 10-6-1868
Standifer, Laura to David Standifer 11-24-1888 (11-25-1888)
Standifer, M. M. to James A. Robertson 4-14-1881 (4-19-1881)
Standifer, Mary to Robert Farrall? 11-6-1874 (11-15-1874)
Standiford, Elizebeth to Richard Smith 5-21-1879 (5-22-1879)
Stanifer, Caroline to Prier? L. S. Crichfield 2-10-1872 (2-15-1872)
Stansberry, Bethina to Hesekah Hopper 1-12-1881 (no return)
Stansberry, Mary C. to William Harper 5-7-1874
Stansberry, Minie to R. H. Yoakum 1-27-1881 (1-30-1881)
Stansberry, Nancy Ann to Azariah Harper 6-22-1874
State, Nanney to Wm. Pearson 2-18-1888 (2-20-1888)
Steel, Lizzy to Jackson Hill 8-25-1888
Steel, Nancy to James Rook? 3-5-1883
Stergeon, Mary to Warrack Butcher 4-11-1871
Sterlin, Hanna C. to O. N. C. Harmon 5-5-1878 (4?-5-1878)
Steward, Jennie to W. L. Cheatham 2-14-1889 (2-25-1889)
Stewart, Mary E. to T. G. Walker 3-6-1888 (3-8-1888)
Stigall, Margret to Lewis Williams 3-27-1878
Stokley?, Roxey to Emond? Kincaid 11-25-1890 (no return)
Stone, Catharine G. to Nathan Dunsmore 9-21-1886 (9-23-1886)
Stone, F. A. to W. M. Jennings 2-2-1880 (no return)
Stone, Linda to J. H. Webb 12-23-1885
Stone, Martha J. C. to N. H. Powell 11-22-1876 (11-23-1876)
Stone, Mary to J. L. Reedy 10-8-1884 (10-11-1884)
Stone, Olley to Tennessee M. Parks 10-15-1870 (10-16-1870)
Stoute, A. M. to James M. Brunton 12-15-1883
Stump, M. J. to James Ghose 1-3-1880
Stump, Moley E. to P. H. Mayes 10-19-1878 (no return)
Sturgeon, Lucinda to Sterling Fugate 10-16-1869 (10-21-1869)

Suil, Nancy C. to C. H. Fraley 6-1-1888 (6-2-1888)
Suits?, R. to R. E. Fugate 3-1-1883
Sulffurdg, Sarah to Hiram Lafard 10-30-1879 (11-2-1879)
Sulfrage, Mary to Elbert Barnes 2-6-1891 (2-8-1891)
Sulfridg, E. C. to Elbert H. Fields 9-2-1879
Sulfridg, Manerva to Samuel Thacker 5-5-1883 (5-6-1883)
Sulfridg, Mary to John Sebolt? 9-25-1880 (10-3-1880)
Sulfridg, Nancy to Henry Baker 5-7-1881 (5-8-1881)
Sulfridge, Caroline to R. N. Nash 8-29-1888 (9-2-1888)
Sulfridge, Laney J. to James Scots? 5-20-1886
Sulfridge, Ollie to C. L. Cuningham 11-7-1887 (11-10-1887)
Sumate, Helan to James K. Gibson 6-19-1880 (6-20-1880)
Summers, Orlena to M. P. Williams 1-15-1886 (1-6?-1886)
Surber, Marry to John Combs 11-24-1880 (no return)
Susong, Molley to John Bishop 9-24-188? (9-26-1886)
Suthern, Sarah A. to Hiam Causby 5-13-1871 (5-16-1871)
Suthers, Angeline to Elbert Sumpter 1-31-1874
Sutten, Matilda to Hugh T. Mountgomery 12-?-1870 (no return)
Sutton, Mary V. to James W. Calor 6-29-1886 (7-8-1886)
Sutton, Mary to James Gordon 5-18-1889
Sutton, Melinda to Henry Sutton 2-25-1885 (2-27-1885)
Sutton, Sarah J. to Wm. Roark 5-16-1871
Sutton, Serelda J. to Allen Brooks 12-10-1874 (12-11-1874)
Swillivan, Mary to George Jones 9-22-1870
Switt?, Matilda E. to Ewens? Walker 10-27-1877 (11-1-1877)
Tague, S. A. to Nathan P. Cupp 4-17-1884 (4-18-1884)
Tallian, Mary to G. B. Deatherage 3-2-1879
Taner, Nancy Jane to John Phelps 1-29-1876 (1-30-1876)
Tanner, Mary to John? Tenaure? 6-18-1870
Tate, Gelana A. to Floid Harrell 8-22-1881 (8-26-1881)
Tate, Marry (Mrs.) to James F. Hall 3-8-1881 (3-20-1881)
Tate, Thursa to Hiram Thomas? 12-?-1870 (12-10-1870)
Tate, Thursey to Harmon Thomas 1-23-1871
Taylor, Lucy J. to James A. Thomsan 11-30-1874 (12-2-1874)
Taylor, Malinda J. to Bery Ellison 3-5-1883 (3-6-1883)
Taylor, Margret J to William Wood 3-1-1878
Taylor, Martha M. to John Fultz 9-1-1873 (9-3-1873)
Taylor, Mary Jane to Wm. L. Jones 8-29-1870
Taylor, Matilda to J. E. Mink 2-?-1880 (2-12-1880)
Taylor, N. J. to S. Hambin 10-23-1890
Taylor, R. A. to G. M. Nelems 11-29-1890
Taylor, Vashti to Fielding Shelton no date (Jan 1885?)
Teague, Mary to Robert F. Russell 10-29-1869 (11-4-1869)
Tennel, Julia A. to John Ridens 6-23-1883 (no return)
Tennels, Margrett M. to James M. Reed 4-24-1882
Terrell, Maggie to Robt. L. Cockerell 2-1-1891
Terry, Matilda to H. V. B. Siler 1-4-1890
Tesnay, Mandy L. E. to William Sumptor 2-19-1872
Testament, Jane to Calvin M. Mink 11-27-1871 (12-30-1871)
Thacker, Jane to S. B. Cook 2-16-1887 (2-17-1887)
Thomas, Alice to William Chadwell 2-26-1885 (2-27-1885)
Thomas, Crese to Stephen Gunn 10-26-1882 (9?-26-1882)
Thomas, Elisabeth to Dudley Gibson 5-17-1889 (5-19-1889)
Thomas, Eliza E. to Campbell Debusk 1-26-1882
Thomas, Emely to Percy G. Lawson 12-23-1874 (12-24-1874)
Thomas, G. F. to S. E. Goin 8-14-1885 (8-15-1885)
Thomas, Lucy to George Hyatt 12-23-1870
Thomas, Margret E. to George W. Lockely 9-29-1875 (no return)
Thomas, Margrett to William Rite 12-21-1880
Thomas, Mary B. to John Holaway 12-24-1888
Thomas, Mary E. to W. L. Dunsmore 7-28-1884 (7-30-1884)
Thomas, Rachel E. to J. T. Ayers 4-4-1882 (no return)
Thompson, Amanda to James Minton 12-10-1890
Thompson, E. E. to Marion M. Drummons 2-10-1886
Thompson, Lizzie B. to David H. Mayse 2-5-1889 (no return)
Thompson, M. J. to Thomas Sutton 10-4-1882 (10-5-1882)
Thompson, Martha to Calven Jones 8-31-1878
Thompson, Martha to Woodson Noe 12-25-1871
Thompson, Nancy A. to William A. Cartwright 8-21-1874
Tiller, Lucy to J. S. Johnson 1-7-1881
Tinnell, Nancy to John Harrison 8-3-1887 (8-7-1887)
Toliver, Lucinda to Wm. Nelson More 8-?-1888 (8-8-1888)
Toliver, Sarah to Wm. Smith 1-2-1888
Tolliver, Elmiriy to David Rillens 10-7-1871 (10-8-1871)
Townsley, John to Montie Brooks 12-3-1887 (12-4-1887)
Townsley, Mary to Wm. Wilson 10-20-1888
Tramel, R. S. to John Meyers 12-12-1878 (12-15-1878)
Travies, Frances E. to James H. Harmon 3-3-1884 (3-6-1884)
Treece, Elizabeth to W. H. Russell 5-31-1889 (no return)
Treece, Hester S. (Miss) to W. S. Carr 5-24-1874 (5-31-1874)
Treece, Hester S. to Wm. Patterson 1-7-1888
Treece, Jane E. to P. G. Fulkerson 12-20-1882 (12-25-1882)
Treece, Mariah to T. T. Hill 12-11-1883 (no return)
Treece, Martha to J. T. Russell 4-10-1888 (4-15-1888)
Treece, Rachel A. to Vincent Moyers 10-30-1883 (11-1-1883)
Treece, S. J. to M. J. Moss 11-21-1877 (no return)
Treece, Sarah to Newton Moyers 10-1-1879 (10-5-1879)

Treece, T. J. to Tandy J. Drummons 2-1-1886
Trent, Elizabeth (Mis) to Hiram Garland 7-23-1881 (7-24-1881)
Trent, Jane to Thos. Minter 6-5-1885? (no return)
Trey?, Margaret Ann to J. L. Wilson 1-28-1874 (no return)
Tucker, Mollie E. to Wesley A. Spradlins 10-29-1877 (10-30-1877)
Tuggle, Sane to B. F. Campbell 4-3-1881
Tullington, Maggie to Thos. Lampkins 4-17-1889 (4-18-1889)
Tumel, Margret M. to Isaac Peerce 1-30-1880 (1-31-1880)
Turner, Caldana to Scott Kincaid 12-25-1879 (1-2-1879?)
Turner, Elizabeth to Garrett Sander 10-21-1882
Turner, F. C. to John Davis 12-11-1880
Turner, Martha J. to J. N. Noe 8-10-1879
Turner, Martha to Zimry William 8-10-1887 (8-11-1887)
Turner, Mary J. to Wm. Watson 2-5-1885? (2-5-1885)
Turner, Matilda to W. A. Campbell 11-16-1882
Turner, Nancy to Landrum Panes? 3-9-1885 (3-10-1885)
Turner, Phaney to Jefferson Rains 6-15-1872 (no return)
Turner, Susan to Jobe Parker 12-31-1879
Tutter, Susan to Samuel Fisher 12-13-1890
Tylor, Vesta to Fielding Shelton 2-14-1885
Tyne, Lewsindey to Cread Grasen 12-25-1879
Underwood, Mary Jane to Silas Myers 1-10-1889? (1-12-1890)
Upton, Lucretia L. to James Young 6-22-1889 (6-23-1889)
Upton, Nancy to Levi Saylor 6-23-1881
Van, Mary J. to Mathew Cadle 10-15-1877
Vanbebber, Esther B. to Joseph H. Yadan 11-29-1879
Vanbebber, M. M. to G. W. Vanbebber 1-26-1879 (2-9-1879)
Vanbebber, Mary J. to Jesse Goforth 11-1-1873 (11-2-1873)
Vanbebber, Mary to John E. Howard 1-4-1869
Vanbebber, Nancy Tenn to Elihu E. Jones 3-1-1882 (3-4-1882)
Vanbebber, Tempy J. to Jackson Stokeley 11-12-1868 (11-27-1868) B
Vance, Louisa to Henry Shelton 2-4-1882 (2-5-1882)
Vanoy, Nancy E. to J. N. Venable 1-26-1884
Vansel, W. T. to M. B. Richardson 1-5-1885 (no return)
Varner, Maggie to John Varner 12-6-1888
Vaughn, Eliza to Balis Laxten 7-28-1879
Vaughn, Jane to James A. Stafford 3-29-1882 (no return)
Vaughn, Laura to Thos. Roberts 9-23-1886
Vaun, Elizabeth to Timothy Roark 8-24-1877
Venable, Matilda J. to James H. Vanay 4-1-1876 (4-2-1876)
Venerable, Elizabeth to Squire Treece 1-29-1876 (1-30-1876)
Venerable, Sarah to B. F. Minton 5-27-1876
Vial, Lizzie to Joe F. Bosworth 8-28-1890
Wade, A. E. to G. D. Jonson 1-18-1879 (1-19-1879)
Wagoner, Marth S. to Wm. Williams 2-26-1885
Waler, Cornely to John Paris 11-1-1879 (11-3-1879)
Walker, Clementine to Wiley P. Burch 10-23-1871 (10-27-1871)
Walker, Joanah to G. W. Bennett 5-30-1880
Walker, Manila A. to J. M. Smith 9-6-1877 (9-9-1877)
Walker, Martha E. to William G. Jessee 6-20-1874 (6-21-1874)
Walker, Martha J. to Wm. Fugate 5-27-1878 (no return)
Walker, Mary J. to J. N. Lewis 11-21-1876 (11-23-1876)
Walker, Ollie to Wiley Bartlett 2-5-1882
Walker, Racheal to Sterling Walp? 4-7-1873 (4-10-1873)
Walker, Sarah to B. L. Meyers 11-3-1873 (no return)
Walker, Sarah to James Owens 4-2-1881
Wallace, Mary L. to Wm. Sullivan 12-22-1890 (12-23-1890)
Wallace, Nancy E. to Richard Gulin 4-20-1888
Waller, Sarah E. to H. P. Daulton 4-12-1888 (4-15-1888)
Wallis, Elisabeth to James Branum 8-22-1874? (8-22-1875)
Waric, Hulda E. to George W. Harison 6-6-1883 (6-7-1883)
Warric, Mary to Henry Rosenbalm 5-17-1883
Warrick, Caley to W. E. Manis 4-16-1889 (5-25-1889)
Washam, Martha J. to James H. Smith 1-26-1872 (1-28-1872)
Waters, Mary H. to W. T. Poor 4-10-1877 (1-27-1878)
Waters, Mary J. to William Sulfridg 10-23-1884
Watson, Celia C. to Isaac B. Johnson 8-1-1874 (no return)
Watson, Martha A. to John W. Billingsley 10-29-1870 (11-2-1870)
Watson, Martha A. to Robert Mayers 11-23-1882
Watson, Martha A. to Robert Myers 11-23-1882 (no return)
Watson, Mary E. to Elias Peters 11-27-1888
Watson, Melvina to John Black 4-21-1885 (4-23-1885)
Watson, Sarah to Thomas Collinsworth 12-23-1868 (12-25-1868)
Waymoreson, Malinia to John M. Mayse 3-6-1872 (3-7-1872)
Weaver, Harriet Lean to King Darris 6-18-1876
Weaver, Martha A. to David Simmon 11-3-1890 (11-4-1890)
Weaver, Mary E. to Henry Carter 2-3-1887 (2-4-1887)
Webb, Celia to Henry Hoskins 4-26-1888 (no return)
Webb, Manerva J. to Calvin Miracle 3-18-1870 (3-17-1870?)
Webb, Martha to Peter Thacker 12-1-1881
Webb, Vina to Thomas Chadwell 2-18-1887 (2-20-1887)
Webe?, M. J. to J. W. Parton 12-31-1880
Welch, Catherine to John N. Rogers 11-22-1872 (11-23-1872)
Welch, Eliza to Marcillus Yoakum 8-12-1872 (no return)
Welch, Fanney to M. F. Caler 4-13-1871 (not executed)
Welch, Louise to George Yoakum 2-24-1870 (2-27-1870)
Welch, Mahulda to Milam Lawson 7-11-1873 (7-13-1873)

Welch, Mahulda to Milum Lawson 7-11-1873 (no return)
Welch, Malissa to John H. Brooks 9-12-1877 (no return)
Welch, Mary A. to W. A. Norel 5-9-1878
Welch, Mary to Robert McBee 9-11-1878 (9-12-1878)
Welch, Nancy to Lewis Thompson 10-24-1888 (10-27-1888)
Welch, Rossie A. to Ewin Brooks 10-24-1890 (10-26-1890)
Welch, Sarah J. to W. H. Hooper 8-17-1889 (8-18-1889)
Welch, ___ to J. P. Loop 4-27-1888 (no return)
Welch?, Mary A. to James Gilbert 10-20-1887 (10-30-1887)
Wells, D. to Thomas Mintar 1-10-1880 (1-3-1880)
Wells, Ellen T. to Preston Dunmore 1-14-1878 (1-15-1878)
Wells, Larrie? to Guss Jennings 7-26-1882 (no return)
Wells, Luretta to Wm. Janeway 1-31-1873 (2-2-1873)
Wells, Martha Margarett to Jesse M. Greenlee 5-22-1869 (5-23-1869)
Wells, Melvina to Peter Muncy 2-12-1875 (2-13-1875)
Welsh, Ellen to Robert Essary 12-24-1890 (12-25-1890)
Wesley, Sallie to John Sweet 10-24-1883 (no return)
West, L. O. to Wm. M. Dotson 2-24-1883
West, Margaret R. to Ancil Epperson 12-15-1888 (12-16-1888)
West, Martha to James Gipson 6-20-1876 (6-25-1876)
West, Mary A. to Pleasant W. Hurst 8-21-1873
West, Mary C. to D. H. Harrell 8-7-1883 (8-9-1883)
West, Matilda to H. H. Overholster 11-14-1884 (11-17-1884)
West, S. J. to James Bunch? 6-1-1884 (6-3-1884)
West, Siller to Wm. D. Harrell 11-22-1878 (11-23-1878)
West, Susan Fin? to J. W. Lawson 4-22-1875 (4-24-1875)
Wester, Louisa to David C. Gibson 2-14-1872 (2-15-1872)
Western, Martha C. to G. S. Sweet 5-7-1888 (5-20-1888)
Wheeler, Faney to David Weatherford 12-8-1873
Wheeler, Frances to Frank Yoakum 3-10-1881 (3-12-1881)
Wheeler, Mary to Fillmore Longman 10-8-1878 (10-12-1878)
Wheeler, Victory to H. D. Shell 12-4-1879 (no return)
Whitacre, Martha J. to John B. Cuningham 10-25-1878
Whitaker, America to David Greer 11-9-1888 (11-11-1888)
Whitaker, Angeline to Robin Brooks 4-3-1874 (no return)
Whitaker, Elizabeth to Joseph Jorden 8-2-1884 (no return)
Whitaker, Jannina to Clinton Whitaker 1-5-1882 (1-8-1881)
Whitaker, Louisey to Nelson Southern 4-23-1879 (4-4?-1879)
Whitaker, Mandy to G. W. Cosby 12-18-1884 (no return)
Whitaker, Margrett to Lewis Fultz 9-17-1880 (9-18-1880)
Whitaker, Mary J. to James England 11-10-1880 (no return)
Whitaker, Ms? A. to B. F. Whitaker 12-31-1878 (1-1-1879)
Whitaker, Rhoda M. to Lafayett England 11-22-1883 (11-23-1883)
White, Alice to Black Kincaid 3-5-1885 (no return)
White, Anne to Zackariah Hodges 11-22-1871 (11-23-1871)
White, Louiza C. to James F. Moss 3-16-1869 (3-21-1869)
White, Margret to Preston Kincaid 4-29-1879
White, Matildy to John Thomas 8-21-1870
White, Mattie R. to T. G. Brown 4-2-1884
Whiteaker, Cornela to Samuel Whiteaker 2-4-1891 (2-5-1891)
Whiteaker, Elizabeth to Calvin Whiteaker 6-16-1870 (6-19-1870)
Whiteaker, Elizabeth to Geo. Whiteaker 1-1-1885 (1-4-1885)
Whiteaker, Elizabeth to John Samler 8-25-1871 (8-27-1871)
Whiteaker, M. L. to J. B. Cunningham 10-24-1877 (no return)
Whitman, Elvira to T. Wm. Poor 5-3-1886 (5-4-1886)
Widby, Rebecca to Henry Sikes 6-23-1887
Widener, Nancy to J. W. Robinson 9-30-1885 (10-3-1885)
Widner, Mary to Wiley Day 2-21-1890 (2-23-1890)
Widner, Tulitha to Joseph Hamby 12-10-1880
Wierman, Mary V. to Charles W. Nash 1-19-1870 (1-20-1870)
Wilaford, M. J. to Andrew Reed 10-19-1882
Wilbern, Martha to John Tandion? 7-24-1881
Wilder, Manda C. to J. D. Travis? 9-19-1871
Wiley, Martha J. to R. B. Payne 3-11-1871 (3-16-1871)
Wilford, Mary to Wm. Reede 9-6-1879 (9-8-1879)
Wilkenson, Sarah to Rufus Cooks 7-3-1884
Wilkerson, Mary A. to John Nelson 12-6-1886 (12-9-1886)
Willialmls, Eliza to Mc. Ramsey 11-7-1868 (11-8-1868)
Williams, Alice J. to Sterling Brooks 1-15-1884 (1-15-1884)
Williams, Cornelia to Levi Brooks 4-4-1885 (4-5-1885)
Williams, Eliza? J. to L.B. Littrell 12-1-1877 (12-2-1877)
Williams, Elizabeth to Wm. Grubb 12-23-1881 (12-24-1881)
Williams, Frances to Lee Thomas 3-7-1876 (3-9-1876)
Williams, George to Simon Cook 9-16-1890
Williams, Lary to John Farmer 9-4-1880 (9-5-1880)
Williams, Lucie to Stepen Kincaid 12-27-1873 (12-28-1873)
Williams, Lucy to N. J. Campbell 1-17-1885 (10-18-1885)
Williams, Marry J. to Solomon Ramsey 8-20-1879
Williams, Martha G. to Elbert Hart 10-17-1871
Williams, Martha to John F. Williams 2-7-1891
Williams, Marthia E. to Andrew Suttan 3-6-1872 (3-7-1872)
Williams, Mary to James Woodard 10-7-1872 (10-11-1872)
Williams, Mary to Thomas Paul 10-1-1887
Williams, Missouri to David Campbell 9-15-1874 (no return)
Williams, P. E. to James L. Meyers 12-27-1884 (no return)
Williams, P. E. to James L. Moyers 12-27-1884
Williams, Priscila to James Payn 8-28-1878?

Williams, Sarah E. to Richard Burks 1-6-1886 (1-28-1886)
Williams, Sarah to John Sandifer 10-9-1886
Williams, Serena J. to E. N. Hamner 1-26-1887 (1-27-1887)
Williams, Vicy to James W. Monday 12-10-1888 (12-11-1888)
Willis, America to Peter Jones 9-17-1885 (9-19-1885)
Willis, Anjaline to Henderson Barnard 1-27-1881 (1-30-1881)
Willis, Jacob to Nancy Nathen 2-7-1886
Willis, Lithy to Daniel Ealy 6-4-1880
Willis, Margrett to John Collins 11-7-1890 (no return)
Willis, Martha Jane to Elisha Gray 8-7-1869 (8-15-1869)
Willis, Mary to Frank Shipman 9-4-1882 (9-7-1882)
Willis, Mary to James R. Carpenter 9-22-1868 (7?-23-1868)
Willis, Melvina to James M. Carpenter 2-19-1874 (2-25-1874)
Willis, Sarah E. to Alexander Hurst 10-19-1868
Willis, Sarrah to John H. Carpenter 8-31-1870 (9-1-1870)
Willis, Thersa to Charlie Wilmot 9-2-1875
Willmot, Martha to D. G. Willis 10-7-1868 (10-8-1868)
Willmouth, Nety to James Hall 4-13-1880
Willright, Manda J. to Perygram Losson 7-31-1882 (no return)
Wills, Elizabeth to William Berry 5-9-1877 (5-10-1877)
Willson, Liza G. to I.? A. Brooks 6-12-1882 (6-13-1882)
Willson, Sarah J. to John Asburn 6-13-1875
Willson, Virginia to R. T. Love 2-23-1890
Wilson, Caroline to Humphrey Brooks 4-7-1882 (no return)
Wilson, Celia to James Toneur 8-14-1887
Wilson, Cola Catharine to Lewis Gib 2-11-1891 (2-12-1891)
Wilson, Cora to Arch Baker 2-7-1891 (2-8-1891)
Wilson, L. J. to R. T. Vann 7-26-1890 (7-27-1890)
Wilson, M. L. to R. H. Perry 3-30-1882 (4-1-1882)
Wilson, Margaret to Wm. P. Owens 5-17-1871 (no return)
Wilson, Martha A. to Lewis Brooks 12-27-1880 (1-1-1881)
Wilson, Mary E. to George Brooks 1-9-1874
Wilson, Orlena to Alwane Mize 8-9-1887 (8-10-1887) B
Wilson, Orlenia to Boston Brooks 7-3-1871 (7-6-1871)
Wilson, S. C. to Thomas M. Tinnel 11-3-1888 (no return)
Wilson, Sarah J. to George W. Pane 12-18-1873 (no return)
Wilson, Sarah M. to J. M. Collins 2-4-1878 (no return)
Wilson, Sopha to John Hamlin 10-9-1884
Wisp?, Nancy to H. C. Lane 11-13-1886 (11-14-1886)
Wolf, Catherine to Wm. M. Reese 7-25-1870 (7-28-1870)
Wolf, Elizabeth to S. F. Grubb 11-3-1883 (11-8-1883)
Wolf, Lucretia to B. F. MacNeal 4-25-1874 (4-26-1874)
Wolfenbarger, Milley to Joseph Surber 1-18-1870 (1-19-1870)
Woodard, A. H. E. to Millerd Myers 7-22-1884 (7-27-1884)
Woods, Martha J. to Smith Parr 8-2-1871 (8-3-1871)
Woodson, Matilda to Andy Claud 8-21-1873
Woodson, Sarah A. to Thos. Ball 10-16-1886 (10-17-1886)
Woodson, William to Angeline Candry 12-15-1878
Woolf, Elizabeth to James Hatfield 12-16-1881 (12-28-1881)
Woolf, Emly to D. J. Surber 5-25-1872
Woolf, Matilda to Calvin Brown 8-17-1889 (8-18-1889)
Woolfenbarger, Sarah to G. G. Cottrell 9-3-1881 (9-4-1881)
Wright, A. C. to David Ausmus 12-31-1878
Wright, Margrett to Danel Hopson 2-10-1883 (2-11-1883)
Wright, Martha J. to John A. Carmack 10-25-1877
Wright, Mary to Carter Fulington 11-5-1884 (11-6-1884)
Wright, Talitha C. to William H. H. Beeler 2-14-1869
Wryly, Numie? to S. F. Hansard 12-29-1885 (12-30-1885)
Wyatt, Sarah to Jame Bray 2-7-1881
Wyley, America to Patton McCrary 9-6-1888 (9-9-1888)
Wyley, Jennie to Hop Gray 1-29-189? (1-30-1891)
Wyley, Ninnie to S. F. Hansard 12-29-1885 (12-30-1885)
Wylie, Nancy C. to P. M. Bolinger 7-24-1890
Wyman, Mary to D. A. Cawood 1-6-1881
Wyrick, Katey to J. C. Arnold 2-9-1884 (2-10-1884)
Wytt, Maggie to Joseph Ferrell 11-27-1884
Yeary, Amand to James W. Yeary 3-2-1883 (3-11-1883)
Yeary, Barbary to Sterling Campbell 10-27-1869 (no return)
Yeary, Mary to George Rowland 1-19-1883 (12-2-1883)
Yeary, Nancy E. (Mrs.) to Moses C. Brooks 9-5-1881 (11-17-1881)
Yoakum, D. B. to John E. Mason 3-7-1881 (3-10-1881)
Yoakum, Elisabeth to H. H. Ritter 12-7-1874 (12-13-1874)
Yoakum, Eliza to John Cawood 7-20-1880 (8-1-1880)
Yoakum, H. M. to A. D. Simmons 12-2-1873 (12-4-1873)
Yoakum, Harret to George Mason 4-27-1874 (5-3-1874)
Yoakum, Juda J. to Felix G. Rogers 11-2-1877 (11-4-1877)
Yoakum, L. J. to James Yoakum 8-21-1880 (9-16-1880)
Yoakum, L. J. to W. S. Large 9-5-1884 (no return)
Yoakum, Louisa L. to William H. Myers 8-25-1879 (8-28-1879)
Yoakum, M. E. to G. W. Woodson 2-7-1880
Yoakum, Mary to D. F. Woulf 8-30-1879 (8-31-1879)
Yoakum, Mary to John Underwood 10-14-1874
Yoakum, Nany to J. P. Ranes 9-5-1884 (no return)
Yoakum, Ollie S. to W. P. Hubard 3-8-1884 (2?-17-1884)
Yoakum, Sallie Ann to Benjamin Bolinger 11-26-1869 (11-28-1869)
Yoakum, Sarah A. to R. W. Hollingsworth 12-3-1873 (11-28-1873?)
Yoakum, Winney to Isreal C. Gibson 3-14-1873

Yodon, Orlena C. to Wm. R. Hansard 2-25-1886
Yokum, M. J. to J. C. Cawood 2-2-1885 (2-8-1885)
York, Elizabeth to R. W. Leffler 2-8-1891
Young, L. C. to Joseph Laine 2-22-1879 (no return)
Young, Lo. to Mat Griffen 3-30-1880 (4-1-1880)
Young, M. L. to Z. G. Cardwell 1-3-1881 (no return)
Young, Manervia to Bowl Lee 2-22-1877
Zeaks, Maria to Emmanuel Collins 4-22-1871 (4-23-1871)
____, Sweet Lucy to Lee Lawson 8-15-1885 (7?-15-1885)
____, Sarah to Elijah Smith 4-6-1877 (no return)

www.ingramcontent.com/pod-product-compliance
Lightning Source LLC
Chambersburg PA
CBHW081258170426
43198CB00017B/2840